Stigma and Culture

THE LEWIS HENRY MORGAN LECTURES / 2008

Presented at
The University of Rochester
Rochester, New York

Stigma and Culture

Last-Place Anxiety in Black America

J. LORAND MATORY
WITH A FOREWORD BY THOMAS P. GIBSON

The University of Chicago Press
Chicago and London

J. Lorand Matory is the Lawrence Richardson Professor of Cultural Anthropology and director of the Center for African and American Research at Duke University. He is the author of two award-winning books, *Sex and the Empire That Is No More* and *Black Atlantic Religion*.

The University of Chicago Press, Chicago 60637
The University of Chicago Press, Ltd., London
© 2015 by The University of Chicago
All rights reserved. Published 2015.
Printed in the United States of America

24 23 22 21 20 19 18 17 16 15   1 2 3 4 5

ISBN-13: 978-0-226-29756-9 (cloth)
ISBN-13: 978-0-226-29773-6 (paper)
ISBN-13: 978-0-226-29787-3 (e-book)

DOI: 10.7208/chicago/9780226297873.001.0001

Library of Congress Cataloging-in-Publication Data

Matory, James Lorand, author.
 Stigma and culture : last-place anxiety in Black America / J. Lorand Matory.
  pages cm
 Includes bibliographical references and index.
  ISBN 978-0-226-29756-9 (cloth : alk. paper) — ISBN 978-0-226-29787-3 (ebook) — ISBN 978-0-226-29773-6 (pbk. : alk. paper) 1. Matory, James Lorand.
 2. African American college teachers. 3. African Americans—Race identity.
 4. Middle class African Americans—Social conditions. I. Title.
  E185.97.M39A3 2015
  305.896′073—dc23
                                        2015008736

♾ This paper meets the requirements of ANSI/NISO Z39.48–1992 (Permanence of Paper).

*This book is dedicated to
My mother,
Deborah Love Matory
April 20, 1928–July 13, 1995;
My father,
William Earle Matory Sr., MD
October 1, 1928–January 26, 2009;
and
Howard University
"The Capstone of Negro Education"
1867–*

Contents

Foreword ix

Introduction 1

1 Three Fathers: How Shall I See You through My Tears? 66

2 The University in Black, White, and Ambivalence: The Hidden Curriculum 116

3 Islands Are Not Isolated: Schools, Scholars, and the Political Economy of Gullah/Geechee Ethnicity 177

4 A Complexion or a Culture? Debate as Identity among African-Descended Indians and Louisiana Creoles of Color 231

5 Islands of the Mind: The Mythical Anthropology of the Caribbean 307

6 Heaven and Hell: American Africans and the Image of Home 370

Conclusion: "Through a Glass, Darkly" 447

Acknowledgments 481
Notes 485
References 491
Index 509

Foreword

The Lewis Henry Morgan Lectures were originally conceived in 1961 by Bernard Cohn, who was then chair of the Department of Anthropology and Sociology at the University of Rochester. A founder of modern cultural anthropology, Morgan was one of Rochester's most famous intellectual figures and a patron of the university; he left a substantial bequest to the university for the founding of a women's college. The lectures named in his honor have now been presented annually for over fifty years and constitute the longest-running such series in North America.

The present volume is based on the Lewis Henry Morgan Lecture that Professor J. Lorand Matory delivered at the University of Rochester in October 2008 with the title "The Other African Americans: Racial Stigma, Ethnicity, and the Hidden Social Curriculum of the University." The lecture was based on ethnographic research Professor Matory had recently completed among the faculty, students, and alumni of Howard University, an institution that has been regarded by its American, Caribbean, and African alumni as the Mecca of black higher education since its founding in 1867. In many ways, he was uniquely qualified to conduct a study of this intellectual elite. Both of his parents were Howard alumni, and his father, William Earle Matory Sr., MD (1928–2009), was professor of Surgery in the College of Medicine from 1971 until his retirement in 1997. The writer has thus known the campus and its neighborhood since his childhood. He has also conducted years of intensive field research in Nigeria (Matory [1994] 2005b) and Brazil (Matory 2005a) since the 1980s.

Professor Matory started this research with the assumption that Howard University had served as a sort of pan-African melting pot, in which "students and faculty originating from countries and regions that conceptualize racial and complexion diversity" in many different ways would "embrace the notion that all people of African descent belong to the same political, marital and extended ethno-cultural category." What he found instead was a deep ambivalence. Despite its overall project of collective racial uplift, Howard University has long served as a major venue of black ethnic differentiation, and this process has only intensified over time.

This discovery led to one of the book's major insights. All hierarchical social systems are polarized between a dominant group whose bodies and way of life are presumed to represent all that is honorable and desirable for human beings in general and a stigmatized group whose bodies and way of life are defined as essentially dishonorable and inferior. These ways of life are regarded as expressions of the intrinsic natures of both the dominant and the stigmatized groups. Ambitious populations are driven to differentiate themselves from the stigmatized pole at the bottom and to align themselves with the privileged pole at the top. One way they do so is to claim that their own group possesses a unique "culture" that may not be of universal value but that is at least superior to the character and lifeway of the stigmatized underclass.

In the hierarchical world order that came into being in the Atlantic Basin over the past five hundred years, the top of the system has been dominated by certain peoples of northwestern European descent and the bottom by people of African descent. Whiteness has come to represent the unmarked pole of inherent privilege and blackness as the marked pole of inherent stigma. European peoples from regions lying to the east and south of this dominant core asserted the unique value of their cultural and ethnic identities in opposition to the universalizing claims of the French Enlightenment and of Anglo-Saxon imperialism. Resisting French cultural imperialism in the seventeenth century and military conquest in the eighteenth, intellectuals like Johann Gottfried von Herder asserted the particularity of Germanic cultural difference in opposition to the universalizing claims of the French Enlightenment. In North America, Jewish and Catholic immigrants from southern and eastern Europe asserted the unique value of their particular ethnic and cultural traditions in opposition both to the universal standard set by the white Anglo-Saxon Protestant elite and to the racially stigmatized descendants of African slaves.

Universities have constituted the primary arena in which socially mobile middle classes everywhere have acquired the cultural capital both to ascend within the social hierarchy defined by the dominant groups and to promote themselves as spokesmen for their own and other, proxy populations that they redefine as "cultures," rather than mere deficient versions of the dominant lifeway. Matory argues that it is no accident that the concept of cultural relativism was developed by African American Polish, German, and Jewish intellectuals such as Alain Locke, Bronislaw Malinowski, Franz Boas, and Ruth Benedict who made their careers in British and Anglo-American universities.

In this book, Professor Matory shows how this process has operated within America's black population. By bringing together the most talented individuals of African descent from many different backgrounds, Howard University has played a central role in the articulation and refinement of the ethnic, genealogical, and cultural markers that define Creoles from Louisiana, Gullahs and Geechees from the southeast coast, American Indians of partly African descent, Jamaicans, Trinidadians, Nigerians, Ghanaians, and many other ethnic groups. What almost all of them have in common is the effort to define themselves in opposition to the negative stereotypes associated with "native" and supposedly typical African Americans. Such ethnic groups thus strive to reclassify themselves as the "middle classes" of a racially stratified system. Few other social theorists have formulated an analytic framework that encompasses race, class, and ethnicity as comprehensively.

But this book is not just an exercise in academic analysis. It is driven by an ethical and political denunciation of the entire system of racial and ethnic differentiation, a system that depends upon the existence of a category of racially stigmatized individuals at its foundation. Everything these individuals do is regarded by the wider society either as an expression of their innate racial inferiority or as an eccentric exception to it. Everything done by individuals belonging to the middling ethnic groups in the system is similarly regarded as an expression of their unique cultural traditions. It is only the unmarked white individuals at the top of the system whose actions are treated either as an expression of universal human propensities or as the expression of their individual character and creativity.

In defiance of this way of thinking, Professor Matory presents us with the life histories of a number of creative individuals who overcame their stigmatized place in this racialized world system and achieved the pinnacle of success in their chosen careers. Ethnography, the documentation of the cultural traditions of particular ethnic groups, gives way to biography, the documentation of the achievements of creative African American individuals. Among these individuals he includes himself, members of his family, family friends, personal friends, professional acquaintances, and public figures. He tells their stories in the first person, as they affected him emotionally and spiritually in the course of his own life. In telling the life stories of those who have been important to him alongside his ethnography of self-proclaimed members of the black ethnic groups he encountered during his field research at Howard University, Professor Matory issues a challenge to all of us who seek to distance ourselves from the stigma of those at the bottom of any social hierarchy by denying their individuality and by claiming membership in some more highly valued collective entity, whether it be a race, an ethnic group, a class station, a region, a nation, or a disability group. Moreover, he shows that universities are a major venue and inspiration for the stigmatized to stratify—and articulate a "cultural" defense of—their own. It is a book written with a rare combination of analytic rigor and personal passion. It is meant to be read in the same way.

Thomas Gibson
Editor, Lewis Henry Morgan Monograph Series
January 2015

Introduction

"We hold these truths to be self-evident, that all men are created equal, that they are endowed by their creator with certain unalienable rights, that among these are Life, Liberty, and the Pursuit of Happiness." The backdrop of the stories that I will tell is that the author of these words—slaveholder Thomas Jefferson, whose text is the foundation of the United States' distinctive legal system and national imaginary—did not intend for these words to apply to people who look like me. And if Black Americans did not enjoy these unalienable rights, it was manifestly obvious—indeed a visible truism—to many newcomers and old residents of this land that people who look like me were not men and that distinguishing oneself from them was the price of the ticket to citizenship.

Hence, the most despised nationalities, castes, and classes from the Old World (not to mention New World natives and mixed-race creoles) sensed that they could entertain the hope of inclusion in this Jeffersonian promissory note only if they could demonstrate that they were historically and categorically different from, opposite to, and agreeably hostile toward people who look like me (Roediger 1989; Barrett and Roediger 2005; Ignatiev 1995).

Yet, at this point in US history, large numbers of immigrants from other lands and people who now recognize and wish to give social effect to their native ancestry look, to many Americans, just like me. No one wants to be directed to the "undeserving" side of racially "segmented assimilation," but what are the options when the signs of that involuntary triage become evident and one's optimism and aspirations are disappointed (see Bashi and McDaniels 1997)? To the degree that one looks African and not northwestern European, he or she is not judged by his or her individual merits and deficits. One is identified as part of a collective, and the strategic advantage of dignifying one's own collective, in contrast to the constituent other, becomes obvious. So Black-looking immigrants and natives face a terrible dilemma—to join forces culturally and socially with the Black "race" of the constituent other in the demand for inclusion or to assert *ethnic* distinction from other black people and exemption from that stigma. Their resolutions are seldom clear, fixed, or painless.[1]

That dilemma is the basic theme of this book, which concerns the self-understandings and performative self-representations of African and West Indian immigrants and transmigrants in the United States, as well as those of US-based triracial isolates and self-described "middle-class" African Americans. Black people are the constituent other of the US nation-state—that one exceptional "race" that was systematically enslaved and denied democratic rights in the world's greatest and most egalitarian democratic republic. We are the internally visible foreigner, in opposition to whom the worthy citizen is defined. This symbolic role imposes a certain fixity upon the public image of African Americans—homogeneous, unchanging, bereft of the characteristics and behaviors that define the normal citizen, and, according to the national mythology, uniquely embodying the characteristics and behaviors inappropriate to the normal citizen.

In a nation-state committed to individual rights, we are the group least entitled to treatment as individuals, to be judged by our individual merits. For us, the individual transcendence of our collective disqualification requires a Herculean, or Sisyphean, effort. Hence, for many black immigrants and natives, the best strategic option seems to be the establishment of an alternative collective identity whose dignity can be highlighted through its distinction from African Americans.

For African Americans, continental Africans long served as this definitively stigmatized constituent other. For example, in urging my cousin and me to cease the riotous noise we had been making during his afternoon nap, my grandfather shouted, "You all sound like a bunch of Africans!" That was in the early 1970s. But still, in 2013, African American attorney and talk-show host Star Jones cast Africans in the same role. In response to a question from CNN reporter Piers Morgan about whether she ever performed a sexually suggestive dance called "twerking," Jones said that no middle-aged black woman "outside the jungles of Africa" would ever perform such a dance.[2] A range of African American cultural projects, from the ardent embrace of Christianity to costly "weaves," rests on the logic that expurgating the African in us is a self-improvement that will persuade whites to acknowledge our citizenship rights and our personal worth. Indeed, having straightened her hair and bleached it, Jones described herself in the broadcast as "blonde."

INTRODUCTION   3

Just as many African Americans use continental Africans as a foil, many black ethnics refashion themselves through "anti–African American" identities. When people feel vulnerable to stereotyping, there is a strong impulse for the stigmatized to deflect those stereotypes onto a group that can be constructed as lower. Indeed, such deflection is internalized in the defensive speech and self-representation of virtually all status-insecure populations.

I describe this process as "ethnological schadenfreude." Much like other stigmatized groups, many immigrant and many native populations of African descent seek exemption from oppression and marginalization by describing themselves as culturally superior to another stigmatized group and gleefully mocking the characteristics that allegedly render that other stigmatized group the *true* constituent other. Many of my interlocutors in this study of ethnological schadenfreude were family friends and neighbors, many of whom were also Howard University students, faculty, alumni, or children of alumni. Because my parents had studied at Howard, my father taught there, and I grew up there, I had long regarded this multiethnic network as an extended family. Hence, my study began with the intention of documenting a world of Black unity, interethnic harmony, and class ambition, in contrast to the mass media's usually anemic portraits of Black America—as collectively poor, socially dysfunctional, and intellectually incompetent. The regional, national, and class diversity that I saw in Howard's sphere of influence came as no surprise. What surprised me is that many of the people that I had seen as extended family saw me and people like me—African Americans—as their antitypes. The account of these processes cannot but be autoethnographic—as much memoir as ethnography. The ways in which these middle-class Black ethnics othered all nonethnic African Americans called attention to the manner in which I had heard middle-class African Americans other working-class African Americans—as a way of seeking upward mobility in a white-dominated world and of disciplining our children into the same pursuit. Through this insight, I came to see the lessons of Bourdieu's study of class hierarchy for the study of ethnogenesis, or the articulation of "culture"-based ethnic identities. What follows is an account of the shared dynamics of class identity and ethnic identity, in which autobiographical memory provides as many lessons as do formal historical investigation and field research.

What anthropologists long called "cultures" are not self-existent units but an ongoing accumulation of momentarily strategic choices among conceivable patterns of action. A person's conduct is shaped not just by his or her autonomous sense of the conceivable possibilities and his or her personal desiderata but also by other people's expectations of a person like him or her, as well as his or her expectations of how people like those around him or her will respond. However, the expectations of people who interact with each other are seldom fully in sync with each other. They debate and struggle, with words and other signs, over what behaviors are acceptable, but not all parties have equal authority to defend or enforce their expectations. Hence, the social field in which these debates take place is hierarchical, and the products of social cooperation are unequally shared. It is in this context that, since the popularization of the Boasian concept of "cultures," people have verbally defined the fixed patterns and standards of thought and conduct of their respective ethnic groups, and they are motivated to do so by a competitive pursuit of approval and opportunity.

The global context in which people name and define their "cultures" was, at the start of the twentieth century, and remains a racially stratified world, in which an ethnoracially unmarked but largely white dominant class exercises disproportionate authority in the classification of others in terms of their "cultures" and yet largely exempts itself from classification in "cultural" and "racial" terms. However, the authority of this class requires consent. The éminence grise behind the articulation of cultures is a "constituent other" population that, no matter how heterogeneous the values and conduct of its members, exemplifies collective unworthiness in the eyes of others. Edward Said (1978) underlined the idea—with a genealogy deep in continental European philosophy and richly developed in Fanon ([1952] 2008)—that Western power and self-understandings are rooted in the construction of a non-Western racial opposite. I submit that this process works not only on a global scale but also within the boundaries of any given nation-state, local community, or "culture." Whereas terms like "the other" and the "constitutive other" tend to emphasize the contrast between the self and the other, I intend, with the alternative term "*constituent* other," to emphasize that this other is internal to the collective self and, in response to the ambition of the person or of the collective, requires expiation. In each local community or population, there is a stigmatized internal subpopulation that serves as the primary constituent other of that social order. The function of stigma in the tandem process of "culture" making and consent to the dominant order is obvious nowhere more than in the binary racial order of the United States, where every immigrant or regional population that seeks to participate in the wider society is assigned its degree of privilege and opportunity based on a demonstration of whether that population is "Black" or not.

"Ethnological schadenfreude," or the pursuit of contrast from and superiority to the constituent other, is a major mechanism in the articulation of "cultures" by the discreditable populations (i.e., populations that are not powerful enough to escape ethnoracial marking). Among such populations, a major mechanism of consent to the dominant order is the continual endeavor to avoid last place by emphasizing their difference from the constituent other and their likeness to the unmarked population. Conversely, a major idiom of dissent or rebellion is the temporary or situational mimicry of (normally stereotyped images of) the constituent other.

Stigma and Culture documents this global phenomenon in what I will argue is its *locus classicus*—in the verbal and other behavioral self-representations of African-descended immigrants and regional ethnic groups at and around US universities. As a precondition of opportunity and honor in US society, each of these populations—African and Afro-Caribbean immigrants, Gullah/Geechees, American Indians of partly African descent, and Louisiana Creoles of color—must either resist the system through the imitation or redefinition of Blackness or, the more common solution, dramatically assert radical "cultural" difference from America's prototypical constituent other, African Americans.

The Demography of the "Invisible"

Among the 37.3 million self-identified non-Hispanic "Blacks" who lived in the United States in 2007, according to the US Census Bureau, 3 million, or 8 percent of the self-identified "Black" population, were foreign born.[3] This figure does not include the numerous people whom others might consider "Black" but who identify themselves as belonging to two or more races or as "some other race."

In 2007, again according to the US Census Bureau,

> Of the foreign-born Black population, 54 percent were born in countries in the Caribbean, including Jamaica (19 percent), Haiti (17 percent), and Trinidad and Tobago (6 percent). An additional 34 percent were born in countries in Africa, including Nigeria (6 percent), Ethiopia (4 percent), and Ghana (3 percent). Approximately 5 percent were born in countries in South America, including Guyana (4 percent), and 4 percent in countries in Central America [which includes, for example, Belize, Costa Rica, Honduras, Mexico and Panama]. Countries from the remaining regions of the world—Europe, Asia, Northern America, and Oceania—when combined represented about 3 percent of the Black foreign-born.[4]

Hence, the most numerous national-origin groups among foreign-born populations of African ancestry in the United States are Jamaicans, Haitians, Trinidadians and Tobagonians, Nigerians, Ethiopians, and Ghanaians. Because of their African ancestry, dark Dominicans, Cubans, and Puerto Ricans also figure prominently among the populations that interest me, although I have met only a few of them at Howard, Harvard, or Duke, the foci of the present account. Such foreign-born populations of African descent in the United States have grown enormously since the Hart-Celler Immigration Act of 1965 and have more than doubled in almost every subsequent decade.

According to Kent (2007), "The foreign-born black population rose nearly seven-fold between 1960 and 1980, and more than tripled between 1980 and 2005. The foreign-born share of all U.S. blacks increased from less than 1 percent to 8 percent during these years" (4). Overall, the number of foreign-born blacks rose from 816,000 in 1980 to 3,578,000 in 2011, most of them having arrived since 1990.[5] During the same time period that the national population as a whole has doubled, the foreign-born black population has more than quadrupled.

The number of specifically African-born people in the United States is relatively small but has grown particularly fast. For example, between 1960 and 2010, the number of specifically African-born people in the United States more or less doubled every decade. As of 2010, 1.6 million African-born people lived in the United States.[6] Undoubtedly, a number of African immigrants were overlooked by the Census Bureau, and a significant number of the children of African immigrants continue to identify themselves *ethnically* as African, just as many children of Caribbean immigrants identify themselves ethnically as Caribbean. Clearly, we are already facing a seismic expansion of the demographic and cultural phenomena detailed in this book, but they highlight a metacultural phenomenon of far broader incidence and significance—the translocal, transnational, and interethnic setting of all ethnogenesis.

Of course, these populations are not, in the anthropological sense, culturally identical to native-born African Americans, but as we shall see, African Americans are also a diverse lot—in class, ancestry, values, and conduct. The point is that the conceptual lines by which black ethnics separate these contiguous and interacting populations into discrete "cultures" follow a supraempirical logic. Indeed, like ethnic boundaries around the world, they tend to articulate the speaker's situational economic interests and political goals.

My analysis compares these immigrant populations—and their children—with a number of *domestic* ethnic groups of partly African descent. These include the phenotypically and culturally highly African-looking Gullah/Geechees, who originated in the Lowcountry, a southeastern region encompassing the coast and islands of southern North Carolina, South Carolina, Georgia, and northern Florida. Other domestic populations—and their diasporas—now recognize and wish to give social effect to their partly European and/or Native American ancestry. These domestic populations—such as the Melungeons, Lumbees, and Saponis of North Carolina and Tennessee; the Nanticokes of Delaware and New Jersey; and the Ramapo Mountain people of New Jersey—have at times been called "little races" (Thompson 1972) or "tri-racial isolates." The Louisiana Creoles of color instantiate a closely related phenomenon, as do the networks of light-skinned, cousin-marrying families that dot the eastern United States, such as the Wessorts of Maryland. Some Wessorts (pronounced "WEE-sorts") have now sought to redefine themselves—or, as they see it, *recover* their identity—as Piscataway or Piscatawa Indians. Though they are of partly African ancestry, these domestic populations are often rancorously divided over the legitimacy of marrying people whom they consider "Black." Of late, it has become particularly profitable and plausible for such populations to claim the treaty rights that they believe had once been accorded to, and then taken away from, their Native American ancestors as a result of their conflation with Black people.

I call all of these African- or partly African-descended immigrant or native populations "black" with a lowercase *b*, though some members of these groups deny that they have any African ancestry. For me, the description of them as "black" with a lowercase *b* simply indicates that their complexions, their features, and the social affiliations of their family members tempt many observers to assume that they are of partly African ancestry, whether or not they do. In the post–civil rights and post-Reaganite era, these apparently mixed-race native ethnics in many ways face the same terrible dilemma that they faced in the post–Civil War and Jim Crow eras—to join forces culturally and socially with others who suffer oppression and the exclusionary stigma of past enslavement or to assert ethnoracial distinction and exemption from that hereditary stigma. The difficulty is that *most* Black people, or African Americans, have non-African ancestors as well. It is therefore difficult for the claimants to exemption from anti-Black racism to assert their exemption purely on racial grounds.

Amid the debate that their claim of difference has generated, the scientific language of an outdated physical anthropology remains available, but the university has more often subsidized a proliferation of "culture" talk and demanded—with varying success—a recasting of the ethical grounds of the earlier anthropometric claims. Instead of claiming racial superiority to "Blacks," as they once did, these avowedly "mixed-race" populations increasingly limit their public talk to claims of being "culturally different" and therefore genealogically and spiritually distinct from African Americans. In other words, "We are different from, not necessarily better than, Black people." Yet their greater willingness to embrace their partly European ancestry than their partly African ancestry reveals a consciousness of a light-dark hierarchy (cf. Fanon [1952] 2008) and an effort to clarify their place of honor and rewards within it. A similar observation might be made of the numerous immigrant populations from Mexico, Central America, Brazil, and the Caribbean, where miscegenation, or *mestizaje*, is valorized, but the preferred trajectory is toward the "whitening" of families and of the national population.

University-inspired "culture" talk—originating, in this case, from a historically Black American university—has also subsidized new claims of dignity and worth by the most "African," and one of the most looked-down-upon, of African American populations: the Gullah/Geechees.

Thus, one major theme of this book is that many African-descended ethnic groups in the United States have adopted the parlance of "culture" to appeal for exemption from the racial stigma that is generally imposed upon African-descended people in the United States, and most of all upon dark, working-class Black Americans. This strategy is at the heart of US anthropology. Franz Boas highlighted the German Romantic concept of "cultures" and established the autonomy of "culture" from "race" in order to give a dignified explanation of why Native Americans, Africans, African Americans, and eastern and southern Europeans—all racially stigmatized populations—were not inferior to but just *impermanently* different from the dominant, culturally unmarked white Anglo-Saxon Protestants. Boasian "culture" dignified subordinated groups, but, ironically, the application of this term continued to index their racial otherness and a history of racial marginalization and political subordination.

Since World War II, anthropologists have been so busy debunking race as a biological reality that we have, by and large, neglected the study of that category's social *consequences* and *uses*. At the same time, other disciplines and the media have often adopted our signature concept—"culture"—as a euphemism for "races." I therefore chart a series of examples of how racial stigma and the desperation to escape it shape collective identity and its "cultural" indexes, highlighting how scholars and schools mediate that process.

However, the American anthropological idea of "cultures" is not the only idiom in which black ethnic populations assert their difference from African Americans. Some black ethnics invoke the vocabulary of British anthropological structural-functionalism—such as "matriliny"—to explain how they can have African ancestry without being Black. In the absence of demonstrable genealogical, phenotypical, or cultural difference, many members of such groups also say they had always felt a latent, invisible, or *spiritual* difference from African Americans. One woman of visibly African descent told me how she knew of the invisible but deeper racial and cultural essence within her: whenever she heard the beat of the Indian drums, she could "feel the blood *boil up* her arms."

Yet many Americans, including African Americans, are oblivious to such black ethnic diversity among them. When I explained to African American students at Howard University that my research concerned "black ethnic diversity in the United States," the plurality of these students responded with something like, "Oh, color? I could tell you something about *that*!" In other words, they were highly familiar with and could understand the need for a scholarly study on how *complexion* influences African Americans' interactions with each other and with non-Blacks. When, instead, I listed the actual populations whose experiences I intended to study, these African Americans typically said that, before entering Howard, they had never known that such non–African American populations existed. They thought all black people were the same, by which these students meant that all black people share the same fundamental collective identity and behavioral norms. In other words, they thought of all "black" people as "Black"—their shared relative density of melanin being a metonym for a shared sense of political and economic marginalization, a fundamentally shared worldview and lifeway and, consequently, a shared set of political interests.

I, too, was once oblivious to the diversity of ethnic self-understandings among people of African descent and the degree of affect behind them. For example, at Harvard College, between 1978 and 1982, I dated the daughter of Jamaican immigrants to New York, whom I thought of as simply African American, or Black, "just like me." Being from New York, she had an even more current sense than I of the dominant and cutting-edge trends in African American music, which was and is central to my conscious conception of Black identity. Only a decade and a half later, when I became interested in this topic, did I ask—with doubt in my voice—whether she had ever thought of herself as ethnically different from me. Instantly, she replied, "Hell, yeah!" If she had ever before given me a hint of her sense of difference, I had failed to notice. I experienced her adolescent tales about her family as reports on a New York variety of the African American experience, only circumstantially different from my Washingtonian variety. We listened ultimately to the same music, danced the same dances, and relished foods from all over the black and nonblack worlds. We both had surgeons for fathers and parents who didn't live together, though mine were divorced and hers had never married. However, just as powerfully as I had assumed we were the same, she had assumed that our being in love did not presuppose that we were, or even cause us to become, coethnics.

Both immigration and the highly visible economic diversification of Black America since the 1970s present empirical challenges to this collective "Black" identity. As Eugene Robinson (2010) points out, almost all people of African descent in the United States want to end racial discrimination, and almost all of us are Democrats. However, we are no longer unanimous in our economic interests. There is a correspondence between, on the one hand, prosperous Black people's efforts to guarantee elite status for our children and, on the other, our condemnation of the alleged behaviors of the quarter of the Black population that is left behind in poverty. Hence, I ultimately compare all of these black ethnic groups to a third and final social category—soi-disant "middle-class" African Americans, who face the same dilemma. Do we join forces with the poor or seek to define our virtues and therefore assert our rights and entitlements in contrast to theirs? Middle-class African Americans have long voted for the interests of our less-privileged racial fellows, partly because we sense the fragility of our distance from their condition (e.g., Dawson 1994). However, our child-rearing practices and daily performances at work involve a self-conscious distancing from white stereotypes about African Americans and from the working-class Black patterns of speech, dress, cuisine, music, bodily movement, and so forth that we think invite, and even justify, that stereotyping. This book is a study of how racial stigma—as a paradigmatic example of all stigma—shapes both ethnic and class identity.

I do not generally capitalize the term "white" because, in most US settings, I observe that most of the people so described think of their color as an unmarked noncategory. Hence, the term "southerner" typically suffices in the description of a white southerner, while such a description of an African-descended person would be perplexing if not modified by the term "Black." It is in this sense that whites are normally an "unmarked" category of southerners and of US Americans generally. And whereas "Black" is a common self-descriptor, white is used as a descriptor by nonwhites and social scientists more than by run-of-the-mill whites. Moreover, since the 1980s, there has been a trend among phenotypical "whites" toward self-description in ethnic terms, such as "Italian," "Irish," and "Jewish," and a deliberate avoidance of the term "white" because of its connotations of unearned privilege (Alba 1990). Where I do capitalize "white," as in the borrowed phrase "traditionally White institutions" (TWIs), I mean to highlight the Black perspective that these institutions were not ethnoracially unmarked or neutral: they were once reserved for a group that had no right to regard itself as the unique paradigm of citizenship or as the monopolist of opportunity.

The Research Setting

The multiple sites that are the setting of this investigation flow, in some ways accidentally, from my biography. Yet they possess the symmetry of a carefully designed experiment. In 1978, during the summer after my senior year in high school, I scooped ice cream for visitors to the Mane Restaurant at the National Zoo in Washington, DC. One day, I was approached by a fortyish Black woman who alternately mopped the floor and worked the french-fry vat.

"You sound like a college boy. Where you go to school?" she asked.

"I'm not in college yet," I replied, "but in the fall I'll be going to Harvard."

"Oh, *Howard*?" she exclaimed. "That's a *good* school!"

This story illuminates the institutionalized history, the assumptions, and the information networks that continue to draw together an international array of black elites who may never before have thought of themselves as racially or ethnically alike. But segregation in the United States had directed them to the dark side of the US educational system. In the United States and in the anglophone Caribbean and Africa, many people admired or still admire a top-tier doctor, a dentist, an engineer, a government minister, or a national president who attended or taught at Howard University and, for that reason, chose to pursue their studies at what Howard alumni come to call the "Capstone of Negro Education" or simply the "Mecca" of Black higher education. Similarly, in his autobiography, Dr. Eric Williams ([1969] 2006), a historian who taught there before eventually becoming the prime minister of his native Trinidad and Tobago, called Howard "the Negro Oxford" (57). In terms of the quality and diversity of its students and the number of its graduate schools, Howard is the preeminent historically Black college or university (HBCU) in the United States and, indeed, the world. Just as important, these verbal representations articulate the spread of a consciousness of Black people as a transnational population aspiring to build a multiclass community that is different from but equal in worth to the dominant, transnational white community. In this hopeful project, Howard is a site of transnational pilgrimage—the global capital of hope and faith among the formerly enslaved, the colonized, and the stigmatized.

I spent the first half of my conscious life at Howard University and most of the second half at the Howard University of the *white* world—Harvard University, the educational Acropolis or New Jerusalem of white America and its sphere of influence. In recent years, I have researched and taught classes about black ethnic diversity in the United States at both institutions.

In these and other selective colleges and universities in the United States, the percentage of black students who are immigrants or the children of immigrants (27 percent) is roughly twice as high as it is in the general population of blacks in the United States (13 percent) (Massey et al. 2007, 245). Moreover, the more selective the institution, the more disproportionate the representation of black immigrants and their children becomes. This fact invites us to consider not only the nature of immigration and the motivations of black ethnics and their children but also the nature of universities in general as communities and cultural worlds.

The moratorium on official segregation in the 1970s, the white reaction against affirmative action in the 1980s, and the election of a Black president in 2008 have given rise to the widespread claim that racism is dead and that black people in the United States no longer have any legitimate grievance. The late German American sociologist Herbert Gans saw something different. According to him, Americans tend to regard their society as classless and have, over the generations, discarded the more conspicuous linguistic, sartorial, taste-based, and other nonracial markers of class status. Gans believed that, for these reasons, race is actually becoming *more* important—not less so—in people's daily judgments about which strangers to trust and which ones to fear (Gans 2005).

Yet, he added, racial classification is not static for every group. Whereas eastern and southern Europeans and Asians were once racialized, marked for subordination, and identified by what was seen as their nonwhite skin color, immigrant waves from such regions with high earnings and the ascent of these populations into the middle class have historically led whites to stop identifying them by skin color at all. The new "color blindness" touted by Reaganites may indeed significantly affect the life chances of assimilated southern European, Middle Eastern, South and East Asian, and Latino immigrants. By contrast, the bearers of sub-Saharan African skin color, hair, and features—whether African-descended natives or immigrants—are indelibly marked by race and actively denied many opportunities to rise from the bottom of the class-status hierarchy. Hence, uniquely for black people, observed Gans, little has changed since the seventeenth century.

African-descended populations in the United States share this experience of permanent constituent otherness with Roma in eastern Europe, untouchables in India, and, in other places, "indigenous" and "aboriginal" populations. Gans added that the marginalization of such groups may endure because it increases the resources available to others. I would add that the presence of a visible and despised other enhances the solidarity of the dominant group and the strength of its leaders, and it neutralizes the potential socially disruptive effects of economic inequality in the racially unmarked population (J. L. Matory 2002). Gans added that the lack of licit opportunity and the continual experience of being stepped over by initially low-status immigrants begins a vicious circle of resentment and criminality among constituent others— especially among males—and increases the majority's impression of a group's "unworthiness." I would add, further, that individual bad behavior always sticks to the general reputation of stigmatized groups more than it does to that of the dominant group.

Against this backdrop, *Stigma and Culture* examines two issues widely neglected in contemporary sociocultural anthropology— (1) the racial context of current forms of ethnogenesis, (2) the hierarchical context of all ethnogenesis, and (3) the sociocultural character of the American university. Ethnogenesis is the making of ethnic groups and the articulation of the "cultures" that substantiate their boundaries. As meeting places and training grounds for the elites of once-marginalized countries, regions, classes, races, religions, genders, and disability groups, universities canonize the historical legacy, the accomplishments, and the normative behavior—in a word, the "cultures" of the groups for which such elites wish to speak. And they do so with one eye toward the practices that distinguish their people from all others, thus justifying the distinctness and solidarity of their core constituency, and the other eye toward the approval of their culturally unmarked rulers and former rulers.

Here I summarize the three arguments that are detailed in the remainder of the introduction. They are the conceptual foundation of the book. The first argument is that, because race is ultimately a local, historically and culturally specific phenomenon, the context of much ethnogenesis today is the movement of people and capital across zones with diverse local logics of hereditary difference and worth. When I say "today," though, I do not mean to imply that this phenomenon started in the 1970s or the 1990s, as much theorizing about globalization and transnationalism would suggest (see J. L. Matory 2005a). W. E. B. Du Bois's canonical articulation in 1903 of the African American spirit followed a period of study in Germany. Gilberto Freyre's canonical 1933 treatise on Brazilian identity followed a period of study in the United States and was a retort to US racism. The literary and cultural nationalist movement known as "Négritude" was Léopold Sédar Senghor's reaction to the racism that he encountered in the late nineteenth and early twentieth centuries while studying and teaching in France. And Mahatma Gandhi's mid-twentieth-century Indian nationalism was rooted in the premise, developed during the period of his residence in South Africa, that Indians deserved better treatment than Africans. The rulers of empires that are expansive enough to generate a correlation between rank and visible phenotypical differences—as far back as the Islamic world of the eighth to the sixteenth century (Lewis 1990)—tend to naturalize that correlation. The ambitions spokespeople of colonized and subordinated groups have long found utility in "cultures" and "culture"-like concepts as a retort.

Hence there is a deeper historical horizon to self-consciously "cultural" ethnogenesis: imperialism and the spread of empire-centered ideas about who has the right to rule. A precursor to the "cultures" concept, Johann Gottfried von Herder's notion of a people's *Geist* was an answer to French imperialism in Europe. Much white creole nationalism in the Americas since the eighteenth century was a reaction to the racialization of the difference between European-born and American-born whites (Anderson [1983] 1991). Much east and southeast Asian nationalism at the start of the twentieth century entailed jockeying for superiority to Africans and likeness to Europeans in the stratified racial taxonomy that its partisans had learned from their Western tutors.

In sum, European imperial expansion, the Declaration of Independence, the civil rights movement, and the Reaganite counterrevolution have been watershed moments in the genesis of ethnic groups, including nations. And a jockeying for rank in translocal and often phenotype-based hierarchies is often the backdrop of such ethnogenesis. Moreover, chronological changes in local racial idioms and other logics of comparative moral worth have probably always shaped ethnogenesis. An equally powerful force shaping ethnogenesis is the movement of populations from one regime of racial hierarchy to another.

The current efflorescence or renaissance of black ethnic identities has many historical precedents, but it may be traced specifically to the effects of desegregation, the acceleration of transnational migration, and the Reaganite counterrevolution against the civil rights movement and social egalitarianism generally. I call this moment a "crisis" of identity in black America because it is a moment of increased dilemma and conflict, not because it is the first such moment or because daily dilemma and conflict have ever been absent from the process of ethnogenesis in other times and places. In common with most of the key moments of ethnogenesis since the nineteenth-century spread of racial science across the European-based empires, this crisis is a reaction to the risk of racial subordination.

My second argument reinforces the well-established anthropological idea that ethnicity is not primordial but contextual, oppositional, protean, and performative. I add to this anthropological commonplace the observation that stigma and the competition for honor and earnings are central to the context shaping the boundaries and cultural markers of ethnic groups. In other words, the setting of ethnogenesis, even in the absence of explicit "race," is and has probably always been hierarchical. However, I will argue that Boasian conceptions of "culture" have become an increasingly popular tool in the plea for collective exemption from last place. The values and behaviors that ethnic spokespeople canonize as definitions of group membership are selected and institutionalized less on the basis of an empirical analysis of antecedent behavioral difference between hereditary populations than on the basis of nostalgia, hope, and the effort to contrast their constituency from the constituent other of the host society. Like descriptions of Howard as "the Negro Oxford" and "the Mecca," culturalist self-representations simultaneously attempt to rescue nonnormative populations from the stigma of inferiority to the unmarked, dominant group and attempt to replace that inferiority with an assertion of parallelism, cosmetic difference but structural similarity, and moral equality with the unmarked, dominant group. Popular culture making is a strategic, political, and hierarchical project, in which diasporic and university populations play a major role. Such popular culture making is less a corruption than a fulfillment of twentieth-century professional anthropology.

Thus my third argument is that one of the most influential contexts of ethnogenesis is the university, which is itself a world of the stigmatized. In sum, it is the upwardly mobile elites of subordinate populations—the very people who have progressively, since the mid-nineteenth century, come to dominate university student populations—who possess the greatest motives to reify definitions of the collective self that remedy their people's stigma and who possess the greatest power to impose their ideas about the defining features of the groups they lead upon broader populations.

Argument 1: The Tension among Diverse Local Racial Regimes Propels Much of Today's Ethnogenesis

W. E. B. Du Bois declared the twentieth century the century of the "color line." In the twenty-first century, the worldwide role of race in ethnogenesis has generated popular debate but little scholarly theorization or investigation. One exception is the volume edited by Clarke and Thomas (2006), which documents the spread of North American ideas about race and African American models of political resistance. But they also document the increased emphasis on culture, as opposed to biology, in the assertion of racial identities. For example, hip-hop music has risen internationally as an idiom for the assertion of collective difference and political assertion. Clarke and Thomas also emphasize the deterritorialization of ethnicity—that is, the spread of ethnic groups far beyond their homelands and their operationalization in diasporic contexts.

It should be added that ethnicity and culture are often idioms of resistance to racialism and of intraracial competition as well. These idioms have been of service in a trend toward increasingly competitive relations among oppressed groups and toward a neoliberal abandonment of the ideal of equal opportunity. Hence, the twenty-first century may be the century of the "ethnic line." African independence in the 1960s began an ever-more ethnicized competition for control over state resources. Since the 1980s, Black and white America have also given increased priority to ethnicity, rather than race, in the articulation of collective belonging and deservingness of middle-class citizenship. And across the Americas, indigenous ethnic groups have, with increasing success, claimed collective rights and resources based upon their local cultural and ancestral differences from the post-Columbian invaders and from other Indian, or First Nations, groups. That is not to say, however, that race has become irrelevant. Ethnicity and its alleged "cultural" markers have been a means for the racially stigmatized to argue for collective exemption from the social disabilities that are the default for their race and for lower echelons of the racially privileged population to deny that they owe their current advantages to a history of racial favoritism.

Yet events in Europe also support the notion that we have entered the century of the ethnic line, when self-ethnicization is an increasingly prominent sequel to racialization. With increased immigration to Europe from Africa, Asia, and Latin America, the diversity within European nation-states is more and more often discussed in racial terms. Hence, even as many US Americans proclaim that we have entered a "postracial" age, much of Europe and Latin America is also growing *more* racialized in its discussions of intranational diversity.[7] However, since the 1990s, as the European Union has prevailed over its constituent nation-states, Europe's subnational ethnic groups, such as Catalans and Swabians, have increasingly advertised their unique cultural qualifications for service to global capital. Nonetheless, even in Europe, dialect and other regional difference shade over into conceptions of permanent hereditary difference and hierarchy, resulting in intermittent genocides. The Balkan wars of the 1990s are only the most famous recent example.

Questions about the universality and the endurance of race are central to today's political and scholarly debates. In the United States, these debates are explicit at the points of encounter between black ethnics and nonethnic Black Americans. For example, perhaps the foremost question troubling Black studies departments that endeavor to accord equal importance to Africa and its various diasporas is this: Is race a universal phenomenon, as objective and as central as gender and class to the analysis of every society and situation?

Or is this US preoccupation only a mistaken and ethnocentric model of how phenotype affects social status everyplace else in the world?

I go back and forth on this question.

On the one hand, conventional wisdom has it that races are empirical units defined by sharp genetic and phenotypical distinctions. Europeans like Carl Linnaeus (1707–78) and Johann Blumenbach (1752–1840) divided the entire human population into three to five major races, which their nineteenth-century successors came to understand as something like large-scale, visually identifiable, and hereditary castes. Twentieth-century biologists long ago demonstrated that the genetic and phenotypical differences among populations are neither sharp nor coterminous enough to make such "races" scientifically credible groupings. Nonetheless, everywhere in the world, people are still treated differently according to others' interpretations of how they look and how their ancestors are presumed to have looked. On this question most scholars of African and African American studies would agree.

Balibar and Wallerstein's *Race, Nation, Class* (1991) directly addresses the role of race, which has, unfortunately, tended to be neglected in the discussion of globalization ever since. The authors argue that, in a world still deeply influenced by European imperialism, "races" are really class positions in the global division of labor. If Europeans are the global upper class, Asians and Latin Americans are its middle class, and Africans and Native Americans are its perennial proletariat and lumpen. A range of phenomena might seem to support Balibar and Wallerstein's phenomenology of race.

However, in the end, this analysis strikes me as too positivist. Omi and Winant (1994) rightly warn us not to reduce "race" to "class." "Race" derives its power to influence human behavior not from its likeness to some supposedly objective roles in the global system of production but from the culture-specific meanings that actors apply to creatively explaining and acting on social difference. Moreover, racial identity and identification appear to outlast and, indeed, to be fortified by Black Americans' entry into the middle class. Blacks who interact with whites daily have more occasions to think about their race, and, as Beverly Daniel Tatum (2003) points out, whites have a far harder time fairly evaluating the credentials of a Black job candidate who ranks near them in qualifications and pay grade than a Black candidate for a position far lower than that of the white evaluators. In many, if not most, whites, Black upward mobility creates cognitive dissonance and provokes competitive feelings and behavior that fortify the social reality of "race."

Moreover, racial classification is subject to diverse perspectives. So the ethnographer must ask: "From whose point of view are races constructed as they are, and what is their analytic worth if they do not correspond with how the populations that are externally described as races think about themselves?" For example, how do the categories "white," "black," "Asian," "Hispanic," and "Native American" map onto the experience and conduct of the black-skinned Sahelians and East African Swahili people who consider themselves "white" on account of their reported descent from the Prophet, not to mention the Syrians and Lebanese who call themselves "white," less in comparison to Europeans than in contrast to Gulf Arabs? How do these Wallersteinian global classes map onto the experience of megapowerful or megarich black people—such as President Barack Obama, American Express CEO Kenneth Chenault, and entertainment mogul Oprah Winfrey—or onto the lives of chronically unemployed Appalachian whites whose lives are, with increasing frequency, washed away by floods of toxic chemicals? And how does "race" explain the extraordinary efficiency with which Yoruba women move root crops from distant farms and across a ragged road system to feed Nigeria's megacities (Guyer 1997)?

So what is universal about the meaning and importance of race, and what is local? In the wake of European imperialism and the massively profitable role of the African slave trade in its unfolding, there are widespread patterns in the mobilization of the European- and US-style racial discourse across the planet. Blackness was long the defining index of inherent disability in the US political economy, as well as the foil in the efforts of many southern European, Asian, and Latin American nations to define themselves as modern. For example, southern European nations have long contended with the dictum that "African begins south of the Alps (or the Pyrenées)," a phrase that highlights the stigma shaping their relations with their northern neighbors. In the nineteenth century, Jews and other European minorities were called "blacks" and "negroes" (Gilman 1993). The northern European identification of contemporary Greeks with the Middle East bears similar ideological effects (Herzfeld 1989). Overlapping nineteenth- and twentieth-century movements—from Brazil and Argentina to Cuba—aimed to whiten their countries through eugenics and the excoriation of both African "blood" and African religions (Helg 1990; Palmié 2002; Ortiz [1906] 1973; Rodrigues [1905] 1945).

Nineteenth-century Asian modernizers took comfort in the idea that, even if they were inferior to their European masters and tutors, at least the science of those tutors declared them superior to the Africans (Dikötter 1997). In the late twentieth century, China supported southern Africans' struggle against the predations of white minority rulers and invited students from allied African nations to study in China. However, those students were frequently harassed by male Chinese students, who resented the government's generosity

INTRODUCTION 19

toward these foreigners, as well as their attractiveness to Chinese women. A little-known fact is that the 1989 prodemocracy protests at Tiananmen Square were rooted in some of the largest and most violent anti-African protests that had taken place in China up until then (e.g., Kristoff 1989). As China seeks to profit from Africa's natural resources, one worries about how local prejudices and European-inspired racism will influence this trade partnership. Several years ago, on a flight from Lagos to London, a fellow passenger from India sought my agreement as he lamented the "terrible poverty in Africa." The notion of ethnological schadenfreude helps me to understand the long-running psychology by which he managed to overlook the nearly unthinkable scale of poverty and malnutrition in his own country. The number of Indians living in misery dwarfs the population of Africa itself.

Only briefly have the media mentioned the historical role of the racist nineteenth-century "Hamitic hypothesis" of the European colonialists and administrators in hardening Tutsi chauvinism and Hutu rage in East Africa's interlacustrine region. This hypothesis constructed aristocratic groups like the Tutsis as "alien races" that had migrated into Africa, introducing civilization from elsewhere. A succession of civil wars in Sudan, where cultural chauvinism and racism have long swirled together, has pitted Arab-identified and African-identified populations against one another in a struggle for dignity and resources. Scholars and journalists debate whether the Janjaweed marauders of Darfur are objectively (read "racially") Arabs or not (Jok 2004). However, despite popular denials of racism throughout the Arab world, these events are part of a pattern. For example, southern and Darfuri Sudanese refugees in Cairo have been subject to continual taunting by their Egyptian Arab hosts. Reports Eve Troutt Powell, "The most painful epithet was 'abid', the Arabic word for 'slave,' a word intended for darker-skinned people of African descent" (Powell 2012, 5). What Frederick Douglass called "the old things of slavery" still haunt the relationship not only between Egypt and Sudan specifically, as Powell points out, but also between the Middle East and Africa generally. In 2011, the quickness of Muammar Qaddafi's opponents to slaughter African migrant workers because some African migrants had served as mercenaries for Qaddafi invites legitimate suspicion of racism. The exploitation and conflicts at the borders of the world's most stigmatized continent with the North African, Middle Eastern, and Asian worlds cannot all be blamed on European racism. However, the combination of ideologies arising from Islamic and European slavery regimes clearly continues to endanger Africans. The assumption of the speaker's superiority to sub-Saharan Africans may be a touchstone of racism all over the world.

With equal and opposite force, subordinate nations, ethnic groups, and generations validate their resistance to domination through the idiom of Blackness. Just as the phenotypically white Boston Tea Partiers of 1773 donned American Indian dress and cosmetics to dramatize their (white) creole anticolonialism, so do armies of non-Black teenagers—from France and Germany to Japan—dramatize their resistance by wearing FUBU ("For Us By Us") clothing, performing hip-hop dance and music, and calling each other "niggaz" (e.g., Treuer 2012; Tate 2003). Greg Tate argues that the black slave was American capitalism's first fetish—both subhuman and superhuman, loathed but continually imitated, a symbol of hipness, virility, and fascinating danger. Whites have long sought to appropriate Black characteristics and styles and to introject these qualities through mimesis, while hiding their Black origins. Tate concludes that whites want from Blacks "everything but the burden." A whole range of racial, ethnic, gender, sexual-orientation, age-based, and disability-based minority groups in the United States have modeled their own struggles for equal opportunity on the African American civil rights and Black Power movements. Indeed, the ravenous appropriation of "Black" style by young, middle-class white men in recent decades appears to address their own alienation amid shifts in the gendered distribution of opportunity and the wage decline affecting most Americans, including middle-class white men.

Western and specifically Anglo-American conceptions of race have been globally influential, and they provide a template for legitimate questions about how hierarchies of opportunity and exploitation are structured and rationalized outside of the West. However, across nations, across regions within the same country, and across classes in the same country, conceptions of the relationship between phenotype and social status still vary widely and radically. Across the cultures of Africa and the African diaspora, people do not all think in the same sociosomatic categories. Hence, when I refer cross-culturally to "race" as an analytic category, I mean a range of local idioms inspired historically by the efforts of *rival* translocal empires to classify the world's population phenotypically, as well as the diverse assertions in which people employ these rival idioms—sometimes with literal and sometimes with metaphorical intent.

The towering peculiarity of the US "race" concept can be either celebrated or criticized with the following joke.

"What do you call a Black man in a three-piece suit?"

"Nigger."

Placed in a global perspective, the dominant binary categories and the very rigidity of Anglo–North American conceptions of "race" are unique. Hence, this riddle is virtually untranslatable into the languages of West Africa and the circum-Caribbean. For example, the meaning of "Black" in US English is as culture-specific as is the meaning of a three-piece suit. In the United States, this attire suggests the male wearer's employment as an executive and/or his conformity to the demands of a formal occasion. That this attire fails to demonstrate a Black wearer's deservingness of respect demonstrates that not even the most proper behavior can rescue a Black man from his inferior status and that his wearing such a suit is ironic: that he could truly occupy a social station or employment status deserving of his interlocutors' respect is inconceivable in this conceptual universe. In sum, Black people do not vary in social status or behavior. But why?

Most biologists agree that the commonplace division of humanity into three to five discrete "races" is mythological. Human phenotypical characteristics—such as skin color, eye color, hair texture, lip shape, buttock size, blood type, and hereditary disease—do vary in their frequencies from one continent or region to another, but these traits do not always covary. Therefore, the division of humanity into races depends upon an arbitrary stipulation about which somatic variations matter and which do not matter for the purposes of the observer. Moreover, the massive coming together of Native Americans, Africans, and Europeans over the past five hundred years has resulted in a rapid remixing of more accustomed but already thoroughly impure gene pools. Even this remixing has been interpreted differently in different societies.

However, the race concept is not simply bad science (pace Boas 1940; Lewontin 1972; Gould 1981) but a performance on one or another empirically perceived "terrain" (Fields 1990), a terrain reshaped over time by successive struggles for honor and dominance in a changing population. Everyone living in the British North American colonies or the United States has had to traverse such a terrain knowledgeably as a condition of personal and familial survival. And for all its historical changes, the bedrock of that terrain has been the unique exclusion of Blacks from the hope of job opportunities, legal protections, political freedoms, and guarantees of personal dignity that every non-Black person has come to expect as a right. Where every other "race" progressed onto an even playing field before Blacks and Blacks could not even get in line, it followed that Blacks were nonnormative people and that we might not be people at all. We were, instead, the paradigm case of unworthiness. This collective paradigm seems impervious to even the mountainous accumulation of accomplishments and contributions by individual Black people.

Not all of the populations in the world that conform to Anglo–North American definitions of "Blackness" enjoy or suffer the same fate everywhere in the world. For example, social scientists vigorously debate whether people of African descent suffer the same kind and degree of material deprivation across the former slaveholding countries of the Americas. Latin Americans and Latin Americanists like Loïc Wacquant and Peter Fry shout "Down with Imperialism!" when North American and North American–influenced scholars (such as Michael Hanchard and Carlos Hasenbalg and his colleagues at Cândido Mendes University) declare that, despite Freyrean claims of "racial democracy" and their "prejudice of having no prejudice at all," Brazilians and Puerto Ricans are just as egregiously racist as Anglo–North Americans and that roughly the same racially coded explanations of social inequality apply to Latin America as to the United States.

Statistically demonstrable similarities among racial regimes in the Western Hemisphere notwithstanding, the reigning interpretations of social experience and the reigning symbolic idioms of comprehensible and persuasive collective social action still clearly vary from one American society to another (see Dzidzienyo and Oboler 2005). For example, Black and white Anglo-Americans are, cross-culturally speaking, unusual in our conviction that a person with even a small proportion of socially recognized African ancestry is "Black." I call this system "binary hypodescent" because, in most of the United States, there are effectively two races (hence "binary")—an unmarked and higher non-Black race and a marked, lower "Black" race—and because children born to parents of different races inherit the identity of the parent with the lower racial status (hence "hypodescent"). Non-Black immigrants to the United States suffer a temporary ambiguity in their racial status. If they avoid marrying Black people and either arrive middle-class or rise into the US middle class, they tend to join the higher-status, unmarked race. Under these conditions, the tradition of white racial endogamy ceases to affect their marital options, such that their children with white partners generally not only remain racially unmarked but become white (Gans 2005).

In some US populations, as well as much of Latin America and Africa, the term "black" and its counterparts in the languages of those regions are usually descriptions of a particular set of *physical characteristics*, of which very dark skin is usually the most important. Tightly curled hair is often equally important, if not more so. I employ the lowercase "black" to denote this meaning—of bearing the physical appearance or presumption of predominantly sub-Saharan African ancestry. On the other hand, in our descriptions of race, mainstream North Americans tend to assume that any degree of African ancestry, independently of one's phenotype, makes a person "Black." In the United States, the "one-drop rule" of hypodescent stipulates that a person can have pale skin, limp hair, blue eyes, thin lips, and a flat bottom and *still* belong to a biological, social, and political category, the term for which, in English, is often capitalized—like a nationality or an ethnonym—as "Black." (Note the contrast to Spanish, French, and Portuguese orthographic conventions, whereby the adjectival form of nationalities and ethnic groups is not capitalized. The capitalization of the US-origin terms "Latino" and "Latina" is thus an orthographic and conceptual hybridization.) In English, the capitalized "Black" tends to suggest that all people of African descent—no matter how few of their ancestors came from Africa in recent centuries—share preeminently important similarities of biology, culture, and political interest, akin to a nationality. And this capitalization, like many other ethnonational self-declarations, stipulates the nearly sacred collective dignity of such a nationality or peoplehood. In that spirit, Black students protesting at the *Harvard Crimson* demanded this capital letter a few years before I became an editor there in 1981. I recall that moment as I decide, in any given instance, on the emic cultural appropriateness of capitalization. "Black" (with the *b* capitalized) essentially refers to a US-based emic identity category that assumes the "one-drop rule" and understands all "black" people to share as set of values, corporate interests, and mutual responsibilities.

I employ the above orthographic distinction between "black" and "Black" for several additional reasons. First, it acknowledges the interaction of competing mythologies about race at the sites of my research. Second, it dramatizes the fact that similar words in the setting of Howard and its alumni networks can convey radically different assumptions, which we will overlook unless we pay careful attention. And, finally, my orthographic choice denaturalizes both usages—blackness and Blackness. They are semiotic, not biological, phenomena.

Even the most basic terms of the conversation about "race" vary from one place or one speaker to another. In Latin America, the closest cognates of the English term "race"—for example, *raza* (Spanish) and *raça* (Portuguese)—are seldom used for the same phenomena as in the anglophone United States. For example, in Mexico and Brazil, one can call policemen collectively a *raza* or *raça*. In Brazil, the preferred term for nongendered, hereditary phenotypical variation is more often "color" (*cor*), a term that, in turn, fails to capture the complex ideology behind what US Americans typically call "race." For example, in the United States there are blond, blue-eyed people of the Black "race," and bittersweet chocolate–colored Tamils are not called "Black." "Race" in the United States is not coterminous with the Latin American Spanish term *color* and Portuguese term *cor*. (I am not sure how a Tamil's *color* is described in Brazil or Mexico.)

Hartigan (2013) further discusses the many ways in which US "race" and

Mexican *raza* differ. In both societies discrimination on the basis of phenotype exists. However, the cultural common sense of each place denies and acknowledges phenotype in different ways. In both countries, complexion corresponds with average levels of education and with income. In Mexico, though, it is indigenous people who, as that country's constituent other, anchor the phenotypical light-dark hierarchy. And, in both countries, cultural characteristics (such as language, eating habits, and residence) affect a person's social classification and status assignment. Yet in Mexico, *raza* is also a term of national unity, alluding to Mexican nationalist José Vasconcelos's concept that Mexicans are a new "cosmic race," produced by the intermarriage of Spaniards, indigenous Mexicans, and Africans (Vasconcelos 1925), though the African constituent tends to be forgotten by Mexican Americans. *Raza* thus alludes to an ideology, dominant everywhere in Latin America but the southern cone, that valorizes miscegenation and prioritizes "culture" (*cultura*) over phenotype and ancestry in the classification of any given person. Hence, in Mexican Spanish, *raza* can refer to all of the people from a given place or region or to a cohort of friends. By contrast, the Anglo-US term "race" implies a taxonomy of biologically separate and fixed types, in which mixed-race people, especially those with African ancestry, tend to be assigned to the lower-status "race," regardless of their learned behaviors, place of birth, profession, or circle of friends.

In most of the Spanish- and Portuguese-speaking circum-Caribbean, the terms for people of various "colors" are highly idiomatic descriptions that identify specific conjunctions of skin color, hair texture, and facial features. For example, in Brazil, a *cabo verde* (literally, a "Cape Verde") is a person with dark skin, limp hair, and European-associated nose shape. And a *sarará* (Brazil) or a *jabao* (Cuba) is someone with beige skin and fleece-like hair.

In much of the anglophone, francophone, and Creole-speaking Caribbean (including nineteenth-century South Carolina and southern Louisiana), a tripartite, or ternary, set of sociosomatic categories is in use. For example, Jamaicans distinguish "blacks," "browns" (or mulattoes), and "whites." A Jamaican brown, or mulatto, is considered as different from a black person as from a white person. Guyana and Trinidad feature a large additional category of South Asian–origin people, and Jamaica has a category of Chinese-descended people who are also recognized as distinct. In Jamaica, "one drop" of Chinese ancestry seems to qualify as Chinese many people who, to me, look unambiguously black. And in Trinidad, a person of combined African and Indian descent—a *dougla*—is recognized as belonging to a further distinct category. In hardly any of these places would President Barack Obama, for example, be considered "black."

Like our Anglo-US system, all of these racial classification systems associate phenotypical diversity with a moral, aesthetic, and social hierarchy—but not the *same* hierarchy under all circumstances. A less African appearance (or, in Mexico, a less "Indian" appearance) is usually regarded as more beautiful and tends to be associated with higher moral status, greater economic privilege, and more access to the levers of political power. However, a dictum widespread in the circum-Caribbean—and strange to most US Americans—is that "money whitens." That is, in Brazil, for example, a wealthy or high-status black (i.e., a phenotypical *preto* or *negro*) person is recognized as a mulatto (*mulato*)—or *moreno* (brown, brunette or swarthy person)—while a wealthy or high-status mulatto is called "white" (*branco*). Conversely, the whiteness of a poor white-skinned person is qualified or mitigated, as in the Brazilian expressions *branco da terra* ("earthy or native white") and *branco da Bahia* ("white from [or relative to the somatic norms of] the [heavily black-populated] state of Bahia"). Consequently, a Brazilian admirer once called me a *moreno claro* (a light brunette), evidently because my education, my relative wealth, and his affection offset the socially degrading implications of my chocolate skin, my African features, and my full-bodied hair. No irony or humor was intended.

On the other hand, in these same Latin American systems, love and intimacy darken. For example, in Latin American Spanish and Portuguese, lovers commonly call each other "my black person" (e.g., *minha nega* [Port. "my black woman"], *mi negro* [Sp. "my black man"]). Moreover, in Cuba and Brazil, the national "somatic norm image" (Hoetink 1967) is brown, so that calling a person "white" implies that he or she is foreign or somehow alien to the national community. And the female exemplars of the national aesthetic ideal are called *mulatas*, even when they are considerably lighter or, more often, darker than the typical phenotypes abstractly associated with that term. The term also implies their sexual availability. Also in contrast to the United States, these Latin American systems normalize sex between white men and dark women, sometimes classifying it as a patriotic contribution to the "whitening" of the nation. In the United States, the public discourse tends to represent dark women as unattractive and sex between the races as immoral.

Many relatively light-complexioned but African-descended people from the English-speaking Caribbean had been accustomed to thinking of their skin color, their Chinese ancestry, or their European ancestry as their most socially salient difference from—and source of superiority to—others in their social world. However, upon immigration to or transmigration through the United States between World War II and the 1980s, the Caribbean's disproportionately "mixed-race" class elites were shocked and estranged by the unique and overwhelming binarism of Jim Crow, the civil rights and Black Power movements, and affirmative action.

Despite overlapping vocabularies and a shared devaluation of dark skin and sub-Saharan African hair and facial features, the social classification systems of the Americas vary with respect to the moments and the ways in which they accord significance to both skin color and comportment. Moreover, these social classificatory systems change over time, partly because of US political influence in Latin America (various forms of US-inspired affirmative action are now practiced in Brazil, Ecuador, and Colombia) and because of the massive immigration of Latin Americans to the United States.

Since the Reaganite neoconservative backlash against affirmative action, the idea of remedying past and present discrimination against racial minorities has taken a backseat in college admissions to the idea that a "diverse" student body simply offers useful life lessons to each of the students. This inventive rationale for inclusion capitulates to the neoconservative premise that the long history of officially unequal access across these "diverse" groups has nothing to do with the current average differences among them and that those current differences are merely "cultural." African-descended immigrants still enter a terrain where the opportunities accorded to dark and light people are clearly different, as they are in the social terrains from which most dark immigrants had originated. But here in the United States, those immigrants are discouraged from talking or even joking about these realities, since the terms "race" and *color*, as well as the history of hierarchy, slavery, debt peonage, prison labor, lynching, unequally funded schools, extralegal expropriation of land, and unequal inheritance, are being judicially banished from consideration by policy makers and educators. The pregnant silences of so-called postracialism (in which the extreme wealth and power of certain individual Blacks is mistaken for proof that the gross inequality of assets and opportunities between the average white and the average Black is a fair reflection of everyone's individual merit and effort) are not worlds apart from the publicly polite racism of Brazil and the Caribbean. However, the racial disparities across the US terrain and the succession of discourses applied to it since the 1960s demand intellectual dexterity on the part of the immigrant who seeks upward mobility. The postracial logic of "culture" and "ethnicity" is an inviting option. A person who represents his or her identity in these terms gains the benefits of being "diverse" without making any obvious confession of racial inferiority and without offending those US American conservatives who would rather not hear about "race" at all.

People who cross the border between different national or postimperial racial regimes often face shocking social reclassifications according to the categories of the host society, and, as Hartigan (2013) points out, among Mexican immigrants to the United States, immigrants often play with, manipulate, or undermine the racial categories of the host country. Are Mexicans white, American Indian, other? Are they Chicanos, Mexican Americans, Hispanics, or Latinos? Are Italians Latinos? Are Argentines? Are African-descended immigrants from Latin America black or Latino? Many nonblack immigrants from Latin America manipulate these ambiguities strategically. However, like their West Indian and African counterparts, Afro-Latinos enjoy a far narrower range of options than do white-looking immigrants. Indeed, Afro-Latinos frequently face rejection by their fellow Latinos and by their country-of-origin-based ethnic groups (e.g., Hernández 2003), a rejection that is undoubtedly motivated by the collective wish of these groups to be seen as more similar to—and therefore more deserving of the same protections and opportunities as—white Americans.

But even dark immigrants make motivated choices that they think make a difference. The light-skinned and freckled son of a dark Jamaican immigrant to Queens, New York, told me what happened when his friends asked him if his family was Black. He asked his mother, and she replied, "I'm Jamaican, not Black." He explains that she came from an elite Jamaican background and refused to see herself as one of the oppressed. But she still takes pride in being the third "brown-skinned person" to be admitted to an elite New York tennis club to which even African American tennis champion Althea Gibson had earlier been denied admission.

Such cross-border adjustments of social perception and self-conception have political and economic implications, but not political and economic ones alone. Transit across borders between African or Caribbean and Anglo-American terrains is often deeply painful and emotionally fraught. For example, dark Afro-Latin Americans face a difficult choice when they come to the United States and realize that, in the eyes of the natives, as one Afro–Puerto Rican woman tells it, "*Mi color me define más que mi cultura*" (My color defines me more than does my culture) (Jorge 1979; see also Hernández 2003).

In another semantic divergence between the meanings we attribute to the most basically cognate terms, Latin Americans tend to use the word *cultura* less for "culture" in the anthropological sense of "conventional and collective way of life" than for "cultivation" or "degree of educational and social refinement." In 2014, in the predominantly Afro-Cuban state of Santiago de Cuba, I was told the story of a professional woman who terribly resents being called *jabá* (the feminine form of *jabao*, a person of African hair texture and/or facial features but light skin color). She reportedly demanded to be called *blanca* ("white") because of her *cultura*. In her mind, she is not *jabá*, much less *negra* ("black"), because she did not grow up with the religion or music that she attributes to lower-status blacks. The white raconteur and the light *mulato* driver fully understood the local logic of her assertion, but the white raconteur reported that he and a black colleague enjoy the woman's discomfort when they call her *jabá*.

Afro-Latin American women in particular have *experienced* the sting of both economic and aesthetic discrimination in their home countries and communities, as when their otherwise loving parents and grandparents curse their hard-to-comb hair. "Damn this hair!" (*¡Maldito sea este pelo!*), the grandmother exclaims, while painfully yanking the hair and scraping the girl's scalp with tines and bristles. Personal acquaintance and friendship can sometimes interrupt this lifelong battering of Afro-Latinas' self-esteem. So as long as they stay in their familiar Dominican, Cuban, or Puerto Rican neighborhoods, men still "throw flowers" (*echarles las flores*, or *piropos*), but these ritual compliments stop when the women enter other Latino or white neighborhoods or middle- and upper-class US venues, such as university campuses, where such compliments are normally forbidden as a form of sexual harassment. Latinas with Negroid features say that, among Latino strangers, they are often told, "You don't *look* . . . [Puerto Rican, Cuban, or what have you]!" On the other hand, these women often report receiving compliments in African American neighborhoods, where there is at least a discourse—since the 1960s—in favor of being "black and proud," as well as a subpopulation that values dark skin and "natural" hair.

There are also native populations in the United States—such as Louisiana Creoles and Indians of partly or possibly African descent—whose movements between their native regions and the broader society are fraught with emotional dangers, cognitive confusion, and economic insecurity. Since the Civil War, Louisiana Creoles of color, Indians of partly African descent, and other "triracial isolates" in the United States have discouraged out-migration from their native regions and practiced cousin marriage in order to *avoid* the curse of falling onto the Black side of the separate and unequal racial binary. The lightest people among these groups could "pass for white" or for some non-US-origin ethnicity. Ironically, through their marital and residential choices, the light-skinned passers had to leave behind families that cherished them above all others, and these "little races," in turn, lost their most cherished members. The group members who are least able to pass are often despised or demeaned by their lighter-skinned kin. Indeed, some such families split in half, with the palest relatives no longer wishing to associate with their slightly darker-skinned kin at all. If the pale ones could not pass for white, at least they could thereby reduce the risk of being regarded as Black.

Ironically, for members of these domestic "little races," as well as most of the Cape Verdean Americans of New England, upward mobility usually required outward mobility and a "confession" of their Blackness. If, in pursuit of a better job, a man or woman migrated to a region where his or her peculiar triracial isolate was unknown, he or she had to work a Negro job; live in a Negro neighborhood; go to a Negro barber or hairdresser; ride in the Negro part of the bus, trolley, or train; keep an eye out for a Negro bathroom; and send the children to Negro schools—at least if he or she was not pale enough to pass for white and bold enough to sever ties with his or her birth family more or less permanently.

At home and in faraway states, Negro schools and universities often were, for most of these partly black Indians and triracial isolates, the most reliable route to upward economic mobility. The home states of these "little races" might have had one or more elementary schools for each of these races but not a high school or a college and definitely not a medical school. If you wanted to move up educationally, you had to either run the family-destroying and potentially embarrassing risk of "passing for white" or concede that you were "Negro" by attending a Negro high school or an HBCU.

To casual readers, these phenomena may seem an artifact of the Jim Crow past, long superseded by desegregation in the 1960s and 1970s. But these stories are often told about the present, partly because the family splits remain. These splits are alive on a large scale in various tribal membership decisions by, for example, the Connecticut Pequots, the New Jersey and Delaware Nanticokes, the Maryland Piscataways and Piscatawas, and, in North Carolina, the Haliwa and Occaneechi Bands of the Saponi Nation. And they are evident in the individual life-changing decisions that living or recently dead people have made to "pass," with no small consequences for their children. In pursuit of a life as "a writer, rather than a black writer," *New York Times* literary critic and editor Anatole Broyard, a child of two Louisiana Creoles of color, abandoned a dark wife and his one darker-skinned sister. He thereby managed to keep his race a secret from his two children with a white woman until just ten days before his death in 1990 (Gates 1997).

Most circum-Caribbean racial environments in the twenty-first century sit uncomfortably between US American binary hypodescent and the historically ternary or spectrum-based logic more familiar in the greater Caribbean. No such environment, however, sits more uncomfortably than New Orleans and its diaspora. In their words and deeds, New Orleans Creoles of color—like the Indians and the "little races" of the eastern United States—are continually debating among themselves and with their neighbors about whether they are a third sociocultural category in a tripartite system or just one culturally and politically meaningless shade struggling for advantage at the disadvantaged end of a binary system. The tension between these models of collective identity is manifest as often in strategic silence or impression management as in angry diatribes, family splits, and self-aggrandizing denunciations of other oppressed individuals or populations. Sometimes, this tension generates great leaders in the struggle against racism, such as West Indian Marcus Garvey and New Orleans Creole A. P. Tureaud (see also W. James 1998). But there remains a deep structural ambivalence. Books, scholars, and schools have been central to the resolution of the emotional dangers, cognitive confusion, and economic insecurity intrinsic to the situation of black ethnics, especially the Creoles.

Like many young nonethnic African Americans today (particularly those in the first generation of their families to attend college), upwardly mobile members of the "triracial isolates" often experience upward mobility as an abandonment or betrayal of their dearly loved home communities. However, a further force that long kept these "little races" isolated was the stigma of cousin marriage. Yet within the universities that seek their uplift and the allied medical institutions that address the insalubrious consequences of inmarriage, members of the "little races" could at least trust that the African part of their ancestry would not disqualify them as human beings. Freedmen's Hospital, where I was born, and its successor, Howard University Hospital, welcomed them, and physicians there report having helped them considerably.

Then there are the Gullah/Geechees of the southeastern Atlantic coast, who originate from one of the oldest sites of tripartite racial classification in the United States. Charleston, South Carolina, and its surrounds were once home to separate communities—and even graveyards—of "blacks," "browns," and "whites." The peculiar economic conditions of the Gullah/Geechees' interaction with neighbors near and far have inspired a very different response to anti-Black and anti-African racism: an early Afrocentric movement that is gradually turning their most extreme stigma into a source of profit and pride. A Howard University scholar spearheaded their effort to show that their linguistic peculiarities constitute a Boasian "culture" rather than a deficiency. Later scholars have helped them to claim a history of great contributions to the wealth of the South and of technological superiority to their supposed racial masters. In some ways, this strategy anticipates the choice of many present-day ethnic groups to redress their marginalization by emphasizing their cultural superiority to other Americans—Black and white.

In Nigeria, by contrast to the circum-Caribbean, "black" skin carries few, if any, moral implications. Rarely does it attract any normative aesthetic judgment, either. And, except among the best-traveled Nigerians or Ghanaians, the capitalized term "Black" corresponds to no social or moral category at all. While some West Africans use skin-bleaching creams, the color of a Nigerian's skin, for example, is not assumed to correlate with his or her social status, earnings, wealth, access to state power, moral worth, political affiliation, ability to dance, sexual talents, spiritual gifts, intelligence, emotional self-awareness, degree of athleticism, or hipness.

Therefore, I do not wish to beg the question of the "blackness"—much less the "Blackness"—of any of the populations discussed here: I simply assume that some of their American interlocutors credit these populations with some African ancestry, even if some members of that population disagree. As my son, Adu, and I attended a powwow of the Occaneechi-Saponi people in Hillsborough, North Carolina, I was surrounded in a dark grove by chocolate-, cinnamon-, graham- and pound-cake-colored women with a range of hair textures. Wearing their deerskin dresses and beaded hairpins, they closed in on me and asked threateningly if I intended to call them "black Indians," as had *Black Indians* (1984) author William Loren Katz. They were not black, they told me; they were Indian.

And there are further reasons not to assume that any such population or any given member thereof is "black" or "Black"—diachronic change and strategic situationality. For example, based upon a survey of selective colleges and universities in the United States, including Howard, Massey et al. (2007) show that, among students who have at some point in the admissions process identified themselves as "Black," immigrants and their children are, once interviewed, considerably less likely than their native-born counterparts to call themselves "Black" or "black" at all, and they are significantly more likely than nonimmigrants and their children to call themselves "other." This discrepancy and diachronic divergence in self-reported racial identity occur despite the fact that the native and immigrant college students in the sample were of similar average socioeconomic status and, according to the interviewers' visual assessment, similar average complexion. These situational shifts in self-concept and self-presentation deserve sympathetic recognition and thoughtful analysis. They illuminate not just the social psychology of mobile populations and how they perceive the structure of opportunity in their lives but also a dynamic feature of collective identity generally that is too often overlooked in objectivist surveys of race and ethnic identity.

In sum, long before I began this project, I had known consciously that different peoples think very differently about what mainstream US Americans call "race." But even the ethnographer's native ideology dies hard. I started out with a hypothesis that I quickly unlearned at Howard. I initially hypothesized that students and faculty originating from countries and regions that conceptualize racial and complexion diversity in ways other than binary hypodescent would, at Howard, embrace the notion that all people of African descent belong to the same political, marital, and extended ethnocultural category. I thought that Howard—and immigration to the United States generally—would smooth out all that diversity of racial self-identification.

I understood that different aspects of one's identity are salient at different times of the day or year. However, I had not fully recognized the degree of cognitive, emotional, and social dissonance that continues to trouble many people who are classified as Black in the United States and also want to be accorded honor and opportunity. I had grown up Black and upper-middle class, so I knew that Blackness was not an economic class distinct from the economic class occupied by my white peers, but black ethnics made me aware that Wallerstein's argument—that race is reducible to core-periphery class relations—is not merely academic; it reflects the tendency of the US academy, the US news industry, and the general population to equate Blackness with poverty and criminality and whiteness with the inevitable middle- and upper-class fulfillment of what is called "the American Dream." Wallerstein's interlocutor Balibar presents a picture truer to the situation that I describe here, in which the fight against Nazism has defanged literal racism, but immigration—and I would add, desegregation—have placed more peoples in face-to-face, toe-to-toe competition (Balibar and Wallerstein 1991). Those previously advantaged by long-distance imperialism and segregation are now in a position to argue only that primordial and indelible "cultural" differences justify keeping the previously subordinate other out of the metropolitan country and out of the competition (e.g., Huntington 1997).

Hence, black ethnics and I both had two potential responses to this new and allegedly "color-blind" logic of hereditary social stratification. We could apply the concept of "culture" to establish the substance of a united front in African-descended people's resistance to domination by our would-be rulers, or we could use it to establish our respective subgroups' unique and individual "cultural" worthiness of white approval and admission to the game.

The racial pseudoscience of the West has spread far amid imperialism, as has the science of "culture," at the hands of imperialism's loyal opposition—the anthropologists. Universities and the mass media have disseminated, in these terms, both a popular logic of oppression and a popular logic of resistance, even telecasting the African American social revolution of the 1950s and 1960s and cybercasting hip-hop across the planet. However, the three to five races that Wallerstein imagined as a Google Earth snapshot of the global class order form not a positivist map or portrait but an idiom—points of reference often borrowed by one faction or another in local debates over collective identity and over the political and economic strategies served by tethering the group's aspirations to one racial point of reference or another.

These processes are global and local, collective and individual. For example, in 1992, with the election of a more Europhile president, the "mixed-race" Republic of Cape Verde changed its flag from the characteristically African and African American red, black, yellow, and green themes to the characteristically European red, white, and blue theme.[8] Tethering one's nation, ethnic group, or region to one racial reference point or another has political and economic implications. For example, these racially coded flag themes dramatize alliances and declare conformity or resistance to existing global hierarchies. The change in the Cape Verdean flag suggests a symbolic shift of sides and an invitation to European investment.

Some racial self-representations are the elective performances of *individuals*, rather than of nations and ethnic groups, as when light-skinned African Americans wear dreadlocks or Afros in a way that disambiguates them. It seems to me that, among scholars of African American studies, light-skinned people are especially prone to do so. Some young white males appear to wear dreadlocks in order to signal their withdrawal—at least temporarily—from the careerist rat race. And although he grew up light-skinned and far away from African Americans, candidate and then President Obama publicly walks with a bop and a lean, talks with a Black liturgical cadence, and often displays himself playing basketball—in recent times a Black-dominated sport—with a group of Black and white male friends (see Alim and Smitherman 2012). Indeed, in his verbal code-switching and his alternation among patronizing "tough talk" to Black America (e.g., his June 2008 lambasting of absent Black fathers), silence about race, and outbursts against racism (e.g., his critique of the policeman who, in 2009, arrested Harvard professor Henry Louis Gates Jr. in his Cambridge home) illustrates this dynamic of ambivalence or strategic dexterity. Thus, to one audience, President Obama reads as "Black," while to another audience he reads as "cool," a manner admired and emulated by generations of white American and European men bored with their own normalcy or mediocrity. It is also possible to read Obama's code-switching as a type of cosmopolitanism that characterizes elites, perhaps transhistorically and all over the world, perhaps today more than ever before (Khan 2012).

In most locales, it is a reliable bet that there is going to be some faction in the debate over the future of any given American social collective that favors a conventionally North American–style, racialist reading of its constituents' identity and fate, as well as some faction that asserts the worth of reading social sameness and difference in terms of a radically different set of points of reference—be it class, ethnicity, or cool. Hence, race should not be regarded as a universal index of identity or a global map distinguishing one continent from another. Rather, US-style racialization is one common discursive strategy among rival discursive strategies in settings across the planet. Racial discourse sometimes serves the locally dominant class (as in Papa Doc's Institut d'Éthnologie) and sometimes the locally subordinate one (as in Rastafarianism). Yet there are classes in between who see themselves as better served—at least some of the time—by ethnicization. These populations "in between" are, to me, the preeminent paradigm case of ethnogenesis in its real-world global and hierarchical context.

These in-between, or middling, populations are continually re-sorting themselves into new alliances and equivalences. For example, the global indigenous rights movement has brought together numerous groups that understand themselves as victims of settler colonialism. Race is a protean and debated factor in these equivalences. Hence, the Puerto Rican representative of a Taino revitalization movement set up her table at several powwows of African-descended Indians that I attended in Maryland and Virginia in 2002. Her display prompted the Jamaican Brown husband of my Virginia Pamunkey and self-described "black Indian" friend Carol to tell me that he, too, has Taino ancestors and therefore appreciated the Puerto Rican Taino's presence at the Chickahominy powwow where we talked.

An elderly graham-cracker-colored Virginian joined the conversation and added his appreciation. He said that he, too, was a Native American, like the Taino woman. Therefore, adding a further translocal logic of alliance and difference, he would rather have his daughter and son marry an Asian than marry any of his intergenerational African American neighbors. According to him, the Bering Strait migrations made Asians and Native Americans the same people—distinct, in his view, from African Americans. In my view, it was equally clear that everyone participating in the conversation that day had African ancestors as well. Privately, Carol—a Howard alumna—voiced the same certainty and expressed her irritation over the pattern of denial among her fellow southeastern Indians. On other occasions, she and her son, then a Howard undergraduate, had reported the violence with which Black-looking Indians had had their identity cards snatched away and been denied entry into the dance circle at various powwows. The design of the Jamaican coat of arms suggests a similar excoriation of blackness from Jamaican national identity. Despite the vastly black majority of that island, the only two human images on it represent Tainos (Cooper 2012).

While Carol seemed quite comfortable hosting me at the Chickahominy powwow, her son apologized for having to avoid lingering near me in public, since doing so could result in his being denied further information by his fellow Indians as he endeavored to complete his undergraduate thesis in Howard's History Department that year.

Thus, mine is a study of how intranationally and internationally mobile and ambitious people respond to being perceived as black spots in a global political and symbolic economy.

Yet the black and brown spots are not the only ones thrown into an identity crisis by recent economic developments. The civil rights movement, the women's rights movement, the OPEC oil embargo of 1973, the "Japan as Number One" scare of the 1980s, and, in the twenty-first century, the rise of China and India have all helped to kill the promise of collective and equal access to prosperity that the US founding fathers seem to have promised to white American men. The oil embargo of 1973 was a crisis for the West but a boom for countries like Nigeria. The International Bauxite Agreement of 1974 added Jamaica, Guyana, Suriname, and Guinea-Conakry to the black nations who thus experienced a new hope that they could pay for the promise of their own independence from European colonialism and for the egalitarian entitlements that their colonizers had once subsidized for European national citizenries through the pillaging of Africa, Asia, and the Americas. Yet the collapse of oil prices and of the bauxite cartel in the late 1970s dashed the hopes of a range of black nations to join the ranks of the wealthy, egalitarian nation-states. But the resulting "brain drain" injected tens of thousands of Africa's and the Caribbean's most educated people into the US social system. The threat of Asian economic dominance, of Islamic "terror," and of the United States' Hispanization have created additional threats to the caste superiority and geographical integrity of the planet's white spots.

Thus, the classification and rank ordering of "races" that arose with the triumph of European imperialism over medieval Islamic imperialism is no longer credible as a literal or singular idiom of collective identity, global social hierarchy, or individual success. However, the anchor of the US social system remains the same. Well into the twenty-first century, African Americans are still invoked as the antitype of brown, yellow, red, and white in-between people's aspirations to upward mobility and as the chief exemplars of resistance to the hierarchical system.

Race, in sum, is less a global map of objective phenotypical variation, continent-based class positions in the global economy, or fixed social identities than a range of local idioms that refer to phenotype. Some of these idioms have spread from their points of origin and become available elsewhere as alternative media of self-representation and alliance building. However, the differences between one local configuration and another—and between the homelands and the host countries of mobile populations—are a constant source of tension and identity crisis. They give shape to a pattern of ethnic identity making that is the subject of my next theoretical argument.[9]

Argument 2: Ethnicity Is Protean, Competitive, and Hierarchical

Because modernists and modernizers long predicted the global homogenization of culture and the decline of ethnic identity, the leading media events—global warming, potential epidemics, and natural disasters notwithstanding—have concerned the proliferation and often murderous juggernaut of ethnic and religious particularism. This book explores one dynamic in this unexpected development. The movement of populations from the site of one racial classification system and into another often creates new varieties of cultural and ethnic assertion, illustrating a competitive flight from stigma that shapes virtually every ethnic identity.

Bourdieu ([1979] 1984) highlighted the role of "taste"—or competency in reading, consuming, and displaying the signs of elite status—as an important idiom of class stratification and of the competitive pursuit of honor. The faith of the lower and middle classes in the superiority of upper-class choices in dress, cuisine, décor, and music keeps the ambitious among them on a hamster wheel in Sisyphean pursuit of what Bourdieu calls "distinction," always too late in apprehending the fashion choices of the upper class and always in flight from imitation by the lower classes.

Stigma and Culture offers evidence that, like taste, ethnogenesis is a competitive and hierarchical process. The drawing of ethnic boundaries around a group and the naming of its shared "culture" regularly occurs against the backdrop of a pervasive suspicion or accusation of the group's inferiority and answers this suspicion or accusation with an exaggeration of the group's differences from some more validly stigmatized group. Ethnic self-fashioning also tends to exaggerate the speaker's group's similarities to an ethnically unmarked dominant group. I call this competitive and hierarchical dimension of ethnogenesis "ethnological schadenfreude" because its partisans take comfort and bolster their own self-esteem by assuring themselves of the even deeper inferiority of some other ethnoracial group. This study of the transnational ingathering of anglophone black populations at Howard University alerted me to the striking parallels between ethnogenesis and the pursuit of class distinction that drove much of my own family life.

A few classic anthropological points about ethnicity serve as a useful backdrop to this argument. Anthropologists have observed that ethnic identity is situational, contrastive, protean, appropriative, and performative.

For example, E. E. Evans-Pritchard (1940) demonstrated one important way in which ethnic and kin-based identity is situational—that is, its segmentary nature. For example, sometimes I present myself as a Duke University person, sometimes as a person from Durham, sometimes as a North Carolinian, and sometimes as an American. In sum, my identity is not constant; it often depends on the nature of the interlocutor at the moment, especially when he or she is an adversary or a rival. Hypothetically, I will choose to identify myself in terms of the largest, the most powerful, or the most prestigious of my potential social identities that also excludes my adversary or rival. I might add a related observation of my own. People in the diaspora of a population are often the ones who first name and most influentially canonize ethnic identities, since they encounter a new type and order of antagonist (J. L. Matory 1999, 2003). Their constructions of their ethnic culture and their homeland are often edited in the service of their goals in the diaspora and in reaction to the forms of stigma that diasporic populations face in the metropolitan host country. These constructions are often reexported, to great effect, back to the homeland. Indeed, they have often been the foundations of territorially nationalist or ethnonationalist movements (J. L. Matory 2005a, 1999; Skinner 1982).

With reference to the Hausa diaspora in the Yoruba city of Ibadan, Nigeria, Abner Cohen (1969) makes the related points that the boundaries and cultural markers of an ethnic identity change in response to historical circumstances. For example, in order to protect their monopoly over the cattle and kola nut trade between northern and southern Nigeria during the 1950s, Hausa traders in Ibadan radically changed the cultural markers that defined belonging in their ethnic group. Before the 1950s, the Hausa people in Ibadan and their Yoruba neighbors had gradually adopted similar religious practices, but the British colonizers had assigned a distinct quarter for the Hausa people to reside in and a Hausa chief to rule it, thus creating an institutional bulwark for the Hausa's economically useful corporate identity, despite the tendency toward religious integration with their Yoruba neighbors.

As independence approached, however, the local Yoruba politicians withdrew the state's financial support for this distinct Hausa quarter and its chief. In this way, Yoruba politicians sought to integrate—or dissolve—the Ibadan Hausa people into the local electorate. With the last institutional bulwark of their social distinction gone, the Hausa merchants feared losing their solidarity as a closed community monopolizing the cattle and kola nut trade. For Cohen, it is the threat to the Ibadan Hausa people's commercial monopoly that explains their sudden and massive conversion to the Tijaniyya Islamic brotherhood. Their conversion restored the Ibadan-based Hausa community's difference from their Yoruba Muslim neighbors and preserved the social closure that had been the basis of their trade monopoly. Ironically, this conversion also created a difference between Ibadan Hausas and their co-ethnics in the north.

In such contexts, it becomes clear that identity is a defensive posture. It is walled and antagonistic to connection and interpenetration. However, its levees remain porous. Neighboring lifeways are open systems that mutually constitute and influence each other through osmosis, complementary contrast, and what Gregory Bateson ([1936] 1958) calls "schismogenesis." Bateson showed, among the Iatmul of New Guinea, how individuals and populations that are told they should be different from each other exaggerate those differences in a mutually complementary way. Moreover, individuals or groups that are competing with each other tend, over time, to grow more and more different from a third party. However, Bateson also observes that, on marked ritual occasions and in ritualized ways, such divergent parties tend to *imitate* each other, much as white Americans imitate Black people during adolescence, on stage, and when invoking communitas and camaraderie with their fellows.

Fredrik Barth (1969) has also pointed out something implicit, as well, in Cohen's work: that cultural difference as such is seldom the cause of ethnic difference. Neighboring populations regularly share an enormous number of collective assumptions and conventions. And each ethnically bounded population is, to a degree, internally diverse in its assumptions, conventions, and conduct. Moreover, unless contiguous ethnic groups work hard to prevent it, they tend to converge more and more over time in their assumptions, conventions, and conduct, such that local behavioral diversity quickly ceases to correlate with ethnicity. Thus, when ethnic boundaries arise or endure, it is usually because some powerful members of that ethnic group benefit materially from a monopoly or a privilege that would diminish in the absence of those boundaries.

Most British and American anthropologists today cite Barth, editor and coauthor of the 1969 volume *Ethnic Groups and Boundaries*, as the great ancestor of these currently prevailing theories of ethnicity. He coined the terms "cultural diacritica" and "cultural differentiae," which suggest that neighboring ethnic groups often distinguish themselves from each other by little more than a small, cosmetic marker of difference and that these groups arise more from the interested effort to preserve some difference of economic niche than from spontaneous or inherent commitment to overall cultural inertia and heritage preservation. Barth further noted that ethnic boundaries tend to be permeable. By adopting the appropriate cosmetic markers, or diacritica, of ethnic identity, people switch into new ethnic categories all the time, and by shedding such diacritica, people equally often abandon their former ethnic categories.

With equal predictability, as Virginia Domínguez (1986) has pointed out, ethnic groups compete to appropriate prestigious but ambiguous potential ancestors, thus asserting the dignity of the group. For the same reasons, they compete for prestigious living members and deny the membership of disreputable coethnics. For example, Hintzen (2003) shows how, through voluntary associations, festivals, and family-centered gatherings, the largely middle-class West Indian, or Caribbean, immigrants on the West Coast of the United States emphasize their difference from what they stereotype as typical African Americans. They do so to such an extent that they deny that their working-class coethnics are "real West Indians" at all. They thus reassure themselves of their collective "cultural" worthiness of prosperity and of their "cultural" deservingness of exemption from the forms of exclusion experienced by African Americans.

The field experiences documented in *Stigma and Culture* suggest at least one major challenge to the Barthian paradigm—that is, regarding Barth's methodological collectivism. In my view, practically speaking, ethnic identities are not so much bounded and mutually exclusive categories in which each person resides during any given period of his or her life as they are a set of situational demands for loyalty and access. Each person has a range of ethnic identity options, as Waters (1990) and Alba (1990) point out for white ethnics in the United States, and these identity options are invoked for specific situational purposes.

Black ethnics, too, have options, though they are not nearly as wide-ranging or profitable as the options available to US-based ethnics of other complexions, hair textures, and facial features. For example, whereas most bourgeois Nigerian immigrants are deeply wedded to the mutually antagonistic sense of being, for example, Yoruba as opposed to Igbo, the children of Yoruba and Igbo immigrants at Harvard tend to join pan-Black organizations but, within them, loudly proclaim their Nigerianness. At multiple events, where the pan-Black organizations happened to honor or recognize a Nigerian, I have heard the Nigerian American contingent—which concentrated at certain tables—shout a long and protracted "Naija!" I have not yet seen enough of the Nigerian community at Duke University to understand why, at a 2010 Black American sorority party honoring the Nigerian legacy of some of the sorority's members and friends, the only collective shout that I heard was "Igbo kwenu!" ("Igbos unite!") and the reply of assent—"Yaa!" In other words, potentially allied black ethnic groups sometimes fuse and sometimes divide themselves. However, it is difficult for black ethnics in the United States to evade assimilation to the less privileged racial segment of segmented assimilation.

Black ethnic choices of alliance do appear to vary according to class aspirations and status. For example, Waters (1999) has observed that in New York City *upwardly mobile* African-descended West Indian immigrants typically emphasize their difference from African Americans, preferring to emphasize their ethnic identities over their potential racial identities, whereas their *non–upwardly mobile* coethnics tend to identify with African Americans. (Of course, there are reasons to suspect that any given Caribbean American's ethnoracial self-presentation will vary situationally, depending on, among other things, whom he or she is speaking to.)

However, for me, a child of the civil rights movement, these strategic uses of difference were surprising. I had conceived of our choices differently. For example, the African American pursuit of citizenship rights is typically represented as achieving its effects by emphasizing the *likeness* of the oppressed to each other and to the oppressor. Martin Luther King asserted the likeness of Black people and their white antagonists with reference to the Jeffersonian dictum "all men are created equal" and to a dream about a commensal "table of brotherhood." In the same spirit, the civil rights protesters performed the case for their likeness to respectable whites by marching in their Sunday, churchgoing best. Except for the color of their skin, they looked like every other Christian, job-holding, middle-class American. Arising in the context of the civil rights movement, the Hart-Celler Immigration and Nationality Act of 1965 also established the idea that potential immigrants from Asia, Africa, and Latin America are no different before the law from European immigrants.

It was also as a child of the Black Power movement that I bridled at the Caribbean strategy of upward mobility through self-differentiation from African Americans. The Black Power movement of the 1960s and the Afrocentrism movement of the 1980s embodied a strategic logic of sameness among black people and collective difference from white people. Through symbols of Africa, a continent then treated as a common denominator of the global Black experience, these movements posited the essential cultural similarity and likeness of political interests among African Americans, Caribbean immigrants, and African immigrants in the United States. It is no surprise that this symbolism of unity reached its crescendo during the 1980s, when the black population of New York City had become more internationally diverse than ever and all of these groups faced the Reaganite backlash against the civil rights movement.

But it is in truth unsurprising that West Indian "ethnicity entrepreneurs" (Kasinitz 1992, 255), who sought power of their own in the city's halls of power, articulated at the same time the notion of West Indian cultural difference from African Americans. In other words, they articulated into being a constituency for which they alone could speak. As in the case of the Ibadan-based Hausa population, new symbolic assertions can create or amplify social divisions in strategic and profitable ways.

Even symbolic assertions of unity with a larger group can entail strategic assertions of difference within the subgroup. Thus, in civil rights marches, wearing a suit carried not only the implication of being "just like" the mainstream Christian white middle class but also the implication of being *unlike* sharecropping Black debt peons, falsely convicted prison laborers, underpaid domestics, and people who, repeatedly passed over for opportunities in the formal economy, sought a livelihood in the underworld. And, in the context of African-inspired religions, possessing more African clothing and other paraphernalia can become a costly demonstration of some priests' superiority to others (J. L. Matory 2005a).

A further strategic, situational, and hierarchical context of black ethnogenesis is what Jean and John Comaroff (2009) call the "commoditization" of ethnicity in a neoliberal age. It is often the best option for those least favored by the formal economy. The populations with the least control over material resources and the means of production—often for reasons that, I might add, are correlated with race—use and modify their "cultures" dramatically in ways meant variously to attract tourists or voyeuristic suburbanites; to prove that they deserve to open a casino; to prove title to an herbal tea or pharmaceutical; or, I might add, to prove that they are more qualified for a low-wage job than are members of another marginalized ethnic group.

For example, the aim of the Occaneechi-Saponi powwow that my son and I attended in Hillsborough, North Carolina, was to celebrate and further legitimize the tribe's recent recognition by the state. Through dress and dance forms borrowed from the Plains Indians (in collaboration with Wild Bill Hickok's Wild West shows) and through a recuperated Indian language, the Occaneechi-Saponis dramatized their worthiness not only of recognition as a distinct community but also of their new access to generous scholarships in the North Carolina state universities. Their lead attorney (who wore buckskin at the powwow) had grown up in my predominantly Black neighborhood in Washington, DC, where he had dressed no differently from his Black peers, and his Gullah/Geechee father practiced medicine at Howard University Hospital. Most of his fellow Occaneechi-Saponis, however, had clearly not shared his upper-middle-class family background or his Black educational advantages. These new benefits potentially made a palpable difference in their lives. Similarly, in 2006, the Gullah/Geechees of the Lowcountry secured federal recognition for a "Gullah-Geechee Cultural Heritage Corridor" extending from Wilmington, North Carolina, to Jacksonville, Florida, which added to the cachet of their distinctive crafts and services and thus empowered them financially and politically to protect their threatened landholdings. Indeed, in pursuit of economic and political benefits, ethnicity entrepreneurs are turning university-based ethnological research into popular ethnic identities, as well as small but life-changing material gains for the disadvantaged.

The case of race and ethnicity at Howard is also chock-full of lessons about the operation of what Pierre Bourdieu calls "distinction" ([1979] 1984). Bourdieu observes that elite class status is marked by the continual adoption of new and hard-to-obtain styles to evade the equally continual imitation of these styles by the middle class. And, as he also might have predicted in this case, slightly higher-ranking social groups often work furiously to demonstrate their "cultural" difference from the immediately lower-ranking group. My hypothesis is that historical changes in ethnic identities, too, follow this pattern of imitating one's superiors in the global ethnoracial hierarchy and of flight from the tastes most recently borrowed by one's supposed inferiors in that hierarchy. Bourdieu also notes that, in evading middle-class imitation and ambition, the uppermost elites sometimes borrow and stylize the practices of the lowest classes. As the most publicly stigmatized and media-depicted lower-status group in the United States, ghetto-dwelling African Americans are a frequent source of such borrowing. As Bateson's concept of schismogenesis reminds us, this highly ritualized and context-specific nature of that borrowing represents a cross-cultural pattern.

Erving Goffman's (1963) work on stigma speaks even more directly to the motive behind many black migrants' emphasis on ethnic distinction. Ethnic identity is useful in the flight from a stigmatized racial status. Goffman also helps us to predict that the cultural diacritica chosen by an ethnicity entrepreneur to define his or her black ethnic group in the United States will tend to resemble the traits admired by white Americans and will be selected to maximize the appearance of that ethnic group's difference from stereotypical African Americans.

Goffman posits that any person who enters a new situation has a "virtual identity"—that is, what people expect him or her to be until they find out otherwise. Observers may later discover the person's "actual identity," based upon the eventual exposure of truths about the person's background, capabilities, and dispositions. Among people who do not fit society's standards, adds Goffman, there are "discreditable" people and "discredited" people. A

INTRODUCTION

person who is discreditable is *potentially* discredited by the exposure of his or her disreputable characteristics. The options of a discreditable person wishing to avoid being discredited include controlling the flow of information so that no one finds out about his or her "defect." An alternative option is behavioral distraction (i.e., "covering") in order to draw people's attention away from the defect. For example, observes Goffman, many blind people wear sunglasses or conscientiously turn their eyes toward the speaker, since their normal disposition to turn their eyes and faces away from the interlocutor is a telltale sign of blindness.

Goffman, like his intellectual grandson Barth, assumes too much voluntarism in most of his examples. Whereas information management and passing are conceivable as effective options for "white"-skinned ethnics, such as most Jewish Americans, for very light-skinned African Americans, and for gays, a blind person is unlikely to throw off the average sighted interlocutor for very long. However, Goffman does help us to understand why black ethnics and dark-skinned middle-class African Americans consciously use accents and diction to demonstrate that we should not be mistaken for the perhaps-more-deserving objects of antiblack prejudice—the poor, uneducated, irresponsible, lazy, thieving, angry, violent, and libidinous monster that has long been conjured up and projected onto ghetto dwellers in order to justify our oppression. In playing up our superior diction, we are "covering." Because we lack the shield of "white" skin, people of African descent in the United States—middle-class, black ethnic, or what have you—tend to play up the power of our clothing, grooming, accents, and verbal self-representations to deflect racial mistreatment, and we blame ghetto dwellers' indiscipline for giving the lie to our efforts.

Yet these performances of covering are as much for other black people as for an immediately present white audience. Quite independently of white racism, people employ grooming and other optional features of self-presentation to gain or maintain status within the group. All other things being equal, though, the visibly stigmatized populations in any given social field tend to strategize more carefully and work harder at this effort. Our discreditability is certainly one reason why. We are both impressed and offended by the degree to which white men can get away with untidy dress and feel unembarrassed about being seen leaving the bathroom without washing their hands. Discreditable people worry much more about such small potential revelations of our unworthiness.

However, visibly stigmatized people often overestimate the degree to which covering achieves the desired goal. One African American administrator at Harvard mocked the efforts of a Mississippian colleague who had spent the three decades since his return from a year at Oxford speaking with a British accent, which he and many Americans regard as prestigious. He appeared to be *covering* the stigma of his Blackness and of his low-status geographical origins. Passed over for a position for which he had prepared and sacrificed mightily, this Mississippian Anglophile reportedly moaned with Churchillian vowels, "I caaaahn't belieeeeve they deniiiiied me thaht promooootion!" That black ethnics and the Black middle class often overestimate the efficacy of our covering does not stop us from trying, hoping, and, with increasing frequency, succeeding. Yet we are highly aware that the strategy still often fails.

Such covering has clearly worked better for many ambitious borderline whites. For example, Harvard's Daniel Patrick Moynihan was born poor and Irish American. Both his own birth family and his transnational ethnic group are wracked with immense social and cultural dysfunctions of their own. But he cleared a path toward his own upward mobility by donning a bow tie and assuming the mantle of ethnoracially unmarked white expertise about Black social dysfunctionality (US Department of Labor 1965).[10] These distractions from Moynihan's own defective background were the perfect one-two punch. This form of covering and its other, violent manifestations are the tried and true path of white immigrant assimilation in the United States. Many borderline white ethnic groups have followed this Irish American model of strategic response to discreditability (e.g., Barrett and Roediger 2005), inflicting unthinkable, expiatory violence on black people who enter their neighborhoods or schools.

Roderick Ferguson (2003) goes further to argue that the sociology propagated by the likes of Robert Park, E. Franklin Frazier, William Julius Wilson, and Daniel Patrick Moynihan is a Foucauldian discourse of domination, structuring the surveillance of and control over "deviant" Black populations by patriarchal white males and by the new Black middle class. This observation indeed complements the view that such sociological discourse strategically masks and aims to neutralize the ethnoracial stigma borne by these upwardly mobile but discreditable Blacks and borderline whites. For upwardly mobile African American sociologists, this discourse clarifies that the problem with their deviant kin, forebears, and former class peers is not hereditary or racial but "cultural" and that these upwardly mobile children of the poor have personally shed that "cultural" problem. A striking number of African American proponents of this argument grew up poor, a fact that increases their authority to speak about and for poor black people but also makes their stake in the argument complicated.

While we were colleagues at Harvard during the 1990s, Professor William Julius Wilson reported the fear and prejudice of white neighbors in his elite

Boston apartment building, suggesting that this discursive and sartorial strategy worked better for Moynihan than it did for him.

In the age of Barack Obama and Oprah Winfrey, culture talk about the "underclass" lends itself to blaming the reactions of the poor to the structural and sometimes intentional foreclosure of their licit options on ignorance and disordered values. The Oscar-winning film *Precious* (2009) puts an exclamation point on this culturalist explanation of Black "underclass" poverty. Since the 1980s, Black conservatives like Thomas Sowell, Clarence Thomas, Ward Connerly, Clarence Pendleton, and John McWhorter have extended these culturalist arguments to their most vituperative extremes, winning them generous sinecures from the "color-blind" institutional advocates of what Bonilla-Silva (2010) called "racism without racists," such as conservative think tanks and the White House under Reagan and George H. W. Bush. (In full disclosure, I was an appointee of the George W. Bush administration, though I hesitate to consider the possibility that my depiction of the nonangelic motives of the oppressed and the oppressor alike may have been useful to the Republicans.)

Goffman observes two further patterns of conduct among the stigmatized that are particularly apposite to my own study. First, the stigmatized "stratify their own.'" For example, observes Goffman, the hard of hearing hate being called "deaf." Similarly, highly assimilated nineteenth- and twentieth-century western European Jews deflected the stereotypes of gentiles about all Jews specifically onto eastern Jews. The cultural incompetency of eastern Jews was identified with their Yiddish vocabulary and accents, which were in turn blamed on their inferior anatomy (Gilman 1993). For his part, German Jew Karl Marx used stereotypes about Jews to discredit rival socialist leaders. Even though Marx himself was so dark that he was nicknamed "the Moor," he lashed his most effective rival, Ferdinand Lassalle, who was also Jewish, with words that were both anti-African and anti-Jewish:

> [B]y the shape of his head and the growth of his hair, he [Lassalle] stems from the Negroes who joined the march of Moses out of Egypt (if his mother or grandmother on his father's side did not mate with a nigger). Now this combination of Jewry and Germanism with the negroid basic substance must bring forth a peculiar product. The pushiness of this lad is also nigger-like. (quoted in Sperber 2013, 411)

In his hair texture, facial features, sympathies, and studio pose, Marx bears no small resemblance to his contemporary Frederick Douglass, a mulatto abolitionist (J. L. Matory unpublished manuscript). In addition, Marx himself seems to have been quite pushy. The stigmatized often cast some subvariety of their own kind as the truly undeserving, in the hope of covering their own all-too-obvious vulnerability to discrimination with a thinly veiled declaration of loyalty to the stigmatizers and of conversion to their cause.

A certain ethnological schadenfreude seems to motivate the resolution with which many Caribbeans at Harvard and Howard declare that they are *not* African Americans and then, en suite, narrate risible tales of African American ridiculousness. I heard a Howardite of Virginian descent, in a similar spirit, attribute the decline of decency and security in his city to the historical influx of Carolinians, implying Black Virginians' great and advantageous difference from Washingtonians of Carolinian origin. And most non-Washingtonian Howard students appear to celebrate their superiority to Washingtonians as a lot, the typical exemplars of whom are taken to be the denizens of the lower–Georgia Avenue crack ally and the teenagers who, at least in 2002, regarded it as fashionable to roll up one pant leg as they moved about the city.

In a similar "stratification of our own," the residents in my upper-middle-class Black neighborhood carefully evaluated each other's complexions, family histories, houses, décor, cars, diction, and children's educational attainments with an eye toward enhancing their own rank at the expense of others'. Only when I began to attend school and make friends west of Rock Creek Park—in the predominantly white Foxhall Road, Tenley Circle, and Spring Valley neighborhoods—did I realize that a gold Mercedes, a Yale degree, the finest diction in the world, a Sixteenth Street mansion, or even a house in Rehoboth Beach did not make us anywhere near white, west-of-the-Park rich. Of course, there was nothing ideal about the lifeways I encountered on the other side of Rock Creek Park, either. I came to know this world well through my high school companions. It was beset by very human insecurities and dangerous compensations of their own, such as suicide, fathers' abandoning their families, divorce, sexual abuse, alcoholism, drug abuse, and economically needless shoplifting. But these are matters for another book.

Although their size and significance is debated, there are some differences between the average socioeconomic status of African Americans, on the one hand, and that of foreign-born blacks, on the other. Most can be explained in terms of the highly selective nature of black immigration. For example, despite the relative poverty of their continent, African immigrants are the most highly educated and the second-highest earning of all the continent-of-origin groups (Speer 1994; Massey et al. 2007, 246; McCabe 2013; Bashi and McDaniel 1997). Many came to the United States specifically in pursuit of higher education or are the product of a brain drain vastly more devastating to Africa than it is fruitful to the United States. And Jamaican immigrants are among the most self-selected of all immigrant populations, coming disproportionately from a skilled middle class with insufficient opportunities for upward mobility at home (Massey et al. 2007, 246).

In addition, John Ogbu (1978) argued that voluntary immigrants to a country and their descendants always outperform the involuntary migrants, the colonized, and their descendants, because they perceive the system as less antagonistic to them. And Mary Waters's and others' research about the New York labor market suggests that this optimism may be a self-fulfilling prophecy. Similarly, Haitian immigrants enjoy a reputation for outworking Dominicans in the Dominican Republic, Dominican immigrants reputedly outwork Puerto Ricans in Puerto Rico, and Hispanic immigrants have a better reputation among US employers than do US-born Latinos.

Eugene Robinson (2010) argues that, although black immigrants tend to come from poor countries, those countries tend to be black-dominated, and there blacks can expect to do anything, as they can in Robinson's own hometown of Orangeburg, South Carolina, the home of a historically Black university. He says that black immigrants and their children tend to be educated and disproportionately come from the segments of their societies most competent to master the system and immigrate, to be optimistic, and to propagate a family history of education. Second, these immigrant populations are culturally prone to respect parents and, in Robinson's view, to grow up in two-parent homes. Third, Robinson asserts, they are immune to stereotype threat—the performance-depressing fear of fulfilling negative stereotypes (Steele 1997). And, unlike African Americans, Robinson concludes, black immigrants know and take pride in their lands of origin. However, for the lack of many of these advantages, the second generation tends to fall off in achievement.

Of course, as Robinson suggests, the selectiveness of black immigration conferred no advantage over the equally selective principles that made elite African American neighborhoods like the North Portal Estates in Washington; Sugar Hill in Harlem; Pontchartrain Park in New Orleans; Anna Street in Norfolk, Virginia; Baldwin Hills in Los Angeles; Robinson's hometown of Orangeburg; and many more such capitals of African American ambition. It is not just the nations of the Caribbean and Africa that have produced upwardly mobile subpopulations. Nor does the proportion of their national populations that is upwardly mobile appear to exceed that of African Americans.

Moreover, Caribbean labor immigration has produced other family situations as well. The many children left behind by immigrating parents are known in the anglophone Caribbean as "barrel children," because barrels full of consumer goods sent from abroad must substitute for the presence of parents. Island dwellers complain that, because they lack adequate supervision and guidance, the "barrel children" are often value-disoriented, undisciplined in school, and criminally violent. For example, Lee Boyd Malvo, the young sniper in the 2002 killing of thirteen unsuspecting strangers in the Washington, DC, area, had been a "barrel child" before his emigration from Jamaica. In 2013, his interview on a Jamaican radio show provoked island-wide discussion of the widespread problem of the "barrel children."

The statistical truth is that, in 2009, 25.8 percent of Black Americans lived in poverty, meaning that 74.2 percent, or nearly three-quarters, did not. Approximately 25.3 percent of Hispanics also lived in poverty, and 9.4 percent of non-Hispanic whites were also poor (US Census Bureau 2013). Thus, one out of ten white Americans lived in poverty, a fact that one would never guess after watching several years of television and films in the United States. On the contrary, one might be excused for believing, as many non-Americans exposed to the US mass media do, that almost all white Americans are rich and almost all Black Americans poor. And, given the visual propaganda on television and in the movies that white Americans prosper by the least effort, it becomes obvious that Black Americans are unwilling to work, inherently deficient in accomplishment, and downright craven in their refusal to engage with the system on its own terms.

The discourse of Caribbean distinction is shaped not only by the disproportions in the mass media's representations of African Americans but also by the motive of the stigmatized to "stratify their own," a motive stronger than the desire to recognize that white Americans with comparable education and skills still enjoy a significant income and wealth advantage over both Caribbean Americans and middle-class African Americans.

My Caribbean interlocutors at Howard and Harvard tended to attribute their self-described success in life causally to what they call "Caribbean culture," and specifically to the ways in which, in their view, that reported "culture" distinguishes them from African Americans—nuclear family structures, emphasis on schooling, propriety in speech and dress, and embrace of British standards. In contrast, my acquaintances in Jamaica and Trinidad, many of them Howard alumni who had graduated in the 1960s and returned home, described these cultural dispositions as "middle-class culture," which they felt distinguished the Caribbean middle class sharply from the impoverished majority population of their islands. Equally fictional or mythological was the tendency of the Caribbean American interlocutors to focus on their superiority to the least accomplished African Americans (such as the denizens of the crack alley), rather than, say, on these Caribbean interlocutors' own shortcomings compared to the most upstanding Black and white Americans.

Sometimes black ethnics' fictional readings of difference are used effectively to discipline children. Many black immigrant parents instruct their children not to "act like African Americans" or to associate with them. For example, one female Jamaican American graduate student at Harvard and a male Haitian American medical student at Howard reported having been kept away from African Americans in general by their mothers. While the Haitian American student's mother was a single parent, the Jamaican American student's mother answered her continued efforts to date an African American boy by criticizing what she regarded as the high incidence of single-parenting in African American households. The Jamaican American student had not been aware that the incidence of single motherhood in Jamaica and other parts of the anglophone Caribbean is even higher than among African Americans. Similarly, a Nigerian pediatrician in the Boston area explained her success at rearing twins—both of whom attended Yale College—by lamenting what she regarded as the error that many other children of African immigrants had, to her mind, fallen into, that "they identify too much with the African Americans."

Of course, this account is not intended to present African Americans as innocent in the practice of ethnological and class schadenfreude. African Americans engage in the strategic stereotyping of black ethnics, just as people from different Caribbean islands and people from different African ethnic groups and countries strategically stereotype each other. Native-born African Americans also engage in the strategic stereotyping of higher or lower classes of native-born African Americans, particularly through the parodic imitation of their accents, diction, and values.

African American schadenfreude will also be treated in the chapters that follow. While members of my mother's upper-middle-class African American extended family identified intensely with the political interests of working-class African American families, the mockery of working-class diction carried a clear message that we were of the race but above the race. It was our job to care for and set an example for poor African Americans, not to be like them. Indeed, every other day, some middle-or upper-class African American luminary—such as Maya Angelou, Bill Cosby, Tyler Perry, or Don Lemon—can be heard on television criticizing the diction or dress of ghetto-dwelling Black people, as though these forms of expression were, in themselves, significant causes of these people's poverty and social marginalization. In sum, black ethnics and soi-disant "middle-class Black" people engage in similar forms of collective self-representation that do not simply innocently report the conventional conduct of earlier generations. Like class distinction, ethnic identity is contextual, oppositional, protean, and performative. But it is also strategic, hierarchical, and responsive to the reality of racial stigmatization.

Stigma and Culture

What are cultures? And how does the study of the stigmatized help answer that question?

US anthropology rests on the concept of "cultures": the notion—rooted in a genealogy of German Romantic thought from Johann Gottfried von Herder to Gustav E. Klemm, Adolf Bastian, and Franz Boas—that different peoples possess different collective assumptions about the nature of the world and ways of feeling and acting within it. In twentieth-century US anthropology, "cultures" were typically conceived of as relatively static systems belonging to spatially bounded populations. And the term carried with it the premise—called "cultural relativism—that every such culture was worthy of equal respect and understanding.

However, since the 1980s, anthropologists have reconsidered the realities of human lifeways in terms of power, representations, and change (e.g., Gupta and Ferguson 1997; Clifford 1988; Abu-Lughod 1991; Asad 1986). We realized that colonial domination and other translocal political and economic processes are not only the conditions under which our field research has taken place but also phenomena that have already changed the lifeways that we intend to observe and describe. Inspired by Edward Said (1978), we also realized that domination shapes the terms in which Western scholars describe other people's lifeways. Postmodern anthropologists recognize that any set of phenomena that we reify as a "culture" is a representational artifact of the conversation that the observer—as the bearer of a particular historically conditioned set of assumptions and perspectives—conducted with his or her particular interlocutors within the observed population. Those interlocutors offer perspectives on themselves and their neighbors that are conditioned by the gender, income, overall wealth, race, age, and so forth of the investigator and of the people being investigated. The conversation and, therefore, the image of the "culture" that results are deeply affected by the specific positionalities of the anthropologist and of his or her interlocutors.

Early-twentieth-century anthropologists are often described as "handmaidens of colonialism," in the sense that our disciplinary forebears—especially the British ones—entered the field as employees of the imperialist and in the service of rendering the administration of the colonized more efficient. It has also been recognized that, among their imperialist contemporaries, the anthropologists of the colonial era tended to be the liberals, advocating the relatively sympathetic description and treatment of the colonized. Nonetheless, late-twentieth-century anthropologists accused our disciplinary forebears of committing an act of hierarchy when they wrote of other people's lifeways as though these lifeways were frozen and internally homogeneous, unlike any lifeway that we ourselves had lived in the West.

Forgotten in this recent disciplinary self-critique are the roots of the "culture" concept in the German nationalist response to French cultural chauvinism. It was at its roots the response of the underdog. The elites of the seventeenth- and eighteenth-century German-speaking principalities treated the aristocratic French lifeway as the single, universal standard of culture, or culturedness. In reaction to domination by these Francophile princes, Herder offered the subaltern idea that each people has its own unique, environmentally determined "national genius" or spirit (*Geist*), a spirit that Gustav E. Klemm came to call *a* "culture"—that is, one of many equally respectable collective lifeways (Herder [1784–91] 1968; Kroeber and Kluckhohn 1952).

Equally important in the history of the term's adoption and use in US anthropology is the central role of borderline whites, particularly Jews like Franz Boas and Melville J. Herskovits, who had a special stake in resisting the biological justification of social inferiority, which had reached a crescendo in late nineteenth-century Europe and the United States. While mainstream anthropological history emphasizes Boas's role in a "salvage anthropology" seeking to capture the nearly lost lifeways of Native Americans, the founding of US cultural anthropology also coincided and overlapped with the Harlem Renaissance, the literary movement at the roots of African American cultural nationalism (Baker 1998). The most famous liaison between these movements is Franz Boas's student Zora Neale Hurston. Boas's students—including not only Hurston but also Melville J. Herskovits, Ruth Landes, and Brazil's Gilberto Freyre—produced an ample and influential body of scholarship on African and African-diaspora "cultures."

A further little-known fact is that it was not Boas but Howard University philosophy professor and doyen of the Harlem Renaissance Alain Locke who first published and very likely coined the term "cultural relativism" (Locke 1924), the signature premise of our field at its mid-twentieth-century height.[11] Boas and several of his students—including Herskovits and Ruth Landes— used the anthropological concept of "culture" to establish that the distinctive lifeways of African American peoples were African-inspired cultures, rather than mere accumulations of deficiency arising from racial inferiority, enslavement, or oppression.[12] W. E. B. Du Bois dialogued and collaborated with Boas in expounding this message. The discursive construction of "cultures" by anthropologists and their interlocutors not only *reflects* local lifeways and their global political-economic context but also regularly *changes* the way that the described populations see or organize themselves. Anthropological portraits of "cultures" regularly become the banners of nationalist and ethnonationalist movements.

Much of the literature on representation has focused on the power of the anthropologist to define other people's "cultures" in ethnocentric and question-begging ways, while much of our attention to culture and power has focused on the ability of metropolitan or local elites to "invent" traditions (e.g., Hobsbawm and Ranger 1983) that naturalize the privileges of the mighty. The present analysis focuses on the "cultural" self-representation of subordinate populations in the context of their competition with other subordinate populations for the favors of the powerful and in the context of their desire to avoid falling into the most abject status. University scholars and students are often directly involved in this project of collective self-positioning.

This analysis highlights the Janus-faced nature of the configurations that are called "cultures." The term describes both (1) the actual patterns of people's collective thought and conduct and (2) the selective canonization of cultural diacritica that are pleasing to the dominant gaze. "Cultures" are samplings of lower-status practice that support, complement, or are neutral to the sovereignty of the rulers. In its culture making, every ethnic grouping but the one at the top and the one at the bottom of the scale endeavors to demonstrate its freedom from the deficiencies that are attributed to the constituent other. The bottommost grouping is defined by its deficiency and the uppermost by the unmarkedness of its way of life. Like the implicitly Francophile lifeway of Herder's time and place, the dominant lifeway is culture *itself*, rather than *a* culture.

Yet every such ethnically unmarked way of life must respond to the rival representations of other empires and to resentful critiques by its class subordinates. The anthropological vocabulary of "culture" can also be an instrument of such critiques. Calling the putatively ethnically neutral elite "a culture" or "an ethnic group" denaturalizes its authority and implies a demand that it be deposed from its role as the standard or prodded out of its sclerotic state.

What is perhaps novel in the current situation is that the universality of today's dominant culture lies less in its qualitative singularity than in its cosmopolitan use of references to and practical mastery of cuisines, languages, and fashions from all over the world. This mastery authorizes the dominant race-class as spokespeople for the rest of the world and as apical coordinators of their production and exchange.

Stigma and Culture largely concerns groups that construct themselves as middling based on the vocabulary of "cultures," in resistance to demeaning classifications of their "race." Thus, "cultures" are strategically constructed in a way deeply inflected by what a Marxist would call "class." They respond to the class aspirations of groups with the ever-present potential for relegation to the lumpen proletariat. But Weberians have long known, as Marxists have long resisted acknowledging, that class is never reducible to economics. Class itself is always inflected through and shaped by gender, complexion, and ethnicity. This book concerns the conjoint processes of class, gender, and ethnic identity formation among the stigmatized; closely examining the case of the university-educated black intelligentsia.

This study of black ethnicity and class distinction is also a paradigm case —begging for cross-cultural application—of culture making as a process of mutual "othering" by subordinate and middling groups. It highlights the process by which, in pursuit of honor and earnings, the discreditable "other" needs to other another. As a member of the other othered by others, I am moved to ask why my group has been useful in this project and how members of my own group engage in similar discursive strategies, successfully or unsuccessfully, to escape stigma, economic marginalization, and physical danger. This is therefore an ethnography not of a bounded culture or ethnic group but of a dialectical process of culture making among ambitious subpopulations of the world's most stigmatized race.

An account of this rhizomatic process (Deleuze and Guattari [1980] 1987) necessarily sets my own African American self-ethnography alongside stories of black ethnic lives and performances. Hintzen and Rahier (2003) have edited a volume of self-ethnographies by black immigrant scholars teaching in predominantly white universities. In many ways complementary to *Stigma and Culture*, that volume strongly illustrates the emic reasoning that I heard repeatedly during my research: because of the different cultures and structural conditions of identity making in their respective homelands, black immigrants are different from Black Americans and rightly resist being lumped together with them (see also Hintzen 2003).

However, there are other dynamics at work. Black ethnic images of their home "cultures" are deeply shaped by the conditions of the diaspora and the host society as well. Arriving in the United States, many black immigrants receive an early warning from white Americans about the importance of avoiding African Americans, on account of our ostensible dangerousness, laziness, or irresponsibility. One contributor to Hintzen and Rahier's *Problematizing Blackness*, Manyika (2003), writes of a broader cross-cultural pattern that I call the "our-blacks-bad-your-blacks-good" phenomenon, which creates favorable conditions in many Western societies for "exotic blacks" (Manyika's term) and encourages those exotic blacks' complicity in the local system of racial oppression:

Africans [in England] often spoke of asserting a visible "African" identity to distinguish themselves from British-born blacks. The distinguishing was done to avoid stereotypes associated with West Indians, exactly as I used to do when I first arrived in England. Such strategic positioning by Africans perpetuated rather than dismissed the stereotypes associated with West Indians. The "I'm black but not from here" syndrome no doubt made conditions worse for West Indians. I have found, in every Western society where I have lived, that non-local blacks are frequently embraced by the majority white population in stark contrast to the hostility that is frequently bestowed on local blacks. (Manyika 2003, 73)

In a personal story, Manyika summarizes the dilemma eventually faced by the "exotic black," a dilemma beyond the reflection of any other contributor to *Problematizing Blackness* besides Noguera:

My study in Bordeaux coincided with the highly publicised controversy over whether Muslim girls should be allowed to wear head veils to school. . . . I felt particularly saddened by the tensions between whites and Arabs but did not feel directly affected by them. This feeling of distance changed, however, on the day that I was attacked by a group of skinheads who mistook me for an Arab. As they began to push and shove, they cursed me for being an Arab and told me to return to where I came from. I was stuck for a way to refute their accusations, and in the few initial seconds wondered whether I should tell them that I was not an Arab and whether that would make me safe. I wondered whether I should claim my Britishness and my Africanness or whether I should stand up for the rights of Arabs.

"Qu'est-ce que vous faites?" I asked them and then switched to English.

"I'm not from here; leave me alone!" I screamed, hoping someone would come to my aid. They laughed at me and told me to stop pretending that I was British and to admit that I was an Arab. . . . It really did not matter where I was from or who I was—in their eyes I was an Arab and that was all that mattered. (Manyika 2003, 74–75)

The cultural self-fashioning of "exotic black" populations in the United States typically serves both the black immigrant's affirmation of his or her superiority to the native Black and the white interlocutor's wish to believe that the marginalization of local black people is grounded in objectivity, rather than racism.

A human foil is still a human, whose complexity is erased by his or her role in the strategic détente of others. In the present volume, self-ethnography not only highlights what is hidden by black ethnics' use of native-born African Americans as a constituent other but also further illustrates the omnipresence of othering among the othered and its general role in culture making. *Stigma and Culture* illustrates a level of double consciousness and a type of dialectical self-revision beyond what Du Bois could have imagined in his magisterial *The Souls of Black Folk*. But like *Souls*, this story resists reduction to any single genre of writing or voice.

This book is not a survey of distinctive immigrant and domestic ethnic groups but a field study of how collective identities are articulated and transformed at a crossroads, the likes of which is indeed the normal context of all cultural history and ethnogenesis. So this is an ethnography of the in-between, of how ethnic groupings emerge and change through the interaction and convergence of populations. As Clifford (1988) points out, identity is conjunctural, not essential, and is often a reaction against disadvantageous forms of assimilation. Like other scholars of transnationalism and historical teleology, Appadurai brings an exquisite turn of phrase to phenomena that he has just recently observed:

> What is new is that this is a world in which both points of departure and points of arrival are in cultural flux, and thus the search for steady points of reference, as critical life-choices are made, can be very difficult. It is in this atmosphere that the invention of tradition (and of ethnicity, kinship and other identity-markers) can become slippery, as the search for certainties is regularly frustrated by the fluidities of transnational communication. As group pasts become increasingly parts of museums, exhibits and collections, both in national and transnational spectacles, culture becomes less what Bourdieu would have called a habitus (a tacit realm of reproducible practices and dispositions) and more an arena for conscious choice, justification and representation, the latter often to multiple, and spatially dislocated audiences. (1990, 18)

But when and where were points of reference ever stable as critical life choices had to be made? To the degree that the reference points were stable, Appadurai suggests, people had no choices and were not making conscious choices about their lifeways. However, people have always been moving, and their points of departure and arrival have always been in flux. The ostensible historical period when actors were not consciously choosing among the available precedents, representing them selectively, and using them as strategic self-justifications is a fiction of modernist nostalgia.

Therefore, the present analysis is focused not on the alleged "roots" of these emergent black ethnic formations in their homelands but on the "rhizomatic" processes by which such ethnic formations have opposed, transformed, swallowed, and ejected each other across historical time and through daily interactions. It was Deleuze and Guattari ([1980] 1987) who reminded us that metaphors like "roots" represent ethnic groups and nations as though they were trees, unilineal in their origins and primordially autonomous from each other. Rhizomes, by contrast, are the root systems of grasses, which stretch not only down into the ground but also across large horizontal spaces. The grass on the west side of the lawn, or the cane on the west side of the field, is connected by its root system to the east side, such that an herbicide applied on one side will also kill the other side. While spokespersons of hierarchical social units would prefer to represent these units as "arborescent," or treelike, in their self-containment and vertical internal structure, the reality is that much cultural history is, like grasses, rhizomatic in its lateral flows and in the mutual constitution of apparently separate units.

A major insight of the literature on transnationalism and globalization is that the lateral demographic and economic influences among contemporaneous nation-states have as profound an influence on any given nation-state as does its local history. My own further premises are that such massive lateral and translocal influences are not new and that, to an even greater degree, the same insight applies to the *ethnic groups* that subdivide or crosscut national spaces (J. L. Matory 2005a). They too influence each other profoundly and, indeed, constitutionally. The history of ethnic groups is necessarily dialectical. Each group, or grouping, is a continually new product of interaction with other groupings and of mutual transformation among them. Here, these premises are tested not only with reference to the special conditions of the world's most stigmatized racial group but also at a globally influential type of institution whose intellectual and social activities have long played a key role in the articulation of self-conscious racial and ethnic identities—the university.

The topic of this book might be summarized as the dialectical and hierarchical nature of ethnogenesis. First, interaction between groups or identities is a foundational condition of identity itself. Second, one of the central dimensions of that interaction—even in a postimperial and post–civil rights era—is stigma, rank, and the strategic pursuit of esteem and opportunities through collective identities. Third, race and ethnicity are interacting dimensions of that pursuit. Ethnicity and its elaboration are characteristic attempts to escape the confines of racial stigma, even when the cultural differences among the stigmatized groups are cosmetic, situational, and historically transient. Conversely, the upward mobility of the members of privileged races is characterized by the shedding of consciously marked ethnic identities.

Argument 3: The University Is a World of the Stigmatized and a Major Venue of Ethnogenesis

Throughout this book, I examine the social setting of the university with the idea that much of its membership and the structure of its intellectual production qualify it as a community of the stigmatized. The university is, indeed, an overlooked paradigm of the "literally-defined world," in which, as Goffman points out, the stigmatized are inclined to produce. For example, university-based Jewish Americans and African Americans publish copiously in the defense of the reputations of their respective ethnic groups. Goffman, himself a Jewish Canadian, identifies lists of friends and enemies and "atrocity tales" as prominent items in these publications. Among the most prominent topics of today's American university debates are allegations of anti-Semitism against critics of Israel and advocates of Palestinian rights. Indeed, the most elite of US universities—including Yale and Harvard—have also invested great energy and resources in validating Black literature, arts, and religion through scholarship.

The elite university is arguably a world of the stigmatized, where the students of the late twentieth and early twenty-first centuries are driven to pursue upward mobility or to rescue themselves from downward mobility. The university is the foremost pathway of outsiders seeking acceptance by their unmarked class, professional, racial, religious, gendered, age-based, and ethnic superiors. It is the site of an alliance between the least moneyed fractions of the upper class and the most ambitious fractions of marginalized and stigmatized social categories, an alliance that inspires both the careful critique of the status quo ante and, usually, a consciously destigmatizing representation of the subaltern.

Stigma and Culture concerns the role of stigma (in the exemplary form of racial stigma) and interethnic competition for honor and income in the process of defining the boundaries and cultural diacritica of ethnic groups. Concretely, it describes the interaction and self-presentation of African and Caribbean immigrants and transmigrants, as well as Louisiana Creoles of color, Gullah/Geechees, and American Indians of partially African ancestry, with nonethnic African Americans at Howard University and in its domestic and international alumni networks. The shared condition of these populations is the unique stigma of inferiority and exclusion suffered by people of African descent in the Atlantic world. The university setting means that the focus of this ethnography is the middle class and the working-class aspirants to this station. It is the setting where I least expected members of these ethnic groups to stereotype the others as unworthy relative to the standards of the dominant society. And the major lessons of this ethnography flow from the fact that I was wrong.

For both the phenotypically privileged and the phenotypically stigmatized, the hidden curriculum of the university can be understood as guidance in the flight from social stigma. The institution is the most effective instrument of social mobility in the contemporary world. It is no mere accident, then, that universities play such a key role in the twentieth- and twenty-first-century rearticulation and, indeed, invention of ethnic identities. Just as universities teach the phenotypically privileged those manners and speech patterns that help to conceal their marginal class and ethnic backgrounds, universities also offer forms of collective organization and the vocabulary of "cultural" self-justification to populations that cannot render their stigmatized phenotypes invisible. One of the largest and fastest-growing types of organization on US college campuses is ethnoracial organizations. As they provide résumé-building opportunities for "leadership" and reify social connections that defy the officially universalizing, objectivist, and rationalist aspirations of the academy, they bespeak a hidden curriculum that remains central to the education of the contemporary bourgeoisie. In this regard, they differ little from but have come to outnumber their ethnoracially unmarked counterparts—the (traditionally white) fraternities and sororities.

Method

As the son of a professor and of two alumni, I literally grew up at Howard University. However, starting in January 2002 and with the support of a grant from the Spencer Foundation, I approached Howard and its alumni in pursuit of the answer to a specific question, about the interaction of racial and ethnic identity in the transnational Black bourgeoisie. I did so also in my additional roles as a visiting professor from Harvard University and a native anthropologist, under the official title of "Distinguished Visiting Scholar" in Howard's Department of History. In this capacity, I spent six months on Howard's campus teaching a seminar based upon five undergraduates', four graduate students', and my own ongoing research about this topic on campus. In 2004, I chaired the external review committee examining the Anthropology Program of the University's Department of Sociology and Anthropology.

Another factor undoubtedly influencing my research is the fact that I am a chocolate-colored, polyglot African American who is easily mistaken, even after years of casual acquaintance, for Caribbean, African, or Latin American. My previous specialty has been the study of West African and Latin American religions, which have given me some distance from the taken-for-granted assumptions with which I grew up at and around Howard. I could not easily be mistaken, however, for a Creole or an Indian, which may have made some confidences easier and some harder for my acquaintances of those social categories.

From January to July 2002, my then seven-year-old son and I lived in a combined graduate and honors undergraduate dormitory at Howard and participated in dormitory activities, such as picnics and talent shows. I mediated, bilingually, in the resolution of a labor dispute between anglophone Black and Spanish-speaking Central American staff in the dormitory. Because I speak Spanish, members of the Central American dormitory staff often spoke with me casually. One day, a Salvadoran friend on the staff, having apparently mistaken me for Cuban, Puerto Rican, or Dominican, told me that Black people (*morenos*) do not like to work, whereupon I proposed to lead a discussion of the misunderstandings within this team of approximately thirty workers. Both management and staff were happy for the opportunity to clear the air. It is unclear whether I resolved this simmering conflict, but the experience enhanced my understandings of the parallel conflict simmering among the university's ethnically diverse black bourgeois denizens as well.

Every day at Howard I dined, debated, and gossiped with students, local alumni, faculty, administrators, and staff. I delivered public lectures about my research and invited public commentary on my observations and inferences, and I explored university archives. Moreover, I had to seek many of the same administrative and medical services at Howard that students and other faculty sought.

My son Adu attended the Oyster Bilingual School / Escuela Biligüe Oyster in a nearby neighborhood, where I learned a good deal about the city's changing demographic and about the preparation of some of the city's ambitious Black American parents for this change. Adu and I had an active social life in the dormitory as well. For example, we frequently exchanged visits with Howard and Oyster students, as well as my largely African American childhood friends and their families.

I also attended parties, parades, and meetings organized by African American, Caribbean, and African professors, students, and alumni, as well as off-campus gatherings organized or attended by all of these populations. These gatherings included ethnic association parties, meetings of expatriate political parties, graduation parties, award ceremonies, and numerous powwows of Indian tribes that appear to have some African ancestry as well—tribes with which several Howard History Department professors and students were affiliated. Many of these professors and students recounted their alienation on account of ideological or skin-color issues. I also spent time regularly with a half dozen self-described Louisiana Creole professors, alumni, and former students. They did not organize themselves or meet publicly on or near campus. They spoke openly to the degree that they had been long-term family friends and colleagues. Others spoke hesitantly, and one friend attributed this hesitancy to the disapproval of her ethnic identity that she always anticipated

FIGURE I.1. Some of my African American childhood friends and their children at Adu's seventh birthday party, held in the Howard Towers dormitory. Photograph by Olubunmi E. Fatoye-Matory.

from her student peers. I also spent a good deal of time talking with restaurateurs from all of these backgrounds and eating in their restaurants.

After my six months on campus, I undertook a month of "deep hanging out" and interviewing among Howard alumni and their families and of archival research in each of four locales: New Orleans (June–July 2002); Port of Spain and San Fernando, Trinidad (July–August 2002); Lagos and Abuja, Nigeria (July–August 2003); and Kingston, Montego Bay, and Ocho Rios, Jamaica (July–August 2004). In between and following these travels, I have kept in touch with my mentors and interlocutors through shared meals, telephone calls, e-mails, and common attendance at university-related social and ceremonial events, such as graduations, retirement dinners, fraternity celebrations, and funerals.

Yet much of the material in this ethnography derives from a lifetime of co-residence and multiple lifetimes of family friendship with the people I write about.

Like any ethnography, this book flows from a dialogue between the described populations and the ethnographer. Much of the material here also derives from the feedback I have received from the nearly 150 undergraduate or graduate students who have attended my classes on this topic and from the hundreds and perhaps thousands of students and colleagues who have attended my public lectures about it. More than twenty of my mentors have read all or portions of this ethnography. Most of these mentors agreed with me wholeheartedly, while some—one southeastern Indian and two Creoles—disagreed with me sharply. But I learned much from their dissent and have included most of it implicitly or explicitly in the text.

A further unusual aspect of this ethnography is that, according to the racial logic of the dominant group in the ethnographic setting, I belong not to a metropolitan elite that is in a position to take its own values and positionality for granted but to an ethnoracial group (African American) that is typically the foil in the competitive self-fashioning of the populations under study (black immigrants, US-based triracial isolates, and Gullah/Geechees). We all bear the same racial stigma but different degrees of access to the now-popular discourse that our distinctive "cultures" should exempt us from that stigma. Like the shoots of a rhizome, we are all affected by the poison cast upon any of us. Perhaps the closest recent counterparts of this ethnography are studies of nonliberal religious women by secular female ethnographers of the same religious backgrounds, whose own attitudes and lifeways are challenged by the religiously devoted women they study (e.g., Mahmood 2005; Ahmad 2009; Fader 2009). To an exceptional degree, the present ethnography gives not just prefatory but central ethnographic and historical attention to the dynamic tension between the ethnographer and his subjects in the depiction and indeed the creation of "cultures."

This book examines ethnic diversity in the African-descended population of the United States, as well as the leading role of universities in the articulation, transformation, and mobilization of the collective identities that shape the priorities and affiliations of the bourgeoisie. Bourdieu ([1979] 1984) highlighted the role of "taste"—or competency in reading, consuming, and displaying the signs of elite status—as an important idiom of class stratification and of the competitive pursuit of honor among proximate strata. The faith of the lower and middle classes in the superiority of upper-class choices in dress, cuisine, décor, and music keeps the ambitious among them on a hamster wheel in Sisyphean pursuit of what Bourdieu calls "distinction," always too late in apprehending the fashion choices of the upper class and always in flight from imitation by the lower classes. Here I offer evidence that, like taste, ethnogenesis—or the articulation of cultures and the making of ethnic groups—is a competitive and hierarchical process. The drawing of ethnic boundaries around a group and the naming of its shared "culture" regularly occurs against the backdrop of a pervasive suspicion or accusation of that group's inferiority and answers this suspicion or accusation with an exaggeration of the group's differences from some more validly stigmatized group and exaggerates the speaker's group's similarities to an ethnically unmarked dominant group. I call this competitive and hierarchical dimension of ethnogenesis "ethnological schadenfreude," because its partisans take comfort and bolster their own self-esteem by assuring themselves of the even-deeper inferiority of some other ethnoracial group. This study of the transnational ingathering of anglophone black populations at Howard University alerted me to the striking parallels between ethnogenesis and the pursuit of class distinction that drove much of my own family life.

This truth is made especially evident in the context of racial stigma. I have chosen to focus my ethnographic study of this phenomenon on historically Black Howard University in Washington, DC. I had expected to see racial solidarity among the subjects of my research, and I did see a great deal of cooperation there. However, my invitation to discuss our intraracial commonalities more often inspired an elaborate explanation of why my black ethnic interlocutors were "culturally" superior to African Americans. At first shocked, I eventually recognized this discourse as a very human response to North American racism, and as a response with similarities to my own home training in class superiority.

Like black America, Howard University comprises dozens of homegrown or immigrant ethnic groups of African descent—among them, Jamaicans, Trinidadians, Nigerians, Ghanaians, Louisiana Creoles of color, Gullahs and Geechees, Indians of partly African descent, and their children. Just as important to Howardites, I discovered, is their wide range of complexions. While their shared African ancestry and a history of racially binary laws and customs in the United States have drawn them together in a shared setting, Howard students, faculty, administrators, and staff have become highly articulate—and indeed imaginative—about the ethnic, genealogical, and cultural differences among themselves. Yet they are not simply reporting antecedent differences. Rather, they invent themselves in dialectical response to the gaze of the ethnically unmarked dominant group and to the strategic self-construction of other populations who also wish to avoid last place.

The empirical setting of this investigation is in some ways unique.

First, almost all of my subjects are Black by North American definitions and something else according to the classificatory conventions of their homelands.

Second, *Stigma and Culture* is set at a time in US history when ethnic identities within all races are proliferating and talk of "race" is being marginalized in US public discourse.

Third, it is set in a university. Among the hypotheses explored here is that Howard follows the contradictory pattern seen in most universities: whereas they are typically chartered to train the bourgeoisie of a particular nation, province, religion, gender or race, they inspire an equal and opposite unofficial articulacy about the ethnoracial or subclass divisions within the university's core constituency. Through not only study but also eating, dancing, club initiation, job referral, dress, publication, gossip, and name-calling, university life is a concentrated multiethnic performance of collective bourgeois class and subclass identity. Thus, at Howard, black ethnics vividly perform and verbally articulate a popular anthropology of what distinguishes them from the stereotypical image of African Americans that they have received and that many of them indeed propagate.

Yet I will argue that a university devoted to the uplift of what is perhaps the world's most stigmatized race is actually a *locus classicus*, where ethnological schadenfreude finds its most memorable and instructive instance, much like taboo and mana in Polynesia, shamanism in central Asia, and caste in India. Black America and its leading educational institution classically illustrate the role of stigma, competition, and hierarchy in the self-making of ethnic groups in most, if not all, places and times.

Based upon half a lifetime of residence at and around Howard, six months of intensive participant observation as a visiting professor in the university's renowned history department, and a month each among alumni in New Orleans, Trinidad, Nigeria, and Jamaica, this ethnography concerns the current processes of racial and ethnic self-construction in the American and transnational black bourgeoisie. Through frequent comparison with the African-descended population of Harvard University (where I have either studied or taught for another half lifetime) and Duke University (where I have now taught for six years), I examine the role of academic and nonacademic ethnology in the pursuit of collective honor and opportunity in a globalizing and reethnicizing world.

Chapter 1, "Three Fathers," describes an African man, a Caribbean man, and an African American man—all recently deceased Howard affiliates—who played paternal roles in my life and illustrate the cosmopolitanness of the black Atlantic elite. Their education, their professional careers, and their marriages coincided with the height of black hopes for unity and uplift in defiance of both colonialism and segregation. Yet their triumphs never fully transcended the obstacles facing African-descended men in a creole world that stigmatizes their phenotype. This chapter charts the role of color, class, and social background in their itinerant pursuit of manhood. In many ways, their choices made me who I am. The intersection among their lives is presented as the social backdrop of my own epistemology. As race men, they provide a temporal and ideological counterpoint to today's narratives of black ethnic distinction that are the ethnographic focus of *Stigma and Culture*, narratives that presuppose the cultural simplicity and inferiority of nonethnic African Americans.

Chapter 2, "The University in Black, White, and Ambivalence," argues that the university is an exemplary world of the stigmatized, who typically create what Goffman called a "literally-defined world" in answer to the national, regional, class, ethnic, racial, gender-related, and disability-related stigmata under which its ambitious denizens struggle. Howard is not unique among universities, most of which were founded to prepare the bureaucratic and professional classes of previously dominated groups coming into their own as nation-states, provinces, regions, races, religions, and genders. The social composition of the twentieth-century university explains a great deal about the shape of the "cultures" that we scholars help to articulate as the charters of ethnic groups and nations.

Ethnic identities refer to habits of interaction and evoke powerful emotions based upon the personal history of people who have shared these habits with others. However, ethnic identities are not primordial; they emerge and change in response to the practical purposes of the people who invoke them as structures of cooperation and badges of honor. Chapter 3, "Islands Are Not Isolated," concerns the recent cosmopolitan and university-inspired genesis of Gullah/Geechee identity, which, in reaction to the stigmatization of the Gullah/Geechees' ruralness and relatively dark complexions, finds a new source of pride in university-based reports of their cultural Africanness and African-derived technological sophistication. I explore the irony that this ethnic identity is deeply indebted to the scholarly efforts of a Howard University professor but has fallen on stony ground among Howard students and alumni. This case demonstrates the cosmopolitan and interclass process by which regional racial categories and economic classes are turned into ethnic groups.

Chapter 4, "A Complexion or a Culture?," concerns American Indians of partly or possibly African descent and Louisiana Creoles of color. These populations overlap significantly with broader networks of the African American bourgeoisie but now employ the anthropological discourse of "culture" to seek distinction and dividends from white-controlled institutions, including universities, state governments, and the Bureau of Indian Affairs. Though many scholars and neighbors believe them to be of partly African ancestry, the premise of black inferiority is deeply embedded in these collective identities. Among themselves, they intensely debate whether revivalist claims that they are distinct "cultures" are really just (or also) instances of anti-Black racism and colorism. I argue that debate itself, rather than specific shared answers to this and other questions, is the chief diacritic of ethnic groups. My person—including my African appearance—became a provocation to several of the intense debates that I document here.

Chapter 5, "Islands of the Mind," concerns the ambivalent response of the largest of these ethnic groupings, Caribbean immigrants, to the US stigmatization of Blackness. For example, what are, in the Caribbean, called "middle-class" values are, in the United States, called "Caribbean culture," in an effort to demonstrate the superiority of Caribbean immigrants and their children to the archetypal object of exclusion from US democracy and economic prosperity, native-born African Americans. Being cast in the role of a foil to the Caribbean success story by people who had known my highly successful African American family and many others for decades was the foremost inspiration behind the theory of "ethnological schadenfreude." The Caribbean case superbly illustrates the hierarchical premises and competitive strategies still embedded in popular and scholarly uses of the "culture" concept. Caribbean American claims to ethnic distinction (like some nonethnic Black people's claims of being "middle-class Black") index upward class mobility and efforts to escape last place in a system of racially bifurcated assimilation.

Despite the fact that Africans are among the immigrants with the highest average socioeconomic status in the United States, they come from the poorest and most stigmatized continent. And their image is not their own. Chapter 6, "Heaven and Hell," documents the self-presentation of Eritreans, Ethiopians, Sudanese, and Nigerian scholars, restaurateurs, security guards, and students at and around Howard, including the writings of the scholars. Their self-presentation must respond to the dueling stereotypes of Africans in the United States—as both prototypes of Black inferiority and symbolic heroes of politically oppositional Black identity. With special reference to the now-supraethnic "Yoruba" identity, this chapter highlights the role of the university and especially that of traditionally White institutions, in transforming black ethic identities.

In the conclusion, I reflect on how it feels to be a fiction and on the lessons of the stigmatized for the discipline of professional anthropology. The competitive pursuit of honor and earnings is a major dynamic in ethnogenesis all over the world, and it regularly relies on the fiction of a constituent other. In the early twenty-first century, America's most stigmatized race is a historically specific case in point, illustrating the role of stigma and hierarchy in the genesis of ethnic groups and the "cultures" that name their boundaries all over the world.

1

Three Fathers: How Shall I See You through My Tears?

Reared in Cambridge, Massachusetts, my then-eighteen-year-old daughter Ayo̩ and then-fourteen-year-old son Adu once told me a joke that Adu's middle-class, biracial friend had told them. Unusually, the boy's father, rather than his mother, is white:

"What's the difference between a black man and a large cheese pizza?"
"A large cheese pizza can feed a family of four."

Though I had grown up in the shadow of Howard University, I cannot say that I found the punch line incomprehensible, but for me the humor lay not in the truth of the scenario but in the joke's verbal embodiment of willful white ignorance. It rests on the same American Dream, or Fantasy, as a hundred-odd television shows that use the imagery of laborlessly rich white Los Angeles and of self-induced Black ghetto desperation to cajole millions of poor and middle-class white people into complacency about the system.

Nonetheless, I feared that, having grown up in the shadow of Harvard and with fewer Black professional role models than I had had, my children were laughing only at the irony of the wordplay and might not be well enough anchored in the reality of Black accomplishment to recognize the lie embedded in this joke about Black men's (in)capacity as breadwinners. The subjects of this chapter made their own way, against the odds—sometimes by enlisting networks of Black male allies and despite their potential marginalization, as dark men or as ethnic outsiders—within those networks.

I begin with this story because it is where I began, with an awareness of the complex humanity of what I learned only later is the world's constituent other—black people; in the United States, especially Black Americans; and, among Black Americans these days, especially Black American men. Just as the "Welfare Queen" was Reagan's most memorable campaign image and slogan, the "absent Black father" is President Obama's wink and a nod to white voters that he shares their common sense about what really ails the world. In truth, our fathers and the fathers of my childhood buddies are complex characters who have applied careful reasoning and hard work to exploit the opportunities that our forebears often sacrificed their lives to create. No person who grew up as I did could mistake Black men for a suitable punch line to a joke congratulating white American men for their unique or uniform competency and dignity as husbands and fathers. I have intimately known too many white fathers and their children to imagine them a collective paragon for any virtues that my fathers lacked. The only difference is that, all other things being equal, their place in the light-dark hierarchy made it a lot easier for them to do the same amount of good for their children.

This chapter is rooted in the felicitous accident that three recently deceased Howard affiliates—one African, one African American, and one Caribbean—have acted as fathers to me. Theirs is also the generation that led the black national independence movements in Africa and the Caribbean and desegregation in the United States. After World War II, they experienced at Howard the largest and most international convergence of Western-educated black people that had ever occurred in history. And they shared a mission to redeem their peoples from political subordination and from the European racial "science" that justified it. For nearly a century, Howard had been a unique, US government–subsidized haven for the most ambitious African Americans within a nation-state where whites were committed to keeping Blacks out of their typically state-subsidized elite-producing institutions.

And even today, no one who grew up in Howard's orbit will find it strange that I love and was loved by a circle of outstanding black men from multiple geographical origins. During the Cold War and until the large-scale desegregation of US universities in the 1970s, Howard became a showcase of the United States' newfound fairness for audiences in the anglophone Caribbean and Africa as well. The Peace Corps and development aid might have impressed the general population of these nations, but Howard is what most impressed the aspiring professional elites. In the race to win the hearts and minds of the newly independent black nation-states, the United States was competing with the Soviet bloc and, consequently, outpaced England, thus both Americanizing the black Atlantic elite and accidentally spreading among them the racial-uplift vocabulary of the civil rights movement.

Yet, as the greatest culturally Western university of the West's most stigmatized population, Howard provided ample opportunity and motive for the stigmatized to "stratify their own." The "color complex," or complexion-based discrimination among people of African descent, was still rampant during the post–World War II era at Howard. In my parents' day, color-coded sororities marked status in a pecking order that spanned virtually all HBCU campuses. Moreover, Howardites, like the personnel of other HBCUs, remain highly conscious of verbal and sartorial signs of class status, which today range from "ghetto" to "bougie" (from "bourgeois"). It is perhaps symptomatic that fashion shows—which showcase and ironically remorph these sartorial signs—are now among the most popular student events at Howard, at other HBCUs, and among the Black students at Harvard as well. Moreover, particularly at Howard, stratifying articulations of ethnicity are as omnipresent and powerful as are the unifying, egalitarian discourses of Black nationalism.

In its subject matter and authorship, this book parallels Frazier ([1957] 1997) and Graham (1999) in documenting the combination of self-love, self-loathing, and ambition that characterizes the Black bourgeoisie. However, the scope of this study extends beyond African Americans and locates these struggles in circum-Atlantic context, identifying the multiethnic character of this class dynamic. These phenomena are also brightly illuminated by Fanon's studies ([1952] 2008, [1961] 2004) of the ambivalent psychology of the colonized and of recently independent national elites—a psychology deeply penetrated by the European colonizers' ideology of black inferiority and by whites' psychological projections of their own sexual and social conflicts onto black people. Like Graham's work, *Stigma and Culture* documents the centrality of university education in defining this the black bourgeoisie since World War II. Beyond the aims of these authors, the present work documents the role of ethnicity and transnationalism in the recent transformation of this class of actors. My aim is neither critique nor encomium but, instead, a fair account of a dilemma. How do people understand themselves when powerful others classify them as collectively worthless? It is often as difficult to embrace and defend one's ascribed collective identity as it is to escape from it.

This chapter offers intimate stories about how three men navigated the symbolic and material shoals of ethnoracial identity in pursuit of benefits for themselves, for their people, and for me. In common, the stories they told to their wives, to their children, and to me reveal their reliance on a class-specific sense of legacy to keep them strong against discouragement and temptation. As dark men in a creole world, though, they faced challenges to their own accomplishments and self-esteem. It is perhaps symptomatic that they all, at least by the end, married light-colored women. Perhaps as a sign of the times or of their relationships with me, the sense of legacy that I heard from them was not coded as ethnic. By contrast, my current research has revealed a present-day population with a disposition to code their past sources of hope and success as "cultures" that allegedly distinguish them from the African American referent of Adu's biracial friend's joke.

My biological father's college and medical-school classmate at Howard, the late Olubadejọ Olurẹmilẹkun Adebẹnọjọ, MD, introduced my parents to each other. When he died on March 3, 1996, his family and friends, in keeping with the tradition of the Nigerian bourgeoisie, took out large ads in several national newspapers commemorating his nearly seventy-two years of life and accomplishments. The several ads that spoke most vividly to me both upset my native conceptions of the dead and either named or created a conviction in me that I now find inescapable. They described my deceased uncle Badejọ as having become òrìṣà àkúnlẹ̀bọ—a "god whom we [now] kneel down to worship."

In life, he had frequently visited my childhood home in Washington, DC, at a time when I did not even know what a Nigerian or a Yoruba was. Since then, I have become a specialist in the study of this West African population and of its influence on the religions of Brazil, Trinidad, Cuba, Haiti, and their immigrant diasporas in the United States. This culture has also become a classical reference in African American cultural nationalism. Uncle Badejọ's readiness to facilitate my professional career and spiritual itinerary might seem serendipitous unless you believe, as I do, that the universe has a habit of paving my way—far beyond anything that I have earned or deserved. His most active role in my life began in 1982, when Nigeria became my second home. As my foremost guardian and guide east of the Atlantic, Uncle Badejọ stood in for my father in the traditional wedding that united me with my Nigerian wife, Bunmi.

The late Dr. Elliot P. Skinner, PhD, was the Franz Boas Professor of Anthropology at Columbia University, but he also frequently served as a visiting professor in the History Department at Howard University, where, during the course of research for this book, I would later do the same. In this regard, he also resembles his most famous compatriot, Trinidadian scholar and politician Eric Williams, who taught there from 1939 to 1948. Elliot and I first met during the Columbia Anthropology Department's unsuccessful efforts to recruit me to its faculty in 1991. However, he never stopped lobbying for me to succeed him as Franz Boas Professor of Anthropology. Since he somehow made my father's acquaintance in the 1990s, I often heard from each of them secondhand accounts of their discussions about and plans for my future.

My biological father, the late William E. Matory Sr., MD, contributed half of my genes, as well as much of the love, labor, and values that have made me who I am. Since his death in 2009 and Professor Skinner's in 2007, they have joined Uncle Badejọ as òrìṣà àkúnlẹ̀bọ (gods whom I kneel down to worship) in my effort to discover and refine who I am, to mobilize at the right times the parts of me that come from them, and to know when the mothers in my life—such as my birth mother Deborah, Aunt Ruth, Aunt Arnzie, Aunt Bette, and Ms. Davidson—set the better example.

This chapter represents my efforts to "see through a glass, darkly" the most intimate embodiments of Howard University in my life. The vale of tears before my eyes is both salty and bitter. The salt would preserve the memory of their love and of their accomplishments. They all modeled the forms of excellence that I then took for granted, and they moved mountains to support my growth.

The subtitle of this chapter is the title of a mournful song from the opera *The Gospel at Colonus* (1985), which retells the story of Oedipus at Colonus in the idiom of African American gospel music. The original play by Sophocles narrates the last days of Oedipus and the fratricidal battle among his sons to inherit his kingdom. Like much that happens at Howard and other post-slavery or postcolonial universities, *The Gospel at Colonus* re-presents Black dilemmas and cultural diacritica in a Western narrative frame.

Within this frame, the accomplishments of these late fathers are undeniable cause for celebration, but there is also bitterness in my tears. These were dark men who made voluntary and involuntary compromises in a creole world. Indeed, some of my New Orleans Creole interlocutors consciously compare the pale-skinned "Old Washington" Black elite to themselves and to the Charleston Browns. And the nonbinary color world they share is in many ways comparable to—and a part of—the Caribbean racial and cultural world known by the term "creole," albeit in its lowercase form. As they struggled for their own and their people's progress, what fears did they have to conquer, what forms of restraint and self-restraint did they adjust to, how did color affect their sense of self-worth, and how did their inner struggles affect their children?

The Boy in the Man

In 1972, when I left Shepherd Elementary School, there were few ideal educational choices for African American children of my class background. The balance of verbal repartee and fisticuffs that characterized Shepherd's playground differed radically from that balance at the more class-integrated Paul Junior High School; hence my quick departure for the almost equally undesirable Congressional School of northern Virginia, where my white homeroom teacher, Mrs. Crenshaw, asked, "Where did you learn to speak that way?" Apparently, my diction—though hardly rare at and around Howard and other HBCUs—knocked uncomfortably against her expectations regarding people of my age and color.

The Maret School suited me well, though I have never managed to outgrow my annoyance at the initial insistence of my white male peers that I play football and basketball for the school. I once expressed my annoyance to a white classmate at an alumni reunion, and he assured me that the pressure had had nothing to do with race. It was just that the school was so small that, without me, they could not have fielded a team. The stigmatized are always on the lookout for slights. But our instincts are not always incorrect. My recollection is that there were always plenty of players on the field, even after I promptly broke my wrist during a preseason practice and became wedded to the bench.

Hindsight might not have led me to interpret my classmates' pleas in racial terms had I not experienced other similarly ambiguous situations, as when the same classmate who denied the role of racial stereotyping in the sports recruitment efforts also expressed surprise that I had outscored him—and indeed everyone else in the class—on the SATs, the main standardized college admissions examination in the United States. After two and a half years in a closely overlapping set of courses, I would not have been surprised had he slightly outperformed me, but I failed to recall any aspect of our respective performances in class that would have made my higher score a surprise to him.

Twelve years ensconced in a predominantly Black world of physicians, dentists, lawyers, accountants, intelligence officers, ambassadors, undertakers, administrators, congressmen, and their children had caused me to think of myself consciously as "the smart one," "the dark one," "the chubby one," or "the child of divorce," depending on the occasion, but never as "the athlete," "the inarticulate one," or "the middling student." Five years in predominantly white secondary schools (I skipped the eighth grade) and four more in a traditionally White undergraduate institution trained me to anticipate at every moment the often-demeaning and sometimes dangerous disjuncture between who I am and what my skin color leads my white interlocutors to expect.

My own double consciousness derives most forcefully from the fact that I come from a medical family (that includes two of my "fathers," my late brother and sister, two biological aunts, two biological cousins, and an army of fictive aunts, uncles, and their children) and from the fact that my education has been divided more or less evenly between the nation's preeminent historically Black university and the nation's preeminent TWI (traditionally White institution). The clinic, the university classroom, and the university clinic are all sites where supposedly objective measures of the self are the most professionally and objectively articulated, intensively monitored, and immutably recorded. For the class of people who normally attend college, the university clinic is the first setting where the young adult encounters official definitions of his or her personal biology and psychic health unmediated by the presence and the decisions of parents.

As a Harvard College sophomore in the winter of 1979, I developed itchy, hyperpigmented bumps on my calves, which a white physician at Harvard University Health Services (HUHS) quickly diagnosed as a sign of lice. On his instructions, I dry-cleaned all of my clothes, at great cost, and applied toxic lice-killing Nix cream to my whole body—but to no avail. On my next visit to Washington, a Howard-trained dermatologist immediately diagnosed folliculitis, caused by winter dryness. Correctly, he predicted that it would go away if I applied urea-based lotion after every shower until the acute inflammation subsided and plain lotion thereafter. This was the first of many occasions when I felt that my family or I had been misrecognized by white physicians at the nation's premier TWI. Over the years, I developed the sense that, when faced with my medical problems, white physicians tended to leap for the most exotic and acute diagnoses and the ones requiring the most radical interventions. I am grateful, though, not to be one of the more statistically representative Black patients who are undertreated when their ailments are actually extreme and life-threatening.

On another occasion, after I joined the Harvard faculty, my excellent white male primary-care physician accepted a job elsewhere, whereupon I chose the next available primary-care physician, who happened to be female. My pediatrician, Aunt Betty, had been an African American woman and the mother of my best friend. During every office visit, however, my new white female physician at the HUHS seemed to tremble with anxiety. She stumbled over her words and often dropped things. When, by the third visit, she had not calmed down, it dawned upon me that something about me was making her nervous, and I could not help but wonder if she feared people of my race and gender. I don't know, but both personal experience and historical evidence made it seem wise for me to seek a new physician.

Years later, and a few months before my tenure decision was announced, I developed a pain in my face that was diagnosed alternately as trigeminal neuralgia and as a migraine. The HUHS physicians prescribed oxygen inhalation, pepper-based capsaicin ointment in the nostrils, and self-injected Imitrex, each prescription failing to resolve the problem more than once or twice. I received tenure at Harvard in 1998, whereupon these excruciating attacks seemed to stop, which led us all to infer that the headaches had resulted

THREE FATHERS 73

FIGURE 1.1. A gathering of Caribbean, African, and African American friends, many of them Howard affiliates, Bethesda, Maryland. Adu is in the middle. Unknown photographer.

from intense psychological pressure. However, another attack came a few years later. As I lay weeping helplessly in the emergency room of Harvard-affiliated Brigham and Women's Hospital, I called my father, just to let him know where I was. Whatever his long-distance suspicions, he had always hesitated to second-guess the opinions of the physicians who were treating me in situ, but on this occasion, he asked if I had been examined for sinusitis—an inflammation of the sinuses, which usually results from infection. Indeed, the Harvard clinicians had neglected this possibility. I had not been so evaluated. A simple course of antibiotics resolved that attack, and I have now been free of this problem for over a decade. On such occasions, I wonder if physicians who have been trained at the most high-powered of urban medical centers aren't looking for the exotic when the ordinary is right in front of their eyes. I wonder if "urban-looking" patients like me don't reflexively reinspire a certain sense of exoticism and experimentalism in such physicians, even after these physicians have practiced medicine for years among college students and professors. I also wonder if the Black and Black-trained physicians at Howard aren't simply less mystified or frightened and are therefore, all other things being equal, more competent in the treatment of a Black patient like me. Moreover, I doubt that Howard-trained or African American physicians generally are as prone to befuddlement when they see white patients.

My daughter Ayọ had a similar experience. When she was nine or ten, a hyperpigmented line appeared across her nose. The HUHS physicians treated it with an assortment of steroidal creams, to no avail. During my research at Howard, however, Ayọ and my wife, Bunmi, came to Washington to visit me and Adu, who lived with me in the dormitory. Together we attended a party honoring the return home of an old Washington-Trinidadian family friend's daughter.

The daughter's African American stepfather, an equally old family friend and former chair of Howard's Pediatrics Department, spontaneously started pushing up his nose with the back of his index finger and asked if our daughter often did something like that. My wife and I exclaimed in unison that she did and then asked how he could possibly have known. "She probably has an allergy" (causing her to rub her nose), he replied. "Take her to an allergist, and he'll tell you what to do," which, of course, we did. The line across her nose is now long gone.

It is difficult to fault HUHS for all of these failures of diagnosis and treatment, partly because I love Harvard and because its goodwill and successes at keeping us well far exceeded its failures. On the other hand, it is difficult not to wonder why Howard produced so many diagnostic and problem-solving successes in those few but repeated cases where HUHS had failed. My late sister, who, until her death, practiced and taught surgical oncology at Brigham and Women's, said that university health services do not hire physicians or serve their patients at the same level of care as university-affiliated hospitals like her own. On the contrary, to my recollection, at least half of our doctors at HUHS held a teaching status or had privileges, like my sister, at the Longwood-area, Harvard-affiliated hospitals. Moreover, I had had similar experiences at both the University Health Services and at Brigham and Women's. Thus, it may still be a reasonable inference—and is at least valuable evidence of Black people's experience of a postsegregation age—that Howard still offers certain advantages to a Black patient with my level of connections. Note that I am fully cognizant of the advantages that my family connections confer upon me as a patient at Howard, but in a truly postracial world, one might expect my being a professor and my daughter's being a professor's daughter at Harvard to confer a similar level of advantage upon us, even in the examination rooms of the white-dominated Harvard University Health Services.

My long-term immersion in the worlds of Howard and Harvard has alerted me to the difference that an HBCU can make in a young man's life. I now kneel down and look back to the lives of the kind of men who made that world, the types of stigma they faced, and their imperfect responses.

Certain truths may be told in the form of generalities about these men.

They traveled from distant places and, at Western-style Howard University, encountered an unprecedented cosmopolitanism and sophistication among other people of African descent. They and their fellow students all brought with them a sense of legacy that guided and buoyed them against the downward pull of segregation, colonialism, and intraracial pigmentocracy. Each man was shaped by a different configuration of oppression and discouragement. However, they shared a sense of purpose that transcended ethnicity and territorial nationality. And, at their level of accomplishment, they also gained backbone from their mission as firsts in the building of new capacities and institutions for black people. On the eve of the civil rights and African independence movements, they all saw themselves as pathbreakers for the collective progress of some racial or national group or another.

They all married not once but twice and did so across regional and ethnic lines. Moreover, their remarriage and childbearing after divorce or the death of the first wife tended to fuel a sense of alienation between themselves and the children of the first wife. Surely this is a pattern uniting middle-class men of all races—the men of the United States, Nigeria, and the Caribbean included. Also following a pattern, it is rare in these circles for such accomplished black men *not* to marry light, long-haired, and/or ethnically exogenous women. Finally, the regional, ethnic, and national worlds that my fathers occupied were never bounded or mutually exclusive. Rather, their shared world was an extensive network crossing rival regimes of race and status, and fraught with creative tensions.

ỌTUNBA OLUBADEJỌ OLURẸMILẸKUN ADEBỌNỌJỌ, MD (APRIL 24, 1924–MARCH 3, 1996)

As I look back on years of being stereotyped by American whites and, even more, by black ethnics, I ask myself how a young African must have felt when he arrived in the United States in 1948, when his brilliance came as a shock. Tarzan movies and missionary propaganda were the main North American sources of information about Africa. On what pillars of identity and camaraderie did Uncle Bandejọ lean? And once he returned to his homeland, what did he make of his experience?

In the preface to the history book written by his own father, Olubadejọ Olurẹmilẹkun Adebọnọjọ wrote, "My father used to say to me as a young student of history many years ago, that everyone knows what history is until he begins to think about it. After that, nobody knows." He added that historians "pick out and record the events that they feel will fit into a particular view that is valued by them and which they would like to share with others who may not necessarily agree with their views" (Adebọnọjọ 1990, v–vi). History is narrated, just as Bourdieu also said of ethnography, in "the logic of the trial." It is a defense against contrary, and usually demeaning, suppositions about the subject. To that I would add that a certain decorum governs the selection of details when the dead still have living partisans, including the other offspring and the siblings, spouses, and friends of the people whose history is being told. The history of the dead is also the history of the living.

My uncle Badejọ was a US board–certified orthopedic surgeon, physiotherapy specialist, author, and Lagos real estate mogul whose list of long-term friends is a who's who of the Yoruba bourgeois elite and an international network of Howard alumni who continually supported each other's endeavors. He brought into the world ten accomplished children—including two attorneys, a pastor, a research chemist, an aeronautical engineer, and a cinematographer—who live in Nigeria, the United States, and the United Kingdom.

He was born to Regina Odubọwale (née Odumọṣu) and H. R. H. Samuel Adegbesan Adebọnọjọ, the *Dagburewe*, or king, of Idọwa, in the Ijẹbu-Ode region of southwestern Nigeria. His maternal grandfather, J. J. Odumọṣu, had been a powerful practitioner of herbal medicine and one of the first, if not the first, convert to Christianity in the Ijẹbu region of Yorubaland. His grandfather's journals are the subject of Uncle Badejọ's first book—*Iwe Iwosan*, or *The Book of Health*, which was self-published during the 1980s.

In his own autobiography, *My Life* (Adebọnọjọ [1994] 1996), Uncle Badejọ attributes the greatest influence on him to his verbally gifted mother, of whom he says he asked questions incessantly. While his elder sister, the late Eva Adebayọ Adelaja, survived to an advanced age, another child died before Uncle Badejọ's birth. Hence, Uncle Badejọ received his middle name, Olurẹmilẹkun, which means "The Lord Relieves Me from Crying."

From 1936 to 1944, Uncle Badejọ attended Ijẹbu-Ode Grammar School, under the principalship of the Reverend A. A. Ẹfunkoya and was lodged in the home of S. O. Odutọla—then the canon and later the bishop of Saint Saviour's Church in Italawajode, Ijẹbu-Ode. In this generation of the Nigerian church, Africans had again managed to take over much of the Anglican Church hierarchy—after their racially motivated displacement by Englishmen in the 1890s (J. L. Matory 1999)—and assumed command over many of the Western-style schools in which the postcolonial Nigerian elite was trained. Uncle Badejọ was at first expected to become a churchman. Why this plan changed is not explicit in his autobiography or clear to his children. From 1945 to 1948, Uncle Badejọ attended the "African Managers in Training Scheme" of the United Africa Company and then enrolled in university evening classes. However, the fact that his next aspiration was business, followed by higher education and then professional school, recapitulates the history of the expanding options for upwardly mobile men in the Anglo-Atlantic world since the nineteenth century (Horowitz 1987).

The reasons Uncle Badejọ chose to travel to the United States, to attend Howard, and to become a physician are equally unclear. Whereas the Nigerian elites who studied abroad normally went to the United Kingdom and the earliest Nigerian universities were modeled on British ones, Uncle Badejọ joined a cutting-edge generation of Nigerians who came to the United States for study. Nigeria's first president, Nnamdi Azikiwe, had graduated from historically Black Lincoln University in 1930, but the number of Nigerians in US universities swelled only after World War II. Uncle Badejọ's autobiography names at least eight Nigerians among his undergraduate contemporaries at Howard (Adebọnọjọ [1994] 1996, 10). For many decades to come, they faced down the competitive claim that US degrees are inferior to or more variable in quality than British ones. (Such crosscutting forms of social and cultural capital subsidize rivalries within even the most corporate and bounded of social groups, such as the nation-state.)

According to his son Lanre, Uncle Badejọ's journey to the United States was facilitated by one Elder Dempsey, but several of his sons also speculate that he received some sort of scholarship for foreign students. However, I have heard over the years that Uncle Badejọ's mother, a prosperous trader in handwoven Yoruba *aṣọ òkè* cloth, also provided significant funding for the three sons she sent abroad for schooling. Uncle Festus would become a pediatrician and Uncle Tọla a general surgeon.

Whatever her financial contributions, Uncle Badejọ's sojourn at Howard, he told his son Lanre, was constantly shaped by his mother's parting words in the Ijẹbu dialect of Yoruba: "*Ranti ọmọ ẹni ti irẹ jẹ. Ma de kọja aye ẹ*" (Remember whose child you are. Do not step outside your proper place in the world). In other words, do not dishonor your family legacy by misbehaving. Honor your forebears by doing good and doing well. Hence, he was on a mission. Legacy—familial, ethnic, regional, or national—are central themes in black migrants' accounts, including my African American birth father's, of their triumph over systematic obstacles. Uncle Badejọ's name was itself undoubtedly a constant reminder to live up to his royal and Christian family legacy. "Olubadejọ" means "The Lord Is Acting in Concert with the Crown," while his surname, "Adebọnọjọ," means "The Crown Is in League with the Arts."

The financial support he received from his mother and the university notwithstanding, "he had to burn the midnight lamp [and] work scrubbing floors to make tuition money" (Lanre Adebọnọjọ, e-mail, March 29, 2009).

Yet even the moral support he received from Howard administrators mattered a great deal to Uncle Badejọ. For example, he wrote and told his children about the close mentorship and profound inspiration he had received from the university registrar, F. D. Wilkinson (Adebọnojọ [1994] 1996,10, 12; Lanre Adebọnojọ, e-mail, March 29, 2009).

Published on the occasion of his seventieth birthday, Uncle Badejọ's autobiography gives no hint of the racial oppression that is the backdrop of Howard's founding and the inspiration behind the civil rights movement, which framed his three major stints in the United States. During the unusually short period of 1948 to 1956, Uncle Badejọ completed his bachelor's degree, medical degree, and an internship at Howard. It was at Howard-affiliated Freedmen's Hospital that he met his first wife, the late Joyce Eleanor Johnson, a light-skinned African American nurse from Enfield, North Carolina (Adebọnojọ [1994] 1996, 10, 15). Her son Ladi has heard that she had Native American ancestry. Indeed, Enfield is the oldest town in Halifax County, one of the two home counties of the Haliwa-Saponi tribe.

It is striking that, in autobiographical hindsight, Uncle Badejọ renamed Freedmen's Hospital "Freedman Hospital," as if unconsciously converting a reminder of the recentness of emancipation in the United States into an innocuous proper noun. During his second stint in the United States, from 1959 to 1962, Uncle Badejọ conducted postgraduate training as a Betsy Barton Fellow in Physical Medicine and Orthopedics at New York University's Rusk Institute of Rehabilitation and at Bellevue Hospital. He received his specialty board certificate (Adebọnojọ [1994] 1996, 10, 15, 16).

Yet his sons Lanre and Henry recall an *oral* history of racial strife that did not appear in his writings. Their father told Lanre, "Black persons could not go anywhere near the White House" (Lanre Adebọnojọ, e-mail, March 29, 2009). Henry adds, "I recall Daddy talking about acts of [civil] disobedience in the nation's capital and students being arrested for standing their ground" (Henry Adebọnojọ, e-mail, April 2, 2009). Yet, by the time of Uncle Badejọ's seventieth birthday, his experience had boiled down to something quite different. His son Henry writes,

> If I were to sum up this part of the remembrance I would say that Howard was a window to the world for Daddy, through his experiences and his study. A place where he met people who looked like him and respected him. People who had burdens on them much like his own . . . to succeed, to be pioneers, to be ground breakers, to be torch bearers. They [Uncle Badejọ and my birth father] must have spoken of some of these things when they were students and must have continued to speak about them as professional men, each wonder-

ing how much of their goals and dreams the other had achieved. It is probably the reason they stayed in touch with each other over many years despite distance. (Henry Adebọnọjọ, e-mail, April 2, 2009)

Uncle Badejọ's autobiography documents his association and friendship with the leading politicians and academics of Nigeria's early postcolonial era, including independence leader and premier of the Western Region Ọbafẹmi Awolọwọ, Lagos state governor Lateef Jakande, Lagos state governor Bọla Ige, geographer Akin Mabogunjẹ, and scholar of religion S. O. Gbadamọsi. Joining these friends and associates in the roll of credits is a small transnational army of Howard faculty and staff who continued to inspire Uncle Badejọ and of fellow Howard alumni who continued to play active roles in his life. Among the Howard faculty mentioned are Africanist historian Leo Hansberry, philosopher and doyen of the Harlem Renaissance Alain Locke, and classicist Frank Snowden (Adebọnọjọ [1994] 1996, 10). Many of the fellow alumni he mentions had lived with him in Cook Hall from 1948 to 1951. Two of these were Charles Epps, future dean of the Medical College, and Andrew Young, future civil rights leader, United Nations ambassador, and mayor of Atlanta. Indeed, according to his son Lanre, Uncle Badejọ "shared a bunk bed with Andrew Young and . . . they used to stay up late on weekends bugging out [having fun] and teasing each other" (e-mail, March 29, 2009). Also listed among these contemporaries and dormitory mates was my own father, who frequently said that Adebọnọjọ and his other Nigerian classmates were brilliant. It is no wonder that the king of his ancestral town chose Uncle Badejọ as his *Ọtunba*, or "Right Hand of the King."

African Americans made up half and Nigerians the other half of the Howard contemporaries whom Uncle Badejọ recalled, thirty-two years later, as his most memorable friends. In his annual holiday letter, Uncle Badejọ recounts my birth father's assistance in securing medical care for him in the United States (Adebọnọjọ [1994] 1996, 26). Uncle Badejọ's short- and long-term experience seems quite different from that of most African and Caribbean students who attended Howard from the 1960s onward. Members of these more recent cohorts tended to live off campus as soon as the university regulations allowed and to live with only fellow Africans or fellow Caribbeans.

Intent on serving his newly independent nation, Uncle Badejọ returned to Nigeria in 1962, acting as chief consultant in physical medicine and rehabilitation and orthopedic surgery (Adebọnọjọ [1994] 1996, 10). During his two years in the Armed Forces Medical Service, he performed active duty in the Nigerian Civil War—also known as the Biafran War—in which Igbo military officers led an attempt at secession by the southeastern region of the country. Between 1971 and 1978, he was the chief medical officer for the Lagos State Ministry of Health and Social Welfare.

In 1973, he suffered the tragic death of his North Carolinian wife, Joyce, leaving eight boy children. She was buried in Lagos. From 1979 to 1982, he served as permanent secretary of health and the environment and secretary of state, from 1982 to 1983, as special adviser on health and the environment for the Lagos state government (Adebọnọjọ [1994] 1996, 10–11). During this period, he married his wife Yewande (née Daniel), a dark and proud Aguda, or descendant of nineteenth-century Afro-Brazilian "returnees" to Lagos. From the time I first met her, in 1982, her hair was always chemically relaxed—a style rare in Nigeria but not uncommon in the Lagosian bourgeoisie of the late twentieth century. *Àǹtí*—that is, Aunt—Yewande and Uncle Badejọ had two boys together. His parenting followed the credo "keep your children busy and keep them with you and keep them out of trouble." He added that he made a point "never to indulge them" (Adebọnọjọ [1994] 1996, 16). He was very proud of the outcome.

After his retirement in 1983, Uncle Badejọ managed his considerable commercial and residential real estate holdings in Lagos, edited and published a history of his native Ijẹbu region written together with his elder brother and his father (Adebọnọjọ 1990), participated actively in the rearing of his minor children, and penned an autobiography (Adebọnọjọ [1994] 1996).

For a professional who has resided in Nigeria since 1962, Uncle Badejọ kept in touch with a surprisingly diverse set of professional colleagues (Adebọnọjọ [1994] 1996, 12). His sons Lanre and Henry explain why. Writes Lanre,

> The impact of Howard on Daddy, as I recall, was to develop a dogged 'sticktoitism'—persevering through to make full use of the opportunity presented. It seems like the rigour of obtaining the golden fleece bonded classmates so much so that, even after Daddy returned to Nigeria, he [had] ongoing dialogue with many of his classmates and visits to the US, knew their whereabouts. The Howard Alum[ni] played a prominent role in his networks because he seemed to be involved in much of the activities both in Nigeria and in the US when he visited. In fact, I recall accompanying daddy to a Howard event in D.C. (1995) at which your late dad was present. May his soul rest in peace. (Lanre Adebọnọjọ, e-mail, March 29, 2009)

Henry adds,

> I don't know much about Daddy's days at Howard, except that it cloaked him in a coat of pride both professional and personal. . . . I remember Daddy's Bison yearbook, ribbed and bound in blue displayed, prominently among his

books. I know Daddy cherished his relationship with his Howard mates, because their names came up frequently enough, but without any specific detail I can share. I list the following names I recall hearing over the years:
Dr. William Matory in Washington DC
Dr. Henry Lucas in San Francisco
Dr. Lorenzo Turner in Cherry Hill, NJ
Dr. William Miles in Rye, NY
Dr. Andrew Young in Atlanta (ibid.)

In my earliest visual memories of Uncle Badejọ, I am wearing pajamas with footsies. Wearing his *agbada* robe of simple, light-colored Austrian lace, he is standing beside a massive brown stereo speaker broadcasting Mantovani and bossa nova in our dining room. I remember hearing from my mother that Uncle Badejọ was a welcome and beloved guest, unlike my father's East Saint Louis confrere Miles Davis, who, according to my mother, would arrive for dinner at the house empty-handed but with his entire band in tow. My father, on the other hand, was grateful for all of these visits. He was at once afraid that this house in the North Portal Estates would cause resentful colleagues to stop referring patients to him and proud of its high-end furnishings. My mother told me that she would move out of the house for the few days after buying them in order to avoid his initial anger. I remember the week of her absence after she replaced the threadbare wall-to-wall pea-green carpeting with a burnt-orange wool pile so dense that it still looked new when we sold the house thirty years later. Dad was at once afraid to stand out and proud when his children did. But he could not decide how to feel about material possessions. His widower father preferred the acquisition of real estate to its furnishing or improvement. Only by the time he married his second wife, a woman with tastes as refined as my mother's, did he develop a tolerance for new cars and conspicuous consumption.

Uncle Badejọ's biography and the annual holiday letter that is published with the posthumous edition of the biography demonstrate a characteristically Yoruba celebration of life's usual trajectory, from its ancestral precursors to death and worshipful transformation into ancestorhood. From early on, Uncle Badejọ knew "whose child he [was]" and acted upon that knowledge. His inborn nobility was the foundation of his mission to create new services and institutions for Nigeria. What is remarkable, though, is the global scope of his empathy and desire to act. It is true that in his final annual letter, he laments interethnic strife, election violence, the corruption ensuing from the oil-based economy, and the disadvantages of privatization for the working class in Nigeria. But his foremost prayer was for a "PEACEFUL WORLD ORDER, in which no human being is oppressed or suppressed and justice for all is pursued" (Adebọnọjọ [1994] 1996, 29–30). He declares his "total commitment and concern for the welfare of our fellow human being[s]" (14). But on the occasion of his seventieth birthday—the last, as he notes, that is biblically promised—he offers some more folksy advice.

First, success requires making choices, and choices involve risk. Don't be afraid of them (14). And finally,

> I do not smoke, I cannot stand it. I drink in moderation. I get enough sleep, not necessarily enough rest. Above all, I avoid stressful situations as much as I can. . . . I plan my daily routine and tried to accomplish as much of it as possible. I learnt early in my days in America that the way to get anything done properly is to do it yourself, but you can still delegate some responsibilities to people you trust with confidence that you will not be let down by them. (17)

ELLIOT PERCIVAL SKINNER
(JUNE 20, 1924–APRIL 1, 2007)

"When you go out to play, always take your own ball," his mother warned him: depend on the whim or largesse of no one (Matory 2009).

In a discipline that long ago eschewed the idea of race, there is much to be learned from the life and career of Elliot P. Skinner, the late Franz Boas Professor Emeritus at Columbia University—where American cultural anthropology began—and doyen of African American anthropology. Among African Americans, anthropology has yet to escape the monstrous shadow of the craniometrists. Consequently, Elliot's protégés were as often diplomats or public-policy makers as career anthropologists. Indeed, it was not without controversy that, in the 1960s, he became the first Black tenured professor at Columbia and then the first Black chair (1972–75) of any academic department in the Ivy League. He did so by bringing his own ball to the game.

I did not know Elliot as well as Uncle Badejọ. But I saw him as a role model, and he saw me as a successor. Among my three fathers, he is the only nonphysician, and as researchers of the black elites of the circum-Atlantic world, we speak the same language, a language seldom heard in our discipline. Nor is our topic often addressed.

Like historian Eric Williams, who would later become prime minister of their shared Trinidadian homeland, Elliot had not studied at Howard but had served as a professor there. Whereas Williams taught there continuously from 1939 to 1948, Elliot conducted several stints of teaching at Howard after 1969. He taught several classes over time in Howard's Department of History—my own host department in 2002—and mentored junior scholars there. He also spent one full year in residence (1995–96) as an Inaugural Fellow of Howard's Ralph Bunche International Affairs Center. There he taught a course, lectured publicly, and mentored thesis students. According to his wife, fellow anthropologist Gwendolyn Mikell, Elliot taught at Howard because "he believed strongly in the responsibility of Black scholars to mentor the next generation, and he was determined to be the one who produced the most Black PhDs." She added, "Of course, he ran competition with [Howard University History professor] Joe Harris for that status (how many stars can exist in that universe?)." She reports that Elliot felt deep affection for Howard. He seemed to regard Howard, above all institutions, as "a ball of our own."

It is difficult to say whether Elliot's appointment to the discipline's most historic professorial chair reveals or reverses the prevailing trends in our field. He reports that, in the infancy of his career, Melville J. Herskovits rejected his application to the anthropology graduate degree program at Northwestern University. A student of Boas and the founder of African studies in the United States, Herskovits reputedly judged black scholars incapable of studying Africa objectively (Cole 2003, 278–80; Yelvington 2006, 71), and with that in mind, he did his best to limit their research and professional options on the continent. Related dimensions of US race relations may help to explain both the distinctive interdisciplinarity of Elliot's engagements—his writings are no less diplomatic history, international affairs, and urban sociology than they are anthropology—and the limited attention his work has received from anthropologists.

Herskovits's reported opinion about black scholars both undershot and overshot the truth. Black scholars in the United States have long found it difficult to ignore the global political context of their studies and to retain the noninterventionist postures that characterized the dominant traditions of mid-twentieth-century anthropology, traditions whose own pretensions of objectivity would later be challenged by the reflexive turn of the discipline in the 1980s (e.g., Harrison and Harrison 1999). For Black anthropologists, Africa was harder to imagine as a mere object of study than as a struggling counterpart or comrade in a global fight. The "native's" endeavors seemed less like living models of prehistory than like the dilemmas, gambles, mistakes, mitigated failures, and partial victories of another victim of racial oppression.

Consequently, Elliot professed his scholarship and measured his successes by standards transcending the academy. He was proud of saying that he had produced more Black PhDs than anyone else in academe—a gift to social progress and not just to the progress of ideas. Beyond that, Elliot himself served as US ambassador to Upper Volta (now Burkina Faso, 1966–69); chairman of the Association of Black American Ambassadors (1988–92); perennial lecturer at the State Department, the Defense Department, and the US Information Service; and mentor to generations of diplomats and public-policy makers. Even in the foreign service, Elliot's linguistic skills reflected a rare degree of commitment to his calling. He spoke fluent French and Moré, the language of Burkina Faso's Mossi people. For his advocacy of Upper Volta's national interests, he received the honorific title of Commandeur de l'Ordre National Voltaique (Commander of the National Order of Upper Volta)—which he considered in every way consistent with his pride in representing the US government.

A man in between disciplines, classes, and cultures, Elliot was bound to innovate in his field and to render sensitive portraits not only of the culturally hybrid empires of West Africa but also of their descendants, who engineered a way to survive and prosper amid enslavement, colonization, and segregation. Like most of my own work, Elliot's opus focuses on the agency of elite and mobile black populations around the Atlantic perimeter. Indeed, their story is his story—the story of people who did not create the rules of the colonial and postcolonial game but found their own ball to kick into play.

Elliot was born on June 20, 1924, in Port of Spain, Trinidad. He came to the United States in 1943, at the height of World War II, and promptly enlisted in the US Army, which gained him American citizenship. After World War II, he enrolled in New York University (NYU), studying anthropology there with John Landgraf, and graduated in 1951. He went on to Columbia, where his main mentor was Morton Fried. There he earned an MA and then a PhD with a dissertation based on fieldwork in British Guiana, on the Caribbean coast of South America (Skinner 1955). This was followed by his two years of initial research on the Mossi. After teaching at Columbia as a visiting assistant professor (1957–59), he moved back to NYU, where he won tenure in 1963, and then rejoined the Columbia department in a permanent position. Apart from leaves of absence, several of which he spent teaching at Howard, he remained at Columbia until his retirement in 1999.

Elliot's story had begun in the multiracial and class-stratified British West Indian colony of Trinidad. His father was a Trinidadian of Barbadian ancestry who was born to a family of landowning craftsmen and merchants. His Trinidadian mother was more modestly born. It is not surprising, then, that his writings luxuriate not only in cross-cultural breadth and attention to black class diversity but also in the humanizing depth with which he reconstructs the daily social and political dilemmas of the medieval Mossi kingdom of Ouagadougou, modern Upper Volta, Ethiopia, Liberia, and Madagascar, as well as those of twentieth-century Black America's itinerant diplomats and race leaders.

Elliot's ambassadorial service crowned his lifelong status as a man "betwixt and between." As a teenager, while working on a US military base in Trinidad, Elliot had admired the African American intellectuals, entertainers, and race leaders whose names and images circulated there. He therefore strategized to follow his émigré father to New York City, where, like the subjects of his political ethnographies, he continually bridged and manipulated the multiple communities and identity claims available to him. He was a Caribbean immigrant to the United States, part of a community that, like Barbadian immigrants to Trinidad, regarded itself as harder-working and higher-status than the local black population, but he chose to define himself primarily as an African American. He became committed to the uplift of Black people generally and to the distinctly African American premise that blacks and mulattoes are family and comrades in arms rather than mutually antagonistic strata in a "white-is-right" hierarchy. However, despite marrying into the African American community, he was frustrated by some African Americans' refusal to accept him as an insider. Moreover, though Elliot felt humiliated by the menial roles accorded to Black people in the US military and was critical of America's devastating Cold War policies in Africa and Vietnam, his national identity was primarily as an American and only secondarily as a Trinidadian.

Elliot wedded pride with pragmatism. He recognized—rather than reviling—the power of power. He not only studied but also played ball on the racially uneven field of the Atlantic perimeter. As if autobiographically, he wrote more often about people's "manipulations," "negotiations," "unofficial activities," "symbolic" interventions, and "back-channel influences" in the pursuit of sovereignty or safety than about the "social structures" or "laws" of society that characterized the conventional ethnographies of his day. In his analyses—perhaps because of the disjuncture between his own ambitions and the opportunities officially allotted to him—fixed social positions gave way to the actor's strategically shifting array of personal, racial, and national personae.

Trained in the 1950s, Elliot wrote with one eye on the Manchester school of Abner Cohen, Victor Turner, and the like—with a high awareness of local social conflict and social dramas—and another on the large-scale dilemmas of political identity faced by black elites in a world of white-controlled nation-states and colonial empires. In Elliot's work, the local social dramas and structural tensions theorized by the Manchester school took place against a macropolitical backdrop. Elliot also anticipated the "historical turn" of anthropology in the 1980s. He invariably took advantage of the extensive written records—including ancient Arabic chronicles of the western Sudan and the diplomatic correspondence of nineteenth-century African American ambassadors in Africa—to reveal his subjects' intellectual complexity, self-awareness, and strategic agency. Such insights were perhaps unavailable but also typically unimagined by the European and Euro-American ethnographers documenting related populations. At least one reason is that Elliot himself grew up with the same hope for change and the same double consciousness (Du Bois [1903] 2007)—and sometimes triple and quadruple consciousness—as the people he studied. It is a fiction knowingly propagated by the sovereign class and faithfully but anxiously embraced by the middle class—out of naïveté or pragmatism—that the current "structures" of life are fixed in law-like ways, that they apply to everybody, and that they look the same from every perspective. Doubts about the fixity, the objectivity, and the rewards of bowing down to this fiction are the hallmark of the sovereign and of the stigmatized. It behooves the ambitious among the stigmatized to act as though they don't know it, but they cannot afford to forget for one minute that the game is rigged.

Elliot is the sole author of three major books, the coauthor or editor of nine, and the author of countless articles. *The Mossi of Burkina Faso* ([1964] 1989) charts the pre-fifteenth-century founding of the Kingdom of Ouagadougou in what is now Burkina Faso, its centuries of expansion, and its twentieth-century adaptation to European dominance and national independence. Elliot's analysis focuses not on frozen political structures but on the continual genealogical debates and shifts of power among the kingdom's constituent principalities. The historical accounts of the conquered, of the conquerors, of Muslim travelers, and of French invaders are used to reconstruct the story of a multiethnic polity with multiple power centers, in which the sovereignty of the Mogho Naba paramount ruler was never a matter of mere rules, tradition, and absolute power but rather a chess-like web of marriages, military alliances, and continual rearticulations of tradition. Inherent dynamism and the rivalry among strategic actors were the structure of this system, which Elliot argued was an enduring example of the political system that had probably also characterized the venerated but now-extinct Sahelian empires of Ghana, Mali, and Songhai.

After reading such a believable account of how power works in the real world, it is difficult to imagine why accounts that depict pre-colonial African politics as rigid machines have remained credible for so long. Such portraits depict African kingdoms as variants on a European bureaucratic ideal, an ideal that fails as a real-world representation of European politics as well. This genre of colonial-era ethnography was in many ways a liberal attempt to show that Africans were not inferior to Europeans, contrary to their image in the Western popular imagination and in critical resistance to the abuse inherent in colonization. The social and even the racial positionality of ethnography's borderline-white pioneers (including the trendsetting Polish anthropologist Bronislaw Malinowski) helps us to understand these pro-African apologetics, just as much as Elliot's prescient historical and practice-oriented approach—twenty years ahead of the trends in our shared discipline—seems to emerge from his own interests as a racial outsider who managed to strategize his way into the heart of power.

African Urban Life: The Story of Ouagadougou (1974) is the most thorough historical and statistical account I have seen of an African city in its precolonial, colonial, and postcolonial phases. It details the twentieth-century transformations that left this administrative center with an ethnically diverse population; a rich social, political, artistic, religious, and educational life; and social arrangements based on a smorgasbord of Western, Middle Eastern, and African cultural models—but with few means of sustaining itself economically. What is most special about the book, however, is Elliot's vivid documentation of the culturally coded but creative and pragmatic choices with which most families make their way under conditions of scarcity. The most intriguing of his accounts detail the reinterpretations of kin reciprocity and of associational life that "high-status" urban Voltaics undertake to ensure their upward mobility and to lighten the weight of their obligations to rural kin. In their homelands as in their diasporas, collective identities depend for their salience and survival on their strategic utility to their most powerful bearers. This study unveils the class diversity and cosmopolitan complexity of African urban life in a manner with few parallels in the ethnographic literature. It is no surprise—though it gave Elliot a sense of vindication—that this book received the African Studies Association's Melville J. Herskovits Prize for the best book of the year. This assessment of the strategic interaction of class aspirations and collective identity also foreshadows the argument of *Stigma and Culture*.

African Americans and U.S. Policy toward Africa: In Defense of Black Nationality, 1850–1924 (1992) self-consciously uncovers the forgotten or marginalized history of an extraordinarily well-educated, politically savvy, and entrepreneurial class of postbellum African Americans who achieved a surprising degree of influence over US and European policy in Africa amid the neoslavery of colonialism and Jim Crow. Implicitly, it places Elliot's own career in historical context. With a unique degree of ethnographic detail, Elliot spotlights the contrasting political strategies of Marcus Garvey and W. E. B. Du Bois, both of whom shared with many African Americans the conviction that uplifting Africa was a necessary precondition for the redemption of the African diaspora. In Elliot's depiction, Garvey, who was a dark Jamaican, boldly declared his antagonism to the European colonialists and to the US American perpetrators of slavery and segregation. By contrast, and with greater success, light-skinned African American W. E. B. Du Bois called for Black unity and African uplift through unavoidable cooperation with those who held most of the guns and the cash—the Europeans and the Euro-Americans.

Two of Elliot's articles were as influential as his books. Through its application and revision of sociologist Georg Simmel's concept of "the stranger," Elliot's "Strangers in West African Societies" (1963) highlighted the normalcy and the diversity of roles accorded to the nonnatives in African societies, inspiring an entire edited volume of writings that illuminated not only the long-running cosmopolitanness of such societies but also the contradictions between, on the one hand, the national sovereignty of postcolonial nations and, on the other, the forms of enduring privilege that European colonialism had conferred upon whites, Asians, Syro-Lebanese, and immigrant Africans (not to mention fictionally "alien races" such at the Tutsis) in African societies.

Elliot's article "The Dialectic between Diasporas and Homelands" (1982) reveals the central but ironic role that Asian, African, and European diasporas have played in the cultural histories and even the nationalist movements of their homelands. This article directly inspired my own study of the mutually transformative "dialogue" between Yorubaland and its diaspora (J. L. Matory 1999, 2005a) and also therefore furnished the central theme of Kevin Yelvington's School of American Research volume, *Afro-Atlantic Dialogues: Anthropology in the Diaspora* (2006), and the edited volume *Transatlantic Caribbean: Dialogues of People, Practices, Ideas* (Kummels et al., 2014). Long before "agency" became the watchword of anthropology and "hybridity" the shibboleth of postcolonial studies, Elliot applied the historian's precision and the novelist's empathy to the symbolically rich strategies of intercultural agents in the black Atlantic world. Again, it is not difficult to recognize the autobiographical roots of this analytical posture or of his influence on my research.

Elliot's insights won him a range of fellowships in anthropology and international relations, from the Fulbright Program, the Woodrow Wilson International Center, the Center for Advanced Study in the Behavioral Sciences, the Social Science Research Council, the Guggenheim Foundation, and the John Hay Whitney Foundation.

However, like my birth father and like many Black scholars, Elliot ultimately measured his success less in terms of abstract intellectual insights than of how those insights benefited a downtrodden race. From lecterns at Columbia University, Howard University, Lincoln University, and the State Department, he trained generations of anthropologists and policy makers, diversifying their ranks exponentially. Yet he recognized that his interventions required a subtle craft. Amid the bass beat of power, the most effective strategy of the righteous, as Du Bois's Africanist diplomacy revealed, is often a minuet. As the American Anthropological Association debated the ethics of anthropologist "embeds" in US-occupied Iraq and the American Psychological Association debated the limits of psychologists' role in torture by US government agencies, Elliot's postambassadorial observation to his students was apposite: "The C.I.A. is everywhere. There's no way to avoid them." You can, however, choose what to say, how to say it, and when to withhold an answer. You can, in short, correct misperceptions and scatter tacks in the path of state-sanctioned misdeeds.

As a professor emeritus, Elliot held court amid the refracted evening glow of the Potomac and a generous wet bar. The locale bespoke the irony and the structural reality of a man in between—a rare anthropologist who had mastered the architecture of elite power, the subtleties of influence, and the cultural hybridity of their exercise in a postimperial world. He denied with his words and yet embraced with a grin his delight in choosing to live out his final years in what he called a "den of iniquity"—the Watergate. There his neighbors included the former Republican senator and presidential candidate Robert Dole and George W. Bush's former national security advisor and then secretary of state, Condoleezza Rice. Like the forms of intersocietal power and influence that Elliot made his expertise, the Watergate condominium complex and the extralegal shenanigans it famously hosted in the early 1970s were built not of squares and angles but of interlocking circles and crescents, laced together by curved, indirectly lit hallways in which the visitor can never see one end from the other. Likewise, Elliot showed us social order not from the perspective of the hereditarily elite classes that wrote the laws of empires and nation-states—or of the middle classes who mistook the law for literal—but from the perspective of those whose survival or obstacle-ridden upward mobility depended on discerning the crooked motives of the lawmakers.

Elliot's interventions appear to draw some of their tactics from the political and performance arts of the black Atlantic, where beauty and effectiveness inhere in syncopating, circumventing, and bending the rectilinear lines of empire and nation-state. The Afro-Brazilian martial art of capoeira, for example, demands the outguessing, outmaneuvering, and subtle distraction of one's opponent. Indeed, at the height of the conflict, capoeira is meant to look like a harmlessly jovial game. Yet the results can be deadly.

Elliot P. Skinner became an ancestor on April 1, 2007. He died a great-grandfather, and in both biography and bibliography, he immortalized the art of capoeira where the Marquess of Queensberry rules.

WILLIAM EARLE MATORY SR., MD
(OCTOBER 1, 1928–JANUARY 26, 2009)

Throughout my years as a professor at Harvard, my birth father frequently asked about the grants in my field that would allow me to "get my own." Much as Elliot's aunt had urged him to do, my father urged me to secure resources of my own so that I would not need to fight with rivals or depend on the goodwill of colleagues and department chairs. Yet a curious inversion distinguishes these two stories from Howard's "greatest generation." On the one hand, Elliot received advice intended for his personal well-being and came to act in the service of our collective racial well-being. On the other, my birth father lived his life self-sacrificially in the service of his race and then encouraged me to pursue personal self-service (Schudel 2009). It had taken a lifetime for Howard to pay him his due.

In common with Uncle Badejọ, my birth father saw himself as deeply defined by networks of male friendship rooted in his college and medical-school careers. When I asked other Howard alumni in the United States, Africa, and the Caribbean whether their networks of fellow alumni had ever opened doors for them in their professional lives, I was shocked by the consistency with which they said no. I say "shocked" because I owe my birth, half a lifetime of superior medical care, my son's access during my research to the best public schooling in Washington, and much of my ease of access during nearly thirty years of international field research to the efficacy of my parents' Howard University–based networks. Those networks have produced more visible effects in my life than has my thirty-seven-year-old connection to Harvard's reputation and networks.

William Earle Matory Sr., MD, distinguished himself as a surgeon, teacher, technical innovator, husband, father, and friend. He was a one-man army in the pursuit of excellent medical care for the disadvantaged and of African American leadership in the US medical establishment. Even his family life gave pause to those who doubted the realism of *The Cosby Show* (1984–92), a hit television series about the family of a Black doctor and his wife, a Black attorney. Dad died on January 26, 2009, at the age of eighty, from coronary heart disease—the nearly predictable affliction of a man determined to prove himself and his race against the legally and customarily inflicted odds. Sherman James (1994) compares such men to John Henry, an object of comparison far more apt, in my experience, than a cheese pizza. According to legend, John Henry was a Black man and a former slave who expertly wielded his hammer to break rocks and clear the way for railroad tunnels. Challenged to race against the operator of a steam engine in completing such a tunnel, he won, but shortly thereafter he "died with the hammer in his hand." These are the wages of having to work twice as hard to advance half as far as one's similarly talented white counterparts. Every Black person I know recites this dictum, and most endeavor to do exactly that. In this regard, I am my father's son: I work four times as hard on anything I do.

Cubans and Brazilians, too, regale a mythical being embodying this character trait of dark black men. The hardest-working god in Cuban Santería/Ocha and in Brazilian Candomblé and Umbanda is the dark-skinned god of iron, technology, and war. The people born under his protection also tend to be dark skinned and to embody his personality traits. Called "Oggún" in Cuba and "Ogum" in Brazil, he works ceaselessly and joylessly. However, without him, civilization itself would be impossible. He is the master of all tools, but the foremost are the sword and the hammer. Bahian priests judge me a son of Ogum, with Oxalá, the usual protector of scholars and the second god in my spiritual ensemble. Oxalá (Obatalá in Cuba) is a gender-ambiguous old man, characterized by coolness and patience. He is closely associated with the color white. But the main rival of Ogum as an archetype of manhood in its prime is Xangô (Changó in Cuba). He is the epicurean and sometimes lazy womanizer and lover of a good party. He is more the ruler than the worker, and in both traditions, he is described as a mulatto. On the other hand, like Xangô, I would rather dance than fight, but being black in the Americas, I don't always have the choice.

Dad served on the Board of Governors of the American College of Surgeons and was one of the first African Americans to chair the Washington, DC, Board of Medicine, which licenses all physicians in the city. From 1977 until his death, he directed Continuing Medical Education for the National Medical Association. This professional organization of African American physicians was founded in 1895, at a time when numerous branches of the American Medical Association (AMA) excluded them. Indeed, the AMA continued to exclude most Black physicians on the basis of their race well into the late twentieth century. His myriad accomplishments notwithstanding, Dad did not join the AMA until 1979.

My father published sixteen scholarly articles—in the *Journal of the National Medical Association*, the *American College of Surgeons Bulletin*, and the *Journal of the American Society of Plastic and Reconstructive Surgery*. He always regretted not having published more. However, he would make an even more important contribution through his filmmaking. Greater still were the fruits of his teaching. Over half a century, according to the Howard University alumni magazine, he trained some four thousand medical students and professionals.

Dad was born in East Saint Louis, Illinois, on October 1, 1928. He was the fifth of six children and, at the time of his death, was the last remaining child of James and Willie Mae Matory. In his life he would experience great accomplishment and equally great sorrow—including the premature loss of his mother and of two adult children. His mother died before his third birthday, whereupon he was sent to Jackson, Mississippi, to be reared by his aunt, Ida Matory, a nurse.

Through stories, Dad conveyed his aunt's lessons to us. For example, as he grew up, Dad was made responsible for the care and feeding of the family milk cow. One day he took the cow out to pasture, but before he could pound the stake for the cow's tether into the ground, he saw a large black snake. He fled in fear and threw down the ax he had been carrying to hammer in the stake. When he tearfully confessed to his aunt that he had lost the ax, she wagged a gentle finger, saying, "Dry your eyes, William, and go get that axe. You can't see with tears in your eyes." This story was usually meant to keep us focused on the goal, even in times of trouble or hardship.

At age eight, my father returned to East Saint Louis, where his father and older sister Helen continued his upbringing in a home next door to the family's shoe repair business.

I often felt mistreated in my father's second marital home and felt perplexed by his refusal to defend me and his insistence that complaint was beneath a person of my accomplishments. To assuage my doubts about his love, he often recalled that he, too, had felt marginalized in his father's house. He had already felt alienated from his birth home by his sojourn in Mississippi, but he was made to feel even more so by the special attention that his younger brother John received from their father. As a child, John had fallen from a playground wall and suffered a debilitating head injury, which required others to monitor him constantly. Others in my own father's household, he urged me, needed greater care than I.

Except for the small middle-class enclave where our cousins live, the East Saint Louis that I have visited since the 1980s has looked like a rust-belt, red-lined slum—the impoverished product of deindustrialization and the federal government's exclusion, or "red-lining," of predominantly Black or racially integrated neighborhoods from federally insured mortgage loans (e.g., Sacks 1994) . However, I do not recall any stories from my father about poverty or discrimination in the East Saint Louis of his birth. I do remember tales of the accomplished people with whom he identified—Miles Davis's dentist father and the school-principal mother of Uncle Ross, a late fellow physician and National Medical Association member who was also my godfather. I knew that my father's father, James—my namesake—was an entrepreneur, but I grasped my father's sense that his university-educated and professional townspeople were, for him, more useful role models. The calling I received from my parents concerned study in the liberal professions.

Against the backdrop of her father-in-law's reported preference for a lighter-skinned daughter-in-law, my mother never quite identified with East Saint Louis. From her I heard of the filth of the city, the smell of the hog-butchering industry, and the mysterious efficacy of the local midwife's massages and patent medicines. Interregional couples, like interethnic ones, often have different investments in the mythology of their respective homelands.

After graduating from Lincoln High School at sixteen, Dad enrolled at Howard University. His journey to the "Capstone of Negro Education" taught him an enduring wonderment and humility. On the train ride to Washington, he was struck with fear when a fellow passenger admired his tweed suit. Rightly or wrongly, he thought the man might have been coming on to him. Soon after his arrival at Howard, he was offered "pizza pie." Never having heard of pizza, he construed the words as "piece of pie." His lack of urbanity, however, did not mean lack of intelligence.

Dad served as the business manager of the campus newspaper, the *Hilltop*, and ran the 880-yard event on the 1947 championship track team. He graduated cum laude with a BS in chemistry in 1949 and received his MD in 1953. In both undergraduate and medical schools, his peers elected him president of the class. This fact makes it difficult for me to believe the depth of the debilitating colorism that many of my Howard interlocutors saw as the bane of his career at the university. I have yet to figure out the consistency among these phenomena except that Dad seems to have been regarded as an extraordinary and exceptional person, like Howard's counterpart to Barack Obama.

It was at Howard that Dad first encountered West Indians, whose British-inflected accents and—to his eyes—sense of superiority to African Americans caused him to doubt the unique legitimacy of the manners he had learned as an aspiring bourgeois gentleman. My father's most anthropological lesson to me conveyed his wonderment that these classy people ate with fork tines down and did not transfer the fork from the left to the right hand before placing food into their mouths. I often wondered whether this story served as a sort of narrative resistance to my mother's domestic authority. Like many ambitious African American women in her day, she was nearly as obsessed with proper table manners as with proper elocution. Dad's encounter with brilliant Nigerian classmates like Uncle Badejọ similarly upset the demeaning misrepresentations of Africans that, in US culture, helped white Americans to justify the second-class citizenship of African Americans and helped African Americans to believe we weren't inferior to *everybody*. So it was with a mixture of Black pride and interethnic rivalry that he and his African American friends joked—in reference to the African students—"They only let the smart ones out!"

Dad became a captain in the United States Air Force, where he served from 1955 to 1957 as the military base surgeon on the Japanese island of Misawa. From 1960 until 2003, Dad made unprecedented contributions to health care and medical training at Howard, helping to maintain its status as the nation's leading HBCU, though he was impressed in later years that Florida Agricultural and Mechanical University was gaining ground. "I don't believe anyone has made a more extensive array of contributions to Howard University College of Medicine in its history than Bill Matory," said LaSalle D. Lefall Jr., MD, professor and former chair of the Department of Surgery. Lefall continued, "He would see things that needed to be done, and he would do them." Nonetheless, if Dad thought himself worthy of the highly accomplished company he kept, he never let on. For all his accomplishments, he kept trying ever harder. Even his all-Black environment compelled him to do so.

From 1960 to 1997, Dad practiced general surgery, focusing on trauma care and colorectal cancer. Early in his career, he and his surgical colleagues at Howard made plans to found a collective private practice, through which they could more effectively control the profits of their labors. However, he was caught unawares one day by the discovery that his colleagues had proceeded with the plan but excluded him. According to my father's support staff, his colleagues had excluded him on account of his dark complexion.

When I heard this story in 2002, I felt that I had finally discovered the source of his continual advice to me over the prior years—"get your own." And that is what he did throughout his career, resulting in incomparable benefits to Howard and to the patients of Freedmen's Hospital and its post-1976 successor, Howard University Hospital. In 1965, he developed the university's program in Continuing Medical Education—the first such program in the Washington area to be certified by the American Medical Association, despite my father's nonmembership in that organization—and served as the program's director until 2003. In 1966, Dad pursued additional training in order to establish and direct the hemodialysis service at Freedmen's Hospital for patients with kidney failure.

In 1970, he founded the university's family practice training program and the Department of Family Practice, serving as its first chair for nine years. After laboring to create and build the department, he lost control of it to his internist colleagues, when the Trinidadian vice president of the university took their side. He never complained about these defeats within my hearing, but

I now attribute his long work hours during the late 1960s and 1970s far more to his efforts to overcome obstacles in his workplace than to his philandering.

My parents' divorce undoubtedly arose from both of these factors and from my mother's frustrated professional aspirations, which she sought to live out through him. According to her reports, he had discouraged her aspirations to attend medical school, reasoning that "one doctor is enough in this family." Thus she sought leadership in the Women's Auxiliary of the Medico-Chirurgical Society of the District of Columbia, in the National Medical Association, and in many other organizations in which my father was active. Consequently, he felt that he had no space of his own. Family friends said that he found her so domineering that he feared he would drown or suffocate if he did not escape.

On the other hand, his dating choices during and after marriage suggest another motive: he felt that he deserved a lighter-skinned woman. My mother reported being told by my father's handicapped brother that their father had urged Dad to divorce her during the early years of their marriage: "When you gonna get ridda dat 'umman?" he would ask Dad, indicating a butter-colored psychiatrist and married friend of my parents as a preferable alternative. Perhaps Dad felt that such a choice would have gained him greater respect from

FIGURE 1.2. *From right*: William E. Matory Sr., MD; South African ambassador to the United States Franklin Sonn and his wife; dean of Howard University College of Medicine Floyd Malveaux, MD, and his wife, Myrna Ruiz Malveaux. Dr. Malveaux is a Louisiana Creole. Unknown photographer.

his color-struck colleagues and might even have exempted him from some of their slights. Ironically, the psychiatrist had feelings for my mother.

"You gotta put a little cream in your coffee," Dad would tell me, with the same whisper, laugh, and gentle elbowing of our ribs that accompanied risqué jokes when he told them to me and, later, my little half brother. Dad's dating choices reflected his advice. After his last dalliance—revealed to my mother by one of Dad's secretaries—she threw all of his clothes onto the front lawn and, with them, the last hope of preserving the marriage. Dad did end up marrying a light-skinned woman, a Filipina—a woman who was not beautiful in any conventional way but was additionally qualified by her financial independence and her lack of children before their marriage. My father was deeply committed to supporting his own children and apparently felt that he could not afford to support another man's offspring, no matter how light skinned their mother.

Things would have been much worse for me if he had married the Louisiana Creole widow of his medical-school classmate. There had been a mutual interest. I became friends with one of her children during my summer 2002 sojourn in New Orleans. I also spent a good deal of time with her older brother, a cream-colored surgeon who reported feeling afraid to be alone with white people. He said that, because they seldom know that he is Black, whites frequently say ugly things about Black people in his presence. Yet he felt no sympathy for me when I reported that the Creole owner of a dress shop near Saint Augustine High School—where I had stopped to pick up a present for my wife—had treated me like a criminal. I thanked the powers of the universe for having spared me the torture of becoming his younger stepbrother. I suddenly realized that this was the kind of conflicted person who—come the inevitable brotherly spat—would have turned my own chocolate blackness into an expletive.

During my research at Howard, my son Adu and I would periodically visit Dad at his stone mansion on upper Sixteenth Street, where I once asked him about an apocryphal story that I had heard on campus. Charles Drew had been a professor of surgery at Howard in the generation before my father arrived there. Young students of "Negro history" like me had heard for years that Drew invented the technique for blood plasma storage, which would subsequently save the lives of countless people. Though butter colored, he was classified as a Negro, and we were told—incorrectly as it turns out—that he died prematurely because, following an auto accident on a southern road, he was, on account of his race, denied the very treatment that he had invented. In the North Portal Estates and in Shepherd Park, where I attended elementary school, I grew up surrounded by a tribe of his daughters, nephews and nieces, grandchildren, great-nephews, and great-nieces, who had, through carefully considered marriages, kept their butter color unadulterated in the subsequent generations. Some of Drew's descendants were humble and kind, while an equal number were clearly possessed by a spirit of self-importance based upon their complexion and their descent from an "Old Washington" family.

All of their houses, though, were smaller and less prominently located than ours. I hardly noticed their superiority complex, because none of them manifested a greater degree of self-importance than my house-proud mother or her elder sister. I was racially proud of Charles Drew, just as I was familially proud of my mother's black, black father—a preacher and the founding bishop of a major statewide church community in Virginia. His was a major route toward upward mobility allowed to dark men without a college education. With the proceeds of his charismatic preaching, he put four Black girls through various professional schools. Two became physicians, one a clinical psychologist, and one a biology professor.

In 2002, I was shocked to hear from interlocutors at Howard that race hero Charles Drew had reputedly favored his light-skinned medical residents, sending only them to integrate the first white-run hospitals that would accept Negro trainees. Whereas others told me this story as a form of protest, my father reacted with equanimity, with what he considered pragmatism, and, in my view, with a sense of low self-worth. He explained it as a merely natural fact that white people find light-skinned people more acceptable than darkskinned people. Therefore, it was a practical and indeed wise decision to send the light-skinned residents first. I hesitate to think about the indignities my father would have asked me to endure from my would-be Creole stepbrother in the pragmatic and wise interest of keeping his marriage peaceful. My father always preferred peace to confrontation, even in the face of unfairness, just as he preferred light skin to dark. On both counts, he seemed to expect me to feel the same. I do not. And my father's marital history is, for me, a map of the roads to avoid.

In Dad's assessment of Drew's reported conduct, I detected the implication that the light-skinned avant-garde thereby opened the doors for subsequent dark-skinned beneficiaries of these opportunities. Indeed, my father conducted part of his later surgical residency in the 1950s at the whitecontrolled Staten Island Public Health Hospital, perhaps having benefited from this strategy. But in light of his apparently complexion-related exclusion from opportunities that he deserved at Howard in the 1960s, I wondered whether he felt that he ever had the right to demand that such mistreatment end. Complexion-based feelings of inferiority and superiority have died hard in African American communities. Even in the 1970s, my mother's elder sister—a cinnamon-colored race-boosting psychiatrist—relentlessly mocked the dark-skinned fiancée of her chocolate-colored son, so much so that he abandoned her in favor a woman the color of banana cream pie, much like that of our grandmother. However, the inner torments of my mother's sister Marilyn related even more to hair than to color. While she had it, her hair stood up instead of swinging. But in pursuit of swinging hair like my mother's, she once applied too strong a lye-based relaxer, which left her with irregular tufts on a scarred scalp for the rest of her life.

His color and hair texture notwithstanding (these issues appear to affect men's careers and marital options a bit less than women's), Dad became a full professor of surgery in 1971 and cofounded the University's Physician Assistant Training Program in 1972. He also personally developed and directed the popular Surgical Pathophysiology, or basic surgery, course that trained thousands of physicians over the nearly thirty years that he taught it. He also established multiple awards—such as the Magnificent Professor Award—to recognize the contributions of his peers.

Until his death, he was working on two other major projects. The first was the establishment of a state-of-the-art surgical skills laboratory and learning center at Howard, borrowing and refining the model of similar centers that he had personally visited in Canada and across the United States. His proposal has become the foundation of a facility at Howard University Hospital that was completed and posthumously named in his honor in 2009. The second major project was an effort to extend the services of the National Medical Association to the Caribbean and Africa, and to reemphasize malaria prevention and clean water in a world of funding often dominated by AIDS-related concerns.

The list of established programs that Dad directed before his retirement is nearly as long as the list of those that he founded. Among them is the Medical Education for National Defense program for mass casualty care, which he ran from 1961 to 1967. And he served on the National Academy of Science / Robert Wood Johnson committee that recommended the nationwide use of "911" for emergency calls. He also directed the university hospital's emergency care area from 1960 to 1982 and its Ambulatory Care Division from 1971 to 1995. He reorganized outpatient services in order to guarantee greater continuity of care—a reform that undoubtedly saved many lives, particularly among indigent and handicapped patients, who otherwise would have lacked alternatives to emergency room care.

Edward E. Cornwell III, MD, current chair of surgery and surgeon in chief at the hospital, described Dad as "an icon in American surgery that transcends all barriers of race, gender and ethnicity." He continued, "Indeed, one would be hard-pressed to name a figure in all of medicine who has made seminal contributions in as many areas of our craft as Matory." My siblings and I grew up with Eddie, who has become an extraordinary trauma and cardiothoracic surgeon in his own right. But he is probably not exaggerating. As the son of a deceased surgeon himself, he might, if he were a lesser man, be inclined to limit his superlatives.

By all agreement, Dad belongs to an ice-cutting generation of firsts in the Black leadership of the non-Black medical establishment. He was the first Black member of the American Association of Surgery of Trauma. From 1977 to 1983, he served as a governor of the American College of Surgeons and as a member of the executive committee of its Board of Governors from 1979 to 1982. He was president of both the Washington chapter of the American College of Surgeons from 1983 to 1984 and of the Washington Academy of Surgery from 1986 to 1987.

Once he entered the leadership of these organizations, he was not simply present; he pushed agendas that reflected his exceptional insights as a physician—emphasizing the importance of continuing medical education for already-licensed physicians and the need for specialists to be continuously on call at any given hospital for the treatment of trauma and burn patients. Dad became famous not only for introducing these innovations at Howard but also for pushing them onto the agenda of the medical establishment nationwide.

During his time in the American College of Surgeons (ACS)—the nation's leading gathering of surgeons and, arguably, the most prestigious organization in all of medicine—Dad not only pursued leadership but also opened leadership opportunities to other African Americans—through filmmaking and networking. From 1972 onward, Dad produced 130 surgical and general medical films to train licensed physicians in new techniques. As a conscious strategy to secure a place of respect for Black surgeons, Dad submitted scores of instructional films for approval by the ACS Motion Picture Committee. These films showcased his own and other Black surgeons' mastery of innovative surgical techniques. Moreover, reports Eddie L. Hoover, MD, editor in chief of the *Journal of the National Medical Association*, "I have observed Matory networking with surgical societies all over this country, lobbying for young African American surgeons in all areas of specialization—and, like me, most of them who were appointed to these prestigious positions had no clue as to how they got there."

After retiring from his surgical practice in 1997, Dad was assistant dean for clinical affairs at the Howard University College of Medicine and assistant medical director for postgraduate affairs at Howard University Hospital until 2002.

While my father was best known for his excellence as a clinician and leader in medical education, he also delighted in the camaraderie of his peers. On his curriculum vitae, alongside the numerous medical societies of which he is a member, appear the proud announcements "Kappa Alpha Psi Fraternity since 1947" and "Sigma Pi Phi Fraternity since 1988." The first is an African American undergraduate fraternity and the second, also known as the "Boulé," an organization of Black professional men at the peak of their professions. He was a Life Member of both organizations. He was also active in the Hellians, Inc., the postgraduate successor to the Kappas, and in Washington, DC's, Cosmos Club, a much-celebrated and predominantly white meeting place for the city's leading journalists and other intellectuals.

My father was very proud of his children's accomplishments and rightly regarded our academic success as an extension of his own. In an era when Black fatherhood is normally described in terms of absence (or cheese pizzas) and as a root cause of what is called "underachievement," all of the above, it should go without saying, is an important sociological corrective. African American families, like Euro-American, African, and Caribbean families, are diverse, but they also live out gendered conventions, fears, dilemmas, and patterns of opportunity and constraint. The tendency of popular and professional sociologists to characterize African American families and African American fathers as deficient is tendentious cultural politics, rather than an observation about the values and resources that African Americans bring to the resolution of their problems. Nor does such cultural politics identify what is culture-specific and ethnocentric about the current distribution of rewards and punishments that make it harder for some people than for others to become effective breadwinners.

My father's family life and his medical career were difficult to separate. Against the downward push of segregation, Dad not only rose to the top of his profession but also prepared a generation of offspring and medical students for the opportunities of the postsegregation era. Like a Nigerian Yoruba, I have come to believe, ọmọ l'aṣọ ayé—"Children are the clothing of our lives." That is, offspring are a parent's greatest production and the most important denominator of his or her identity. As I wish for my children's lives to be central to the stories that are told about me after I die, so I shall conclude this story of my father's life.

Along with my mother, Deborah Love Matory, he gave life to my older brother, William Earle Jr., and my older sister, Yvedt, both of whom spent a great deal of time with him in the surgical laboratory at Howard. We were all equally driven by our mother's disappointed ambitions and by the will not to be outperformed by each other.

My brother Earle graduated from class-diverse and predominantly Black Calvin Coolidge High School with a cohort of brilliant and ambitious peers who integrated the elite, predominantly white universities of the Northeast. Earle belonged to the class of 1972 at Yale. His years there marked the denouement of the social and political crisis that released Black people from Jim Crow and, even more effectively, released white American women from their own counterpart of the same. When I was eight or nine, I ran across an essay he had written for a freshman composition class. In writing, he raged and cursed about racism and manhood, focusing on the significance of the term "motherfucker." Like much information that third-world nationalists mobilize in the construction of their insurgent identities, this report had probably derived from a white-published book or a white-financed movie. However, it was only years later that I wondered where in the cocoon of upper Northwest Washington he had encountered the racism that he raged about and how he had become an authority on these paragons of indecency who, according to Earle's report, were despised for having sex with their own mothers. The Yale professor rewarded Earle's insights with an A. Somehow I doubt that a Howard professor of that era would have reinforced this particular genre of insurgent identity making.

Earle's own racial nationalism and my father's financial situation brought him back to Howard for medical school. After his divorce, my father was supporting two households, so he appealed to Earle to spare him the burden of a Yale medical-school tuition. But he did buy Earle a Corvair, on the right rear window of which Earle pasted a decal of the red, black, and green Black nationalist flag. Unlike my sister and me, who attended TWIs from junior high onward, Earle never had a non-Black friend, though his Black friends came in all complexions. Though I tend to side with Black people and other oppressed groups collectively, I like nice individuals of all colors as much as I dislike mean individuals of any color. Moreover, in daily interactions, I tend to find privileged people less touchy and easier to deal with than underprivileged people. The dominant can be heartless when their dominance is challenged, but it is also true, as a matter of course, that hurt people hurt people. For all his own economic privilege, Earle simply mistrusted the racially privileged.

Whatever his feelings about white people, my brother respected the social capital that he felt the Ivy League uniquely conferred. So his capitulation to Dad's financial concerns was, for him, a sacrifice.

One day, less than a year into my flight from a predominantly working-class Black junior high school, where I was bullied, to a predominantly white private school, I sat bored in the backseat of his Corvair. As he and my mother talked in the front seat, I unthinkingly etched the letters F-U-C-K into the Black nationalist flag decal. He asked me why I had done it, but an answer was beyond my conscious reach. Eleven years my senior, Earle offered some replacement for the male parenting and kindness that my father could then offer only nonresidentially. Earle never said another word about my spontaneous reverse graffiti on his car window.

The mid-1970s were years of economic crisis and declining opportunities for most African Americans, but Earle prospered. After graduating from Howard, he conducted his residencies in predominantly white university hospitals—Harvard's Beth Israel and Saint Francis Memorial in San Francisco. He became a plastic surgeon and professor of surgery at the University of Massachusetts and later moved to establish private surgical practice in Orange County, California. Earle also published a surgery textbook called *Ethnic Considerations in Facial Aesthetic Surgery* (1998), which was based upon the premise that Northern European aesthetic ideals should not be assumed universal or applied in aesthetic surgery for other racial and ethnic groups, such as Asian, Black, or Mediterranean people; there is a distinct aesthetic ideal for each of these populations, he argued. Earle was perplexed by my argument that there is nothing natural or apolitical about these newly proposed, group-specific ideals.

Nonetheless, Earle was a man of caring and consistency. On the Christmas Eve when I was eleven, in the midst of our parents' incendiary divorce, Earle took me on a last-minute run to the toy store, asking me to help him choose presents that our then-seven-year-old cousin Wade might like. I did my duty, albeit with some measure of jealousy and resentment, only to find these presents under our Christmas tree the next morning wrapped up for me. Earle had wanted to make sure that I had a happy Christmas, even if our parents had lacked the presence of mind to do so themselves. Stories like this, about older brothers, cousins, and neighbors who give of themselves to guide and care for African American boys can be heard in even the most desperate Black neighborhoods and under the most dire circumstances, but these are not the stories that sociologists typically want to hear or tell about us (Burton and Stack 2014).

Throughout the years of his surgical training, Earle also acted as a surrogate father to four disadvantaged African American children—three brothers and a sister—from Roxbury. He took them and me camping and deep-sea fishing. We went to family restaurants and pizza parlors together. The ill manners and physical aggressiveness of two of the boys never bothered Earle. He commanded their respect in ways that I could not. I did not speak their language. Earle's model, however, was not sufficient to keep all of them out of the criminal justice system. For a time, he dated a white woman with a similarly troubled white daughter. Earle was clearly a stabilizing influence in her life as well. He and the café au lait African American woman he eventually married adopted two butter-colored boys, who loved him deeply. He loved them, too. He was an assiduous parent. However, my coffee-brown wife and I have often wondered why the two beautiful chocolate-colored boys that the couple had previously brought to Thanksgiving dinner had not been worthy of the same love and investment.

Unlike Earle, Yvedt attended an elite private high school—Sidwell Friends—and she refused to consider attending Howard. Instead, she completed her BA and her MD at Yale and became a surgical oncologist and a professor of surgery at Harvard. Sidwell left her with a lifelong circle of white, Black, and Asian-white multiracial friends. In her last years, her best friends were an intergenerationally wealthy white female neighbor and a circle of dark African American women physicians, some of whom she had grown up with and some of whom she had mentored during medical school.

Yvedt loved Yale—where she was introduced, and she introduced me, to the love of African art through Robert Farris Thompson. She was also proud of Yale. Her diplomas were the focal point of her medical office at Brigham and Women's. But she never abandoned her passion for art. She collected not only African wood and bronze statuary but also Japanese paintings, ceramics, puppets, and cloth. Born in Misawa, Japan, she also shared our mother's love of Japanese food, furniture, painting, and ceramics.

Class identity was as important to Yvedt as it had been to our mother. To that, she added a certain public demonstration of racelessness (Fordham 1996). On the one hand, she identified deeply with African and African American art. On the other hand, she was highly offended when white classmates at Yale wrongly assumed that she was on a scholarship, and she insisted that she would have made it independently of the civil rights movement. At Yale and in other predominantly white environments, she was not one to greet another Black person solely on account of his or her shared race. Yvedt had milk-chocolate skin, lamb's wool hair, pillowy lips, and a bonbon nose. But months after her death, the online *AfroCentric News* published a list of "Notable Black" people married to non-Black spouses (Fikes 2000). On this list, her husband Randall Kennedy, a professor at Harvard Law School, was identified as a "Notable Black" and she as his "Non-Black" spouse. I do not know whether the author of this list inferred this misclassification from Randall's unpredictable political stances or from the author's own inability to imagine a Black woman having attained Yvedt's position in life and having occupied it so seamlessly. Had she still been alive, I would have teased her about this slander, and she would have laughed with both chagrin and satisfaction.

Despite her cosmopolitanism, she was ambivalent about her name. When she learned that we had facetiously named my two-year-old daughter's Black doll "Tameika Chanté"—almost all of the human images in our home are black, and deliberately so—Yvedt spontaneously exclaimed, "I *hate* those names!" Thereafter, I enjoyed reminding her that the apparently German- or Dutch-inspired modification of her first name also reflected a characteristically African American inventiveness with names. Similarly, in order to produce Yvedt's middle name, Lové, our mother had taken her own maiden name and added an acute accent to the *é*, as if to turn the name into a French participial adjective meaning "beloved." Our mother was nearly as proud of her limited French and German skills as she was of her Japanese. (Because I enjoyed tweaking Yvedt's class anxiety, I never mentioned my thought that our mother's inventiveness suggested considerably greater intercultural literacy and a higher class station than the working-class "Tameika Chanté.") After hearing my analysis, Yvedt and her husband made every effort to delete the acute accent from her middle name, even on her funeral program.

Both of my full siblings died in 2005—Earle of complications from diabetes and Yvedt, ironically, of metastatic melanoma. She had spent most of her professional life healing other people's cancer. Several of my white female colleagues at Harvard told me that she had saved their lives. Before and after she died, they also told me of her extraordinary warmth and kindness toward them. Her fellow Black graduates of Yale medical school, under the leadership of two African American women, have organized an endowed annual Grand Rounds lecture in her honor at the medical school. Yearly, it brings in some of the nation's leading surgeons to address the Yale medical faculty and house staff in her honor.

I spent nearly as much time as Earle and Yvedt in Dad's surgical lab, but mostly pleading for the lives of the dogs and guinea pigs on which the Howard medical students—and my siblings—first learned their craft. I sensed that, while congratulating me for my own nonmedical successes, my father blamed the circumstances of my initial exposure to surgery for my choosing a nonmedical career.

I attended mostly white Maret School, perplexing my father that I could be a Black nationalist and also have so many white friends. Most of my Black childhood friends spread out among the predominantly white private schools in the area, and when my father could not traverse the city to pick me up, I commuted for more than an hour and a half each way by public bus. The child who came of age in between my father's marriages and in the jaws of the resulting financial crisis, I was the only one of my father's children without a car in high school and college. Consequently, I also became the most independent. In addition, I received some urging from my brother. When I told Earle that I intended to go to Yale, like him, my sister and my aunt Marilyn's children, he replied, "Are you kidding?" All sentiment aside, Yale was, to him, second best. So he is the reason that I received my BA in 1982 from Harvard instead. My 1991 PhD, also in anthropology, came from the University of Chicago. I recently left a tenured full professorship in anthropology and African and African American studies at Harvard to become the chair of African and African American Studies and the Lawrence Richardson Professor of Cultural Anthropology at Duke University. (Such endowed chairs indicate the university's special recognition of the scholar's accomplishments.) I now direct the Center for African and African American Research there. For my full siblings, the study of Black humanity, complexity, and dignity was an undergraduate phase and light armor in the pursuit of high-earning careers. For me, it became a career goal.

I like my name and believe that it manifests the same subversive Black creativity in naming as my sister's. Lorand is the Hungarian Magyar version of "Lawrence." Naturally, it leaves even colleagues who have met me guessing about my national origins. My mother's elder sister, the psychiatrist, borrowed it from a Hungarian psychiatrist living in Switzerland, whose name or published work she apparently admired—Sandor Lorand, MD. Although many potential employers read them as a sign of unworthiness, African American names are often defiantly cosmopolitan, disrupting the boundaries of Americanness and even of race. The particular names in our family reflect the broader stock of cultural knowledge available to the Black bourgeoisie. But, like other African American names, they also invoke a world of status and amplify a vision of transnational connections that transcend the United States' definition of us as an antitype and a problem.

Dad's second wife was a professor of obstetrics and gynecology who practiced for thirty-four years at Howard University Hospital, until her retirement in 2007. Their son attended the Saint Albans School, a favorite of Republican congresspeople for their male children and, in my observation, a soul-crushing hell for once-spirited Black boys. My brother-in-law, the Harvard law professor, is an alumnus of the same school. So is my childhood best friend Clark, who is now a physician and emergency room director. On the homeward-bound bus trip from a swim meet, Clark had teased a fat white boy, who then retorted, "Nigger!" over and over again to every taunt my friend could think of, ultimately reducing my friend to helpless tears. No adult on the bus put a stop to it.

My father had never been active in the schools of my mother's children. Perhaps his struggle at Howard kept him too busy. But some combination of personal maturation and an awareness that his third son was alone and helpless across real enemy lines led him to become highly active at Saint Albans. Indeed, he became a trustee of the school. The sacrifice entailed was plain to me. Dad had always been self-conscious around white people. His discomfort was evident in a deliberate and ceremonious speech pattern seemingly intent on avoiding grammatical errors. In his native element, he freely code-switched, as bourgeois Black men tend to do, in order to invoke respect and camaraderie, each in its proper moment. As my childhood friend Clark, the emergency room physician, taught me in adulthood, a Black man who wants both authority over and cooperation from other Black people simply cannot be effective without this skill. He and I know that I am a bit incompetent in this regard. However, like the Jamaican Patwa of most middle-class islanders, my childhood friend's African American Vernacular English (AAVE), too, is deeply impoverished and adopted with a degree of ambivalence.

Long before he came to advocate code-switching, Clark told me a joke at the expense of AAVE speakers that confessed a collective racial shame:

"What has six legs and goes 'Ho-de-do. Ho-de-do. Ho-de-do'?"

"Three Black men running for the elevator."

Like Bill Cosby and Maya Angelou, my mother disagreed with Clark regarding the worth of vernacular speech, her perspective perhaps shaped by a different but equally gender-based set of opportunities and expectations. One day, according to her, my mother and father had stopped at a gas station in East Saint Louis for repairs. Apparently in order to invoke camaraderie with the Black mechanic and thereby ensure the thoroughness and the economy of the diagnosis and repair, my father stood beside the mechanic under the open hood and exchanged both observations and humor in AAVE. However, when he reentered the repaired car and drove off, my mother chided him with thinned lips: "Bill, *these people* do not expect you to talk like *them*! You're a *doctor*!"

My father's two marriages were in many ways a progressive induction into the bourgeois style of his generation. He gradually became accustomed to unapologetic luxury and the affect of privilege, at least in his spouses and children. Conversely, in my teens and twenties, I, too, began to code-switch, but like many elite Black young people, I did so jocularly. But by then my father could see neither humor nor social efficacy in the effort. He shouted on more than one occasion, "I didn't send you to Harvard to talk like that!" I still joke in AAVE. My sister stopped in her early twenties.

Dad faced down a good deal of racial and class anxiety in order to ease my little half brother's way through Saint Albans, but with no obvious benefits. The school did little to guide or support my half brother as college approached. But Saint Albans was not the only source of my half brother's problems. For example, though his Filipina mother deeply loved and admired our father, she never had a positive thing to say about other Black people. She felt angry about not being accepted socially by Washington's Black elite, an exclusion that she attributed to their loyalty to my mother. However, her own tendency toward rudeness and derogatory talk about her working-class Black patients may be an indication of the real problem. My mother's own assertiveness may have rewarded a lighter-skinned woman, but it did not make her uniformly popular in Black elite circles, either.

Because of her insecurity and lack of tact, my stepmother Consuela inadvertently amplified her children's sense of inferiority to my mother's children. On several occasions at the dinner table, she said to our father, in my half siblings' presence, "Bill, don't blame me if my kids aren't as smart as yours." Since high school, my half brother Michael and half sister Victoria have felt terribly anxious about being compared with my mother's children, such that my half sister refused to apply to Yale and Harvard, and Michael once asked me to get out of the family photograph commemorating our father's birthday.

After Saint Albans's failure, it was our father's networks in the Black elite of Washington that ultimately opened the necessary doors for my younger half brother, who transferred from one of the Pennsylvania teachers' colleges to Georgetown University, where he received his bachelor's degree. Ultimately, Michael chose the career path of his mother's father, who had been a colonel in the Philippine military under US-backed dictator Ferdinand Marcos. My half-brother chose the US Marines, because, he told Dad, "I want to be the best!" Unfortunately, he chose a bad moment to do so. He served under traumatizing conditions in Kuwait, Iraq, and Afghanistan, but he has risen to the rank of captain. On the occasion of the family photo, Michael had organized the birthday party for our father at a Washington, DC, officers' club in order to highlight himself and his accomplishments in the military, and he did not appear to want my mother's children to be present at all.

Like her brother, Victoria attended a private Black elementary school run by our neighbor. Later, like Yvedt, she attended Sidwell Friends, where she and her mother resented the degree to which she was regarded as a Black child. In an apparently white liberal effort to affirm the racial identity by which most people would recognize her, teachers encouraged her to do a social studies report on an African country. She preferred to do her report on the Philippines and wished to be considered Asian. All of our Black family friends, though, comment that Dad's genes must be very strong, because no one could tell visually that my half siblings have any Asian ancestry. Victoria graduated from Columbia University and Howard University Law School, where she grew more accustomed to the rewards of being part Black. Indeed, she came at times to call herself "Black" but also seems to have taken comfort in regarding her mixed background as a point of distinction correlated with her good grades in law school. She is smart, though. Extraordinarily, she passed the New York State Bar Examination on her first attempt, reportedly an unusual feat. It is also a testament to Howard's excellence.

Often guests in our home, Dad's surgical trainees likened themselves to his children—albeit his "academic" children, according to Eddie Cornwell—just as conscious as we were of Dad's gentle but effective ways of teaching, guiding, and inspiring. They awarded our father the Student Council Teaching and Leadership Award in 1962, 1982, and 1984. Perhaps Dad's medical trainees did not realize how apt the comparison between his biological and his academic children was. His biological children often competed with each other as harshly and strategically as junior physicians contesting for head surgical resident. Some of us competed headlong. Some of us tried to avoid comparison by refusing to apply to the most selective colleges or by going into uncharted professional fields. Some even tried to recover lost dignity by appealing to higher-status racial identities. Everyone but my full sister felt not quite unconditionally loved or respected enough, but we all had something to prove. In our own bourgeois way, our family reflects and inflects the racial dynamics of the broader society, and our approaches to race and racism outside the home reflect intrafamilial dynamics. However, every white and black ethnic family I know well encompasses a similarly complex configuration of love, ambivalence, and rivalry.

However, except for the occasional outburst by my half sister or half brother, all of this was well under wraps on public occasions. At holiday gatherings with his natural and his academic children, Dad would accept one glass of wine, to toast his family and guests, but his cup was never empty—in any sense. First, he was deeply and abidingly generous. Second, like Uncle Badejǫ, he disliked the effects of alcohol. He was proud to say that he had never seen his father drunk. (It is a striking testament to the power of his model that I am the only one of his children who drinks alcohol. Although I found it off-putting in high school, I learned to value this style of masculine social communion from a Native American friend after high school and from white friends in college. When I drink now, I remember their camaraderie.)

Until the end, Dad did not regard his life as his own; he lived it modestly and in the service of others. Yet Dad never felt that he was finished growing or building. Having once told me that he had never been to Africa, didn't want to go to Africa, and had left nothing in Africa, he became, in his later years, a diligent advocate of the continent. He gave me credit for changing his mind.

Even as his knees wore out and his heart faltered, he traveled to South Africa, Nigeria, and Cuba, offering his skills and those of the National Medical Association in the service of better disease prevention and health care in both Africa and the Caribbean. It is no wonder that the National Cathedral conducted for this princely healer a "Category 1" memorial service—a category normally reserved for heads of state and national officials

In the last half decade of his life, Dad clearly presaged his death. His 2002 written instructions for his funeral had warned that his love and sharing—rather than any material assets—would be his main legacy to his children. (I discovered only later that this warning was intended chiefly for my mother's children.) "Love to All," he concluded. "My deepest gratitude to All My Children, Deborah and Rita."

Here, in summary, I have recalled the lives of three men, the sweat of whose hands made the clay that I am—one Nigerian, one Trinidadian, and one (my birth father) African American. Their lives and mine intertwined at Howard University. This chapter establishes the autoethnographic refrain of the entire book, wherein my family's Howard connections illustrate the networking and cosmopolitan self-positioning of a broad swath of the anglophone Afro-Atlantic bourgeoisie.

In *The Gospel at Colonus*, Oedipus has suffered exile for crimes he did not mean to commit. He achieves inner peace only by forgiving the wrongs done to him and acknowledging the power of the gods. The song "How Shall I See You through My Tears?" commemorates the moment when he is reunited with loved ones he thought he would never see again. Here I tell the story of three men in exile, who, like many men of their kind, have been denied their full and just rewards. Their foibles are in many ways the destiny of black men and Black institutions in a creole world. In my initial efforts to understand black ethnicity, I had not expected to see them, but, now that my eyes are open, I want the world to see them and to see that they have been a blessing to the world. As I tell their story and mine, I locate the workings of stigma, colorism, and ethnological schadenfreude in the intimate context of people who were not fated to do well but who nonetheless did good.

The story of my three fathers is not a simple one reducible to the structures or strategies of complexion, race, or ethnicity. Its protagonists are neither the angels nor the devils that men are inclined to turn their fathers into. Even less are they the punch lines of a joke or the monsters that sociologists, reporters, and film directors prefer. Rather, they are real and exemplary black men.

They are the makers and not merely the victims of history, but we cannot understand their dreams, their accomplishments, or their failures without acknowledging the forms of ethnoracial stigma, educational opportunity, and identity options that structured their choices. They have made their choices with a conscious awareness of Black diversity and shared stigma as well.

The great men and felicitous relationships described in this chapter came of age at a time of relative harmony of purpose in the circum-Atlantic black bourgeoisie—the period of the civil rights movement and the decolonization of Africa and the Caribbean. I have told the story of a circle of conviviality that I took for granted before I began my exploration of ethnic diversity beyond my accustomed circles. There, since 2002, I discovered a more complex but equally human dynamic shaped by the age of Reaganism and by the often violently divisive postcolonial realpolitik of African and Caribbean nation-states. Black interethnic rivalry before the white gaze and the zero-sum pursuit of honor among the dominated were not new to the 1980s and 1990s, but I sense their acceleration and observe its results in the twenty-first century. This acceleration coincides with the resurgence of white American ethnic identity, the global explosion of ethnonationalism, and, since 1993, the resurgence of ethnic and regional identities because of the weakening of the nation-state within the framework of the European Union. The rise of black ethnicity is epochal, but it reveals some shared features of ethnogenesis in all times and places.

The growth of black ethnicity also reveals economic changes that have affected black men's abilities to take care of their families and their opportunities to see themselves as effective leaders of their communities. The nihilism of current media images of "Black" culture and, therefore, of the foil against which black ethnic identities are invented relate to the declining ability of working-class African American men to take care of their families and the decline of any connection they see between education and their likelihood of finding gainful, licit employment. These changes in working-class African American life are not cultural essences or uniquely African American phenomena. They have been followed by similar changes in the Caribbean, Africa, and white America, in all of which the male-female ratios in college are declining. The forms of compensatory hypermasculinity dramatized by male hip-hop artists today are but falsely attributed to African American "culture" as a whole, timeless essence or to African American culture alone. Instead, the archetype performed by these artists is a harbinger of and model for behavioral patterns found across races and ethnic groups. For example, the same violent hypermasculinity is also found in today's Caribbean dancehall music and in the musical tastes of suburban white males, who actually drive the US music market and finance the selective promotion of Black artists willing to mime the most exaggeratedly and unrepresentatively nihilistic stereotypes about the racially marginalized.

In Contrast: Black Immigrant Self-Making in the Twenty-First Century

These portraits of Howardites and the relationships they represent are far too complex to yield a single conclusion. They are a dense portrait of life—indeed, of three interlocking lives that have shaped my own personal life and perspective. These portraits bespeak a long and loving rapport and identification across ethnic, national, and imperial boundaries—a rapport and identification that were common in the Howard where I grew up and remain so.

However, these portraits become more meaningful in the context of the perspectives of other authors with a different experience of both the past and the present. *Problematizing Blackness* (2003) is a volume of "self-ethnographies" edited by Percy C. Hintzen and Jean Muteba Rahier and written largely by African-origin or African-descended professors teaching in predominantly white American universities.

The sites of my own research are broader: they include the HBCU world as well. In a way, the essays in *Problematizing Blackness* provide a temporal counterpoint to the ideas and lives of my three fathers, who all came of age during the civil rights movement and the struggle for independence from British rule in Africa and the Caribbean. By contrast, most of the contributors to *Problematizing Blackness* speak from a neoliberal age when the Hart-Celler Act and the collectivist, antiracist activism of the 1950s, 1960s, and 1970s are a distant memory, even among those who remember them at all. The majority of black immigrants has entered the United States since 1990.

Problematizing Blackness ends with a critical summary and response by a US-born son of black immigrants. Collectively, all but this last of the collection's authors express their discomfort at their "invisibility"—that is, having their differences from African Americans overlooked by white Americans (see Bryce-Laporte 1972) and oppressively denied by African Americans. The authors highlight a range of differences between the systems of social inclusion, exclusion, and stratification from which they originate and the United States. With reference to these differences, they assert their personal individuality, in contrast to the stereotypes imposed on them as black people by American whites and the army-like loyalty and conformity demanded by Black Americans.

Virtually all of the authors express their shock at the extremely binary logic and what they regard as the constant salience of dichotomously construed racial identities in the United States. Their vivid immigrant "self-ethnographies," then, chart the existential crises that these authors have suffered since immigrating to the United States and their resistance to the efforts of white and Black Americans to confine them to certain racially prescribed identities and roles. These authors narrate the complex mental and social lives that they lived before immigration to the United States, often contrasting these with the ostensible simplicity and conformism of African American mental and social lives. The editors frame these "self-ethnographies" as a politically progressive denial of racial binarism and a critique of racial solidarity as a politically primitive failure of imagination.

For example, the two fully Nigerian contributors paint pictures of a homeland free of social constraints on their personal identities and opportunities. The Caribbean-born contributors to this volume, on the other hand, tend to assert that race mattered *less* in their homelands than in the United States. They explain that racially hybrid parentage, complexion, economic class, education, and the ambiguous ideological entailments of national independence all modify a person's social status in their respective Caribbean homelands and cause everyone's racial identity to vary situationally. Consequently, racial classification in their homelands is not binary, fixed, or entirely determined by African ancestry. In short, in the Caribbean, a person of African descent can employ various means to transcend the definitional inferiority assigned to the aspect of them that is black. In the anglophone Caribbean, the emphatic display of conformity to "British" values is foremost among these means (Hintzen 2003).

These authors tend to concur that African Americans, because they accept the binary racial order of the United States, are more submissive and less accomplished than are black immigrants in general and that, in an age of massive transnationalism, racially binary identities have become outmoded.

However, several of the contributors agree that the resistance of black immigrants to identification with Black Americans is not *merely* an artifact of transnationalism or of some primordial differences between their subjectivity and that of African Americans. These contributors add that many black immigrants have actually adopted white American prejudices and white American advice that, if they want to get ahead, they should avoid Black Americans. Moreover, the current US discourse of "multiculturalism" encourages ethnic self-identification. Finally, to many immigrants, it seems only practical to steer clear of the working-class truculence and oppositionality that they attribute to African American culture as a whole.

On the other hand, asked to provide an overview, Pedro Noguera, a *son* of Jamaican and Trinidadian immigrant parents, criticizes the failure of the other contributors to take sides in what he has concluded is indeed a binarily coded struggle. He accuses his cocontributors of a failure to acknowledge that the binarily coded struggle of Black Americans is the very reason that black immigrants were able to come to the United States and prosper as they have done. He blames their solipsistic withdrawal from this struggle on the selfish ethos of our times and on their not having been born in the United States as he was. He suggests that their children will think very differently about their racial identities and loyalties.

Today, many black immigrants seem to feel that their relationship to African Americans is more one of competition than of alliance, much less identity of culture, political position, or economic interests. I would prefer to regard the attitudes of my father's generation as a product of their good sense. But the attitudes of their day also resulted from the conditions of colonialism and segregation, in which opportunities for members of their disadvantaged race were more uniformly closed. As the doors opened for a few, racial unity became more difficult to sustain (Wright 1997; Wright, Taylor, and Moghaddam 1990). In the context of Brazil, Carl Degler (1971) wrote of the "mulatto escape hatch"—that is, the material advantages conferred upon mulattoes, allowing them to escape the worst cruelties of racialized oppression and thereby reducing their incentive to struggle against the racialized hierarchy itself. Even if Degler and others have exaggerated the earnings differential between Brazilian *mulatos* and *negros*, the psychological and social effects of the mulatto escape hatch are as real in Brazil as are those of racial binarism in the United States. By extension, one might identify, in the US and European settings of black immigrant life, the workings of an "ethnic escape hatch."

Not all of these essays, however, equally deserve Noguera's criticism. If they are not all activist in their posture, they still reveal the human complexities and dilemmas that are the context of even the bravest and most militant activism. For example, Nigerian-born but non-Yoruba and mixed-race contributor Sarah Manyika looks back upon her schooling in Nigeria and her experiences in Europe and southern Africa to recognize what may have been extremely racialized forms of exclusion and hierarchy in all of those places. In perhaps the most emotionally honest of these essays, she also describes the privileges accorded to "exotic blacks" in many Western settings and the painful dilemmas with which such dilemmas have confronted her.

I write as a generational peer of these scholars, as a person who assumed his first full-time teaching position in 1991, but also as a person who finds it difficult to separate my Americanness from the racial, ethnic, and class hybridity of the community of men and women that has produced me—at

Howard, in my neighborhood, and in my family. My mother's mother was reportedly descended from Native Americans (the truth of this claim is less important than its role in a long-running debate that structures the identities of many African Americans). My parents were introduced to each other by a Nigerian Yoruba man. Of both foreign and domestic birth, my childhood neighbors were diverse in ways far more complex than the concerted sense of Blackness that I believe we shared and more heterogeneous in their characters than most of the authors of *Problematizing Blackness* recognize. Moreover, our Blackness was neither primordial nor fixed. Nor were our respective ethnic identities. This hybrid ethnography defies the simplification to which Black Americanness is subject in the ethnological schadenfreude of many whites and black ethnics.

I am not saying that my family is typical of African American, middle-class African American, or even upper-middle-class African American families from Washington, DC, or from the mid-Atlantic coast, where my network of friends and active family connections has always been concentrated. Indeed, the typicality of *any* family is a function of the typifier's narrowness of interests or lack of discernment. Yet my family and I were clearly shaped by a history of social arrangements, concepts, opportunities, barriers, and strategies familiar to millions of African Americans.

Much the same kind of qualified generalization could be made about the black ethnic populations with whom this book is concerned. By reason of those same qualifications, the translation of their histories into assertions about Caribbean, African, Creole, or Native American "cultures" is no simple or empirical matter. Such a translation is invariably an act of prescriptive will—that is, of goal-oriented representation and stipulation in a culturally hybrid and economically competitive context. Like other people's "culture" making, black ethnogenesis is a self-authorization in what Bourdieu calls the "logic of the trial" ([1979] 1984, 476–84), a fact that makes these self-representations not false but dialogical, selective, self-flattering, and self-promoting.

Of such stigmatized populations as homosexuals and Jews, Bourdieu writes,

> [S]ocial identity is the stake in the struggle in which the stigmatized individual or group, and more generally, any individual or group insofar as he or it is a potential object of categorization, can only retaliate against the partial perception which limits it to one of its characteristics, and, more generally, by struggling to impose the taxonomy most favourable to its characteristics, or at least give to the dominant taxonomy the content most flattering to what it has and what it is. ([1979] 1984, 475–76)

Hence, the isolation of one of a person's characteristics and the choice to classify him or her according to it is not simply a form of observation or knowledge. It is a judgment and an act of power by an interested observer or group of observers. And so is the choice of the observed person to accept and redefine the category or to reject it and choose another category of self-classification. Everyone wants to be classified in the most advantageous way and to classify others in a way that confers advantages upon the classifier. The daily language of social classification is like the language of the prosecution or the defense in a trial. It is partisan. It is always a selective observation about its object, based upon an interested choice of what to emphasize in the person or group's character and a judgment about which actions and what time period in the person or group's existence to emphasize. On the other hand, in these few cited pages of *Distinction*, Bourdieu seems to regard the distanced, leisurely discourse propagated by academic observers of social groups as disinterested. On the contrary, we scholars also have a set of stakes in the trial. As we pursue the ideal of disinterested analysis, it is good that we seek the fullest range of evidence and subject it to the most careful syllogistic logic and experimentation, but it is also wise to acknowledge our stakes and make them part of the evidence that we scrutinize.

Nothing that I have said about my three fathers or about my family is consciously untrue or exaggerated. It is meant to reveal a multidimensional truth and not merely to defend the image of any person or group. If anything, this collective self-portrait leads me to question the realism of the bounded groupings presupposed by the black ethnic construction of "cultures." Nonetheless, there is no reason to suppose that my ethnology is more or less interested than anybody else's. Like the black ethnic "cultures" that I analyze below, this ethnography/memoir is a portrait rendered in answer to a pervasive doubt about the worth of my person and my people, as well as a question about the my group's collective worthiness of opportunities and rewards that an ethnically unnamed, dominant population is assumed to merit without explanation or justification. The reader will have to apply his or her critical judgment and personal experience to the judgment of whether I have been truthful and fair, because some self-representations are neither.

The next chapter examines one of the main institutional generators of opportunity and choice for the transnational Black bourgeoisie. The university is a "literally-defined" world of the stigmatized, and the representations called "cultures" are, to a great degree, the products of its socially conditioned epistemology.

2

The University in Black, White, and Ambivalence: The Hidden Curriculum

A permanent sense of inadequacy and obligation drove my birth father, like me, to a steady stream of accomplishments. Yet he felt most comfortable with understatement about his accomplishments. For all of his practical contributions to Howard University and to the health of Black people, he regretted having published little and seemed to doubt his capacity to excel according to this measure of achievement. In the hierarchy within and among universities, writing is valued over oral and practical instruction, just as theory is valued over practice, abstraction over concreteness and encyclopedic documentation, and publication over clinical work. Moreover, universities rank themselves and obsess about outsiders' ranking of them. Founded to address the needs of an abused population emancipated only recently and with virtually no education or assets, Howard and other HBCUs have always been torn between the impulses to satisfy the immediate needs of the oppressed and the standards set by people who, on the backs of Blacks, had liberated themselves from material need and displayed that freedom through their very abstract erudition.

On the other hand, I grew up free of material want but was, once set adrift in the white world and enrolled in traditionally White "Research I" universities, all the more consciously burdened with the indelible stigma of slave ancestry. Exercised by the supposition that I was a lice carrier or an athlete, I adopted a strategy similar to that of many West Indians at Howard, though the collective fortress of my ambitions was more racial than ethnic. Also, like my mother, I tend to feel that I have more to lose by concealing my own and other Black people's accomplishments than by letting them show. After all, television is a twenty-four-hour propaganda machine advertising the normalcy of white wealth, genius, and ingenuity and of Black poverty, criminality, and brute physicality. If intellectually accomplished and materially comfortable Black people do not present themselves honestly, then who will? Every Black person bears the burden of representing his or her race, fearing that every error or lapse will confirm the stereotypes self-interestedly propagated by the majority. At the same time, we hope that every personal accomplishment by us or by other Blacks will lift the defamatory veil a bit, improving the overall reputation and material condition of the race. Like Sisyphus, though, we struggle uphill against the reality that prejudice and interest defy empirical experience and against the fear that our shortcomings will always count more than our successes. Such are the unenviable dilemmas of the stigmatized.

Black people may be among the most obvious exemplars of this phenomenon, but I observed the same even among my white male Harvard classmates and faculty colleagues, who also suffered from their consciousness of outsiderness, owing variously to their rural, southern, new-money, Jewish, lower-middle-class, non-Harvard, or uneducated familial roots. The pursuit of tenure and the years of worrying that one has not accomplished enough tend to stick with the best of us. When a person without a Harvard degree receives tenure at Harvard, he or she is reminded of the inferiority of his or her background. Before the award of tenure can be conferred, a recipient without a Harvard degree is given an honorary one, suggesting that no one without a Harvard degree is worthy of tenure at Harvard. However, I have yet to hear of a colleague who has refused this honor. Moreover, even for a famous and well-published Harvard professor, it is inevitable that one's department will, before long, hire someone more famous and better published. In the university, there is no perch safe from dishonor and, indeed, stigma—the most common of which is the stigma of not having published in a while or of being "past one's peak."

When Duke invited me from Harvard to chair the Department of African and African American Studies and to establish the Center for African and African American Research, I accepted the offer on condition that that the dean give us the resources to hire five academic stars, in order to set our department on the path to being better than Harvard's or any other department. However, as soon as I arrived, I heard of complaints about my salary and about the offices and other resources that had been assigned to me. Then I heard from an alliance of tenured associate and full professors that they had changed their minds: now they wanted to hire only untenured assistant professors. They did not like the Harvard-style "star system." It would ruin the morale and sense of community in the department. The foremost spokesman of this position pooh-poohed the quality of Harvard's department, though it has, since the 1990s, been widely regarded as the best. Yet as soon as he received a fellowship to spend a semester at the research center of that department, he leapt at the opportunity. Hierarchy is threatening to those at risk of being overshadowed but irresistible to those with the opportunity to climb.

Both Black and white Americans are skeptical of academic intelligence and tend to regard displays of it as insulting to the democratic premise that everyone's information, thoughts, values, and vote are of equal worth. Add to that the mix of pride and resentment that many members of downtrodden populations tend to feel for their upwardly mobile fellows. They are regarded alternately as heroes, brownnosers, and betrayers. By breaking ranks, they undermine the solidarity of the oppressed and disrupt the circle of commiseration. The self-presentation of highly educated members of pariah groups arises from a compromise between the wish to rise and, at the same time, to preserve the safety of their fellow pariahs' loyalty. There is, however, an additional difficulty under which the racially stigmatized suffer in an exemplary way. Many whites not only overlook Black intellectual excellence but also resent displays of it that they cannot deny. It is easier for whites to credit Black people with excellence in areas that can be discussed—albeit falsely—as merely natural physical gifts, such as sports and sex. Yet investment in these areas of allowed accomplishment is no more essential to the collective lifeways of the stigmatized than is the very common decision to defy them.

In the *corpus inscriptionum* (Malinowski 1922, 24) of racism, the signs marking waiting rooms, service counters, and water fountains "White Only" or "For Colored" are the most widely remembered in the mass media. But another, statistically rarer sign is described more often in the oral histories of segregation that I heard in Howard's sphere of influence. According to these accounts, the sign at the beach or over the service counter reads, "No Niggers, Dogs, or Jews Allowed." According to the mother of a Chinese friend, similar signs in white-dominated parts of old Shanghai once read, "No Chinese or Dogs Allowed." Such vivid taxonomies of dishonor are hard to forget. Neither in leisure nor at school, at Virginia Beach or in the shadow of Howard, could a person of color avoid the irony of the "separate but equal" doctrine enshrined in US law by the 1896 *Plessy v. Ferguson* Supreme Court case. America mouthed the words of universal human equality but, in practice, equated the constituent other with four-legged animals. In the presence of such signs, many poor or borderline whites must have felt a delectable schadenfreude. The feelings of many black ethnics and middle-class Blacks were surprisingly mixed. This book details the complexity of their responses.

For example, the stigmatized are hyperaware—noticing, scanning, and creating a cover to conceal their discreditable status. The most active participants in this process are the discreditable, or imaginably middling, groups, who still regard it as possible to distinguish themselves from the people in last place. Making an example of the ironic likeness among Blacks, Jews, the deaf, and the blind, Jewish Canadian psychologist Erving Goffman observed that the stigmatized tend to craft a "literally-defined world" around themselves, an observation that helps us to understand not only the success of magazines like *Ebony*, *Jet*, and *Essence* and the endurance of the HBCU but also the role of the university in general in contemporary society. Consistent with Goffman's observation, every previously downtrodden region, religion, nation, or race aspires to found its own publications and universities and, there, *retell* its own story. The university is a context in which the stigmatized—of whatever region, religion, nation, race, or gender—seek to intellectualize their way out of the dilemmas of dishonor, self-alienation, and ambivalence. Let it be remembered that most universities in the world were founded in the service of stigmatized local elites seeking independence from and equality with currently superior imperial or national elites of another ethnicity, religion, gender, class, or region. Yet the measures of excellence in scholarship—including the authoritative language of publication, the most prestigious venues of publication, and the scholars whom it is necessary to cite—persist long beyond political independence or jurisdictional distinctness from the metropolis.

The political capital of the jurisdiction and its most prestigious university are often in different cities but are typically in the same *region* of the jurisdiction. Thus, the stratification of "power/knowledge" (Foucault 1980) can be mapped geographically. And just as ambitious populations within a jurisdiction imitate the accent or dialect of the capital, ambitious academics imitate the standards set by the more metropolitan universities and their ambition is to migrate there.

Like the masking of regional accents and dialects, scholarly "rationality" is what Goffman might call the perfect "disidentifier," a cover drawing attention away from the nonnormative characteristics of the discreditable and the discredited. Scholarly "rationality" is also often the retelling of social reality from the vantage of the discreditable but in the language of dominant class.

Irish American Harvard University professor Daniel Patrick Moynihan was perhaps the perfect exemplar of this strategy of the stigmatized. Like those of many white and black ethnics, Moynihan's efforts at disidentification relied in equal measure on adopting the language of the ethnically unmarked dominant class and dramatizing his superiority to the Black constituent other. In a process much like ritual scapegoating, Moynihan's covering of the stigmatized aspects of his own lower-class Irish background involved displacing that stigma onto Black people and using his verbal and sartorial performance of metropolitan expertise about us to fake his own invulnerability to the same stigma. I am tempted to apply this model and Moynihan's example to his entire discipline, but a conscientious review of the sociological literature is beyond the scope of this book. The arguments and analyses of scholars certainly reveal important truths and often solve material problems, but they also embody the "logic of the trial" (Bourdieu [1979] 1984, 476), asserting and defending the analyst's desired place of dignity in a hierarchical world, fraught with the constant risk of discreditation. Even the finest scholarly insights are enriched by the recognition of this motivational backdrop (J. L. Matory unpublished manuscript).

The University as a "Literally Defined World"

The improvement of the group's collective image and the evasion of ever-anticipated defamation are major motives in the efforts by the stigmatized to rewrite their role in the world. Stigmatizing attack and riposte are defining mechanisms of collective identity in every population because any population can be stigmatized by another population under some circumstances. Yet Black people in the United States exhibit these processes paradigmatically. Except perhaps for homosexuals, African Americans are the American social category for whom the anticipation of defamation is the most constant reality.

Universities are often ground zero for the most authoritative and socially definitive attacks and ripostes. For example, in 1967, Harvard's Christopher Jencks and David Riesman published in the *Harvard Educational Review* what they regarded as an innocent and objective critique of "the American Negro College," describing these institutions, with the exception of the "Negro Ivy League" (Fisk, Spelman, Morehouse, Hampton, Tuskegee, Dillard, Howard, and so forth), as "academic disaster areas" (Jencks and Riesman 1967a). (Moynihan presented his critique of the Black family as similarly innocent.) However, because it is a historically Black university, even scholars at Howard and Black scholars at Harvard felt drawn into this whirlpool of stigma and riposte. In response to Jencks and Riesman, Black academics and political leaders mounted a swift defense in the press, culminating in the publication of *Black Colleges in America*, edited by Black Harvard professor Charles V. Willie and lecturer Ronald R. Edmunds (1978).

For Goffman, the stigmatized and the normal are not separate and opposite types of people. Rather, they are opposite *perspectives*, since everyone is deficient and ashamed in some context that demands or normalizes a quality that he or she lacks. This observation raises for me a general question about the American university—no matter what its complexion, gender, religion, or regional base. Are universities paradigmatic communities of the stigmatized?

From the nineteenth century until the 1960s, the culture of hereditarily privileged white fraternity boys—which Helen Lefkowitz Horowitz (1987) calls "college life"—cut the dominant figure on US university campuses. However, much of the student population of universities since the nineteenth century—and an ever-growing proportion of that population over time—consisted of individuals whose social disadvantages made education their best chance for upward mobility, such as poor white boys, Jewish immigrants, and working-class veterans of World War II. So rapidly has this proportion of the college population grown since the 1970s that it now represents the demographically and culturally dominant element on campus.

I would add that, despite the university's pretense of valuing well-roundedness, the rise of the standardized test is symptomatic of an overall development in which the university favors prospective students and faculty members who have mastered the skills of solitary cogitation and production at the expense of camaraderie and teamwork, which were favored by the elite family connections and the buddy system that previously drove most college admissions and "college life." Compared with the wider society, scholars are now disproportionately the products of sheltered, socially isolated, or asthmatic childhoods. Out of this alienation arises the critical consciousness that is quintessential to the contemporary liberal arts. Our disposition to question and deconstruct received wisdom might just typify the perspective of the stigmatized. Of course, these observations do not apply equally to all tertiary institutions or to all parts of the admissions pool. The more elite the institution, the more applicable this characterization is, but family connections and "legacies" still shape admissions to most universities. However, particularly since the late 1960s, universities are less and less dominated by the George W. Bush type of family insider and team player (with its gentlemen's Cs and resentment of "grinds" and grade grubbers) and more and more by racial and gender outsiders (such as Jewish people, black people, Asians, women, and gay people) who feel that education is their best bet for a chance to break into a system long bent on reserving most slots for straight and gentile white males.

In sum, Howard raises for me the hypothesis that all American universities—and particularly the most elite among them—are communities of the stigmatized and that the knowledge we create, the values we enact, the solutions we propose, and the powers we confer are all shaped, literally or metaphorically, by stigma. Even more than most disciplines, my discipline of anthropology, at least in its twentieth-century, antiracist incarnation, was founded by stigmatized, not-so-white whites—Poles, Czechs, and Jews—who had a personal stake in redefining or erasing antecedent boundaries between the supposedly civilized and the supposedly savage, and in rescuing themselves and the rest of us from permanent hereditary stigma. These are the people I call "borderline whites."

As American democracy's defining example and symbol of exclusion, Blackness is an exemplary stigma and the HBCU a *locus classicus* of self-fashioning under the conditions of stigma. A black person's choice to attend college suggests the hopefulness that, like a Jewish person, a Slav, or a poor white Anglo-Saxon Protestant, he or she is discreditable, rather than discredited, that there is some way to cover the potentially disqualifying stigma and some place where people will not automatically notice that disqualification.

One major contention of this book is that my "not-so-white" discipline has pursued a boundary-clarifying mission and has, for that reason, furnished the boundary-clarifying vocabulary suitable to the projects of many African-descended ethnic groups in the United States. In these negotiations, the boundary-clarifying terms of ethnicity are also the terms by which the boundaries of Blackness become permeable or potentially escapable. For example, many black ethnic groups have adopted the Tylorean/Boasian parlance of "cultures"—each one a set of supposedly shared values and practices that sharply distinguish one bounded population from other such bounded populations near or far. Black ethnics have even adopted the vocabulary of structural-functionalist anthropology, such as "matriliny," or the tracing of descent exclusively through the mother's line—an attribution that the partially African-descended Indians of the southeast employ to argue that their paternal descent from Africans does not stop them from being Indian. Black ethnics have employed our disciplinary vocabulary to appeal for exemption from the racial stigma of which native, nonethnic African Americans are treated as the appropriate and paradigmatic targets.

In the 1950s, most black natives and immigrants were what Horowitz (1987) calls "outsiders" in the university—the children of noncollege graduates in hot but unequal pursuit of upward mobility and even of collectively national or racial "uplift," as the race men once called it. Back then, both black immigrants and Black natives at Howard recognized themselves as suffering under global white supremacy. However, immigrants and natives were outsiders to different degrees. On the one hand, native, nonethnic African Americans reveled in a system of historically Black fraternities and a network of long-term camaraderie. On the other hand, like the working-class Protestant outsiders of the nineteenth century and the working-class Jewish outsiders at the TWIs during the early- to mid-twentieth century, the African and Caribbean immigrant and transmigrant students of the 1950s were generally uninterested in joining the fraternities and sororities that then dominated campus social life.

However, in other ways, mid-twentieth-century black ethnics were more similar to their African American peers than are their counterparts in the twenty-first century. In the 1950s, because of the two groups' similar class and racial status, twentieth-century black ethnics had far less of a reason to distinguish themselves sharply from African Americans than do black ethnics today. If anything, African American students during the 1950s tended to look down upon their international peers. Even more often than now, African Americans insinuated that their African and Caribbean peers lived in trees and wore grass skirts. African Americans were often eager to distance themselves from the craven primitivity that they had seen in Tarzan movies. Nonetheless, these African American students had to admit that their African and Caribbean peers were often smart. Like the returning American World War II veterans, the international students tended to be older than most of their classmates, and, having had to work to earn their passage, room, and board, they were often more goal and professionally oriented. Another motivation for black unity during the 1960s was that many African Americans vicariously identified with the recent independence of African and Caribbean nations.

However, in the twenty-first century, when I began my formal research, most of the African and Caribbean immigrants in US universities are, like most students, what Horowitz calls "new outsiders"—people driven by the fear of downward mobility and the desire for a reliable and prosperous career, rather than by a passion for ideas and risky intellectual or political explorations. That is, because of immigration policies favoring professionals and students, black ethnics are disproportionately the children of people of considerably above-average income, who, as a result of economic and political crises in their homelands and of their parents' years of struggle with American racism, are petrified in the face of potential downward mobility in the United States. This fear appears to have heightened their incentive to distance themselves from African Americans and to stereotype African Americans as socially disabled and culturally incompetent.

Moreover, since the 1980s, at the same time that black immigration to the United States was rising sharply, a new consensus was emerging in the media and in white popular culture that racism was a thing of the past and that deficiency of character was the main extant reason for the endurance of disproportionately high levels of Black poverty in the United States. And a series of US Supreme Court decisions—starting with *Regents of the University of California v. Bakke* (1978)—undermined university admissions policies that, in compensation for past and present racial discrimination, give Black people preferential treatment in admissions. Instead, university admissions committees justified their targeted admission of historically underrepresented populations in terms of the educational value of "diversity," a quality that could operate independently of race or any history of forcible exclusion. "Cultural" diversity became an asset just as it became rude—an act of "playing the race card"—to mention race or racism at all.

The US university is a world of the stigmatized, and it is no accident that "cultures" have become one of its most popular idioms of self-fashioning.

On the Nonuniversality of the University: College as a Culture

Scholars live in the university as fish live in water. We seldom recognize or study it as a distinctive cultural space, shaped as it is by an unnatural and culture-specific symbolic language, an increasingly transnational population, an increasingly shared official curriculum, and, to purloin a phrase from John Gatto, a "hidden curriculum" as well. In the context of primary and secondary schools, Gatto's (2005) term describes the forms of social control, as opposed to mere information delivery, that conventional school pedagogy engineers. I am also indebted to Paul Willis's observations about the complementary behavior of students and teachers that drives working-class boys into working-class self-expectations and jobs (Willis 1977). Central to the hidden curriculum of US universities is a dialogical process of ethnoracial class formation among students. For me, this dialectic includes the competitive struggles for dignity among the subgroups of the stigmatized.

This curriculum is not only hidden but, in many ways, contrary to the official curriculum. Something in the structure of American universities induces their inhabitants to speak, and even more often to perform, a message opposite the message the institution itself ratifies in its charter and other official pronouncements. For example, in their ethnographic studies of American public state universities, Moffatt (1989) and Nathan (2005) discovered that, to the same degree that university officials preach in favor of the life of the mind, students articulate and perform careerism. To the degree that officials urge personal responsibility, students construct their lives in terms of "fun" and "freedom."

Students reach a range of compromise strategies. However, in these compromises—contrary to the hopes of professors and administrators—reflection, long-term learning, and figuring out the best philosophy on life are not what occupies most of the students' time. These public state university students spend a part of the week—Monday through Wednesday or Thursday—

studying hard and abiding by the rules of the professors. However, many students at these TWIs use the long weekend—from Thursday night to Sunday night—to get drunk. In short, many US students—and perhaps the majority—"grind" and then self-medicate in a weekly cycle. They are honest when they can afford to be, but they cheat when their credentials depend on it. Nowadays, it seems, people cheat less often to help their peers, as they did in the past, and more often to help themselves. This shift is consistent with the straitened conditions of postgraduate economic survival in a neoliberal age, and it parallels the rise of ethnic distinction over racial solidarity. Students do help each other to plan their schedules, to balance hard against easy courses, to figure out the easiest major that is likely to get them into professional school, to identify the easiest professors, and to do just what the professor says they should do to maximize their grades.

However, since the 1970s, the principle of individual striving has prevailed more and more over the principle of horizontal camaraderie and fun that, according to Horowitz (1987), dominated student life from the nineteenth century until the 1950s. Increasingly, horizontal solidarity is embraced only when it mechanically serves some anticipated career goal, such as "demonstrating leadership." Harvard officials report that this is the motive behind the proliferation of student ethnic organizations—black and nonblack.

If our students' choices appear superficial, the best that can be said of the university's pedagogy is that it is contradictory. In the elite private university, we professors urge our students to innovate and rethink things (we say) for the sake of their living a reflective life, but we compel them to risk expressing novel ideas on pain of a bad grade that could cost them their future livelihoods. Moreover, the architecture, the attire worn and ritual formulae uttered at graduation and convocation ceremonies, and the archaic terms we use to describe university officials endorse not innovation but the power of antiquity and stability, or at least its simulacrum—as our colonial and fake American University Gothic architecture suggests. While elite universities ask their students to eschew materialism and careerism, our immaculately kept lawns and gardens, the naming of campus buildings and endowed chairs after rich donors, and spiraling tuition costs advertise the importance of cash. The grading and credit system and the intensity of time-based regimentation in the university suggest, more than anything else, the regimes of a prison or of a bank. Students face multiple dilemmas in their use of time and energy between careerism and the life of the mind and between individuality and solidarity. And the choices they make are often the opposite of what university professors and administrators think we are urging.

The Changing University in the Changing Global Economy

Before the 1970s, we could entertain the fantasy that our walled-off campus quads structured a liminal space at a distance from the world, a four-year initiatic retreat, or spiritual health spa between childhood and adulthood, when a young person could engage in pure transformative reflection and fun. However, at the beginning of the 1970s, white liberal protesters were shot down at Kent State, and the oil crisis taught the subsequent generations of undergraduates that they were no longer guaranteed either four years of freedom or the level of adulthood prosperity that their parents had enjoyed. From then on, the university became less and less a liminal phase and more and more a continuation of the struggle against the post–oil crisis vortex of downward mobility, a struggle that began in high school and might—just might—end with retirement, assuming that we don't suffer long-term unemployment and our reverse mortgages don't run out before we die.

If four years in the university provides a moment of reflection, it is a live performative reflection on the lifelong dilemma whose consequences are heightened in a neoliberal age—do you strive individually or embrace horizontal solidarity? On the one hand, the official university primarily favors applicants and rewards the kind of student who can work by herself and for herself and then show the boss what she has done on her own. (It has become almost a cliché that teamworking techie entrepreneurs drop out before graduating.) But then we arrange for the individualist student to live with a thousands-strong four-year family of peers suffering similar forms of alienation, subordination, discomfort, and unpaid servitude. Their selective and instrumental solidarity often reflects the contradictory nature of their assignment. Another common result of this contradiction is suicide.

Despite some dissimilarity of contents and motives, all types of US university share a similar dialectics, to which my time at Howard alerted me. To those dilemmas and dialectics I have already discussed, I add the observation that universities in general induce more verbal self-identification than virtually any other institution on the planet—as much a prisons and almost as much as hospitals. They do so through, for example, SAT registration forms, admissions and financial aid applications, interviews, customs procedures, introductions during orientation period, identity cards, examination blue books, club membership rolls, medical records, and transcripts. Moreover, contrary to what most faculty and students care to remember about elite, private and ethnically unmarked institutions like Duke or Harvard, most universities were chartered expressly to produce and unify the bourgeois leadership of one specific nation, region, language group, ethnoracial group, gender, or disability group. And even Duke retains the shadow of its history as a regional institution reproducing the southern (white) elite, just as Harvard reproduced and disproportionately reproduces the northeastern white elite. Yet it is equally obvious that universities induce students to declare identities and found organizations that oppose, subdivide, internally rank, and name the internal heterogeneity of the nation, region, linguistic group, ethnoracial group, or gender that the university is intended to serve.

Though many of the same observations might apply to Howard, this book is not a study of white students at white schools, and the issues at Howard are a bit different. The HBCU requires more specific consideration. Because they have been brought together based upon a shared and powerful racial stigma, the dilemmas of HBCU students also differ from those of white students at TWIs.

Moreover, as far as I have been able to discover, there is no existing ethnography of an HBCU. The vast majority of the ethnography of schooling and Black people concerns secondary schools, where the students typically fit a very different profile from those in HBCUs. On the one hand, the primary concern of the high-school-based ethnography—in the United States and, unknown to Caribbean immigrants, the Caribbean alike (e.g., Miller 1991, Parry 2000)—seems to be young African-descended people's rejection of academic endeavors. In sum, fully aware that education is necessary for individual upward mobility in a white-dominated world, working-class black kids—especially boys—wonder whether education is not also a betrayal of their own oppressed people, a surrender of their autonomy, and a self-denigrating capitulation to the oppressor's insulting values. And they tend to suspect that conformity in school emasculates them. Moreover, like their working-class white peers, they must ask themselves if their degrees can ever earn them as much as their parents' union jobs had earned them during better economic times (see, e.g., Fordham 1996; Ogbu 2003; Fordham and Ogbu 1986).

In the 1950s and 1960s, sociologists tended to argue that working-class children—quite independently of class—suffered from their lack of so-called middle-class traits, such as "individualism . . . [and] ability to defer gratification." Once these young people were "labeled as failures, and placed in terminal tracks," the argument went, they became frustrated, and they established an antischool culture that "inverts the image of the rule-abiding, obedient and hardworking student by granting peer approval to the rule-breaker, the insolent, and the hedonist" (Davies 1999, 193). "Among males, rebellion was epitomized by fighting, confrontation with authority figures . . . , smoking and drinking, and sexual bravado." Girls rebelled by flaunting their emerging sexuality, and a disengaging from academic concerns in favor of a preoccupation with romantic relationships" (193).

Particular authors emphasized the value that the working class placed upon "toughness," in contrast to the school's emphasis on "self-control," intellect, and "discipline." Stinchcombe (1964) emphasized the male-gendered component of such rebellion, suggesting that it was a conventional response by academically unsuccessful *boys* across classes. Also crosscutting classes, observed Coleman (1961) was an adolescent culture "bound by shared interests in consumerism, peer popularity, and other youthful pursuits" (Davies 1999, 193).

Downes (1966) observed that white working-class British in the 1960s, in contrast to their American counterparts, lived in a cultural milieu that did not nurture dreams of upward mobility, leading the youth of this class to perceive school as irrelevant to their future. (In fact, the US cultural milieu, at that time and now, has presented many similar obstacles and much similar discouragement to Black American upward mobility.) Being too young to begin full-time employment, working-class youth tended to adopt delinquency as a "cure for boredom."

Since the 1970s, a generation of European, Canadian, Australian, and US sociologists led by Paul Willis has argued that the antischool culture of many working-class populations arises not from a cultural deficit but from the informal culture of the working class, whose main themes include solidarity over competitiveness, an antagonism to institutional authority, and pride in manual labor—as opposed to the "pencil-pushing" culture that the school shares with the bureaucratic and professional world of the middle class (Davies 1999, 195).

Of course, much working-class resistance to the middle-class school culture of the English Midlands is also driven by anger—predictably misdirected toward nonwhite Britons, gays, and women (Willis 1977). The misogyny, homophobia, and antiwhite dimensions of much US rap music and its Caribbean counterparts are too obvious to require detailed illustration here: rap often projects an ambivalence about "bitches," "hos," and "batty boys" (a derogatory Jamaican term for gay people) even deeper than its ambivalence about "niggaz." Indeed, if one substituted the word "race" for "class," the aforementioned descriptions of white European and North American subcultures would intuitively sound like apt descriptions of popular culture in North America today. Clearly, *some* of the North American counterparts of British working-class youth suffer the same hopelessness about their potential for upward mobility. Because of the tough sentencing standards for crack-related convictions and racial discrimination in sentencing generally,

Black and Latino youth are overrepresented not only among the hopeless but also among the incarcerated (see Cose 2002, 103). These are among the causes and the fruits of what sociologists have called "oppositional culture."

My conversations with Howard students, alumni, and neighbors suggest a highly fraught relationship among racial, class, and gender identity. For example, a young man who speaks too "proper," dresses too neatly, appears to study too hard in school, walks too symmetrically, uses too little profanity, eats yogurt or quiche, crosses his legs like scissors, or carries books home from school makes himself vulnerable to assault or name-calling that questions his sexual orientation. Bourdieu observes of European working-class boys and men, as well, that their conformity to middle-class expectations invites accusations of homosexuality from their peers ([1979] 1984, 382–84). The hypermasculinity and misogyny at the backdrop of these accusations are reactions to the pervasive doubt about the manhood, dignity, and self-determination of working-class and otherwise stigmatized men. All other things being equal, a boy's willingness to invest in school success is a measure of his independence from standard measures of masculinity or his insulation from the demands of male camaraderie.

I have seen evidence of this phenomenon among Black, Latino, and white boys in the Cambridge and Durham public high schools. However, school success is reportedly more consistent with popularity among white boys than among Black and Latino boys. These fruits are hardly confined to one race or ethnic group, but it is a reasonable hypothesis that in these Western, urban societies, the degree and duration of a population's marginalization correlates with the intensity of the oppositional culture that it generates.

Graduate students in my class at Howard were highly articulate about the prohibitions that surround working-class male conduct and are required to guarantee one's safety. If one hasn't mastered them, one is even unlikely to be picked for a team at the basketball court. Students said that verbal expression not intent on putting another male down or on charming a woman must be kept to a minimum. On the other hand, swift and decisive physical reactions to any challenge are encouraged. My students disapproved of my advice after my son got in trouble for hitting a boy back at the Oyster Bilingual School. I advised Adu that the person who hits back is more likely to be caught than is the person who struck first. Therefore, if ever struck again, he should fearlessly scream his assailant's name while telling him to stop—for example, "GEOOORGE! Stop hitting me!" That way, everyone would know who was guilty and who was innocent, and the teacher would have to intervene on Adu's side. Moreover, his verbal display of fearlessness would, by itself, remove him as a desirable target of any bully.

"Oh, no! No, no, no!" my students chided. "He should hit the kid back!"

"What if the other kid is stronger and ends up injuring Adu?" I asked, incredulous. "Plus, he could get kicked out of school!"

"Well, at least he went down fighting!" They laughed, as if to say, "It may not be ideal, but that's the way it is." Indeed, fourteen years later, both of my children still laugh over this advice.

Especially for working-class boys, school seems to pose a special challenge, in that they are conventionally allowed more freedom to move about outside the home free of supervision than are their sisters. So the intense supervision and hierarchy of the classroom are more threatening to their gendered self-conception. Indeed, black boys of every ethnicity in urban schools are understood to get into a lot more trouble (or to be persecuted much more) than are girls. It is particularly obvious in racially integrated schools that black boys—also across ethnicities—are diagnosed disproportionately with attention deficit / hyperactivity disorder and other mental or emotional disorders (e.g., Cose 2002, 91), and they appear far less likely than white boys to receive the appropriate medical and psychological intervention as a result.

The key to success for Black males, my childhood friend Clark told me, is learning how to code-switch—in speech and conduct. It is plainly, simply, and rightly the socially competent thing to do. Though it may not be sufficient for everyone, it worked for him. Similarly, in the Black working-class high school that she studied, Fordham (1996) shows that boys who also play team sports are not criticized by their peers for working hard in school. Their conspicuous demonstration of peer camaraderie and masculine physicality seems to avert the accusation that they are homosexual or "acting white." Yet working-class boys are not alone. A little-known fact is that the gender gap in educational achievement is highest among the rich. "The largest educational gender gap is among families in the top 25 percent of the earnings distribution, where women lead men by 13 percent in graduation rates, compared to just a 2 percent advantage for women from the lowest income families" (Coontz 2012).

Upper-class white male anti-intellectualism is not a new phenomenon. Consider how shamelessly George W. Bush bragged in his commencement address to the Yale College class of 2001, "And to the C students I say, you, too, can be President of the United States." He added for emphasis that he and his accomplished classmate Richard Brodhead, then the dean of Yale College and now the president of Duke University, "put a lot of time in at the Sterling Library, in the reading room where they have those big leather couches. [Laughter] We had a mutual understanding. Dick wouldn't read aloud, and

I wouldn't snore. [Laughter]" (Bush 2001). I suspect that this combination of folksy self-mockery and thumbing his nose at "book smarts" went over especially well in middle America, where Bush long enjoyed great popularity. It is a form of code-switching and image management—a euphemization of enormous personal power. However, it is also a confession that the source of such power is not intellect or hard work but hereditary social capital.

This culture of the "gentleman's C" had been entirely normal among the New England elite before the 1970s—even among women. For example, a female white Anglo-Saxon Protestant friend from the town of Andover, Massachusetts, who attended Smith College in the early 1960s told me that, at that time, it was considered tasteless and "Jewish" to strive too hard for good grades. As insulting terms for studious people, the terms "nerd" and "wonk" were still current among my white adolescent and adult peers at Maret and Harvard (and in movies about white teenagers) long before I ever heard them among Black peers. Nor did I witness nearly as much drinking and drug use among my Black high school and college peers as among my white ones.

On the other hand, the HBCUs represent a major and little-publicized setting where Black people, for all our ambivalence, have also defined education and professional ambition as a "Black thing"—indeed, as a Black weapon against white oppression. In this way, the dilemmas of the HBCU student remain somewhat different from those of urban public high school students, of working-class white high schoolers, and of rich whites at TWIs. HBCU students must strategically choose the forms of collective solidarity that most favor their upward mobility. They seem to feel less free than TWI students to present themselves merely as individuals, but the idioms of their collectivist self-presentation are carefully selected and judged. At Howard, the first principle of self-presentation for men and for women is that both purely "ghetto" and purely "bougie" are undesirable styles of self-presentation. "Ghetto" is regarded as trashy, and "bougie" as both fake and elitist. And while one might hear a woman being called either name, men know better than even to risk being called "bougie." Or perhaps that description of a man (that is, a "real" man) is inconceivable.

These are matters of taste, which Bourdieu deconstructs, defining it not as an inborn and individual awareness of what is intrinsically beautiful but as a mode of self-presentation that results from one's class-specific and intergenerational degree of exposure to the latest knowledge, behaviors, and consumer preferences of the highest elite echelon (Bourdieu [1979] 1984). Bourdieu assumes that middling classes and ambitious members of the lower class continuously imitate the knowledge, behaviors, and consumer preferences of their class superiors but that their lateness in adopting the most current forms of elite taste, as well as the nervous performance that results, gives away the inescapable inferiority of the lower to the higher classes. Bourdieu observes that the working class, and especially the men among them, often resent and resist the higher classes and therefore resist the trickle-down of taste.

As a multiclass category, African Americans inflect this logic in a distinctive way. Especially afraid of losing the alliance of their working-class allies and clients, middle-class and elite African Americans "hedge our bets" by code-switching and by constantly seeking the right register along an acrolect-basilect, or "bougie"-"ghetto," continuum as we communicate with other African Americans. The ideal manner of situational code-switching and stylistic hybridity is known to some as "bougetto."

In race-targeted universities, students who have arrived from places with idioms of racial, or sociophenotypical, classification unlike those of the United States often appropriate the cultural capital of the elite classes at home and advertise it as a mark of *ethnic* distinction, thus elevating their status either within the inescapable racial categories of the United States or as an ethnic exemption from the forms of social disability that attach to that racial category.

Whether at HBCUs or at TWIs, professors, too, seek advantage by fudging, or disidentifying, our class status. We possess great cultural capital but relatively little economic capital. We recognize—and even set—the standards of taste of our economic superiors, and we authorize their children's access to their parents' class. We know and aspire to "quality," but we can seldom afford to consume it—except during university-funded postlecture dinners at upscale restaurants—and we either look down upon or perform an ironic distance from those lacking the education to know the difference. We are also often highly ambivalent about our economic superiors. Yet we are happy to move up in the hierarchy of universities to those institutions that the rich favor for their children, thus fetching a higher salary for ourselves. Or, sometimes, we exchange the higher status of a top university affiliation for a higher salary at a lower-status institution, as I did. The capitalist logic of the competitive recruitment system is obvious, but it—and capitalism generally—are often resented by the professors who lack the capital to engage in these exchanges.

Universities and professors, like ethnic groups and their members, exist in a field of competition for resources and rank. It is not surprising that the ranking of ethnic groups is one idiom and mechanism of such ranking. Historically Black Howard University is thus doubly rich in such lessons about the "communities of the stigmatized."

Reading the Race: Contradiction Ritualized

While elite universities encourage the questioning of received wisdom, they also create taken-for-granted frames of experience and self-performance. Rituals such as commencement exercises and the convocation dramatize the structure of identity and consciousness upon which the university is premised. Within a European-modeled framework, Howardites intermittently and with increasing frequency assert their distinctive racial identity and collective purpose. For example, the Howard University commencement exercises of 2002 began with European classical music, the US national anthem, and then a Negro spiritual.

Dressed in the medieval European attire that typifies high ceremony at universities in the anglophone world, President H. Patrick Swygert outlined

FIGURE 2.1. Howard University Commencement Convocation, 2002. President Swygert is on the left side of the screen, and the commencement oratrix, Atlanta mayor Shirley Clarke Franklin, is at the center. Photograph by the author.

FIGURE 2.2. Graduates. Note the stole made of Ghanaian Ashanti kente cloth, a prominent symbol of African American pride at university commencements and in the pulpit. Photograph by the author.

the central themes in all of the subsequent speeches—"African American" accomplishment and responsibility to provide leadership in the "world community." I do not recall any mention of Africans or Afro-Caribbeans in his speech, but Professor Belton—an espresso-colored Trinidadian American—said that President Swygert was the first president he had heard speak of "the African diaspora." Indeed, at the 2002 commencement, I heard his multiple references to Africa as "the motherland." On the other hand, though I have seen them for sale at the Gospel-Spreading Bible Bookstore on Georgia Avenue, I noticed few of the kente-cloth stoles bearing inscriptions like "Class of 2002" that I expect to see as a matter of course on African American college graduands at Harvard and Duke, where the relative paucity of African-descended people and the fact that the university leadership is not Black seem to occasion greater unity across the black student population. The United

States is a major market for Ghanaian kente because the colorful cloth has become an African American sign of Black pride and pan-African unity.

At Howard, however, the university leadership consciously signals its "African Americanness," seemingly unaware that many black immigrants and their children feel excluded by this term and its US-centered symbolism. Jesse Jackson launched the term "African American" in 1988 as a homeland- and cultures-based alternative to "Black." For most native-born Black Americans, it includes all people of African descent in the United States, eliding differences of recent immigrant or old triracial isolate origins. When they wish to distinguish themselves from native-born populations, however, Caribbean Americans and recent African immigrants, along with their children, reject this term as a reference to them. They thus reject the notion that Black Americans and the US logic of binary hypodescent are the paradigm of all African-descended populations and communal identities.

On the other hand, Black Americans who employ this term seldom realize that they are communicating this notion. We take for granted the unity of Blackness as we define it. For example, invoking African American youth and radio vernacular, President Swygert spoke of giving "shout-outs" to various constituencies deserving of special recognition, and, with a hand gesture, he saluted his fellow members of the Omega Psi Phi fraternity—and by extension all members of Black Greek-letter societies, which have few non-US-born members. From the dais, the term "African American," African American Vernacular English, and the African American Greek-letter societies were intended to stand as tropes for the collective identity and aspirations of all black people.

However, audience members could not but reflect upon ethnic, class, and color diversity, as well as "taste." Speaking to me, some in the audience criticized as "ghetto" those graduands who wave at the camera during commemorative photos. In Anglo-US society generally, communication between adults and teenagers is fraught with its own difficulties. That is, some parents and teachers who want to preserve their authority but also solicit voluntary assent from young people try to speak youth dialect to achieve these results. However, they must be careful. Such attempts can look fake and, because older people are usually late in adopting this fast-changing language, invite ridicule. These difficulties in adult-youth communication are amplified among African Americans and, I would hypothesize, among all stigmatized populations. So some of my young African American companions at the commencement criticized President Swygert's diction, saying that his use of vernacular merely compromised his "rep" as "bougie," or elite, a reputation that they apparently expect him to preserve.

Professor Belton and his African American wife, Margaret, watched the graduation on cable television. His wife is a highly accomplished scholar from Chicago, but her mother has Louisiana Creole roots and, though she is Nilla Wafer–colored, her father comes from a proudly black, Black, and anticlerical family long determined to keep itself free of white blood. Her father's family thus remains opposed to the union that produced her. Professor Belton and his wife told me that, while watching the commencement, they had scanned the crowd and the dais to assess the average and the range of complexions present. It was clear to these friends, as it was to a group of light-skinned alumni I met at the graduation, that Howard's student population is becoming darker over time. For some people, including these visiting alumni, this change is a source of distress. For others, it is more distressing that the complexion range on the dais is not changing quite as fast as that of the audience.

To much of the audience, the commencement exercises are a snapshot of "our people" at our best and a focus of anxiety about whether the university is producing a leadership class, or what W. E. B. Du Bois called a "Talented Tenth," that represents us well and cares about our cause. Like the photos of leading social institutions in African American and Caribbean communities, such snapshots are carefully monitored as evidence of complexion-related inequality and disunity, and of our collective progress—or failure—at overcoming colorism.

What I noticed from my seat in the audience was not just the complexion diversity but also the flamboyant sartorial diversity of the dark audience. An astonishing number of families I saw at this ceremony included women with West African wrap skirts and towering, flowerlike taffeta head ties, suggesting the families' origins in the swathe of countries between Sierra Leone and Cameroon on the Gulf of Guinea. A far smaller number wore the Habesha *kemis*, the typical female attire of Eritrea and Ethiopia.

Because of the university's racially defined mission, the diversity of Howard's student body, faculty, and administration takes almost all outsiders and many newcomers by surprise. While Howard disproportionately attracts students who would be called "Black" in the binary system of the United States, the university includes students, faculty, alumni, and staff of all races and of innumerable nationalities, including people of African descent who have never previously called themselves "Black" or "black." Among them are not only Nigerians and Afro-Trinidadians but also Jewish Americans, South Asian Indians, North Africans, Filipinos, Central Americans, and, particularly in the 1980s, Iranian refugees. Not only *Afro*-Caribbeans but also *Indo*-Caribbeans from Guyana and Trinidad have long seen Howard as "their" university as well. For example, Afro-Trinidadian Eric Williams became the first prime minister of Trinidad after having taught at Howard, while Indo-Guyanese Cheddi Jagan attended Howard before becoming the first prime minister of Guyana. During my six months at Howard, I heard a vivid popular anthropology of ethnic and regional difference.

There was no more common trope of black ethnic self-representation on campus than "the lazy African American" (or, in the perception of the Central American workers in my dormitory, "the lazy black person [*moreno*]" generally). But how could even such constitutional US American clichés resist the opposite empirical reality that Howard represents? At Howard, black immigrants are daily surrounded by a whole range of African American characters and considerably outnumbered by a university-educated, professional, and productive subset thereof.

The trope of the "lazy" native may well be endemic to the immigrant situation. Barbadian immigrants to Trinidad reportedly call the natives "lazy," as do Haitian immigrants in the Dominican Republic, Dominican immigrants in Puerto Rico, and Caribbean and African immigrants in the United States—most gleefully in reference to African Americans. The a priori definition of white Americans as the apical group and the paradigm of rightness—and a gargantuan media apparatus presenting African Americans as their definitional opposite—largely exempt white American natives from this chain of accusation and make all black people available as the constituent other for the Central American workers at Howard.

But a further, dialectical structure of meaning making—endemic to universities—may also be at work here. Just as students at the TWIs studied by Moffat and Nathan fashion identities and conduct opposite the priorities of their professors and administrators, Howard students see and act upon complexion hierarchy and ethnic diversity to the same degree that the university's official pronouncements emphasize racial unity.

The Architecture of Embrace and Distancing

The negotiation of distance, alliance, and dignity among the stigmatized is not entirely verbal or dramatized in rituals alone. In the HBCU, embrace and distancing often occur in physical, sartorial, and culinary performances and in the architectural structuring of space. The heart of Howard's campus is a grassy quadrangle called "the Quad"—on one of the highest hilltops in what was called, during the time that I grew up, "Chocolate City." The African Studies building, Rankin Chapel, the Administration Building, Douglass Hall (the History Department building), the Fine Arts Department building, the Theater Department building, the Blackburn student social center, and

FIGURE 2.3. Founders Library, Howard University, 2002. Photograph by the author.

Founders Library form the walls of this Quad. Founders Library is the architectural anchor of the Quad, and it is proudly described on campus as the world's premier collection of books about the black world.

Faded photographs of Black students, professors, and administrators line the walls of most of these buildings. On the inner field the Quad, benches, oak trees, and a sundial mark the gathering places of various Greek-letter societies and of the Caribbean students, who, in a way, form a distinct fraternity of their own. These landmarks are the sites of regular ritual performances and the daily exchange of news and social commentary. Diagonal pathways lace the buildings together, and in 2002 these paths were constantly traversed by students on cellular telephones—years before they became a frequent sight on Harvard's campus—while an American flag snapped like a rifle report overhead.

Just to the north of the Quad are the Texas-sized sports field, a dormitory, and an indoor swimming pool; and to the west and southwest, a series of professional schools—Business, Social Work, and Architecture. These schools all sit at the crest of what is called "The Hill." Descending The Hill toward the south, one passes the School of Engineering, the natural sciences quadrangle, and the university health service. No street on The Hill leads anywhere but to or from a campus building. Unless you have business with the university, you have no reason to be on one of these roads, and your presence stands out. The

Hill is the only hill nearby, so the gradient leading up to this citadel of Black learning and bourgeois identity is intimidating to all but those who share in its mission. At the bottom of The Hill is old Freedmen's Hospital, where my siblings and I were born. It has since become a faculty office building. The old Wonder Bread bakery has turned in to a computer center, which houses, on the Georgia Avenue side, a row of retail shops.

The medical area stretches out still farther to the south, beyond the first through street on campus. It includes the National Genome Research Project, the Colleges of Medicine, Pharmacy, and Dentistry, a state-of-the art medical library, the Center for Sickle Cell Disease, and the colossal Howard University Hospital, Freedman's successor.

Several dormitories sit at the western and southern edges of the medical area, but passage to these dormitories is considered dangerous. They neighbor public housing projects and are far from the four lanes of Georgia Avenue, which rush along the western side of the campus, and from equally wide U Street, which extends westward from the south side. On Georgia Avenue, south of U Street, a series of shops, a Metro subway station, and the Howard University Visitors' Center struggle to reclaim a skid row/crack alley that extends several blocks before hitting a blockade at the walls of McCullough Homes, a stately moderate-income housing project managed by the United House of Prayer for All People—a nationwide Black Pentecostal church

FIGURE 2.4. The crest of the Hill, Howard University. Photograph by the author.

FIGURE 2.5. Map of the Howard University campus. Reprinted with the permission of Howard University Communications and Marketing.

founded in 1919 by a Cape Verdean immigrant named "Daddy Grace." Its current bishop's home is miles from here, a mansion backed by deep woods, two blocks down North Portal Drive from the house where I grew up.

In 2002, my son Adu and I lived in the Towers—a graduate and undergraduate dormitory across Georgia Avenue from campus. The barking of the "Qs"—President Swygert's Omega Psi Phi fraternity brothers—often thundered through the courtyard of East Tower, inviting everyone to watch the "stomps," or "step shows." I watched from Adu's bedroom window. The Qs conveyed the impression of an exclusive, well-ordered, and stylishly dangerous pack. To me, the omega signs branded on the arms of fully fledged brothers—call it proud flesh or a keloid—suggested equal measures of collective self-possession and slavishness. We all knew, from the carved tablet atop his desk, that even the building manager of the Towers was a Q.

Most of my Caribbean acquaintances on campus preferred to keep their distance from these organizations. For them, the keloids encapsulated the type of conformity and waste of time that they would rather avoid. Like most fraternities on most campuses, the Black American Greek-letter societies exact a cost in time and, during the initiation (or "pledge"), grades. As in initiations to adulthood and to secret societies all over the world, including white fraternity initiations at TWIs, the associated rituals sometimes result in severe injury or death. In these cases, the university takes disciplinary action.

FIGURE 2.6. The Towers dormitory, where Adu and I lived in 2002. Photograph by the author.

But the payoff is often a lifetime of camaraderie, which my father, too, knew well and loved deeply.

It is difficult not to see Howard's architecture and landscape as a symbolic reflection of American racial history. If you approach The Hill from the south, as most African Americans did in past generations, you rise in altitude as you climb northward toward the center of campus. The Hill stands far from the city's shorter but more politically powerful hill—Capitol Hill. However, *The Hill* has afforded a safe haven for the Black elites of the nation and of the world to write alternative narratives of dignity and progress, as well as whisper narratives of mutual one-upmanship. Whereas the preeminent ritual narration of African American progress retraces the upward flight from the mire of southern slavery and the centers of Jim Crow oppression, the city's largest annual ritual display at the time of my research was the Caribbean Day Parade down Georgia Avenue in June. It, too, culminated at Howard. However, to the shimmering peal of steel drums, the feathered dancers of a dozen island-based fraternal clubs descended from the *north*, laughing all the way. (Because of the organizers' outstanding debts to the city, the parade has not taken place since 2011.)

The chief media in the parade's dramatization of social sameness and difference—like those of the powwows of the mixed-race Indians of Maryland, Virginia, and North Carolina; the Creole balls of Los Angeles; and the cotillions of the African American upper-middle class—are clothing, music, dance, and food.

Like the city's enormous Black middle class itself, these momentous convergences on The Hill—affecting populations and nations all around the black Atlantic—are almost entirely ignored in mainstream press coverage of events "inside the Beltway."

When and Where I Entered

In 1966, my aunt Arnzie—whom I called "Aunty Arnzie"—took frequent weekend breaks from her premedical studies at Howard to visit my mother and the rest of my birth family on North Portal Drive, at the top of Sixteenth Street. My mother Deborah, father Bill, brother Earle, and sister Yvedt lived surrounded by birches, hollies, magnolias, dogwoods, plum trees, forsythias, and azaleas in a 1950s rambler whose Frank Lloyd Wright–inspired architect had built it into the wave of a small hill and christened it "the Merrimac." Its name derives from a lost Union battleship.[1] Some called our neighborhood the Gold Coast, in honor of its simultaneous wealth and Blackness, but others, like my mother, distinguished our particular subdivision as the Platinum Coast—newer, "swankier," farther north, and more recently colonized by the Black bourgeoisie than the army of brick colonials that preceded it on Sixteenth Street. As if we had settled virgin forest, our streets were named for flowers and trees, but our houses were postwar modern, and the earlier, largely Jewish colonizers, except for a few, had retreated before us into wealthier Bethesda and Potomac, Maryland. Our kind had not yet planted a forest of multimillion-dollar McMansions in Prince George's County, which we did during the 1980s, turning it from a lower-middle-class white domain into the wealthiest Black county in the country. When I was growing up, most of the synagogues of the Gold Coast would not become churches for another decade, but the Washington Ethical Society, a branch of a secular Jewish New York–based organization, would long remain, for me, a more delightful and memorable Sunday experience than was "hincty" Mount Zion Baptist Church.

Like Aunty Arnzie, both of my parents had attended Howard—where my mother received her bachelor's degree in chemistry and her master's in psychology in the 1950s. With his bachelor's and medical degrees from Howard, my father both taught and practiced surgery there. On the Gold and Platinum Coasts, most of my friends were the indulged but ambitious scions of surgeons, pediatricians, cardiologists, diplomats, intelligence agents, accountants, attorneys, judges, dentists, professors, the owner of the private primary school that my half siblings later attended, and the owner of Chili Bowl Ben's restaurant. Most of our parents had also attended Howard during the 1940s. But until my Aunt Arnzie dragged us into the gravity of Howard undergraduate life in the 1960s, our house contained more European and Japanese art than African or Haitian, since my father had served as the resident surgeon on an Air Force base in occupied Misawa, Japan, where Yvedt was born.

Inside the Merrimac, I grew up among the clean, mid-twentieth-century-modern lines of Herman Miller, Mies van der Rohe, Knoll, Arno Saarinen, and Arne Jacobsen, alongside Japanese lacquer, Bose, and bossa nova. Not even the classical touches in the décor—the Italian traditional dining set and a tangerine velour-upholstered Louis XV bergère—gave any hint of nostalgia for pre–World War II British or US society. Not one piece of her own mother's Victorian furniture or tastes moved with us to the North Portal Estates. But Mom did collect Crown Derby and Limoges china, which she acquired, along with her nine-piece silver table settings, from a Virginia antique mall called Thieves' Market and sometimes directly from a Black servant of Virginia's declining gentry—apparently a congregant of one of Granddaddy's many churches. I don't know how Annie had come by it. Only in time did Mom add ebony, ivory, and mahogany sculptures from Kenya, Nigeria, and Haiti.

Mom worked throughout her marriage to Dad. A chemistry major and a premed in college, she transmuted her premarital aspirations into a postmarital career as a clinical psychologist. She got her master's degree, too, at Howard and then worked, successively or simultaneously, as a professor of psychology at the University of the District of Columbia, a director of handicapped services in the DC Public Schools, a child psychologist, a director of various District of Columbia city government health and welfare programs, and a Democratic Party fund-raiser and organizer. She was a highly competent planner and administrator. A small staff of large women—some from my grandparents' church and some hired independently—worked in our house, helping my mother to take care of us and to "entertain." Mom competitively entertained the fellow members of "Med Wives"—the wives of the Medico-Chirurgical Society of the District of Columbia—and the complexion-coded battles for rank always sizzled beneath the well-polished surface of things. The bridge party in the 2011 film *The Help* looked strikingly familiar, except that some of the help in my mother's house was white—in truth, she called herself "Portuguese"—and all of the guests were some shade of Black. The guests never spoke unkindly to or about the staff within their hearing, but my mother did privately describe the most intimate of these helpers as possessing "low-normal" intelligence.

Mom wore every kind of precious stone and metal on her neck or her fingers, but she had a specific preference for black mink, Bruno Magli shoes, Cadillac and Mercedes, Sauternes, and J. Ruiz y Cía sherry, which she called "J. Ruizy." When she attended Maggie Walker High School in Richmond, Virginia—named after a Black Virginian who was the first woman of any race to found a chartered bank in the United States—the best students in US schools were tracked toward French rather than Spanish. To this day, her White Shoulders is the only kind of perfume that I can tolerate near me. Most brands irritate my sinuses, reminding me of the crucifying headaches that accompanied the run-up to tenure. When my mother drove me to nursery school, White Shoulders was my last whiff of maternal comfort before she left me screaming, crying, and vomiting in the clutches of my daytime captors. Well into high school, I could not imagine a happier place to be than my house and the miles of Rock Creek and woodland that surrounded it.

My mother did not, as far as I know, chase brand names in merchandise. Rather, she marked her status by the *places* where she shopped and commanded respect—Saks Fifth Avenue, Lord and Taylor, Neiman Marcus, Gump's. She refused ever to shop at Garfinckel's because, she told me, this posh Washington-area chain had, at some earlier time, denied Black people the right to try on hats before buying them. By contrast, she and some other mothers staged a fashion show at the Saks in Chevy Chase, Maryland, featuring their own teenage daughters as the runway models. Integrating these stores was a class-specific element of my mother's role in the civil rights movement. During the late 1960s, I had no idea what a new lesson I was being taught about myself and my proper role in society as she addressed the almost uniformly white sales staff of these posh retailers with the casual assumption that they would serve her promptly and well.

In 1968, Don Freeman wrote and illustrated a book called *Corduroy*, about the adventure of a similar Black middle-class mother and daughter—Lisa—in such a high-end department store. The well-dressed mother is preparing to leave with her bags full of costly purchases when Lisa suddenly fixates on a little teddy bear—the eponymous Corduroy himself—with a button missing from his overalls. But the mother rejects Corduroy on account of this defect. Previously unaware of the defect, Corduroy searches the store that night for his missing button, but without success. The next day, though, Lisa empties her piggy bank, returns to the store, and buys Corduroy. Both Lisa and Corduroy are then relieved to have finally found a friend. Lisa then secures a new button to repair Corduroy's defect.

Corduroy was and is staple reading for the children in our family and networks because we tend to seek out materials that bolster both our children's racially assaulted self-esteem and their love of reading. Only from the present standpoint do the clothing and the themes in Freeman's book call attention to the specifics of the late-1960s bourgeois ethos in which I grew up. The subtext of this story is signaled visually rather than verbally, and this subtext has only gradually mapped itself onto my early shopping experiences as I write this book. I do not know if I was subliminally aware of it then, but the artfulness of both Don Freeman and my mother lay in keeping that subtext subconscious for me. The little brown-furred Corduroy and the two brown-skinned shoppers share a condition of defectiveness and, for that reason, are friendless in this otherwise all-white space of consumer luxury. And money is insufficient to solve the problem. Corduroy searched this consumer wonderland for a material cure, and so did Lisa's mother. The chemical processing of the mother's and the daughter's hair seems a further effort to resolve the same problem. Lisa's insistence on buying and fixing that teddy bear with love was, in the idiom of post–World War II consumerism, an act of self-love.

By the latter half of elementary school, rather than go home at the end of school, I would do my homework at the home of one housewife neighbor or another until my mother came home from work. She no longer had regular "help" around the house, from which fact I infer, in hindsight, that my father had stopped paying for it, the first in a series of visible signs that their marriage was breaking down. Also in hindsight, I notice that the mothers who were at home at that hour of the day and who could therefore receive me were typically the color of vanilla ice cream. Only in 2002 did I discover that many of these vanilla wives lacked college degrees. According to my mother, who heard the words as braggadocio, one of them reported that she dared not go downtown during the 1968 riots because she would surely be mistaken for a white woman. Half of the wives in the North Portal Estates were her color and the other half cinnamon or darker. But among the working moms, cinnamon and chocolate outnumbered vanilla by five to one. It was the vanilla moms who came to school occasionally to serve as playground guards. My cinnamon mother came less often but with greater distinction—to give talks about sex education, science, or careers. As I waited in their homes after school, her vanilla peers were neither kind nor unkind to me. They largely went about their personal and family business as though I were not there.

Though she made rich gumbos and New Orleans–style pralines, my mother's default meals consisted of spicy T-bone steak or eye of round, corn or sweet potato pudding, and Birds Eye frozen vegetables. Her butter-rich lemon Bundt pound cake surely contributed to my late-childhood weight gain, but I never acquired a taste for her holiday fruitcakes, soaked and resoaked for months in Jim Beam and dark Bacardí. We often ate in Japanese restaurants, like Sakura in Silver Spring and Japan Inn in Georgetown, where she practiced her Japanese with the waitresses and chefs, and we steered clear of any restaurant that she had ever known to be segregated. My mother kept an immaculate house, but she was unwilling to take care of my father's ailing sister when she moved into what we called the "maid's room," though we had never had a live-in. My mother explained her refusal in terms of Aunt Cutie's intolerance of my childhood noisemaking, but until he died, this refusal remained one of my father's most heartfelt grievances.

Mom read and reread *House Beautiful* and *Architectural Digest*, though the divorce allowed her only to dream of refurbishing and refurnishing. But gradually her interest in charity grew. Starting in the late 1970s, she annually organized her friends to deliver Thanksgiving and Christmas food baskets to underserved families, an operation that my friend Terry inherited and now leads. I inherited the mid-twentieth-century modern furniture, just in time for it to come back into fashion, since, over the prior thirty years, alimony, child support, and her spotty professional income after the divorce were never sufficient for her to replace it.

Like Aunty Arnzie, my mother was cinnamon colored but took great pride, until chemotherapy in her mid-fifties thinned it, in her naturally pendulous hair. Whatever traces of Africa remained in it were easily, if malodorously, extirpated with an electric hot comb. There were times when Aunt Arnzie identified such hair and their mother's butter-colored skin as evidence that her roots in Toano, Virginia, were Indian. During her nephrology residency in El Paso, Arnzie attended powwows of various southwestern tribes and bought a papoose, which hung in my grandmother's living room for decades after Arnzie abandoned the idea of using it to carry her own infant daughter.

Yet my mother's pendulous hair was apparently insufficient to get us invited into Washington's high-color Jack and Jill Club, where more acceptable Black bourgeois mothers gathered to train their children in the mission of social superiority and Black racial uplift—"Talented Tenth"-style (Du Bois 1903). Years after my mother died, a family friend the color of french vanilla ice cream offered one reason why my mother had chosen, as a postgraduate adult, to pledge Delta Sigma Theta: Mom doubted that the Washington-area Alpha Kappa Alphas would have admitted a woman of her skin tone. Until I began these investigations in 2002, I had had no idea of the complexion-based forms of exclusion that my family had experienced among others of our race. Such slights were loudly ignored, at least in the children's presence. Perhaps, compared to the snarling police dogs on the Edmund Pettus Bridge, these forms of exclusion seemed impassable. Thus, I received more of my training in privilege and taste at Saks Fifth Avenue, Lord and Taylor, the backseat of a Cadillac or a Mercedes, Shepherd Elementary School, my mother's Scrabble board, Deborah's Hayride to Christmas and, soon after desegregation, the most expensive private high school in the city (*Washington Post* 1995).

We could afford it because my mother and her mother had married highly accomplished dark men. My mother's butter-colored mother had married a man as coffee-black and regal as an Asantehene. He had worked his way up from the shipyards of Newport News, Virginia, to the leadership of the Virginia state diocese of the Church of God in Christ, most of whose buildings he himself had acquired through the deft financing and refinancing of mortgage loans from white-owned banks in the segregated South. Words, however, were the coin of his realm. At home, after the church had emptied, he, his four daughters, and two sons would debate politics, literature, and semantic nuance until my grandmother, "Mother Dear," interrupted their verbal momentum with a shoe thrown down the stairs. Family friends sometimes attribute my verbal ability to an inheritance from my mother's father. Some even wonder why I did not become a preacher like him. Granddaddy imagined a different future for me. Periodically, while passing through a room where I sat, ate, or played, he would call out to me, "My doctor!" Only today can I imagine the pains that he anticipated my healing. His goal for his daughters and for me was no different from the one favored by many Jewish,

Caribbean, and African immigrants for their offspring—a career in medicine. He was announcing his expectation that I defy the social disabilities and limitations that afflicted his own generation of dark men.

My father was an excellent breadwinner, but I always knew my mother's people better than his. Like me, my father worked late at night and, unlike me, through many of our family vacations. (We do field research instead of vacations.) So my remembrance of things past, like that of the partly African-descended Indians and Louisiana Creoles of color studied in this book, derives largely from my mother's people. And as I rethink these experiences as charters of my personal ambition and ripostes to the derogatory oversimplifications projected onto us as constituent others, I find myself citing the habitus of my mother's people and their own strategic, arriviste responses to the constraints of race in their day. I am struck that, for Uncle Badejọ and Elliot Skinner, too, it was their mothers' parting dicta that they reported as the guideposts of their adulthood.

Looming over the sanctuary of each of Granddaddy's churches was a portrait of a blonde and blue-eyed version of Jesus whom the congregants called "God" and whose image would have been a sufficient deterrent to my interest in my grandfather's occupation, even if he had not pointed me toward medicine. Much more alluring to me, though, was the portrait of the Church of God in Christ founder, Bishop Mason, surrounded by the pieces of driftwood that reportedly inspired his visions and sermons, as well as the congregants shouting and speaking in unknown tongues under the inspiration of the Holy Ghost. In some ways, my scholarly research on similar phenomena in Africa and Latin America is a personal quest that began in those sweltering Pentecostal sanctuaries, and the language that I use to fathom and justify this research is a way of holding spirit temporarily at bay. The professoriate was my compromise, one not so anathema to Granddaddy's reasoned Pentecostalism. The occasions when he spoke in tongues were rare enough to be remarked upon, and he privately confessed skepticism about those pastors who frequently and casually asserted that God had spoken to them. "I've been saved [i.e., committed to Christ and bound for heaven] for thirty years," he said, "and God has never spoken to me!"

A migrant from East Saint Louis, Illinois, my father, too, is unmistakably black, which invited not only disdain but, at times, a small measure of pride from his Howard colleagues. His Wonder Bread–colored surgical chief once beamed that my father had won a prestigious residency at a predominantly white hospital, saying, "We're real proud of you, Bill. No one will ever doubt where your smarts come from!" In other words, his accomplishments could not be credited to "white blood"; his successes and honors belonged unambiguously to their shared and unfairly humbled race. (In professional circles, I often run into this physician's children, one of whom was my student and another of whom is a leading international correspondent for the *New York Times*.)

Ambitious herself, my mother regretted giving in to the Victorian paternalism that reportedly made Dad ask her not to attend medical school. According to Mom, Dad ended the discussion with the fiat "One doctor is enough in the family." Years later, when Aunt Arnzie's first husband, an army officer, issued a similar command, my mother was undoubtedly among the advocates of the swift divorce that followed.

I often wonder by what mistake my father married my mother. I knew, from the tears he shed after her death, from the stunning pink-granite headstone that he bought for her grave, and from the instructions he wrote me for his own funeral, that he loved her. But I had never known him to date any other woman as dark as she or, except for his second wife, anyone as highly educated. When they can afford it, men emasculated by racial stigma tend to seek psychological relief and upward mobility through the acquisition of their tormentors' women—black men through Caucasoid women, Jews through the "blonde shiksa goddess," and Hutus through Tutsi women. Mom did have the hair, but I have always suspected that the marriage resulted from an unplanned pregnancy. However, years later, upon interrogation, my mother produced the right sequence of dates for their marriage and my elder brother's birth. I still wonder if an unwanted and accidentally terminated—or fictive—pregnancy preceded the one that produced Earle.

For my siblings' and my educational and professional success, I credit not only the Howard-generated environment of high expectations and my father's quiet persistence but also my mother's efforts to compensate for her own color- and gender-blocked personal ambitions. Not only her own children but also her neighbors' children, her youngest sister, her divorcee neighbors, my wife, and several of my white friends internalized the urgency of her push for education and excellence. She has counterparts in the coming-of-age stories of my black ethnic friends, who tend to speak, however, as though such personalities were unlikely to be African American. Our networks were actually full of such American "tiger moms" (cf. Chua 2011). Organizations like Jack and Jill and Tots and Teens were the products of their coordination and ambition for their children. But I have yet to meet any Black American, black ethnic, or white American women with my mother's track record.

Back at Howard in the 1960s, Aunty Arnzie set her eye on medicine and more. Before becoming a nephrologist, she and her newly Afro-clad friend Rose set out to be the first Howard Campus Queens able to win the title without passing the infamous "brown paper bag test," according to which club memberships and other honors in many Negro communities were reserved for people with skin lighter than such a bag. Though today's Howardites report that no one broke this barrier until the early 1970s, Aunt Arnzie brought the wind of Black pride through the French doors of our basement, where she rehearsed me in its slogans.

"What is your nationality?" she would shout with the fervor of a protester and the smile of a cheerleader. Like a rocket, on tippy toes with my arms to my side, I dutifully blasted back, "I am an Afro-American!"

"Say it out loud!" she intoned, her head and neck diving with emphasis. "I'm Black, and I'm proud!" I answered, like the children's chorus on James Brown's 1968 hit by the same name. Only then I would find out whether, that week, she had brought me Hostess chocolate-covered cupcakes, orange-covered cupcakes, or Twinkies from the Wonder Bread bakery shop on Georgia Avenue. These are likely the years when my plump phase began, perhaps another foreshadowing of my career as an academic. I still regard sweets as a suitable self-reward for successful intellectual work.

Much more memorably, though, these were the years when Aunty Arnzie persuaded my parents to stop razing my hair down to stubble. Instead, soon followed by my older brother and sister, I grew an Afro. All of my parents' children had come out as dark as milk chocolate, with hair like lamb's wool. Perceived from an intimate proximity, though, Earle's hair and mine curl like astrakhan—undoubtedly my maternal grandmother's contribution. Since the beginning of her professional life, our sister Yvedt had always chemically processed her hair, making its natural texture harder to recall.

Yet from the age of five, I found the African in me the most interesting. My *Corduroy* was a tattered copy of *The Illustrated Book about Africa* (1959), and my childhood playmates included not only Black self-reported descendants of Francis Scott Key and Thomas Jefferson but also the children of ambassadors from Zambia, Chad, Rwanda, and Somalia. (I cannot but also remember a kindhearted Vietnamese foster child in the neighborhood, though I do not recall which family he lived with. Only in later years did I infer that the stream of scars on his face and down his arms had probably been etched by US napalm.) But it would not be until the late 1970s that I perceived my Africanness in political terms, as a cris de coeur about the cruel hypocrisy of white American foreign policy in South Africa.

In the early 1970s, a cousin of mine, who was born in and still frequented Liberia, brought me "African pennies"—like rusty, twisted cocktail stirrers—and, once, a python skin. Though generous and brilliant—she was the first female class orator at Yale College—she understood me little enough to think the skin would appeal to my love of animals. I would have preferred a live snake, to join my tegu lizards and anoles, tortoises and terrapins, hamsters, gerbils and guinea pigs, frogs and toads, red-tailed sharks, piranhas, ghost fish, lionfish, sea anemones, clown fish, and batfish. Unbeknownst to me until later, whenever one of the dozen family friends whom I called "aunt" would offer to buy me a new pet, my mother made it clear that snakes, birds, and monkeys were beyond her limit. Up until high school, when my interests shifted to race and politics, she and my father ferried me across Washington's most distant suburbs in pursuit of species I had hunted down through the pet shops section of the Yellow Pages. Visits to the Southeast Pet Shop on Capitol Hill and to Gifford's Ice Cream Parlor in Silver Spring were the rewards my father gave for my tolerance of our well-upholstered and air-conditioned but excruciatingly boring middle-class Mount Zion Baptist Church. As my mother and her friends nursed Cuba libres out of leopard-pattern tumblers, the Knoll chairs and table in our basement gave a perfect view of my playful tomato clown fish, my goldfish-eating piranhas, and my bonsai collection.

While we occasionally played football or basketball and liked music, my friends also had a range of other passions as idiosyncratic as mine. My friend Clark, for example, collected hundreds of Hot Wheels model cars and during his teen years transitioned to go-carts and minibikes. After thirty-five years of immersion in white people's and ten years of black ethnic stereotypes about African American boys, I often look back and feel a peculiar sense of disorientation. How can it be, I ask myself, that we were Black American boys and were not one-dimensional poster children for sports, incivility, violence, inarticulacy, and other sorts of conformity to the lowest expectations. Were we real? The question seems odd, but other boys and men ask it, too. And some eventually concede that they can "be real" or "keep it real" only by accepting others' definition of them as athletes and thugs and that their agency is limited to oppositional assertion of the dignity of those roles.

In hindsight, I recognize the suddenly lowered expectations—or, indeed, hostility toward Black distinction—that I experienced at some TWIs, as when Mrs. Crenshaw, at my first predominantly white school, asked where I learned to speak "that way." She later wrote my parents a letter complaining that I was "very inteligent [sic]" but that my vocabulary alienated the other children. Why did she not welcome my vocabulary and use it to enrich her classroom?

My son Adu suffered similar experiences with the virtually monochromatic faculty of the integrated and liberal Cambridge Public Schools. He entered prekindergarten smart, capable, and curious. One day, at age four, he asked the teacher to give him some multiplication problems, and she obliged: $0 \times 0 =, 1 \times 1 =, 2 \times 2 =$, up to $10 \times 10 =$. Adu got all of the answers right,

100 percent. During a parent-teacher-student breakfast, he proudly showed his work to my wife and me. However, as the teacher rushed past our table, on the way to addressing some other urgent hosting duty, she paused long enough to say, "Oh, those are some math problems Adu asked me to give him, and I was so worried. I was so worried!" Fearing that my son would feel discouraged, I called no attention to her words (I was practicing that same kind of loud silence that my mother had employed to deal with the complexion problem in our Black bourgeois world, in the hope that the child would not notice the insult). As Adu's teacher passed by again, I rebounded, "Oh, [teacher's name], this is wonderful work. We are so proud of what Adu has done here! You were saying?" Though I opened a mile-wide door for her to affirm my son's efforts and to encourage his school-appropriate behavior, she instead detailed her *worry* about the fact that he had refused to go out to the playground with the other children until he had finished his math.

On another day, she asked her four- and five-year-old students to string beads in a pattern. Unlike any of the other students, Adu grasped the concept and executed it perfectly. He strung five yellow beads, five black beads, five red beads, and five blue beads, then five yellow, five black, five red, five blue, and so on until he had completed an approximately seventeen-inch necklace with precisely four segments of four colors each. It was mathematically and visually elegant. In addition to understanding the concept of pattern, he had perhaps seen me stringing bead necklaces and bracelets in imitation of Cuban *santero* art and thus understood the technique. Then the teacher had the children execute crayon drawings of the pattern on paper. In time for the parent-teacher conferences, the teacher posted the bead strands and drawings on a cork board, which she then showed my wife and me. She explained the project to us: "I wanted to teach the concept of patterns, so I had the students string beads in a pattern and then draw the pattern." She concluded pitifully, "And Adu just couldn't draw it. He just cooooo*uuuuullllldddddnnnn'tttt draaaaaw the paaaatterrrrn*!" with downcast eyes, she wagged her head, as if in sympathy for Adu's hopeless case.

Admittedly, the crayon drawing was not particularly good. *None* of the prekindergartners had successfully *drawn* anything that one could call a pattern. (Even as adults, most people find crayons hard to draw with.) But Adu was the only child who had strung beads in anything like a pattern, and his pattern was as perfect as it was complex. Yet his teacher could not see—or was unwilling to see—his accomplishment. I was reminded of Paul Willis's (1977) observations about how teachers signal their expectations of working-class boys in the English Midlands and channel them, intergenerationally, toward unfulfilling, working-class jobs. Adu's pre-K teacher, like mine in the seventh grade, was signaling her racialized expectations. Fortunately, both of us had "tiger" parents who would not let such microaggressions go unanswered (Guha 2003).

Most people would rightly regard this hardworking, goodwilled Jewish female teacher as liberal, and I have no doubt that she cares about her students. Indeed, she reportedly gifted $100,000 to the single Black mother of three children in the school in order to help her buy a house. It is a confusing lesson that some members of hereditarily privileged or borderline white groups are comfortable with largesse toward those they see as their social inferiors, but they can be, at the same time, very uncomfortable with signs of ambition, high social rank, or intellectual superiority among those ostensible inferiors.

Among the signals that touch a child are casual remarks, which may or may not translate into conscious memories, about the worth of the child, about the social category to which he or she belongs, and therefore about his or her proper life trajectory. It took me decades to get past the frozen-body Europhile pretensions of "classical" music as it is propagated in the United States, but, at my father's request and with his financial support, I put my children in Suzuki violin classes at the Longy School of Music in Cambridge. And for a decade, I took classes there, as well. During my research in Washington, we enrolled in the Levine School of Music and, along with Adu, attended master classes whenever possible. One day, a master violinist decided to begin the class without tuning his instrument to the highest standard but, instead, just "good enough for jazz." Though he bore a number on his arm that suggested he was a Holocaust survivor, he dismissed as groundless my complaint about this gratuitous put-down of an African American musical genre. That the expression was commonplace in his world, as I later learned, made him insist that his offhand remark was as innocent as it was inoffensive. He did not care that it diminished my ability to learn from and enjoy his lesson. What was clear to me was that this borderline-white immigrant had learned the lesson of many of his predecessors—that a sense of superiority to African Americans and their creations was his entitlement, even if he knew nothing about playing good jazz.

Howard is an institution of and for Black people, and its leadership assumes that people of African descent share qualities that make a shared institution important—historical disadvantage, a mission to uplift the disadvantaged, and consequently, a similar perspective on reality. For such reasons, many stigmatized minorities, disability groups, and women see great advantage in schools run by and for their own. Howard students and alumni regularly report a sense of caring, high expectations, and shared mission that they either missed or feared they would miss in predominantly white and white-run schools.

There is no denying, however, the Eurocentric foundations of Howard's curriculum. For example, Howard's Music Department has long given greater priority to Western classical than to jazz or any other African-inspired music. Black people's progress within Western society—including expertise in "classical" music—is Howard's preeminent goal. Power and status lie in the mimesis of elite white American manners, speech, writing, and modes of analysis. Despite its general commitment to Black progress within the framework of Western culture, economics, and politics, the university has also intermittently embraced African-inspired culture as a common legacy of Black people. For example, in recent years, the Department of Fine Arts has displayed African art in a dozen front-hall vitrines—much of it from the collection of the late philosophy professor and expositor of the Harlem Renaissance Alain Locke—just off the foyer. The collection seems to have repeatedly come and gone from this space since the 1920s.

During the 1960s and 1970s, the Western-inspired scholasticism of the official Howard, the insurgent Black nationalism of Howard's student body, and the transnational social connections of its alumni made an alternative but hybrid "cultural" sense of self easily available to me and to others of my class. For my sister Yvedt and me, Nigeria, Ghana, and Senegal became sites of both pilgrimage and research, much as Europe would become for our white peers at Sidwell Friends, Saint Albans, and the Maret School. I learned of the Afro-Cuban Santería, or Ocha, religion from an Afro-Cuban professor of Spanish at Howard and of the Afro-Brazilian Candomblé, Batuque, and Umbanda religions from the Moorland-Spingarn Collection at Howard's Founders Library. My mother's friend and fellow Howard alumna Aunt Ruth introduced me not only to the Moorland-Spingarn Collection but also to the Martin Luther King Jr. Library, the main branch of the District of Columbia's public library system, and to the Montgomery County, Maryland, library near my house. These information sources empowered me to challenge the versions of US history taught in my traditionally White but liberal private school. Fortunately, my Maret history teacher Leonard King, a secular Jew and lifelong "ABD" (all but dissertation), rewarded my racially insurgent use of the tools that he and my Aunt Ruth had given me. When I repeatedly interrupted class to dissent from William Styron's fictionalized and bestializing representation of antislavery rebel Nat Turner, Mr. King shouted in mild annoyance, "Shut up, Matory, and write me a paper about it!" I did so, and he gave me an A. When I am compelled to look back and explain why I am irreducible to a constituent-other stick figure and when I tell my children didactic tales about what they should be, I often tell these stories about Mr. King and Aunt Ruth—stigmatized people with uplift agendas of their own.

The University as Social Triage and Stratification

By the etymology of its name and the objectivist pretensions of its historical reputation, the university is usually presumed to produce and disseminate culturally neutral knowledge and to make its denizens quantitatively more "cultured" by neutralizing their culture-specific and qualitatively divergent vernacular "cultures" or worldviews. At most, universities are typically expected to *document*, rather than propagate, particular cultures. Yet most universities were chartered to produce the cultured elite and the bourgeois leadership of one specific nation, region, language group, ethnoracial group, religion, or gender, as were many primary and secondary schools.

As is well known, school districts in the segregated South regularly assigned Negroes to one set of primary schools and whites to another. Schools perform a class-based triage as well. In my half generation, Shepherd Elementary School represented an ingathering of Washington's Black professional-class children, as had Amidon Elementary in my elder siblings' cohort and my neighbor Ms. Davenport's Tots' School did in my junior half siblings' time. However, pockets of the segregated South had also recognized a third racial category, such as the Lumbees, Melungeons, Saponis, and Louisiana Creoles of color. The state or the Catholic Church in their home neighborhoods established schools where these groups predominated. If no secondary school specific to a third racial category was available, the Indian children in some cases attended Indian schools in Oklahoma but, in most cases, had to choose between attending the Negro high school and not attending high school at all. After 1915, the founding of Xavier University brought together college-bound Creoles of color from New Orleans, the bayou country, and the Cane River region, but until desegregation, those who wished to attend professional schools had to attend historically Black Howard or Fisk University or one of the northern TWIs that admitted Negroes and—in student housing assignments, for example—treated all people of partly African descent as Negro. Now that Xavier's student body has blackened and Blackened, several New Orleans Creoles told me, *avoiding* Xavier has almost become an index of Creole ethnicity. However, the university administration remains uniformly Creole.

In other words, schools and universities in the US South and every place in the world are a social triage system, aggregating students voluntarily or involuntarily into a progressively smaller number of officially recognized collective identities. Even when the choice is voluntary, people of a class, nation, region, religion, language group, ethnoracial group, or gender vastly outnumbered at any given school or university tend to avoid that school or university or, if they choose to attend that school or university, often feel painfully out of place. For example, in my undergraduate days at Harvard, working-class white students there reported great discomfort and alienation. African American and black ethnic peers of mine from the North Portal Estates who attended Duke have reported feeling the same way there.

The aggregated identities of higher educational institutions—such as the multiregional Creoleness assembled at Xavier, the multiethnic Blackness assembled at Howard, and the multicounty North Carolinianness assembled at the University of North Carolina, Chapel Hill—are welcomed by many, but such aggregated identities are also transformative and potentially threatening to the communities that these students leave behind. These aggregations inspire new conversations, new diction, new social alliances and oppositions, new hierarchies, and new modes of fashion, hairdressing, dancing, marrying, eating, and seeing the world. From Howard University, Aunty Arnzie brought such novelties into my childhood home. The university absorbs, assembles, and transforms but seldom obliterates ethnic division.

Universities are triage units where locally and regionally recognized ethnoracial categories are folded into nationally and internationally recognized ones, and these categories often reemerge in radically new forms. For example, at Howard, northern Muslim and southern Christian Nigerians; Cape Verdeans and Ethiopians; "Negro" and "red" Trinidadians; "black" and "brown" Jamaicans; New Orleans, Cane River, and bayou Creoles; Pamunkeys, Saponis, Mattaponis, Piscataways, Piscatawas, Nanticokes, and Pequots; Tapscotts, Nickens, Proctors, and Savoys all potentially turn Black, in ways that distinguish them forevermore, in both class and racial identity, from many of their kin and childhood friends. Yet they can also become "African," "Caribbean," or "*just* Black" (a.k.a. "*regular* Black"). In some cases, they also become "halfie" (Abu-Lughod 1991) experts on behalf of—or even in the leadership of—local ethnic "revivals" and boundary revisions back home. Particular historical events have also given new salience to a postethnic category at Howard and in its alumni networks—such as "international students," whose new sense of "us" aggregates Caribbeans with Africans, opposing them not only to African Americans but also to their US-born coethnics.

Certain institutions, such as Oxford, Cambridge, Yale, and Harvard, assemble empire-wide elites that presume themselves so universal that they possess no national, ethnoracial, or regional name. The spectrum from the most local to the most imperially central educational institutions is also typically a hierarchy corresponding to the increasing age and socioeconomic class of the students, the increasing age of the institution, the decreasing practicality and the increasingly theoretical nature of the instructional material, the decreasing emphasis on classroom teaching, and the increasing importance of research and publication in judging professorial accomplishment.

As initiatic institutions, universities carefully organize and mobilize hierarchically arranged time-based cohorts of the bourgeoisie and create the conditions for them to revise the historical narratives of—and therefore to charter and argue in favor of new values, legal rights, alliances, and occupational foci for—the now-translocal communities that produced the students and made their schooling possible. Each university seeks to elevate itself in the hierarchy of universities and its students in the parallel social hierarchy of the planet, counting on the accomplishments, the enthusiasm, and, in the United States, the donations of those cohorts to raise the reputation of the university and of the social category for which it stands.

The Mission and the Appeal of the HBCU

The HBCUs were typically founded with state or missionary support, including that of African American missionaries, to educate recently freed people, who were denied access, by reason of race, to the far more numerous and better-funded TWIs. Though similar institutions were founded to educate American Indians and many TWIs had long admitted Indians, many HBCUs admitted Indians as well. Virginia's historically Black Hampton Normal and Agricultural Institute, now Hampton University, had been modeled on the institutions established by white missionaries for native Hawaiians, and it also hosted a major population of Native American students, particularly from the western United States. However, dormitories were segregated, and Hampton does not appear to have generated much fellow feeling between Native American and African American students (Baker 2010). Thus, the HBCU is the product of a transnational and transracial nineteenth-century phenomenon—charitably founded institutions intent on creating the westernized leadership of downtrodden ethnoracial groups.

Racially targeted educational institutions ask of their members critical questions that are central to this book. What are the options and responsibilities of the elites of oppressed groups? How does white or ethnoracially unmarked power impinge on the education of nonwhite or ethnoracially marked minds? What is the need for and what are the dividends of a group-specific educational environment, particularly in the wake of legal desegregation and official gender equality? What is the duty of a group-specific university to the members of other groups? This question has been particularly pressing for African Americans and Jews because, as present-day and recently historical constituent others, both groups often perceive the abridgement of any group's rights and opportunities as a slippery slope toward their own degradation or annihilation. What is the duty of HBCUs to non-US blacks and to Americans of oppressed groups that do not regard themselves as Black?

As of 2004, around the time of my residency at Howard, there were 108 HBCUs in the United States (Williams and Ashley 2004, xix). At that time, Williams and Ashley observed,

> HBCUs still graduate 70 percent of all black physicians and dentists and half of all black engineers in the United States. Tuskegee University alone produces 80 percent of the African Americans practicing veterinary medicine, while Florida A&M University has outranked Harvard in the number of National Achievement scholars among top black high school students that it has recruited and enrolled. And while only 20 percent of college-bound African American students initially choose to attend HBCUs, nearly one-third of the bachelor's degrees awarded to black graduates come from traditionally black schools. (2)

At elite scholarly conferences, when I deliver talks about the topic of this book, I am invariably approached by a half dozen Black colleagues who reveal that, previously unbeknownst to me, they had received a degree from Howard or some other HBCU. The report I have heard from current Howard undergraduates and alumni appears to be true: they feel that, after leaving Howard, graduates have the confidence to go anywhere they please.

Howard's annually published informational booklet emphasizes knowledge in the service of society, particularly through the enfranchisement of African Americans and other marginalized groups:

> The mission of Howard University as a comprehensive, research-oriented, predominantly African-American university is to provide an educational experience of exceptional quality at reasonable cost to students of high academic potential. Particular emphasis is placed upon providing educational opportunities for African-American men and women and *for other historically disenfranchised groups*. Furthermore, Howard University is dedicated to attracting, sustaining, and developing a cadre of faculty who, through their teaching and research, are committed to producing distinguished and compassionate graduates who seek solutions to human and social problems in the United States and throughout the world. (Howard University 2002, 5; emphasis mine)

Howard University seems to have been officially committed, for longer than most of its white peer institutions, to social activism informed by scholarship. Such social activism has only recently become a growth area in Harvard's and Duke's curricula, a movement that might be understood partly as a reaction against the perceived marginalization of the humanities in US colleges and universities. In social activism, the humanities and the softer social sciences have found new purpose and a grounds to new appeal for dwindling funds. By contrast, social activism has long been a deep raison d'être of HBCUs and was among the founding principles of departments of African and African American studies in the TWIs.

From 1947 to 1956, the preeminent historian of African American history, the late John Hope Franklin, taught in Howard's Department of History. Alongside a delegation of his disciplinary peers, he joined the civil rights marches of the 1960s, but most important, he used the discipline of history to confront the United States with the truth about its injustices toward African Americans (Y. Williams 1998).[2] Howard-trained and -based lawyers and sociologists designed the plaintiff's legal strategy in *Brown v. Board of Education*, the US Supreme Court case that overturned the doctrine of "separate but equal" facilities for Blacks and whites. Ironically, the argument of Howard Law School graduate, plaintiff's attorney, and future Supreme Court justice Thurgood Marshall and his team affirmed the logic that African American distinctiveness resulted largely from official oppression and marginalization by whites—in short, from an imposed social and cultural disability (Baker 1998). Their argument won the day. This argument, like Howard's mission statement, highlights what is socially disadvantageous about Blackness.

This argument contrasts with the one proffered by Du Bois ([1903] 2007), which highlights not just Black disadvantage but also the unique moral, intellectual, and spiritual vantage of the African American. During his studies in Berlin (1892–94), Du Bois was clearly inspired by the legacy of Johann Gottfried von Herder and the early nineteenth-century German-speaking burgers who, in avowing the virtue of their distinctive national legacy, also disavowed the notion that the Germans merely occupied some deficient stage in the acquisition of a putatively universal but French-centered culture. While Du Bois acknowledged the African cultural legacy in African American religion, it was Herskovits and his Boasian colleagues who mounted the case that African American "culture" was distinctive and valid on account of its African heritage (Herskovits [1941] 1958). Historically, this set of arguments has met with deep ambivalence at Howard. Nonetheless, in recent years, many Howard students and alumni—including two white ones—have told me that they chose Howard because they wanted to learn "the Black perspective" on the world and on the academic disciplines. Howard Business School, for example, specializes in entrepreneurship and focuses on African American case studies. Indeed, the online university-wide core curriculum of Howard, instituted in 2001, is visually dominated by courses with this orientation (Howard University, "University-Wide Core Curriculum-Howard University," http://www.howard.edu/academics/corecurriculum.htm). The university thus requires students to think about the history and literature of Black people and encourages thoughtfulness, albeit in less culture-specific terms, about our written, oral, and sartorial self-presentation.

Students also reported wanting to experience the forms of personal support and affirmation that they expected uniquely from a Black school. Indeed, many Howard students told me that their professors take an exceptionally personal interest in the students' success. Howard self-consciously trains an elite to excel despite its racial encumbrances and to speak and fight for its embattled people. Thus, Howard researchers and service professionals give a special degree of attention to problems disproportionately afflicting Black people—such as hypertension-induced kidney failure, AIDS, and sickle-cell anemia. Having received, for most of my life, health care from both Howard and Harvard clinicians, I can attest to the difference it makes to be treated by Black physicians and taught by people who regard my success as a product, an element, and a precondition to their own individual and collective success. With this principle in mind, one colleague in Howard's History Department verbally lashed me for basing my career at Harvard rather than Howard. She judged it a dereliction of my duty to Black people.

Yet Howardites are equally articulate in reporting the administrative difficulties of being at Howard and, reportedly, at most HBCUs. In reply, administrators say that they constantly work on these problems and have resolved many of them through computerization and online enrollment. Students—and visiting professors—who do not learn to address clerical staff in a suitable mesolect and with both charm and deference will face roadblocks to tuition payment, registration, parking permits, financial aid, paychecks, transcripts, identification cards, and so forth (see also, e.g., Y. Williams 1998). HBCUs are not an idyll of racial solidarity and mutual support. They teach harsh lessons about humility in working with people of lesser class status, earnings, or credentials. (My move from Harvard to Duke has taught me similar lessons.) Young people who have missed this lesson in their home training quickly receive it and many others at Howard. Consequently, Howard alumni who complain about these issues regularly follow up with the report that these travails at Howard uniquely equipped them to "succeed anywhere."

However, it is, in my view, a mistake to attribute these lessons uniquely to HBCUs. Financial officers at Duke and Harvard seem to delight in showing professors who is really the boss. Many Duke faculty resent the benefits given to professors recruited from more elite institutions. For example, one of the highest-ranking administrators at Duke, another recruit from the Ivy League, warned me that if I wanted the cooperation of my new colleagues at Duke, I should never preface a suggestion or a proposal by saying that it had been done that way at Harvard. At most, I might refer to "my previous institution." Professors are as touchy as any stigmatized population about hints that they are outranked by someone of their social class. TWIs are also worlds of the stigmatized.

Black Any Way You Want to Be

The president of Howard at the time of my research, H. Patrick Swygert, reportedly said, "At Howard, you can be Black any way you want to be." Despite the premise of the university's Blackness and of its mission to uplift the oppressed, President Swygert deftly undermined the idea that all Blacks must think and act alike. The ethic of intragroup homogeneity motivates much adolescent behavior in all races but is especially coercive in the lives of the stigmatized. Among working-class African American adolescents, the demand for conformity in the face of a domineering and demeaning enemy is often punitive and army-like (of course, Willis [1997] observes the same about white English adolescents). President Swygert's pithy adage reminds one that, where Blacks are in the majority, we can feel freer to try any area of study, any sport, any hobby, any clothing or hairstyle, any music, any strategy of social uplift, any political party, and so forth without fear of confronting someone else's stereotypical view that we are not "keeping it real," being Black enough, or being loyal enough to the interests of the race. Black people are legitimately diverse. They can disagree and debate. Black people are dark and light skinned; Republicans and Democrats; "ghetto" and "bougie"; Christian and Muslim; gay, straight, and on the "down low"; Nigerians, Ethiopians, Jamaicans, Trinidadians, Creoles, Gullahs/Geechees, and Indians; non-Greeks and Greeks—Alphas, Kappas, Omegas, Sigmas, AKAs, and Deltas. Like ethnic groups and worshippers of Yoruba-inspired gods, each African American Greek-letter society is alleged to have its own normative personality type, complexion, region of demographic concentration, and professional focus. Where black people do not have to deal with the immediate social and psychological encumbrances of being someone else's constituent other, a far fuller range of human possibilities seems available. Again, however, the HBCU is not an idyll, since its diversity is internally stratified and its own internal choice of constituent others reflects the prejudices of the wider society, as when lighter-skinned medical interns were reportedly chosen for the first available residencies at traditionally White hospitals.

African American anthropologist and Spelman alumnus Kamela Heyward-Rotimi reminds me that the denizens of HBCUs may not be any more tolerant of diversity than other people from their home communities. But at an HBCU, a bright young Black person can count on meeting and finding affirmation among an elevated concentration of other bright young Black people who share his or her idiosyncrasies.

For these reasons, many Howard faculty, administrators, and students say that they are there because they prefer to be "Black any way they want to be"—or at least not immediately subject to a white majority's dictates about the limits of who they can be. Many students also find Howard the most affordable of their possible choices, but few attend Howard for that reason alone. Some wish to learn about the world from a "Black" perspective. Some prefer to attend college or graduate school where their relatives and respected neighbors went and where they expect their fellow alumni to show an interest in their careers. Some wish to avoid the stereotyping, marginalization, and other forms of discrimination that they anticipate at TWIs. Most faculty and administrators could work elsewhere for better pay and with greater administrative support, but they chose to go to and stay at Howard because, they say, "It's the best we've got." They want to support Black and other disadvantaged students and want to do so in an institution under the control of the intended beneficiaries.

Howard has approximately eleven hundred faculty members (Strauss and Kinzie 2007) and a student population of ten to twelve thousand, up from five to six thousand in the 1950s and 1960s. Thus, unlike some HBCUs, Howard has grown, rather than shrunk, in the wake of legal desegregation. In 2001, Howard had 8,864 students from the United States. Among US students, the largest numbers came from Maryland (2,027), the District of Columbia (1,044), New York (859), and California (638).[3] Thus, strikingly, the coasts are overrepresented and the South underrepresented in Howard's student body (Ranimor A. Manning, Office of University Research and Planning, personal communication, June 25, 2002). Howard undergraduates from the United States are highly attentive to their states and regions of origin, which are reflected in sartorial style, preferred music, preferred parties, and membership in state-based clubs.

The non-US presence at Howard is difficult to count, since many faculty and students hesitate, for fear of deportation, to register their national origins officially, and the university tends to accommodate their discomfort. A general pattern of change, however, can be inferred from the available statistics. According to the latest statistics available during the time of my research, the number of foreign-born students had grown progressively from the Depression until the collapse of oil prices in the 1980s. Howard's foreign student population spiked between 1934 and 1940 (during the Depression) and between the 1950s and the 1970s (amid the post–World War II expansion of US global influence and the "cultural" diplomacy of the Cold War). However, the numbers remained high in the 1980s. In 1982–83, approximately sixteen hundred of the eleven thousand students, or 14.5 percent of Howard students, reported being foreign nationals (Ranimor A. Manning, personal communication, June 25, 2002), and during the 1989–90 school year, international students constituted 15 percent of the student body. However, the numbers dropped sharply after 1989–90, when the US Congress forced Howard to increase tuitions and apply a sizable surcharge to the tuitions of international students. The causes and the consequences of the surcharge dramatically illustrate the situational dynamics of identity in an HBCU and deserve careful attention.

For the diverse populations that pass through it, is the HBCU a fork in the road, or does everybody merge ethnically? A tale that I heard repeatedly during my research suggests that the matter may be more complex, more dialectical. Plutarchus is said to have coined the term "syncretism" in the first century CE to describe the process by which the otherwise fractious Cretans would quickly unite to fend off attackers from the outside. Just as wars and feuds demonstrate and continually rearrange social order among Plutarch's Cretans and Evans-Pritchard's Nuer (1940), protests are both defining moments in the social order of US universities and classrooms of the hidden curriculum.

One such protest took place at Howard in 1989. University president James Cheek had appointed Lee Atwater—a strategist for the Republican National Committee—to Howard's Board of Trustees. A Republican himself, President Cheek had apparently appointed Atwater in the hope of further expanding Howard's access to federal funds. Through similar tactical alliances over the course of his long presidency, Cheek had expanded Howard's building stock and number of academic programs significantly. However, the appointment of Atwater was particularly risky. Atwater dramatically embodied the US ambivalence about Blackness, but Cheek was willing to tap that ambivalence for the advantage of his university.

Like many white Americans, Atwater was a great admirer and, like some, a competent performer of African American rhythm and blues music. He had even performed and recorded with B. B. King. But he was also willing to play political chicken with Black lives. A protégé of once-segregationist senator

Strom Thurmond, Atwater is accused of almost single-handedly directing the Republican Party's savvy counterassault against the civil rights movement, employing a modern and subtle form of race-baiting to capture southern white voters for the Republican Party. Atwater's most famous contribution to this strategy was the infamous Willie Horton ads in support of the 1988 presidential bid of George H. W. Bush. In those ads, images of a convicted Black rapist from Massachusetts who committed murder while on prison furlough were used to discredit the presidential candidacy of Democratic Massachusetts governor Michael Dukakis. At the same time, the ads played on a stereotype about African American men that had led to the extrajudicial execution of hundreds of innocents from the late nineteenth century to the mid-twentieth. It was difficult for people of African descent in the United States not to believe that the Republican National Committee, under Atwater's leadership, had deliberately stoked white fear, disregarded a history of white villainy, and indeed put Black lives at further risk. Atwater's desire to win at any cost seemed craven. However, before his death from brain cancer in 1991, Atwater converted to Roman Catholicism and repented for what even he confessed was ruthless race-baiting. But he had set his party on a course that has yet to be reversed.

In 1989, foreign-born black and Black American students had joined together against this shared antagonist and in the defense of a shared racial interest. Cheek's appointment of Atwater to the board was the last and the worst appointment of his presidency. The student protests successfully unseated Atwater. However, these protests also invited retaliation—a retaliation that targeted foreign-born students because they were reportedly accused of having led the protests. Ironically, it was the highest-ranking immigrant on campus who, in the face of these protests, stood firm for law and order. As in many cases at Howard, both the establishment and the antiestablishment alliances cut across ethnic lines. As the university's interim president, Trinidadian physician Carlton P. Alexis called the city police on the protesting students, though Washington mayor Marion Barry arrived just in time to call them off. Whereas Alexis had once been considered President Cheek's inevitable successor, his decision to call the police on the protesters was held against him, and his 1990 candidacy for university president failed. (Not until 2014 would a non-US-born person become president—Dr. Wayne A. I. Frederick, a Howard-trained surgeon also from Trinidad.)

In fall 1989, the majority-Democratic 101st US Congress forced the university to increase the tuition for foreign students by 10 percent in fall 1990, by 30 percent in fall 1991, and by 50 percent in fall 1992. President Cheek opposed the congressional mandate for a surcharge on foreign students, and he in fact bragged about the benefits of Howard's substantial number of African and Caribbean students almost since the university's founding in 1867:

> We have been cultivating friendships where they didn't [previously] exist. . . . There are very few countries where I can't pick up the phone and speak to someone in a high-level position . . . who is a Howard graduate. . . . It is in our national interest that we continue to do what we have done for 120 years. (Feinberg 1988)

In 1992, the president of the Howard University African Students Association would add, "Howard has been able to turn out leaders in Africa and the Caribbean. . . . These students are tomorrow's leaders, and if they are not properly prepared, what kind of partners are they going to be?" (Masters 1992).

During the 1987–88 school year, according to the *Washington Post*, "international students" represented between 16 percent and 20 percent of Howard's student population (Feinberg 1988; Diallo 1989). As a percentage of the student population, international students had already declined to 15 percent by the 1989–90 school year—because of falling oil prices and unstable currency exchange rates—but the tuition surcharge sent the percentages plummeting further still. In the years between 1989–90 (the last year before the surcharge began) and 1993–94, the percentage of international students in the student body fell from 15 percent to 11 percent, dropping by more than a quarter (Howard University 1994; Diallo 1989; Elder 1988; Masters 1992; Feinberg 1988; Lamar 1889; Wilgoren 1990). Yet at least one out of ten Howard students was still foreign born.

It is not clear to me when the surcharge was rescinded (though it was certainly in 1992 or later), but five years later, a Howard University self-study in 1999 reported that the percentage of these students had begun to rebound and was expected soon thereafter to reach "Howard's more traditional 16 percent of the student body" ("Howard University Self Study 1999," cited in Ponterotto et al. 2001, 857). However, many foreign-born alumni, their children, and current "international" students remain aggrieved and incorrectly blame the Howard administration for the surcharge. They interpret it as a sign of unwelcome, which may limit the success of this rebound (Masters 1992; "Howard University Self-Study 1999" quoted in Ponterotto et al. 2001, 857).

At the time of my interviews, twelve years after the protests, foreign administrators, students, and alumni tended to interpret these events along newly transformed and perhaps postethnic lines. Several foreign-born professors and alumni who remained in the United States asserted proudly that the foreign students had *led* the protests, offering this assertion as evidence of the political docility that many Caribbean Americans attribute to African

Americans, and of the bravery and leadership that they attribute to themselves (see also W. James 1998). During my post-2002 interviews, foreign alumni abroad and current international students tended to agree that African American administrators instituted the surcharge out of an ongoing animus toward foreign-born students in general. "I don't think they want us anymore," was the conclusion that several non-US-born students and alumni offered me. This "us" aggregated Caribbeans with Africans and, by aggregating US-born children of Caribbeans and Africans with African Americans, also separated the US-born from their foreign-born coethnics.

Most African American officials may be unaware of the feeling of alienation among international students. My late father, an African American medical-school professor, told me that the faculty and the administration greatly value the international students and that he regarded the decline in foreign student numbers as a terrible loss to Howard. First, many of them are excellent students, contributing to the quality and reputation of a Howard education. Second, when they return to their homelands and assume leadership, they carry forth Howard's main mission—the uplift of the Black race and of other downtrodden peoples.

This episode and its fallout are perhaps the perfect example of how the primary identity categories that people bring to the university are transformed, subdivided, and merged into novel forms, as a result of structural aspects of university life, specific events, and their changing interpretation. In 2002, amid their shared sense of alienation, Caribbean students and the much-reduced number of continental African students found common ground in the story of the surcharge. They displayed their new unity at Caribbean Students Association parties, which students reported were also the parties most frequently attracting Africans on campus. Also uniting these groups were virtually identical Caribbean and African narratives of being asked by African Americans if they live in trees or have television in their countries. Thus, as Evans-Pritchard's *The Nuer* (1940) also suggests, alliances are protean and have a shifting rationale—even in the university. The syncretic culture produced by Howard is less a settled conclusion than an ever-shifting set of alliances, in which invented cultural repertoires and symbolic performances furnish convergent but still heterogeneous vocabularies of action.

And the university has provided the architecture for these alliances. Many students gather together in the university-funded Office of International Student Services. There, in 2002, the students, the university administrator (an African American woman married to a Ghanaian), and a very active and polyglot white student employee monitored the visa difficulties, the financial conditions, and the culture clashes experienced by foreign-born students.

Thus, the university administration and the students have together given heightened salience to the now quasi-ethnic or postethnic category "international students." By the logic of the hidden curriculum, however, it is unsurprising that the centralized gathering of foreign students and the statistics gathered about them in this office also structure rivalries among national-origin groups, the most vocal form of which is competition over national test score averages and admissions numbers.

As of 2001–2, when I taught my class at Howard, 1,306 out of Howard's total 10,690 enrolled students—or 11 percent—were foreign nationals. Africa and the Caribbean have long been the best-represented foreign regions. Caribbeans then outnumbered Africans. Among international students, 525 came from Africa and 613 from the greater Caribbean (including Bermuda, Guyana, and the Virgin Islands). The 2001–2 student body included 224 Jamaicans, 170 people from Trinidad and Tobago, and 39 from Barbados, as well as 174 Nigerians, 73 Ghanaians, 50 Kenyans, and 33 Ethiopians (not including the 6 Eritreans). Twenty Britons, 17 Chinese, 11 Indians, and 11 Saudis also attended Howard at the time. Nigerians were more concentrated in the School of Engineering than in other professional schools. (Indeed, the chair of the Chemical Engineering Department was a Nigerian Yoruba and a major leader in Yoruba transnational politics.) But the Business School had the highest proportion of foreign students. Barbadians were particularly drawn to this school. During the post–World War II period, the School of Dentistry hosted a concentration of Caribbean students. For example, in the class of 1953, when my father graduated from the School of Medicine, 6 of his 66 classmates had come from the Caribbean, including 1 from Puerto Rico. By contrast, 10 of the 47 students in the dental school that year were Caribbeans (*Bison* yearbook 1953). In 2002, the most remarkable disproportion was the concentration of Canadian students in the dental school, where the 19 Canadians represent over 5 percent of the enrollment.

In recent decades, the female-to-male ratio among Howard students has grown at remarkable rates, anticipating similar trends among white students nationally and at the TWIs. Among Howard students who are US citizens, women have long outnumbered men. For example, in 1976–77, there were 4,496 female students and 4,144 male students. In 2000–1, the 5,719 female US citizens outnumbered the 3,145 male US citizens by a factor of nearly two to one: for every nine US female students at Howard, there were five US male students. Universities in the Caribbean are affected by a similar and similarly growing gender imbalance, an imbalance far less evident among Caribbean students at Howard. However, female Caribbean students did outnumber their male counterparts at Howard by a small measure. By contrast to both the Caribbean and the African American examples, African male students outnumbered African female students at Howard. A decline in the proportion of male students is evident across all of these populations. Whereas in 1976–77 male international students outnumbered their female counterparts by a factor of 2.5 to 1, in 2000–1, these male and female foreign student populations had reached rough parity, with the 660 men outnumbering the 646 women by a mere 14 souls. Currently, among Howard's 10,573 students overall, women outnumber men by *more than two to one*. Men account for only 32.4 percent of the student body.[4]

In the US as a whole, the growing educational gender gap in favor of females is particularly pronounced among the *most* stigmatized populations (people of African descent) and the *least* (wealthy Americans), but the trend is both national and global. In 2012, women earned almost 60 percent of the college degrees awarded in the United States, up from one-third in 1960. However, in the overall US student population, women are still, on average, choosing majors that destine them for lower earnings. Observes Stephanie Coontz, "[G]ender integration in college majors has stalled since the mid-1990s, and, in some fields, women have lost ground" (Coontz 2012). On average, not only women but also Black students and domestically born students appear to be underrepresented in engineering and the hard sciences and overrepresented in the social sciences and the humanities. However, Howard bucks some of these national trends. For example, in Howard's medical school, women significantly outnumber men.[5]

Of the estimated eighty thousand living Howard alumni, only a few are actively in touch with the alumni office (Nairobi K. Adams, personal communication, June 20, 2002), but Howard alumni networks are, I discovered, important among the overlapping networks that structure the lives of a significant minority of the Black bourgeoisie in the District of Columbia, New Orleans, Port of Spain, Kingston, and Montego Bay. In Lagos, Howard alumni networks are, relative to the city's enormous population, small but close knit.

Whenever I reported my interest in "ethnic diversity in the black population of Howard," Jamaican, Trinidadian, Barbadian, Nigerian, Ghanaian, Ethiopian, Gullah/Geechee, partly African-descended Indian and Louisiana Creole students, alumni, faculty, and staff—unlike their African American counterparts—tended to understand my interest immediately. Their sense of ethnic distinctiveness is highly motivated and frequently rehearsed. On the other hand, nonethnic African Americans at Howard tend to be more vocal about the diversity of skin color and hair texture among Black people, which, many complain, regularly correlate—albeit unofficially—with club memberships, likelihood and quality of employment, and dating options at Howard.

Except for a period in the 1990s when—as I was told by one light-skinned man—an explosion of dark-skinned male leads in Hollywood movies gave dark men a dating advantage at Howard, the advantage has typically gone to light-skinned men and women. In the twenty-first century, as when my father studied and trained at Howard, light-skinned people were assumed to have a better and broader range of opportunities on both sides of the slowly fading color line. In recent years, President Obama's election has been taken as a case in point. White and Black Americans take it as no surprise that the first "Black" president of the United States is light-skinned and that his Black parent was not a native-born African American but what Manyika (2003) calls an "exotic black." (However, among African Americans, it was not his Kenyan parentage but his biracialness that created suspicion about his loyalties. Hence, Obama was legitimized by his choice to marry a dark wife.)

On the other hand, more than a few of the light-skinned citizens of the university community are descended from quasi-ethnic Maryland or Virginia networks of families who once married their cousins in fulfillment of their perceived "duty" to keep the family light-skinned. At times, these and other such populations have understood themselves less as light-skinned Black people than as Indians or as Louisiana Creoles.

A statistical census of these ambiguous populations would be difficult. However, they, too, illustrate a dialectic of race, class, gender, and ethnicity that is central to my argument about the conflicting pull of ethnological schadenfreude and lifeboat collectivism among the stigmatized. On the confusing field of status competition at and around Howard, the strategies of these native-born populations of partly African descent vary greatly. Ambitious dark men tend to work hard and marry "up" in color. Ambitious dark women tend to seek escape from their devalued position through exceptional levels of education and taste. Both of these strategies are evident in my family. However, the seemingly permanent abridgement of opportunity leads some constituent others to valorize the image of the "bad man," the numbers runner, or the gangster, who is sometimes a woman. This character is as well established among European lower classes, the descendants of the enslaved in the Caribbean, and white ethnics in the United States as it is among African Americans. At Howard and in the precarious elements of the African American middle class in general, these contrasting models of success are expressed in the styles of self-presentation known as "bougie," "ghetto," and "bougetto." On this complex terrain of competition, light-skinned people and wealthy

Blacks who need the loyalty of the dark and the poor have a special incentive to master "bougetto" style. But some native-born people of African descent at Howard also quietly prepare the ground for ethnic, or cultural, assertions of distinction that deny the need for alliance.

The HBCU in the Naming of the Black Bourgeois Self

The university is the preeminent initiatic structure in US society and a moral testing ground. Students tend to choose and be chosen by a university that bespeaks their social identities and personal aspirations. Like Howard, most universities name themselves as the gathering place and training ground of the future elite of some ethnoracial or other specifiable demographic subgroup. Of what social category does the student imagine him or herself a future leader or articulate servant? From what social category of mentor or subclass peer group does he or she imagine receiving empathy and the most useful, applicable, and comprehensible knowledge and personal contacts? And each student must test his or her aspirations against the norms of the race, class, and class subechelons that the university articulates.

Among the likenesses that bring people together in college are also similar resolutions of widespread value conflicts—between the pursuit of distinction and egalitarianism, between competitiveness and cooperation, between "escape" from the lower-status group and the service of its collective needs, between rebelliousness or manipulation of the system and conformity or capitulation to the system, between ambition and fun, between the life of the mind and careerism. Those born rich and those born to struggle are likely to resolve these dilemmas differently, as are natives and immigrants, as well as light-skinned and dark-skinned people. The setting of *Stigma and Culture* highlights these universal dilemmas against the backdrop of the struggle of the most ambitious among the stigmatized to avoid last place.

Hundreds of miles away from parental authority for the first time, students must make scores of affiliative choices, regarding classes, roommates, sports team memberships, and club memberships. Some such choices are limited by the student's personal competency, and every student's schedule is idiosyncratic. However, most choices are shaped by consultation with trusted others. At Howard, these networks of trust are often ethnically and color coded.

In the context of racial stigma, the choice to prioritize a black ethnic identity or to pursue Black racial solidarity strikes many people of African descent in the United States as a moral one, akin to the contrast between egoism and loyalty, between stealing from or adding to the proceeds of others' liberation struggle. The phrase that for me best encapsulates the ambivalent performance of color, race, and ethnicity at the nation's leading historically Black university is "We are of the race, for the race, but above the race." Black ethnics appear to share this self-figuration with much of the color-class elite among nonethnic, native African Americans. This ambiguity of identity is performed as articulately as it is verbalized, and the performances are judged scrupulously on Howard's campus. According to what I take to be the ideal among African American students at Howard, not only must one balance "ghetto" and "bougie" in one's musical tastes and attire, but one must also be both book wise and streetwise, both collectivist and individualistic, both erudite and vernacular. (On a similar form of code-switching in Caribbean culture, see Reisman [1970].) One must be able to communicate respectfully with both the rich and the poor. One must pursue a lucrative career and have social fun along the way, equally conscious of one's rights and responsibilities.

The families of first-generation college students—a significant proportion of Howard's population—often fail to understand the purpose of college, and they often resent the bourgeois ways of thinking and speaking that their upwardly mobile sons and daughters must adopt in college. Some of their parents have experienced the economic and social benefits of labor unions and, even amid the rapid decline of unions, see the individualistic pursuit of wealth as a materially or morally inferior choice. For their part, first-generation students are often embarrassed by the speech and manners that they brought from home and must readopt when they return home. Moreover, the elite university is the place where the constant scrutiny of a person's intelligence reaches its height. Hence, not even upper-class inheritance and connections can entirely rescue a person from the shame of demonstrable ignorance and ill-preparedness. The personnel and the modes of knowledge of the university are fraught with anxieties about the past—about the adequacy of one's family pedigree, of one's high school, of one's academic preparedness, and of one's ethnic, national, or regional group. Like migration, school attendance induces students to recognize their home cultures as marked and, usually, to reimagine the home culture as an emblem of the self that one needs to embrace or struggle against in order to secure acceptance among the privileged.

Psychiatric residents in training at the Howard University student clinic tell me that resolving these contradictory demands is difficult and sometimes results in extreme performances—such as those of financially comfortable, straight-A students who turn tricks on the side and brilliant boys who feel that girls will ignore them unless they act and dress like "thugs." Such performers sometimes end up in the teeth of the law. While few cases are this extreme, perhaps even these extreme cases represent the resolution of the typical quandary of middle-class Americans of all races: we seek the signs of class distinction but are also embarrassed by them. Perhaps more than most Americans, African Americans fear that too much class distinction will both invite white assault and isolate one from the protection of Black comrades. In the post–civil rights era, light-skinned men seem to feel particularly intense pressure to demonstrate their vernacular credentials and worthiness of belonging among Black people. Solidarity is perhaps the foremost weapon of the weak, and it is difficult to give up.

However, the moral choices of the upwardly mobile immigrant or transmigrant do not appear to be conditioned as intensely by the same compunctions about upward mobility, by the same historically conditioned fear of white American brutality, or by the same confidence that other people of African descent will come to the rescue when necessary. Indeed, black immigrants tend to be more motivated by the great loss of symbolic status that they tend to suffer when tarred for the first time, upon migration to the United States, by the dark side of US racial binarism. The official curriculum of Howard stipulates the embrace of binary hypodescent and of collective racial uplift as the solution, whereas Howard's hidden curriculum propagates a vivid mythology of subracial difference as an alternative escape route from racism. As Nathan (2005) and Moffatt (1989) suggest, such student contrarianism is not unique to the HBCUs. Yet, if all universities are worlds of the stigmatized, the denizens of the HBCU suffer under a higher degree of such stigma because of the high visibility of racial stigma. When the doors to upward mobility are open to only a few, cheating and gaming the system are better options for the invisibly stigmatized. For populations under constant and inescapable scrutiny, ethnological schadenfreude is the more attractive means of nosing one's way through the door.

"Cultures" and "Rules": Fictions of Fixity

At its foundation, the university is an exemplary world of the stigmatized, who—in answer to the class, ethnic, racial, gender, and disability-related stigmata under which its ambitious denizens struggle—create what Goffman (1963) calls a "literally-defined world," where people defensively publish the evidence of their collective dignity. Yet, within this world, they are also driven to "stratify their own." From this self-stratification arises a range of moral dilemmas. Howard is not unique among universities, most of which were founded to prepare the bureaucratic and professional classes of previously dominated groups coming into their own. But there are other reasons to think of universities as exemplary worlds of the stigmatized. It is not typically the most popular high school students who end up in the best universities.

Rather, it is the asthmatics, the people whose mothers supervised them the most closely, and the ones who have been overly diagnosed with learning or emotional disabilities, giving them access to the most constructive medical and psychological interventions. The university is the main site where the class-marginal have a chance to elevate their fates in the world. It helps ethnic and lower-class whites to acquire nonethnic, middle-class diction, manners, and marital partners. It inspires queer and racially marginalized students to form alliances that affirm and support them. In answer to the historical exclusion of stigmatized racial minorities, the university engineers "diversity" and offers the vocabulary for potentially sympathetic accounts of these "cultural" others. University departments of anthropology, ethnic studies, and area studies promote the concept of "cultures," which affirms and empowers the stigmatized.

In the United States at least, white Anglo-Saxon Protestants do not tend to be described as an "ethnic group" or their conventional practices and ways of thinking as a "culture." Their ethnicity and lifeways tend to be treated as an unmarked norm. It is in this sense that "cultures" and "ethnicity" are the vocabulary of the stigmatized in their efforts to separate themselves from the indelibly discredited races. "Cultures" are also the markers of white or potentially white groups that have yet to be fully included. Thus, in many ways, ethnicity marks a loyal opposition. Yet it can also mark Foucauldian forms of resistance that implicitly embody the power/knowledge, or categories of action, stipulated by the powerful. "Cultures" and "ethnicity" are also a vocabulary compatible with the "new cultural racism," according to which neoconservatives like Samuel Huntington explain in ostensibly color-blind terms why some populations do belong and others do not belong in our midst.

The idea of "cultures" as discrete, internally homogeneous, and countable entities is largely dead in my discipline, as dead as the concept of "races." But I still believe in the analytical worth of "cultures." For me, "culture" is not the pre-Klemmian, pre-Tylorean, and pre-Boasian "humanistic" notion that all human self-cultivation converges on a single standard of thought and behavior—a conception that has been dead in my discipline for even longer.

Because "cultures" tend to be attributed to the low by the high and by the ambitious spokespeople of the low, "cultures," as I understand them, are products of an interclass and translocal dialogue. Each "culture" is the ever-changing pattern of actions that people undertake because those actions are advantageous and because antecedent actions in a population have made the present pattern of action conceivable or justifiable. What is conceivable to people in one position within a social field—that is, any given age, gender, class, race, disability category, region, nation, empire, and so forth—may not be as easily conceivable by or for a person in another position. And some people have greater material power to justify their actions than do others.

Moreover, as Bourdieu ([1972] 1985) suggests, most people's portraits of their own "cultures" focus on outstanding cases—both the morally exemplary and the odd, much like the typical characters and scenarios on US television. Almost all insiders' reports of their "cultures" are virtually blind to statistical norms and to certain massive phenomena that are normally taken for granted. References to "cultures" are always comparative, and comparisons between "cultures" are always highly motivated. In conversations with insiders, references to foreign cultures are often used to criticize aspects of the home culture that the speaker wants, self-interestedly, to change. In conversations with outsiders, descriptions of the home culture are usually intended to aggrandize the speaker for his or her ethnic dignity or to demonstrate personal superiority to his or her rivals. The accuracy of such popular ethnology is also limited by the speaker's class-, gender-, and race-limited awareness of both the home and the host societies.

My own professional interpretation of the "cultures" concept and of elite North American university life also arises from a specific social position. I am not, for example, a freshman trying to follow the official rules so that I can graduate on time. Nor am I a short-term visitor in need of a map to navigate the campus. I am a senior professor and research center director highly aware of the creativity with which I design the "rules" for students in any given class, with which colleagues make "agreements" and then break them, and with which financial officers and deans confronted with new situations improvise decisions based upon a congeries of factors impossible to reduce to any rule book, map, or formula. In a major university, no one could possibly memorize all of the rules and precedents, so rules are invoked mostly when a disagreement between equals or an ambiguity requires adjudication. Many other actions are permitted largely because no one has called special attention to them and they "feel" OK to the most powerful people or networks of allies who are aware of them.

Yet authority and order within the university, as in any bureaucracy, depend on subordinates' belief that we are all simply following a set of anonymous rules applied equally to anyone of a given rule-determined status. One of Duke's highest-ranking deans, who has also served in a similar position elsewhere, told me that the majority of his time is devoted to conflict resolution. Over my years at Harvard, Duke, and Howard, I have witnessed and participated in a range of such conflicts. Many of them reveal that actors in any given office normally act in ways only loosely shaped by their official job description. So the holders of officially complementary offices fight over who owns the right to make certain decisions.

Moreover, the scattered sets of official rules simply do not address most of the actions and interactions that take place on campus. The "rules" are the accumulation of resolutions when powerful people or constituencies have felt uncomfortable about the way in which something previously ungoverned by rules took place. Once that discomfort is resolved or the uncomfortable situation forgotten, the broader, cross-situational implications of the rule are also generally forgotten—until some other powerful person hunts for a bureaucratic reason to justify his or her bad "feeling" and strategizes to get it redressed. At my level in the university, when equally powerful or determined parties conflict over what is allowable, there is often no mediator with sufficient interest or sufficiently greater power to settle the conflict. In such cases, the higher-ranking parties do their best to ignore the conflict or offer profitable distractions to each party, such that the acute manifestations of the conflict go away or are postponed. Delay and inaction are among the favorite tools of crisis management.

Whatever the tool employed, it is a matter of high priority to keep the continual conflicts at the top invisible to lower-ranking participants in the system. The disruption of the image that the rules are fixed, impersonal, and ancient would delegitimize the system and undermine the authority of its leaders. Perhaps that is why twentieth- and twenty-first-century elite universities—which endeavor to change their students and pay professors to design new ways of thinking and acting—still punctuate every school year with invented but ever more changeless- and rigid-*looking* ceremonies. Implicit in the system is the fear that, if the rules did not seem to be anchored in some nearly Mosaic revelation, all authority would be lost.

Like "the rules," "cultures" are the patterns of collective life seen from the position of low rank. The idea of "cultures" conceals the processes of selective precedent-citation improvisation, and conflict that generated "the rules" of collective life in the first place. What I describe as "culture"—in the singular—is the processes of citation, improvisation, and conflict that are social life in hierarchical settings. One of the products of this improvisation and conflict, particularly at the middle and less-empowered levels of the global social hierarchy, is the strategic discursive representations called—in the plural—"cultures." Just as university culture is rooted in conflict and improvisation, so "cultures" are improvised arguments in a debate about the rightful trajectory of populations. Of course, one could imagine a student-written ethnography of the "rules" of university life that contains just as much useful truth, but, like Elliot Skinner before me, I am motivated to write about the stratified networks through which people who did not write "the rules" adapt, manipulate, and work around them. Unlike most anthropological ethnographies, this one is not tinged with encomium, which natives of the "culture" are inclined to demand. Nor, like most American sociology of race relations, is it intended as a critique. Rather, it is an account of what I see as I attempt to understand my world from the vantage of an elevated position in the academy, as well as in the US class hierarchy, and a degraded position in the global racial hierarchy.

The next chapter concerns people who, partly because they look like me, have been accorded a very low value in Howard's logic of Black ambition. Historically, they are perhaps Howard's foremost constituent other, and they have sought relief from their stigma through Tylorean/Boasian concept of "culture." Yet Howard also played a central role in turning this rural antitype of the university's own educational ideals into the most worthily "African" of African American ethnic groups. In many ways, the emergent Gullah/Geechee ethnic group showcases an ambivalence essential to cultural nationalism and universities alike. The fictions of Gullah/Geechee "culture" embody not only the aspirations of the United States' blackest population but also the limits of Howard's and the rest of the Western academy's ability to recognize its dignity. The chapters to come detail the great variety of black ethnic groupings at Howard and in its alumni networks, as well as the dialectical quality of their mutual transformation and reification.

3

Islands Are Not Isolated: Schools, Scholars, and the Political Economy of Gullah/Geechee Ethnicity

Stigma shapes not only the hidden curriculum but also its intellectual output.

African American Howard graduates from the 1940s and 1950s advised me against using the terms "Gullah" and "Geechee" as I had done. In their time, the terms had been spoken only behind the backs of their classmates from the coastal North Carolina, South Carolina, Georgia, and Florida Lowcountry, since these terms carried the implication of rural backwardness and intellectual deficiency—the very qualities that the university's culturally unmarked but highly Western-inspired project of "racial uplift" had been designed to counteract. Yet, thanks to the efforts of Howard alumnus and former Howard professor Lorenzo D. Turner in the 1930s, the Gullah/Geechee poster child of Black American cultural deficiency has since become the classical Greece of African American civilization and is gradually becoming a proud ethnic identity in its own right.

This chapter concerns the interclass and translocal genesis of what is often represented as Black North America's most archaic, isolated, authentic, and, indeed, foundational ethnic group. This chapter also documents the role of schools and universities—Howard University prominently among them—in this inventive response to racial stigma and constituent othering. In sum, Gullah/Geechee identity illustrates the fact that ethnic identities emerge not from isolation but from translocal interaction and stigma. Among these interactions are the ethnoracial lumping and splitting practices of schools and the role of the university in training elites and naming their folk constituencies.

A Black North Carolinian, Lorenzo D. Turner earned his BA from Howard in 1914 and taught in its Department of English from 1917 to 1928, serving as chair for the last eight of those years. During that time, he also earned his 1926 PhD in English from the University of Chicago. He subsequently taught at Fisk, where he designed one of the first programs in African studies, and at Roosevelt University in Chicago, where he served as chairman of a new African Studies Program. But Turner's interests, like Skinner's, were not limited to the academic. He cofounded the Peace Corps training program to prepare young volunteers for service in Africa.[1]

Though he began his research on the Gullah/Geechees only in 1929, after leaving Howard, his influential book *Africanisms in the Gullah Dialect* (1949) embodies an ambivalence endemic to the university and perhaps nowhere more so than to Howard. Indeed, Howard highlights the ambivalence inherent in all cultural nationalist projects. The cultural and racial distinctiveness of the "folk" justifies the autonomy of the group for which the elite scions of those "folk" wish to speak. But it is the Western middle-class cultural qualifications of those elite scions—such as literacy, colorless and abstract forms of speech, clothing styles inimical to manual labor, monogamy, individualistic orientations toward school work and spending, and respect for monetary debt, private property, intergenerational concentration of wealth, and the other hereditary media of upper-class dignity—that qualify these elite scions as *spokespeople* for and *political leaders* of their "folk." This story has been repeated in cultural and political nationalisms (and their host universities) the world over and in the protonationalist documents penned by novelists, anthropologists, and linguists.

Turner's book reconsiders a range of Black language varieties long judged incorrect and inferior—and no one was probably more convinced of their incorrectness and inferiority than were the majority of the Howardites during Turner's time. Turner offered the alternative view that these Black language varieties were a "dialect," or sublanguage, with a legitimate but distinctive standard of its own. It is perhaps the perspective of the stigmatized that causes university scholars to favor value-neutral and egalitarian uses of terms like "culture" and "dialect." But it is equally obvious that institutions like Howard officially condemn the actual *speaking* of "dialect," in the more everyday pejorative sense of that word. In turn, such universities advocate "culture" in the laudatory, humanistic sense of conformity to the single high-class and ethnoracially unmarked standard of excellence. By their own peculiar sort of compromise, universities teach us to regard the "culture" of the "folk" as something to be written about and the dialect-speaking "folk" themselves as people who need to keep quiet and be spoken for. Universities construct the assimilated bourgeoisie of a regional population as its spokespeople and representatives in the halls of ethnically unmarked power. A range of such interclass processes regularly drives ethnogenesis.

Gullah/Geechees at Howard

Unbeknownst to me until recently, I had known two Gullah/Geechee physicians all of my life—two cousins from the South Carolina seacoast. Only in 2002, when I began to ask questions, did I hear of their distinctive heritage. Our families' lives had been deeply intertwined—through their attendance at Howard and through a fraternity, a sorority, and an adult women's club, as well as the friendship and dating that had linked our families. Being Gullah/Geechee seemed to hold little intrinsic interest for them, and they seemed unaware of the copious ethnological literature about their people. Indeed, the aspects of Gullah/Geecheeness they emphasized were often the (possibly compensatory) opposite of what had been emphasized in that university-based literature for nearly a century. Their words also mildly challenge the premises of the warning I received from others—that Gullah/Geechees are simply backwater people, naturally embarrassed by their deficiency.

For example, while one cousin proudly devoted most of our conversations to the recently discovered Indianness of his erstwhile African American wife, the other spent most of our conversation detailing, with equal pride, his own European ancestry. Indeed, while the literature emphasizes the phenotypical Africanness of this population, the physiognomy of one cousin and the complexion of the other do suggest much European ancestry. The one cousin I asked about Penn School and Center, which the literature identifies as the educational capital of the South Carolina Gullah/Geechees, said that he had never attended or even heard of it. The ethnonym preferred by the lighter-skinned cousin—"Geechee"—seems to ratify their shared slant on what made this identity acceptable, though not necessarily amiable, to them. Whereas the term "Gullah" usually refers only to the Black population of the Lowcountry, "Geechee" has at times referred exclusively to the region's white population (Dale Rosengarten, personal communication, May 2, 2007). Perhaps consistently, this family friend warned me that, while the term "Geechee" was acceptable to him, the term "Gullah" was indeed offensive.

In my first job—at the Howard University print shop in 1974—my closest coworker had come, unambiguously black, from the same region. He embodied a much more usual scholarly image of the Gullah/Geechee. Thirteen years old when I first met him, I was perhaps half his age. He never named himself ethnically, and he seldom spoke. However, his few words were well chosen for utility or spot-on humor, though seldom at anyone else's expense. As he trained me in both printing skills and proper workplace conduct, he often cited Penn Center, on South Carolina's Saint Helena Island, as the source of his authority. Years later, I discovered that Penn Center and Saint Helena Island sit at the heartland of a regional way of life that is today being called, with increasing pride, "Gullah/Geechee."

Judging by his northern Florida origins and distinctive speech pattern, I infer that one high-ranking dean, with whom I have regularly interacted since 2002, is also eligible for this new ethnic designation, but he himself never said so.

In 2002, my best friend among the Howard Gullah/Geechees—let us call her Margaret—also "got her start" at Penn Center and then attended another HBCU, South Carolina State University, in Eugene Robinson's hometown of Orangeburg, because her father thought it unsafe for her to attend a faraway urban school like Howard. But Howard was the target of her greatest admiration and aspirations. She is now the academic program coordinator of Howard's Science, Engineering, and Mathematics Program. Away from home and buoyant with nostalgia, she has come to embrace the identity, and she has her own ideas about its proper indices. "Gullah," she says, describes not the people but only the language and the "culture." While there is little consensus, I use the term "Gullah/Geechee" to describe all of the populations and practices eligible for either term, except when my interlocutor prefers some other term.

In response to my request for instruction, Margaret excitedly reproduces Gullah parlance to illustrate that it is both different and beautiful, and not "funny" or wrong, as many people think. She recalls that, before the Charleston City Market became "all gentrified," selling high-priced arts and crafts to tourists, it housed a lively fresh produce and fish market. Female hawkers there would shout out to their younger potential customers, "Daughdah! Daughdah!" or to peers, "Cousin! Cousin! Wanna bah some fush?" On the one hand, Margaret's mother (like mine) emphasized the importance of culturally unmarked middle-class-style American English diction. On the other hand, her father and other men in her family were highly educated and accomplished, but even the one who was a high school principal regularly split verbs and simply did not care. Margaret says that, for most people in her world, subject-verb agreement was not considered a substantial enough issue to worry about. Intelligence, she summarized, is what mattered.

Her conclusion opened my eyes to the arbitrariness of the conviction that had been the oxygen of my upbringing—that split verbs were a sign of intellectual retardation and an embarrassment to the race. But my father, too, had been more likely to break grammatical rules than my mother. Lower-status or ethnoracially stigmatized men in many Western societies regard unmitigated conformity to middle-class linguistic and other social conventions as emasculating. In groups of lower-status males, the consistent observance of standard grammar and the refusal to code-switch can be read as a refusal of egalitarian camaraderie, as slavishness to one's class or status superiors, and even as signs of homosexuality.

Indeed, conformity to such grammatical rules—to which one might add the avoidance of split infinitives, of the word "irregardless," and of "myriad" as a noun—may contribute more to political self-positioning than to clarity. Even the "Queen's English" has a deeply impoverished conjugation system compared to its Germanic and Romance substrate languages. So even the "Queen's English" is only slightly more precise (or, rather, redundant) than AAVE and Gullah in its indication of who is performing an action. However, by this dubious standard, one would have to acknowledge that even the "best" English is *far* less precise than the worst German, Spanish, French, or Portuguese. The real social work performed by consistent subject-verb agreement in English is that it indicates intergenerational belonging in the urban middle or upper class or the consistency of one's efforts to please those classes. Like table manners, subject-verb agreement is a shibboleth. In middle-class African American populations, it embodies the never-far-from-conscious prayer that, if we speak "properly," the ethnically unmarked dominant class will open the door for us. In Caribbean English, this and the correct pronunciation of initial *h*'s embody a similar prayer.

It also struck me that, except for the Geechee cousins, both of whom married people from other regions of the United States, none of my Gullah/Geechee friends at Howard knew each other. Nor did they share an agreed-upon name for or definition of their population. At Howard, there is a disagreement over not only the nomenclature but also the diacritica of this emergent ethnic group. Though Penn School and Howard have been critical to the recent genesis of the Gullah/Geechee ethnic identity, Howard's campus itself has been stony ground for the emergence of a local Gullah/Geechee ethnic community.

Postslavery and postcolonial universities tend to dress up the ethnic groups, regions, nations, and religions that they re-present in the "cover" (Goffman 1963) of Western middle-class language, necessarily silencing any ethnic distinction that is defined by its dialectal difference. Insofar as universities dignify the ethnonational or religious groups that they re-present, they also treat the vernacular-speaking folk as mascots, rather than agents, of the group and their lifeway as a source of raw symbolic images, rather than as legitimate standards guiding daily life for those who are pursuing individual and collective upward mobility. Hence, at Howard, Gullah/Geechees were and are not typically expected to take pride in or unite around their cultural distinctiveness. To do so, they would have to speak, and their class-conscious, diction-obsessed peers would indeed find it "funny," if not risible.

However, just after his departure from Howard, Lorenzo Turner gave the Gullah/Geechees of the southeastern seacoast homeland a means to redefine their collective self as a triumphant redoubt of African culture abroad, rather than as the products of an inability to assimilate to a supposedly universal but truly Euro-American middle-class ideal (for a similar case, see Holsey 2008, 79–80). Thus the university has both facilitated the individual effort to shed Gullah/Geechee distinctiveness and helped to articulate what makes the Gullah/Geechees back home a bona fide collective in their own right.

The Dialectics of Invention: Empire, Nation, Race, and Ethnicity

In the wake of Benedict Anderson's *Imagined Communities* (1983), most scholars have been convinced that nation-states and the imagined communities they engender emerged from recent centuries of economic and ideological change. Nation-states are not typically administrative structures that grew out of primordially bounded, culturally well-defined, and ethnically self-conscious prestate communities. Instead, nation-states emerged from novel communications technologies and from intraimperial rivalries that made it profitable for provincial leaders to imagine a more local set of boundaries and a new peoplehood within them. If provincial leaders were to achieve a dignity equal to that of the empire's ranking bureaucrats, they would need to help define their respective provinces as peoples in their own right, with distinct and worthy spirits, lifeways, and biologies all their own. It was in such terms that Johann Gottfried von Herder first imagined a German peoplehood that was not simply an inferior facsimile of the singular French "culture" so slavishly imitated by the rulers of the German-speaking principalities.

Races are as unnatural and novel as nations. In various ways, Gould (1981), Omi and Winant (1994), Fields (1990), Fredrickson (1982), and others have demonstrated that races are biologically fictional but have become units of social action through the efforts of dominant populations to use scientific language, laws, and occupational monopolies to privilege themselves. In reaction, subordinated populations have embraced and used the fictional categories of race to resist domination and, much like the independence leaders of nation-states, to reimagine the boundaries and cultural diacritica of their peoplehoods.

Ranger (1983) and Peel ([1989] 1993) have shown in Africa, Yancey, Ericksen, and Juliani (1976) have shown in the United States, and I have shown in the black Atlantic world generally (J. L. Matory 2005a, 1999) that ethnic groups do not typically emerge from the inertia of primordially distinct cultures either. Ethnic groups are not units that merely maintain their unity while modernity inserts them into pluralistic national and international environments. Instead, ethnic groups emerge from imposed administrative units, resistance to domination, competition for status, commercial rivalries, dynamic cultural exchanges, and divisions of economic and political labor, all of which result from the convergence and interaction of populations. Moreover, ethnic groups are not timelessly fixed. The boundaries between, the defining cultural features of, and the names of ethnic groupings regularly change over time. Indeed, many configurations of boundaries, cultural diacritica, and names that are presented as primordial are quite new.

Unconsidered in this "invention of tradition" school of thought is the racial context of such invention. The invention of national and ethnic identities often contests imperialist assertions of the racial inferiority of the secessionist national or ethnic group. But it can do so either by asserting the dignity of the whole race or by asserting the secessionist group's difference from the inferior race. The relationship between races and ethnic groups is in many ways similar to that between empires and nations. Each pair of entities arises from a competition between centralizing and secessionist leaders, often with rival economic and political interests. Each set of leaders attempts to reify and primordialize a set of reasons why its jurisdiction is uniquely real and legitimate.

Gullah/Geechee, black Indian, Louisiana Creole, Caribbean-immigrant, and African-immigrant ethnic identities are equally shaped by racial stigma, invention, selective reference to vernacular practice, and the tendentious motives of university scholars. However, the emergent Gullah/Geechee ethnic group is unique in the degree to which it accords a positive value to Africa and to African ancestry. Below, I explore the cosmopolitan roots—or rhizomes (Deleuze and Guattari [1980] 1987)—of what is now often characterized as Black America's most African subculture and ethnic group and as a living ancestor to present-day African American culture at large. Its Africanness and its emergent ethnic self-awareness are the products not of primordial isolation and inertia, as has often been assumed, but of its extensive interaction with schools, scholars, and the interethnic dynamics of global capitalism. Indeed, the flawed premise that African culture in the Americas can survive only when its bearers are isolated from European influence is an artifact of university scholars' ambivalence about the vernacular cultures for which they presume to speak.

Schooling, Aggregation, and Resistance

Schools aggregate diverse populations and at each level of the student's progress from preschool to professional school unite the young elites of a higher-order regional or ethnonational grouping. Yet at each level, schools create the incentive for students to declare the greater salience of the ethnonational identity represented by the next-lower level of school.

With their bricks, mortar, and cast-off equipment, segregated Black American schools not only monumentalized the pariah status of African Americans but also provided a powerful, albeit supervised and guided, setting for Black teamwork and the articulation of oppositional strategies in authoritative, middle-class language. They brought together as peers in the classroom and on the playground children whose families might previously have thought themselves immiscibly different in class, complexion and hair texture, ancestry, occupation, and religion. A measure of the power of such community- and culture-building institutions is that classmates are more likely to speak with the school-homogenized accents of their state-defined racial peers than with the often-diverse accents, dialects, or languages of their parents.

In various parts of the South, the schools were not just segregated binarily. For example, in the mid-twentieth century, Creole children gathered together in the local Catholic schools, such as the Epiphany and Corpus Christi elementary schools, Xavier Prep high school, and Xavier University. The choices of other "little races" (Thompson 1972) and mixed-race Indian populations were typically more limited. For example, the University of North Carolina at Pembroke was founded in 1887 as Croatan Normal School in order to train Native American public school teachers. Like the racially segregated Indian churches that emerged in the postbellum period, such schools embodied the state's refusal to admit most Native American and partly Native American students to white schools, as well as the anxiety of these often partly African-descended Indians to preserve their difference from the main target group of the degrading and rights-denying practices of Jim Crow—the Negroes.

The complexion-coded Saint Mary's College and King's College in Port of Spain, Trinidad, and Queen's Royal College of Kingston, Jamaica, also reflect histories of nonbinary racial division. In 2002, Saint Mary's College high school was still reputed to serve a largely "French Creole" student body, whereas King's College and Queen's Royal College were later founded specifically to give dark black boys the same opportunities. These schools and their alumni networks attract fierce intergenerational loyalty and inspire enthusiastic rivalry.

While the more heavily Christian southern half of Nigeria had quickly and massively embraced Western education as a strategy of upward mobility, the largely Muslim northern half of that British colony was more resistant. In 1922, colonial officials founded Katsina Training College, which later became Barewa College, specifically in order to attract and train the sons of the northern emirs. Barewa College assembled and trained a new northern military and administrative elite, contrasting in identity with the southern elite and concerted in its effort to dominate the entire postcolonial nation. The Barewa Old Boys Association—that is, the alumni group—justifiably calls its alma mater "the 'cradle of Nigerian leadership'" (Barewa Old Boys Association 2001, iii). The Old Boys Association has been central among the overlapping networks facilitating northern hegemony during most of the history of postindependence Nigeria.

These schools have, to various degrees, also been feeder schools to Howard, leading to the aggregated "Blackness" that Howard officially reifies and targets for collective uplift. High school alumni networks remain alive at Howard, but the shared fact of coming from Nigeria, coming from Jamaica or Trinidad, or coming from a British-inspired examination system often becomes the more salient fact in the "big pond" of Howard. Hence, school-related identities follow the same shifting, segmentary logic as ideal Nuer lineages, clans, and tribes (Evans-Pritchard 1940). However, not all secondary schools lead equally to Howard. For example, the typically dark boys from Port of Spain's King's College are far better represented at Howard than are the typically light-skinned boys from Saint Mary's College.

Other differences were correlated with the disproportionately dark population that Howard attracted from the Caribbean. These young Caribbean men who come to Howard are the least likely to have come from the business class and the most likely to regard education as their only route to prosperity. Until the late 1960s or so, the blackest Jamaican and Trinidadian boys regarded themselves as the most academically ambitious and talented. Speaking to me during the first decade of the twenty-first century, dark middle-aged Trinis recalled that the light-skinned "French Creole" boys looked down upon them but also paid them to do their homework. At the time, they reported, the South Asian–origin Indians of Trinidad also tended to be academically undistinguished. Thus, the high school–to-university school sequence is a triage system, sorting people out according to color, class fraction, and ethnicity. However, like medical triage, it aggregates its subjects by a top-down logic, a logic ultimately governed by a culturally unmarked dominant class and then reminds its subjects about an order of ethnoracial difference between Blackness and the social group united by the high school.

Penn School, the predecessor to Penn Center, aggregated populations of the Lowcountry—from southeastern North Carolina to northern Florida—and scores of barrier islands that had once been known primarily for the distinction of being "backwoods" or "country." Only by the efforts of the directors of Penn School and a small army of southern white folklorists, basket merchants, and tourist boards; northern white missionaries, scholars, and museum directors; a Black Howard University professor; and returnees from the Gullah/Geechee diaspora in the North did these speakers of diverse dialects and lifeways come to be recognized as a "culture" and as the classical ancestor to African American "culture" generally. The absence of a self-conscious and self-named Gullah/Geechee community at Howard University tells us a great deal about the divergence between the priorities of Howard's founders and leaders, on the one hand, and those of the people who invented Gullah/Geechee "culture," on the other.

The Gullah/Geechees and the Janus Face of the University

Rural African American folkways have been an object of ambivalence at Howard, which has historically sought, through the liberal arts, to produce what W. E. B. Du Bois called "the Talented Tenth." Carter G. Woodson's complaint in *The Mis-education of the Negro* ([1933] 1977)—that Negro schools train their students in traditions other than their own and in skills useless to their communities—seemed obliquely aimed at Howard, a university that neighbored Woodson's own headquarters. The truth, however, is more subtle.

In 2002, Howard University's annually revised official portrait of itself, *Facts*, reported the history of the school's foundation:

> In November 1866, shortly after the end of the Civil War, members of the First Congregational Society of Washington considered establishing a theological seminary for the education of African-American clergymen. Within a few weeks, the concept had expanded to include a provision for establishing a university. Within two years, the University consisted of the Colleges of Liberal Arts and Medicine. The new institution was named for General Oliver O. Howard, a Civil War hero, who was both a founder of the University and, at the time, Commissioner of the Freedmen's Bureau.
>
> The University charter, as enacted by Congress and subsequently approved by President Andrew Johnson on March 2, 1867, designated Howard University as "a university for the education of youth in the liberal arts and sciences."
>
> In 1879, Congress approved a special appropriation for the University. The charter was amended in 1928 to authorize an annual federal appropriation for

construction, development, improvement and maintenance of the University. (Howard University 2002, 11)

While many elite US universities began as seminaries and, during the nineteenth century, became liberal arts colleges, Howard experienced its theological phase only as an idea and quickly emerged, under US federal government protection, as the preeminent training ground for the nonhereditary leadership and professional class of its target population. Howard's schools of medicine and law have undoubtedly furnished Black America with indispensable tools of survival and progress. However, European and Euro-American standards of knowledge and utility started out and remained central to Howard's educational project, as they did in colonial and postcolonial universities worldwide, a fact that helps to explain, though not justify, the resistance of the northern emirs and, more recently, the murderous attacks of the Taliban in Afghanistan and of the Boko Haram movement in Nigeria on state-operated schools. Insofar as the West remained or remains dominant in these regions, upward mobility has depended on mastering European modes of knowledge and administration—in short "power/knowledge" (Foucault 1980). In the black Atlantic world, the irony that postcolonial liberation was led by the most assimilated and depended on a confession that the prior lifeway of the target population was inferior became most evident in the 1950s, during a wave of national independence movements ultimately institutionalized by Western-schooled bureaucrats. But there is hardly a more Anglophile institution in *any* former British colony—including the United States—than the universities. Indeed, the finest of US universities slavishly mock the administrative vocabulary, the titles, the architecture, the ceremonies, and the garb of medieval Oxford and Cambridge. For example, so committed are Harvard and Yale to British symbolic credentials that they retain the term "masters" for the resident faculty heads of the student residences, ignoring the more salient meaning of this term in the history of the United States—the head of a slaveholding estate. Marcus Garvey would describe such internalization of the former colonizer's models as "mental slavery."

Similarly, the History Department at Howard now annually hosts a ceremony initiating its best students in the national history honors society, Phi Alpha Theta. Following a standard script, each of four professors personifies, narrates, and lights a candle representing one historical period—"classical," "medieval," "Renaissance," or "modern." More appropriate to a European historical experience than to an African or African-diaspora experience, this periodization narrates a retrospective view by the elites of Western Europe and its diaspora about the changing, but always defining, role of Greece and Rome in the cultural history of the whole world.

As an anthropologist of Africa and its diaspora, as well as a historian manqué, I am more accustomed to classifying the history of the world according to other phases and dynamics, such as the advents of sedentary agriculture and of iron smelting, the Bantu expansion, the desiccation of the Sahara, the Islamic contact period, the Atlantic slave trade, colonization, emancipation, the linked movements for national independence, civil rights, Black Power and Afrocentrism, the oil boom/crisis, and neoliberalism. As standards of historical periodization have multiplied in the academy, Howard at times continues to espouse Black dignity with reference to the standards that the dominant political class takes for granted, even as elite TWIs have challenged those standards. It is riskier for the stigmatized than for the privileged to be the first to break old rules. In general, the postmodern multiplication and relativization of such standards is often experienced as a threat by ethno-racially stigmatized intellectuals, who have worked hard to reify and dignify their peoples according to the dominant standard. Only for the populations securely rooted at the crest of the hill is it tolerable that the slopes being scaled by others have become amorphously muddy.

I was honored to be asked to deliver the keynote address at Howard's Phi Alpha Theta initiation ceremony on April 22, 2002. Though I had not anticipated the nature of the ceremony or the surprise it gave me at a historically Black university, I delivered an address called "Who Is the Subject of History?," which began with the following summary:

> All historical narration requires a subject position, and even the best history is as much about the present subject position of its present-day authors as it is about what actually happened in the past. In my opinion, it is but a slight exaggeration to say that every historical narration invents and reifies a subject position that is foreign to most of the historical actors described in it.

My colleagues spoke kindly of my address, but it was not until 2010 that I worked up the courage to ask one of my History Department colleagues why the subject position invented and reified in Phi Alpha Theta ceremony had been embraced without any critique or irony. My colleague explained without self-justification or apology that there had been no discussion of the issue in the department because the ceremony had been received as natural. The text of the ceremony had been written by and inherited from the national historical honor society, "inerrant" and for verbatim recitation. Membership in this society "was an unquestioned honor, nationwide," my colleague said, adding, "I'd participated in many of them before. I'd been a member of it since I was a wee student." As an expression of Black pride in scholarship, Howard's Phi Alpha Theta initiation ceremony might reveal either or both of the following: the cosmopolitan self-confidence or the naturalized alienation of the Black subject reified by the historically Black university.

This case dramatically illustrates the dynamics that shape all universities. Whereas much of post-1960s hostility toward universities in the United States is rooted in the right-wing premise that universities are the instruments of left-wing mind control, university programs are also funded to the degree that they attract the approval of politicians, state bureaucrats, and corporate philanthropists and to the degree that they are subscribed to by career-minded students. Professors and administrators are not entirely free to state the truth as they see it. Conformity to politically dominant ideas and the appearance of political neutrality (which are usually one and the same thing) are rewarded. Even the most insurgent university pedagogy is deeply compromised, syncretic, and ironic.

As every anthropologist knows, signs that come from one place can embody very different meanings when articulated from another place or position. For example, "freedom" meant one thing to the nineteenth-century Confederate advocates of "states' rights" and the late-twentieth-century neoconservatives (such as Reagan, who regarded communism, and not apartheid, as a threat to "freedom") and, on the other hand, quite another thing to the nineteenth-century abolitionists and the 1960s civil rights protesters. Similarly, the Greek letters by which Black American fraternities and sororities typically name themselves have been embroidered with vernacular and African-looking dance moves, or "stomps," entirely alien to the "college life" of white American fraternities and sororities.

Even music education at Howard has always favored European classical over African American classical music, or jazz. For example, one Trinidadian American professor and alumnus offered as proof of this observation the report that, when he nominated even the jazz legend Miles Davis for an honorary doctorate, the university ignored him. Even the forms of "Negro spiritual" featured at Howard's public ceremonies are performed in the operatic, "concert-hall" style popularized by the Fisk Jubilee Singers in the early twentieth century as it sought donations from white potential benefactors.

Periodically, the self-censorship of professors fails, and the administration intervenes to restore the ethos of unspoken compromise. In the 1970s, professor and psychiatrist Frances Cress Welsing was denied tenure at Howard because she argued that white racism resulted from the fear, implicit in the one-drop rule, that the white race was vulnerable to extinction in the face of the more powerful genes of Blacks and other nonwhites (see Welsing 1991). Like other minority schools, Howard negotiates between the aspirations of the minority and the demands of the majority-dominated market and state. After all, Howard receives a significant—and, as we have seen, fragile—proportion of its annual budget from the US Congress.

The epistemology and the social order of the university are a compromise between those of the folk it speaks for and those of the ethnically unmarked elites who authorize upward mobility by the elite scions of the folk. Yet it is also in the nature of university professors and students to test the limits of their funders' power. Hence, even though the single most influential student of Gullah/Geechee cultural history was a Howard alumnus and former Howard English professor, an ethnic community typically defined by its paucity of non-African ancestors, the richness and Africanness of its vernacular culture, and the non-European influences on its language would never take root on Howard's campus.

Assimilation to white middle-class appearance and linguistic and sartorial standards is, in the view of the racially stigmatized, the best available disidentifier and the price of progress toward safety, prosperity, and power. Embedded in the structure of the postslavery and the postcolonial university is the premise that ethnic, regional, national, and religious topics are legitimate objects of study—indeed, legitimate emblems of the social group chiefly served by the university—but that Western analytical, narrative, and other metalinguistic frames are superior and unique vehicles of intelligence, truth, and professional qualification. The failure of Afrocentric Gullah/Geechee ethnogenesis, the success of Anglophile Caribbean ethnogenesis, and the ambiguous performance of Louisiana Creole and black Indian ethnogenesis on campus all teach us something about the nature of Howard—its feeder schools, racial focus, class focus, political priorities, and financial sponsorship, as well as the sources of stigma that drove its founding and drive its daily workings.

Roots/Rhizomes/Dialogue:
On the Coevalness of the Gullah/Geechees

Whereas the conventional wisdom constructs the Gullah/Geechees as the "roots" of African American culture, "rhizome" might better capture the dialogical genesis of this culture in its broader Afro-Atlantic context. Perhaps the virtue of the related "dialogue" metaphor (J. L. Matory 2005a) is that it highlights the diversity of local solutions to the dilemma underlying an ongoing translocal conversation. In itself, the scholarship on the Gullah/Geechees holds further lessons about the nature of ethnogenesis and the editing processes that interclass dialogue imposes upon it.

The Gullah/Geechee people are the *locus classicus* for the study of "African survivals" in North American culture. As such, they have been saddled with the duty to generate universal principles for the explanation of Africans' acculturation, adaptation, and cultural resistance in the Western Hemisphere, and they provide the main North American test case for explanatory principles generated elsewhere in the Americas. Yet the well-studied Gullah/Geechee case, like the Afro-Atlantic world generally, holds untapped lessons about the historical genesis of cultures and ethnic identities worldwide. Is isolation the normal precondition and conservator of cultural and ethnic distinctiveness? And do the enslaved and their descendants choose their ancestors' ways and identities mainly when and where isolation from the dominant class has made the culturally unmarked alternatives of the metropolis unavailable? The existing literature on the Gullah/Geechee people of the southeastern US coast and islands says yes to these questions, which also stand at the heart of both black Atlantic and global cultural history.

On the other hand, students of so-called globalization and its precedents have increasingly recognized the long-distance flows of people, ideas, and resources that, far from eliminating sociocultural difference, have enhanced and transformed it (see J. L. Matory 2005a, 73–114). And there are cosmopolitan spaces where nonassimilation and linguistic distinctiveness are effective social capital. Where it is profitable, distinctiveness is consciously created. For example, the people who became Italian Americans constructed a new but Old World–inspired ethnic identity in the midst of intensive commercial, political, and educational interaction with other ethnic groups. Indeed, in US cities, they were often surrounded and brutalized by Irish immigrants with the same religion (Barrett and Roediger 2005). An ethnic identity consolidating the mutually antagonistic regional populations and diverse dialects of the Italian peninsula was, arguably, not a mere survival of European conditions but a creature of immigration and of the multiethnic and pluri-racial American condition. The simultaneous arrivals from diverse parts of the Italian peninsula in the same urban US neighborhoods created opportunities to work together in the same industries and to cooperate in the service of their domestic needs (e.g., Yancey, Ericksen, and Juliani 1976).

Even more deliberately, the Yoruba revivalist kingdom of Oyotunji, in Beaufort County, South Carolina, has created a new African American subculture based on a deft blend of the signifying practices of Cuban priests of Ocha, Africanist anthropologists, African American political nationalists, and tourists of all colors. Oyotunji gains symbolic capital by dignifying a cultural standard that, unlike the mass culture in the United States, normalizes Blackness. But they also hope to draw tourist dollars and must speak a language understood by potential tourists. A roadside sign announces the presence of "Oyotunji African Village . . . As Seen on T.V.!"

Similarly, I argue that Gullah/Geechee culture is an evolving product of interaction rather than of primordial isolation. The formalization of its defining boundaries is the product of deliberate work, much of it taking place in nearby schools and faraway universities. What most scholars describe as the lapse of Gullah/Geechee isolation since the 1950s has threatened some aspects of Gullah/Geechee cultural reproduction but vastly enhanced others. Moreover, this so-called lapse of isolation was actually one of multiple historical changes over time in the terms of Gullah/Geechee interaction with others. The critical feature of this latest change might not be the loss of *isolation* as such but the *loss of land and of access to maritime resources*, which are not and should not be necessary results of increased interaction. Here I will consider the uncertain evidence that the recent dispersion and out-migration of some Gullah/Geechees threatens the endurance of their creole language variety. However, I will also offer evidence that out-migration and subsequent return—along with tourism and the proliferation of outsiders' scholarship about this population—have precipitated an unprecedented degree of cultural self-awareness, canonization of tradition, and pride, as well as profit, in Gullah/Geechee speech, foodways, handicrafts, and history. "Gullah/Geechee culture," as such, is a product of *interaction and return*, and, far from dying out, "Gullah/Geechee culture" has now become a potent university-subsidized weapon in the struggle to maintain landownership and access to resources. Perhaps for the same reasons, it is an ineffective vehicle for the propagation of bourgeois identity within the university: as evidence of an indigenist claim to collective land rights, it relies on an image of ethnographic changelessness and nonassimilation to Euro-American bourgeois norms.

In sum, the following revision of Gullah/Geechee cultural history challenges a central explanatory principle in the literature—that isolation is the cause of Gullah/Geechee ethnic distinctiveness and the necessary precondition of African cultural "survival" in the United States. This revision arises from the inconsistent evidence found within that literature, as well as the comparative example of multiple black Atlantic cases, in which the colonized and the enslaved have created distinctive African-inspired cultures and identities amid daily dealings with non-Africans and in full knowledge of non-African cultural alternatives. This argument also highlights and calls for self-consciousness about the Eurocentric logic of much cultural nationalism, including the forms articulated by black ethnics in the United States and propagated by the Howard University curriculum.

By way of comparison, the West African Yoruba ethnic identity came about in the mid-nineteenth century not as a result of the isolation of the Yoruba's ancestors from other populations but as a direct result of their encounters with Hausa people (who coined the name "Yoruba" in reference to the largest proto-Yoruba polity, Ọyọ), slave traders (who classified the captives who embarked at Lagos as though they belonged to a single peoplehood), the British Royal Navy (which rescued thousands of Ọ̀yọ́, Èkìtì, Ẹ̀gbá, Ẹ̀gbádò, Ìjẹ̀bú, and other "recaptives" and settled them together in Freetown), returnees from Freetown (who reduced to writing a language variety comprehensible to all of these antecedent populations), and African returnees from Cuba and Brazil (who settled and virtually built the core of Lagos, the cultural capital of the emergent Yoruba identity). In fact, even the regions of today's Yorubaland that are most isolated from European influence have, for many centuries, been crossroads of mutual influence and intercourse with the ancestors of the Nupe, the Hausa, and the other peoples of the Islamic world (J. L. Matory 1999), not to mention the Ewe, Gen, Aja, and Fon speakers, the Edo speakers, the Itsekiri and others. Ojo (2009) adds that, in the nineteenth century, the southward flight of multiple ethnic groups from northern, Fulani conquerors and regional wars promoted a mixing of the previously separated populations who came to be called "Yoruba." This convergence under duress further consolidated the new identity.

The foremost symbol of Yoruba ethnic identity, which did not exist before the mid-1800s, has been the reduction of the diverse and sometimes mutually unintelligible Ọ̀yọ́, Ìjẹ̀bú, Èkìtì, Ẹ̀gbádò, and Ẹ̀gbá—as well as the diasporan Sierra Leonean Aku, Cuban Lucumí, and Brazilian Nagô—language varieties to a single, hybrid language written in Roman script. The Bible written in this language by bilingual Anglophile black missionaries from Freetown and the cultural nationalist literature of the Lagosian Cultural Renaissance, written in response to a rising tide of British racism in the 1890s, were charters of Yoruba culture and identity as we know them now. Cross-culturally, Bible translations by university-educated scholars have often been canonical, establishing the linguistic standards of previously amorphous dialect clusters and thus defining both the boundaries of nations and ethnic groups and the standards by which educated elites from these groups distinguish themselves from their provincial class inferiors (J. L. Matory 1999).

Equally surprising is the case of the Afro-Brazilian Candomblé religion. Often identified as the most powerful manifestation of African culture in the Americas, Candomblé is as much indebted to an ongoing dialogue among priests, trans-Atlantic merchants, Lagosian cultural nationalists, Brazilian nationalists, and American feminists as it is to the alleged memory of a pristine and isolated African past (J. L. Matory 2005a).

Such classical exemplars of Black Atlantic culture demonstrate three cross-cultural facts of social life. First, the units of collective action and meaning making that we call "cultures" are not self-existent entities. They are not "islands" of sui generis distinction and internal homogeneity awaiting subsequent discovery by outsiders. Rather, each is a unique intersection, interpretation, adaptation, convergence of translocal flows, and family of interpretations thereof.

Second, the typical telltale signs of ethnicity—that is, the consciousness and enforcement of hereditary difference through endogamy and child rearing—become a named reality only when and where one population has a material incentive to distinguish itself intergenerationally from a copresent population.

Third, the copresence of populations regularly results in each group's imitating the other's practices. Cultural distinction is therefore an act of will and of selective attention. Hence, isolation is neither the norm of culture making nor even a possible condition of ethnic identity formation. Much less is isolation the normal condition of cultural or ethnic endurance.

The people who today embrace the "Gullah/Geechee" designation perhaps provide the most surprising example of these cross-cultural patterns. According to historian Dale Rosengarten, this term, which implies that the Gullahs and the Geechees are essentially the same people or are simply geographical variants of the same African-descended ethnic group, is a recent coinage (according to her, Georgians historically favored the term "Geechees"). In the past, according to Rosengarten, some local people have actually used the term "Gullah" to contrast the local black population with the local white one, which the same local people call "Geechees." Moreover, the use of "Gullah" and "Geechee" as self-ascribed identities came about only in the past thirty years (Dale Rosengarten, personal communication, May 2, 2007).

There is much ambiguity in the meaning of these terms and much debate over their dignity. In 1970, for example, when a program produced by South Carolina Educational Television described the local tradition of artistic basketry as "Gullah," most of the basket sewers—the producers of the most highly prized material emblem of this emergent identity—vehemently objected. They took the term as an insult referring to their despised rural social status. The disambiguation and dignification of these terms have been products of literacy, of cross-class and cross-cultural conversation, and of the encroaching threat to Gullah/Geechee landholdings.

In the early nineteenth century, "Gullah" was used to describe a person from Angola. For example, "Gullah Jack" was the name of a conspirator in Denmark Vesey's 1822 slave insurrection in Charleston. Since the 1890s, a period that Hobsbawm and Ranger (1983) credit with a worldwide proliferation of "invented" identities, local white populations have regarded the referent population as possessing a distinctive lifeway and folklore worthy of a distinct name and worthy of study (Dale Rosengarten, personal communication, May 2, 2007). Researchers in the twentieth century applied "Gullah" not only to the distinctive coastal language but also to a whole range of customs and beliefs related to religion, cuisine, domestic architecture, basketry, and other crafts, as well as "intangible traits, such as motor habits, modes of behavior, and social institutions" (Bascom 1941, 48–49). Hence, as in the Yoruba case, outsiders were the first to identify the Lowcountry population as a single culture and ethnic group. Insiders' self-conception as such followed decades of interaction with these outsiders and nowadays frequently cites as exemplary the forms of cultural conduct first canonized by outsider scholars and missionaries. It is not unusual for an ethnonym now fully embraced by its referents to have started as an epithet first applied by outsiders. Indeed, the Hausa people's use of the term "Yoruba" was originally derogatory.

According to Eltis et al. (1999), 165,429 enslaved Africans disembarked in the Carolinas and Georgia between the late 1600s and 1866. Among their descendants are the approximately 500,000 people who today speak the distinctive Gullah/Geechee language variety in the Sea Islands, the southeastern coast, and their diaspora in other parts of the United States (Pollitzer 2005b, D7; Hargrove 2005, F11). The Gullah/Geechee people descend from the enslaved Africans who built and sustained the lucrative rice plantations in the marshy coastlands and inland estuaries between the Cape Fear River in North Carolina and the Saint John's River near Jacksonville, Florida—collectively called the "Lowcountry." These enslaved Africans also built and sustained the indigo and long-staple cotton farms of the seventy-nine offshore barrier islands of Georgia and South Carolina.

Though the Sea Islands are generally represented as the heartland of the Gullah/Geechees' distinctive culture, the Gullah/Geechee people represent a significant proportion of the African American population in the thirty-mile-wide coastal strip of the mainland from southern North Carolina to northern Georgia. Gullah/Geechee-speakers are most concentrated in the rural areas and small towns of South Carolina, such as Sandy Island, Planterville, and McClellanville. However, major populations are found also in Georgetown and Charleston in South Carolina and in Savannah, Georgia, as well as northern Florida, Oklahoma, and New York City (National Park Service 2005; Opala n.d.; Dale Rosengarten, personal communication, March 26, 2007).

The shared premise of much scholarship on the Gullah/Geechee people— and the major reason they receive so much attention—is that they are reputedly the most culturally and genetically African among the descendants of populations enslaved in the United States (National Park Service 2005, 13, 100; Pollitzer 2005a). Indeed, scholars have traced the terms "Gullah" and "Geechee" to various African origins—above all among the peoples of West and West-Central Africa. On the one hand, the term "Geechee" has been linked to the Ogeechee River in coastal Georgia (Sengova 2006, 214; Hargrove 2005, F4) and to the "Kissi" (pronounced GEE-see) people of Liberia (L. Turner [1949] 1973, 194). On the other hand, "Gullah" might derive from the name of the "Gola" people of what is now Liberia, one subregion of the West African rice belt from which South Carolinian rice planters actively sought to acquire skilled rice growers, or from "Galo," the Sierra Leonean Mende people's term for the Vai people (L. Turner [1949] 1973, 194; Creel 1988, 17–18; Opala n.d.). Both the Vai and the Mende now live in the rice-growing lands of Sierra Leone. Alternatively, "Gullah" might derive from "Ngola"—the source of the term "Angola" and the title of the ruler of the Mbundu people in what is now Angola. The Mbundu people may have grown even more rice than did their more famously rice-growing West African contemporaries (Wood 1974, 59). The European and Euro-American slave traffickers attached the label "Angola" to the largest ethnically named category of people forcibly brought through the port of Charleston (Creel 1988, 15, 30–31, 37; Wood 1974, 59, 302, 333–41; Joyner [1984] 1985: 14, 205–6). Despite the well-documented use of this term since the early nineteenth century to captives from Angola, and for reasons that I will discuss below, the "Angola" people are systematically neglected in current discussions of the African roots of Gullah/Geechee culture. In sum, the social connections and research venues of non-Gullah/Geechee, university-trained researchers have given a new and selective focus to the Gullah/Geechees' own sense of their historical roots and of their contemporary African kinship networks.

Turning Shame into Name:
On the Exemplary Africanness of the Gullah/Geechee Culture

The objections of Howard sociologist E. Franklin Frazier notwithstanding (1942, 1943, [1957] 1974), Melville J. Herskovits ([1941] 1958) established the principle that African American cultural distinctiveness might be traced to a distinctively African cultural legacy—rather than to African Americans' deficient acquisition of the Euro-American standard, whether by reason of black intellectual inferiority or white oppression. Like Howard University law professor and jurist Thurgood Marshall, Frazier attributed African American distinctiveness to the effects of slavery and discrimination. On the other hand, inspired by Herskovits, formerly Howard-based linguist Lorenzo Turner ([1949] 1973); anthropologists William Bascom (1941) and Joseph Opala (n.d.); historians Peter Wood (1974), Daniel C. Littlefield ([1981] 1991), and Dale Rosengarten ([1986] 1987); geographer Judith A. Carney (2001); art historian John Michael Vlach (1990); and others have assembled copious evidence that not only the language of the Gullah/Geechees but also their eighteenth-century ancestors' rice-growing skills, their manufacture and use of baskets, their rice-processing mortars and pestles, their methods of animal husbandry, their fishing tools and techniques, their sacred music and rituals of burial and worship, their folktales, their magical practices, and their devotion to their kin are deeply indebted to West and West-Central African precedents.

For example, the ancestors of the Gullah/Geechees are identified as the originators of free-range cattle keeping in North America, which proved more adaptive to the Lowcountry landscape than did the time-honored English methods, as well as the skills in rice growing and processing that made that agricultural industry possible (Wood 1974, 30–31). The Gullah/Geechees' apparently distinctive beliefs about affliction and death, as well as the medical and ritual practices they have employed in their management, are also widely assumed to derive from African sources (Bascom 1941, 49; Creel 1988; Opala n.d., "Gullah Customs and Traditions"; Pollitzer 2005b, D31–D33; Hargrove 2005, F25; Joyner [1984] 1985, 138, 142–43, 150–55), though some scholars have documented important European and Euro-American models for African-looking Gullah/Geechee practices and important Euro-American suppliers of their raw materials. Equally evident are the long-running interaction of the Gullah/Geechees with other African American populations and the cosmopolitan *creativity* of Gullah/Geechee healing practices (C. Long 2001, esp. 95–96, 122, 150–51, 249; Chireau 2003, 215–16).

Gullah/Geechee people are most famous in the scholarly literature for their distinctive language variety—Gullah, or Sea Island Creole—which, despite its largely English-derived lexicon, is difficult for most English-speaking Americans to understand. Scholars recognize the Gullah language as a creole deeply influenced by West African phonetics, vocabulary, grammar, naming practices, and narrative forms (L. Turner [1949] 1973; Mufwene and Gilman 1987; *The Language You Cry In* 1998; National Park Service 2005, 55–58; Pollitzer 2005b, D20–D28; Hargrove 2005, F6–F11; Sengova 2006; Joyner [1984] 1985, 209–10).

While some scholars emphasize the qualitative difference between Gullah/Geechee language and culture and those of other Black North Americans (Hargrove 2005, F3, F6, F7; Sengova 2006), Herskovits established the comparative framework within which the Gullah/Geechees' cultural history is usually assessed. Assuming that the cultures of the West African Fon, Yoruba, and Ashanti (as reconstructed in the "ethnographic present") represent the extant base line, or starting point, of African American cultural history, Herskovits's "ethnohistorical" method, or "social laboratory," posits that less acculturated African-diaspora groups, such as Afro-Bahians and Surinamese Maroons, reveal the stages and intermediate forms through which African cultural traditions had been "transmuted" into their counterparts among more highly acculturated African-diaspora groups, such as the African Americans of the United States. Thus, as one such intermediate form, spirit possession in the Afro-Brazilian Candomblé religion could be taken to demonstrate the African derivation of "shouting," or the behavior of those "filled with the Holy Spirit," in Gullah/Geechee and other Black North American churches, like my maternal grandfather's Church of God in Christ (Herskovits [1941] 1958, 220–21). According to Herskovits's "scale of intensity of Africanisms," Black North Americans in general were a step ahead of various less acculturated Caribbean and Latin American populations of African descent. Moreover, he regarded the Black Americans in northern US cities as a step ahead of those in the South—prominently including the Gullah/Geechees (J. L. Matory 2005a, 11). Dozens of scholars have usefully employed Herskovits's "ethnohistorical" method in the study of African American culture and acculturation to Euro-American lifeways.

Since Gullah/Geechee ways appear to be the most conspicuously African of African American lifeways, scholars of African American culture tend to look to Gullah/Geechee culture for the classical origins of African American language, religious practice, sacred music, dance, and cuisine in general. For example, since the mid-nineteenth century, travelers and northern teachers among the Gullah/Geechees have described an African-looking ritual called the "ring shout." Following the normal church, or "praise house," service, fully ordained members of the praise house often engaged in an accelerating circle dance, accompanied by singing and clapping. The ring shout culminated in the ecstatic descent of the Holy Spirit (e.g., Creel 1988, 297–301; Southern [1971] 1983, 169–71; National Park Service 2005, 69–70; Hargrove 2005, F12–F13). Generations of African Americanist scholars have represented the ring shout, along with the call-and-response pattern of Gullah/Geechee spirituals, as the classical forms of African American religious practice, musical performance, and even political community building (e.g., Sobel [1979] 1988, 140–48; Stuckey 1987; Creel 1988; Gomez 1998; R. Long 2005, 103).[2]

Herskovits and his generation of anthropologists were interested in the conditions that caused some colonized or formerly enslaved populations to assimilate European culture faster or slower than others. Why, they asked, did the Gullah/Geechees and their ancestors "retain" so much more African culture than did other African American populations? Researchers have offered multiple explanations.

First, the South Carolina landscape is said to resemble that of the West African Rice Coast, allowing the African captives to adapt their own technically sophisticated African methods of exploiting the coastal salt marshes to their own and their masters' needs (e.g., *Family across the Sea* 1991).

Second, the Lowcountry hosted a range of tropical diseases to which Africans were more resistant than whites, keeping the local white population seasonally itinerant and generally small in numbers (e.g., Creel 1988, 34; Pollitzer 2005b, D3-D4, D9; Wood 1974, 63-91). Moreover, the demands of rice production created plantations with some of the largest numbers of enslaved people in North America. At the time of the British North American colonies' War of Independence, half of all South Carolinians were of African descent (Wood 1974, xvi; Joyner 1985, 205), and they were concentrated on the Lowcountry coast and neighboring islands. The colonial and antebellum Lowcountry had the highest concentration of black people with the least frequent exposure to whites in mainland North America, thus facilitating the "survival" of African culture.

The third reason commonly given for the intensity of Africanisms (and for the relative purity of African ancestry) among the Gullah/Geechees is that Africans continued arriving in South Carolina until an unusually late date by North American standards—1858 (e.g., Creel 1988, 193; National Park Service 2005, 51) or 1866 (Eltis et al. 1999). Hence, in the Lowcountry, African culture was repeatedly renewed from its sources until the eve of the Civil War or even later.

Fourth, the unusual terms of slave labor in the Lowcountry are said to have contributed to the retention of African culture. In most of the South, enslaved people worked in gangs in which no field worker's duties were finished until the workday of the entire gang had ended. On the Lowcountry rice plantations, by contrast, each worker was assigned a "task," or a specific amount of work. If the enslaved person completed it quickly and efficiently, he or she could use the surplus time to assist others, cultivate his or her private plot, or engage in leisure activities that embodied his or her own African cultural preferences, rather than the master's European ones (e.g., National Park Service 2005, 37-41; Joyner 1985, 127-34). Carney (2001) believes that the "task" system itself originated in Africa.

Isolation?

The foregoing multifactor explanation of Gullah/Geechee cultural history leaves hardly a base uncovered and has a great deal to truth to recommend it. Yet it is usually marred by a misleading summary and refrain—a shibboleth so common in the literature that scholars have overlooked its inconsistency with, for example, the well-publicized facts of the waterborne trade in the Lowcountry and of the century-old boom in Gullah/Geechee commercial basketry for non–Gullah/Geechee homemakers, tourists, and museums. This shibboleth is "isolation." In explanations for the endurance and intensity of Africanness in the culture of the Geechee/Gullahs, hardly any word arises more often.[3] For example, Turner writes, "The African speech habits of the earliest Gullahs were being constantly strengthened throughout the eighteenth century and the first half of the nineteenth by contact with the speech of native Africans who were coming direct from Africa and who were sharing with the older Gullahs the *isolation* of the Sea Islands—a condition which obviously made easier the retention of Africanisms in that area than in places where Negroes had less direct contact with Africa and lived less *isolated* lives" (L. Turner [1949] 1973, 5; emphasis mine). Writes David DeCamp, "Gullah remained a relatively pure creole because its speakers were so geographically and socioeconomically *isolated*" (quoted in Turner [1949] 1973, ix; emphasis mine).

Other authors have extended the principle that isolation preserves creole languages to their reasoning about the creation and survival of Gullah/Geechee culture generally. Thus, William Pollitzer writes, "Their *isolation* on the Sea Islands permitted development of their unique culture" (Pollitzer 2005b, D9; emphasis mine). Indeed, the authors of the most comprehensive study of Gullah/Geechee culture to date also make the most comprehensive and absolute claim: "The *isolation* of sea island communities from outsiders was *vital* to the survival of Gullah/Geechee community cultures" (National Park Service 2005, 13; emphasis mine).

The term "isolation" summarizes the alleged effects of the geographical distance of the Sea Islanders from the mainland, the flight of colonial-era planters during the season of mosquito-borne diseases, the year-round paucity of whites (until recently) on the Sea Islands, and legal segregation. Such isolation is represented as the major obstacle to the forms of acculturation that would otherwise, according to this theory, have wiped out African-inspired culture in the Lowcountry. African culture and the creolized forms in which it is most evident are thus represented as products of conservatism and as inherently less appealing or powerful than the culturally unmarked but truly European-inspired lifeways that—had they been highly visible to the ancestors of the Gullah/Geechees—would have replaced their African-inspired culture.

This assumption illustrates the ambivalence of the HBCU and of the university generally toward the "folk." These institutions appreciate the distinctive lifeways of the "folk" for whom they speak, but they assume that the adopted language and conduct of the university-educated *assimilé* are uniquely practical, attractive, metropolitan, and useful to the group. The "folk" are dignified by the university scholar, but only as mascots in the ethnonationalist, developmentalist project. However, the main problem with the isolation hypothesis is not political or ethical but empirical.

The case for the principle that isolation contributes to *linguistic* distinction seems, intuitively, stronger than the case for its role in other forms of cultural distinction, but various real-world cases undermine even the linguistic principle. For example, it is well known that dialects diversify and proliferate the most within the often small and demographically concentrated confines of their geographical origin, not where large distances allow the greatest separation among the speakers of different dialects. Moreover, creole languages like Haitian Kreyòl, Jamaican Patwa, and Cape Verdean Kriolu thrive in the poor Black neighborhoods of the eastern United States, where they are transformed from the symbols of poverty and low status, which they had been in their respective homelands, into symbols of national pride in the diaspora and of distinction from and superiority to the immigrants' even more stigmatized African American neighbors. At Howard, in what I take to be the same spirit, two Jamaican students living in the East Tower dormitory with Adu and me often loudly dominated the elevator space with their Patwa. Once they entered, no other conversation could happen in the shared chamber. In such cases, the management of *interaction* with the people of other languages and cultures, rather than the fact of *isolation* from them, has kept African-influenced creole languages very much alive.[4]

For its part, AAVE has now been marketed and disseminated across class, regional, and national boundaries through the global music industry. Such cosmopolitan marketing has resulted not in the death of this distinctive language variety but in its elaboration and the constant, creative renewal of its lexical difference from "standard" American English. For at least the past fifty years, no American young person or adult man has been considered hip or culturally up to date without being able to speak a little of this distinctive dialect. But, like upper-class culture, it continually changes in order to avoid the homogenizing consequences of imitation by the masses. As a result, AAVE is very different from one generation to the next.

It is even less obvious that actual cases of isolation among African-diaspora cultures have, as a general rule, resulted in or from cultural conservatism. Indeed, among African-diaspora cultures, some of the most radical cultural inventiveness and transformation is observed among relatively isolated populations, such as Haitian peasants (see, for example, Métraux ([1959] 1972) and the Surinam Maroons (e.g., Price and Price 1999; Bastide [1967] 1971; J. L. Matory 2005a). On the other hand, movements advocating the preservation or restoration of unadulteratedly African religion in the Americas tend to originate and flourish most at the lively cultural and commercial crossroads that are Bahia, São Paulo, Miami, and New York. Also consider the highly visible case of Hasidic Jews in New York City and Israel. Will alone is sufficient to keep them culturally and socially distinct from numerous in-crowding neighbors. Cultural conservativism and restorationism (which, once naturalized by its protagonists, looks like conservatism) seem to hold the greatest appeal not for isolated populations but for populations that have a powerful set of nearby demographic or political forces to fight against. A hypothesis with much evidence to recommend it is that populations make a conscious effort to restore or not to change old ways chiefly when they are at risk of being overwhelmed or materially disadvantaged by absorption into their cosmopolitan surroundings.

Yet in the study of Gullah/Geechee language and culture generally, most authors invoke "isolation" as a preeminent cause of Gullah/Geechee linguistic and cultural Africanness. On the contrary, it seems to me that it is not isolation but the distinctive terms of the Gullah/Geechees' interaction—as landowners, merchants, pupils, subjects of a philanthropic "experiment" in social uplift, symbols in the folkloric self-fashioning of other populations, and lobbyists for land rights or for their own distinctive role in the marketplace—that are producing a proudly distinctive, modern, and no less African-inspired identity. Hence, in this chapter, I both question the degree to which the Gullah/Geechees and their ancestors have been isolated and propose that the Africanness of their lifeway and of their ethnic identity are indebted more to this population's cosmopolitanness and dynamism than to its isolation. And schooling has been a critical element of that cosmopolitanism.

This chapter challenges the premise—hitherto adduced even more confidently in the Gullah/Geechee case than in the equally dubious cases of Cuban Ocha, Brazilian Candomblé, Louisiana Creole culture, and Nigerian Yoruba identity—that isolation is the chief factor preserving African-inspired culture and producing distinctive ethnic identities generally in a post-Columbian world. This argument also compels us to rethink the nature of Native American, Caribbean, and African cultural distinction, further topics of the chapters to come. The assumption that even *relative* isolation and, by extension, ignorance about non-African alternatives are the normal conditions for the "retention" of African culture in the Americas belies not only the particulars of Gullah/Geechee history—including the cosmopolitan history of Gullah/Geechee rice technology and commerce—but also the overall historical patterns of the black Atlantic world.[5]

For example, colonial and antebellum South Carolina was more actively engaged with the world economy than were most other British North American colonies and their successor states—through its early provisioning of ships and of Caribbean sugar plantations, the slave trade and the maritime trade in rice, indigo, and highly prized long-staple cotton (Littlefield 1991, 2). Far from isolated, this region in the seventeenth and eighteenth centuries received major transshipments of people and ideas not only from diverse ports of West and West-Central Africa but also from the anglophone Caribbean and, at the turn of the nineteenth century, from Haiti, as islanders of all colors fled the Haitian Revolution (Wood 1974, 6; National Park Service 2005, 21; C. Long 2001, 89; Joyner 1985, 205, 207). In the seventeenth and eighteenth centuries, South Carolina was not one of the least-connected but one of the best-connected British colonies and US states.

Far from being isolated, the eighteenth-century incubator of Gullah/Geechee culture was home to not only the bearers of a vast array of African cultures but also French Huguenots and English Quakers, Scots, Irish, Swiss, Dutch, Sephardic Jews, Bahamians and Barbadians, and Creek and Cherokee Indians (Joyner 1985, 207; Meinig 1986, 176–90; Pollitzer [1999] 2005a, 7). The Gullah/Geechees' ancestors were also well aware of the proximity of the Spanish in Florida, among whom runaways knew they could find safe haven (National Park Service 2005, 23–26). The Lowcountry African population included excellent speakers of English, Spanish, Portuguese, French, German, Dutch, and Chickasaw (Littlefield 1991, 132–34). One 1763 runaway slave advertisement describes, for example, "a Negro man named LUKE . . . [who] has been used to the seas [and] speaks English, French, Spanish and Dutch" (Dutarque 1983, 231).

The enslaved were not only intelligent but also mobile. Few of them belonged from birth to death to one master; thus any given captive might know, influence, and be influenced by several plantation subcultures (Wood 1974, 253; cf. Ojo 2009). Captives sometimes moved long distances—as a condition of their service to their masters, as a function of their social lives, and sometimes in temporary or permanent flight from slavery (e.g., Littlefield

1991, 133). In the eighteenth century, *mariners* constituted 9 percent of South Carolina's skilled slaves, and they greatly facilitated the mobility of Black nonsailors as well (Bolster 1997, 21–23, 155–56).

Contrary to the supposition that nineteenth-century antebellum Gullah/Geechees were isolated, they appear to have participated actively in a circum-Caribbean maritime flow of people and revolutionary ideas (see Gaspar and Geggus 1997). For example, the National Park Service reports: "One of the best-known rebellions was attempted in 1821 [*sic*]. Denmark Vesey, a literate and charismatic free Negro who lived in Charleston, planned the insurrection. *He was familiar with the Haitian slave revolt and kept in touch with black leaders there.* Vesey recruited a band of between 6,600 and 9,000 Negro men during the four years of planning. They met in secrecy at a farm which *could be reached by water* so that they could avoid the slave patrols" (National Park Service 2005, 26; emphasis mine; the actual date of the planned revolt was 1822).

A setting in which Vesey and his prominent coconspirator "Gullah Jack" could communicate with the leaders of the Haitian Revolution and coordinate the convergence of thousands of men by boat would be difficult to describe as "isolated." Not until after the defeat of Vesey's conspiracy were the Black seamen who disembarked in Charleston imprisoned to prevent their movement about the city (National Park Service 2005, 26–27). They had previously enjoyed considerable freedom of movement and interaction with the city's diverse population.

Not even after 1822 could locally enslaved and free people be kept from moving about and crisscrossing the numerous local waterways of the region. Indeed, the local economy depended on their mobility. The barrier-island-protected creeks, salt flats, and rivers of what would become Gullah/Geechee country afforded its inhabitants considerable mobility among the islands and between the islands and the cosmopolitan cities of the mainland. The enslaved and their free descendants long used these waterways to move about and to barter and sell their farm and maritime produce, as well as their basketry, all across the region (e.g., National Park Service 2005, 38, 45; Hargrove 2005, F23; Rosengarten [1986] 1987, 22–25). Consequently, Richard Long (2005) describes the Charleston Market as a "geographical extension and high profile site" of "the Gullah world" (103). It strikes me as odd, in principle, that a coastal people, whose homeland neighbors a major port and is crisscrossed by highly navigable marshes and rivers, would be considered isolated relative to, say, to residents of the inland mountains, valleys, forests, and prairies where some Black North American settlements are found. Navigable water does not isolate islands, and islands are not really insular. Like the Mississippi

River, the Mediterranean Sea, the Indian Ocean, the River Niger, and even the Sahara Desert, the navigable tidewaters of the Lowcountry have long facilitated long-distance connections.

Moreover, even the most African-looking of Gullah/Geechee cultural projects have flourished amid long-distance commercial contact with a far-flung clientele of non-Gullah/Geechees. For example, the most famous Gullah/Geechee "root doctors" are said to have possessed imported African ritual objects (Pinckney [1998] 2003, 50, 92), which suggests anything but isolation (pace Pinckney [1998] 2003, 7). Root doctors employed herbs and performed rituals to heal their clients physically, to protect them from harm, and to harm their own and their clients' enemies. Even at the postbellum height of the Gullah/Geechees' putative isolation, highways and ferries brought cars full of non-Gullah/Geechee clients from distant states to consult with root doctors in their supposedly isolated island redoubts (Pinckney 2003, 94, 93, 104; C. Long 2001, 94), and their Gullah/Geechee magic was well amplified by complementary European and Euro-American spell books, such as *The Great Book of Magical Art, Hindu Magic, and East Indian Occultism* (1902) by Lauron William De Laurence and *The Sixth and Seventh Books of Moses* (1910) (C. Long 2001, 14–16, 121–22). During the early 1980s, the latter book was even available for purchase in the bookstore of the University of Ibadan in Nigeria, suggesting that some West Africans, too, found such texts congenial to their spiritual practices and that black Atlantic spirituality is cosmopolitan, even at its putative "roots." The US Postal Service severely limited Gullah/Geechee isolation, making such books easily available in the Lowcountry and making Lowcountry magic available all across the country (Pinckney 2003, 93–94; C. Long 2001, 150–51).[6] The *appearance* of remoteness and exotic origin is an extremely common element of credible magic—no less among Gullah/Geechee root doctors than among West African Yoruba healers. This appearance is easily conflated with isolation, but it actually bespeaks the opposite.

Despite his mystique of isolation, the most famous Gullah/Geechee root doctor, Dr. Buzzard (Mr. Stephaney Robinson), specialized in the resolution of court cases, and he possessed a sophisticated knowledge of how to circumvent the state's efforts to restrict his practice (Pinckney [1998] 2003, 93, 99). On the other hand, Dr. Buzzard's colleague and contemporary Dr. Bug (Mr. Peter Murray) was caught supplying "roots" to cause his clients heart palpitations. Of his case, Pinckney writes, "After the arrest and incarceration of Dr. Bug for helping Gullah draftees fail their physicals for induction into the military, dozens, and perhaps hundreds, of young men went to root doctors in an effort to foreshorten World War II before their inductions. It is commonly believed that the atomic bomb was the result" (58). Thus, Gullah/Geechee root work thrived not in isolation but—like much else in Gullah/Geechee cultural history—in the context and consciousness of state law and of international politics, history, and business.

During and after the US Civil War, the ancestors of the Gullah/Geechees had experienced an earlier and more intensive engagement with northern military officials, administrators, missionaries, and teachers (through the famous "Port Royal Experiment") than virtually any other southern population. Since then, no African American population has participated in the social-scientific, musical, and literary projects of a more diverse array of partisan outsiders than have the Gullah/Geechees. These outsiders have included, over time, officials of the Freedmen's Bureau, nostalgic southern white folklorists, fiction writers, curio merchants, commercial gallery owners, northern white philanthropists, Black and white schoolteachers, ministers of the African Methodist Episcopal Church, museum staff, Broadway musicians and composers, and non-Gullah/Geechee African American scholars (National Park Service 2005, 71, 82, 102; Hargrove 2005, F32). The Gullah/Geechees' only rivals of similarly small demographic size are the Louisiana Creoles of color, who illustrate the similarly axiom-breaking combination of a highly African-influenced culture and a long history of maritime commerce and travel, early occupation by the Union army, intensive study by outsider artists, folklorists, teachers, and social scientists, and a strong sense of ethnic distinctness amid vast interaction with ethnic others.

Conventional explanations of the postbellum "preservation" of the Gullah/Geechees' distinctive and African-inspired culture similarly overlook evidence of the geographical mobility and extraracial social dynamics in that culture. While at least one widely cited author dates Gullah/Geechee "isolation" from the eighteenth century (Pollitzer 2005b, D20), most authors who specify a time period suggest that the Gullah/Geechees' ancestors were most intensely "isolated" after the Civil War, when they experienced a stability of population, practice, and belief that was disrupted only by the construction of bridges between the Sea Islands and the mainland in the 1950s. After the fifties, new resorts and suburbs displaced many Gullah/Geechees from their land and diminished their opportunities for self-employment in the fishing industry. Instead, they had to take wage-paying jobs in better-capitalized companies (e.g., National Park Service 2005, 82; Hargrove 2005, F5, F36–F40; Pollitzer 2005b, D49).

However, there are alternative ways of reading the effects of these events on Gullah/Geechee cultural history. Far from creating or restoring Gullah/Geechee isolation, the postbellum period was characterized by new types of movement in and out of the Gullah/Geechee zone—on the part of nostalgic southern whites (such as Ambrose Gonzales, DuBose Heyward, and Julia Peterkin), Afro-Philadelphian teacher and writer Charlotte Forten, Afro-North Carolinian professor Lorenzo Dow Turner, basket wholesalers and retailers, and the Gullah/Geechee merchants of Sea Island produce and seafood, who sold their merchandise from a range of venues in Charleston, including the famous Charleston Market. Such movement was the raw material of much shame and pride, of exploitation and opportunity, of offensive stereotyping and retrospective canonization among generations of Gullah/Geechees. Gullah/Geechee culture has emerged from dynamic crosscurrents, not a still backwater. Since the colonial period, Gullah/Geechee merchants and labor migrants—slave and free—have repeatedly left and returned to the region. Since the civil rights movement, some have left and returned as the most vociferous spokespersons of Gullah/Geechee cultural nationalism (National Park Service 2005, 52, 84, 95–96). Indeed, the most prestigious and celebrated of the living basket sewers is a returnee from New York, Mary Jackson (Rosengarten, Rosengarten, and Schildkrout 2008, 142).

Not only the ideas of university scholars but also the Lowcountry schools themselves have helped to foster the distinctive and African ways of the Gullah/Geechees. Schooling, at institutions like Penn School and at universities far away, has done more to staff the leadership and provide the techniques critical to a revival movement than to encourage the abandonment of Gullah/Geechee distinctiveness (e.g., Rosengarten [1986] 1987, 25–27, 29; National Park Service 2005, 118).[7]

It was in 1862 that a largely white group of northern philanthropists, missionaries, and teachers founded, on Saint Helena Island, the Penn Normal School—predecessor to the Penn Normal Industrial and Agricultural School and to its successor, Penn Center, Inc. Penn School was founded to educate the recently freed people of the region in the trades (Hargrove 2005, F32; Rosengarten [1986] 1987, 25–30). Penn School trained its students in carpentry, cobbling, harness making, blacksmithing, wheelwrighting, and basketry—all in conformity to Booker T. Washington's gospel of "industrial education," not W. E. B. Du Bois's aim to train a "Talented Tenth" of race leaders through the liberal arts. Penn's avowed aim was to keep people on the land by giving them reasons to stay there. Teaching them updated agricultural methods, supplementing farm work with income from craft production, and extending financial credit were intended to create an environment of "economic independence and dignified living in their rural communities" (Rosengarten, Rosengarten, and Schildkrout 2008, 129). To Penn's founders, ruralness was not a deficiency but a superior moral and economic option. In some ways,

Gullah/Geechee society is rooted in the same experimental utopianism that drove the founding of new rural communities throughout the United States in the nineteenth century.

To the same degree that the Du Boisian aims of Howard were unfriendly to the Gullah/Geechee self-identity propagated by Penn, its students, and its faculty, Penn School laid some of the cornerstones of that identity by preserving, elaborating, and enshrining the distinctive basketry of this region. They did so by labeling it African and thus establishing it as a venerable connection to a past that had not been otherwise validated and to a rural lifeway now endorsed by missionaries, merchants, scholars, and artists (cf. R. Williams [1973] 1975).

Further, the recent acceleration of communication, transportation, and migration, which have often been blamed for reducing Gullah/Geechee isolation and therefore endangering this people's cultural survival, has actually inspired an *increase* in the Africanness of Gullah/Geechee basketry forms. The basket sewers of Mount Pleasant, South Carolina, now model some of their baskets on forms seen in books about Africa or on crafts brought from Africa by Gullah/Geechee travelers (Rosengarten [1986] 1987, 43; Rosengarten, Rosengarten, and Schildkrout 2008, 143–44). Indeed, the recent proliferation of grassroots lobbying organizations devoted to the rescue of Gullah/Geechee "culture" is less evidence that Gullah/Geechee lifeways are in danger than an instance of the enduring cosmopolitanism and growing strength of an ethnic group ever more comfortable with its cultural distinctiveness and at home in the global "ecumene," or smorgasbord of cultural symbols (Hannerz 1996). Indeed, as the textile factories decamped from the Carolinas to the Third World and the Gullah/Geechees lost out in competition with better-capitalized fishermen and farmers, the sale of "culture," based upon the university-derived and carefully managed imagery of Gullah/Geechee difference, has become one of the better remaining sources of income.

A Comparison

The assumption that isolation explains the "retention" of African culture in the Americas finds little support in the study of the Caribbean and South America, though scholars of the African diaspora have seldom questioned this assumption. For example, Roger Bastide (1983, 242–43) describes Bahia as exceptional in being a large city that retained its African religion with relative purity. Herskovits recognizes Paramaribo, Port-au-Prince, and Bahia as similarly exceptional ([1941] 1958: 115–16, 120, 124). And Newbell Niles Puckett ([1926] 1969: 10–11) represents New Orleans as exceptional. Rather than "exceptions," these numerous urban cases might better be seen as disproving any simple rule (J. L. Matory 2001, 36, 41n5).

Yet this persistent assumption requires especially conscious and critical attention because of what its Western scholarly advocates unreflectively imply about African culture: that people choose African ways of doing things only when they are unaware of non-African alternatives. Two generations of scholarship on the importance of African technology in South Carolina agriculture—including that of Peter H. Wood (1974), John Vlach ([1978] 1990), Daniel Littlefield ([1981] 1991), and Judith Carney (2001)—ought by now to have eliminated this assumption from the intellectual tool kit of African diaspora scholarship.

Moreover, the emphasis on isolation in the genesis of Gullah/Geechee identity places the cart before the horse in the general analysis of how ethnic identities come about in the first place. The isolation model posits that people recognize their difference from others primarily when and where those others are *absent*. In fact, one population tends to recognize and classify its difference from another population *only* when the first population interacts and competes enough with the second population—or has enough power to exclude it from key opportunities—for the imaginable differences between the two populations to make a strategically *useful* difference. That is, ethnic groups arise when populations are close enough to each other to need and value the same things yet different enough in resources, specialties, or political status to form rival or complementary teams in pursuit of them (e.g., Cohen 1969; Barth 1969; Skinner 1975; Schildkrout 1978; Domínguez 1989; Handler 1988). Ethnicity emerges, by its very nature, in *shared* spaces.

Similarly, it might be argued that cultural difference typically arises from the differential interpretation and use of overlapping knowledge, behaviors, and resources. Indeed, as William Bascom (1941) observes, the most prolific Africanisms among the Gullahs (and, I might add, other African-diaspora populations) are not practices and beliefs that primordially *distinguished* Africans from Europeans but areas of *overlap*, or congruence, between African and European cultures. Writes Bascom:

> There were a number of institutions common to both regions [Africa and Europe], including a complex economic system based on money, markets, and middlemen, as well as a large number of crafts among which iron-working was important; a well developed system of government based on kings, and courts of law in which cases were tried by specialists (lawyers) and in which ordeals were employed to decide certain cases; a religious system with a complex hierarchy of priests and deities; a common stock of folklore and a common emphasis on moralizing elements and proverbs. Aside from writing, the

wheel, the plow, and Christianity, most of the distinctive traits of Western civilization seem to have followed the industrial revolution.... Since most African traits of a specific nature have disappeared [among the Gullah/Geechees], what is to be found is, for the most part, a series of institutions which differ from the European forms only in their African flavor. (43–44)

For example, Gullah/Geechee beliefs about hags and ghosts highlight parallels between African and European conceptions (Creel 1988, 313–22; Joyner 1985, 142, 150–51, 153; Pinckney [1998] 2003; C. Long 2001, 14–16).[8] Likewise, both the British Isles and West Africa offer vivid precedents for "shouting," or the ecstatic experience of the divine presence during worship. For example, the nickname "Quakers" for the Society of Friends was inspired by the reputedly convulsive physical gestures observed among the seventeenth-century members of the sect when visited by the Holy Spirit (*Oxford English Dictionary* 1971, 2:2382). One might find these phenomena in different degrees of frequency among Gullahs/Geechees and their white neighbors, but these relative degrees of frequency have long shifted amid changing religious trends and revival movements. For example, the Quakers no longer "quake." Conversely, the banjo—an instrument of African origin—is now played more often by white than by Black Americans. The appeal of *The Great Book of Magical Art, Hindu Magic, and East Indian Occultism* (1902) to Gullah/Geechees and to the many African peoples who converged in Ibadan, Nigeria, in the 1980s begs for explanation in similar terms.

In language, too, similar phonemes, terms, and syntactical structures from the European and African substrate languages of African-diaspora creoles often reinforce each other and even provide pragmatically useful opportunities for creative ambiguity (Reisman 1970; Mufwene and Gilman 1987, 131). For example, the *r*-less word endings of both Gullah and the white brogue of Charleston appear equally indebted to the phonetics of Niger-Congo languages and those of the southern English dialects spoken by most early British settlers of South Carolina (Hunt 2007, 145). In a further example, the Gullah/Geechee phrase *dafa fat*, meaning "excessively fat," has been interpreted etymologically both as "done for fat" (suggesting, in English terms, the fatally deleterious character of the condition) and as a cognate of the West African Vai term *dafa* (meaning "mouth full") added to the English term "fat" (L. Turner [1949] 1973, 14).

African-inspired culture in the Americas often draws strength from its similarities to European-inspired culture or, as in the case of African rice cultivation, its superiority to European techniques in the service of non-Gullah/Geechee, Euro-American needs—in short, from its practitioners' proximity to, rather than isolation from, non-African overlords, neighbors, and clients who needed their skills. Various authors even argue that conversion to Christianity facilitated, rather than halted, the spread of African-inspired magico-religious practices (e.g., Chireau 2003, 53–54; Pinckney [1998] 2003, 73, 111). In many settings, African-inspired medical care has been regarded as more effective and trustworthy than its Euro-American alternatives (e.g., Joyner 1985, 148; Pinckney [1998] 2003, 40). Indeed, whites who live alongside Gullah/Geechees have regularly embraced African-inspired beliefs, behaviors, and expressive genres (e.g., Pinckney [1998] 2003: 17, 97–109, 111; Ritterhouse 2003; C. Long 2001, 150–51 passim; Philips 1990). The Euro-American appropriation of the banjo, rock and roll, hip-hop, and AAVE are similar but more widely discussed examples.

Likewise, the "survival" of foodways seldom depends on the isolation of the people who invented them. For example, Carney (2001, 116) demonstrates the West African origins of the much-advertised cross-racial preference for grain separation—as opposed to stickiness—in US rice cuisine. Moreover, the mapping of ethnic and regional diversity structures the marketing of prepared food in virtually all societies. And recipes travel. For example, thanks to my friend Henrietta Snype of Mount Pleasant, South Carolina, my Cambridge friends and my family acquired a powerful penchant for "swimps and gwits," seasoned to traditional perfection with Lipton Onion Soup Mix. Consequently, we now participate in the propagation of an ethnic identity, a cuisine, and a language that few of us had previously known to exist. In multi-ethnic contexts, distinctive foods and ways of preparing them can also serve as signposts of separation between social groups—both as a rallying point for in-group unity and as a means of excluding those who eat differently—since it is difficult to befriend or marry people bound by different dietary rules and intolerant of different tastes or smells. Thus, cosmopolitan settings spread the knowledge of any given food culture and amplify the semantic and social value of diverse culinary conventions.

Even the most intensive genre of Gullah/Geechee Africanisms relies for its meaning and much of its usefulness upon the copresence of whites and other non-Gullah speakers. By far, the most numerous cognates of African words in Gullah—as identified by Lorenzo Turner and his Niger-Congo-speaking collaborators at London's School of African and Oriental Studies—are "basket names." These are Gullah/Geechee personal names known only to family members and other Gullah/Geechees, in contrast to the English names that are used with strangers, at school, or in written communications (L. Turner [1949] 1973: 40). Thus, the semantic meaning and pragmatic function of "basket names" assumes and depends on the existence of an outsider audience that insiders have occasion to exclude. Gullah/Geechees are, according to Mufwene and Gilman (1987), "generally bidialectal in various varieties of local or standard English" (130). Thus, Gullah/Geechee names and language generally are used not for the lack of an alternative but, often, in order deliberately to convey in-group intimacy or to prevent monolingual English-speakers from understanding a private communication (e.g., Pollitzer 2005b, D29; Sengova 2006, 226; L. Turner [1949] 1973, 11–13). Moreover, as an English or AAVE speaker chooses between a Germanic-origin and a Greek- or Latin-origin term of similar meaning (e.g., "woman" vs. "female" and "white" vs. "Caucasian"), a Gullah/Geechee speaker may undoubtedly use the contrast between Gullah/Geechee words or phrases and English words or phrases of similar meaning to convey finely nuanced messages about his or her thoughts, social relationships, and pragmatic intentions. And just as multiple Iberian dialects have survived centuries of Castilian dominance, Gullah is likely to survive and remain useful in countless projects of meaning making and situational community building in a multiethnic and multicultural world.[9]

Africanisms and White Identity

I would add the general observation that the most vibrant and populous African-inspired cultures in the Americas are not the ones isolated from mainstream Euro-American cultures but those that most effectively employed Western communication and transportation technologies to communicate regularly with Old World Africans (e.g., J. L. Matory 1999). And these African-diaspora cultures are often the ones that look so different from metropolitan Western culture that, as emblems of local authenticity, they become useful in the identity politics of local white elites resisting domination or marginalization by more metropolitan whites. In Brazil, for example, the "socially white"[10] elites of the Northeast, such as psychiatrist Raymundo Nina Rodrigues, anthropologist Gilberto Freyre, and journalist Édison Carneiro, championed Afro-Bahian culture as an emblem of their own legitimacy—and that of Brazil as a whole—in resistance to the Europhile pretensions of the economically dominant white elites of São Paulo and the presumptively Western culture of the United States. The Northeast had once been the economic, political, and cultural center of Brazil. White northeastern regionalists contested their own marginalization by proclaiming the unique authenticity of northeastern black culture and its superiority to the black cultures of São Paulo and the United States, as well as northeastern Brazil's allegedly exemplary embrace of racial hybridity. For proof, these light-colored champions of Afro-Bahian culture often cited information from—and lauded the remarkable professional accomplishments of—the black Brazilian merchants and pilgrims who used steamships to shuttle between prestigiously anglophone Lagos and lusophone Bahia in the nineteenth century. Rodrigues, Freyre, and Carneiro also cited the books published in English by the Yoruba cultural nationalists of Lagos (J. L. Matory 1999).

Similarly, in the wake of the 1898 US invasion of Cuba, Fernando Ortiz made Afro-Cuban culture into an icon of Cuban autonomy and dignity. Postbellum white New Orleanian writers George Washington Cable, Robert Tallant, and Lyle Saxon, among others, documented and sometimes exaggerated the mystery and sensuality of Creole New Orleans. Subsequent generations of white New Orleanians have even understood and marketed themselves to tourists as the scions of a sybaritic aristocracy—cosmopolitan, French-inspired, African-seduced, and just too sophisticated to embrace the moral and racial purism of Protestant America. In the face of US domination and racial chauvinism, Mexican indigenism and the Haitian Bureau d'Éthnologie recounted similar allegories, inferring from the distinctive "folk" cultures of their respective nations the dignity of Mexico and Haiti and the rightfulness of their desire for freedom from US domination (J. L. Matory 2005a, 149–87). Both the global fame of sub-Saharan African sculpture and its influence on Black American art, décor, and politics—in my birth home as well—are indebted to its early-twentieth-century appropriation by Parisian cubists and fauvists, who sought an elixir for Europe's aesthetic and spiritual exhaustion.

Like the conquered or superseded white elites of southern Louisiana, northeastern Brazil, and Mexico and even the elite francophone blacks and mulattoes of Haiti, the conquered whites of Charleston have avidly documented, celebrated, protected, and at times even subsidized the distinctive and African-inspired "folk" cultures of their dark local subordinates. Generations of postbellum documentation, fictionalization, and performance of Gullah/Geechee culture by nostalgic southern whites—who in turn inspired DuBose Heyward and George and Ira Gershwin's 1935 opera *Porgy and Bess* and Walt Disney's film *Song of the South* (1946)—have canonized Gullah/Geechee culture as a classical emblem of southern white cultural identity and moral goodness, particularly in the face of a perceived assault on local institutions by northern white generals, capitalists, and federal judges demanding an end to segregation. Many prominent southern whites—such as Georgian Joel Chandler Harris, Mississippian Newbell Niles Puckett, South Carolinian DuBose Heyward, and Charleston's all-white Society for the Preservation of Spirituals—linked their nostalgia for the Old South to this careful documentation of a distinctly Black regional culture (J. L. Matory 2005a, 296–97; see also Pinckney [1998] 2003, 55–56).

The Society for the Preservation of Spirituals is the most dramatic Lowcountry example. Made up exclusively of the children, grandchildren, and great-grandchildren of slaveholding South Carolinian planters, the society endeavored, from around 1923 until recently, to preserve the nineteenth-century, pre–"concert hall" versions of the Negro spirituals that the Gullah/Geechees themselves had progressively abandoned. The Fisk Jubilee Singers—of Nashville's historically Black Fisk University—pioneered the conversion of such "folk"-derived spirituals into written form and operatic voice, apparently intent on rendering them respectable and worthy of a high-status concert-hall audience of white potential donors. This form of the spiritual has since become the standard form among African Americans, including performers at Howard University's official gatherings. Not only did the all-white society study, record, and transcribe what it understood to be the antecedent and "authentic" forms of the spiritual, but it also performed them in carefully reproduced Gullah/Geechee language (J. L. Matory 2005a, 297, 341–42n3).

Rearranging Roots

The particular African origins that these superseded white elites tend to attribute to their emblematic local Black subordinates seldom correspond to the actual demographic proportions among the African captives taken to that American region. The African homeland attributed to these Black mascot populations is usually one of a few African peoples—such as the Yoruba, the Ashanti (the most famous subgroup of the Akan speakers), and the Fon (or Dahomean) kingdoms—that have been accorded special prestige in the Africanist anthropological literature and only then in the folkloric musings of cosmopolitan intellectuals who speak for the dignity of their respective races, regions, and nations. Such selective and sometimes fictional genealogical reconstructions helped to demonstrate the superiority of even the superseded white creole elite's native region to the native regions of their own conquerors, imperialists, and reformers (J. L. Matory 2005a, 38–72; 1999; Littlefield [1981] 1991, 174–75).

The prestigious African forebears of African-diaspora cultures are often identified through writings like those of Northwestern University professor Melville J. Herskovits (1958), British military officer and ethnologist A. B. Ellis ([1894] 1964), or Peace Corps anthropologist Joseph Opala (n.d.). All three of these scholars derived their ideas from a dialogue with elite black intellectuals who had their own prior intellectual and political agendas—W. E. B. Du Bois and the writers of the Harlem Renaissance in the case of Herskovits, the Lagosian Cultural Renaissance in the case of Ellis, and in the case of Opala, the Sierra Leone–Gullah Research Committee at Fourah Bay College (J. L. Matory 2005a, 1999; Sengova 2006, 216). The Lagosian Cultural Renaissance forcefully dignified the emergent Yoruba culture in particular and explains a great deal of pale-skinned Latin American elites' knowledge of, pride in, and exaggeration of their regional black subordinates' Yoruba and Dahomean Fon roots (J. L. Matory 1999). The Kongo and other West Central African origins of the plurality of African American captives are almost never accorded the same attention or dignity.

White regionalists are not the only people, however, who propagate selective genealogies. African American Lorenzo Turner's emphasis (e.g., [1949] 1973, 247, 292) on the Yoruba antecedents of Gullah language is probably indebted to Herskovits's disproportionate emphasis on West Africa's most famous kingdoms, as well as to the overrepresentation of certain British-colonized peoples among the scholars at the School of Oriental and African Studies, where Turner sought help in identifying the African origins of Gullah terms. Intentionally or not, ethnic genealogies are often remade under the influence of present-day social relationships and of scholarly misjudgments and political priorities.

In historical fact, the plurality of the Gullah/Geechees' African ancestors have been identified reliably as Angolan and West-Central African, but the scholarly literature dignifying the African origins of South Carolina's rice culture gives little attention to the Gullah/Geechees' Angolan and West-Central African roots. The most studied African rice-producing region—between the Senegambia and Liberia—has now become the more prestigious origin, and within that region, Sierra Leone is the place where Euro-American anthropologist and former Peace Corps volunteer Joseph Opala had the social and intellectual ties necessary to activate the resulting kinship networks. Similarly, Turner had conducted his overseas research in London, Sierra Leone, and Jamaica, neglecting both Angola and Liberia, whose language variety actually has a greater claim to kinship with Gullah/Geechee than does Sierra Leonean Krio. A new and growing kinship between the Gullah/Geechees and the peoples of Sierra Leone has now been made real by multiple official visits between these two communities and by two deeply moving documentaries—*Family across the Sea* (1991), produced under the sponsorship of South Carolina Educational Television, and *The Language You Cry In* (1998).

In the light of this selective activation of Gullah/Geechee cultural history, it is especially striking that Littlefield's inventory of the eighteenth-century African runaways in South Carolina ([1981] 1991, 118–23, 129–31)—from which we can infer the overall demography of the captive African population—includes no Yoruba people (though the one "Nego" might be a "Nago" Yoruba), no Gola people (the Sierra Leonean people often credited with the origin of the term "Gullah"), no Mende people (the most populous ethnic group in Sierra Leone), and no Baga people (the ethnic group from Guinea-Conakry credited with the most likely precedents for the tidal rice-growing techniques that made South Carolina prosper—see, e.g., Carney 2001, 19). It is also surprising, given the popular interpretation that Gullah/Geechee language derives form Sierra Leonean Krio, that Gullah/Geechee pronunciation and intonation more closely resemble Liberian English than Krio (Sengova 2006, 225; J. L. Matory 2006; J. L. Matory 2005a, 295–98). In my view, the similarities among Krio, Gullah, and Liberian English are indebted not to Gullah's having its roots in Krio but rather to the parallel, hybrid circumstances of their genesis and the migration of freed African Americans to Sierra Leone and Liberia in the mid-nineteenth century.

In sum, the activities of university-trained and usually nonindigenous scholars and the local appropriation of their scholarship have actually turned the course of history—by reshaping the self-understandings, priorities, and community-building efforts of contemporary Gullah/Geechees and other peoples of the African diaspora.

Dialogue

This late-twentieth-century rearrangement of Gullah/Geechee roots illustrates the motivated intercultural *dialogue* (Matory 2005a, 2006) that produces cultures and ethnic identities in all real-world social fields.

For example, Gullahs/Geechees have not always been conscious of the historically traceable worthiness of their lifeway (in a word, their pedigree) or of the importance of their African ancestors' technological contributions to the region's agriculture. However, dialogue has changed their minds. Most Gullah/Geechee children have grown up believing that the language of their forebears and, by extension, their own is just an inferior version of American English—hence the pejorative connotations of the term "Gullah" or "Geechee" for many of my interlocutors at Howard. Indeed, coastal Georgian Clarence Thomas attributes his own relative silence on the Supreme Court bench to his having attended schools where his Gullah/Geechee language variety was considered inferior (National Park Service 2005, 56).

On the other hand, Howard University–inspired scholarship has played a major role in the recent Gullah/Geechee embrace of Africa and the tandem recognition of Gullah/Geechee as a creole language rather than merely a deficient form of English. Perhaps counterintuitively, such scholarship has done more than any degree of Gullah/Geechee isolation to change Gullah/Geechee lifeways from a marker of low class status into a culture and a self-ascribed ethnic identity—through cosmopolitan processes of formalization, textualization, canonization, and commercialization.

Moreover, far from having "preserved" their African culture through isolation, Gullah/Geechees "discovered" their Africanness, amplified it, and gave it a new social reality in the late twentieth century. Arguably, this *prise de conscience* had its roots in Lowcountry people's conversations with outsider Lorenzo Dow Turner and in his scholarly dialogue with the bilingual African and Africanist intellectuals he met at London's School of African and Oriental Studies.

In turn, Turner's project was indebted to the aim of borderline-white anthropologist Melville J. Herskovits to rescue African Americans from the stigma that he called "the myth of the Negro past." This myth was the established white American view that Black Americans have no culture or historical legacy to speak of, a view used to justify the continued dehumanization and disenfranchisement of African Americans and of those immigrants who could not quickly enough distance themselves from us. Both Herskovits and his admirer Turner enlisted the Gullah/Geechees in a project of African American redemption—a project that extended Johann Gottfried von Herder's eighteenth-century redemption of the German speakers from their reputation of inferiority to the French and Franz Boas's twentieth-century project to redeem southern European, eastern European, and Jewish immigrants from their reputation of inferiority to anti-immigrant Anglo-Saxon "Know Nothings." Using the pro-African and pro-Black ethnohistorical logic of Boas's student Herskovits, Turner's work appropriated and reworked the antecedent efforts of nostalgic southern white writers and of the northern-supported educators at Penn School.

Penn played a major role in propagating and defining production standards for Gullah/Geechee crafts and folk arts, such as "native island" basketry (e.g., Rosengarten [1986] 1987, 25–30; L. Turner [1949] 1973, xv; National Park Service 2005, 118). The school's efforts to cultivate Gullah/Geechee basketry did not occur in local isolation but coincided with the nationwide arts-and-crafts movement, which, during the Depression years, promoted rural handicrafts (Rosengarten [1986] 1987, 27). In turn, the basket sewers and merchants along the tourist corridor of US Highway 17 in the vicinity of Mount Pleasant, South Carolina, have capitalized on the dignity and academic "cover" (Goffman 1963) that Turner's transoceanic, interethnic dialogue gave to their African heritage. This heritage became an advertising point recommending Gullah/Geechee crafts to potential buyers—most of them white. The emergent Africanness and dignity of Gullah/Geechee culture have also become a rallying point for the Gullah/Geechees' resistance to displacement from their lands and from coastal resources (including the sea grass upon which the basketry depends), as well as the grounds for an increasingly targeted and mutually beneficial alliance with the war-ravaged people of Sierra Leone. Such were the cosmopolitan forces that helped to make the coiled basket into today's preeminent visual symbol of Gullah/Geechee cultural distinctiveness and ethnic identity. A magnificent traveling exhibit and museum catalog are among the latest spectacular results (Rosengarten, Rosengarten, and Schildkrout 2008). Like schools, museums are major inventors of cultures and of the collective political units they substantiate.

Penn Center also hosted the 1988 visit of Sierra Leone's president Joseph Momo, which resulted in the visit of two Gullah/Geechee delegations to Sierra Leone during the 1990s. Those visits also resulted in the popular impression that Sierra Leonean Krio is the origin of Gullah/Geechee language, in the lobbying efforts of Gullah/Geechees to assist Sierra Leoneans during and after their recent civil war (1991–2002), and even in the recent declaration that the Gullah/Geechees are the "Mende people of South Carolina" (Sengova 2006, 219–32; J. L. Matory 2005a: 295–96, 341n1)—that is, the diaspora of Sierra Leone's largest ethnic group. In fact, the great similarity between Liberian English and Gullah gives more evidence of the South Carolinian roots of Liberian English than of the Sierra Leonean or Mende origins of Gullah. Yet these creative constructions of cultural genealogy are the most recent African-inspired products of a transoceanic, interethnic dialogue led by Howard alumnus and former English professor Lorenzo Dow Turner. And they all began at the very height of this Lowcountry population's alleged isolation.

Turner himself was a major agent of this transoceanic, interethnic dialogue, as his transformative scholarly work in the 1940s did not begin and end with his research stint in the Sea Islands. As an African American from North Carolina, he famously achieved a level of access to private Gullah practices and parlance that had been denied to previous, white researchers. Yet his unique degree of access demonstrates not that the Gullah/Geechees lived in a world apart from whites but that they lived in close enough proximity to whites to mistrust them and to have established a convention of excluding them from certain information. My best Gullah/Geechee friend at Howard reports that her coethnics still smile broadly at whites but, out of deep mistrust, reveal nothing of their inner feelings and thoughts. The Gullah/Geechees had been engaged in a centuries-old and highly active dialogue with their masters and managers, employers, customers, neighbors, teachers, missionaries, and researchers. However, their linguistic pragmatics involved a careful differentiation between how they communicated with ethnoracial insiders and ethnoracial outsiders.

Gullah/Geechee culture has undergone a further characteristic moment in the consolidation of ethnic groups and the canonization of their cultures—the publication of a vernacular Bible. Appropriately for this culture, *De Nyew Testament* (2005) is printed not in Gullah alone but with the King James English version alongside the Gullah translation. Gullah/Geechee culture is, after all, characterized by a bilingual field or creole continuum—that is, a range of forms between the most creolized, or basilectal, and the most "standard," or acrolectal. As speakers choose a form along this spectrum, they mark the formality or intimacy of the occasion (see, e.g., Reisman 1970). What makes the *De Nyew Testament* canonical is not just that it legitimizes the language and therefore provides a symbolic foundation of a new Gullah/Geechee peoplehood but also that it establishes *one* version of the internally heterogeneous Gullah/Geechee linguistic field as a standard worthy of the sacred and of the official. In practice, Gullah varies from island to island, just as the so-called dialects of Yoruba vary from region to region.

Similarly, the translation of the Bible into Yoruba required an artificial homogenization of these dialects and thus created a previously nonexistent and now school-taught standard around which the Èkìtì, the Ọ̀yọ́, the Ìjẹ̀bú, the Ẹ̀gbá, the Ẹ̀gbádò, and so forth can and do now rally as an emblem of collective sameness in the face of rivalry with Igbo and Hausa people—Nigeria's other major ethnic groups. Standard Yoruba distinguishes the educated, the urban, and the well-traveled from marginalized local populations. Time will tell which of these cross-cultural patterns will yet flower in the emergent Gullah/Geechee culture and ethnic group.

The Gullah/Geechee Renaissance

This cosmopolitan dialogue is the root of what might be called a Gullah/Geechee Renaissance, which, like all renaissances and revitalization movements, is as much a novel invention as a rebirth (see National Park Service 2005, 93–98). Among its most remarkable inventions is that a Gullah/Geechee returnee from New York has been "enstooled"—borrowing the Ghanaian parlance of the Ashanti and other Akan speakers and that of New York–area African American practitioners of Akan religion—as "Chieftess of the Gullah/Geechee Nation" (National Park Service 2005, 96). In 1996, Marquetta L. Goodwine, a native of Saint Helena Island, then residing in Brooklyn, founded the Gullah/Geechee Island Coalition, an organization designed to promote and preserve Gullah/Geechee culture through "land re-acquisition

FIGURE 3.1. "Queen Quet" of the Gullah/Geechee nation attending a festival for the Yoruba god Shango at Oyotunji Village, Sheldon, South Carolina. Photograph by the author.

and maintenance," and to celebrate this culture "through artistic and educational means electronically and via 'grassroots scholarship.'" Describing the southeastern coast of the United States as the "Gullah/Geechee nation," Ms. Goodwine—also known as "Queen Quet"—took her people's case before the First International Conference on the Right of Self-Determination and to the United Nations in Geneva in 2000 (National Park Service 2005, 95–96; Hargrove 2005, F31–F32; Sengova 2006, 235–42).

This renaissance has, since the early 1990s, included a boom in Gullah/Geechee literary and artistic production (Sengova 2006, 242–43; National Park Service 2005, 59–71). Often educated and media-savvy, Gullah/Geechee writers, singers, painters, craftspeople, educators, and lobbyists have taken their message of Gullah/Geechee peoplehood and cultural distinctiveness to the multiethnic press, television stations, the Internet, municipal and county governments, the US Congress, the United Nations, public schools, tourism bureaus, and commercial galleries.

In 2006, as a result of cooperation among the National Park Service and organizations like the Gullah/Geechee Sea Island Coalition, as well as the initiative of African American congressman James Clyburn, a white-dominated and English-speaking US Congress officially designated the southeastern coast and its islands as a cultural and ecological "preservation" zone known as the "Gullah/Geechee Cultural Heritage Corridor" and established a commission for its management. Congress thus funded an effort to coordinate

Gullah/Geechee educational institutions, Gullah/Geechee activist groups, and non-Gullah/Geechee institutions that propagate academic knowledge about this emergent culture (Joyner 2007). The planning for this legislation resulted in the publication and the international, online dissemination of the most comprehensive and democratic documentation of Gullah/Geechee life to date (National Park Service 2005).

This National Park Service document legitimizes a political constituency and affirms its worth to the tourism industry. The text does not, however, deflect the interest of real estate developers and tax assessors who refuse to exempt family land from the taxable increases in land value that result from the building of resorts in the area. Gullah/Geechee landowners remain vulnerable, but their university-endorsed claim to a distinctive "culture" makes it possible for them to defend themselves not only through ethnic organization and lobbying but also by leveling charges of "cultural genocide" against county officials (Severson 2012).

So, without minimizing the tragedy of Gullah/Geechee land loss, it might be said that Gullah/Geechee culture and ethnic identity are more alive than ever before, and the source of the Gullah/Geechee Renaissance has been anything but isolation or inertia. The success of this national legislation and a range of local legislation proves the power of a competitive threat to create and energize identities. More concretely, it also demonstrates the growing skill of Gullah/Geechee organizations at educating the multiethnic and multiracial public, lobbying regional officials to secure Gullah/Geechee landholdings, and pressuring non-Gullah/Geechee landholders and businesses to allow Gullah/Geechees access to ancestral sites and raw materials for their basketry. For some Gullah/Geechees, these successes are a further step in the direction of nation building. Thus, the African-inspired culture and ethnic identity of the Gullah/Geechees have emerged not from conservative isolation but from progressive and strategic dialogue—much of it guided and legitimized by the work of Lorenzo Dow Turner and his university-trained successors Margaret Washington Creel, Charles Joyner, Daniel C. Littlefield, Salikoko Mufwene, Joseph Opala, Dale Rosengarten, and Joko Sengova.

In sum, what has made the Gullah/Geechee an ethnic group and might yet make it into a credible nation? Their distinctive livelihood—as, preeminently, the enslaved farmers of rice, indigo, and long-staple cotton—was largely an economic class distinction that made a secret in-group language as useful as the unmarked language of communication with the oppressor class. After the Civil War, the Gullah/Geechees shared a common status as landed yeoman farmers under continual threat of land expropriation; as fishermen; as seafood and produce merchants; and, often, as pupils and alumni of Penn School and Center. Their distinctive livelihood, their common economic status, and the utility of their lifeway in numerous elite projects—and not their isolation from whites—preserved, invigorated, and transformed their distinctive crafts, in-group language, and church-based form of self-government.

As long as some islands, such as Johns, Wadmalaw, and Saint Helena, retain major Gullah-speaking populations and mainland populations (such as Mount Pleasant's) continue to profit from the distinctive, tour guide– and road-sign-ratified "authenticity" of their African-inspired craft (see National Park Service 2005, 65), there is little danger that even the unscrupulous displacement of some island populations will cause this distinctive ethnic identity to disappear. Alongside the return of émigré cultural nationalists and the emergence of a professional class of Gullah/Geechee cultural educators (choirs, storytellers, and school presenters), the loss of certain islands is likely to help centralize, standardize, and canonize this ethnic identity. Indeed, some Gullah/Geechee organizations have now proposed to regulate the performance and presentation of their culture (Hargrove 2005, F33). If such regulation comes to pass, Gullah/Geechee culture as such will have achieved a degree of reality and authority unprecedented even at the end of a hundred years of alleged isolation. But the behavioral substratum of this newly reified culture will also have changed profoundly.

In the film *The Language You Cry In* (1998), we are shown a group of Gullah/Geechee visitors to Bunce Island, the island off the coast of Sierra Leone where westward-bound captives from the mainland had trodden for the last time on African soil. There the American visitors tearfully receive a lecture from white American anthropologist Joseph Opala about the horrors their putative ancestors had experienced on the island. One visitor reports that she has finally "discovered" her culture, a culture that she had never known about. The irony of "cultures" these days—and perhaps as long as there have been diasporas and the motive to make cultural canons—is that they are not as much lived or known by their members as they are "discovered," "revealed," or "asserted" in dialogue with outsiders. Moreover, cultures regularly find their most ardent champions among erstwhile members of the group who have moved far away, faced misrecognition or denigration by outsiders, read the dignifying or value-neutral anthropological accounts of their ancestral distinctiveness, and returned in the role of spokespersons for an identity with little previous salience, pride of place, and usefulness among those who stayed at home.

On the Worth of African Culture in the Americas

As agricultural technicians, forced- or free-labor migrants, seamen, merchants, rebels, diplomats, and pupils, Gullah/Geechees have fashioned a transnational ethnic identity based on the dignity of the world's most denigrated continent and of their previously low-status language variety. They have done so not in isolation from the flow of people and ideas across regions, races, and classes but in the face of racial stigma and in the midstream of a black Atlantic exchange. Contrary to the premise that "Africanisms" depend on isolation and the invisibility of an alternative, much evidence in the Gullah/Geechee literature suggests that Africans and non-Africans who live and work together sometimes prefer African ways of doing things to non-African ways. We can no longer be content with the assumption that Africanisms "survive" chiefly in spheres of social life that lack or have outlived a useful material purpose (see J. L. Matory 2001; 2005a, 277), in spheres exempt from white interest, or in the neglected interstices between the larger arrangements that whites did care to police (pace, e.g., Mintz and Price [1976] 1992, 38–41).

African technologies and ways of building community have often been directly useful to both the Gullah/Geechees and their non-Gullah/Geechee contemporaries. For example, the eighteenth-century white planters who self-consciously experimented with rice varieties and ways of cultivating them either knew about or could have researched the relevant Italian, Chinese, Malagasy, Native American, Dutch, or English techniques (Littlefield [1981] 1991, 104–5), but they preferred to adopt and elaborate on West African techniques.

Not only free whites but also enslaved and free Africans had choices. The availability of time away from whites would certainly have furnished the conditions for a creativity rooted in African, European, and Native American precedents. Such freedom, though, could hardly be summarized as isolation, since the enslaved still had to learn a great deal about their masters' language and standards. Moreover, the proceeds of the captives' creative work—in cooking, song and dance, ritual, private garden cultivation, quilting, and storytelling, for example—were openly observable, thoroughly documented, and frequently mimicked by whites, except when the African captives and their descendants consciously decided to keep secrets. And secrecy, after all, presumes not isolation from a potential observer but the continual threat of his or her presence.

Indeed, as Mufwene (1991, 233) observes, some of the most insistent, or "fanatic," speakers of basilectal Gullah are not the ones *least* exposed to the acrolectal alternative but the ones *most* exposed—that is, "those who once moved out of the islands and then came back." He adds, "Some are among those residents reverting back, or holding on, to it because they feel their identity threatened" (232).[11]

Dissent

Even those most committed to the received wisdom about the origins of Gullah/Geechee distinctiveness will concede that this population has indeed always interacted with the outside world. But they will ask me to concede that the Gullah/Geechees were at least *relatively* isolated compared to other Black North American populations and that this *relative* degree of isolation must be the explanation for Gullah/Geechee cultural distinctiveness. Yet I maintain that the need of past writers to exaggerate the isolation of this people's ancestors results from the weakness of this causal model in the first place. In my view, neither absolute nor relative isolation but, instead, a specific and qualitatively important form of cosmopolitanism explains the emergence of this ethnic identity and the African-inspired canonical forms that it has taken.

Rather than emphasizing that the Gullah/Geechees' ancestors were isolated before the bridge building of the 1950s, I posit that the waterways that structured Gullah/Geechee ancestral lifeways made transportation *easier* than in many nonmaritime regions of the United States during the same pre-1950s era. What has made the Gullah/Geechees and their postbellum ancestors culturally African is less their lack of exposure to the outside world than their relative freedom—as landowners, merchants, and clients of Penn School—to choose the occasions of their mobility and the terms of their self-presentation. The loss of land and of access to some economically profitable means of self-representation and livelihood is indeed a threat to Gullah/Geechee prosperity, but that very threat has amplified the incentive to organize, reify, canonize, propagate, regulate, and enforce the African-inspired terms of the Gullah/Geechees' local and extraterritorial cultural unity. The disbanding of the Hausa chieftaincy in Ibadan during the early 1950s had similar results. In the Gullah/Geechee case, university-educated writers and scholars—especially Black, conquered white, or not-so-white ones—have provided many of the textual charters of this population's ethnic self-recognition.

In response to this argument, one expert on the Gullah/Geechees was willing to concede that the eighteenth-century colonial period and the post–World War II era have been influential periods of nonisolation, but he maintains that the twentieth-century era of segregation blocked Gullah/Geechee access to goods, credit, education, government, power, and status. In my view, the literal meaning of "segregation" suggests isolation but conceals the highly interactive nature of that way of life. Segregation did less to isolate Blacks from whites than to fix the stigmatizing and hierarchical but nonetheless *complementary* terms of the races' close interaction in the same spaces and industries. Segregation not only allowed for but also assumed and resulted in powerful and sometimes highly intimate forms of mutual influence, though the material benefits thereof were distributed with deliberate inequality (see, e.g., Hunt 2007). By giving whites most of the profits for Black-white interaction, segregation actually created an incentive for Blacks to imitate whites and not vice versa. Indeed, it created a further incentive for whites to exaggerate their physical and cultural difference from Black people and continually to invent new signs of difference, or cultural differentiae, to prove their worthiness of superior profits. Yet even this pursuit of distinction often involved the obsessive and ironic mockery of Black people's speech, music, and dance—a phenomenon that Bateson ([1936] 1958) calls "schismogenesis." In these performances, ironic mockery has always involuntarily shaded into long-term imitation. Once imitated, Black people often innovated, keeping one step ahead.

For strategic and aesthetic reasons, the trajectory of cultural exchange and identity transformation has never been simple. What might now be called "Gullah/Geechee culture" is the cosmopolitan strategy of a US population whose usual complexion and rural livelihood make it highly vulnerable to stigma within Howard's sphere of influence. With their livelihood under threat, they have found the wherewithal to market the signs of their valuable place in the material and symbolic universe of a powerful array of outsiders.

This chapter in no way denies the importance of Gullah/Geechee people's efforts to retain their hereditary lands and access to maritime resources. Poverty and proletarianization are neither ennobling nor Africanizing, which fact leads to the main theoretical claims of this chapter. First, ethnic identities arise not from isolation but from interaction among populations. The rural peasantry is no more the source of a people's distinctive and "authentic" lifeway than are its urban merchants, lobbyists, and outsider ethnographers. Second, there is no reason, in the New World or the Old, to assume that people choose the lifeways of the oppressed chiefly or even normally because they are isolated from the lifeways of the oppressor. In the Gullah/Geechee case, it is not isolation from Euro-American alternatives but, instead, the people's command of profitable African skills and symbols, their access to the landed and maritime resources, their access to markets and schools, and their ambivalent relationship to local white populations that enabled and, indeed, subsidized a preference for African-inspired culture.

A General Theory

I propose a dialogical theory of culture and ethnic identity (J. L. Matory 2006, 2005a). Whatever is culturally distinctive about any population on the Atlantic perimeter or anywhere else in the world has resulted not from isolation but from the local conditions of transoceanic, multicultural, and interclass dialogue across the centuries. How else did cowry shells from the Maldive Islands, Venetian beads, and Dutch schnapps become such important symbols in and of West African cultures, far exceeding their current importance in their non-African lands of origin? How else did the banjo, an instrument of African origin, become central to the racial and class identity of poor hinterland whites in the United States? How else did corn-based polenta in northern Italy and tomato sauce in southern Italy—both made from American cultigens—acquire such defining roles in these European cuisines? Proximate ethnic groups and even those separated by oceans tend to imitate each other extensively (Roach 1996). Peoples develop patterns of collective behavior that complement those of the populations they live beside, trade with, govern, or are governed by. If any unit is called "*a* culture" (thus making cultures *countable*), any given culture is the unit constituted by the complementary and overlapping lifeways of populations and classes that exchange with each other. It is through a dialectical and competitive process of inheritance, innovation, imitation, evasion of imitation, and flight from stigma that locally proximate populations and their spokespeople sort out widely available symbolic repertoires into formally contrasting and bounded cultural units. A dialogical theory posits that cultural differences do not endure simply out of stubbornness, resistance, or natural stasis. They endure and have meaning because they are more useful—as practical tools, as symbolic means of guaranteeing the loyalty of a useful alliance, or as a means of rationalizing monopolistic advantage—than are the cultural alternatives modeled by neighbors.

Ethnic groups, for their part, are not the same as cultures. Ethnic groups are seldom internally homogeneous in their lifeways or without major behavioral and educational overlaps with neighboring ethnic groups. Ethnic groups are the populations—often occupation- or class-inflected—that are named or choose to name themselves in contradistinction to proximate populations, despite the significant diversity of lifeways *within* each ethnic group and despite the significant overlap and *complementarity among* the collective lifeways of neighboring ethnic groups. Hence, ethnicity arises less from isolation than from the pursuit or defense of a distinctive role in the production and exchange system or in the political hierarchy of a system where there is a hereditary division of labor and of privilege.

Diverse geographical origins and languages are but part of the roots of ethnic difference because, first, the differences of belief and practice between *groups that are rarely in contact with each other* are not usually recognized by those groups as salient. People notice or articulate ethnic difference, act upon it, and define its socio-cultured criteria only when other groups are close enough for there to be an occasion to exclude members of those other groups from some right or privilege. Second, people who live close together or even interact very quickly learn to act and think in similar ways, unless there is a good, profitable reason not to do so—such as monopolizing certain marital partners, productive resources, areas of commerce, residential privileges, political honors or titles, spheres of authority, and so forth. "Cultures" are the reification of socially and symbolically useful difference. They are the products, not the causes, of ethnic differentiation.

Moreover, "survival," "retention," and "preservation" seldom aptly describe the history of cultures or of ethnic groups. Collective practice and identity are as strategic as they are habitual. Not only the Gullah/Geechees but three other cases mentioned in this chapter lead us to the same conclusions: (1) North America's other famous African American ethnic group (that is, the Louisiana Creoles of color), (2) Yoruba culture and ethnic identity in nineteenth-century coastal West Africa, and (3) the African-inspired Candomblé religion in Bahia, Brazil. What is distinctive about the Gullah/Geechees is not isolation from other population groups but their disproportionate ownership, relative to other African Americans, of their own land. As self-employed people and people with a stake in maintaining their collective control over certain land and maritime resources, they could and did make the choice to cultivate an in-group language variety—a means to and a symbol of some people's inclusion in and others' exclusion from the in-group's collective resources.

Gullah/Geechee cultural history provides lessons not only about the strategic and situational nature of ethnic identity but also about the complex and dialectical political economy of subaltern cultural reproduction, in which material and cultural power are seldom isomorphic. While money and firepower undoubtedly confer disproportionate power over the selective reproduction of culture, materially strong and materially weak classes often find a shared advantage in propagating and dignifying the distinctive practices and identities of the weak. Material power facilitates the broadcasting of one's culture, but the African diaspora thoroughly demonstrates the seductive power of exogeneity and of code-switching as low-tech alternatives to the cultural orthodoxies, technical inadequacies, and emotional discontents of the strong. In the contemporary United States, many well-meaning social scientists and policy makers are still too quick to dismiss the technical, linguistic, and ritual alternatives generated by the weak as deficiencies or as the results of ignorance about the alternatives. On the contrary, African-inspired American subcultures are often a thoughtfully honed and historically crafted wedge, prying open the narrow spaces of agency and authority allotted to the weak.

This chapter examines the political and cultural economy that has generated the emergent Gullah/Geechee ethnic identity on the southeastern US coast and its diaspora. I offer here a foundational lesson about the situationality, the segmentary character, the motivating economic interests, and the performative nature of ethnic identities. This identity illustrates a further common phenomenon: the prominence of schools and scholars in ethnogenesis. It is no surprise that it was a Howard University–associated scholar who weighed in on behalf of this most stigmatized subgroup of the most stigmatized race. Yet he and his followers have also reproduced the assumption equally at the heart of the university and of US racism—that the culture of the folk is symbolically important for its bourgeois coethnics or conationals but is both archaic and incapable of surviving modernity and progress.

The contradictory reasoning in the scholarly literature about Gullah/Geechee ethnogenesis also reflects the interclass compromise at the heart of ethnogenetic processes all over the world. The "folk" become mascots in a project well beyond their control, and the profits they derive from it are usually meager. On the other hand, those meager benefits often depend on bourgeois sponsorship. For example, the study and classification of Gullah/Geechee language are made possible by the university-based skills, traditions, and equipment of linguistic analysis; by the expectation of collaboration among scholars from different universities, even on different continents; and by foundation funding. The transformation of the Gullah/Geechees into an ethnic group and a culture depended on an altitude and geographical breadth of comparative overview entirely inaccessible to the "folk" themselves except when they are collaborating with university scholars. In my observation, such dialogical ethnogenesis is closer to a rule than to an exception.

Complexion and class status affect the formation of ethnic identities, their internal hierarchies, and their options in the pursuit of status relative to other ethnic groups. This observation about African-descended ethnic groups places in high relief what could probably be said about all ethnic groups today. So the tools of individual and collective self-improvement crafted by rural landowners and at a trade school like Penn were quite different from, for example, those crafted at Saint Augustine High School in New Orleans or in the examination schools of Kingston and Port of Spain, which have propelled many New Orleans Creoles of color and black Caribbeans into Howard's student body, faculty, and administration. Nonetheless, one of Howard's highest-ranking deans at the time of my research seems to be from the southernmost reaches of Gullah/Geechee society, as is one of the leading physicians in the Employee Health Service. The dean is a warm and unpretentious man, which makes his Gullah-inflected speech disarming. Moreover, his longevity in office suggests that he conducts his job with great administrative and political savvy.

Though I was surprised by the degree to which our family friend in Employee Health emphasized the mixed-race background of his people, I should not have been. The scholarly literature and most of my Gullah/Geechee interlocutors emphasize that they collectively look very black. But Howard in the mid-twentieth century may have been inviting and available only to a particular subset of Gullah/Geechees. This family friend in Employee Health is the color of Nilla Wafers, and he is the father of a young man who helped to lead his butter-colored but avowedly African American mother's people toward recognition as an Indian tribe in North Carolina. In emphasizing the racial hybridity of his ethnic group, this physician is perhaps reacting to the discomfort that his daughters report feeling sometimes in large-scale encounters with his Gullah/Geechee birth family. One of his daughters told me that she and her sisters feel uncomfortable about standing out so visibly at family gatherings on account of their light skin. Their father's own self-representation appears to reflect a degree of empathy with them. Thus, in this family, Gullah/Geechee and black Indian identities not only combine but also reshape each other. His self-representation also appears to repair the usual contrast between the Gullah/Geechee category and the Talented Tenth—the first normally being the dark poster child of the "folk" to be spoken for and the latter (at least in the Americas) being the light-skinned spokespeople.

The revolutionary spirit of anglophone black West Indians has long combined resentment of the oppressor with an admiration for his tools. In that spirit, former Howard University professor Eric Williams led Trinidad to independence with the cry, "Massa day done!"—"The master's day is over!" Spoken in the language of the masses, it was clearly a cry for dignity both racial and national, a cry also uttered by other alumni of American HBCUs, such as Nigerian independence leader Nnamdi Azikiwe and Ghanaian independence leader Kwame Nkrumah. Yet African American Howard alumni and students, from the 1940s until the present, report among African and particularly Caribbean peers a powerfully Anglophile sense of superiority to Black Americans. A sense of superiority to other oppressed groups is also one of the weapons of the weak, which some immigrant and black ethnic students at Howard rejected as counterproductive. Others learned to wield it well.

The chapters that follow document several black ethnic responses to racial stigma that are very different from the Gullah/Geechees' embrace of African dignity and vernacular speech.

Africa is the world's most despised continent, but Gullah/Geechee identity instantiates its recuperation as a symbol of hope in the African diaspora. The next chapter illustrates the dialogical theory of culture and ethnic identity with reference to Louisiana Creoles of color and American Indians of partly African ancestry, whose characteristic response to the stigma attached to Blackness is not to valorize it but seek honor and profit by denying it. Africa and the contested worth of its genetic and cultural contributions to US civilization are the linchpin of both scholarly ambivalence and the Gullah/Geechee cultural revival. The contested worth of Africa is also the implicit axis of Louisiana Creole and southeastern Indian ethnogenesis today. However, these collective identities are, in the end, constituted less by clearly marked boundaries and cultural diacritica than by the debates about who they really are.

4

A Complexion or a Culture? Debate as Identity among African-Descended Indians and Louisiana Creoles of Color

A shallowly buried corpse still haunts domestic "African American" identity: Are all of the descendants of "colored" people Black, or was the very term a nineteenth-century bureaucratic weapon intended to reduce the remaining eastern Indian tribes, the Louisiana Creoles of color, and other "triracial isolates"—or "little races"—to the rock-bottom status of Black people? Since then, segregation, intermarriage, cultural exchange, the struggle against segregation, and even the new "color-blind" racism have done much to create a shared subculture and community among these populations, but the aspiration to escape last place remains.

Neither their cultural convergences with Black America nor the civil rights alliance fully extinguished the social subnetworks of schooling, friendship, and marriage that some now interpret as signs of ethnic distinction. Many erstwhile members of the "little races" have, for generations, lived and died, celebrated and mourned, played, fought, and often intermarried with their soi-disant Black neighbors. Many have dismissed their "little races" as relics of past self-hatred and self-delusion, while others have launched full-scale revival movements that reject Blackness altogether and reclaim autonomous "cultures" of their own. Others, still, commute between beloved Black communities, such as Howard, and equally beloved triracial isolate enclaves.

During this research, I joined a score of such Howardites in their interstate transmigrations between these communities. I watched as they changed their clothing, their speech patterns, their food choices, and even their willingness to sit, stand, or talk with me. I experienced something similar when, in 2003, I invited myself along to Friday prayers with a Hausa Muslim Howard alumnus in Abuja, Nigeria. In his government office and in the privacy of his home, I received the deference and hospitality due to a learned visitor and a fictive fellow-

Howard "old boy." However, as soon as we crossed the threshold of the mosque's grounds, my host disappeared without even a "see you later." After prayers, we departed so quickly that I inferred he did not wish to be seen with me.

Perhaps he simply did not like to mix the "old boy" anthropologist affairs with his piety. Perhaps he suddenly remembered an urgent appointment. Or, just perhaps, the growing tension between the Ummah and the West over suspicions about the distribution of flawed vaccines in northern Nigeria and over 9/11 made the public knowledge of his association with me more uncomfortable at the mosque than at the office. The fault lines that he and my American "little race" interlocutors crossed during these spatial transitions seemed similarly anxiety producing—for them and for me.

Each of the "little races" discussed in this chapter is internally heterogeneous. What defines each one as an ethnic group is less a "culture" in the Tylorean/Boasian anthropological sense—with agreed-upon norms of proper thought, feeling, and behavior—than a communal debate over whether or not it should "recover" its non-Black ethnic identity and rights and by what logic. What any such "little race" tends to share is less a uniform set of cultural diacritica (or distinguishing features), as Barth and Cohen would suggest, than a set of focal venues for their debate over what might distinguish them from Blacks and an effort by one side to "revive" a set of symbols suitable to mark that distinction.

Many of my transmigrant "little-race" friends and mentors say they suffered physical and emotional violence as a result of their ambiguous appearance and their ambivalent positions in this debate. And I myself suffered the reminder that—neither as a participant-observer anthropologist nor as a long-term family friend—could I cross every boundary safely. The unclarity of these boundaries made them into battlegrounds.

Of course, the post-Boasian, dialogical phenomenology of "cultures" that I outlined in the last chapter does nothing to disqualify the "little races" from claiming the status of "cultures." Indeed, their extreme case might illustrate a further feature of all or most "cultures": they are constituted less by consensus than by debate. This chapter illustrates foremost the role of contestation and debate in ethnogenesis. I learned the most from conflicts that resulted from the deep discomfort of some members of the "little races" with the very presence of people who look like my son and me.

The "Little Races"

Native Americans east of the Mississippi are a diverse lot, as are the Creoles of color, whose ancestral heartland is southern Louisiana. The Native American peoples I studied include Cherokees, Choctaws, Saponis, Seminoles, Rappahannocks, Mattaponis, the Nanticokes, Piscataways, Piscatawas, Pamunkeys, Chickahominies, and numerous "fringe people," the term by which some of my Native friends describe the self-recognized Indians who are members of no particular tribe (see also Rountree 1990; indeed, this book was strongly recommended to me by my two most important Virginia Indian mentors. It therefore figures prominently in my portrait of this literally-defined world). Creoles of color—typically the descendants of French- or Spanish-speaking antebellum free people or of the enslaved arrivals from Saint Domingue after the Haitian Revolution—are also diverse. Historically, New Orleans Creoles, the "Cane River" Creoles of Natchitoches, and the Bayou Country Creoles of Opelousas have diverged in their language, cuisine, musical tastes, sense of historical legacy, and place in an intra-Creole status hierarchy. For example, the members of these different Creole subgroups identify different languages as the mother tongues of their ancestors: in declining order of prestige, Continental French, Cajun French, or the Louisiana "Negro" creole, inspired by the vernacular spoken by late-eighteenth- and early-nineteenth-century arrivals from Saint Domingue. In the hierarchy separating urban from rural Creoles, lower echelons seem unaware of how anathema their language and musical varieties are to the Creole ethnic identity of their more urban class superiors.

For a time after the Louisiana Purchase of 1803, the typically mixed-race free ancestors of today's Creoles occupied a middle rank between blacks and whites. However, like the white descendants of Louisiana's French and Spanish colonizers, they were under pressure to assimilate the culture—including the racial classificatory system—of their Anglo-American colonizers. Yet, like many later Caribbean or African immigrants, the Creoles of color struggled mightily to resist their reduction to the status of American Blacks. Nineteenth-century Louisiana free people of color generated a lively French- and African-inspired literary, culinary, artistic, and musical tradition (e.g., Kein 2000a). However, since the Civil War, much of the history of the Louisiana Creoles of color has resulted from a convergence of their legal status, political interests, socioeconomic indicators, educational histories, cuisine, language, and music with those of intergenerationally English-speaking Americans of African ancestry (e.g., Brasseaux, Fontenot, and Oubre 1994, 110–11). Even the forms of color-caste endogamy practiced in their self-defense against the downward racial mobility imposed by Jim Crow have knitted them into the broader interstate networks of non-Creole African American life. A similar history characterizes many Native American populations east of the Mississippi.

Marriage, education, and labor migration have created Louisiana Creole and Indian diasporas that are often deeply embedded in African American neighborhoods, universities, and kin networks across the country. It is sometimes difficult to distinguish these diasporic populations from the lighter-skinned class echelons of the broader African American population, while darker-skinned out-migrants from these local triracial enclaves seldom have any chance of remaining aloof from Blackness. Until the 1970s, the phenotypical evidence of Creoles' and southeastern Indians' partially African ancestry often made it impossible for outwardly and upwardly mobile members of these populations to dwell or study outside of African American society. Moreover, according to my early-twenty-first-century New Orleans Creole mentors, whatever language their ancestors spoke and however white they may look, "As soon as a Creole opens his mouth [to speak], you can tell he's Black!" Such is the degree of intergenerational proximity and mutual influence between Creoles of color and other people of African descent in Louisiana. That is not to say, however, that their social networks and venues of debate always dissolved indistinguishably into the African American mass.

One could write several whole books about Louisiana Creole networks or about the Native tribes—state-recognized and unrecognized—that neighbor or overlap with African American communities. They all differ from each other in many ways. Indeed, in each of the "literally-defined" worlds of these discreditable populations, many books and articles have already been written about what distinguished them from Black people, and these publications are known and actively discussed by the triracial public. The present chapter contributes to this literature but has an altogether different purpose: to clarify the role of "literally-defined" debate in ethnogenesis globally. The revivalist movements of the "little races" are a case in point.

James Clifford's widely cited chapter "Identity in Mashpee" (1988) details the efforts of a partly African-descended population on Cape Cod to claim white-colonized land in the name of their "Indian" tribe and uses this case to refute the "organic" model of collective identity—long supposed by anthropologists and state officials alike—whereby the endurance of an ethnic group is defined by the continuity, fixity, and changelessness of the "culture" that it practices. In Clifford's observation, the social continuity of the Mashpee tribe lay in the repeated substitution of one cultural diacritic for another over time. That Clifford makes this observation in the context of a court case in which the realness and the continuity of the tribe is being debated is, to me, not an accident but part of the dialogical and contention-based essence of ethnic identities generally. Ethnic groups do not simply exist or not exist, in objectivist fashion. Rather, contestation over their realness, their membership, and their cultural diacritica is an essential element of collective identities. And ethnogenesis, like taste, occurs in the "logic of the trial."

Nor is it incidental, in my argument, that the Mashpee Indians are part African. In US history, the reality or the allegation of African ancestry is virtually the prototypical excuse to deprive a population of honor and resources in favor of a white or wannabe-white rival. And every such group must figure out, as a precondition to claiming or reclaiming honor and resources, how to redefine its hereditary relationship to Africa. Ever discredited or potentially discredited by their African ancestry, Louisiana Creoles of color and most of the Indian populations east of the Mississippi also powerfully illustrate the role of stigma and interethnic hierarchy in ethnogenesis.

This chapter explores the motives and the conduct by which populations group and regroup themselves—and debate every regrouping—in a world where such populations have lived together intensely with others and where neighbors share a great deal of their cultural repertoires in common. In common, Louisiana Creoles of color and Indians of partially African ancestry are indigenous to the United States and have hundreds of years of history on this continent. Moreover, unlike the Gullah/Geechees, many of these Creoles and Indians feel equipped to claim that they are not Black at all. Yet after centuries of state-driven social and cultural convergence with African Americans, the ethnic revival movements of these populations face the suspicion that they are not simply seeking to recover an innocently distinctive and endangered cultural legacy but are, rather, seeking a sense of superiority to their African American neighbors. Their options for demonstrating their cultural difference from and superiority to African Americans necessarily differ from those of most recent immigrants from Africa or the anglophone Caribbean and of their children. Among the options of the triracial isolates is the assertion of racial difference.

Unlike most of the existing literature about Creoles and Indians of partly African ancestry, the present chapter is more ethnographic than historical. It documents the role of education and debate in ethnogenesis and of situationality in the daily invocation of ethnic identity. The university has served at least two purposes in the lives of these ambiguous-looking and always discreditable groups, both related to the careful information management that the discreditable must master. First, universities furnish the anthropological discourses of cultural difference that potentially rescue the "little races" both from Blackness and from the almost equally stigmatizing accusation that they are anti-Black racists. Separation from Blacks is more easily justified when the boundary is named in terms of the anthropological concept of "culture" than when it is named in terms of skin color and hair texture. At the same time, the university models mainstream bourgeois diction and taste (i.e., "culture" in the nonanthropological sense), as well as the social alliances to which bourgeois diction and taste afford access. "Culture," in both senses, is the public language of the "literally-defined world" of the discreditable. In this incubator of upward mobility—the university—transmigrant elites must use this language to redefine both their race and their class, often through the process of defining the "folk" for whom they speak, as well as this elite's *assimilé* qualifications to speak for them and to profit from their leadership.

Ironically, the arrival of these Creoles and Indians in the university reflects and amplifies their cultural likeness to the normative population of the university. Moreover, far away from home, they are no longer as identifiable by their distinctive family names or home neighborhoods. Under such conditions, phenotype becomes increasingly important in the collective self-definition of "little races." At home, the phenotypical heterogeneity of their small local communities is no obstacle to mutual recognition and solidarity. However, in the diaspora of such communities, and at moments when they are under scrutiny by outsiders, and during revival movements that reassemble long-dispersed groups, coethnics with certain phenotypes hear phrases like one that Afro–Puerto Ricans report hearing in the United States: "You don't *look* Puerto Rican!" (Jorge 1979). In the case of Louisiana Creoles and many east-of-the-Mississippi Native American communities, that means, effectively, that the people with the dark skin and tightly curled hair get pushed out, particularly at times when the home community is under scrutiny by outsiders who have the right to deny official recognition for the group and those who regulate the distribution of limited resources.

In 2002, I reentered Howard through an extensive network of my students and friends, my own childhood neighbors, my late mother's friends, and my father's friends, colleagues, trainees, and employees. Many had known me since before I had known myself. From some, a history of long-term love and mutual confidence earned me a remarkable degree of honesty about the supersensitive topic of this chapter. For example, one childhood neighbor revealed, with a laugh and in their presence, her inference that her parents are cousins—members of a quasi-ethnic network, or little race, of northern Virginians who, out of a sense of "duty," married their cousins in order to keep their families light skinned and distinct from their black neighbors.

She is surely aware of the widespread Washingtonian contempt for the Maryland families who engage in the same practices and are famous for the resulting birth defects—such as the weak dental enamel that results in the premature loss of their teeth. Yet segregation meant that Howard-affiliated Freedmen's Hospital was among the few places where they could receive medical treatment. However, a number of these families have recently sought recognition not as an epidemiological oddity or as people who hate being

A COMPLEXION OR A CULTURE? 237

FIGURE 4.1. Piscatawa Powwow, Waldorf, Maryland, 2002. Photograph by the author.

Black but as Piscataway Indians. Anthropologically, they now argue that their practice of cousin marriage is not a racially motivated perversion but further proof of their descent from Maryland Indians who, in their understanding of history, are the ancestral source of that marital practice.

In fact, cousin marriage was common among Euro-Americans as well during the nineteenth century but came under criticism by democratizers who associated it with aristocracy (McKinnon 2015). Of course, the demand that they marry outside of the tiny kinship circles that preserved class distinction did not extend to the idea of marrying outside of the white race. In effect, the white democratizers were extending aristocratic status to the entire white race. In this context, the enduring or heightened preference for cousin marriage among the little races seems a natural reaction to their rock and a hard place: exclusion from marriage to whites and the prospect of being cast into the bondage that late-nineteenth-century Klan violence, land expropriation, vagrancy laws, the convict lease system, and Jim Crow—which white southerners called "the Redemption"—were reimposing on anyone in the South who could, by actual descent or association, be identified as Black. Historical revisionists and tribal revivalists tend to explain cousin marriage as evidence of the endurance of a primordial Native American tradition. But, by the end of the nineteenth century, the impulse to endogamy among these populations was clearly—and probably above all—an effort to erase their long history of intermarriage with African Americans. And this motive endures. Less intuitively understandable but key to the argument of this book is that these populations directed and continue to reserve their deepest anger, resentment, and even violence not for the whites who actually deprived them of the rights but for the people they consider Black.

In a manner typical of these new (or resurrected) eastern tribes, one particular Maryland family or set of families tried to monopolize membership in the government-recognized tribe. The state-recognized Piscataways managed to secure a court order barring the use of the name by the excluded families, which then deleted the *y* in order to advertise their powwow legally. The most common type of tribal split divides the branch of the family with more white ancestors, which branch is usually the first to be recognized by the state, from the branch with more visibly African ancestry, which branch, if it is ever recognized, is usually the last.

The debate over the legitimacy of the dark family or tribe members regularly and rancorously splits families. So deeply did my childhood next-door neighbor trust me that she even detailed the rancorous split between the olive-complected and the caramel-colored branches her Virginia-based extended family, confident that the idea was too silly and our mutual regard too great for me to take the information personally. Of course, she was right.

Indians, Blacks, and "Black Indians"

In another case, the neighborhood networks that bound my little-race interlocutors and me guaranteed tolerance for my investigation but stopped far short of guaranteeing a warm reception. Though I was a childhood classmate and friend of Derek's sister's at largely Black and elite Shepherd Elementary School and our fathers were close colleagues, there was still ample room for fruitful misunderstanding. Features like my son's and mine had literally threatened the survival of many southeastern Indian peoples for centuries, and, rightly or wrongly, I attributed our unsettling experience at the Occaneechi-Saponi powwow to this fact.

In August 2002, more because of information from Derek's mother than because of his willing invitation, Adu and I attended the annual powwow of the Occaneechi Band of the Saponi Nation (OBSN) in Hillsborough, North Carolina—not far from Halifax County, where Uncle Badejọ's first wife had been born. The OBSN is a small band centered in the so-called Texas Community of Alamance County, North Carolina, but much of the band's population is also found in Orange and Caswell Counties. This landmark event celebrated the long-awaited recognition of this partly African-descended tribe by the State of North Carolina.

Derek's father is one of the two South Carolina Geechee cousins who had trained in medicine alongside my father at Howard and, until her recent retirement, practiced medicine in the same department as my stepmother. Though Derek's sisters and his mother, in the mother's own words, "still claim African American," both sisters accepted tribal membership cards for themselves and their children. The dividends include full-tuition scholarships to North Carolina state universities and colleges.

Though she "claims African American," Derek's sister Felicia admits that, among her father's dark Geechee relatives, she feels like a "spectacle." Indeed, many Indians of partly African ancestry and New Orleans Creoles of color feel uncomfortable in settings where they are significantly outnumbered by darker people. They report feeling most comfortable around people of a similar complexion. The privileges of being a light-skinned person among African Americans are material and emotional. However, they are frequently offset by dark people's resentment of those privileges or perhaps at times by the mere discomfort of standing out.

A native of Mebane, North Carolina, Derek's mother is aware of her Indian ancestry but is also a prominent insider of elite Black Washington, DC. Like her daughters, she had married a Black man—in her case, a Geechee physician mentioned in the last chapter. Like him, the two daughters became physicians. Derek's mother and at least one of his sisters also achieved membership in the Links, the most elite of African American women's service organizations. The mother's Nilla Wafer color was undoubtedly an advantage in pledging, as it had been with respect to her marital options. Light-colored women tend to get the choicest of Black mates, just as Derek's mother's mother and my mother's mother had done. However, Indians of partly African descent like Derek do not feel that their professionally and economically elite Black paternity makes them any less Indian.

With his caramel skin and wavy hair, Derek did not stand out physically in the multicolored, upper-middle-class Black neighborhood where we grew up. In the upward race from once-poor Georgetown or still-poor Anacostia to the North Portal Estates and beyond, Washington's nineteenth-century mulattoes had enjoyed a significant head start. Nor was it unusual that Derek was darker than his sisters; brothers often are. However, in our 2002 interview, he reported always having felt inwardly different from African Americans and having experienced some antagonism in the neighborhood for what he perceives as his non–African American looks. Indeed, many of my light-skinned

FIGURE 4.2. Dancers at the 2002 powwow of the Occaneechi Band of the Saponi Nation, Hillsborough, North Carolina. The full diversity of complexions that I saw at this powwow does not appear in the photographs on the band's website. Photograph by the author.

friends and acquaintances—Indian or not—report such antagonism from dark people (and some dark friends report having witnessed it). But Derek says that it was his inner feeling of difference, and not the potential material rewards, that motivated him to act upon his mother's Indian heritage. Beginning in the 1990s, Derek joined a decade-old effort by his kin in Mebane to gain state recognition for their status as the Occaneechi Band of the Saponi Nation. It is clear to me that his intervention made a significant difference.

According to Derek, North Carolina has the largest population of "non-reservated Indians"—that is, Indians without a sovereign territorial reservation—east of the Mississippi. Hence, the state is the heartland of the southeastern Indian populations that were displaced from their land, stripped of treaty rights, moved about, consolidated into one tribal alliance and then another, and assimilated under involuntary terms into a racially stratified system not of their own making. Virtually all of them had intermarried to some degree or another with neighboring African Americans, whites, and descendants of other Indians. However, a vivid and diverse mythology and an ever-changing vocabulary emerged to explain their ambiguous relationship to the overwhelmingly binary Anglo-American logic of race. In the region encompassing southern Virginia, North Carolina, and eastern Tennessee, overlapping populations of such triracial isolates have been called "Melun-

A COMPLEXION OR A CULTURE? 241

geons," "Lumbees," and "Croatans," a term now regarded as derogatory. Outsiders sometimes lump together sets of triracial isolates that do not recognize themselves in terms of these rubrics.

Such mythology identifies them variously as descendants of the white lumbermen from Lumberton, North Carolina, who had patronized Black prostitutes; of Portuguese or Turkish settlers; or of the marooned pirates associated with Sir Walter Raleigh. The favored myths deny in any way possible the rights-killing presence of African ancestry (e.g., Sider 1993; N. Kennedy 1997; Dromgoole 1891), and the story about Black prostitutes may have been invented to defame both them and African Americans generally. Derek has not heard any of these terms and mythologies applied to the Occaneechi-Saponis, except their having been described in the past as "Croatans" and as "Portuguese."

DNA testing on the descendants of those families who were called "Melungeons" in Tennessee's Hawkins and Hancock Counties during the 1800s and early 1900s revealed them to be "the offspring of sub-Saharan African men and white women of northern and central European origin" (Loller 2012). This study proves nothing about the ancestry of the Occaneechi Band of the Saponi Nation. But I wondered initially if this backdrop could explain why both my son and I felt so bad after leaving the 2002 Occaneechi-Saponi powwow. Things were far more complicated than I had realized, and the tension between Derek's perspective and mine taught me a lesson that deserves careful consideration.

At the end of a long, sweltering August day, the ceremony had already passed its crescendo as I chatted with Derek, the tribal chairwoman, and another female member of the band at the reception table. They sat behind it, under an open-walled party tent, while I stood on the other side and in the wilting 4:00 p.m. sun. Indeed, I had been standing continuously since Adu's and my arrival at noon.

A half hour into our conversation, I asked them if I could sit with them, in an empty chair behind the now-inactive sign-in table. Their fifteen seconds of silence and exchange of sidelong glances made it clear that careful thought went into their reply. With synchronized nods, they declined my request. "I'm afraid that won't be possible at this time," said the chairwoman.

Our conversation came to an abrupt halt. I hoped in vain that we could all pretend that nothing had just happened, allowing our previously lively conversation to proceed. But after five minutes of silence, I wandered off, feeling as embarrassed for my family friend as for myself. For that reason, it took me twelve years to work up the courage to ask Derek what was going through his head at the time.

Soon after sunset, I was approached by Emma Smith, whom I had first met at a Chickahominy powwow in Charles City, Virginia. Emma was herself a Virginia Indian with a graham-cracker complexion and soft features that also suggested African ancestry. She wore a radiant white buckskin dress accented with bead patterns and fringes that danced even as she stood still. As a crowd of curious women supervised our conversation, Emma railed against William Loren Katz for having misrepresented her kind by titling his 1984 book *Black Indians*.

I do not know how many of the women in this gathering were Occaneechi-Saponis, as opposed to visitors from other tribes. According to Derek, their refusal to acknowledge that one could be both Black and Indian is inconsistent with the history and the ideals of his tribe.

With Black church-like hums of affirmation, eye-rolling exasperation, and sharply pointed fingers targeting me in accusation, several women of apparently mixed African and non-African ancestry told me that they are not Black and should not be described as such. They are Indian. I feared for my safety in this darkening glade beside the fairgrounds, as they asked—with a good measure of accusation—whether *I* intended to describe them as "Black Indians." As I assured them that I was there only to find out how they described themselves and would reproduce it faithfully, they gave me some breathing room. However, talking to each other as much as to me, they continued to explain, from every position around me, why they are not Black.

And are proud not to be. For example, Emma told me later on the telephone that nineteenth-century shipper and "back-to-Africa" activist Paul Cuffe, enslaved nineteenth-century Virginian revolutionary Nat Turner, twentieth-century Harlem Renaissance writer Langston Hughes, and the descendants of the antebellum "free people of color" in general were actually Indians, wrongly swept up in the dragnet of the "one-drop rule." She added that African Americans fear losing these erstwhile members of their race because the Black race would otherwise have no accomplishments of its own. Though Emma's were the most strongly worded that I have heard, similar competition for prestigious ancestors and assertions of African American inferiority were common among my southeastern Indian and Louisiana Creole interlocutors, not to mention their Caribbean immigrant counterparts.

At the Hillsborough powwow, I had encouraged my son Adu, then seven, to go and play with the other children while I talked with the adults. Like most elite parents, I consider up-close exposure to social and cultural diversity an important part of his education. A happy and gentle boy, he has always made friends easily, in Cambridge, Durham, Washington, New York, Bahia, and Berlin. Looking for a reason to feel happy during the drive home, I asked if he had had a good time. Not at all, he said. The children had been mean to him and called him names. Rather than ask for further details, I changed the subject, not wanting this experience to take root in his beautiful little soul.

In 2013, I contacted Derek and his sisters again to ask them, like a score of my most important mentors during this research project, to read the nearly finished manuscript. Doing so was particularly important in his case because I wanted to make sure that I did not embarrass him or misrepresent him regarding a situation that had hurt my feelings. At first, he responded angrily. But because of e-mail difficulties amid my departure for a year-long leave of absence in Berlin, months intervened before I searched for and saw his e-mail. As he himself observed about the conflicts between "white-Indian" and "black-Indian" tribes, time cools things down. And our nearly three-hour transatlantic Skype call was perhaps the densest learning experience of my field research on this topic.

In the earlier e-mail Derek had corrected several factual errors in my account and said that I had chosen a bad day to conduct interviews and annoyed people at the powwow with my questions. He recalled that a sometime chairman of the tribe had been so annoyed that he threatened to sue me if I published anything he said, an incident that I do not recall. In response to my tale about standing at the tribal registration table, Derek wrote, "It was Tribal policy that *only* Tribal members could sit in the Tribal booth area during pow wows," adding, "This policy applied to *EVERY* non-member and not just you." He said that I had been biased and, by failing to conduct follow-up interviews, had simply used my superficial information to confirm what I already believed.

As a fellow stigmatized person, I could empathize. As Goffman (1963) has pointed out, information management can be a life-and-death matter for the discreditable. I was not out to embarrass Derek but to get at the shared root of our respective situations. Perhaps his having read only the sections of the manuscript that spoke about him and his band made that fact difficult to realize.

Fortunately, the delay in my reply to Derek and our subsequent e-mail exchange allowed us both to measure the situation carefully. I reminded him that the reason I sent the manuscript to him in the first place is that I do not want to and must not embarrass him. And I respect his right to reply. It also helped that we could by then remember the depth and the importance of the social connections between us. In a shared community that matters to us, we are both implicated by the words that I publish.

Consequently, in August 2014, twelve years after that powwow, we both spoke with candor and love. He told me that *he* had not regarded my questions in 2002 as inappropriate, but their timing was bad. Like me, the people

I had annoyed were hot, and doubly so because they were wearing buckskin. Like me, they were tired, and doubly so because they had been working on a massive public event. More important, the band's leaders had just completed a brutal battle for recognition and faced both commission and journalistic adversaries continually trying to debunk their legitimate case for recognition by harping on race. They were sick of the questions, and they were mistrustful of my motives because I was a "stranger."

I balked at the word "stranger," saying that his mother had asked me to call him, I had called him, and he had "invited" me, indicating a hotel for my son and me and giving me careful directions. He balked at the word "invited." Though he had told the tribal council that I was coming, he hadn't told everybody. Indeed, when I'd spoken to him before the powwow, I had not sensed that he was anxious for me to attend.

I explained to him that, had he or any of his family come to visit or attend an event in my university or anyplace else that I considered my home, I would have made sure they were comfortable. Hindsight is twenty-twenty, I said, so I'm not blaming anyone for the imperfections we all have. But even if the chairwoman couldn't let me sit in the shade, she or Derek could have explained the rule and offered me a glass of cold water and an appropriate place to sit. I had felt that such lack of empathy for me might have to do with the general history of anti-Black sentiment in the southeastern tribes. He said no. There are Occaneechi-Saponis with dreadlocks and skin as dark as mine who, on that very day, had sat as prominently under that tent as any other member. He apologized and said that he had felt especially bad about my son's experience. I thanked him and admitted that, unfortunately, such things, which are sometimes inspired by children's early intuition that their dark fellows don't deserve the same love as their light ones, can happen in any of our communities. I valued his apology, but I also learned from the exchange that the state recognition of the Occaneechi Band of the Saponi Nation had represented a major triumph against a very real anti-African bias among the southeastern Indian nations, in no small part because of the efforts of Derek and his great-grandfather.

Derek's basic lesson to me was this: However culturally hybrid and imperfect in their genesis, southeastern tribal communities have a persistence and integrity worthy of respect. But this lesson easily segued into my own; yes, he belongs to a bounded Indian community in the North Carolina Piedmont, but he also belongs to my community—the Northwest Washington world of Black physicians, attorneys, accountants, diplomats, and secret service agents that gave boys like us a sense of our infinite possibilities. We could, in sum, be "Black any way we wanted to be." In the real world, people's membership in communities is dictated not by unique and discrete cultures but by their situational choice to recognize a common experience and common interests. Our nearly three-hour conversation was, to me, a testament to the fact that his being an Indian did not stop him from also being my little brother, bound by a network of relationship that is, to me, just as special as any other.

The additional details that he generously offered were more than just corrections. They were vivid and honest reflections that reveal humanity and heroism under difficult circumstances.

Recognition by the state takes place under the authority of the North Carolina Commission of Indian Affairs, which is made up of representatives of the already recognized tribes, as well as representatives of several Indian organizations. It is dominated by the largest "non-reservated" tribe, the Lumbees, who are triracial but reputedly highly conflicted about that fact. The state's largest tribe with a reservation, the Eastern Band of the Cherokee Nation, keeps its distance from these battles. Some local Indian-descended populations, such as the Lumbees and the Haliwa-Saponis, may have found it easier than the Occaneechi-Saponis to secure state recognition, and some of their leaders appear to have been hostile toward partly African-descended aspirants to such recognition.[1] It would contaminate their own claims to the legitimacy of their recognition as Indians, of their access to the few federal grants available to state-recognized Indian tribes, and of their potential claim to the colonial-era treaty rights of their forebears, should such tribes ever attempt to make those claims through the courts. Among the leaders of the fight for the recognition of the partly African-descended Occaneechi-Saponis was my former neighbor Derek. He fully recognizes that his mother and the "Texas Community" from which she hails are "triracial" and avows that the effort to deny their recognition as "both Black and Indian" is a form of racism on the part of "white-Indians."

Derek cares deeply about his people and was inspired by conversations with Texas Community elders to research the Tutelo-Saponi language that was spoken by their Indian forebears. With the initial help of a Howard University linguist, who happened to be white, Derek began to reconstruct a language that, according to Hazel (1991), no one had likely spoken in a century (and perhaps two centuries). And he did so based upon songs and word lists gathered while a group of eighteenth-century Saponi refugees dwelled among the Iroquois in what is now New York State.

Because Derek recommends Hazel (1991) as a source on OBSN history, information from that article is used here to supplement this summary of Derek's Skyped tutelage. Revivalists among both the southeastern Indians and the Louisiana Creoles frequently refer to scholarly publications and orally refer to their content as they argue the reality of their widely doubted peoplehoods.

The last documented pre-twentieth-century reference to a distinct Saponi tribe was in 1763 (Hazel 1991, 12). Amid the vicissitudes of war, state violence, missionization, alliances with the Catawba and the Iroquois, the flight from Virginia segregationist laws, and the pursuit of a better life, the tribe as a whole has moved in and out of Virginia, and some kin of the families now identified as members of the OBSN—including the Bunches, the Haitcocks, the Jeffrieses, the Whitmores, the Stewards, the Watkins, and so forth—took refuge in New York State among the Iroquois or migrated to Tennessee; Ohio; Kansas; Washington, DC; and other parts of the country. Some, like Derek himself, have returned to Alamance County or migrate to and from other residences.

As a tribe and as a set of families, the Occaneechi-Saponis may have had a highly distinctive lifestyle in the mid-eighteenth century, but by the mid-nineteenth, available records suggest that they spoke and dressed much like their Black and white neighbors. Moreover, the state classified them according to legal categories—such as "colored," "free colored" and "mulatto"—that were also assigned to free Black Americans, categories that also created an ambiguity about their entitlement to prior treaty rights and to exemption from the indignities imposed upon most southeastern Black people in the nineteenth century. However, Derek proudly affirms that, before and during the nineteenth century, some people of African descent did marry into the Occaneechi-Saponi community. Some whites married in, as well, so some members of the tribe descend from Indians and Europeans alone. However, the difference between partly European and partly African ancestry is immaterial to one's status as an Occaneechi-Saponi and should, in his view, be immaterial to one's recognition as an Indian of any tribe.

Hazel (1991) reports that following multiple migrations, the "Texas community was intact by 1820" (15). The state called its residents "Free Colored" in the 1800s and "Free Negro" in 1830, but the "Free Negro" list "enumerates nearly all of the families that were ancestral to present-day Indian communities in other parts of North Carolina such as the Lumbee, Coharie, and Meherrin" (15). Hence, among these southeastern tribes, African ancestry is not unique to the Occaneechi-Saponis. If African ancestry does not disqualify the Lumbees as Indian, it should not disqualify the Occaneechi-Saponis either. Numerous nineteenth-century Indian court testimonies and petitions documented by Hazel capitulate to the white racist assumption that no one with an African or an enslaved ancestor could be legitimately Indian. However, according to Derek and the North Carolina Commission of Indian Affairs, it is not their racial purity that establishes their continuity with the tribes of their Indian forebears but their social and "cultural" continuity, some of which was evident in the nineteenth century. After all, most of the state-recognized tribe members admit to having numerous white ancestors. If part-white tribes are not disqualified, why should part-black tribes be?

Writes Hazel, "Although much of the traditional culture had been lost by the time of the Civil War, some traditions, particularly ones dealing with food gathering and wild plant use continued" (1991, 22). The Occaneechi-Saponis were particularly well known as trappers and herbal healers. Yet the social continuity of this Indian community came to rely less on the endurance of these occupational distinctions than on a novel reaction to a political force that emerged in the late nineteenth century—racial segregation.

In the twentieth century, much as in the Virginia case, the best-known forms of North Carolina Indian communities' continuity with their Indian forebears were churches. Two distinctly Indian churches were founded "around the turn of the twentieth century" (Hazel 1991, 23), which it should be noted was when state and collective white violence against African Americans were, in the wake of Reconstruction's failure, reaching a crescendo. Based on the example of Virginia, there is good reason to believe that Indians who once worshiped alongside African Americans felt the need to seek higher, safer ground. Schools, too, were a refuge. The Martin, Patillo, and Crawford schools fell under the "colored schools" division of the segregated county school system, but they remained largely Indian. When school officials decided to merge the Martin School into the mostly Negro Pleasant Grove School, Indian parents objected forcefully. They eventually gave in on account of the superior facilities of Pleasant Grove (ibid).

It is my view that, as Cohen (1969) points out, the political or economic advantages of maintaining (or, I might add, creating) ethnic distinction are often what motivates people to exhume obsolete names and practices, to project new significance onto differences of little antecedent importance, to borrow exogenous practices in order to reinforce old social distinctions, and to invent entirely new cultural diacritica. Ethnic identities are protean and strategic invocations, not primordial and self-existent realities. And I regard the Occaneechi-Saponis, as well as all of the southeastern tribes that I visited, as a case in point.

But Derek underlines the fact of social continuity. In sum, even if their dress, speech, foodways, and, eventually, schools did converge with those of their Black and white neighbors, a "core community" of Occaneechi-Saponis did maintain a corporate existence throughout the nineteenth century and up until today. Nor in this regard are they any different from their "white-

Indian" counterparts. Moreover, the fact that they have only recently adopted the celebratory powwow style of the western Indians—and, I might add, adopted or readopted buckskin as ceremonial attire to mark their social distinctiveness—make them no different from scores of other Indian tribes around the country. Derek is right.

And he usefully amplifies Cohen's point, arguing that political and economic interest can also motivate an ethnic group's adversaries to *deny* social distinctions that are very real and persistent. For example, facing competition from the casinos of what Derek regards as legitimate "Black-Indian" tribes in New York State, Donald Trump vociferously asserts that these tribes are "Black" and therefore *not* Indian at all.

Derek is not sure whether he agrees with me, though, about the following general assessment. I do not believe that people have an intrinsic desire to remain culturally different from other people. On the contrary, most people like to try the sensuously attractive or prestigious behaviors of neighboring populations, unless we are subject to some material incentive *not* to do so.

But then we get to the real crux of the debate. It is a live debate among southeastern Indians, into which I stepped only accidentally.

As Derek and I relaxed into brotherly candor, he acknowledged that the anti-Black racism engendered by nineteenth-century white racism has become a habit in southeastern Indian communities, which often victimize their darker members for a historical crime that is not their own.

I would summarize the backdrop as follows: In the face of a crime not their own, the Indians of the southeastern United States face a painful dilemma. They were once independent peoples, with values and practices of their own and the footing to bargain with other peoples as equals. But an overwhelming European settler colonialism imposed both private property and a racial hierarchy of rights. Withdrawing from this system was nearly impossible, but to the extent that it was possible, withdrawal typically meant survival at subsistence level, unless neighboring whites used one's partly African ancestry as an excuse to strip away one's little remaining land and other treaty rights, which meant a fate worse than subsistence—that is, dispersion and homeless poverty. On the other hand, integration into the system meant not only greater prosperity but symbolic degradation—entering the system in last place, alongside Black people. In either case, the Black constituent other was a living, breathing symbol that Indians had few attractive choices.

But as it turns out, Derek has been a pathbreaker in demanding equal treatment before the North Carolina Commission of Indian Affairs for "white-Indians" (the ones whose non-Indian ancestors are primarily white) and "Black-Indians" (the ones whose non-Indian ancestors are primarily

Black). Indeed, he comes from a long line of fighters against anti-Black racism in southeastern Indian families and communities.

For example, in the 1930s, when members of the Texas community petitioned for an Indian school separated from the Black school, they may have been seeking to preserve their distinct legacy as Indians, but they were doing so in complicity with the racism of the state and at the expense of their Black-Indian relatives. Derek's Occaneechi-Saponi great-grandfather was a "white-Indian"—that is, a descendant of Europeans and Native Americans. He fathered children by his first wife, who was also "white-Indian." After she died, he married a "Black-Indian" woman and fathered children by her as well. Derek's line descends from this foremother. When the great-grandfather was approached to sign the Indian school petition, he refused because he knew that, according to the policies of the state and the intent of the petitioners, "white-Indians" like his first set of children would be admitted, while "Black-Indians" like his second set of children would be rejected.

Writes Derek in an email to me:

> [T]he petition failed. A White Alamance County, NC School Superintendent, Mr. AC [sic] Younts . . . wrote the BIA [Bureau of Indian Affairs] and convinced them that the Texas people were "colored" and did not need an Indian School. In spite of the BIA's own written statements and conclusion of Indianness, they agreed with Mr. Younts and referred the Texas leaders to the NC [colored] School system. Was it due to the Texans possessing too much "Black blood" (racism) or was it an economic reason—that Alamance County did not want to pay for a third, separate school system (as required under NC law) for its Indian population? The answer is probably a combination of both of these reasons. (e-mail from Derek to the author, August 31, 2014)

Derek agrees that southeastern Indians' flight from the forms of white racist oppression suffered above all by African Americans may be one of the reasons that they maintained their distinct communities. And he observes perspicaciously that desegregation, far from reducing concern about race, made many southeastern Indians *more* anxious to demonstrate their distinction from African Americans.

A member of the whiter-looking Haliwa-Saponi tribe once stage-whispered a question to someone else while Derek was in the room. He "wondered" why Derek had attended an HBCU, implying that he must therefore be Black and therefore *not* Indian. Like Derek's gossiping antagonist, the members of the North Carolina Commission of Indian Affairs cannot mention aloud their wish to exclude partly African Indians from tribal recognition, even as they try to rig the recognition criteria against it.

When I first talked to Derek about this issue in 2002, he was not as boldly vociferous as he is now, but he has since found his voice. Derek now says out loud, to anyone who wants to know, that he is proudly both Black and Indian. And he cites historical evidence of the alliance he embodies and recommends as a model for his contemporaries. He tells me that, in a conspiracy that occurred sometime between 1726 and 1729, African Americans and Saponi Indians in Virginia were allies against white oppression. He is a product of love among three races and of the HBCUs in particular, which have nurtured Blacks, Indians, and "Black-Indians" for a century and a half. Like Walter Benjamin, he would tap history as a source of our better selves. Derek notes that his own tribe accords full rights and pride of place to its members regardless of their complexion, hair texture, or hair style. And he has noted the progress of other tribes in doing the same.

However, perhaps because of their awareness of enduring anti-Black bias in the official and unofficial recognition of Indian tribes, not all members of the OBSN appear to be comfortable publicizing the African ancestry of many tribe members. For example, in "A Brief History of the Occaneechi Band of the Saponi Nation," which appears on the OBSN official website, "formal marriages and common-law relationships between Indians and their European neighbors" are mentioned explicitly, while the African ancestry of the band goes unmentioned (www.obsn.org/a-brief-history, downloaded August 23, 2014). And in my observation, black-looking people are underrepresented on the OBSN website relative to the number of such people I saw and photographed at the 2002 powwow.

But Derek avows, I think correctly, that conscientious people like him and his great-grandfather are making a difference. In multiple eastern tribes, black-looking Indians tribes are gaining recognition, and black-looking individuals are gaining the tribal memberships that they were once denied. Moreover, tribes once split along the "white-Indian"/"black-Indian" divide are now reuniting. Some of the federally recognized tribes that once used blood quantum to determine membership are now even rethinking this standard, which Derek considers racist, because, otherwise, they will end up with no members at all. In that spirit, Derek says that membership in the OBSN is determined not just by genealogy but also by continuous residence or continual long-term involvement in the community.

Derek said he regretted how he had initially expressed anger toward me. He'd been burned many times by journalists and anthropologists. But he respects my family and me. We go back a long way. And he respects my having sent him the manuscript for review, even though, he said, I didn't have to do so. I said I did, on ethical grounds. I owed him that respect. Moreover, I knew that I could not understand this experience without the benefit of his perspective, which I vowed to publish alongside my own. And he said repeatedly that the story I am telling needs to be told.

Our community of agreement and debate thickened and personalized the network of social ties that had all along linked not only us personally but also the southeastern Indians, the Gullah/Geechees, and African Americans collectively. But that doesn't make Derek any less Indian.

Slavery, Racism, and "Document Genocide"

Some southeastern Indians take a less subtle posture, asserting that a person cannot be both Black and Indian. Among the Virginia and North Carolina Indians who taught me, Emma was the most vocal partisan of this position. She blames the mistaken labeling of their forebears as Black on eugenicist and Virginia State Registrar of Vital Statistics W. A. Plecker, who, in the 1920s, committed what she and some other southeastern Indians call "document genocide" against these accomplished Indians by reclassifying both Indians and Negroes in Virginia as "colored" (see also, e.g., Lovett 2002, 208). Indeed, participants in the Chickahominy powwow told me that the new law was harshly enforced. Back then, they told me, "If you said you were an Indian, they would kill you."

David Treuer (2012) summarized the general experience of American Indians in this way: they were stripped of their land, forcibly assimilated, idealized as noble savages, and forced to look that way in order to be accepted as Indian. But Native Americans of partly African descent—and, by extension, many tribes who remained in the southeast after the Indian Removal Act of 1830—suffered a distinctive permutation of these events.

The series of legal and administrative reclassifications that took place in Virginia was subtle, revealing that Indians were far from the true target of exclusion amid the racial narrowing of citizenship during what Southern white supremacists called the "Redemption." Up until 1910, a free Virginian who was officially less than a quarter Negro was legally white, so that some of Sally Hemings and Thomas Jefferson's descendants were legally white. The Racial Integrity Act of 1924 redefined anyone with a single nonwhite ancestor as colored—with the explicit *exception* of some descendants of Native Americans. Certain highly influential white families—the so-called First Families of Virginia—had proudly proclaimed their descent from Pocahontas and yet were exempted from reclassification as "colored" (Maillard 2007; Jacques 2011). Above all, the State of Virginia's new exclusions targeted not Indians per se but African ancestry and any suspicion thereof.

Thus deprived of their distinctive legal category, treaty rights, and institutions, ambitious Indians who appeared to be part black had to attend HBCUs, live in Negro neighborhoods, and marry other people classified as "colored." However, in the view of today's Virginia and North Carolina Indians of partly African ancestry, those marriages, school assignments, and residential conditions did not invalidate their Indianness. Like Derek, Emma herself had attended an HBCU, but unlike the rest of her family and Derek, she was emphatically *not* Black.

Though angry about Plecker's official "push" in the 1920s, some eastern Indians equally fear the great "pull" of Blackness for their children. Young Delaware Nanticokes, for example, are said to find Blackness more "modern, cooler," because they associate it with popular culture. Those who choose to be Indian feel that they are outvoted by their peers and less popular. In New Jersey, young Nanticokes often assimilate as Puerto Rican. (The New Jersey Nanticokes are a product of their ancestors' decision to part ways with their darker-skinned Delaware cousins.) Those who then moved to California assimilate as Chicano. "They take on an entire persona," observed Piscataway leader Gabrielle Tayac, who is also a curator at the Smithsonian Institution's National Museum of the American Indian. Often propelling these moves, says Gaby, is a growing hatred of whites.

I encountered the warmest of receptions among Gaby's tribe, the Piscataways, and their cousins the Piscatawas in Maryland, and I do not seem to be alone in that experience. A group of Black friends and family who also embrace their Native American legacy whom I encountered at the Piscatawa powwows reported that they, too, received a warm reception there. Happy to learn of my research, they performed a spontaneous circle dance after the powwow had ended. Several of the dancers wore Indian moccasins and hair adornments, and two of them wore African-style clothing as well. One of them wore dreadlocks.

The history of Howard University's largesse toward their ancestors may help to explain the goodwill of the Piscataways and the Piscatawas. But economics offers an additional possible factor. The county that these peoples call home is also home to the African American population with the highest average income in the United States, higher than the average white income in the county. Unsurprisingly, Black people dominate the county government. Like the District of Columbia's Gold Coast, where I grew up, Prince George's County is one of the places where it is the most difficult to look down upon African Americans or see us as a constituent other.

On the other hand, close inspection reveals a deep resentment of Black people in most of the cultural and genealogical self-fashioning that I witnessed

FIGURE 4.3. A circle of Black Indian family and friends dancing spontaneously after a Piscatawa powwow, Waldorf, Maryland, 2002. Photograph by the author.

among Virginia and North Carolina Indians. Emma's hyperbolic claims about the Indian source of most putatively African American accomplishment is arrayed chiefly against African Americans' collective possessiveness about mixed-race people, but it is also defense against what self-described Black Indian Howard legacy student Curtis Howe describes as "the last stand of Jim Crow—the Indian reservation." No less than the Cherokees in their recent vote to disenfranchise the descendants of their African American slaves and advocates (Evans 2007; *New York Times* 2007a, 2007b) and the Seminoles in their similar action in 2000 (Glaberson 2001), the light-skinned and part-white claimants to Indian treaty rights in the eastern United States have sometimes violently denied their part-black cousins' access to the same rights.[2]

Many of the southeastern tribes had enslaved Black people and, in recent years, have proved even more anxious than whites to exclude the descendants of the enslaved from the benefits of citizenship. At the Chickahominy powwow that I attended in Charles City, Virginia, in 2002, belt buckles and other paraphernalia featuring the Confederate flag were common at the vending tables.

In recent years, I have discussed the Cherokees' and the Seminoles' votes with numerous Native Americans from federally recognized tribes. To a person, they have invoked the argument that, whether others agree or disagree with the choice, the sovereignty of those nations guarantees them the right to define membership as they wish. Among these prosovereignty interlocutors was the Cherokee tribal attorney married to the daughter of a Louisiana Creole dean at Howard. The dean's other daughter is a CNN cable news anchorwoman of the sort that the network then seemed to favor for their racially ambiguous appearance. I have always wanted to ask how these Natives would feel if Black and white Americans applied the principle of sovereignty and voted Native Americans out of their US citizenship. In hierarchical systems, a dense web of social connections often unites the discreditable with the discredited. However, their social proximity and similarity of condition often inspire asymmetrical antipathy where I had expected mutual empathy.

From the early 1970s until the sale of my mother's house in 1993, a poster of Ungloghe Luta—Red Shirt—of the Oglala Dakota hung on my bedroom wall. And he long hung on the wall of the sitting room outside my bedroom in Durham. The Edward Sheriff Curtis photo exemplified for me the beauty, dignity, and tragedy of others who had lost the war against European imperialism and white racism. Red Shirt was on my wall because he represented a part of me. (Not unlike many African American intellectuals, I have long felt the same way about Palestinians.)

During the summer after high school, my half-white, half-Wichita friend Ken reflected some of the glow of Curtis's portrait. Our friendship arose from a combination of mutual curiosity, shared iconoclasm, and our both being very different from our working-class African American coworkers at the National Zoo's Mane Restaurant. It was because of him that I learned to enjoy beer as a medium of brotherly communion. I had never seen the appeal of such communion with my equally beer-loving white peers at the Maret School. Like the other Black kids in my life, I liked to dance and preferred the resulting endorphin- and pheromone-based high. Ken and I parted ways after the summer of 1978 but stayed in touch for a few years through hours-long phone calls.

The summer after my sophomore year at Harvard, I proposed to visit him, but he warned me not to come. In his native Anadarko, Oklahoma, he said, the Indians "would treat you really bad." I didn't believe they could treat me any worse than had my white high school classmates, who had actually done nothing worse than pressuring me to play sports and, in the case of one borderline-white boy, conspicuously underestimating my intelligence (after I received the highest SAT scores in the class, he declared, as if he had witnessed the unthinkable, "Randy, you did better on your SATs that *I* did!"). I had not then been aware of the much greater intensity of feeling—both negative and positive—that other oppressed races in the United States often feel toward Black Americans. Ken stopped just short of calling me naïve.

I never saw Ken again. In the late 1990s, he appears to have died from the effects of alcoholism. Like my own full brother and sister, he died young. He could hardly have been over forty-five, providing some ambiguous evidence of the point made to me by one Virginia Indian about why she thought it more a matter of need than of racial chauvinism for Native Americans to declare themselves. Contrary to Emma's claims of Indian superiority to African Americans, Native American poverty levels, health problems, and death rates greatly exceed those of Black people and virtually every other population in the United States, and they need to lobby for more targeted public intervention.

Ken's mother, too, had been an alcoholic, and I sensed that he had grown up poor. Only after the Cherokee and Seminole votes did I come to believe that his refusal of my visit was anything other than an effort to keep his bourgeois friend from witnessing his family's poverty.

The roots of the animus of the Oklahoma tribes toward Black people are apparently deep. In the Negro history books of my youth, the Black "Buffalo Soldiers" were celebrated for their prowess as Indian fighters and for the admiration that Native Americans reportedly expressed by giving them this name. Smithsonian museum curator John Whittington Franklin and his late father, renowned historian and former Howard University history professor John Hope Franklin, are the descendants of people enslaved by the Choctaws. Having lived in Oklahoma, John Whittington reported that many contemporary Native Americans actually feel great anger toward the Black killers of their ancestors and also, consequently, toward Black people in general. Recently, the younger Franklin collaborated with Smithsonian curator and Piscataway tribe member Gaby Tayac on a National Museum of the American Indian exhibition about Black-Indian relations. Recall that Gaby's people long received their medical treatment at Howard, giving her greater reasons to support this call for interracial alliance.

Back in the southeastern United States, the African American threat to Native Americans was nonmilitary. But the animus is still sometimes violent. At Virginia powwows, lighter-skinned Indians are accused of snatching away the tribal identity cards of Black-looking Indians. To many southeastern Indians, including dark ones, any verbal or physical association with people of African descent is defamatory—the surest route to losing their recent battles to recover long-ignored treaty rights and a sense of personal dignity. My family friend Derek reports that the part-white Haliwa-Saponis, who were the first band to achieve North Carolina state recognition, hate the darker Occaneechi band with a passion. However, the pattern does not stop there.

Against this chauvinism among part-white Indians, Emma's reappropriation of Paul Cuffe, Nat Turner, and Langston Hughes as Indians establishes dark Indians' superiority to Blacks and declares dark Indians a desirable catch for any race or tribe. Like many members of black immigrant groups, triracial isolates, and Indian groups, Emma seems to reserve her greatest anger not for the white racists who have oppressed Indians and Black people or for the Indian racists who have enslaved or excluded people of African ancestry but for the nonethnic African Americans who are viewed as dragging down the groups who are unwillingly associated with them (see Dromgoole 1891 for a similar nineteenth-century phenomenon). White supremacy has always relied on such interested consent by the governed.

Some Europeans, many Indians, and most of the Africans in seventeenth-century Maryland, Virginia, and the Carolinas occupied an unfree status. However, after Bacon's Rebellion in 1676, involuntary lifelong servitude was increasingly racialized and legally restricted to people of African descent (Fields 1990). Though often abrogated or ignored, various treaties promised freedom, property rights, and a degree of political autonomy to some southeastern Indian populations. However, the colonies, their successor states, and the federal government always reserved far greater rights for whites than for nonwhites in this region. Whereas the "one-drop" rule operated to exclude most racially mixed individuals from the privileges of whiteness, a certain fraction of recognized white or Indian ancestry, sometimes as little as seven-eighths and sometimes as much as fifteen-sixteenths, was sufficient in Virginia to exempt a person from the most despised and legally encumbered status—that is, Blackness.

However, the fraction of white or Indian ancestry needed to exempt a person from Blackness tended to increase over time. Moreover, practically speaking, it was difficult for any African-descended person to disprove the Blackness of all but one of eight great-grandparents or all but one of sixteen great-great-grandparents. Since the beginning of European and African settlement in North America, there had always been significant sexual contact among whites, Indians, and Black people. However, these increasingly harsh laws, combined with the vast and forcible removal of most southeastern Indians to the West in the mid-nineteenth century, made the remaining Indians ever more vulnerable to redefinition as "people of color," legally indistinguishable from African Americans and ever more penalized by that racial status. At least one Virginia Indian group that had willingly intermarried and allied with African Americans—the Gingaskin tribe—was forced from its reservation and, with no place else to go, merged into the local Black community (Rountree 1990, 184).

During the civil rights movement, though some southeastern Indians allied with African Americans to pursue equal rights for all, the most common reactions recorded by Rountree (1990) in Virginia and Sider (1993) in North Carolina were anti-Black hatred and intensified efforts by Indians to distinguish themselves from African Americans. This reaction has a long history. For example, Hugh Jones wrote in his early-eighteenth-century chronicle that the Indians "hate, and despise the very sight of a Negroe; . . . . and fear and revere the whites" (quoted in Rountree 1990, 155).

After the emancipation of the enslaved, as the force of Jim Crow segregation grew in the late nineteenth century, churches that had, before the Civil War, simultaneously welcomed Black, white, and Indian worshippers split up. Often the earliest distinctly tribal institutions in recorded memory, separate "Indian churches" were founded with the expressed intent to avoid association with Blacks (Rountree 1990, 188, 200). In other words, the most widespread Indian response to white-imposed segregation was to segregate themselves, in turn, as dramatically and as institutionally as possible from Black people.

They regularly fought for distinct schools, as well, which they secured with lesser frequency. Writes Rountree,

> Indian children were welcome only in the black schools. Therefore, to preserve their "Indianness" in their own and in outsiders' eyes, the Indians had to refuse to allow their children to enter those black schools. . . . [T]he Indians had to raise even higher the barriers between themselves and their black neighbors, which naturally caused resentment on the part of the blacks, who regarded the Indians as fellow oppressed people. (1990, 200–1)

Rather than fight segregation in public transportation, Virginia Indians typically fought to be recognized as "white." Their victory was what required them to begin issuing tribal identification cards. With such cards, they could avoid prosecution for riding in "white" train cars (Rountree 1990, 212). Starting in 1889, these highly mixed-race populations had campaigned, with the encouragement and help of Smithsonian anthropologist James Mooney and University of Pennsylvania anthropologist Frank G. Speck, to prove legally, and probably counterfactually, that they had no African ancestry at all. (Mooney and most Virginia whites believed that these populations did have some degree of African ancestry.) By the time of the Civil War, they had lost their distinctive languages and come to share much ancestry and normative conduct with their Negro and white neighbors. However, those mixed-race populations that could plausibly use what Rountree calls "oral history and hearsay" to distinguish themselves from the constituent other made desperate efforts to do so, particularly as whites erected the fortress of anti-Black segregation, or "Jim Crow." The state-recognized Pamunkeys even refused to accept a "colored" teacher assigned by the state to teach in their school.

In the structure of Jim Crow, Virginia whites made little effort to distinguish populations with nonwhite "blood" from each other, and few of these populations were recognized in any way by law. However, in their ethnological efforts to recover native history before it was lost, Smithsonian anthropologists turned a spotlight on these and similar populations in Maryland, Delaware, and North Carolina. They did not just document the memory of Indian ethnonyms, place names, surviving cultural traits, and extant social groupings. Mooney and Speck actually encouraged and in some cases directed the proliferation of self-proclaimed Indian tribes and public performances in which these populations advertised their distinctiveness. They also encouraged the founding of more distinctly "Indian" churches, the production of written membership rolls, and the invention of hybrid forms of dress that reified the difference between these mixed-race populations and "colored" populations that lacked the means or the desire to deny their African ancestry. The widespread national and international ethnological expositions of the day were a preferred venue of these performances. But the fact remained that a large part of Virginia's unambiguously "Negro" population was also of mixed racial ancestry, and such performances of difference from Blackness were as interested as they were inventive and novel. Even during the civil rights movement of the 1950s and 1960s, many Virginia Indians—deeply impoverished and poorly schooled as they were—opposed school desegregation and, to a person, says Rountree, refused to participate, for fear of being branded with the low social status of Black people in case the Black struggle for equality failed (1990, 202–18, 241).

Moreover, in hierarchical systems, "last-place anxiety" (Tajfel and Turner 1979) is a powerful impulse to complicity. The average person's fear of coming up last is more compelling than his or her resentment of the hierarchy that has cast him or her as second worst. Indeed, social psychologists Tajfel and Turner (1979) show that in intergroup competitions for resources, most people consider it more important to maintain superiority over another group than to maximize both groups' resources and create a situation of equality. In various studies, "subjects are randomly classified as members of two non-overlapping groups." Nothing else about the other members of the in-group or of the out-group is known to the subject, who knows of no conflict of interest or previous history of conflict between these random groups (Tajfel and Turner 1979, 38). The authors conclude,

> There is a good deal of evidence that . . . maximum difference (M.D.) is more important to the subjects than maximizing in-group profit (M.I.P.). Thus, they seem to be competing with the out-group, rather than following a strategy of simple economic gain for members of the in-group. (39)

That is, suppose that researchers assigned the research subject to Group A and told that subject of the existence of another group, Group B. Each subject was then given two options. On the one hand, according to the "maximum-payoff" option, the subject could give twenty dollars to each member of Group A (the in-group), on condition that he or she also give twenty dollars to each member of Group B (the out-group). On the other hand, the "maximum-difference" option was to give each member of Group A *more* resources than the subject gave to each member of Group B. For example, in the "maximum-difference" option, each member of in-group A might receive only ten dollars (i.e., less than the "maximum payoff") but receive the satisfaction of giving each member of out-group B only five dollars. In this range of experiments, the vast majority of the research subjects chose the "maximum-difference" option over the "maximum-payoff" option.

Much to my surprise, these psychological experiments demonstrate people's willingness to accept net material losses in exchange for establishing or preserving their superiority to another group of subordinate people. In that spirit, many Virginia Indian groups were even willing to deny their children schooling if segregation required them to attend school with Black children and thereby risk confessing the Indians' collective likeness, under the label "colored," to Black people and social equality with them (Rountree 1990, 200). The same principle seems to apply to the distribution of honor in many hierarchical settings. Virginia Indians were willing to accept a system that devalued them as long as they could claim superiority to Black people. Honor, even more than cash, is subject to a zero-sum calculation, as equal honor to all is actually no honor at all—which helps us to understand why a research subject might take a cut in net material receipts in exchange for the right to impose an even bigger cut on the members of a different social group. *Relative* wealth is a greater signifier of honor than the *absolute amount* of cash.

The anthropological record documents numerous societies in which equality among members of the in-group is highly valued—where, for example, resources are conscientiously shared or the ideal moment to end a game is when there is a tie. However, long-lasting collective identities tend to develop around the distinctive resources and honors to which nonmembers of the internally egalitarian group are denied access. Hence, the collective assertion of superiority to another group might, logically, rise *in proportion to* the ideology of in-group equality. It seems to me, though, that every in-group has its own de facto forms of internal inequality. However, the awareness of the in-group's superiority to an out-group masks such de facto in-group inequality and promotes in-group loyalty and satisfaction (J. L. Matory 2002). In a probative contemporary case, the Republican call in 2011 for its base to "take America back" from President Obama was a program to restore whiteness to its place of exclusive honor *instead* of reducing income inequality among whites. Equally probative is the willingness of so many poor southern whites and Indians to wave the flag of the Confederacy, long after the rich slaveholders and their descendants visited disaster upon those poor whites and Indians through the Trail of Tears and a disastrous war.

One might be tempted to believe that antecedent cultural differences between Indians and Blacks in Virginia and the inherent devotion of Indians to the preservation of their distinctive culture were the real motives behind their self-distancing from Black people. However, during the antebellum and Jim Crow eras, the organized Virginia Indian groups were far more militantly and officially opposed to intermarriage with Blacks than to intermarriage with whites. In 1889, the most widely known Virginia Indian tribe, the Pamunkeys, had about a hundred members in residence, communal land, governance by a chief, extensive commerce with their non-Indian neighbors, and no distinctive language of their own (Rountree 1990, 203–5). Even amid the cultural renaissance that Mooney and Speck inspired, their new "Indian" attire was largely Victorian with feather accents. Many of the performances encouraged by Mooney and Speck also called upon the powerful imagery of Pocahontas, whose storied romance with early English settler John Smith commemorates cooperation between Indians and whites, refuting the latter-day notion that Virginia Indians had simply wanted to preserve their racial and cultural autonomy all along. Amalgamation with whites was as desired as amalgamation with Blacks was feared.

As in the case of the Hausa community of Ibadan in the 1950s, the maintenance of a distinct culture had not been a priority until a changing political and legal situation threatened to diminish group members' access to certain honors and resources. By comparison, the culturally more distinctive western tribes, who had no stake in Virginia's turn-of-the-century reorganization of the racial hierarchy, gladly sent their youth for advanced education alongside ambitious young Black people at Virginia's Hampton Institute (Baker 1998). Today's southeastern Indians clearly feel ambivalent toward whites as well, and many told me that they wish to be neither Black nor white. However, their all-too-human identification with the victor and general tendency to "cover" their cultural and biological kinship with African Americans with feathers and buckskin remain clear. The three Howard affiliates who most facilitated my access to the world of the southeastern Indians belong to an exceptional and brave subgroup. However, it should be noted that Emma, the most vocal advocate of Indian superiority and difference from African Americans, is also an HBCU graduate.

Despite its "cultural" emphasis, the southeastern Indian renaissance has a racial component as well. A soi-disant black Indian Howard alumna and descendant of the Pamunkeys, Carol Squanto served as my main guide at the Chickahominy powwow in May 2002. She traveled with her mother, also a Howard alumna; her Jamaican "brown" husband, who also described himself as a "Taino"; and her son Curtis, my other main guide.

Carol identified "big block heads and fleshy noses" as the distinguishing physical features of the Virginia Indians. Typically, she added, they were also "reserved" and "taciturn." As she had told me on many other occasions, she was fully aware of the partly African ancestry of the Virginia tribes, as well as most members' denial of that ancestry and resentment of its public acknowledgment. She believed, however, that the long-term in-marriage of these "triracial isolates" (her term) had produced a degree of demographic stability that made them worthy of designation as Indian tribes. Indeed, the convergence of tribally and racially diverse populations is the foundation of numerous long-recognized tribes, such as the Seminoles.

Derek and the family of Carol were not alone among my acquaintances who acknowledged and embraced the notion of their jointly African and Native American legacy. Largely because of the HBCUs, they are among the most Western-educated partisans in this fiery debate. But they are ill-equipped to silence the racially polarizing arguments of the rank and file. Hence, while Carol considered herself a Black Indian, her like-colored neighbor at the Chickahominy powwow did not share that view of himself. He showed me the black-and-white reproduction, taped to the side of his van, of an early-colonial lithograph featuring Virginia Indians. He and Carol employed it as proof that the contemporary Virginia Indians' African-looking features had also characterized the precontact Virginia Indians and were therefore not in themselves proof of African ancestry.

The owner of the poster and the van was sixtyish and Nilla Wafer colored. He dreamed of bringing western Indians to Virginia to marry the local people and thus renew the Virginians' Indian blood. He hoped, furthermore, that, if his children did not marry other Indians, they would marry "from one of the other Asiatic races." He said he would accept whomever they love, but he would definitely prefer "one of the Asiatic races." At the same powwow, I later heard from a thick-haired, Hershey's-colored champion of a shawl dancer, who called herself a "full-blooded Cherokee, with not a single Black ancestor!" As if to underline the danger of my doubting her words, she informed me, with a hand lingering on her waistband sheath, that Indian women always carry a knife and that "the women are more dangerous than the men." She repeated herself for emphasis.

But it was not the doubts of people like me that she needed defending from. In 2007, the Cherokee nation voted to terminate the citizenship rights of the often mixed-race descendants of its former African American captives. The Congressional Black Caucus ardently defended the so-called freedmen, leading the charge to cut off federal funds to that nation until the freedmen's rights were restored (Lee-St. John 2007).

Many of the cultural and phenotypical diacritica of southeastern Indianness strikingly resembled features of my own matrilaterally Virginian family, but ones that we had almost never employed for those purposes. Carol, the Black Indian Howard alumna, strongly urged me to buy and enjoy plenty of the "Indian" foods that were available for sale along one side of the powwow grounds, to "support" the event. The local Indian specialty, she urged, is cake, and it is especially good. On the tables, I saw pound cake and several varieties of frosted layer cake, from which I chose the coconut because it reminded me of the kind that my own "fleshy-nosed" maternal grandmother from Toano, Virginia, used to make. I still did not like the coconut, just the dense yellow cake. The "Indian succotash" that was available seemed to contain the same type of kernel corn and lima beans that my mother had served, when I was a child, from a frozen Birds Eye bag, but this succotash included a creamy and slightly glutinous sauce. It may also have contained kidney beans. Regrettably, since I had not yet noticed the symbolic centrality of food types among all of the ethnic groups I was researching, I neglected to taste it for closer comparison. But as Bascom pointed out in reference to the Africanness of the Gullah/Geechee culture, the similarity between Indian and African American or Euro-American food might be exactly what enables Indians to preserve their lifeways and ethnic identity rather than what disproves its continuity. Perhaps in a sense unintended by Bascom, Gullah/Geechee and, as we shall see, Creole cuisines—much like bagels and moo-shi pork—remain diacritica of an ethnic group long after they have become part of the dietary repertoire and cosmopolitan self-fashioning of other populations.

Names, too. During summer breaks from college, my closest circle of friends consisted of several secular Jewish classmates from Harvard and one from Wesleyan. Feeling left out among people I loved, I told them that I was Jewish, that the original Jews were not white, and that, in the end, I was more Jewish than they. The mother of one such classmate, Ms. Stein, believed me because, after all, my mother's name was "Deborah." I didn't bother to tell her about the rest of the names in my Pentecostal and Baptist African American family had come from Hebrew, Greek, Latin, French, Magyar, Anglo-Saxon, and, in sum, African American Vernacular English. The cultural repertoire of any given ethnoracial group comes from all sorts of places.

Conversely, foods and names that are generic in their land of origin can become symbols of a specific subgroup abroad. For example, bagels, smoked salmon, braided loaves of egg bread (*Zopf* [High German], *Challah* [Yiddish]), chicken soup with large doughy dumplings (*Knödel* [High German], *Kneidalaj* [Yiddish]), and even gefilte fish (*gefüllte Fisch* [High German]) appear to be as generically German in Germany as they are specifically Jewish in the United States, Brazil, and Argentina.[3]

Hence, neither the rich sensorium nor even a sign system as intensely important as naming are the measure of an ethnic group's reality. Social practices and artifacts become a "culture" less because they are unique to a specific population than because a person or population has the incentive and the occasion to imagine them as diacritica of a bounded group.

For the lack of palatable alternatives at the Chickahominy powwow, my son ordered the whole fried chicken leg on the absorbent Sunbeam white bread, the likes of which had also been sold by Hershey's-toned Black women in the kitchen of my grandparents' Herald of His Coming Church of God in Christ in Norfolk, Virginia. However, in an effort to avoid hypertension, obesity, and diabetes, people of my African American family and class had largely abandoned the African-inspired technique of deep-fat frying a generation ago. Like our roughage- and colon cancer–conscious upper-middle-class white countrymen, we had come to favor whole-grain breads and to regard white bread and fried food as signs of poverty and provincialism. Consequently, the fried chicken was a new and disagreeable experience for Adu. For similar reasons, at the Occaneechi-Saponi powwow, we avoided the "Lumbee Frosty Drink," the cheese and chili nachos, and the fry bread being sold from an old ice cream truck emblazoned with the phrase "Indian Food." By contrast, we had long interpreted these foods as a variety of cheap "American" carnival foods that we avoided on account of our education and our ability to afford healthier and higher status alternatives.

The cultural diacritica of ethnic distinction are less often distinct objects or practices than the selective showcasing of objects and practices shared with other groups. These objects and practices often become emic symbols of ethnicity at the same time that they are being abandoned by upwardly mobile classes and turned into litotic antisymbols of elevated class identity, or "taste."

The Howard Band

The lives of Black Indian transmigrants were as conflicted and debated at Howard as they were in their homeland communities. Like many other African-descended people at Howard, Indians on campus employ the nearby lower-class African American population of Washington as a foil to their own identities. Carol's son Curtis had grown up in the nearby Washington neighborhood of Columbia Heights and in suburban Columbia, Maryland, the same community where professional Louisiana Creole families, like that of the Howard dean, have concentrated themselves. Columbia was planned and built in the late 1960s as a racially, religiously, and class diverse community—an alternative to the received racially exclusionary blueprint of the post–World War II US suburb. But Curtis emphatically identified his own and his family's origins as Virginian. He saw his typological opposite when he turned toward the crack addicts of lower Georgia Avenue, then a block south of Howard's campus. When he named their type and the cause of their inadequacy, he could not well blame their flaws on their African Americanness, as did, for example, a local Eritrean restaurateur and a Ghanaian guard at the nearby CVS drugstore, since Curtis regards himself as not only Indian but also African American. Nor could he blame the crack addicts' deficiencies on their being Washingtonians, as do many non-Washingtonian African American students at Howard. The more logical and self-flattering option for Curtis was therefore to blame the disorder of lower Georgia Avenue on "the people from North and South Carolina," alluding to the diverse migrant streams that turned Washington predominantly Black after World War II and kept it so until recently. The Virginians have tended to regard themselves as culturally and phenotypically superior to the Carolinians. I was surprised by this state-based chauvinism. However, when I heard it, I felt the delight of recognition: human beings are endlessly creative, flexible, and arbitrary in their attempts to convince themselves of their superiority to other groups of people.

My experiences during this research project have often reminded me of Dr. Seuss's book *The Sneetches and Other Stories* (1961), published the year I was born. In the title story of the book, there is a bipedal species of creature known as "sneetches." And the sneetches with stars on their bellies feel infinitely superior to the sneetches without stars on their bellies, until an inventor comes along with a machine that can, for a fee, apply stars to the bellies of starless sneetches. Once the formerly prestigious star has become commonplace, the inventor advertises that, for an additional fee, his machine can remove the star from the bellies of the original star-bellied sneetches, thus restoring their claim to distinction and superiority. And they fall for it. In the end, as everyone chases after distinction—paying to have the star removed, then restored, and the removed again—the inventor gets rich. However, in the confusion, it becomes impossible to tell who is superior, and the sneetches all just decide that the snobbish pursuit of superiority to others is futile and silly.

Ethnic identity markers among human beings, perhaps like stars among sneetches, are not reducible to chits in a zero-sum struggle for honor and wealth. They are also loaded with reminders of all that is happy and sad in our family histories and other long-term webs of social relationship, like Proust's tea and *petites madeleines*. But the same tea and *madeleine* cakes can pop up in the memories of coethnics and strangers, like the *arroz con pollo* that my Panamanian friend was shocked to discover I, too, had grown up eating. Similarly, I had always thought of "Go Down, Moses" as a Negro spiritual, only to find out that my best friend on the Harvard faculty and her family thought of it as a Passover song. It is not difference but the will to difference that attaches nostalgia to the collective politics of "culture."

Curtis was a quiet and thoughtful young man. The subject of his senior thesis in history at Howard was the Virginia Indians. He took his Blackness seriously as well. His mother had sent him to an urban Afrocentric elementary school, where he learned, in addition to the usual math, science, and English lessons, a great deal about Egypt, Kwanzaa, and great Black heroes past and present. However, he also felt bullied by his peers on account of his graham-cracker color and floppy hair. However, he liked and trusted me, as I did him. At the crowded powwows, Curtis spoke to me conspiratorially, conscious of what he perceived as the anti-Black racism of Virginia Indians and anxious to prevent them from knowing that his historical research had revealed information that they would not like. His very association with me at the powwows entailed the risk of blowing his cover. So once he had welcomed me and explained the basics of my surroundings, he would leave me on my own. I understood.

Curtis attended Howard on a full alumni scholarship and would graduate with high honors. His academic success notwithstanding, Curtis did not seem to feel a part of the university or of the surrounding neighborhood. Because he lived between his family's two homes, he was seldom on campus. I also infer that he avoided the History Department because of an episode of undignified treatment by a professor. One day when Curtis, his alumna mother Carol, his alumna grandmother, and his brother were visiting, one dark Caribbean professor blustered, "I see your brother took a little more from the Motherland," referring to the brother's more evidently African features.

Many African-descended peoples in the Americas regret their African features, to the extent that parents and grandparents often—in the manner of *Sophie's Choice*—favor the offspring with less African features, and the more African-looking offspring feel resentful. I failed to ask why the more African-looking brother was absent from the powwows I attended with the rest of his family. This Caribbean professor's words were particularly shocking because US people, and particularly university-educated ones, tend to regard public comments about other people's physical appearance as rude. Moreover, color-based resentment among African-descended siblings in the United States is common and was hurtful for the professor to stoke. Attempting to repair the damage, as I have also done following untoward remarks by my children's teachers, the mother replied, "It's his Indian spirit that matters! And their accomplishments!" In midstream, she had sensed that both of her sons were under attack. Months and years later, the family still referred to this episode as "the Incident." News of it had even spread to the African American Department chair, who tried to conceal his joy that he was, on this rare occasion, above the usual fray.

Curtis had more than once suffered the consequences of his ethnoracial ambiguity, or at least he read his experiences through it. For example, he had once been called "nigger" at his predominantly white school, but the Black kids had not stuck up for him. He said that boys and men with his features are regarded as effeminate and unattractive, a sentiment underlined by the proliferation of dark-black male Hollywood stars and hip-hop artists during the 1990s. From Denzel Washington to Jay Z, we became the archetype of sexy, dangerous masculinity. Thus, even though he actually looked to me like a smart and strikingly handsome Black boy, Curtis carefully avoided public attention. Instead, he observed others carefully—with more fear than judgment, except toward the black Indian women he says are called "lighty-brighty." He criticized them for trading on their light skin color to marry successful dark men. I am not sure whether my friend was more bothered by being left out of this pattern of partnering or by the antiblack female aesthetic hierarchy and insincere gold digging that he thought the strategy of the "lighty-brighties" revealed.

Curtis and I sometimes had brunch at a Pamunkey Indian–owned diner two blocks away from campus. One of the owner's two restaurants in the neighborhood, it was the louder—with more of a neighborhood-based clientele. The soaring exterior wall facing the vacant lot where we parked featured a three-story-tall portrait depicting its owner with a slender physique, blue eyes, skin the color of pancake batter, and a towering white hat. In truth, the owner inside was pear shaped with chestnut eyes, and considerably darker and shorter than his portrait. His skin is actually closer in color to a well-done pancake.

The menu was unreformed southern—pancakes with Karo syrup, fried bone-in Virginia ham, link sausages, scrapple, home fries, eggs scrambled with American pasteurized processed cheese food product, and so forth. Everything but the sweet tea was fried. Both the smell and the texture of old grease clung to the skin. The working-class African Americans who ate there tend to think of it as "down-home cooking," unaware that the Pamunkey owner and his fellow Indian patrons consider it Indian food. To me, the Karo syrup, the American pasteurized processed cheese food product, and the smell of pork lard made this cuisine "greasy spoon" and lower class. The facsimiles of it occasionally reproduced in the Matory kitchen for the sake of racial nostalgia would have featured, instead, real maple syrup, sharp cheddar cheese or mozzarella, and canola oil—and even that at a minimum.

From his post at the cash register, the fat owner shouted with contemptuous humor at his dark cooks and waitresses. They laughed and joked back, but never in terms that suggested their right to return his insults in kind. Curtis whispered to me with disapproval that the owner sometimes unabashedly calls his employees "niggers." When I asked our waitress if it was true, she replied with an unworried chortle, "Yeah, but we don't pay him no mind, cuz he Black, too. Don't nobody care what he say he is, cuz he Black just like us." Less sanguine, I have now removed Ungloghe Luta from the wall of my home.

This Pamunkey restaurateur's other establishment, across the street from Howard University Hospital, served a more professional and university-based Black clientele. It was quiet, clean, and free of the greasy smell. There I never saw the owner or heard his shouting. Like many Louisiana Creole public figures of my acquaintance, he has chosen where and when to make an issue of his ethnoracial difference. Graduations, especially, seem to invite conspicuous ethnic displays. Curtis's Howard-alumna grandmother reportedly wore full Indian regalia to his graduation. Yet she was vastly outnumbered by those in West African taffeta head ties and the Ethiopian/Eritrean Habesha *kemis*.

Creoles and Light-Skinned Black People

As an ethnic category in Louisiana, "Creole" first referred to the native-born inhabitants of the territory acquired in the 1803 Louisiana Purchase. Among its referents were chiefly people of Indian, African, Spanish, and French ancestry, often in various combinations. A century of cohabitation among these groups before the Louisiana Purchase had created a distinctive pattern of life and relative freedom from the suffocating racial binarism of the English-speaking southern region of the United States, where "free Negro" was a status so highly encumbered as to be a virtual oxymoron. Many of the New Orleanians who are today recognized by others as Creole also claim descent from the free and mixed-race refugees from the Haitian Revolution of 1791–1804, which occurred at almost the same time as the Louisiana Purchase itself.

Over the course of the nineteenth century, members of this compound population who thought themselves racially eligible for the rights of whites tended to abandon the ethnonym "Creole" for fear of being mistaken for Black (Domínguez 1986). Like the southeastern Indians, they sought to avoid the cascading loss of rights afflicting even free people of African descent over the course of the nineteenth century. Since then, the potential claimants to these distinctive historical genealogies—Black, Indian, Creole, white, Haitian-American, and so forth—have continually made strategic choices about when and how to invoke them. For example, Creole of color professionals and politicians who depend on Black clienteles and allies tend to avoid public mentions of their Creoleness, and one Creole-descended mayor of New Orleans called himself "Haitian American" in the context of an effort to encourage Caribbean politicians and merchants to ship their merchandise through the port of that city.

The diversity of local histories and of individual strategies has meant that, from one region of southern Louisiana to another, well into the twenty-first century, Creoles vary in the residential, linguistic, musical, and phenotypical standards by which they recognize themselves and each other as Creole. French and Spanish surnames are a common but not indispensable index, or distinguishing characteristic, of Creoleness. Similarly, most but not all Creoles are Catholics, and most but not all Creoles have some non-African physical features. Most also have some ancestors who spoke some French or some lexically French-based creole language. During my research, since 2002, I met people who identify themselves or each other as Creole not only from New Orleans, the Louisiana bayou region, and Louisiana's Cane River area but also from Mississippi, Oklahoma, California, and the Washington, DC, area. No single territory of origin or residence is agreed upon as a necessary or sufficient index of Creoleness. Nor is there agreement on how many of the multiple typically Creole characteristics are necessary to prove that an otherwise unknown person is a Creole. Yet in the literally- and hearsay-defined world of New Orleans Creoledom and its diaspora, these questions are continually debated.

In this chapter I limit my observations to the social network of professional-, political-, and business-class Creoles in New Orleans, their confreres at Howard, and the offspring of those confreres, who are among the most influential of Americans—Black or white. They would be a poor source of generalizations about Louisiana Creoles as a whole, but they are the most politically powerful and the most respected subset thereof. They are the heirs of a long history of education and literacy among the few and of their forebears' widespread involvement and excellence in the building trades.

Like other Creoles, these elite, New Orleans Creoles share a nostalgia about childhood attendance at certain churches, about residence in once predominantly Creole neighborhoods, about certain French or Creole language expressions they heard as children, and about an eighteenth- and nineteenth-century family history of *plaçage* (i.e., women's contracting officially as mistresses to wealthy white men). But for my Creole mentors, these are nostalgic remembrances of things past rather than reports of present-day conduct. My Creole interlocutors report an intervening period of cousin marriage, which is no longer as common as it used to be. At least before Hurricane Katrina in 2005, there were a few public places where elite Creoles of color still gathered to see and be seen and to sort out quietly who belongs and who doesn't. At the top of the list were two restaurants—Dooky Chase and Pampy's.

"Culture" versus Color

In anthropology, the faux pas of the ethnographer are often the occasions of the greatest learning. That is, they reveal the assumptions—as well as the sacred cows and the culture-specific emotional conflicts—of one's interlocutors, about which the anthropologist had previously been ignorant. The field researcher's expression of a contrary assumption or casual mention of an open secret sometimes elicits explosive anger, from which the ethnographer receives an important lesson. In my first and only conversation with him, University of Arkansas English professor Raymond DuPlessis (a pseudonym) told me that Creoles were a "culture," which, in his writings, he insists is not limited to any particular skin color but which endeavored to preserve itself through endogamy. His scholarly writings further identify the group as a product of the unfair white male privilege to dictate the social classification, moral worth, and material opportunities of others. However, he accepts the group's centuries-old reality as a noble and culturally distinctive fait accompli.

Among the defining indices of Creole culture, this well-connected New Orleans Creole told me by telephone, are Catholicism; church attendance at Corpus Christi, Saint Monica's, or Epiphany; membership in the Knights of Peter Claver lay brotherhood; the possession of a French or Spanish surname;

residence in the Seventh Ward; and attendance at Xavier University. He identified the publications of George Washington Cable as an important element in the cultural self-awareness of Creoles. He also named the edited volume of Sybil Kein, *Creole: The History and Legacy of Louisiana's Free People of Color* (2000a), and the publications of Gwendolyn Midlo Hall as authoritative accounts of Creole "culture."

Indeed, in the "literally-defined world" of New Orleans Creoles, certain books are ubiquitous. Among these are also Mary Gehman's *Free People of Color of New Orleans* (1994), *Gumbo Ya-Ya* (1945) by the Louisiana Writers' Project, and the edited volume of Arnold R. Hirsch and Joseph Logsdon, *Creole New Orleans: Race and Americanization* (1992). In a few homes, I saw, always in English translation, Rodolph Lucien Desdunes's *Our People and Our History: A Tribute to the Creole People of Color in Memory of the Great Men They Have Given Us and of the Good Works They Have Accomplished* ([1911] 1973). Some people in New Orleans and at Howard appeared to use them actively as reference books in establishing their own genealogies, but in all cases, the books, as physical objects, served as nonverbal emblems of the value that their owners accord to their distinctive ancestry and their regional way of life.

For a literature scholar, the typical characteristics that DuPlessis says identify Creoles may read like a "culture," but for most anthropologists, they read like the cultural diacritica of an "ethnic group," the more comprehensive Tylorean/Boasian culture of which actually overlaps enormously with that of neighboring groups and whose boundaries are regularly permeable to the departure of old and the entry of new personnel (Barth 1969; Domínguez 1986). Virginia Domínguez observes such permeability in the boundaries around urban Louisiana Creole identity, but she describes the distinguishing cultural diacritica as more like a "family resemblance" than like a fixed definition of membership. That is, a *preponderance* of the following characteristics is what makes one a New Orleans Creole: being Roman Catholic, having a French or Spanish surname; speaking French; eating a distinctive cuisine of hybrid African, European, and Native American origins; having grown up in the Seventh Ward of New Orleans; having attended Corpus Christi Church and Saint Augustine's High School; moral propriety; and being of the skilled or professional class.

But in my observation, admission to the Creole ethnic category seldom requires even that loose standard of "family resemblance." And many additional characteristics feature in my friends' debates. Unlike Domínguez in her pre-1986 research, I never heard New Orleans Creoles in 2002 suggest that speaking French was a usual or typical marker of being Creole today. Moreover, far from emphasizing propriety, my friends' sense of their own sophistication seemed to entail a delight in Latin American–style flirtation and fin-de-siècle free love, in contrast to the prudish ways of Protestant, "redneck" northern Louisiana. In agreement with Domínguez, I also found the presence of some Caucasoid features an important diacritic of Creole ethnicity. Unlike the Creole nationalists, I would not characterize the difference between New Orleans Creoles and their non-Creole African American neighbors as the difference between two separate "cultures" (I would not even describe the difference between Black and white Americans as that). Yet it is also plain to me that the meaning of the term "Creole" has changed greatly over time and that it varies according to the class and regional background of the speaker. Used by different people and under different historical circumstances, it does not always refer to the same people and things.

However, Raymond DuPlessis gave his own educational biography as evidence of the distinctiveness of Creole culture and identity from African American life. Hungry for adventure, DuPlessis left New Orleans in 1967 to attend undergraduate school in a predominantly white Catholic university in the North. Approximately the age of my late brother Earle, he said he does not know any Creole of his generation who attended an HBCU outside of New Orleans. Those who wanted to attend an HBCU attended Xavier. Thus he describes his nephew as "iconoclastic" for having attended Atlanta's historically Black Morehouse College, and he says that he does not know any Creole alumni of Howard. This last report is perhaps, to my mind, a measure of his relative unfamiliarity with the medical and dental community in New Orleans, which I came to know extensively. It might also reflect his strategic denial of the long-term and intensive overlap between Creole and African American networks.

In truth, few of my brother's friends and class peers from Washington attended HBCUs, either, as the elite TWIs had just flung open their doors for the likes of Earle and DuPlessis to walk through. Earle's choice hardly meant that he did not feel "Black," and his attendance at Howard Medical School had not been his first choice. At that time, talented young Creoles were, not unlike Earle, making a series of racially fraught choices of their own about the schools best matched to their social and professional aspirations. The boundaries of elite New Orleans Creoleness were and are, as Barth would put it, permeable. And, in many cases, they resemble the boundaries around the nationwide African American elite. Or, to put it another way, the self-positioning of ambitious, upper-middle-class Creoles and that of ambitious, upper-middle-class nonethnic African Americans do not appear to be as opposed as DuPlessis suggests. What is still under debate, however, is the relative importance of phenotype and "culture" among the diacritica of Creoleness.

Like Indians of partly African ancestry, Creoles of color often claim accomplished African Americans or persons of overlapping identities as exclusively their own. For example, in our telephone conversation, DuPlessis mentioned that Howard alumnus (and Uncle Badejọ's roommate) Andrew Young is Creole—though, to my understanding, he conformed to *none* of the "cultural" indexes previously listed by DuPlessis himself. DuPlessis then added, plausibly, that Young's family had frequently socialized with Creole dentists (Young's father had been a dentist) and that Young had grown up in a circle of doctors' and lawyers' sons who, DuPlessis implied, were therefore largely Creole. In an apparent slip of the tongue, he added that an English surname is problematic only when a person is "dark" and that Young "looks Creole," apparently therefore exempting him from exclusion on the grounds of his English surname. Recalling Young's skin as graham-cracker colored, I asked if Creoles were typically so dark, whereupon DuPlessis shouted at me that he was sick of such colorist assumptions about Creoleness and that my misapprehension must have resulted from the poverty of my previous reading. In fact, like most of my inquiries in the field, my question had followed from DuPlessis's own words. Despite his earlier denial that Creoleness corresponded to any particular color or phenotype, it was DuPlessis who said that a person could "look Creole." My faux pas was that I had called attention to an open secret.

It emerged in time that DuPlessis had been leery from the start of our conversation. Following his outburst, he alerted me that he would not have talked to me at all were it not for my friendship with the mutual white friend who had introduced us, and he declared my pursuing the issue of Young's color an indication of the usual offensive misconception that non-Creoles bring to inquiries about Creoles. "It's not really about complexion; it's about culture." After hanging up on me, he lambasted me thoroughly in an e-mail to our mutual friend. He urged that our friend convey to me "the sophistication of the New Orleanians." He continued, "N[ew] O[rleans] Creole's [*sic*] have a very strong sense of history and identity" and urged our mutual friend to "try to impress upon him [me] the level of cultural sophistication that is normal for the New Orleans Creole."

As our mutual friend pointed out, our blowup was a "perfect storm" of disciplinary, status, and ethnic tensions. Whereas I saw myself as seeking an emic view of Creole identity, DuPlessis apparently assumed I was a resentful African American enemy to his ethnic identity. Whereas he wanted us as two scholars to discuss the literature on Creole culture and history—or, if you will, the Creoles' "literally-defined world"—I wanted his personal experiential and emotional take on it. Being regarded as an "informant" took on a hierarchical implication especially because of the status differences between our respective universities and our ranks within them. The status gap between the source of his PhD and his current teaching appointment suggested poor postgraduate output. Whereas I thought I was according him the respect of an insider with inerrant expertise on his experience, he thought I was depriving him of his status as a professor and expert on the literature about Creoles. Never having wanted my experience to be ignored in favor of existing scholarly representations of what African American males are supposed to be like, I thought I was showing him friendship. A range of conditions appear to have made it impossible for him to feel that way about me. Nonetheless, our conversation taught me a great deal. Like southeastern Indianness, Creoleness is as ambiguous as it is contentious.

DuPlessis is not alone among the revisionist Creole scholars who insist that complexion is irrelevant to this purely "cultural" category. However, without admitting it, DuPlessis had taught me something about the permeability of the Creole ethnic category. The further lesson of DuPlessis's ire—like Derek's initial anger—is that the *right to speak the open secrets of the group* is a further index, or diacritic, of in-group status. To put it another way, membership in virtually any social category is marked by the hiding of such open secrets from outsiders (see also Herzfeld [1997] 2005 and J. L. Matory 2003).

Pride and Shame: How Creoles Stratify Their Own and Redraw Their Ethnic Boundaries

Indeed, the culturally coded boundaries of elite New Orleans Creoleness are, in my observation of photos and conversations, particularly permeable to the inward flow of the light skinned, the educated, and the prosperous, and to the outward flow of the dark skinned, the woolly haired, and the impoverished. For example, two close Creole friends told me that, no matter how many other Creole family resemblances you possess, if you live in the public housing projects, you are not a Creole. The three of us had a good laugh about the self-serving and self-aggrandizing nature of such Creole reasoning. But this ejection of discredited group members is common among black ethnics and is not normally regarded as hypocritical. Similarly, Hintzen (2003) reports that the middle-class Caribbeans of California deny that their working-class fellows are "real West Indians" at all; they are reclassified as African Americans. In Nigeria, Yoruba people have a proverb that identifies the pursuit of honor as a universal motive in the setting of boundaries around the ethnic or other social group: "*Ìjẹ̀bú t'ó gbẹran l'ójà, ara wa kọ́, Ìjẹ̀bú t'ó kọ pẹ́tẹ̀ẹ̀sì, ara wa ni*" (An Ìjẹ̀bú [i.e., member of Uncle Badejọ's linguistically distinctive Yoruba subgroup] who steals an animal in the market is not one of us; an Ìjẹ̀bú who builds a magnificent house is one of us).

My close Creole friends' humor and DuPlessis's ire reveal tandem features of the Creole flight from stigma. On the one hand, many Creoles relish the idea of their superiority to "black" people. On the other hand, the racism that attaches that superiority to Caucasoid features also leaves the Creoles themselves vulnerable to discreditation. On account of the element of their ancestry and phenotypes that *is* black, Creoles have been vulnerable to job discrimination and, therefore, poverty and shame. Thus, an affirmation of their superiority to blacks is also a confession of their inferiority to whites and the legitimacy of white discrimination against Creoles.

Even within their local networks, Creoles are vulnerable to the pain of not looking sufficiently Caucasoid. After a 1997 lecture at New Orleans's Tulane University, I dined with members of the host department and some of their spouses, one of whom was a copper-colored woman whose stylishly short hair languished in capital S's rather than sitting in *o*'s or dangling in *j*'s and *l*'s. I do not know whether the transliteration was chemical or genetic. When I learned that she was the only native New Orleanian at the table, I asked the fortyish woman about her upbringing. Without any further question from me, she spoke of the wide circle of cousins who played together with delight, about the foods they enjoyed, about the Creole grandmother who combed their hair, about the shame she—like dark *puertorriqueñas* and *dominicanas*—had been made to feel about her hair texture and skin color, and about the adults' preference for her lighter-skinned cousins. I wanted my eyes to show sympathy without gravity, but as she slumped down and her face crumpled into rivulets of tears, I could do nothing but pass the cleanest napkin at hand and hope that the conversation at the other end of the table would keep any embarrassing attention away from her.

My companion was one of many New Orleanians who reported traumatic relationships with their Creole maternal grandmothers. Like many southeastern Indians, most of the Creoles I know focus on their matrilineal ancestry—that is, their mothers' and maternal grandmothers' forebears—to demonstrate their own ethnic bona fides and to illustrate what they regard as the defining attitudes and behaviors of their ethnic group. Illustrating these attitudes and behaviors, one Creole friend told me that her grandmother called the light-skinned grandchildren the "blessed ones." Another told me about the time that she brought home a dark boyfriend. Once he had left, the grandmother told her "not to bring that black man back into my house." Another grandmother barred even the initial entry of the black suitor. Holding her broom in the doorway, as if prepared to sweep away dirt, she told her granddaughter, "Get that nigger off my porch!" Creole nationalists tend to deny the reality or diminish the importance of these phenomena. It is certainly easier for the light descendants than for the dark descendants of Creoles to disregard them. In his online photos, DuPlessis looks like someone who could easily pass for white.

Another prominent Creole scholar, a retired professor, acknowledges Creole racism, but, given what she regards as the universality of racism, she denies that this racism is an especially salient element of Creole culture. However, unlike DuPlessis, she *does* regard ancestry and appearance as defining elements of Creole ethnic identity. For example, this scholar told me that Creoles are racially mixed and that non-Creole African Americans are not. On the contrary, Howard-based Creoles shared with me their consciousness of the significant population of non-Creole African Americans in Washington, DC; Charleston, South Carolina; Virginia; and Maryland who appear just as racially "mixed" as Louisiana Creoles. In my view, Atlanta, New York, Chicago, and Los Angeles are no exceptions. There are numerous light-skinned and European-featured people in every region of the United States who consider themselves Black.

This Creole professor argues that Creole culture should not be defined by its racism: "Don't all cultures discriminate aesthetically against African features?" she asked rhetorically. Though I have found Africans, Europeans, and Latin Americans considerably more varied than North Americans in their appreciation of black beauty, this scholar is probably correct with reference to the *dominant* trends in the United States and Latin America.

Indeed, anti-African bodily aesthetics are a point of overlap between anything that might be called Creole culture and its African American counterpart, though the Creole manifestation of these aesthetics is certainly more extreme. For example, three of my four best childhood friends (who range from graham to cinnamon colored) married butter-colored women. However, one of these friends said that his choice had been based purely on love and contrary to his usual physical preferences. The fourth of my best childhood friends was that butter-colored descendant of Francis Scott Key, and all of his partners have been dark—the African American mother of his child, his Ethiopian wife, and his Nigerian boyfriends. My Nigerian wife looks like chocolate, our daughter like dark caramel, and our son like coffee. Their beauty often makes me stop and stare. Indeed, we named our son "Adumarado̩n," a Yoruba praise name for velvety-black people. It means, "Blackness Makes the Body Radiant" and demonstrates a Yoruba aesthetic value of considerable antiquity and contemporary endurance. My sense is that Nigerians who regard white or extremely light people as more beautiful are as exceptional in their country as I am in my own—that is to say, not common but not rare, either. In Nigeria, skin bleaching with hydroquinone is becoming more common, but most Nigerians of my acquaintance find white people ugly. People all over the black world express a preference for rounded hips, which they associate with black women, and express distaste for the effect of aging on white skin and of wetness on white people's smell. Even in Europe, there has long been a taste for Black beauty, and its paragons—from Josephine Baker to Naomi Campbell to Alek Wek—seem to grow blacker over time. Our then-twenty-two-year-old caramel-skinned daughter Ayọ received a great deal of romantic male attention when we lived in Berlin. I received a similar level of attention in London and Paris during the 1980s. In sum, anti-African aesthetic racism is common but by no means universal or unmitigated in the regions where I have lived and conducted research for this book. The case of New Orleans Creoles is extreme.

During my six months on Howard's campus in 2002, I conducted interviews with over a dozen Creoles of color. I spent many an afternoon or evening dining with Creole physicians and both interviewing and doing business with a Creole restaurateur who had begun but not completed her bachelor's degree at Howard. I had known most of these physicians for decades without, however, knowing that they were Creole. I had perceived them simply as part of my people—normal Black people, albeit light-skinned ones, if I had been pressed.

Only in 2002 did I discover that, like Professor DuPlessis, most Louisiana Creole Howard students and faculty members hesitate to discuss with African Americans their sense of difference, since the Creoles involved in such discussions expect to be assaulted verbally with the accusation that they are merely fetishizing their light skin and long hair as badges of superiority. Assured by the depth of our family connections or my accepting demeanor, numerous Creoles spoke to me extensively. Except for two, though, they all tended to speak cautiously.

During one monthlong and multiple weeklong stays in New Orleans, I interviewed, attended church, dined, went dancing, or lived with scores of Howard-affiliated people who were recognized by their peers as Creole. These included a former mayor (the husband of my half-Mexican, half–African American Howard-alumna godsister), his university-administrator mother, and his brother; several university professors; and a dozen Howard-trained physicians and dentists, their families, and their friends. I have also dined with and interviewed a dozen non-Howard-affiliated professors, secondary-

FIGURE 4.4. Creole friends and family at home. Photograph by the author.

school educators, and activists of Creole descent, though many of them patently rejected the identity. I explored the Amistad collection at Tulane University, and I received a brief but deeply informative introduction to the Xavier University archives by head archivist Lester Sullivan, who is himself descended from people he called "white Creoles."

I was honored, as well, to interview, dine with, and play violin with non-Howard-affiliated professor, poet, musician, and self-described "Creole nationalist" Melissa Shapiro. According to her website at the University of Minnesota, where she is professor emerita, she "largely created the field of Creole Studies through her early publications and presentations." At Minnesota, Shapiro taught under the name Mercedes Bates but tells me that she adopted the name Melissa Shapiro in recognition of her partly Jewish ancestry. She has published poetry, lore, and scholarship. She has also recorded a half dozen CDs of "Creole music." Among the genres that Shapiro performs as representative of Creoleness is Zydeco, which most of my elite New Orleans Creole acquaintances regard as anathema to their collective identity. However, like their typically white Cajun neighbors, rural Creoles appear to regard Zydeco as emblematic of their community. Shapiro says that she grew up underprivileged, which may account for some of the differences between her sense of the Creole musical canon and that of my friends.

Nonetheless, Professor Shapiro is in many ways like Queen Kwet of the

Gullah/Geechee nation. After returning from a long sojourn far from the heartland of her ambiguous ethnic group, she has almost single-handedly led a local revival of Creole identity. Not all would-be Creoles agree with the radicalism of the difference she asserts between Creoles and African Americans or the fervor with which she sometimes proclaims it. However, in my view, the intensity that she has added to the debate is itself a public reactivation of the social network that is Creoleness.

Discretion or Extinction?

I also interviewed and spent time at the originally non-Creole but now ethnically mixed Zulu Social Aid and Pleasure Club, in a number of non-Creole spiritual churches, and with the continental French owner and two African American tour guides at Creole Tours, a Creole-themed tour company based in the French Quarter. One of the tour guides is the light-brown and Afrophile daughter of former Virginia governor Douglas Wilder, my father's friend and Kappa Alpha Psi fraternity brother.

I discovered that, far from indicating a misunderstanding on my part, my queries about the role of color in DuPlessis's identification of Creoles went right to the heart of a painful debate among Creoles, and with their neighbors, about whether Creoles are (1) a "separate" and "completely different culture," as Melissa Shapiro believes; (2) an intermediate third category in a ternary racial system; or (3) a largely complexion-defined segment of the Black race. In some ways, this quandary recapitulates the historical difference between the culture (in the Tylorean/Boasian sense) that the multiple races of Creoles may justifiably be said to have shared in the early eighteenth century, and the complexion-coded, pan—African American social network of which upwardly mobile Creoles are a well integrated part today.

But matters may not be so simple. Ethnic identities and the will to cultivate or generate their cultural diacritica can long outlast apparent overall cultural assimilation. Howard-based Creoles who grew up in or who have visited California describe a great deal of religious, ceremonial, culinary, commercial, and social effervescence among Louisiana-born Creoles in late-twentieth-century Los Angeles. California Creoles, they said, still attended the same churches; sponsored "Creole balls"; sent for seafood, hot boudin sausage (stuffed with pork blood, rice, meat, and spices), and filé (or ground sassafras root) from New Orleans; and held their rites of passage in the same rental venues, much like many immigrant communities from abroad.

Professor Shapiro's efforts to revive, relegitimize, and publicize a "separate" Louisiana Creole "culture" may find particularly receptive ground amid the post-Katrina dispersion of Creoles. However, my New Orleans Creole friends who have returned there since Hurricane Katrina tell me that property owners like themselves are more likely to have returned than non–property owners and that, in this class of people, they detect no increased interest in the Creole legacy. If anything, interest in the conventional venues of Creole interaction, such as the Pampy's and Dooky Chase restaurants, has declined.

At Harvard in 2006, I witnessed one surprising instance of Creole self-declaration, apparently emboldened by the explosion of non-US black ethnic groups on campus. Annually, the undergraduate Black Men's Forum hosted a corporate-sponsored banquet in a luxurious downtown hotel celebrating Black women at Harvard. In the next semester, the undergraduate Association of Black Harvard Women would similarly honor Black men at Harvard. Around 2006, the Black Men's Forum took a moment to honor that year's president of the Association of Black Scientists and Engineers (ABSE). Just as the mass of Nigerian students in attendance had repeatedly called "Naija!" when one of their own was honored, a lone young man called out, in honor of the ABSE president, "My Creole sister!"

As demographically insignificant as this shout-out might seem, it is unimaginable to me that it could happen in New Orleans—or at Howard. Even before Katrina, according to Shapiro and my Howard-affiliated informants, such public effervescence in the Creole population had fizzled out in New Orleans. One self-described "Creole nationalist" professor blames what she regards as the "extinction" of New Orleans Creole "culture" on the African American majority. I, on the other hand, would substitute the word "ethnicity" for "culture" and "discretion" for "extinction." Creole food, for example, has not become extinct. Rather, like Chinese cuisine and European/Jewish bagels in the United States, it has become a cuisine enjoyed by many groups. Creole cuisine has become a symbol of identity and collective difference for broader groups, such as New Orleanians and African Americans generally. What has declined are the opportunities and the willingness of erstwhile Creole people in New Orleans to come together and display their difference publicly. Too many members of the African American majority upon whom elite Creoles depend for votes and customers resent public assertions of Creole identity as assertions of not just difference but also superiority.

This Creole nationalist blaming of the African American majority for the near extinction of Creoledom adds a dimension to my understanding of DuPlessis's preemptive mistrust and explosive anger. While many African Americans are quick to perceive the colorism in Creole identity, elite Creoles below the class echelon of physicians and politicians (much like their counterparts among the Indians of partly African ancestry) perceive the African American embrace of the little races as an existential threat to the ethnic groupings that these professors at middling universities could hope to publish studies of, revive, speak for, and lead. Higher-class would-be Creoles, of the sort who have served as mayors of New Orleans and president of the National Urban League (i.e., the echelon of Ernest "Dutch" and Marc Morial), could find only disadvantage in the public advocacy of Creole nationalism.

For his part, DuPlessis thinks New Orleans Creole culture is very much alive. And there may be a reason he disagrees with Shapiro. His e-mail to our shared white friend reveals his acquaintance with the significant number of sophisticated and educated New Orleanians who move in Creole circles without necessarily proclaiming their Creoleness publicly. DuPlessis is the brother of a prominent politician. Having grown up more modestly, Shapiro does not share DuPlessis's kin connections to or depth of acquaintance with the Creole political class. On the other hand, Howard alumni networks thrust me firmly into the middle of this and other elite classes of Creoles.

DuPlessis predicted that the "sophisticated" New Orleans Creoles would not talk to me. If he correctly suspected reasons for which they would not speak to me, he poorly understood the reasons why they would. The members of the most powerful Creole social networks in New Orleans—which include the mayors, doctors, dentists, lawyers, judges, newspaper editors, and restaurateurs—move fluidly between Creole social networks and non-Creole African American networks. Through institutions like Howard, the Boulé professional men's fraternity, the Jack and Jill mothers' and children's organization, the National Urban League, the NAACP, and others, they regularly meet, depend on, fight for, and marry other African Americans—particularly light-skinned people or, less often, but very much like southeastern Indian women, highly accomplished dark-skinned men. As the son of a Howard alumnus and professor of surgery (not to mention a tenured Harvard professor in my own right), I was an honored guest and semi-insider before I had arrived. Indeed, I intuit that I had come close to becoming the stepbrother of one of my two closest Creole friends in New Orleans.

Nonetheless, Professor DuPlessis's early reaction to me revealed the tensions implicit in this ethnic identity, the difficulties inherent in investigating it, and the error of assuming that Creoles are a self-existent or "separate" ethnic group. It is the very uncertainty of and debates around the ontological status of this group that keep their networks alive. Unlike electoral politics or the retailing of medical, dental, and legal services, university teaching does not require the maximization of one's own ethnoracial constituency. In fact, in the pursuit of tenure, an advantage goes to those who specialize in minute but novel research topics, and, once received, tenure sharply reduces the need

A COMPLEXION OR A CULTURE? 281

to satisfy many people at all. However, it is risky to write and teach on topics that may offend major campus constituencies—such as the study of Creoles at Howard or the study of Palestinians at Harvard or Columbia. On the other hand, studying Creoleness is relatively unthreatening at the University of Minnesota or the University of Arkansas.

By identifying my acquaintances (wherever literary clarity allows) as people who were *recognized by their peers as Creole*, I hint that I do not recall meeting any college-educated New Orleans residents, apart from Professor Shapiro (who had only recently moved back from a lengthy teaching career at the University of Minnesota), who described *him or herself* as "Creole." The only men in New Orleans who said yes when I asked if they were Creoles were working class—the occasional taxi driver, for example. By contrast, a highly placed Creole politician quoted his brother as follows: "Creole is a state of mind [pregnant pause]—a *fucked-up* state of mind!" A number of other people identified as Creole also quoted the brother in these terms. Another well-known dark Creole activist who had attended Xavier declared point blank, "Being Creole has nothing to do with a cultural difference. It's just a claim to white privilege" (personal communication, July 16, 2002). It should be noted that, despite his harsh critiques of Creole identity, this New Orleans Creole descendant is himself married to a light-colored "Cane River" Creole from Baton Rouge.

Whenever I asked an educated New Orleanian woman if she was Creole, she would say something like, "I don't know. It depends on what you mean by 'Creole,'" whereupon her female companions proceeded to read her: "Girl, you know you Creole. Look at your hair, your color. And I know your mama; she grew up with my mother in the Seventh Ward. And didn't they go to Corpus Christi [Church]?"

The object of this phenotypical and historical reading would typically glow with pride, much like a Yoruba person being regaled with her family *oriki*, or attributive poetry. "Afflatus" is Karin Barber's (1991) term for this involuntary bodily affect. In New Orleans, Creoles recognize each other, but educated and high-profile Creoles—such as bankers, politicians, and physicians—publicly tend to declare themselves African American. For example, Pampy was the cinnamon-brown, smoky-voiced owner of the gourmet Creole restaurant and New Orleans watering hole that bore his name and was, in 2002, the preeminent place for elite would-be Creoles and elite African Americans to see and be seen. In color, he was closer to the softly glimmering mahogany bar and paneling than to most of the women who engaged in the "you-know-you-Creole" game. Perhaps, despite his complexion, his commercial success made him worthy of claiming. But he himself said Creoleness is "dead."

Overhearing this claim, however, a physician trained by my father and identified by others as Creole whispered to me, "But you see he married another Creole anyway!" This combined rejection of, reticence about, and quiet pride in Creole identity may have resulted from their fear that I might disapprove of Creole identity, but I doubt it. I sensed that this double or triple consciousness is essential to a tight-knit network that defines itself in an unsettled dialogue with white Americans and with other African Americans over color, genealogy, and class.

However, it is a network that would be difficult to characterize as a "separate" or "completely different culture" of the sort imagined by Shapiro and DuPlessis. This network is defined by its own uncertainty about the distinctness of its own reality. Are they a fortress against Blackness defended by their grandmothers' brooms and curses? The favored politicians and wives of Black society? Or just a population of people who monitor each other's outward social trajectories because, Creole or not, they shared a loose multifamily network and thus a faint remembrance of things past? Because so few of my mentors who were identified by others as Creole identified themselves as such, the reader should take all of my references to "Creoles" to mean "people identified by others as Creole." Where this parlance proves too cumbersome, I simply call them "Creole," but the above qualifications of the term still apply.

When populations have lived side by side and participated in the same institutions for hundreds of years, as have Creoles and non-Creole African Americans, claims of complete cultural difference are more wish or speech act than observation. As far away as Washington, I had eaten the signature Creole dishes—gumbo and jambalaya—scores of times at my own African American mother's and my aunt Ruth's African American dinner tables. But a wish or a speech act is all it takes to create an ethnic identity, as long as the right people are ready to go along. One could invent a diacritic by which to distinguish Creole from not-really-Creole gumbo. For example, my mother's gumbo was always thickened with okra rather than filé—both of which styles I have enjoyed in New Orleans gumbos. Hypothetically, because it is less well known and harder to obtain, filé could be useful in the distinction making of a Creole "ethnicity entrepreneur" (Kasinitz 1992). However, I have never heard this particular distinction employed as a cultural diacritic.

For most anthropologists, a "culture" is a comprehensive way of thinking and of conducting life. Eating spaghetti every Wednesday, eating chitterlings or gumbo once a year, or marching in the Saint Patrick's Day Parade may in some places suffice as proof of one's membership in an ethnic group, but none of these performances is even nearly sufficient to define one's lifeway as a distinct culture—much less a "separate" and "completely different" one.

In an age of massive and continual movement of people, images, and ideas among the most distant places on the planet, many anthropologists doubt the view that *any* cultures are still distinct from each other (e.g., Hannerz 1996; Clifford 1988).

Ambiguity as a Cultural Diacritic

Given the fact of historical change, the very loose family resemblances normally employed in the identification of Creoles seem, by Barthian standards, insufficient—or at least long out of date—as descriptions of what makes Creoles a group today. The most commonly proffered indexes of Creoleness are now performed by very few Creoles. Few Creoles now live in the Seventh Ward, which, long before Hurricane Katrina, had reportedly been "taken over" by non-Creole African American renters. In the 1960s, Pontchartrain Park became a point of convergence between the Creole and non-Creole African American elites, just as New Orleans East hosted a similar convergence in more recent years. Moreover, while Xavier University's ranking administrators remain Creole, attending Xavier, rather than a predominantly white college, is now almost a sign that one is *not* a New Orleans Creole. By 2002, Creoles were in the minority at Xavier—only about a third of the students, according to Sullivan. Xavier is now not only predominantly dark and non-Creole Black in its student body but also reputedly the greatest producer of successful African American medical-school applicants in the country.

The highest-ranking Creoles regularly defy the "textbook" indexes of Creoleness. Many of the most prominent Creole families have either German or Welsh names (such as Haydel and Jones) rather than French or Spanish ones. In New Orleans, the costly seafood ingredients that typify Creole cuisine—the most elaborate, enduring, and public of Creole-identified practices—prohibit daily consumption. It generally appears on holidays or in restaurants, where the non-Creole customers generally outnumber the Creoles. Creoles are still a minority among Catholics of African descent in the United States, and amid both interregional migration and rapidly declining church attendance in the United States, churchgoing Catholicism becomes even less significant as a diacritic of Creoleness. Finally, Shapiro includes within the category of Creole culture a range of magical practices and powers that my other New Orleans Creole friends say are but falsely attributed to them.

It is striking, though, that Creoles share their reputation for magical powers with the Gullah/Geechees. Why? Both of these populations dwell near the greatest North American ports of the Atlantic slave trade. Moreover, as Mary Douglas, Victor Turner, and Peter Fry have all pointed out, these groups' defiance of normal standard social categories—or what Arnold van Gennep would call their "liminality"—suits them to attributions of magical expertise. But the definition of the "liminal" depends on one's point of view. It is no surprise that some of my Gullah/Geechee friends credit seers from North Carolina's mixed-race Lumbee Indian tribe with magical gifts and speak of the long lines of clients waiting for their services. In other words, from the Gullah/Geechee perspective, it is now my family friend Derek's people—the faraway and racially ambiguous North Carolina Indians—who seem endowed with magical powers.

In the absence of any remaining residential, school-based, linguistic, or culinary indexes of distinctness, the parlance of "culture" seems an effort to resurrect distant-past forms of cultural distinctiveness as proof that the color-coded boundaries of their privileged social networks are ethically justifiable.

On the other hand, the most privileged categories of New Orleans Creoles gain no advantage by naming and claiming their ethnic distinctness, boundedness, and cultural frozenness in time. Indeed, the boundaries of the Creole elite are highly porous to anyone with the right skin color. Among the potential hereditary claimants to Creoleness, it is only those with precarious sources of income and honor who seek a boost through the reification and proclamation of their Creoleness—the poor, the diasporic, and the professors.

To recap, many light-skinned and previously non-Creole African Americans are assimilated (voluntarily or involuntarily) into the New Orleans Creole political and medical elite, and Creole cuisine has spread far beyond the Creole ethnic group. Certain minor speech patterns and religious proclivities among some of my upper-middle-class Creole interlocutors did strike me as distinctive. For example, several people alerted me to the fact that some beloved elders of theirs used the term "bay," meaning "baby," to address friends and loved ones. Their delighted laughter about this observation suggested a combination of nostalgia and embarrassment. The middle aged, the young, and the college educated did not seem to employ this locution, except in playful imitation of their elders, much as my sister Yvedt and I ironically mimicked AAVE.

In its rhythm and pronunciation, Creole speech—like that of the southeastern Indians—is indistinguishable from the code-switching and the post-Creole continuum between the speech of university-educated African Americans and the African American Vernacular English of their respective regions. When asked about the existence of distinctive Creole parlance, both the topic and the definitional uncertainty of Creoles' answers were revealing. Several fortyish friends (i.e., of my age at the time) could recall the complexion-related terms *ma-rine-y* and *briqué*, but they had to ask their then sixtyish and seventyish mothers for the definitions. Even most of their mothers seemed uncertain. Most of the cultural phenomena that Creole nationalists identify as distinctly Creole are now remembrances of things past, proud evocations of a time when some whites considered their ancestors something other than Blacks, enabling a few of them to accomplish things that even fewer other people of African descent could.

This sort of "salvage" ethnology is perhaps the defining feature of early-twentieth-century anthropology and of twenty-first-century ethnogenesis among the little races. In the case of the eastern Indian populations, the early-twentieth-century anthropologist or linguist would approach a population whose ancestors' language was no longer spoken and ask if any words whatsoever were left over. The lists so generated tended to be short. For example, in the early 1840s, a century and a half before the southeastern Indian revivals of the 1990s and 2000s, Reverend E. A. Dalrymple "was able to collect only 17 words from the two oldest women" on the Pamunkey reservation (Rountree 1990, 188).

However, in the absence of obvious sociocultural distinctions from African Americans or white Americans, even New Orleans Creoles with nothing against Black people sometimes wonder who they are. One of my two best New Orleans Creole friends, Cherie K., is a cinnamon-colored woman, in her late thirties when I did my research, with obsidian-black tresses. I attended mass with her once at her regular church, which was not among those regarded as typically Creole. At church, she told me that her best friends and regular companions there were not other Creoles but a circle of "elderly white ladies." One day, as she sat in church with these friends, one of them leaned over and whispered into her ear, "Watch your purse! A Black boy just came in!" Over the course of our thirteen-year friendship, my friend repeated this experience several times with great perplexity, even though the experience had apparently occurred years before we met. The first thing she said was that the quotation revealed the racism of her elderly white pewmates. But the quizzical tilt of her head and her squinting glance toward some invisible thought bubble asked, "What do they think I am, if not Black?" I intuited that even her own thoughts about the matter were uncertain. Upon reading these passages of the manuscript, Cherie K. affirmed that my intuition was correct.

Having grown up in Washington and in the North Portal Estates, I do not find the appearance of most Creoles ambiguous, but many Creoles interpret experiences like Cherie K.'s church incident as evidence that others assume they are white or at least non-Black. However, many unambiguously Black people are also addressed by un-self-conscious white people in much the same way that Cherie K. was. In my experience, sometimes they are not looking at me when they speak their prejudices. One day when I was visiting a Maret School friend in his gentrifying Capitol Hill neighborhood, I asked whether he was friends with the guys with whom I had just exchanged greetings as I entered his yard. "No," he said. As if suddenly entranced by a spot on the wall behind me, he added, "These Black kids are so mean." He repeated the phrase a few times, with the same peculiar demonstrative adjective that objectified all "Black kids," rather than specifying these particular kids, whose apparent meanness, I infer, was more closely related to the class-based conditions of their encounter with my friend than to their color. I tapped my friend on his shoulder, to exorcise the spirit that was possessing him, and asked if he remembered whom he was talking to. He did a double take and said, "What?" Either he did not think of me as Black, or he simply failed to notice the contradiction between our friendship and the social category that, to him, explained his neighbors' meanness. Neither of us yet had the vocabulary to describe the devastating social effects and minor retaliations that arose from the gentrification of Capitol Hill.

Other visibly Black African Americans in similar situations report a common cliché in the white interlocutor's subsequent explanation: "Oh, I wasn't talking about you! You're different. You're so smart/well-groomed/educated/decent. You're just like us. You're not *really* Black!" (After reading this passage, my Black Panamanian American friend at Duke wrote, "We all get this."). My late sister, my daughter, and my son have also been on the receiving end of such insulting words, which suppose that normative Blacks are the antitype of everything that whites value and like to imagine is statistically normative among them. For example, white and, less often, Black commentators have expressed shock about our middle-class diction and school orientation, the presence of Oriental rugs in our homes, or even Adu's wearing a National Public Radio jersey. The takeaway is that Blackness comes in only one kind, and it is defined by deficiency and subaltern otherness.

Cherie K.'s best friends are Creole, but in the context of our friendship, she also seemed to feel comfortably and perhaps situationally Black. The kind of Blackness that both of us instantiate—bourgeois, educated, antiracist, socially liberal, and culturally omnivorous—differs little from the elite membership of her would-be Creole networks. Yet in many situations, she faces definitions and expectations that leave her looking or feeling uncomfortably out of place and without a category.

In a further example, Cherie K. loves Black Protestant revivals and enjoys listening to Black preachers of the "prosperity gospel," such as the Reverend Creflo Dollar. She felt some desire for and identification with this massively public and self-confident Black Protestant community. But events reminded her that she is alien to that world. At one revival, she was invited for coaching in the gifts of the Holy Spirit. Several Black women surrounded and massaged her, praying and enjoining her to speak in tongues. And Cherie K. really wanted it to happen. In voices intended to relax her inhibitions, the church women repeatedly urged her, "Let it go. Just let it go. Let it go. Just let it go." Instead of feeling relaxed, my friend felt self-conscious about disappointing their expectations, and nothing came.

The women persisted for what seemed like forever. So rather than disappoint, Cherie K. released a stream of "Mumina mumina mumina. MUMINA MUMINA MUMINA!" She was relieved, and so were her tutors. "That's right," the women said. "You see? That wasn't too hard, was it?"

We both laughed over the tale, but we were also both deeply discomfited by this illustration of the contradictory set of desires and expectations faced by Creoles (and, I might add, other nonnormative black populations) in the United States. For example, Protestantism—and charismatic forms thereof—are often treated as normative or defining cultural features of American "Blackness." They can be fascinating for those who want to feel more like cultural insiders, but the pressure to conform to this ethnoracial diacritic can be off-putting to Black atheists and aspirants to middle-class rationalism and respectability. And although I spent my childhood summers surrounded by the gifts of the Holy Spirit, the enormous crowds and the money orientation of the prosperity gospel megachurches are foreign to me.

In any ethnoracial group, the standards of belonging are a matter of debate and of situational variation. So membership requires a shifting set of performances, all of which are subject to be judged inauthentic by one beloved community or another. Perhaps the most empirical sign and implicit diacritic of Creole identity is the heightened experience of ambiguity. Of course, this ambiguity is a variant on the experience of unrealness felt by all of the many people whose human complexity conflicts with the demands of group solidarity or with their definition as a constituent other.

Like most of the Black adults I know, I am long past worrying whether my behavior and character are "Black enough" in anyone else's eyes. But since I began this research, I have regularly shaken my head in confusion over the tension between the sociological and mass-media representations of "Black boys" and the Black boy that I was. Am I simply inventing that boy? Was the diversity of my interests an oddity? Like black ethnics and like the more prototypical constituent other, I feel required by this imposed oddness to formulate a reactive self-construction, not only to convince others of my worth, but also to anchor myself against internal confusion. Macroscopically, these are among the functions of "culture" talk as well.

In New Orleans and at Howard, people who regard each other as Creole daily rehearse their ambiguity and debate the terms of self-classification by monitoring each other's educational histories, marriages, divorces, political careers, restaurant appearances, legal travails, and so forth. These conversations involve a deep caring about the people discussed and a sense that even the speaker is implicated by the actions of the person being discussed. These ongoing biographical rumors, as well as the questions and expressions of surprise they inspire, involve a constant testing of the moral, educational, and phenotypical boundaries of the Creole network.

Creoles and the School Triage

When Creoles try to figure out if an unknown person shares their identity or belongs in their networks, the names of certain schools come up regularly. If someone attended Valena C. Jones Elementary School, McDonough 35, Corpus Christi School, Epiphany School, or Xavier Preparatory School, there is good reason to suspect some further personal or family connection to that person. In accounts of Creoles' educational histories, contrary to DuPlessis's experience, the HBCUs attended by Creoles still roll off of the tongues of my other interlocutors; TWIs are more often conflated with each other. What remains clear is that the choice of a college is read as an indication of one's bona fides as a New Orleans Creole. But the hermeneutics are subtle. Attending a TWI leaves open the possibility that one is a Creole separatist and nationalist, whereas a Black university can suggest either the abandonment of Creoleness or the view that Creoles are a type of Black people.

Like other matters Creole, the ethnic status of Xavier University is debated. While it is clearly a Roman Catholic university and therefore attractive to Creoles of color, my friends debate whether it is a Creole university. The scholarly literature reports that, before 1968, the university was associated with or even dominated by Creoles (Domínguez 1986, 173; Kein 2000a, xiv). Hence, older Creoles in New Orleans and my Creole mentors at Howard also identify Xavier as a Creole institution, though perhaps more in its administration and symbolically core population than in absolute numbers. Because it is the preeminent local Catholic university targeting people of color, Xavier has long been a point of convergence for some classes of Creole. On the other hand, my middle-aged and younger Creole-descended friends in New Orleans are equally certain that Xavier has never been a Creole institution, just a Black Catholic university that many Creoles, in acknowledgment of their Blackness, happened to attend.

However one imagines Xavier's connection to Creoleness, says University archivist Lester Sullivan, the student body has always been predominantly dark. Indeed, Sullivan showed me class photographs from the 1910s teeming with cinnamon- to chocolate-brown but wavy-haired people (I do not know whether the source of those waves is chemical or hereditary). Among the photographed students, French surnames predominated. Since the 1930s, the student body has been predominantly Protestant, and by 2002, it was only about one-third Catholic (Lester Sullivan, personal communication, July 10, 2002).

These images from the 1910s suggest that there were once many dark Creoles, that they were once more central to Creole communities and institutions than they are now, and that education was important to them, perhaps for the same reasons that dark Caribbean men disproportionately pursued education in the mid-twentieth century. However, dark Creoles have largely been pushed out of their erstwhile group, much as dark Latinos in the United States are being pushed out of their ethnic groups. Having grown up in the mid-twentieth century, one pound cake–colored Creole-descended poet and activist told me of her family, "We weren't the cream of the Creoles; there were Creoles who wouldn't have anything to do with us cuz we were too dark." And her family passed on the discrimination. Her parents would not allow her sisters or her to bring home black friends. A butter-colored Creole woman who had grown up a few years later told me that, then, "You weren't allowed to be Creole if you were too dark." "Creole but dark" was the sort of phrase that my Creole generational peers used to describe exceptional cousins of theirs, followed by an obligatory description of their redemptively non-African-looking hair and then a mention that some few of those cousins possessed neither the characteristic hair nor the characteristic complexion. Creoleness might once have included people of all complexions, as DuPlessis says about the present, but over time Creoleness tended to shed its legally white members, its unambiguously black ones, and, through a long history of intermarriage with light-skinned African Americans, any consistent or reliable correlation with French or Spanish surnames.

If the somatic norm image (Hoetink 1967) of Creoleness has changed, Xavier's student body has changed even more. Amid a changing national and local ethos, Xavier faculty and students fought over and ultimately rejected the term "Creole," and the networks of family belonging associated with that term became less and less central to the university community (Domínguez 1986, 173). However, at least until the desegregation of the TWIs, Creoles continued to nest themselves in this and other African American structures of educational opportunity, and they brought their ever more color-coded sense of social identity and belonging with them.

My elite Creole family friends and mentors at Howard demonstrated the process whereby many Creole Xavier graduates have long wedded their fortunes to those of other African Americans by attending Howard Medical School or Meharry Medical College in Nashville, Tennessee. Indeed, the deans of both medical schools at the time of my research were Creole. Thus, universities historically presented upwardly mobile young people with a choice: to remain wedded to their small racially intermediate community or wed their future to the elite of a more encompassing but differently defined community.

In the post–civil rights era, TWIs may be the only convenient and profitable places to make unambiguous assertions of Creole cultural distinction. By contrast, in elite New Orleans and at Howard, Creoleness has become a debate about the contemporary realness of a color-coded network deeply embedded in the broader African American professional class.

The Ambiguities of Mating and Marriage

As the classical analysis of ethnicity would lead us to expect, Creoles pay close attention to each other's marriages. However, the sense in which Creoles are endogamous combines the secret with the fictive. Elite New Orleans Creoles, even college-aged ones, regularly marry each other, but they are no more likely to announce that fact publicly than they are to declare themselves Creole. The consequent estrangement of non-Creole African American friends and clients would be costly. It is also common for them to marry selected types of non-Creoles. In my circle of acquaintances, many Creole men were married to light-skinned non-Creole women, including African Americans, Puerto Ricans, Mexicans, Syrians, Pakistanis, or Jews and other white Americans, though the vast majority of non-Creole spouses was made up of light-skinned African Americans. Light-skinned outsiders are embraced as coethnics without discussion or resistance. However, such ethnic adoption is virtually impossible for the dark-skinned spouses of Creoles.

The complaints of one acquaintance underline the preeminent principle of mate selection, and that principle is not "cultural" in any classical, nonracist sense. A male Creole admissions officer at Xavier complained that "buddies" of his who see him with a dark girl say obliquely, "Oh, so you like her? Be careful who you marry. You know, you can fool around, but, for God's sake, don't marry one of them. . . . You can fool around, but why do you have to go around with her in public?" For his "buddies," color, not culture, is the issue. When they consider dating dark people, many Creoles, like some non-Creole African Americans, are urged to "consider the children"—that they not turn out too dark on account of an unwise mating choice. Pitifully, my own mahogany-handsome father and his own ebony father appeared to have held similar sentiments. My cinnamon-colored psychiatrist aunt—my mother's sister—offered the same advice to her chocolaty son when he fell in love with an equally chocolaty woman. Ironically, my sentiments are more like those of my father's light-skinned surgical chief. I have always wanted my children to be superdark and superaccomplished, leaving no doubt about the ancestral source of their brilliance or their beauty.

On the other hand, many Creole women, like southeastern Indian women, either marry highly successful nonethnic and dark Black men or partner extramaritally with white men whose educational and professional accomplishments pale—no pun intended—before their own. Such was almost the case of the niece of my New Orleans Creole friend Cherie M. Though Cherie M. looks like butter, her older brother is a prominent, bronze-colored judge with an expressed preference for "Creole-looking" mates. His honey-colored daughter had graduated from Yale College and was on her way to University of Michigan medical school. At the time, she was dating an Italian American holder of a bachelor's degree from the State University of New York at Buffalo, a school of vastly lower ranking.

One night over dinner with the entire family at Pampy's, the young man grew very annoyed over my matter-of-fact reference to "white-skin privilege," or the unearned social and material advantages that tend to accrue to whites simply on account of their skin color. We spent much of the evening debating the sufficiency of his claim to have "earned everything I've got." I had not intentionally alluded to his luck in dating, but perhaps he sensed the implication and resented the reminder. Over the subsequent thirteen years of my friendship with Cherie M. and Cherie K., this episode has gradually morphed from a source of embarrassment into one of entertainment. Cherie M.'s niece is now a physician, but the relationship did not last. She remains single. This increasingly common experience among African American female professionals is especially striking because, when they could not find a Creole husband, Creole women once had their pick of dark and highly accomplished Black husbands. Now, however, both Creole and non-Creole Black men have easy access to unaccomplished white wives, a choice that they often seem to prefer.

In the generation of Cherie M.'s parents and mine, it is not uncommon for Creoles at Howard and in New Orleans to marry or partner with a dark person as a second, nonreproductive spouse. But these relationships are often unstable. Despite the expectations of their parents and peers, many Creoles and Indians are clearly attracted to and fall in love with dark people. However, their partnerships are more often premarital and postmarital than marital or reproductive. Despite the increased flexibility of their tastes in men, my middle-aged and younger Creole women friends seem to be encountering the same shortage of eligible and willing heterosexual partners as African American women in general. They admit, though, that they still have an unfair advantage over dark women.

The Horrors of Ambiguity: Creole Lore

In my observation, the most outstanding and universal feature of Creole culture, in the Tylorean/Boasian sense of "culture," is a predilection for Gothic storytelling. These tales are also the intimate side of the *debate* over what matters, which debate *I* call "culture." Among my elite and "sophisticated" acquaintances, the contemporary counterpart of the ghost stories and spells in the famous 1945 volume by the Louisiana Writers' Project, *Gumbo Ya-Ya*—and of the myriad novels about Creole women's Machiavellian and magical antebellum couplings with rich white men—is a genre of tales about the origins and the horrors of my acquaintances' own phenotypical in-betweenness.

On the one hand, the people identified by their peers as Creoles tend to recount their genealogies mechanically, syllogistically, and cautiously, emphasizing the Europeans, Indians, and nineteenth-century free people among their forebears. Though the qualifier "free" implies the presence of ancestry eligible for enslavement, New Orleans Creoles of color never mentioned African ancestors to me. Similarly, the carefully charted genealogy of one bayou country Creole physician at Howard is covered with notes revealing which ancestors were French, Spanish, German, or Indian. With eyebrows arched, shoulders and palms raised toward the heavens, he once whispered to me, "But we can't find the color," rendering questionable the default presumption that his family had any African ancestors at all. "We've looked, and we just can't find the color." Nonetheless, this physician was visibly colored. Moreover, he long remained wedded to Howard, and Howard lovingly wedded to him. After decades of service to Howard, however, he took an undoubtedly more lucrative job with a prominent pharmaceutical company.

Somewhat like the Gullah/Geechees, the Cane River Creoles take a different position with regard to their ancestry. The Metoyer family, for example, proudly recalls its African-born foremother, whose sexual charms and entrepreneurialism made her the founder of a slave-driven plantation empire and of a light-colored dynasty of rich and refined planters (see, for example, Mills 1977).

On the other hand, with fiery stillness and a mood of painful, irresolv-

A COMPLEXION OR A CULTURE? 293

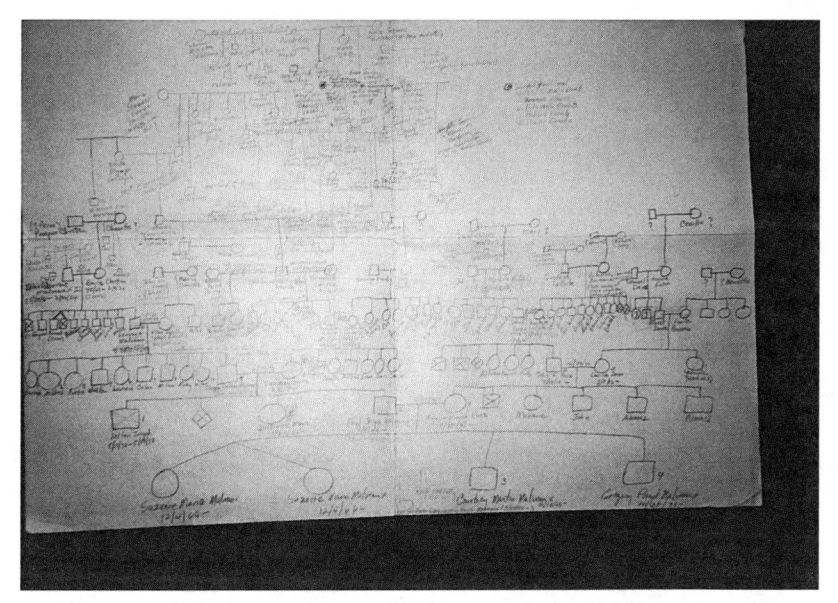

FIGURE 4.5. A Creole family tree, Washington, DC. Photograph by the author.

able dilemma, New Orleans Creoles tell a genre of Gothic horror stories about their hellish limbo between a nostalgically remembered eighteenth-century Latin American color-caste continuum and a twenty-first-century Anglo-Saxon binarism. Though they have certainly heard these stories many times, their family room and dining table audiences sit breathless and with hands clenching their armrests. My landlady, for example, was a gingerbread-colored woman who managed a major part of her dark, non-Creole father's mortuary and limousine business. She frequently swung her head and flicked her thin, pencil-length dreads out of her eyes, shelving them behind her ears, as if in imitation of her long-haired Creole mother or a blonde in a shampoo commercial. Through savvy investment and sharpness, she had extended the family's funeral home empire by acquiring the stretch of "Creole cottages" where I lived, in the historically Creole Tremé neighborhood. Built by Creole craftsmen, this neighborhood had, in the years before Hurricane Katrina, undergone a wave of renovation and gentrification. Fortunately, it survived the storm. A light-skinned African American with a light Creole wife and my dark Creole landlord had the most stunning houses in the neighborhood.

Although my Howard-alumna godsister had introduced us, my landlady was, upon our first meeting, businesslike to the point of gruffness. However, she eventually invited me into the lively and tight-knit circle of her sisters and their children. Their Sunday brunch of eggs, hot sausage, pancakes, cantaloupe and honeydew, strawberries, orange juice, and pecan sticky buns was a bigger spread than I had ever seen in my family, except on holidays, but the foods were no different. The quality of the laughter and intergenerational respect reminded me of better times in my own mother's own allegedly "free-issue" family. (Like many Creoles, my mother liked to believe that her mother's people had never been enslaved, and she selectively constructed a family tree to prove it.) The matrilateral focus of extended family life and the matrilateral emphasis of ethnic and genealogical identity inheritance struck me as common features of Creole and African-descended Indian, as well as the non-Indian and non-Creole African American, populations that I knew best.

My landlady's sisters and their children switched fluidly between ceremonious standard English and lively African American Vernacular, the eldest sister often adding the affectionate term "bay" to the end of her sentences. I noticed, though, that my landlady was the darkest of the sisters. She was clearly the most enterprising, the quietest, and least fun-loving—all perhaps for the same reason. She had clearly not been one of the "blessed ones." When she finally opened up to me, she recounted with the greatest poignancy a type of story that I had heard a dozen times before and have heard a dozen times since.

Many Creoles report having relatives who "pass for white," as did *New Yorker* literary critic and would-be Creole Anatole Broyard. Some did so temporarily and others permanently. Among their motives, I was told, was the pursuit of better pay and freedom from the choiceless prison of segregation. Broyard wanted to be accepted as a brilliant writer, not a brilliant Negro writer, confined to the small world of topics on which Negroes were allowed to profess expertise. When she was a child, my landlady's mother's brother was "passing for white" in a Los Angeles neighborhood. She recalls their occasional family visits to his California home, when her light-colored Creole mother would rush in to deliver Christmas presents to her brother and his family but would instruct her dark, non-Creole husband and the multihued children to stay in the car, without explanation and despite the children's pleas to see their cousins. After the mother ran back out of her brother's house, the New Orleans family would drive away in mournful silence. On the other hand, when that mother's passing brother and his conjugal family visited New Orleans, they received generous hospitality. Yes, my landlady answered quietly, as if ashamed, the lack of reciprocity and the reason for it did bother her.

But my landlady was actually lucky to know her cousins at all. On the eve of adulthood, my friend Cherie K. felt frustrated at *never having met* her California cousins. Her mother had forbidden contact, apparently by agreement with the brother, but my friend accidentally discovered their telephone number. When Cherie K. called her uncle's house, a prepubescent girl answered. When she realized that the girl knew nothing of her New Orleans family, my friend inferred that the girl thought she was white. Most controversial, as she told this story at a family dinner where I was a guest, was Cherie K.'s final act of protest. "You're Black!" she told the girl. "Don't you know you're Black?" At the dinner table where we sat, my friend's mother pursed her lips (they were thin enough to disappear) and exhaled audibly in annoyance—whether at Cherie K.'s audacity in telling the story to a relative stranger, or at the fact of her brother's continued estrangement, I do not know.

It should also be noted that members of the cousin-marrying little races in the eastern United States report similar horrors around racial ambiguity and inescapable irony. One neighbor from such a little-race family background told me of a relative who got a job scrubbing the floors of a white-owned apartment building in Washington. When the building manager noticed his light skin color, he sent the relative to man the elevator on the grounds that it was undignified for a white man to kneel on the ground scrubbing the floor. However, when the relative revealed that he was Black, he was fired from the elevator job, which was considered too good for a Black man.

Also common in New Orleans are the tales of passers who moved away and did not return home until the day of their mothers' funerals.[4] In the iterations of the tale that I have heard, the bereaved passer would usually sneak in late through the side door of the church and then sneak back out before the end of the funeral, never to be seen again.

The paper-bag test is another narrative theme endlessly repeated. The politically prominent Knights of Peter Claver lay brotherhood, for example, is said to have had a paper-bag-colored covering on the table at its entrance. As a man filled out his application for admission, the color of the unsuspecting applicant's hand was cleverly compared to that of the table cover. After he left, any application submitted by too dark a hand was thrown directly into the trash. The irony is that, according to some of my mentors (others deny it), the backroom strategizing that has produced all four of New Orleans's publicly Black mayors is said to have taken place within the Knights' four walls. The first three—Dutch Morial, Sidney Barthelemy, and Marc Morial—are identified by most Creoles as Creole. Uncertain Creoles regard Mayor Ray Nagin's membership in the Knights of Peter Claver as evidence that he, too, is Creole. The similarly prestigious and influential Autocrat Social & Pleasure Club is said to have had a paper-bag test *and* a comb test. While Shapiro does not doubt that Creoles practice magic, she is more skeptical about these omnipresent and obsessive tales, dismissing them as mere urban legend. Similar

FIGURE 4.6. Autocrat Social & Pleasure Club, New Orleans, 2002. Photograph by the author.

tales are told about the past admission policies of some sororities on the campus of Howard University.

Of enduring metaphorical significance are Creoles' tales of sneaking into the white section of segregated movie theaters but still having to endure the painful and distracting fear of detection. Other tales recount the similar experiences of sitting in the Negro section of the streetcar and being told to move, of hearing hateful comments about Black people from the white woman at the next locker outside the gym showers, and of entering a party where everyone else is white. In this last setting, they constantly anticipate insults (from whites who cannot tell that they are Black) regarding that invisible but socially and legally defining part of themselves that is Black. To me, the most painful part of the tale is the raconteur's fear of speaking up.

It reminds me of the scene in Steven Spielberg's *Saving Private Ryan* (1998) in which a Nazi soldier slowly plunges a dagger into the chest of an American GI as the victim's Jewish American fellow soldier stands by, afraid to act. Afterward, as the Nazi looks him directly in the eye and calmly walks away, the surviving GI stands there catatonic, only apparently unscathed. While I expected the Creole raconteurs to feel guilt about their inability defend their race, what I actually heard was the crushed self-esteem that resulted from not being able to refute the insult, of having to smile as though they agreed with the premise of their own partial or essential worthlessness.

A dagger through the invisible soul hurts worse and hurts longer than one through the heart.

The son of my father's Creole would-be wife became a surgeon. My would-be stepbrother was among those who told me that he feels uncomfortable not only in a room where he is the only Black person but also in a room full of dark Black people: "One time I went to a party [in Alabama, where there are no Creoles, he said], and everybody was black, black, black. I felt completely out of place." When I asked why, he said, "It was like if you were Shaquille O'Neal in a room full of midgets.... It's like if I showed up in a tuxedo, and everybody else showed up in jeans." He wasn't afraid, though, "because the guys with me were pretty tough." I was more surprised by his unreflective *candor* about his feelings of superiority to dark Black people than about his feelings per se. I became so accustomed to such vocalizations in New Orleans that, when asked by even welcoming Creole friends, I openly vowed that I would never bring my family to visit that city. Were my dark children present to hear such poetically vivid and unreflectively racist talk, from people they would have to call "uncle" and "aunt," I could not let it go unanswered. No dagger would plunge into my children's souls while I stood by silently.

It was also news to me that my would-be stepbrother felt physically threatened in the presence of dark Black men. However, many Creole and African-descended Indian women—not to mention light-skinned nonethnic African American women—also report discomfort with dark women, partly based on a childhood history of verbal taunts and hair pulling. In much of the Americas, people of African descent have inflicted great pain on each other over the issue of complexion. It calls forth the hatred of what many light and dark people have agreed is the feeling of essential worthlessness we share as a result of not being white.

A highly accomplished surgeon and professor at a prestigious local university, my would-be stepbrother has been unfailingly generous to me during my multiple stints in New Orleans, opening his home and wallet and clearing his busy calendar to assure my comfort. But in the midst of our hours of food and fun, we always return to the same conversation—a virtual repeat of conversations that I had with my father when he was alive about the degree of fairness that I have the right to expect from the world. I often wondered whether he, like my father, was reminding me about my own lack of worth or projecting onto me his doubts about his own worth.

Over dinner at his home one day, I told my would-be stepbrother, his wife, his sister Cherie M., and our mutual friend Cherie K.—all but his cream-colored Puerto Rican partner were Creole—about the humiliation I had suffered in a dress shop on the way back from interviews at Saint Augustine High

School in the historically Creole Seventh Ward. The school was once heavily Creole but is now occupied almost entirely by ambitious, talented, and dark non-Creole boys. The Treasure Trove did not look like much through its rusty metal grates and cloudy windows, but there seemed some chance that I had found an opportunity to buy a present for my wife, who, for that month, was back in Cambridge taking care of the kids alone. The opportunity carried the additional benefit that I could patronize a business that, perhaps mistakenly, I thought of as Black owned. Like my late father, I endeavor to do so whenever I can.

In most places in the Afro-Atlantic world, people peg me within moments of our interaction as a professor, some other kind of teacher, or, occasionally, a physician. But not in the Seventh Ward of New Orleans. Completely ineffective that day were the dress, carriage, and diction that I and much of the Black bourgeoisie use to advertise our respectability and to forestall the indignities we expect white merchants and police to heap upon the Black poor.

When I tried to open the shop door, I discovered that it was locked, even though the presence of the shopkeeper, two young attendants, and two customers inside suggested that the store was open. Everyone inside was pecan brown. It was even hotter that day in New Orleans than at the Hillsborough powwow. After an interminable minute of the shopkeeper and her attendants' staring at me from across the shop and through the door, one young woman finally came to the door. She looked through the dirty glass and shouted, "Can I help you?" Wearing beige gabardine slacks from Bloomingdale's, a Brooks Brothers tennis shirt, a Skagen watch, invisible-frame eyeglasses, and a leather Coach backpack for my notebooks and camera, I brought with me to the Seventh Ward the illusion that I looked like an Ivy League professor—albeit an unusually stylish one—stopping to browse for a gift for his wife. So I answered with the simple and obvious "Yes, I'd like to come in."

But before opening the door, the young woman and the shopkeeper deliberated out loud for another thirty seconds, while I stood in the ninety-degree heat. When she finally let me in, I entered and started looking around, the same way that my mother had demonstrated "browsing" at Saks and Lord and Taylor ever since, at age six, I had unknowingly helped to integrate these high-end Chevy Chase department stores. I had no idea that my presence and my dollars would be so much less welcome in a ramshackle Creole-owned shop in the Seventh Ward where all of the dresses hung inside plastic bags to keep the dust off.

I felt proud that I had been polite enough not to walk out as soon as I noticed the polyester quality of the merchandise. But then the shopkeeper barked, "You're gonna have to leave your bag behind the counter!" Astonished that she answered my charity with authoritarian rudeness, I furrowed my brow at her for a moment and said calmly, "On second thought, I don't think I'll be patronizing your shop."

As soon as I began my story, my Creole dinner companions knew where I had been and whose shop it was. They had known the mother and her two daughters—then on summer break from elite colleges—for years. One of the Creole women at the dinner said it was awful and exclaimed, "That woman is crazy!" My host's sister Cherie M. looked at me with sadness and said she was sorry that had happened to me. She planned to talk to the shopkeeper to find out what happened. On the other hand, my would-be stepbrother told me why he could sort of understand and why I should, too.

He complains all the time about the racism of his white surgeon colleagues and of other whites who, without realizing that he is Black, say awful things about Black people in his presence. Yet he thought I should understand that the Seventh Ward—which, the Creole conventional wisdom has it, had gone downhill because of all of the non-Creole Black renters—had become a pretty dangerous place, and so the woman had to be careful about being robbed. He nodded indefinitely when I asked him if I looked to him like a robber. I argued that a clothing dealer ought to be able to size up the ensemble of my haircut, my dentition, my glasses, my watch, my clothing, my shoes, and my diction quickly enough to know better.

I might halfway expect a white shopkeeper to be blinded by my color and miss every other sign of who I am. But a Black shopkeeper? I told him I had *never* been treated that rudely by a white shopkeeper and was shocked to have had my first such encounter with a person who, as far as I was concerned, looked like me. In principle, I know that Black people can make the same misjudgments about their own kind as do white people, but I am far more accustomed to such ironies in Latin America than in the United States. In São Paulo, a black policeman had once moved to draw his gun on my wife, my infant daughter, and me as we pulled up to our hotel in a taxi. The lesson of this story, including the shopkeeper's lack of remorse after Cherie M. spoke to her about why she had treated a tenured Harvard professor and friend of a friend that way, is that the pecan-brown shopkeeper did not regard me as a person of her own kind. Indeed, all the evidence of my class superiority notwithstanding, my skin color and African features made me her constituent other. And it is difficult for me not to conclude that my host's lack of sympathy means that he feels the same way. Regardless of our class similarity and the family connections between us, he and I do not seem to him equally worthy of the same benefit of the doubt when it comes to a reasonable stranger's judgment about our respectability or potential for criminality. I am tempted to call his and my father's ethic the *Sophie's Choice* (1979) "pragmatism" of the stigmatized. The Polish protagonist of William Styron's novel, Sophie, has a non-Aryan-looking girl child and an Aryan-looking boy child. A physician at Auschwitz, where she is interned, tells her that she may keep only one child. She has to choose which one to abandon to an uncertain fate. She feels anguish but chooses to keep the Aryan-looking boy child. The difference is that my father and my would-be stepbrother felt no anguish. Like the Gothic tales that Creoles tell, my tale of the Treasure Trove concerns a hereditary curse and an irresolvable terror faced by its characters—the terror of ambiguity. The similarity among these tales could easily be construed as a cultural likeness between my Creole interlocutors and me. But in this regard, we also bear a "family resemblance" to Jews, Poles, and other in-between populations.

The Politics of Choice

Judgments about ethnic sameness and difference are not always verbal, fixed, or equally evident to all viewers. The New Orleans diaspora Creole scholars Raymond DuPlessis and Melissa Shapiro are as publicly vocal about their Creoleness as New Orleans's three or four Creole mayors—including the brother of DuPlessis—have been cagey about theirs. Indeed, New Orleans's first mayor of acknowledged African descent, Ernest "Dutch" Morial, appears to have proclaimed his Blackness fervently, at least in the presence of Blacks. One of my Creole-descended friends wrote:

> Dutch Morial['s] reputation was really as a BLACK mayor and one who won fair, square and quite openly. Maybe some creoles claimed him [as Creole], but the identity he embraced was very definitely black, and black people in the city, those without a creole heritage or what have you, related to him thusly. (female Creole-descended friend and former Harvard student, e-mail, January 11, 2011)

Yet Morial's appearance would have allowed him to pass for white, and he may have taken advantage of that fact. Hence, one dark Creole-descended activist and Xavier alumnus who said he had known Morial personally added, "When Dutch was in the company of whites, he'd never deny being white" (personal communication, July 16, 2002).

Cherie K.'s father had been Morial's roommate at Louisiana State University Law School, where, in 1954, Morial was described as the first Black graduate (Hirsch 1992, 291). She offers her own interpretation of his motivations. She may be hinting at a contrast between Morial's private and public self-representations:

Yes Dutch referred to himself as black *publicly*. He came into power during the Civil Rights Movement and it was more important for him to be inclusive and not try to separate himself as Creole. (Cherie K., e-mail, January 12, 2011; emphasis mine)

When one depends on the votes or friendship of African Americans, it would appear unstrategic to publicize this potentially elitist or complexion-related form of ethnic difference—hence one Creole nationalist scholar's worries about the African American–induced "extinction" of the Creoles. Among African American constituents, clients, bosses, teachers, mentors, friends, and potential second spouses, the history of Creole contempt for even their own dark-skinned and fleece-headed grandchildren is often too well known and too pitiful to deny. But, as Shapiro pointed out to me, Creoles are hardly the only people suffering from such internalized racism.

Nor have Creole-diaspora activists and scholars—including DuPlessis—been remiss in challenging American racism, colorism, and contempt for Africa. For example, Kein (2000c) has emphasized the African heritage of Creole cuisine. One Creole professor of fine arts at Howard has focused his publishing career not on the rich nineteenth-century tradition of Creole studio arts—as one might expect from the usual tendency of Creolophiles to emphasize elite, distant-past ancestors—but on the equally rich nineteenth- and twentieth-century African American art of quilting. Virtually every wall and shelf of this Howard professor's house is covered with African carvings. His own beautiful paintings—he himself is a talented artist—typically depict dark people with dignity and heart. At least before Hurricane Katrina, he returned yearly to lead art projects at his Seventh Ward alma mater, Saint Augustine High.

Nonetheless, he is privately fascinated by what he suspects are the commonalities of experience and culture among New Orleans Creoles, "old" Washington's light-colored African American elites, and the Charleston Browns—nineteenth-century mulatto scions of white wealth, whose living descendants my colleague has so far, much to his disappointment, failed to locate during his visits to South Carolina.

What emerges from my discussions with elite New Orleanians and the professional-class Creole diaspora is a structural contrast between the motives of Creole professors in TWIs far away from New Orleans and those of Creole politicians, physicians, and other elites who depend on Black colleagues, voters, and clients. The former group tends to reify Creoleness as a distinct culture, identifying it as the property of a specific ethnic group. Sometimes deliberately and sometimes accidentally, they tend to mention that a light skin color, straight hair, and light-colored eyes typify this group in contrast to African Americans. However, they are at pains to argue, in the antiracist precincts of the contemporary academy, that the defining differences between Creoles and African Americans are not racial but "cultural"—that is, linguistic, literary, culinary, residential, and religious. Yet most of their evidence concerns distant-past personalities and practices. Creole enthusiasts thus exhume a legacy rather than identify what makes today's Creoles culturally distinctive in the Tylorean or Boasian sense.

Like other black ethnic proclamations about their "cultures," this is the vision of a lifeway frozen in time and internally homogeneous, one that denies change because of an omnipresent feature of such change—namely, mutual imitation among populations that are visible to each other, as well as the homogenizing results of blacks' common subjection to Jim Crow and other circumstances. The black ethnic speaker tends to see such change as costly to his or her inherited dignity and hoped-for privileges. The dissolution of the supposedly distinct culture has coincided with the group's assimilation into the lower segment of US assimilation. It resembles the transformation of "tribals" into "pariahs" within the Indian caste system. In the US American case, the frozen portraits of black ethnic "cultures" are usually paired with and logically dependent on an equally frozen and internally homogeneous portrait of the depravity of the constituent other, the nonethnic African American. Both portraits are as rigid as a university commencement ceremony. The authority that flows from them depends on their appearance of changelessness.

On the other hand, Creole-descended politicians, physicians, and other elites who depend on Black voters and clients avoid public discussion of their Creoleness and limit the term "Creole" to descriptions of food and of other people. Nonetheless, these elites participate in a network of fellow descendants of Creoles that shades indistinctly into much broader networks of light-skinned or professional-class African Americans.

Many elite New Orleans Creoles recognize the patterns of their own participation in African American institutions. For example, some Creole men told me that their fellow male Creoles tend to join the Kappa Alpha Psi fraternity more often than others. My father, too, was a Kappa. It is a measure of the Creoles' assimilation into broader African American society and classificatory logic that they have tended to join not the fraternity of the intellectuals (Alpha Phi Alpha) or of the hypermasculine "dogs" (Omega Psi Phi) but that of the "pretty boys." By contrast, as we will see in the next chapter, Caribbean-born men have tended not to join the African American Greek-letter societies at all.

For both Creole nationalists and Creole-born Black assimilationists, the identification of any given person as "Creole" is less a fixed and categorical reality than a guessing game and a debate. In common, these practices of inference, discovery, and struggle are less lists of fixed diacritica or even family resemblances than a search for common memories, places where paths might have crossed, and places where one does not feel visually out of place, all of which provide evidence of belonging in the same social and affective network. Memories of forebears who used "Creole" as a self-description, memories of peers and forebears who adamantly rejected this form of self-description, and Gothic tales of forebears who languished in the hell of their ambiguity are equally salient and probative evidence of shared belonging in this network.

Are Creoles an ethnic group? Is there a distinct Creole culture? Perhaps so, but these terms were certainly more applicable 150 years ago than they are today. And at least in its elite New Orleans and Howard University variants, membership in that network is not—or is no longer—defined by a separate residential area or by a set of names, practices, beliefs, or foods that it monopolizes. Rather, it is defined by erstwhile Creole people's unique confusion, an internal debate, and a degree of defensiveness over whether they count as a distinct group and over who belongs to it. By calling their confusion unique, I do not mean to say that they are wrong to be collectively uncertain, but that they illustrate a most extreme form of the debating that perhaps shapes all ethnic identities and an extreme case of the personal confusion of people who can profitably claim to be insiders to multiple rights-bearing groups—that is, the confusion of most people in the world. To a degree, all collective identities in the world entail a degree of such confusion. But some populations have more choices—or more painful choices—than do others.

The nostalgia of the definitions given to Creoleness by university scholars Shapiro and DuPlessis does not prove that they are wrong. Theirs is one exceptionally fervent faction within the debate that—like the feud among Evans-Pritchard's Nuer (1940)—continually calls this social network into existence. The signature contribution of Shapiro and DuPlessis to this ethnography is that they reveal the distinctive function of the university in clarifying what is not clear, in disambiguating what is ambiguous, and in reifying phenomena that can then justify books, grants, research institutes, and, sometimes, tribes or nation-states. To a degree, they also reveal the difference between Howard and TWIs as venues of culture making.

Given the nature of Howard's population, I have interacted with three domestic populations of mostly or partly African ancestry—Gullah/Geechees, southeastern Indians, and Louisiana Creoles of color—in this order of increasing intensity. In a way that made my research difficult and its lessons all the more fruitful, my African physical appearance is an important and antagonistic symbol in the self-figuration of the latter two populations. This chapter has benefited especially from sharp conflicts with two of my little-race mentors, illuminating for me the conflictual nature of ethnogenesis generally.

One of the defining features of ethnic identities and networks is that they are venues of debate about who belongs and who does not. My presence and my questions about southeastern Indians and Louisiana Creoles precipitated a ready-made anger in some of their partisans, calling attention to debates endemic in these populations about whether the identities they propagate refer to "cultures" or to stigma-driven appeals to escape from last place in a light-to-dark hierarchy.

Like Gullah/Geechee ethnogenesis, these cases clearly illustrate the proteanness of the cultural diacritica that, Barth argued, define membership in ethnic groups. They illustrate the fact that the competitive pursuit of earnings and honor shapes these efforts to classify people. They illustrate the role of schools as sites of social triage—dividing, aggregating, and rearranging the personnel of ethnoracial categories and identifying their leadership. And they call attention to the role of universities in authorizing—in terms of "cultures"—the social categories to be spoken for by university-educated elites.

In addition, the emergent southeastern Indian tribes specifically illustrate the role of museums and salvage anthropology in the resurrection of corporate groups, as well as the role of laws and courts in adjudicating their boundaries and diacritica. On the other hand, the Louisiana Creoles specifically illustrate the diverse stakes that ethnic spokespeople in different professions and professors from different types of university (i.e., TWIs vs. HBCUs) bring to the debate over which ethnoracial categories are legitimate and who gets to speak for them. These cases are especially rich in the lesson that the little races that leaders reify as ethnic groups are highly permeable, and elite New Orleans Creoles so powerfully embody this principle that it may be more useful to call them a boundaryless "network" than an "ethnic group." Indeed, it may be useful to regard networking as an alternative descriptor of the permeability that Barth attributes to ethnic groups.

But above all, this chapter illustrates the defining role of debate and contestation in ethnogenesis. If there was once a time when the southeastern Indian tribes and the Louisiana Creoles had plausible claims to Tylorean/Boasian "cultures" distinct from those of their Black and white American neighbors, it is centuries past. Changes in state laws compelled them to interact daily and intensively with whites and, above all, Blacks. While some members of these populations have united with African Americans in the pursuit of individual and collective upward mobility, others have sought to restore distinction, in ways motivated variously, over time, by the Afro-phobic logic of slavery and Jim Crow, the nationwide post-Reaganite resurgence of ethnicity, swelling international migration, and the potential for the descendants of Native Americans to recover the material benefits of their ancestors' treaties.

Any outsider who speaks of these dilemmas and debates is likely to invite anger because he or she appears to be taking sides. But taking sides is not my goal. Rather, I see in these cases strong evidence that the debate itself—indeed, the irresolvable fixation on specific dilemmas—is the phenomenal diacritic of these human communities and of many others as well. And at the crux of these particular debates is the question of what to do with people who look like me—the African American constituent other. Will we be a foil, a model, or an ally?

Since the Hart-Celler Act of 1964 opened the floodgates of the brain drain from Africa and the Caribbean, the color of Howard, of other elite universities, and of the African American professional class in general has shifted all the more rapidly from 6:00 p.m. to midnight. The US Black elite is darkening further still.

The transition has not always and everywhere been smooth. For example, from 1996 until at least 2001, historically Black Virginia State University was wracked by charges and countercharges of discrimination between African and African American professors (*Journal of Blacks in Higher Education* 2001; Timberg 2000). In 2004, Harvard professors Henry Louis Gates Jr. and Lani Guinier questioned whether affirmative action at Harvard was benefiting the right people, when, according to their estimate, two-thirds of the university's "black" undergraduates were, to quote the *New York Times*' summary, "West Indian and African immigrants or their children, or to a lesser extent, children of biracial couples" (Rimer and Arenson 2004).

Their meeting of minds on this topic is striking. Gates is a light-skinned African American, and Guinier is the biracial child of a Jamaican immigrant. While one other normally outspoken Harvard colleague, Jamaican immigrant Orlando Patterson, recommended that we "let sleeping dogs lie" (Rimer and Arenson 2004), Gates and Guinier recommended a more selective distribution of access to the collective benefits of affirmative action, based upon the distinction between people whose four grandparents were born of slave parentage in this country and others who lack this pedigree. The then president of Harvard, Lawrence Summers, refused to comment on the matter. And as far as I know, no university in the United States has followed Gates and Guinier's recommendation. However, Gates and Guinier have broken the taboo on what is, for many, a fearsomely divisive and worrisome topic.

Yet, also as far as I am aware, no one has questioned the belonging of

Louisiana Creoles of color and black Indians in the core group of affirmative-action beneficiaries. Other critics of race-based affirmative action have wondered, however, whether middle- and upper-class Black people deserve this remedy. It is difficult to predict where this new parsing of collective identity and the hierarchy of rights to material rewards will end up.

The next chapter documents an elite immigrant reply, according to which Caribbean immigrants are, by reason of "culture," and not class or race, more deserving of the rewards of US citizenship than are African Americans. Ethnogenesis is normally a project not only of debate but also competitive one-upmanship. Perhaps it is Caribbean American ethnogenesis that best illustrates this point.

5

Islands of the Mind: The Mythical Anthropology of the Caribbean

My first teaching job was at Phillips Academy in Andover, Massachusetts, during the summer of 1982, when I graduated from Harvard College, and in the school year of 1983–84, after my Rotary year in Nigeria. Teaching English literature and religion, I worked with extraordinary students and colleagues, the most influential of whom sought my opinion on how to diversify the curriculum and enhance the experience of nonwhite students. The colonial brick of the buildings gave discreet cover to the mountain of lucre that endowed this establishment. Little of that wealth was made available for my comfort while I served as one of four faithful adult spokespeople for the race among a faculty of over one hundred. At the end of the day, I went home alone to an apartment furnished with the castoffs of older colleagues.

Only as I write now do I recognize that the two senior colleagues who had integrated Andover long before the other recent college graduate and I arrived were a married couple of Louisiana Creoles. From the welcome that they gave me and their advocacy on behalf of nonwhite people, I could not distinguish them from any of the other light-skinned neighbors with whom I had grown up. Indeed, his honey tone did not strike me as light, and the African facial features of his wife meant more to me than her wheat-colored and freckled skin.

It was this Creole couple that made me aware of the concern on campus about the swimming requirement. But it was perhaps the presumption of our at least partially shared biology that turned this theme into a private and particularly distressing conversation among us. Like several of our kindly white colleagues, they were at a loss for solutions to the problem that so many of our Black students were failing the required swimming test. A white assistant dean had wondered aloud whether it was a bone-density issue. For my part, I was at a loss to explain what made my kind of Black people different from the ones who had been admitted to or noticed at Andover.

I had learned to swim rather well—at Howard and at Camp Letts, an integrated YMCA summer camp in Edgewater, Maryland. In fact, that skill became my salvation after the research for this book caused me to regain so much weight after a pretty slender adolescence and young adulthood. Much of my field research took place in restaurants with students and at the dinner tables of Howard alumni and professors. Only by swimming two miles a day for a year and a half did I take off the resulting twenty-six pounds. In the North Portal Estates, all the children of our chocolaty-black and dense-boned next-door neighbors, my cinnamon-brown best friend and pediatrician's son and his walnut-colored brother, and several other neighbors swam for predominantly Black local teams and for their predominantly white private high schools. Swimming pools were the focus of family vacations for my matrilateral cousins and me. In scores of recently integrated hotels and motels, we would thunder down hallways and unhinge doors in a race for the pool. So at Andover I was forced to ask myself for the first time how I had escaped my race's reputation for incapacity: "Are Washingtonian Black people different?"

The next time I asked myself that question was after the publication of Fordham and Ogbu's 1986 article "Black Students' School Success: Coping with the Burden of 'Acting White.'" The article reports that—beyond inferior schooling and the paucity of material rewards for school completion—certain psychological coping strategies by Black students further limit their striving for academic success. Fordham and Ogbu argue that many African American students develop identities resistant to their oppressors, and they consequently dismiss the striving for academic success as a "white" characteristic. Consequently, they accuse the academic achievers among themselves of "acting white" and thus betraying their oppressed race.

The Fordham and Ogbu article gave ethnographic substance to Ogbu's earlier cross-cultural comparison of colonized, lower-caste, and involuntary-migrant minorities (e.g., Ogbu 1978). This earlier work had shown that populations in these structural positions regularly underperform in school, whereas, when they and their parents immigrate voluntarily to other countries, they perform just as well as immigrants from the privileged classes of their home countries and better than the structurally subordinated populations of their host countries. Ogbu illustrated this phenomenon with reference to, for example, Koreans and members of the Eta caste in Japan who voluntarily immigrate to the United States and lower-caste Hindus in India who voluntarily immigrate to the United States, in contrast to involuntarily colonized or enslaved Native Americans, Puerto Ricans, African Americans, and so forth.

Yet the colonized and the enslaved are not alone in their deliberate resistance to the demands of school. As Bourdieu ([1979] 1984) points out in the context of class hierarchy, camaraderie is the prime psychological weapon of lower-status groups generally, so many working-class Europeans also discourage and harshly punish such individualistic and camaraderie-disrupting pursuit of upward mobility. Before Black American youth, and especially Black boys, became the focus of this literature of lamentation, the same phenomenon was documented in predominantly white European, Canadian, and US schools as well (Fordham 1996).

Ogbu's former student Signithia Fordham detailed a further instance of this phenomenon in one Black high school in southeast Washington, DC, where the structurally subordinated descendants of involuntary immigrants found academic achievement antagonistic to their racial identity. Though the research had been based in my hometown, I managed to convince myself that that this particular southeast DC school was an exception. In the Washington-area public and private schools that I had attended up until just four years before Fordham's research, I had never heard the expression "acting white." Recalling the 1970s, some of my friends who had remained in public schools longer than I said that they had been teased for "acting rich" or "stuck up," for being "bookworms" or "teachers' pets," or merely for being "high-yellow" or "red-bone," which terms for skin color they took for insults. Some of my interlocutors said they simply felt out of place in these settings for having light skin or straight hair. On the other hand, many of these peers reported learning how to code-switch between formal English and vernacular dialect in order to deflect potential antagonism toward people of their class, complexion, or level of ambition. But none of them recalled being accused of "acting white" either.

I do not recall being teased much while I was in my public elementary school—I was taller and wider than most of my peers. Perhaps for that reason, and because I attended relatively class-homogeneous private schools from the second month of seventh grade onward, I felt little pressure to code-switch, and I now regard myself as incompetent at that linguistic skill. I speak Spanish, French, Portuguese, and Yoruba fluently, but I experience a block when it comes to varying the class register of my speech.

Far from feeling that Black people were especially resistant to school, most of my Black friends in private schools and I noticed the lack of academic seriousness among a sizable minority of our white peers, who drank beer, smoked marijuana, and enthusiastically popped pills from their mothers' medicine cabinets. I recalled that those of us who did not simply take for granted the expectation that we succeed were endowed with the fervor that we must constantly use our academic skills to stop white people from holding back our race. In our neighborhood, academic success and professional ambition were requirements of our Blackness, but this Black-inspired fervor sometimes affected our white friends as well.

However, it was insufficient to save all of my white friends. Somehow, my Maret schoolmate Gary had touched my mother's heart, despite his willingness, on one occasion, to tease her about our home décor. I was shocked by her tolerant laughter when Gary compared the high-modern shelves in our kitchen to the auto parts racks in his father's used car dealership. I had never witnessed such a sign of friendship between my mother and a white person. I enjoyed Gary's company as much when he was stoned as when he was straight. He was always iconoclastic and lighthearted. But his merchant-class Jewish parents worried about his future and sent him to a boarding school with a drug-rehabilitation program. When his dormitory caught fire, he could not flee in time. When she heard the news that Gary had died of smoke inhalation, my mother wept, as I weep now at the memory.

I also have a very dear and trust-fund-rich white Washingtonian friend, the son of a congressman. He recounts the story that, when he had dropped out of college and was adrift, my mother told him, "I don't want Randy hanging out with people who can't finish college." He reports that he returned to college the next semester. He is too modest to add that he later graduated summa cum laude and was inducted into the Phi Beta Kappa honors society. With some evidence, I regarded—and still regard—Washington as a Black success factory, with considerable benefits for our white friends as well.

In 1997, as an associate professor and resident scholar in Harvard's Leverett House, an undergraduate dormitory, I led an undergraduate discussion group about Fordham and Ogbu's article. Unfortunately, there were no other Washingtonians in the group to counterbalance my generation- and neighborhood-specific account. But everyone else in the group—which was drawn from Harvard's disproportionately New York–based undergraduate population—had indeed heard the expression "acting white" and knew of its vile effects. My reasoning and my emotions together led me to believe—and to defend my self-esteem with the inference—that Washington's uniquely Black-dominated and HBCU-influenced "culture" had quarantined my city from this pestilence. I was not immediately equipped to recognize the likely effect of class diversity, historical change, and diversity across schools and families in explaining the difference between my experience and that of Fordham and

Ogbu's southeast Washingtonian subjects. It remains possible that I was correctly identifying the specific effects of relative wealth and the proximity of an HBCU in Northwest Washington, in contrast to distant Southeast, an effect that Eugene Robinson saw similarly around South Carolina State University.

On the other hand, now that I force myself, I can think of five North Portal Estates peers, out of scores, who did not finish college. One brilliant and bespectacled butter-colored boy thought it unnecessary, and he developed a successful career in international business, focusing on Nigerian telecommunications (he is now even more deeply immersed in Nigerian life than I am). A French-vanilla boy went to jail as part of a family-based car-theft ring, and psychiatric problems incapacitated one straight-haired, Nilla Wafer boy, himself the son of a psychiatrist. A buttery friend of my sister's—a daughter of the married Virginia cousins—reportedly experimented with drugs and dropped out of Howard. And the biggest childhood discipline problem in the neighborhood was a creamy boy who reportedly looked down upon dark people, but I know nothing of his adult trajectory. To me, these cases seem infinitesimally few, and none seemed directly explicable in terms of the "acting white" phenomenon.

If anything, the majority of my least educationally driven neighbors were also the whitest-looking, and some of the worst-behaved boys at overwhelmingly Black Shepherd Elementary School were actually white. This fact reminds me of what dark Caribbean men of my father's and elder brother's generations said about their academically complacent Trinidadian French Creole and Jamaican Brown classmates. The dark boys believed that educational excellence was their *only* path to success; they could not count on teacher favoritism or the inheritance of a family business. In both the Caribbean and the US cases, I also infer that the dark boys' accomplishments in school and the liberal professions eventually compensated, on the mating market, for their disfavored skin color.

In my nostalgic memories, I am still unable to account for why *any* upper-middle-class Black Washingtonian would steal cars or drop out of Howard. Hence, my oversimple recollection of my hometown still exemplifies for me my own infinite possibilities. I mobilize that recollection, as well, to convince my children of their own "cultural," hereditary, and therefore inevitable potential. In this regard, I am little different from the Caribbean students, faculty, and parents at Howard who explained and perhaps even motivated their successes in terms of what made them collectively different from Black Americans.

This chapter concerns the mythological discourse of "cultural" difference under conditions of migration, racial stigmatization, and class similarity—

FIGURE 5.1. A successful Howard alumnus and engineer at his home, Port of Spain, Trinidad. Photograph by the author.

that is, how Howard students, alumni, faculty, administrators, and staff of foreign or ethnically marked domestic origins represent themselves collectively in reaction to racial stigmatization in the United States. They vacillate between, on the one hand, the performance of difference from and superiority to nonethnic African Americans and, on the other hand, the performance of fraternal similarity to us. By calling the structure of these self-representations mythological, or even fictional, I presuppose not that these self-representations are less true than the strategic and sometimes literal African American supposition that all Black people are or should be alike and that likeness is a precondition for unity in the struggle against racism. Rather, the terms "mythological" and "fictional" are intended to indicate that these self-representations are the actors' situational, strategic, and selective *stipulations* or *charters* of collective selfhood, rather than merely empirical observations about the typical behavior and values of their coethnics. Like the retrospective reflections that Andover demanded of me, immigrants' construction of Caribbean "culture" is powerfully shaped by a reaction against the most insulting suppositions that Americans impose on the foremost local exemplar of Blackness—native-born African Americans.

Caribbeans who end up at Howard also characteristically end up embracing the North American notion that they are Black. They are often vocal and adamant in their defense of Black people generally. For added measure, they look to their Caribbean homeland for proof that *their* kind of Black people—West Indians, or Caribbeans—are different from the Black people who are legitimately vulnerable to the stereotypes. In fact, the argument goes, West Indians contribute to Black dignity by disproving that all Black people are like African Americans. And the difference is typically described as their distinctive "culture." Some Caribbean Americans offer the most classical and extreme prototype of ethnological schadenfreude that I encountered in the course of my research. At the same time, Caribbean Americans like Marcus Garvey, J. A. Rogers, and Stokely Carmichael / Kwame Turé have been among the most vocal defenders of Black racial dignity.

Ethnicity and Distinction

Much is known about the shape of ethnicity cross-culturally. People from any given place tend to share many symbols, assumptions, and interests in common. Yet anyone with the vaguest knowledge of the self-reported differences between Igbos and Yorubas, Black and white Americans, Iraqi Sunnis and Shiites, or Northern Irish Protestants and Catholics knows that proximate populations are more conscious of the symbols, assumptions, and interests that *divide* them than of those that *unite* them. In the diaspora of any of these territorially based populations, many such cultural differences are made less important by the migrants' shared differences from the host population, by the perceived incivility of the hosts, and by the usefulness of advice and service from those conationals who arrived earlier and are therefore relatively knowledgeable. They share similar worries about kinsmen back in the homeland, as well as a similar desire to return there. A Yoruba proverb says, "It is because of the rain that doves and chickens were brought together [in the same coop]"—*Òjò tó rọ̀ ló jẹ́ ká kó ẹyẹlé pọ̀ mádìẹ*. That is, similar adversity unites previously dissimilar parties.

This relativity of political scale is not limited to the diaspora. Hence, a person visiting the Ekiti state capital of Ado might think of herself primarily as a villager from Ayede but, while teaching at the University of Ibadan, think of herself primarily as an Ekiti person. In the context of a fight with an Igbo, the same Ayede person might consider herself Yoruba. In the context of the struggle against northern Nigerian political dominance, she is as likely to consider herself a southern Nigerian and seek to coordinate resistance along those geographical lines. Questioned by a seemingly naïve or aggressive African American in Washington, DC, she is more likely to identify herself simply as Nigerian, or even African, and look to any other Nigerian or continental African for sympathy in the face of such an alienating encounter.

As Evans-Pritchard (1940) discovered in the case of the Nuer people, identity is, in this way, often segmentary, and its political scale shifts situationally. The shape of personal and collective identity is dictated less by an enduring essence than by the affiliations of the actor's immediate antagonist. In other words, conflicts bring social order and personal identity to life, such that, in a fight with a crowd of white Americans, a Black American is reminded of her Blackness and is strategically tempted to invoke her commonality of identity with other Black people to raise a collective defense. Yet in a fight (or competition) with another Black American, she must locate an identity of a lower order or a crosscutting identity that excludes her antagonist, such as fellow family member, fellow "middle-class" person, fellow dark-skinned person, fellow woman, or fellow New Yorker. In a fight with a Briton or a Jamaican, she may invoke solidarity with all her fellow Americans, and in a fight with a Black man, she might call upon the sisterhood of all women. And as every US filmgoer knows, there is nothing like an alien invasion from another planet to remind us that all of humanity is one.

As Fredrik Barth (1969) and Abner Cohen (1969) have pointed out, cultural difference as such is seldom the cause of ethnic difference, or the enactment of distinct peoplehoods. Neighboring populations regularly share an enormous proportion of their collective assumptions and conventions in common. And each ethnically bounded population is, to a degree, internally diverse in its assumptions and conventions. Moreover, unless contiguous ethnic groups work hard to prevent it, they tend to converge over time in their assumptions and behavioral conventions. Thus, when ethnic boundaries arise or endure, it is usually because some powerful erstwhile members of that ethnic group benefit materially or psychologically from a monopoly or a privilege that would diminish in the absence of those boundaries. Following Kasinitz (1992), I describe these leading actors as "ethnicity entrepreneurs."[1]

Bourdieu's ([1979] 1984) observations about class distinction and the function of "taste" also illuminate the dynamics of ethnicity. Most middling classes or subclasses invest enormous energy in demonstrating through style, diction, and school affiliation their likeness to higher social classes and, even more, in highlighting their differences from and superiority to the next-lower class or subclass. Similarly, many upwardly mobile Afro-Caribbean immigrants invest considerable effort in describing what favorably distinguishes them from African Americans and in the maintenance and display of the diacritical parlance, or accents, that can be used to distinguish them from African Americans when it is useful to do so. Goffman might describe these as efforts by discreditable people to "cover" through situationally sensitive information management. Of course, members of the white American and white immigrant working class have historically gone to vastly more dramatic and violent lengths to distinguish themselves from Black people and thus to "cover" their own low social status among white people (Ignatiev 1995; Roediger 1990; Morrison 1993). These efforts might be better described as "expiation"—ridding themselves and their neighborhoods of the part of themselves that is vulnerable to being judged unworthy of assimilation to the upper racial segment of US society.

Implicit in the whiteness studies literature, as in the present case, is that much consequential signaling of ethnonational and racial sameness and difference occurs not just in words but in ritual, sartorial, danced, gestural, culinary, and sometimes martial performances (Hall 1983; Lott 1993; Domínguez 1989; Handler 1988). Such performances are often competitive and intent on creating, preserving, or modifying a hierarchical relationship among the performers' respective ethnic groups. Equally important is the fact that, like class difference, ethnoracial difference in the United States is often performed for a third-party audience—that is, a normally unmarked ethnoracial group or class that outranks both groups of performers and has the power to dispense or withhold wealth and honor.

Universities produce, reproduce, and reify collective identities in myriad ways. Through application forms, scholarship forms, identification cards, grade records, and ethnoracial organizations, universities induce more verbal classification and self-classification than perhaps any other institution in the world. But many nonverbal phenomena in the university are also read as signs of social difference. For example, among Howard undergraduates in 2002, sports teams and majors were taken to display the difference between African Americans and non–African Americans. To many Howardites in 2002, swimming and soccer suggested the athlete's foreignness. The more natural or applied the science, the fewer US Americans were found there as majors, just as at TWIs like Duke. Not only are students conscious of this tendency, but some exaggerate it to the point of treating the matter categorically.

So, for example, one African American student told me that his peers in the Engineering School make him feel out of place. In his mind, they were saying, "What are *you* doing here?" At Howard, these differences are read in terms of campus geography, since the liberal arts buildings sit high on "The Hill," the science buildings at the middle, and the medical complex at the foot. Given the increasing numbers of non-Americans and non-Blacks encountered as one descends The Hill, many locals read ethnicity and architecture on campus isomorphically. Thus, at Howard and elsewhere, mythological stipulations and charters of ethnic difference are articulated not only in words but also in proxemics and performances, among the most vivid of which are culinary.

Universities are food factories. Busy and childless young people with few cooking facilities subsidize a plethora of eating establishments, which both mime the mythology of ethnic difference on campus and give social form to its stipulations.

Racial Embrace and Ethnic Distinction in the University

Long before I began my research at Howard, I had known that different peoples think very differently about what mainstream US Americans call "race." However, I hypothesized that students and faculty originating from countries and regions that conceptualize racial and complexion diversity in terms other than binary hypodescent would—at Howard—embrace the notion that all people of African descent belong to the same political, marital, and extended cultural category. I thought Howard—and immigration to the United States generally—would smooth out all that diversity of ideas about race.

Indeed, I heard proof in the following story told by a man who served as the president of the Howard University Caribbean Students Association (CSA) for several years during the late 1940s. Mr. Leonard Bartlett (a pseudonym) was a "brown" man, a term by which Jamaicans describe their typically intergenerational and middle-class mulatto population. We first broke bread—and *roti*—together in suburban Silver Spring at the Negril restaurant, which he told me was, like the branch next to Howard on Georgia Avenue, owned by a "Chinese Jamaican" alumnus. I had looked for him from 2002 until 2010, without knowingly seeing him. Eventually, family connections revealed another set of details about him. His sister had married my childhood neighbor—the son of a Howard-trained dentist and of my mother's dear friend and sorority sister, another Howard alumna. She told me that the owner of Negril was also the son of a very wealthy Jamaican cardiologist practicing at Howard University Hospital. Our first meeting was like a family reunion. I count it as a major lesson about Jamaican American racial classifications that the name, speech, manners, skin color, and facial features of this "Chinese Jamaican" Howard alumnus would not have distinguished him from the gingerbread-colored people whom most of my childhood neighbors would call "African American."

Over curry goat and coco bread at Negril, this CSA president emeritus told me of his introduction to US racial binarism and colorism. In the 1950s, he learned that in the United States his privileged class background, his selective taste, and his whole-wheat color conferred no advantage that his "race" could not undo. I duplicate here my paraphrase of his words from my field notes:

My British schoolmaster in Jamaica had shown me Stepin Fetchit [a film actor, born of West Indian parents, who played a lazy buffoonish African American in multiple films from the 1930s to the 1950s] and asked me if I wanted to be like that. "No," I said. He said, "So don't associate with those people."

However, like me at the door of the Treasure Trove in New Orleans, Mr. Bartlett received an epiphany about his place in the local taxonomy of race at the door of a down-market commercial establishment. The former CSA president said that, during his freshman year at Howard, he was hungry at the end of a day of classes. So he walked down Georgia Avenue toward U Street in search of a restaurant. The first one that he saw was across from the old trolley station, but as he headed for the door, a group of "dirty white men" emerged from a construction site that he called "a hole in the ground" and entered the same restaurant. Having originated from a respectable and status-conscious home, he then dared not enter that restaurant. So he marched farther down Georgia Avenue, where he found nothing else open. Without a viable alternative, he furtively backtracked to the diner near the trolley station. In fear that someone would see him and report back to his mother that he had disgraced himself by eating in such a place, he turned up the collar of his trench coat, like a sleuth, before entering.

He then stood at the counter, waiting and waiting. When he finally rapped on the countertop, a white man in a grease-stained apron emerged and pointed out a sign above the grill and said, "Can't you read, nigger? 'No Niggers, Dogs or Jews Allowed!'"

From this story, Mr. Bartlett concluded: "If there's one great lesson that America has taught me, it's this, and I will always be grateful to America for this lesson: You might be brown or as black as the night, but we are all the same. Bartlett then laughed at the irony: "I'd been *ashamed* to be seen in there." Pride in his interstitial position in the British colonial color hierarchy had closed his eyes to the essence of even that system—the relativization of the humanity of *all* African-descended people. Jim Crow opened his eyes.

However, over the course of my multiple meals and conversations with Mr. Bartlett, the arc of his narrative led beyond the themes of pan-Africanism and unity across color castes. He ultimately detailed the strategy by which he had modified and even inverted the old color hierarchies that Howard in fact shared with the British West Indies. The account of his ingenious challenge to the pigmentocracy reified a new set of *ethnic* divisions.

When Mr. Bartlett first arrived at Howard, student government had been monopolized by a small group of African American fraternities and sororities with an almost exclusively light-skinned membership. Under his leadership, he reported, the leaders of several predominantly dark-skinned Greek-letter societies joined together with the Caribbean Students Association and the African Students Association to pool their votes and win the election for student-body directorate. For years thereafter, he said, each of the three main offices in Howard student government—president, vice president, and treasurer—rotated among members of these three insurgent groups.

In Mr. Bartlett's triumphal story, region-of-origin-based ethnicity—that is, the supranational "African" and "Caribbean" ethnic groups—came to matter more than it ever had in the actors' respective native countries. In this ingenious putsch, complexion-coded hierarchies were not erased but were almost inverted.

I have some doubts about the literal truth of Mr. Bartlett's story. My father had been the very dark president of the undergraduate class of 1948 and of the medical class of 1953. In none of my many conversations with him would he confirm these reports. Of course, everyone's memory is partial and selective, and my father was relatively sanguine about colorism at Howard. However, many Howardites share with Mr. Bartlett the exaggerated impression that, until their generation, Howard's pigmentocracy had been absolute.

This narrative trope serves a special function, though, in Mr. Bartlett's account. It bolsters a common Caribbean American mode of recollection that African Americans had been utterly docile to American forms of racial oppression until confident Caribbean immigrants came along to wake them from their long political slumber. This theme recurs in the stories that Louisiana Creoles and their advocates tell about their superiority to non-Creole African Americans (e.g., Hirsch and Logsdon 1992).

Nevertheless, I was still surprised by the third theme that emerged over the course of our conversations. These emergent but now-naturalized region-of-origin-based ethnic divisions had a hierarchy implicit among them. The CSA president offered in passing that Caribbean Americans are more accomplished than African Americans on account of their immigrant ambition. Indeed, he added, *all* of the most accomplished black Americans are Caribbean. He mentioned Malcolm X (born of a Grenadian mother and an African American father), Judge Constance Baker Motley, Stokely Carmichael (a.k.a. Kwame Turé), and Shirley Chisholm (advocating the same argument, other Caribbean American mentors of mine also mentioned Marcus Garvey and *NewsHour* host Gwen Ifill). Unlike my American Indian interlocutor Emma Smith, Mr. Bartlett prefaced his allegation of African American underachievement with an empathetic history of how badly African Americans had been beaten down by their white countrymen. We were not to be blamed for our underaccomplishment. He wagged his head in pity, much as my son's kindergarten teacher had done.

Perhaps some explanation emerges from the following encounter. A deeply activist and race-loving alumnus who had returned to live in Jamaica told me that his Caribbean contemporaries at Howard during the 1960s and 1970s lovingly regarded accomplished African Americans as individuals who had "escaped" the norm. (Of course, the alternative possibility is that those accomplished individuals represent one end of the normal bell curve in any group.) He said he had simply never thought about it when I asked if he did not also regard Caribbeans who managed to attend university and professional school in the United States as exceptions who had similarly "escaped" the life pattern of their countrymen. My father and his contemporaries had proffered a similarly ego-satisfying (and racism-ratifying) reason for their Nigerian classmates' intelligence: "They only let the smart ones out!" These Caribbean men's pity for African Americans had much in common with the many less empathetic explanations that I have heard since 2002, which suggests that the black ethnic person naturally deserves some sort of esteem that ordinary African Americans do not deserve and did not earn.

Mr. Bartlett's ultimate line of reasoning surprised me because, at Howard, Mr. Bartlett—a retired laboratory technician—was daily surrounded by native-born African American doctors, lawyers, professors, and administrators far more accomplished than he. As Mr. Bartlett and others narrated their contrasting visions of Caribbean and African American "cultures," it never seems to have struck them as ironic that they were narrating this vision to an African American Harvard professor, whose surgeon father and psychologist mother many of them had known personally or by reputation for decades. Nor was my type of African American family rare in Washington. They crowded Georgia Avenue daily on their commutes to Howard; to the DC Public Schools; to their medical, dental, and legal offices; and to their corner offices throughout Federal Triangle.

Perhaps one reason for the candor of such Caribbean testimonies is that, to many of these interlocutors, I look, speak, and have accomplished as they wish to believe that they collectively do. Therefore, like Andrew Young among the Louisiana Creoles, I *must* be one of them, notwithstanding all of the well-known facts to the contrary. Add to that the fact that I have shown an interest in their story and that I look like the average Caribbean-origin Howardite. It is also possible that what I have described as "candor" is actually defensiveness. Perhaps some of my interlocutors feel outnumbered, overpowered, and stereotyped by the African American majority around them and, knowing my family's and my own history, wish to preempt what they assume will be my possible unawareness that the Caribbean, *too*, has produced greatness. This discourse may be a direct form of resistance to African American dominance at Howard, where many Caribbeans feel that they do not enjoy the degree of authority that they deserve. My African American father's words about his Nigerian classmates give evidence of some African American resistance to acknowledging the talents of our foreign-born peers.

Indeed, much of the resistance that I encountered as the chair of African and African American Studies at Duke came from African American professors who felt that faculty recruitment should prioritize Black US American studies over African, Caribbean, and Latin American studies and that US racial binarism should be the analytical model for all racially coded aggression throughout the world. And these African American colleagues did have the power to enforce those priorities. Fortunately, these are not the sentiments of all African American professors or of all such departments. The prevailing sentiments at my previous institution were very different.

The black ethnic narrative theme to the effect that "all of the people who are mistaken for accomplished African Americans are *actually* members of our ethnic group" conveys the feel of overkill and ulterior motive. Even if I am not judged guilty of the same degree of exaggeration, some readers will judge my reports of my family and our kind immodest, which I cannot deny. I present myself, too, as an exemplar of a common set of responses to stigma and discreditability. Overkill and immodesty are equally omnipresent elements of ethnological schadenfreude.

Washington is rife with black poverty, but so is Kingston and, by 2002, it would have required a powerful act of will to overlook the extraordinary number and quality of Black American professionals in the city, like Vernon Jordan and Condoleezza Rice—not to mention W. E. B. Du Bois, Ralph Bunche, Martin Luther King Jr., Thurgood Marshall, Oprah Winfrey, Toni Morrison, Judith Jameson, Spike Lee, Henry Lewis Gates, William Julius Wilson, Ken Chenault, etc. But stellar and even minimally successful African Americans were as invisible to this immigrant anthropology as we were to the Daniel Patrick Moynihan's sociology and as we remain in his discipline. And Mr. Bartlett was not alone in ignoring the deep poverty of the majority in their respective homelands. He joined Emma Smith and Daniel Patrick Moynihan in this psychologically palliative oversight.

Ethnological schadenfreude is an underrecognized "weapon of the weak" (Scott 1985), honed to a sharp edge by the British-trained class-consciousness of many anglophone Caribbean immigrants. The obsessive (re)appropriation of prestigious ancestors and coethnics embodies the same motive, and its most vivid example arose from a Caribbean / African American dialogue in New York City, since African Americans too have sought to identify presumptively white heroes who were "actually" Black—including the pharaohs, Aesop, Mozart, the "five Black Presidents" of the United States, Alexandre Dumas, Aleksandr Pushkin, and so forth. But the logic is strikingly different from what we have seen so far. I learned about many of these figures and the evidence of their Blackness from J. A. Rogers's two-volume *World's Great Men of Color* (1946–47), which Aunt Ruth made sure was on my bookshelf. A participant in the Harlem Renaissance, the Jamaican American author and journalist set out to prove that Black people had contributed more to history than was normally recognized. As I became a man of color, Aunt Ruth stocked my "literally-defined world" with these and many other such books—as a shield, a sword, and a mirror.

In one biography, Mr. Bartlett's stories reflect both the mixed feelings and the changing history of black immigrants' entry into selective US colleges and universities. Contrary to my initial hypothesis and the first story that Mr. Bartlett told me, what I later discovered was this: even in the midst of a single major cooperative project—that is, Black uplift and Howard University itself—and an unpredictable array of interethnic alliances around institution building, political insurrection, and study, there is a profusion of talk, organizations, residential arrangements, ritual displays, and culinary elaborations of black diversity and interethnic hierarchy. Because they lack the shield of whiteness, people of African descent in the United States—be they middle class, black ethnic, or what have you—tend to play up the power of our clothing, accents, and verbal self-representations to deflect the mistreatment accorded to low-status people. These self-presentations are intended to demonstrate distinction, or unique worthiness, against the default white American assumption of black worthlessness and often in deliberate contrast to some large category of African Americans who truly deserve that assumption.

In the context of the stigma that attaches to African ancestry generally, Louisiana Creoles, partly African-descended Indians and Nigerians, but, above all, Jamaicans and Trinidadians have elaborated a fictional anthropology of difference from African Americans that bears but the faintest relationship to verifiable generalizations about the lifeways of any of their homelands. Yet this fictional anthropology is not merely a set of false verbal reports. It is both spoken and performed. It is a challenge to biological racism, asserting that some of us are *different* by reason of local history and social training. It is also a highly effective means of disciplining and inspiring children. It answers the same needs that my mother, my aunt Ruth, and Howard University consciously addressed—by similar means but with differently selected beneficiaries.

I chose to conduct most of my research, however, not in spaces directly dominated by whites or in the East Coast urban ghettoes, where recently arrived black immigrants of diverse classes (but with little hard currency to pay rents elsewhere) are likely to have landed first and where they are exposed primarily to the poorest African Americans. Some of these black immigrants were our housekeepers when I was growing up, and many were our patients. But few would have had much access to the world of the African American professional class. For that reason, I chose to conduct this research in a space where I thought no one could overlook that class. I thought Howard was the perfect test case of whether African-descended people would unite in the absence of significant disparities of class, education, and ambition. Howard University is the self-described "Capstone of Negro Education" and the "Mecca" of Black intellect, where the most highly ambitious and race-loving members of all of these groups have gathered. No one here, I thought, would assume that Black Americans are credible antitypes for the success and citizenship of others.

But I was wrong. Stigma and stereotype resist empirical correction, particularly when their articulation can be used to clarify the speaker's worthiness of exemption from stigma and stereotype and to demonstrate his or her proximity to the elite group. Indeed, discreditable people have as great a stake in expiating and crucifying the discredited as they do in sticking their necks out to join in a concerted resistance. Cases on *both* extremes—among closeted gays, religious converts, mixed-race people, racially ambiguous whites such as Irish and Jews, and culturally ambiguous people, or assimilés—are common enough to be called clichés. Similarly, bullied children seem to know instinctively that when they enter a new school, it is useful to bully someone else first. But some bullied children stick up for their fellow victims. The more common situation is probably profound ambivalence and contradictory behavior and declarations that correlate, albeit unreliably, with situational self-interest. People can't always figure out where their interest lies.

These patterns are probably universal across human situations. But Howard demonstrates the special consequences of intraclass competition for earnings and honor, as well as the relative absence of the ethnoracially unmarked audience. As we will see further in chapter 6, black ethnics at Howard have produced a "literally-defined world" that looks quite different from the one produced by their counterparts at TWIs. On the other hand, at Howard, the student and faculty *performances* of black ethnic difference are more frequent and more dramatic than at most TWIs.

Cooking Up Difference:
Child-Rearing as Performative Ethnology

At Howard, the average African American freshman's expectation of Black racial homogeneity and mutual sympathy gives way to the sophomore's high consciousness of Black intraracial diversity and competition. However, the sophomore's consciousness of what makes his or her subgroup different from other varieties of African-descended people is not a simple recapitulation of the lifeway of the homeland (or hometown) and its observable contrast to the lifeways of other homelands, though ethnic self-consciousness usually speaks as though it were.

For example, what upwardly mobile Jamaican Americans describe as "Jamaican," "West Indian," or "Caribbean culture"—that is, speaking the Queen's English, living in monogamous nuclear families, hardworking ambition, and exam school orientation—is, in Jamaica, described not as "Jamaican culture" but as "middle-class values," which are assumed to *distinguish* the bearer from the vast majority of his or her countrymen. There is no comparing the average Caribbean immigrant to the average resident of his or her native island. For example, even relatively poor Caribbean students at Howard in the mid-twentieth century came from that minority of these islands' population with at least temporary access to major sums of cash. Since they had to show the US consulate that they possessed the means of paying tuition and living costs in the United States, many Caribbean alumni of Howard report having borrowed money from relatives and friends for temporary deposit in their bank accounts. Visa in hand, they could return the borrowed money and then work to raise their own funds in the United States. In any national population, such people would have to be considered exceptionally education oriented, well connected, ambitious, trustworthy, and adventurous.

Nonetheless, in the United States, what immigrants call "Jamaican," "West Indian," or "Caribbean culture" tends to be contrasted with a generalization about African Americans as a whole based upon the subset of that population that seems most opposite to the speaker's ideals. For example, at both Howard and Harvard, many children of immigrants told me that their mothers studiously isolated them from African Americans and told them not to "behave like African Americans." One Jamaican American Harvard graduate student from New York City specified that her mother was systematically unfriendly toward her African American friends because, in the mother's view, African American children grew up in single-parent homes.

Such black stereotyping is as unempirical as any stereotyping by whites. This "Jamerican" New Yorker at first recalled that all of her family's Jamaican friends lived in two-parent homes until she paused and remembered that her mother simply *did not know* that one of her Jamaican American girlfriends also has a single mother. Moreover, my Jamerican interlocutor recalled, her mother accepted her African American boyfriend *only* because she discovered that he had two parents at home. However, his case did not appear to alter the mother's general impression of African American children and their families as a whole. So effective was her mother's lesson that my student was incredulous when I pointed out that unwed and single parenting are as common in Jamaica and the rest of the West Indies as among African Americans, if not more so. In an effort to repair her mother's stereotyped contrast, my informant speculated that this phenomenon among Caribbean families might be recent. I assured her that it is not (e.g., Smith 1962; Higman 1975).

These black ethnic mythologies are unusually articulated not with malevolence but with pathos, ambivalent identification, or resignation. The family forms and child-rearing strategies of middle-class Caribbean Americans are in many ways indistinguishable from those of middle-class native-born African Americans, except that Caribbean Americans tend to attribute their differences from other Black families to ethnicity rather than class.

In 2010, I had lunch at the Cuban Revolution restaurant in Durham with a dear colleague at Duke University. At fifty-seven, she had fresh and darkly beautiful skin, which varies from milk chocolate to a cinnamon blush around her cheeks, and she speaks with an unremarkably northern middle-class US accent. Her name always invited me to pronounce it with a Spanish accent, though I had never heard her do so. So I felt self-conscious and affected when speaking it—in between worlds when I wasn't getting any hint that I should be.

In the restaurant, she ordered *arroz con pollo*—rice with chicken—in an American accent. When I commented that my African American mother used to cook that a lot, she said her mother did, too. Did her mother add ginger root, as did my Filipina stepmother? No, because her kids didn't like it. She asked where I was from, adding, "From someplace where they cook *arroz con pollo*?" (suddenly with a Spanish accent). "No, I'm from Washington, DC," I replied. I didn't go into my view that recipes travel and that the foodways and other cultural practices that supposedly derive from one "culture" or another really just become cultural diacritica when someone wills them to be so. I wanted her to talk.

It turned out that her parents are Panamanians. Her mother, of the same color as my friend, has two Jamaican parents. Her father is a bit lighter. His father had come from Antigua, also in the Caribbean. My friend had not known her paternal grandmother. All of her grandparents had gone to Panama to work on the canal. But whereas the father had grown up in the Canal Zone, with all of its US-style segregation and other racial indignities, the mother had grown up closer to Panama City, in a neighborhood with Spanish-speaking people of all shades and continental origins. Both of my friend's parents are fully bilingual, but I speak better Spanish than my friend.

Her father having completed his bachelor's degree and her mother having nearly completed hers in Panama, the father applied in the late 1940s to various traditionally White medical schools in the United States, only to be rejected by all of them. So he decided to apply for dental school at Howard. He had always been interested in dentistry. He got in and enjoyed the experience enormously.

Saddled with tuition debts, he enlisted in the army to pay them off. The young family was posted to Fort Dix, in New Jersey. Eventually, in order to buy a house, they moved to Deptford, New Jersey, an hour and a half away. He commuted to Fort Dix with a white fellow officer—her father would eventually retire as a full colonel—who lived in the same town. In 1956, when my friend reached the age of five, the parents announced they were ready to take her to school. Recognizing the specialness of the occasion, she asked to wear her patent leather shoes. My friend laughed at the irony of wearing patent leather with her play clothes.

In the summer days just before she started kindergarten, her father automatically took her to the school where he had seen his white friend drop off his son during their shared morning commutes. But as they walked up the school stairs, a white man appeared, raising the flat of his right hand to the father and daughter, as if simultaneously stopping illegal traffic and holding up a mirror to their black faces. "Colored don't attend school here," he said, tersely reducing their humanity and a child's aspirations to the shade of a peculiarly US stoplight. He detoured them to the correct school for their kind.

The father drove up a dusty, dead-end road toward a building that, at the time, my friend was not old enough to recognize as dilapidated. Nor did she know that it lacked indoor plumbing. Decades later, with tears in his eyes, her father expressed surprise that she remembered the day. "Yes," I interrupted, "it's the kind of moment you don't want to call attention to, because you hope that your children will overlook it." That is, they will overlook the messages of personal limitation that the dominant society tries to impose. "No," she replied, her parents didn't really avoid the conversation about such matters. At the moment, though I had learned something from the interruption, I regretted the possibility that my intervention would be mistaken for confirmation of some untrue stereotype about the ineffectual way that African Americans deal or dealt with such situations. She told her father that she remembers that day because the dust on the road made her father ask the girl to roll up her window. When she couldn't work the crank, he reached over to close the window for her.

He left her in the car as he entered the school. When he emerged, my friend asked excitedly, "Am I going to school here?" Her father said nothing. After deliberating at home, the parents made arrangements for my friend to live with a Black family on the Fort Dix military post, where, though separated all week from her tearful mother, she could attend a school that President Eisenhower had integrated along with the US Army. My friend was at first relieved at the prospect of not having to fight with her little sister all week long, but the host couple also had a child her sister's age, with whom she would have to fight instead. She said her parents had nothing against sending her to a Black school; her father just wasn't going to send her to one without indoor plumbing.

The family eventually moved to Willingboro, New Jersey, a Levittown development community. I noted with surprise that, unlike some of the other postwar housing tracts built by Levitt and Sons construction company, this one was integrated. My friend then noted that her father was the only "African American"—then she corrects herself—"black dentist" in the town. I guess that, like many black immigrants, my friend regards "African American" as ambiguous. One has the option to describe a native-born or an immigrant black person as an "African American." But when it comes down to it, the paradigmatic referent of "African American" is a native-born person descended from native-born grandparents. In this regard, her father is "black," but not "African American."

In the tenth grade, my friend had a white male guidance counselor who asked, with a skeptical contortion of his face, why she wanted to go to college. The counselor recommended stenography instead. She explained to him that she had always wanted to go to college, she might want to become a physician, and had A's in every class *but* typing. Why would she want to become a stenographer? When she told the story, weeping, at the dinner table, her mother stood up and, spinning around with her hands on her head, cursed the counselor, raged against the system, and insisted that they all go to the school and set the counselor straight.

My friend remembers her father's hulking physical presence as he folded his arms around the tornado of his wife's rage and said, "Calm down. Calm down. I think it's time for us to tell them [my friend and her younger sister and brother]." They were moving to Germany.

My friend celebrates two major blessings in her life. First, though she was angry about having to move to Germany, the move allowed her to travel overseas and see the world—a world beyond the US racial restrictions in which she would otherwise have stewed for her entire life. (The US "melting pot" has always meant different things for black and nonblack immigrants.) Among her valuable experiences in Germany was an encounter with a white female guidance counselor on the military base, who, upon seeing her grades, said she could get into the college of her choice. Her mother announced that she was going to college even if they "had to buy the college." But, like the parents of my Gullah/Geechee friend, they discouraged her from attending Howard, worried that sending her to a big city like Washington would be like "throwing [her] to the wolves." My friend eventually got into Radcliffe but, because a health condition required her to be near her family, chose to attend Douglass College of Rutgers University.

She also learned a new perspective on her struggle with low expectations in the United States. A white female classmate who had attended high school with her at Fort Dix and had moved to Germany at the same time offered her own thoughts on the white male counselor, saying, "That had nothing to do with race." That counselor had also shamelessly promoted the white girl's academically underperforming brother, all on account of his sex. (Because I was the one who brought up the possibility that sexism accounts for some of her discouraging experiences, I am not certain of the priority that she herself gives to these respective explanations of marginalization in her life. Until she sent her Black son to a white liberal school, my late surgeon sister had always said that she felt more affected by sexism than racism. Surgery is reputed to be an especially macho field.)

My Duke colleague and friend recounts the second blessing she received from moving to Germany with some embarrassment, because she realizes that some people find this analysis offensive. She is aware of the tension between native- and foreign-born blacks in the United States. Many of the foreign-born think they are superior to the native-born, and, she notes, there has been a controversy about the proportion of black university students who are foreign-born or immediately descended from the foreign-born. Without any intention to stoke such tensions, my friend explained that, for ethnic reasons, not only had she done well in school, but she also plays three instruments—the violin, the piano, and the organ. She still regularly gets contracts to play the organ for various churches, though she is now a PhD, a well-liked instructor, and a high-ranking administrator at Duke. She recalls that when she asked her mother if she could stop taking music lessons, the mother said no. Pointing at the white children playing outside, she told my friend that those kids could *afford* not to practice. Whatever they do or don't prepare for in life, "the world is their oyster." "You, on the other hand, have to prepare twice as well for life in order to get what you deserve," she told her daughter. "You will not only practice all three instruments, but you're going to enjoy it." Her parents made her do more than "the white *and* the Black kids" she knew.

I know of few Caribbean American, Caribbean, or African American families who required their children to practice three instruments. But, for example, the lengths to which the parents of former secretary of state Condoleezza Rice pursued her musical education hardly make her an alien to middle-class Black America. These two women's own extraordinary persistence and excellence embody the advice that most African Americans have heard from our parents (see McWhorter 2010). In his youth, my own father played the violin, and my mother continued to play the piano in adulthood. My sister and I both took clarinet and piano, though Yvedt alone stuck with piano. Just the week before she died and as a parting gift of encouragement to her own pianist son, Yvedt performed in concert the Allegro of Mozart's Sonata in G, K. 283.

Our father provided an early subsidy for my children's string lessons. They enrolled in piano classes as well. Ayọ is an excellent violinist and has now graduated from Harvard College. Since he was a high school junior, Adu has played the viola semiprofessionally. I took up violin alongside them, pursuing a lifelong ambition, and added the cello seven years later. However, carpal tunnel syndrome and the directorship of Duke's Center for African and African American Research have temporarily sidelined me.

I mentioned to my Panamanian American friend that every middle-class African American parent I know preaches the same lesson as her mother, only in more aphoristic language: "Child, you have to work twice as hard to get half as far" as your white peers, "so get down to work." I hoped that I had said little enough not to appear defensive. But I was telling the truth. Many African Americans follow this dictum in one or more areas of our lives, sometimes resulting in the syndrome that African American epidemiologist and social psychologist Sherman James (1994) calls "John Henryism." Many of us simply excel.

My friend concluded by quoting two African American women from her racially heterogeneous circle of friends. Their mothers had discouraged these ambitious African American women from attending medical school. "It's a big mistake," they were told. "You need to settle down, get married, and have children." It was the mother of my friend who sat them down and gave them the backbone to pursue their dreams. Those friends, she said, have always credited my friend's determination and confidence to the fact that her parents "didn't grow up here"—that is, steeped in the paralyzing racism of the United States.

I did not mention that my African American mother had played the same role as her mother in the lives of dozens of people—Black and white—and that such a role might not be confined to or caused by being non–African American. The implication of the story that African American mothers in general prefer domestic careers for their daughters runs contrary to the behavior of all the Black American mothers and grandmothers I have known. The similar advice I have heard attributed to African Americans reportedly came from husbands and a brother—never a mother or a father. For example, my brother encouraged my sister to consider the health of her marriage and her own biological clock before taking a prestigious medical residency at Sloan Kettering in New York. As a Harvard law professor, her husband taught and lived in Cambridge. My sister was irate and attributed the advice not to African American culture or even sexism per se but to sibling rivalry tinged with sexism. She felt she could have it all. And she did, but all too briefly.

Even after a large Pentecostal church wedding, my aunt Arnzie divorced her first husband, an army officer, because he discouraged her from attending medical school. My mother's father made sure that all of his four daughters earned graduate degrees, neglecting, according to my uncle, the education of his two sons because his greatest fear was that his daughters, if uneducated, would have to work as housekeepers and tolerate sexual abuse from white men. It is perhaps partly for this reason that African American women have long enjoyed high rates of education, not to mention employment, relative to African American men.

Nonetheless, after years of research on black ethnics in the United States, I am deeply familiar with the portrait of African Americanness at the backdrop of my friend's family biography. It is a sympathetically painted foil to the ambition and accomplishment that then implicitly typifies the ethnic group of the non–African American raconteur. But it is not only unsubtle but, to me, almost wholly unrecognizable as a description of the African Americans I know.

After I wrote my initial account of our lunch conversation and shared it with my friend, she wrote back to correct some details, which I have corrected above, and emphasized that she had never identified her parents' enthusiastic encouragement of her own and her friends' educational and professional ambitions with ethnicity until her native-parentage African American friends *themselves* did so. Both of these friends became family physicians, and one broke new paths in leadership for both her race and her gender.

Surely these women's accomplishments owe at least as much to their own family backgrounds as they do to the influence of my friend's parents, but it is also true that the mythology about model minorities is not propagated by those minorities alone. Similarly the stereotype that Black people are good at sports and at sex is not propagated by whites alone or by Blacks alone. Black people have come to internalize white stereotypes and even to take pride in and derive motivation from them. In the 1980s, America relished *The Cosby Show*, but many African Americans declared this program about professional-class Black people unreal. Conversely, in the 1990s, the unrepresentative words and behaviors of rap musicians were taken to be uniquely "real." And comedian Dave Chappelle's humor about some crack-strewn streets of Southeast Washington, DC, in the 1980s sells better than novelist and Yale law professor Stephen Carter's writings about the equally real but color-struck and competitive world of Northwest Washingtonian doctors, lawyers, and judges (e.g., Carter 2002). In 2010, during his conversations with me here as a guest of the Center for African and African American Research at Duke, Academy Award–winning filmmaker Lee Daniels declared film characters like Precious—the illiterate, HIV-infected victim of serial rape and child abuse—more normative and representative of Black America than the physician and the lawyer who headed Cosby's television family. Daniels and I have clearly had different experiences and seen different statistics, which is further evidence of an intra-Black diversity all too easily forgotten by some.

These images serve myriad nonliteral and nonempirical projects. They clarify the boundaries of US citizenship, making it more permeable to not-so-white whites, Asians, Latin Americans, and not-so-Black blacks than to drylongso African Americans. These images can also be used by Black Americans eager to sell music and films. Like bedtime and Gothic dinnertime stories, no matter how horrible, they appeal to listeners insofar as they incant a familiar theme. They can be used to inspire pity and social intervention. And, like the "Indian" garb worn by the participants in the Boston Tea Party of 1773 and the female attire donned by male rebels in early modern Europe (Davis 1978), the conventional media persona of the Black American can be donned to dramatize and embolden the performer's own resistance to the normal restrictions on his or her emotions and conduct—no matter what the performer's race or nationality. Yet these images make it difficult for real African Americans and real Native Americans to escape the presumption of conformity to those images. Discrimination by others and internalized stereotypes can both become self-fulfilling prophecies.

Yet the more common reality is that these images make careful reasoning difficult, even for otherwise reasonable people. Once insiders and outsiders make the initial mistake of prematurely drawing a relationship of causality or mutual dependency between two outlying variables, it is often difficult for them to disconnect those two variables. For example, if one of the few Poles I know is a criminal, I am likely to suspect that Poles are disproportionately criminal. On the other hand, if I am Irish, I am unlikely to invest as much causal or other logical weight in the equivalent proportion of Irish people I know who are criminals. Likewise, many straight people casually equate homosexuality with pedophilia and would never stereotype straight men as a group on account of the equivalent proportion of heterosexual men who molest children. On the other hand, having internalized the sense of stigma, African Americans are often quick to attribute the misdeeds of other African Americans to their Blackness.

One day at lunch at our house, a Black congressman and my mother lamented the irresponsible campaign behavior of a mayoral candidate. To her emphatic agreement, the congressman declared, "That ain't nothin' but nigga business!" Teenage literalist and racial nationalist that I was, I objected. With the benefit of Herzfeld's ([1997] 2005) insight about "cultural intimacy," I later realized that such private self-deprecation—and the maintenance of its privacy—is a performative feature of virtually all nationalisms and other collective identities. Nonetheless, I regarded the terms of their critique as unfair. Being always already stigmatized makes a whole group automatically and collectively guilty of the bad behavior of a few members of the group, while members of the ethnoracially and culturally unmarked populations walk around with their virtual identities (Goffman 1963) uncontaminated by the negative deeds of even large numbers of their ethnoracial fellows.

Black immigrants are indeed a highly self-selected lot. But the willfully propagated "model minority" ideology of my Caribbean interlocutors tends to obscure, for example, the prominence of the Shower Posse and other Jamaican gangs in the murderous drug trade, just as white men's powerful public presentation of themselves as normal frees them from the stigma suffered by the sizable minority among them, as reported in scores of newspaper articles in the past two decades, who use meth and oxycodone, rob banks, murder their wives and girlfriends, use guns to commit mass murder in elementary and high schools, favor rumor and religion over science, habitually binge-drink to the point of vomiting, or start wars that can never be finished. It can be a profound learning experience for white Americans to visit Europe, where their white skin does not shield them from collective stereotyping with reference to such behaviors.

Moreover, the native-born African American population is full of its own self-selecting subpopulations, and there is no reason to believe that these self-selecting populations are smaller in proportion to the African American population at large than, say, successful Caribbean immigrants are to the Caribbean population at large, or successful Panamanian immigrants are to the Panamanian population at large.

Whatever her sense of difference from African Americans, my friend did, as a postgraduate, join the Alpha Kappa Alpha sorority—a choice that I find uncommon among anglophone black Caribbeans of her generation, at Howard or elsewhere. Indeed, she brought her mother and her sister in as well. By contrast, joining African American Greek-letter societies has nowadays become a very common choice among African- and Caribbean-ethnic Duke undergraduates.

"Are You Representing?"

At Howard, "you can be Black any way you want to be," but you are also reminded that your behavior reflects upon Black people in general. In 2002, the electronic billboard in my dormitory flashed to each exiting resident the rhetorical question, "Are You Representing?" or the statement "Make sure you represent . . . the big Bisons . . . Howard University."

The students in my "Other African Americans" class at Howard defined "representing" as "performing or showing your best in order to honor your group." It differs from "flossin'," which is individual and personal showing off, and from "frontin'," which was, by then, an outdated term for putting on a false show. These terms embody the dilemma of social actors in virtually every society: How does one pursue individual distinction in the dominant system without offending the collectivity? To what degree must personal credit be attributed to the group? Conversely, to what degree is personal shame blamed upon the group? And what are the uses of fiction and image management? For members of stigmatized populations, the options have a particular slant, and the decisions are necessarily more emotionally fraught.

For example, middle-class African Americans tend to feel personally embarrassed by the misbehavior or improper diction of other African Americans and personally proud of the exceptional accomplishments of our fellows. Many of us regard our own accomplishments as disproof of white people's stereotypes about Black people in general and fear that our personal failures prove those stereotypes. Conversely, instances in which non–African Americans offend us or unfairly evaluate our work and conduct are often attributed to those non–African Americans' prejudices about us collectively. We tend to feel that, because we are a stigmatized minority in our home society, each of us represents all of us. And there is a great deal of pressure to represent the group well. Misbehavior and improper speech are viewed as one way of discrediting the race. Our sense of purpose makes many of us more serious about schoolwork and more goal oriented than our white peers. On the other hand, the burden of belonging to a group that we know is stigmatized can impair performance by demanding dysfunctional communalism or by adding anxiety. Relative to Black people, all other things being equal, white people can count on being judged as individuals and are unhindered by the need to "represent"—or by the fear of badly representing their whole group. However, all other things are never equal; everyone belongs to a group that bears the burden of some negative stereotype. Black people in US society, however, are perhaps the most visibly defining exemplar of this dynamic.

As African American social psychologist Claude Steele (1997) demonstrates, a reminder to even a high-performing person that he or she belongs to a group that is stereotyped as inadequate in any given field of performance—such as women in math and the physical sciences and African Americans in many intellectual domains—dramatically depresses his or her performance on standardized tests in comparison with his or her performance when there has been no such reminder. What Steele calls "stereotype threat"—the fear of being negatively stereotyped, judged, or treated stereotypically, or conforming to the stereotype in an area where one cares about doing well—can affect the members of any group about whom a negative stereotype exists, such as skateboarders, older adults, white men, and gang members, in the areas of endeavor where that group is negatively stereotyped.

Another hurdle faced by ambitious members of stigmatized groups is that conspicuously outperforming one's fellows is sometimes resented, as it makes people who are already feeling inferior feel even more inferior. This fact amplifies African Americans' anger over foreign blacks' assertions of superiority. Honor is a zero-sum game, with particularly intense implications for the discredited, because, for us, there is so little honor to go around. Low-status, or discredited, people often resent the ambitions and success of their fellows even more than they resent the ambitions and success of hereditarily high-status people. African Americans describe cases in which other African Americans enviously impede one's own progress as the "crabs in a barrel" phenomenon: those who appear to be trying to climb out of a shared status of discredit must be clawed back down.

For the most stigmatized populations, the pursuit of social mobility without the loss of coethnic or same-class approval requires enormous tact, subterfuge, or what might be described, in an extension of Goffman's intended meaning, as "covering." In the eyes of other low-status people, ambition can be a stigmatized quality. On the other hand, subgroups that can construct a sense of community around their shared superiority to the rest of the stigmatized group effectively shield themselves from some of the pressure against individual social mobility. It is difficult for the stigmatized, who are vulnerable to discrimination by their class superiors, to abandon the camaraderie of their class of origin without at least defining a new subclass that will back them. The logic of Jim Crow and of today's mass media offers poor whites a subclass identity that can justify ambition. "Whiteness," or the obligation to be collectively better than Black people, has facilitated collective white upward mobility through the unions. But it also offers poor but ambitious whites an alternative to the lost solidarity of their working-class fellows.

The sentiment behind the exhortations on the East Tower electronic billboard is familiar to any middle-class African American anticipating an interaction with non-Blacks, but the question suggests an additional implication for so-called model minorities, such as anglophone Caribbeans. Because superiority to other stigmatized populations is presumed to inhere in one's group, one suffers under the additional, collective pressure not to lose caste. For example, a black Trinidadian secretary in the History Department, who often attended my class, reported that whenever she sees a young fellow Trini misbehaving on campus, she scolds, "Oh, no, you are *not* a Trinidadian!" Under similar circumstances, she might also have said to any Howard student, "Oh, no, you are *not* a Howard student!" Her irony is immediately clear, effective, and, she thinks, corrective. That is, the empirical fact at hand is that some Trinidadians and some Howard students do misbehave. This negative copula is, then, normative—a performative utterance (Austin 1962) that creates a reality rather than an observation. These myths of primordial cultural difference among black populations are not merely bad anthropology; they are social fictions and self-fulfilling prophecies—symbolic strategies of disciplining young people's behavior and naturalizing collective differences of morality or capacity.

They do not, however, necessarily imply that coethnics will or should get along with each other. At Howard, coethnics are often identified as each other's greatest nemeses within a department and can be found on rival sides in any given conflict. Unlike the ethnic classifications described by Evans-Pritchard (1940), Barth (1969), and Cohen (1969), these myths of difference are more often invoked to explain the success or worthiness of individuals than to unite groups in action. Expected similarity of worth or ability often heightens competition rather than reducing it. As Goffman (1963) points out, the hard of hearing fervently protest their superiority to the deaf.

Representing the Caribbean

Yet the myths of ethnic difference propagated by Caribbean immigrants anxious to climb over African Americans on the US social ladder will shock the scholar or observant visitor to the black ethnic homeland. These myths of ethnic difference include both the underreporting of racism in the Caribbean and the idealization of white American power. For example, in order to explain what she regards as the radical difference in self-confidence between African Americans and Caribbean Americans, one Grenadian American professor at Howard who had grown up in Trinidad repeatedly told me that there is no racism or colorism on that island. Indeed, I am often told by Caribbean Americans that, in their home countries, it is not color at all but only class that matters. This conviction matters so much to some Caribbean Americans that they sometimes become loud and even physical in its defense. At one dinner party where I offered evidence to the contrary, my Trinidadian-Grenadian host got up and, towering over me, snatched a napkin from my hand and threw it in my face while shouting that she was right. The balance of play and violence in her conduct was difficult for me to discern.

While over the course of our decade of conversations my Howard colleague has come to moderate her position, Howard alumni I talked to in Trinidad and Jamaica during the 2000s were immediately vocal about their contrary experience during the same historical period described by my Trinidadian-Grenadian professor friend. A dozen Howard alumni in Trinidad described to me experiences of complexion-related exclusion from jobs, particularly in the banking industry, until the 1970s. But like African American recollections of past colorism in the Greek-letter societies at Howard, these Caribbean traumas were not really experienced as past. In Jamaica and Trinidad, casual and unguarded conversation among my dark interlocutors still attributed much wealth, station, and undeserved privilege to "brownness" (in Jamaica) and "Creoleness" (in Trinidad). Even successful dark men seethed over the opportunities that they said they had lost over the years to less intellectually and academically qualified boys of lighter complexion.

To be sure, Caribbean racism and US racism are different. Among other things, much of the former occurs in the complete physical absence of whites. For example, a Trinidadian sophomore at Howard who described himself as "red," or light skinned, told me that the "best-looking boys" attend his high school alma mater—the historically "French Creole" Saint Mary's School—and that his parents were aghast that he announced his intention to attend Howard. "You'll be the lightest one there!" they exclaimed. At the end of his story, he laughed with a mixture of embarrassment and derision, not sure of what I thought he should feel about their prediction.

The Trinidadian sister-in-law of a Howard medical professor who temporarily lodged my family in her country reported the widespread use of the term "niggeritis" among people of all colors and classes in Trinidad to describe the laziness that sets in after a good, heavy meal. (Aaron McGruder's animated series *The Boondocks* [1999–2014] abbreviated the term as "the 'itis.") Hence, in Trinidad as elsewhere, even the demonstration of universally human traits is taken to prove the defectiveness of the stigmatized. My Trinidadian hostess introduced the term in the context of her discomfort at a wedding of ethnically Syrian Trinidadians, where this graham-cracker-colored woman with African features and floppy hair reported being the only non-Syrian-looking guest. In her presence, her Syrian companions used the term "niggeritis" to express their satisfaction with the meal. Howard-trained physicians of African descent on the island angrily tell me that most of them have left the island, since, according to them, Indo-Trinidadians now monopolize the medical licensing board and discriminate against Afro-Trinidadian physicians. As of 2002, the two main political parties in Trinidad were roughly divided along the same racial lines. Trinidad is hardly free of racism.

Like many Jamaican and African American women, dark Trinidadian women gnash their teeth in complaint over what they regard as the preference of successful men for light-colored women. Conversely, my best Trinidadian—or "Trinbagonian"—friend at Howard, Philip, was a Hershey's-dark and handsome undergraduate in engineering who refused to date any more light-skinned, or "red," girls. He had been burned too many times, he said. He now dates only "negroes."

Moreover, though he comes from the island of Trinidad, the term he consistently used for his nationality consciously recognized the equality of the two main islands that give the country its official name, "Trinidad and Tobago." In this regard, he differs from most of his fellow Trinidadians. Tobago, the smaller and racially darker island, usually goes unmentioned in casual conversations about the nation and its people. That island tends to be spoken of in a patronizing tone, as quaint and relaxing, in contrast to the racial and cultural "cosmopolitanness" that is proudly attributed to the larger island. Whereas Trinidadians tend to describe themselves as "cosmopolitan" and "mix" (i.e., racially mixed), they also tend to regard Tobagonians as more phenotypically African and therefore more culturally parochial. My dark Trinidadian friend's laborious and self-conscious name for his nation is clearly a reaction to the contemptuous dismissal of blackness that he perceives among his countrymen.

In defiance of the marginalization of his island and of his dark color, one cinnamon-colored male colleague of mine in the History Department goes a bit further than Philip, militantly and as frequently as possible declaring that he is "not a Trinidadian." "I am a Tobagonian," and, hammering his index finger like an exclamation point into the tabletop, he rhythmically incants, "TO-BA-GO-NI-AN!"

When I returned in 2010 to discuss this manuscript with my 2002 hosts in the department, this colleague gave further information that illuminated his earlier commentary on the relative Africanness of black Indian Curtis Howe and his brother. He urged me to recognize, as I had actually already noticed and written, that relations between Trinidad and Tobago are strained. Trinidadians, he said, historically regard Tobagonians as "ugly and stupid" on account of the greater purity of their African ancestry. Indeed, a visiting African had once told this colleague that the smaller island's culture was "just like" the visitor's African culture. This colleague's commentary on the black Indian brothers might then be taken as heartfelt and compensatory praise for Curtis's brother––a Tobagonian-inspired and African-endorsed attack on the antiblack racism common to Trinidad and the Indian tribes of the southeastern United States. This is perhaps the most vivid conversation about multiple consciousness that I witnessed during my research. The complex dialectics of black ethnic identity at Howard are on full display here.

Cooper (2012) also shows that Jamaica, the foremost Caribbean nation sending students and emigrants to the United States, tends to emphasize its racial mixedness at the expense of its predominantly African genetic and preeminently black cultural heritage. The Jamaican coat of arms, which shows two Taino Indians and the motto, in Latin, "Out of many, one people," deliberately effaces the massively African majority of the island and implies the nation's nonblackness. (Recall from chapter 4 that Carol's Jamaican "brown" husband described himself as a "Taino." I wish that I had asked him more about this identity.) There are places and historical periods in the Anglo-Caribbean where South Asian–origin Indians have been assigned a lowly place in the ethnic hierarchy of value—as in Jamaica—but the devaluation of "covering" of blackness is a shared core principle of Caribbean and US national identities. Despite all of these realities, Caribbean immigrants and their children in the United States tend to highlight the contrast between black ethnics and African Americans by idealizing of race relations in the Caribbean.

On the other hand, the equal and opposite idealization of *North American* race relations often serves the same rhetorical purpose. Some claim that, because of the nonracist character of Caribbean "culture," Caribbeans get along with white people better than Black Americans do. Ultimately blaming Black-white tension in the United States on Black Americans' obtuse unwillingness to get along with whites, many Trinidadian and Jamaican transmigrants judge that African Americans exaggerate the prevalence of white American racism as an excuse for African Americans' own laziness. This perception undoubtedly results partly from the relative kindness that "exotic" blacks receive in many Western societies. I have experienced the same phenomenon in Brazil. One dear white Brazilian friend often tells me, "You American blacks are different. You study, you work hard. Our blacks are different. I tell them to go to school. I tell them to dress up decently and get a job. And what do they do? They just hang out in the street and smoke marijuana." But black immigrants and transmigrants often speak in the voice of the dominant Whites. As a dinner guest at the home of a graham-cracker-brown Trinidadian man who, in the United States, had worked for a time as a security guard, I heard that African Americans are the ones who don't go to school, dress up decently, or get a job; we're the ones who hang out in the street all day taking drugs. That some Caribbeans recognize and are willing to take advantage of the "your-blacks-good-our-blacks-bad" phenomenon is documented in both Europe and the United States. Both Kasinitz (1992) and Manyika (2003) describe cases in which "exotic" blacks consciously take advantage of this white prejudice.

While some short-term residents of a land are consciously aware and take advantage of local forms of racism at the expense of people of their own color, it is possible for an immigrant unfamiliar with the local gestural signs of racial hostility to overlook them. One experience in Trinidad reminded me of how easily an outsider might fail to perceive even the local forms of racial discrimination that are directly impinging upon him or her. At my insistence, the "dougla"—or part-Indo- and part-Afro-Trinidadian—son of a Howard alumnus took me to a festival of the Indo-Trinidadian-influenced soca music called "chutney." We had wandered through the open-air venue for an hour before we stopped to watch the onstage action. I was perplexed when the Indo-Trinidadian boyfriend of an Indo-Trinidadian woman dancing in the audience repeatedly and anxiously signaled for the woman to move away from us and toward him. The woman had had no interaction with my friend and me. Nonetheless, my companion later explained that the source of the boyfriend's anxiety had been obvious to him. Hadn't I perceived the hostile stares that had followed us from the moment we entered the festival grounds? No, I had not.

In reaction to the local Indo-Trinidadian hostility to Afro-Trinidadians, my limited experience might have inclined me to emphasize the "cultural" virtues that make African Americans easier to get along with. And if exempted by a powerful licensing board from the discrimination that natives of my color experience, I might also infer the superiority of American Blacks in general and accuse Afro-Trinidadians of a moral problem.

The mythological anthropology of black ethnic difference also includes the premise that education and hard work are uniquely undervalued by African Americans. Among Americans of all races, the rates of university education have historically declined when, with the proliferation of degree holders, the income benefit of the degree has declined (Lowenstein 2007). African American commitment to progress through education is especially remarkable in light of fact that the income benefits from education have always been lower for Blacks than for whites (see, e.g., Perry 2003).

The employment advantages conferred by education are real, but the opportunity also remains proportionate to the degree that one's own group is in power. People tend to recognize talent among individuals of the in-group before they recognize equal talent in individuals of the out-group (Tajfel and Turner 1979; Wright 1997). Of course, this tendency is offset a bit by stigmatized people's internalized skepticism about their own group's talents. That is, potential employers belonging to stigmatized groups cannot be counted on to favor their own to the same degree as normative employers. Education is costly in cash and in the postponement of pleasure. Hence, race, class, gender, and location factor into anyone's reasonable cost-benefit analysis of education, and it is difficult to attribute one fixed degree of commitment to education to any given culture as a whole.

All over the Atlantic world, working-class people ask themselves whether the hard work of education will yield—for people with stigmatized accents, genders, skin color, and caste statuses—opportunities proportionate to the delays in gratification that education requires and to the length of time that stigmatized minorities can expect to live. The relationship between educational opportunities and job opportunities has always varied according to skin color and gender. However, postindependence politics in the Third World, the international women's movement, the series of oil booms and crises since the early 1970s, and the liberalization of US immigration law have also continually reshaped the equation and the strategic choices of Nigerians, Trinidadians, and Jamaicans—not just African Americans.

For example, oil-producing Trinidad, oil-producing Nigeria, and bauxite-producing Jamaica invested enormously in standardized exam-based schooling when independence and mineral revenues allowed a vast expansion in their state bureaucracies. High scores were a ticket to high-paying government jobs. However, in Nigeria today, for example, Igbo boys disproportionately choose petty commerce over education because they reportedly believe that the Hausa- and Yoruba-dominated state bureaucracy has shut them out.

Even among those Nigerian ethnic groups and genders that find university credentials useful, the buying of grades and cheating on examinations have reportedly become the norm rather than the exception. Howard alumni who are secondary-school educators in Jamaica and Trinidad also report a sharp drop in school discipline and academic commitment on those islands in recent years. Nathan (2005) reports rampant cheating in today's white American state universities as well, and a Duke administrator confirmed a "definite increase" in cheating at my home university. Like the Nigerian 419-ers and Wall Street's "Masters of the Universe," American college students are learning to work the system. In the eyes of many, production and conscientious service pay too little. Designing one good app or a new derivative tricky enough to circumvent the federal financial regulators, as well as massive campaign contributions to politicians who can then be counted on to bail you out after the resulting market collapse, look like smarter options than years of conscientious study or block-by-block building.

In early postindependence Trinidad and Tobago, dark black boys were reportedly often among the top scorers on the state-administered standardized exams—a measure not only of their brilliance but also of their deficit of alternative routes to prosperity. Howard alumni who graduated from Trinidadian high schools in the 1960s and early 1970s report having been paid to do the homework of scions of the light-colored French Creole business elite. Back then, it was not the Indo-Trinidadian girls but the black Trinidadian males who were best known for their intelligence and commitment to education. Dark Howard alumni from this generation described the children of the French Creoles, by contrast, as either unintelligent or uninterested in education because their fortunes awaited them in business, not bureaucracy or the professions. It is a good bet that, as they outachieve all other social groups in Trinidad and Tobago today, Indo-Trinidadian girls are responding to their own sense of the limitations on their options.

Nowadays, young Afro-Trinidadians—especially boys—are rare in the scholarship-winning ranks of performance on the Caribbean-wide standardized exams. In Jamaica, too, the boys have so rapidly fallen behind the girls that the University of the West Indies campus at Mona, the state bureaucracy, and the professions in Jamaica are reportedly becoming all-female domains. Some educators blame the phenomenon on the desire for quick cash and easy consumption in a setting where the drug dons provide influential models of high living without the patience of the educational marathon. Others blame the influence of MTV or the consumerism and indiscipline of the "barrel children" left behind by their labor émigré parents in the United States. The "barrel children" are so named because of the barrels of Nike, Adidas, Fubu,

Timberland, and other attire shipped home by guilty absentee parents. Amid such rapid cultural change and exchange between the Caribbean and the United States, reified and timeless notions of "Caribbean culture" have limited value as explanations but great utility in adult immigrants' projects of self-encouragement and in the disciplining of their US-born children.

They also serve in efforts to cultivate advantageous relations with white Americans. Jamaican American and former secretary of state Colin Powell grew up in the Bronx, and he is perhaps the most public spokesperson for what he describes as "an extraordinary record of accomplishment by West Indians," as contrasted with African Americans, in the United States (Powell with Persico [1995] 2003, 22–23). In his 1995 autobiography, Powell stands up for the dignity of Blackness, commending some West Indians and African Americans for recent efforts to recover their African culture. However, far more of his account is devoted to a lay sociology of what allegedly distinguishes him, as a Jamaican American, from African Americans in general and makes him and his kind more worthy citizens and candidates for political office. Powell attributes his success to an upbringing in the Bronx by a nuclear family, which he misrepresents as typically Jamaican. In his view, the islanders of the anglophone Caribbean developed the "attitudes of independence, self-responsibility, and self-worth" lacking in African Americans because of the earlier date of Caribbean abolition, the relative absence of white supervision, the relative equality of rights between black and white, high-quality and mandatory education, and the embrace of British culture in the islands. In further explanation of Caribbean American success, Powell gives secondary credit to the West Indian "emotional and psychological" advantage of not having been brought to the United States in chains. In sum, Powell, too, combines pity for African Americans in general with a conflation between the conditions and responses available to middle-class Jamaicans, on the one hand, and to Jamaicans as a whole, on the other.

In Jamaica, to paraphrase the words of Howard University president H. Patrick Swygert, you can be Jamaican any way you want to be. When people are in the majority, outside the context of interethnic competition, and beyond the obvious supervision of their status superiors, their sense of the local sociocultural landscape becomes more nuanced. Their verbal representation of their collective way of life is less defensive, more attentive to diversity, and more critical of their numerous compatriots who do not share their values. Of course, interclass competition on the island—or within any given ethnic group—also encourages people to idealize their own class and to generalize ungenerously about the class nipping at its heels for power and prestige. On the other hand, in diasporic contexts, ethnicity or nationality is the more functional logic of social solidarity and competitive distinction. In the diaspora, talk of class diversity in the culture of the homeland is subordinated to a logic of "cultural" distinction from one's ethnic rivals in the pursuit of the approval from the ethnically unmarked dominant class—the white American political class, in the context of Powell's political autobiography.

I empathize with Powell's position, though. Far away from my home and faced with the speculations of a white administrator at Andover about the possibly biological sources of Black incapacity in the swimming pool, I instinctively referred back to the avidly swimming upper-middle-class segment of Washingtonian society in which I had grown up, and I generalized my class-specific experience to Washington as a whole. My first thought was that, if these allegations about Black incapacity were true, there must be something "culturally" different about my homeland, Washington, DC. Mind you, it was beyond the race-focused US American imagination of all of us that poor and working-class white students at Andover may have been failing the test at higher rates than the middle- and upper-middle-class Black students.

In contrast to Powell, a resident of the Jamaican diaspora, my largely middle-class interlocutors in Jamaica complained constantly about the diversity of values and behavior among their countrymen—including the "rude" culture of dancehall, a long-standing working-class norm of nonmarital polygyny and absent fatherhood, the extraordinary violence of the "garrison" towns run by drug dons, marijuana consumption, the glue sniffing and food begging of children near some areas frequented by tourists, the violence and authoritarianism of working-class parenting, and the heavy drinking in the "rum shops," all of which are associated with populous "downtown" Kingston. "Uptown," on the other side of high walls encrusted with jagged glass, one finds a norm of legal monogamy, parents passionately preparing their children for the highly competitive exam schools, piano recitals, and high tea. There are, in the rural areas, practitioners of the African-inspired Pukumina religion and, in the cities, High Church Anglicanism. In Jamaica, there are people who habitually show up late and people who normally arrive on time. There are the deep and creative "Patwa" language of Jamaica's impoverished majority and the "Queen's English" of the ruling class. Between these extremes is a very steep color and class hierarchy, a very deep popular resentment, and an often surly service class. Immigrant reports of the home culture often knowingly depend on the unlikelihood that the host country audience has ever visited or will ever visit and examine conditions in the home culture at close quarters. Such reports often contrast sharply with the jeremiads about the home country heard in gatherings of immigrants from the home country and of people they consider insiders.

During my 2005 stay in Kingston (one of several since the late 1960s), my own family transacted with several male professional drivers who expected prompt pay despite repeated lateness, no-shows, and failure to follow instructions. It might be easy to describe them as "lazy" and, for those with a stake in proving American or African American superiority, to describe the whole culture in such terms. But such an argument would merely illustrate the mythological anthropology that I am describing here. Powell's second-generation paean to his parents' home culture is colored by both nostalgia and, amid his deliberations about whether to run for president, an effort to reassure white American voters that he is not really African American. Moreover, it is likely that his parents employed half-true accounts of life "back home" to discipline and encourage him. But nostalgia and racial appeasement clearly occlude his sociological vision and erase from his ethnology the lower-class majority of the island, which has produced the island's most original and extraordinary contributions to the world. Like the creativity of the African American working class, those accomplishments arose in direct challenge to class oppression, racial stigma, and linguistic marginalization and bear little connection to the Anglophile, middle-class "brown" values that Powell attributes to island culture as a whole.

Among black immigrants to the United States, it has become conventional to describe African Americans as constitutionally "lazy," which is exactly how local Afro-Caribbean laborers were described when South Asian laborers were brought into the Caribbean to replace them, obviating the need to address Afro-Caribbean demands for better labor conditions. The premise of black Trinidadian laziness implicit in the term "niggeritis" (or "the 'itis," for short) ignores the history of racially unequal rewards for labor and demeans black accomplishment on the island. This passing on of stigma amid labor competition is a common phenomenon, as, for example, when Haitians in the Dominican Republic reportedly describe Dominicans as lazy, while Dominicans in Puerto Rico describe Puerto Ricans as lazy. In a similarly strategic response, some Central American workers at Howard attribute laziness to all black workers, regardless of their ethnicity. Since the 1940s, federally subsidized programs to bring guest workers, or *braceros*, from Mexico have been used to break the back of African American agricultural workers' demands for humane wages and labor conditions. The accusation that African American workers are "lazy" has been helpful to the interests of both white farmers and Latino migrant workers.

Black immigrants' ultimate appeal to a cultural explanation of the labor market—rather than a structural one in which they are willing if dependent actors—is an empowering and sometimes deliberate self-promotion over native-born African American workers. And many white American employers find this appeal convincing (see Waters [1999, 98–103] for a further discussion of the uses, flaws, and consequences of the cultural explanation). Thus, the struggle over enduring racial inequalities in the job market and in the social benefits of labor is postponed for another generation.

However, black immigrants are not the only parties with a stake in their culturalist arguments. Waters (1999) reviews seven decades of scholarship—beginning with Ira Reid's *The Negro Immigrant* (1939)—debating whether Caribbean immigrants and their children outperform African Americans economically. She observes:

> [T]he estimates of, and explanations for, West Indian success tend to mirror political differences. Conservative writers such as Thomas Sowell are likely to see big differences and to stress cultural explanations. Liberal writers such as Stephen Steinberg are likely to see little or no differences and to stress structural explanations for the differences they find. (96)

The foremost motive of conservatives has been to use the comparison to demonstrate that some deficiency in the collective values and dispositions of African Americans, rather than racism, is the actual cause of African Americans' disadvantaged position in US society.

Waters summarizes the overall empirical evidence, including her own statistical and ethnographic study of New York City during the 1990s, as follows:

> West Indians [in the United States] may no longer earn more than African Americans when background characteristics are statistically controlled, and there is some question of whether [West Indians] ever were overrepresented in entrepreneurial activities. . . . Nevertheless, there are still some ways in which West Indians outperform African Americans. They are more likely to be employed, less likely to be on public assistance, and more likely to have husband-wife two-earner households. And, while earlier immigrant cohorts have higher education than later ones, West Indians are recognized as having higher educational aspirations in American society, especially among the second generation. (1999, 98–99)

Waters documents several explanations for these West Indian successes. Immigration selects for the ambitious and the optimistic. Psychologically, rather than comparing their wages to those of privileged populations in the host country, they are grateful to be able to earn more and educate their children better than they could have done at home. Moreover, they are less likely to reject and resent low-status jobs in the host country because their sense of personal status is still rooted in the home country. They benefit from immigrant chains of communication about job availability. And, according to

Waters's study of low-wage work in New York City, white employers prefer immigrant workers, partly because they believe West Indians' stereotypes about their ancestral culture and values and partly because immigrants are more willing to accommodate the flexible and noncontractual demands of their employers. Low-skill West Indian employees and white employers share an interest in believing that native Black job expectations result from a cultural deficiency, and American stereotypes that have existed since the days of slavery are available as sources of ideological support (Waters 1999, 98–118). Ironically, these same stereotypes are available in the Caribbean to describe the native-born black people in that region as well.

The dividends of being classified as an exceptional immigrant subgroup of a stigmatized race are more than economic. They are psychological as well. Even a self-ascribed reputation for exceptionalism gives backbone. The contrary case of Caribbeans in England and Canada, who are often stereotyped as underachieving, suggests the further benefit of contrast to an even more stigmatized group—a role that African Americans play for Caribbeans in the United States. Like the royalty of a tiny principality, the petty elites of Black America—both immigrant and indigenous—often display an hauteur exceeding that of whites many times richer than they. Colin Powell begins his exegesis of West Indian superiority with the following observation: "American blacks sometimes regard Americans of West Indian origin as uppity and arrogant" (Powell with Persico [1995] 2003, 22; see also Frazier [1957] 1997 on the reported arrogance of the Black American bourgeoisie). Powell seems not to realize that, surrounded by an often-petulant lower-class majority, middle-class people in Jamaica also contend with the accusation of arrogance, but those who wish to avoid verbal and physical assault, as well as exaggerated prices in the market, modulate the class register of their speech and behavior to avoid this accusation. The large middle-class of the highly class- and value-diverse Black American population suffers under the same suspicion of arrogance from its less affluent coethnics. Like middle-class Jamaicans, middle-class African Americans code-switch in order to deflect this suspicion. However, in the interethnic settings that Powell implicitly describes and the interracial settings where he sought political traction for himself, he appears to have decided that the advantages of being seen as superior to native-born African Americans exceed the advantages of apparent solidarity with African Americans. Like Barack Obama, he assumed that he could count on Black Americans to support him, even if he insulted us in front of his white audience. Yet ethnological schadenfreude is a double-edged sword. Joining in the condemnation of the discredited only temporarily relieves the discreditable of their stigma. In the long term, though, it reinforces the power of a stereotype that a less vulnerable rival will one day use against the discreditable.

The discreditable often seek to escape their condition by proclaiming their likeness to a third party whose worth they think their audience will not doubt. Thus, black ethnic claims of dignity are layered with symbolic connections not only to their distant homelands but also to their British and French imperial masters. For example, anglophone Caribbean self-esteem is often articulated through a powerful Anglophilia that impresses white Americans, since white Americans themselves tend to feel inferior to the English. For example, Caribbeans affronted by Jim Crow in the early twentieth century often reportedly shouted, "I am a subject of the British Empire! I shall report this to my consulate!" They did so despite the fact that, in their island homelands they were treated as inferior by the British, their earlier emancipation notwithstanding (e.g., Hintzen 2003). In 2002, a "red" Trinidadian interlocutor of mine at Howard boasted of the fact that, at his Port of Spain school, even the judge of the local piano competition was flown in from England. Like Powell, he regarded the neocolonial centrality of England in the local standards of excellence as proof that his school and even Trinidad as a whole were excellent. Sharing with white Americans a sense of inferiority to the British, such Jamaicans and Trinidadians seem unaware of the tremendous variability in the quality of English schools, and of English piano judges as well. In his autoethnography, Guayanese immigrant Percy Hintzen (2003) shows how personal contact with the real English people in his homeland undid his own sense of inferiority to the British. But Powell and my "red" Trini interlocutor demonstrate the enduring utility of British infallibility. It is difficult for most white Americans to deny, and it reflects well on a discreditable person who can claim association with it.

My favorite illustration of the tethering of the myth of Caribbean superiority to the taken-for-granted myth of English superiority is a joke recounted at a gathering of Howard alumni that a very kind Howard alumna hosted in Kingston on my behalf:

> One day, George [W.] Bush was visiting Buckingham Palace and said to Queen Elizabeth, "Mrs. Queen." [The audience of the joke has already begun to laugh and roll its eyes at Mr. Bush's abysmal ignorance of the etiquette of the Court of St. James in addressing Her Majesty.]
>
> "Mrs. Queen," he repeats buffoonishly, "looks like you got a pretty well-organized country here. Everything seems to work. Howja do it?"
>
> The queen replies with a slow and majestic drawl, "Well, Mr. Bush, the main trick is to select intelligent subordinates. Allow me to demonstrate."
>
> Whereupon she calls out, "Mr. Blair! Mr. Blair!"

When Tony Blair enters the room, he bows gently. "Your Highness?"

"Mr. Blair, a riddle. Who is it? This person is the child of your mother and of your father but is neither your sister nor your brother? Who is it?"

"Of course, Your Majesty," replied Mr. Blair, "it is I!"

Elated by this simple lesson in leadership, Bush returned to the White House, immediately calling Dick Cheney into his office. "Hey, Dick! Gotta question for ya! Gotta question for ya! This person's the child of yer mother and yer father, but it's notcher brother or yer sister. Who is it?" he asks, followed by a self-satisfied, shoulder-twitching snigger.

At a loss, Cheney rocks from one foot to the other, saying "Ummmm. Ummmm. I know, Mr. President. I know. Just gimme a minute." He then rushes out of the room to ask somebody who would know.

"Uh, Colin" [referring to Jamaican American Colin Powell, who was then the US secretary of state]. "Uh, Colin, gotta a question for ya. Can you help me out here? This person is the child of yer mother and yer father, but it's notcher brother or yer sister. Who is it?"

Without skipping a beat, Powell immediately and calmly answers, "Why, of course, Dick, it's me."

"All right! I got it!" shouts Cheney with glee, wringing his hands fiendishly and rushing back to the Oval Office.

"I got it, Mr. President. I got it. This person's the child of yer mother and yer father, but it's notcher sister or yer brother. Why, it's . . . ," and the raconteur paused for dramatic effect, "Colin Powell!"

"No, you idiot," replies Bush. "It's Tony Blair!"

Such, in contrast to the casual intelligence of the British and the Caribbeans, is the empty-headed buffoonery then at the helm of the world's accidentally greatest power. Of course, as a superseded world power that had to be rescued by the United States during World War II, the British themselves nurse a sense of inferiority that they palliate with a similar genre of jokes.

In the United States, African Americans have been particularly useful in the projects of immigrant ethnic groups to establish their "whiteness" and worthiness to partake in the "American Dream"—particularly among the Irish, the Jews, the Italians, and all manner of southern or eastern Europeans whose whiteness had not been firmly established in Europe (Roediger 1989; Morrison 1993; Sacks 1994; Ignatiev 1995). West Indian ethnogenesis instantiates and amplifies this strategy.

One is reminded of the symbolic use of other East and Southeast Asians in Japanese nationalism, at a time when the reigning international "science" had established that all Asians were inferior to whites (Dikötter 1997; Kristoff 1995). While presuming to speak for and rule in the interests of the nearby Asian Other, the Japanese also tortured their Asian "little brothers." In turn, the degradation of the Asian Other served as an important trope in the establishment of Japanese equality with the Europeans.

Similarly, Ethiopians take enormous pride in having evaded European colonization, a fact that distinguishes them sharply from their comparison group—that is, Africans and other groups successfully targeted for conquest by Europeans. As among middle-class Jamaicans, Caribbean immigrants in the United States, and middle-class African Americans, the sense of being the best of one's (stigmatized) kind is tremendously gratifying, establishing the actor's superiority to some whites as well. The Jamaican joke about George W. Bush is a case in point. The arguments come in various forms: that we are cleaner, craftier, less naïve, more intuitive, more sincere, more musically and sexually talented, and so forth. The recollection of such rhetoric is useful to the stigmatized when they face assault or failure in white-dominated environments. One Ethiopian graduate student at Harvard told me that, on more than one occasion, it had given her the strength to go on. She could identify the forms of overcompensation embedded in the childhood lessons she had received about Ethiopian superiority to other Africans and to whites—overcompensation in the face of poverty, famine, and the nation's dysfunctional politics. But the emotional lesson continued to serve its purpose. Caribbeans and Ethiopians in the US refer to their specific regional or national histories in order to substantiate this compensatory rhetoric, with the assumption that these histories distinguish them from some normative type of black person. On the other hand, many middle-class African Americans propagate a similar rhetoric, but with the premise that all black people in the United States share in this form of superiority to whites.

For ethnic groups of African descent in the United States, the main physical and ethical difficulty with ethnological schadenfreude is the ultimate difficulty of establishing their physical difference from the descendants of US slaves and maintaining that physical difference among their children.

Recipes for Sameness and Difference

At Caribbean and African student gatherings and the southeastern Indian powwows to which I was invited by students, music, dance, art, and food were important media in the performance of social difference from or likeness to others. Moreover, much of Howard's rental property and of the nearby architecture on Georgia Avenue and U Street is occupied by purveyors of clothing, music, books, and food, which are important props of performative identity assertions on campus. These displays of "culture" and taste enable performers to supersede the more visible and indelible similarities imposed by race. Most TWIs surround or are surrounded by bars and pizza parlors. Sometimes the fraternity houses themselves substitute for bars. As far as I have noticed, however, there has not been a single bar or pizza parlor near Howard's campus since I began my formal research and began paying attention in 2002. Universities create a profusion of food, and the menus are in some ways a map of any given university community's social priorities.

For me, pizza reads like an edible sign of the anti-institutional, anti-professorial, anti-intellectual, and antihierarchical student ethic that Helen Lefkowitz Horowitz (1987) calls "college life." It is an equally evocative metonym of social unity in general and of what Victor Turner ([1966] 1995) calls "communitas"—a ritual, calendrical, or historical moment of social equality in an otherwise hierarchical social unit, a moment that invigorates the society but could result in either the transformation or the reinforcement of the antecedent social order. In the spirit of communitas, pizza is round, antiarchitectural. It is like road pizza—broken down and without a detectable skeleton. It also mimes Durkheim's mechanical solidarity, in which all of the social and spatial divisions look alike. It is easily divisible into fungible segments, like a communion wafer. Indeed, eating pizza is like a communion.

It is no wonder that pizza figured so prominently in my father's tale about his introduction to the university. It remains the preeminent culinary sign of "college life"—such as the egalitarian networking within fraternities, which was central to his experience on Howard's campus and remained central even at his funeral, where his cohort of the Kappas performed a fraternal farewell.

Pizza is the opposite of the built-up, multilayered, and twisted-all-around architecture of the expensive nouvelle cuisine—sitting on a plate covered with inscrutable sauce writing—favored by professors, particularly at Harvard and Duke, where university expense accounts subsidize its extravagance.

Similarly, beer embodies a literal and a Durkheimian effervescence. It is also antiarchitectural—no umbrellas, no ice, no straws. It induces the forgetting of historical legacies, class hierarchies, and interpersonal boundaries. It is easily shared in pitchers, kegs, or bongs—funnels fitted with one or several symmetrically arranged hoses, used to force the drinkers to swallow large quantities of beer rapidly in a competitive race to horizontality. Servings of beer do not need to be prepared one by one, just tapped and poured. The only hierarchy involved is that people under eighteen or twenty-one are officially excluded from this communion. However, a major mythic and ritual theme in white American youth culture and films about it is the crafty circumvention of even this form of exclusion and hierarchy.

A white male Harvard student once told me of the egalitarian and brotherly trust demonstrated and consolidated when you and your friends are drunk to the point of vomiting and insanity and yet your buddies still make sure you get home safely. In fact, your buddies often serve as your sole source of memory about the evening, the accounts of which, I have observed, continue to circulate and fascinate for decades. In similar bonding rituals, added a prospective Cultural Anthropology Department graduate student at Duke, white coeds hold back the hair of a girlfriend who is vomiting in the toilet or rescue her from drunken sexual encounters that she would otherwise later regret. These episodes can be a test of the fraternal or sororal bond as well. One dear childhood friend and Black fraternity member told me that, against his advice, his son chose to join a white Greek-letter society. One night when the son had joined in the ritual drinking, his fraternity brothers left him on the street overnight in a puddle of his own vomit. The young man was devastated. His father said, "I told you so."

By contrast, the consumables of choice for the wonks, grinds, and other acolytes of professorial meritocracy at TWIs are individually and privately consumed—coffee, Ritalin, Adderal, and antidepressants. It is perhaps a sign that, among the "millenials," stimulants are as dominant today as the anti-anxiety medication Valium (celebrated by the Rolling Stones as "Mother's Little Helper") and the antidepressants Prozac, Wellbutrin, Celexa, Paxil, and Zoloft were in their parents' and grandparents' baby-boomer generation. So kaleidoscopically varied and common were these little helpers that my white high school peers at the Maret School named them by color and shape rather than pharmaceutical names.

Amid the progress of what David Harvey calls "time-space compression," more productivity is demanded—and faster—of each successive generation. The "outsider," "wonk" drugs of the millennial generation answer and require the hierarchy-satisfying demands of Starbuck's prices and psychiatrists' diagnostic criteria. They leave behind no traces of communal friendship or personal transcendence to commemorate. They facilitate the competitive pursuit of individual achievement. Howard has a Starbuck's, but I suspect that Howard runs on less Ritalin than do most TWIs.

In the HBCU, the dilemmas of hierarchy and communitas and their alimentary symbols are arranged along different axes. The racially stigmatized bear the burden of always representing or being represented by a group. Even upward mobility requires the excuse of a group whose norms require such mobility or whose needs are served by it. Among white Americans, ethnicity has, until recently, tended to correlate negatively with individual professional self-promotion and upward class mobility, as a string of American movies about the white ethnic working class (including *Saturday Night Fever* [1977] and *Mystic River* [2003]) demonstrate. White upward class mobility is generally associated with the abandonment of marked ethnic and class identities. On the other hand, ethnicity and other collectivist substitutes for Black racial identity have to the same degree tended to correlate with upward mobility among people of African descent in the United States. Hence, rather than pizza parlors and beer joints, the altars of commensality that surround Howard are chiefly black ethnic restaurants—Ethiopian, Eritrean, Ghanaian, Jamaican, Trinidadian, Louisiana Creole, black Indian, and Black Hebrew Israelite. Howard students do order pizzas for delivery from Domino's and Papa John's, but not, apparently, often enough to justify the opening of a nearby branch of those chains.

It is ethnic restaurants that festoon the edges of Howard's campus, subsidized by the convergence of numerous immigrant ethnic groups, young university professionals with cash, childless students, the shortage of on-campus kitchens, and fire codes that forbid cooking in most dormitory rooms. Their menus further illustrate the diasporic transformation of homeland cultures, as well as the new forms of social alliance and separation that these transformations mythologically facilitate—during off-campus dates, girls' nights out, dinners after a late sports practice, and catered campus parties. They also represent an increasingly central alternative to the egalitarianism of "college life."

The alternative to "college life" that they pose is hierarchical, grade oriented, and socially stratifying. The individualized units in which ethnic food is selected and served in the restaurants that supply it are an apt metaphor of the ways in which black ethnics at Howard use ethnic identities less as forms of collective organization than as evidence of individual distinction. The contrast between the student-favored cuisines of Howard and those of most TWIs is symbolically consistent with the zeal of the stigmatized to "stratify their own." The cuisines favored by professors at TWIs embody the cultural logic of the stigmatized, consistent with the hypertrophy of status distinctions among professors and among universities, in which each faculty member and each university is conscious of ranking below others or being at risk of a fall. The dining options of professionals at Howard are more hybrid. The faculty dining room is an up-market, carpeted cafeteria, where the steam table features delicious but mass-produced food, not plated works of edible architecture and scripture. And there are no nouvelle cuisine restaurants nearby. A related but nonculinary element of this ethos is that Howard pedagogy is weighted toward service and conscious of the insufficiency of theoretical abstraction.

The creation and reorganization of ethnicity in the Howard-area restaurant market parallels the reclassification of racial and ethnic populations on campus. For example, in 2002, Tropicana—the Jamaican Eatery—served not only typically Jamaican coco bread and Irish moss drink but also Indo-Trinidadian roti—curried meat in elastic mille-feuille flat bread. Tropicana did not serve roast breadfruit, yams, or any of the other "provisions" conventionally associated with Jamaican folk cuisine on the island. The Trinidadian-owned Islander restaurant on U Street served rice-based pilau and chicken in brown sauce, the likes of which I never encountered in the restaurants of Trinidad because, I was told, they are considered domestic food, unworthy of purchase. However, on some days, the ground and seasoned leaf dish known as callaloo was available at the Islander. It was much meatier, and much saltier, than anything I tasted in Trinidad. Here, Trinidadian home cooking is dressed up on tablecloths. The owner, Miss Addie Green, was vocally committed to high standards in everything she did. When, at the end of our first encounter, I asked if she had a professional card that I could take, she lambasted me for the "culture of low expectations" whereby I could even have conceived of the possibility that she did not have one. The discreditable are extremely sensitive to possible hints of being doubted or tested. Moreover, she had clearly taken upon herself the obligation to exemplify high standards for her public and for her people.

Besides callaloo and pilau, few foods are regarded in Trinidad as typical of the nation. Consistent with its continually verbalized self-representation as "cosmopolitan" in race and culture, Trinidad seems to cook up a welter of Indian, "Negro," Chinese, and British dishes, which, like "American" cuisine, is seldom recognized or presented as a whole inside its home country. (When the term "American" appears on a restaurant signboard or menu in the United States, it is usually a down-market restaurant serving the cuisine of a nonblack but alien-looking and alien-sounding population that fears its citizenship will be questioned (e.g., "Chinese American," "Polynesian American," and "Lebanese American"). For black retailers and for entrepreneurs targeting the culturally omnivorous class elite and the ethnic market, a greater advantage lies in the advertisement of completely non-American "authenticity." In fact, the more specific and inaccessible the named regional origin of the cuisine, the more prestigious. The Islander menu presents an idiosyncratic whole from which my Trinidadian student friend Philip's most redolent home culinary memory was entirely missing: shark and bake—fried blacktip shark meat, or other white fish, on oily bread—usually eaten at the beach. He asked me to make sure to eat some on his behalf when I got to Trinidad.

In sum, memories and reproductions of "home" in restaurants abroad are always selective, creative in their conflations, decontextualizing, and subject to the limits of commercial availability. In ethnic restaurants in the diaspora, menus can embody the ethnicity entrepreneur's ambitions to upward mobility and the claim of not only difference but also "distinction" (Bourdieu [1979] 1984) from the more ordinary and easily pegged coracial locals in the US symbolic universe.

More obvious is the power of food to trigger nostalgic remembrances of things past, becoming a simulacrum of intraethnic communality in the diaspora. For example, a light-skinned, bourgeois Haitian student in my "Other African Americans" class at Harvard told me, well before the 2010 earthquake, that no Haitian food tastes better than the kind cooked over coals by a woman surrounded by smoldering trash heaps. Hyperbole did not reduce the sincerity of his point, which received nods of affirmation from his dark and class-diverse Haitian classmates. After my Lewis Henry Morgan Lecture, which was the basis of this book, a Jamaican student at the host institution, the University of Rochester, told me that, while in the United States, she relishes rice and peas and ackee and saltfish, a high-fat tree-born fruit scrambled with shredded codfish. But when her father comes from Jamaica to visit her in Rochester, he is appalled by her plebeian eating habits. She adds that, in Jamaica, she would never buy "food in a box"—that is, in the sort of carry-out container in which she buys food here for consumption in her apartment. I imagine that she would not walk around eating "Jamaican" meat patties in public, either. In England and in much of the Anglophile Third World, people delight in mocking the mobile and public eating of Americans, even as they progressively adopt the same putatively lower-class-looking habits.

Both of these stories illustrate the Janus-faced nature of ethnic identity. Whereas sit-down ethnic restaurants dress up foreign cuisines for competitive purposes, diaspora cuisine also has a class-leveling, populist, and nostalgic modality. One kind of cuisine is intended to articulate collective reputation, respect, and hierarchy, while the other articulates intimacy and egalitarian community, normally to an in-house audience. I read the light-skinned Haitian man's public declaration of his food nostalgia as an invitation to intimacy with his dark Haitian classmates and the Jamaican father's advice to his daughter as a reminder that she needs to "represent" her family and her nation abroad.

I encountered the most striking socioculinary alliance in a Louisiana Creole restaurant and catering service operated by a pita-beige Louisiana Creole woman who had attended Howard for two years, until her father stopped paying her tuition. A nutmeg-brown, dreadlocked man from Trinidad was her husband and business partner. She served po'boy sandwiches, which are less Creole than New Orleanian generally, and a range of more canonical Creole foods, such as filé gumbo, along with a smattering of Indo-Trinidadian dishes, such as curry goat roti. She spoke of her menu as though she were trying to justify to her skeptical father her own marriage—"I've been to Trinidad, and really the *cultures* are very similar. There are Creoles there too. The food. The Mardi Gras. They're Catholic" (emphasis mine). I, on the other hand, recall few similarities between the cuisine of New Orleans and the cuisine*s* (plural) of Trinidad. During my sojourn in New Orleans in the summer of 2002, Creole society boasted a restaurant-based haute cuisine—which bespoke the shared respectability of both elite Creoles and elite non-Creole African Americans—the likes of which I was unable to identify in Trinidad. Pampy's served plated art in surroundings of leather, brass, and voile. Finally, this Washington Creole restaurateur's husband in no way resembles, or appeared to identify with, the reputedly aloof and light-colored French Creoles of his home island.

The half dozen Eritrean restaurateurs of U Street make a point of offering spaghetti and spumoni on their menus, which offerings—in commemoration of Eritrea's colonization by Italy—serve to distinguish them from their Ethiopian counterparts. As *opponents* of Eritrean secession from Ethiopia in 1993, most Ethiopian Americans verbally minimize the difference between Ethiopians and Eritreans. "We are the same people," they tend to say. Indeed, both populations answer to the ethnonym "Habesha." This term derives from the ancient Ge'ez language, which remains the language of liturgy for both groups. "Habesha" refers chiefly to the speakers of Amharic and Tigrinya but can at times also extend to Somali and Gurage speakers. However, it can also be used to exclude a whole range of Ethiopians from consideration, marginalizing them from the dominant national identity or from a claim to civilization. Culinary fictions can serve other strategic purposes as well. An Eritrean restaurateur once told me with great authority, "We Africans like to eat raw meat," which generalization would come as a great and upsetting surprise to my Nigerian Yoruba friends, who typically roast or fry every speck of red—except for the copious ground hot pepper—out of their meat. The Eritrean restaurateur also told me that, in Africa, women do not take their husbands' surnames. Actually, my Ekiti wife's father reacted with great surprise to the fact that I had "allowed" her even to hyphenate her postmarital surname. I can only surmise that this businessman has a financial stake in representing the whole of Africa for African American lovers of "the motherland" like me. Ironically, most of the Africans on Howard's campus regard Ethiopians and Eritreans as aloof and generally unwilling to identify with other Africans. The authority and the dignity of ethnic spokespeople rely on nonempirical generalizations about the in-group. Like the ethnonym "Habesha," campus culinary fictions can be as intent on separation as upon conflation and alliance. Menus document the aspirations of ethnicity entrepreneurs for their group, as well as assertions about its boundaries.

In sum, food can be a highly flexible symbol of competitive respectability or a projection of horizontal alliance building. But in the diaspora, it is seldom an innocent replication of the foodways of the homeland. In the Howard University and Washingtonian diaspora of black immigrant groups, the diacritical behaviors of one class at home can become the standards of a whole nation abroad, foods can become detached from their class origins, the symbols of private life at home can become the symbols of public life abroad, the symbols of a whole region or continent can become the symbols of one country, and vice versa. The HBCU and the commerce that it subsidizes dramatize unprecedented horizontal alliances and, above all, vertical hierarchies—in effect, new ethnic identities with novel canons and newly class-defined culinary diacritica.

In common, these hybridized diasporic cuisines ultimately run up against the implicit moral and economic question of whether to embrace the nearby African American constituent other or step up to a higher rank on her back. For example, some Caribbean American students embroidered the small differences between Caribbean macaroni and cheese and African American macaroni and cheese with powerful aesthetic and moral judgment. For a time, one circle of Caribbean American and second-generation African girlfriends at Harvard operated what they described as a pan-African catering service. Their perennial joke was that all you have to do to make African American "soul food" is slather gallons of sweet barbeque sauce on everything. They laughed uproariously as they revealed the simple "trick," clearly enjoying their shared insightfulness and superiority. This is the humor of ethnological schadenfreude.

In fact, the African American cuisine on and around Howard's campus in 2002 varied tremendously. The least common denominator of cuisine among all student ethnic groups on campus seemed to be the burgers, hot dogs, potato chips, and fries served in the basement of the Blackburn Center, the social hub of the College of Arts and Sciences. The high-status, cafeteria-style dining room upstairs, mainly for faculty, served not only ribs with sweet barbeque sauce but also greens or green beans simmered with smoked meats, spicy broiled fish, corn niblets, mashed potatoes, leafy salads, sweet-and-sour cold bean medleys, candied yams, baked potatoes, corn bread, black-eyed peas, collard greens and kale, fruit cobblers, carrot cake, strawberry shortcake, sweet tea, and hot coffee. A Louisiana-made but Mexican-inspired African American staple, Tabasco pepper sauce was always available, and both salt and ground black pepper sat on each table. Sweet, savory, sour, bitter, piquant, and umami were equally on offer. While my African American colleagues and I would, if asked, probably have called this smorgasbord "soul food," I imagine that the same array of dishes appears on the holiday tables of elite southern whites as well.

For its chefs and consumers, the diacritical taste of this cuisine is not the sweet elements, which it shares with white American cuisines, but vinegar and red pepper, as well as its defiant recuperation and dignification of once-throwaway meats, the recuperation of which, by analogy, dignifies the cuisine's stigmatized consumers.

A half-century-old parallel African American cuisine has also long been available just off campus. Today, that low-sodium, low-fat, dairy-free, and semivegetarian variant on soul food is served in a Black Hebrew Israelite restaurant called Everlasting Life, across from the Business School. Though this culinary variant and its accompanying mythology are precedented in the Nation of Islam, the Black Hebrew Israelites are African Americans who regard Black people as the true descendants of the ancient Israelites and appear to model their lifestyle upon their interpretation of this genealogy. Many of them transmigrate between the United States and the town of Demona in modern Israel. Instead of embracing the symbols of past slavery and recuperating them, this cuisine invalidates slavery as the historically defining aspect of Blackness. Admirers and merchants of this cuisine regard it as superior to ordinary African American cuisine in terms of healthfulness and distance from the slavery-infused and Christian-associated symbolism of the pig and its nether parts. Indeed, in their view, right eating will lead to immortality. The parts of the pig used in soul food—such as pig's feet, ears, and intestines—are said to have been castoffs, too lowly for the white master to eat. The Black Hebrew Israelites are part of an African American tradition that embraces Palestine and the Arabian Peninsula as parts of the geographical and cultural continent of Africa, with the understanding that the original Jews and the Judeo-Christian and Islamic traditions are Black and African. This cuisine performs the vision that Black people are not former slaves but the original "Chosen People." In sum, this is a cuisine of spiritual and indeed social upward mobility, which also speaks in ethnic terms.

Thus "healthy" cuisine also includes a prescription for biblical-looking gender relations and, thus, for the repair of what is regarded as American social dysfunction. At their Georgia Avenue restaurant, a disproportionate number of female servers and patrons wore their hair "natural"—that is, chemically unprocessed and trimmed short, braided, or dreadlocked. At

Everlasting Life, uninformed or careless female visitors are advised to cover their legs and to dress properly during their next visit.

This cuisine and its associated cultural practices represent an additional strategic response to stigma. The Black Hebrew Israelites accept that the present lifeway of African Americans is, like the pig, contemptible. Therefore, they endeavor to reconstruct and recover a cultural past that deserves respect. However, in this revivalist cuisine, the implicit rival for respect is not other black ethnic groups but European-descended whites, who are alleged to have imposed the current degrading foodways (and gender relations) on Black people. If anything, both the high-status campus dining room cuisine and this insurgent, off-campus revisionist cuisine tend to incorporate Caribbean and Creole dishes at their margins rather than depicting those cuisines as the contemptible opposite of African American cuisine. For example, Jamaican-inspired jerk chicken was sometimes available in the Blackburn Center's upstairs dining room. Its piquancy makes it a coethnic variant of Black cuisine.

I do not mean to imply, however, that this African American culinary pan-Africanism is free of chauvinism. It involves an appropriation and subordination of other cuisines. Moreover, the verbiage of African American contempt for black ethnics is, in nonculinary contexts, remembered and fluently quoted by its black ethnic targets. Caribbean and African students report being asked by their fellow students if they live in trees and wear grass skirts or, doubtfully, if they have television in their countries. Some international students found it equally offensive that African American students doubt their familiarity with the current pantheon of African American hip-hop stars, such as Jay Z, who, in 2002, was still a novelty to me.

Like the 2002 commencement address of Howard University president H. Patrick Swygert, Howard's version of African American cuisine classifies black ethnics as indistinct from African Americans, as marked subsets of our Black superset. Indeed, I called my class about these populations "The Other African Americans" and had intended to give this book the same title, before it was appropriated by another author. One result of this African American identity imperialism is that African Americans deny themselves a distinct club, interest group, and propaganda operation. Bourgeois African Americans tend to consider such intraracial separatism crude. For their part, black ethnics tend both to relish the opportunity to distinguish themselves from the low social status of African Americans and to resent exclusion from those aspects of African American culture that the media propagate as cool, such as the music of Jay Z.

To be sure, some black immigrant performances of collective similarity

FIGURE 5.2. Celebrant at the Caribbean Day Parade in Washington, DC, June 29, 2002. The seven outstanding "Trinbagonians" named on her T-shirt are analogized to the seven great colonial mansions surrounding the central park of Port of Spain, the national capital of Trinidad and Tobago. Photograph by the author.

and difference make no comparative reference whatsoever to African Americans, but they still reflect the will of the stigmatized to stratify their own. For example, the musical playlist of the Howard Caribbean Students Association parties dramatizes the rivalry between Jamaicans and Trinidadians for cultural hegemony in the English-speaking Caribbean, political power in the CSA, and relative success at exam-based admission to Howard. After a period of strife over whether the single playlist included a fair balance of Trinidadian soca, on the one hand, and Jamaican reggae and dancehall, on the other, the CSA leadership made the Solomonic decision to divide up the spoils of the entire Caribbean between their two islands. They hired two separate deejays for each party—one Trini and one Jamaican.

Though they would alternate several times in the evening, each would play for half the total duration of the party. The associated dance styles differed visibly (few party dances are as spectacular as Jamaican "wining"). When it was the Trinis' turn, they reminisced and sang along with the soca songs, each of which evoked fond memories of the Trini Carnival of a particular year. (Few musical genres are as witty and ribald as calypso, of which soca is a subtype.) Shared comprehension of the double entendres and insider references to Trinidadian politics is a favorite genre of egalitarian communion between musicians and audiences. What I cannot confirm is the report of several CSA members that, whenever the Jamaican music came on, all the Trinis sat down and that whenever the Trini music came on, all of the Jamaicans sat down: Howard Jamaicans and Trinidadians look alike to me. Thus, in the context of the competition for honor and resources, even interisland differences—like the

FIGURE 5.3. Ensemble dancers in elaborate feathered costumes are the main theme of Caribbean Day parades in the United States and carnival parades in the Caribbean. This kind of sensual interlude is common. Photograph by the author.

difference between reggae and soca—are seldom perceived as morally neutral. They are the idiom of symbolically loaded boycotts on the dance floor. Even when the hierarchy is difficult to settle, ethnogenesis is a competitive process.

The breadth of inclusion and the naming of ethnic identities also have competitive implications. My friend Philip's commitment to describing his conationals is a case in point. The inclusive way that he named his nation and its people was probably at least partly intended to maximize his voting bloc. My friend was one of the two leading Trinidadian officers of the Caribbean Students Association.

Philip's discourse further illustrates the Janus-faced character of ethnic and even national identities. And its performance can be dramatic. The inward face of nationalist performance that affirms solidarity within the group tends to involve "rude" and "raw" dancing, the wearing of "natural" hair (such as dreads), the consumption of street food, and the celebration of lumpen lifestyles, as in Jamaican dancehall, Caribbean / African American gangsta rap, and films about gangsterism, such as *The Harder They Come* (1972) and *Shottas* (2002). Even Oxford-educated Eric Williams speaks its internal egalitarianism in basilect: "Massa day done!" On the other hand, the outward face of national "culture" speaks itself in Anglophilia, exam schools, piano competitions, and "tablecloth" cuisine. Despite his brief paean to Jamaica's cultural debt to Africa, this is the Caribbean "culture" of which Colin Powell spoke. It is real, but far from the whole picture.

Native and immigrant communities face structurally similar dilemmas but enact strategically different permutations of hierarchy and solidarity, lumping and splitting, code-switching, Janus-faced identities, and deft alternation between "taste" and vulgarity. However, for immigrant groups, the fewer one's economic means and the closer one is to the marked race of the constituent other, the greater the incentive to declare oneself "culturally" distinct from that other by naming the ethnic "culture" according to its most acrolectal forms.

Can We Talk? The Languages of Sameness and Difference

Even more frequently than ethnic cuisine and dance, speech continually replays and aims to resolve the dilemmas of sameness and difference among the stigmatized. Actors deliberately and situationally choose between idioms of hierarchy and solidarity. Particularly among the stigmatized, the linguistic boundaries between classes must be negotiated as delicately as those between ethnic groups. The potential for insult is always great. Like light skin, scholastic diction is highly valued at Howard, but it can be mistaken for a sign of preten-

ISLANDS OF THE MIND 361

sion, effeminacy, and disloyalty to the group, particularly if the speaker cannot switch at the appropriate moment into the vernacular dialect of the group whose assent is sought—whether AAVE or, for example, Jamaican Patwa.

Light-skinned Jamaican prime minister Edward Seaga (1980–89) was famous for his eloquence in Patwa and ethnographic expertise on the Afro-Jamaican Pukumina religion. Likewise, light-skinned African Americans—especially men—are required to display their racial loyalty and "down"-ness actively, a pattern that helps me to understand why the butter-colored Black people and even the whites in my neighborhood were overrepresented among the wildest children and the least academically accomplished adults of my peer group. They had the most to prove in terms of group loyalty and, in the case of the males, in terms of masculinity. Their efforts at bourgeois self-promotion were the most easily interpreted as effeminate and disloyal to the collective.

However, like slang, vernacular speech is risky for a nonnative speaker to employ. Even the high-class coethnics of native vernacular speakers must be very careful.

For example, Philip and my other Trinbagonian companions at the Caribbean Day Parade told me that my own and other African Americans' deliberate attempts to learn Caribbean creole language varieties are regarded as inauthentic and potentially offensive. Caribbean students in my "Other

FIGURE 5.4. Crowd at the 2002 Caribbean Day Parade in Washington, DC, 2002. Photograph by the author.

African Americans" class at Harvard suggested three reasons for my Howard companions' sensitivity.

First, in the Caribbean, middle-class people employ their nations' creole languages in intimate, familiar, and emotionally direct communications. To them, the effort of nonnative speakers to speak those languages implies a false familiarity with the context, a false understanding of who appropriately speaks those languages to whom, and, usually, an erroneous evaluation of the particular nonnative creole language learner's degree of intimacy with the Caribbean interlocutor.

Second, outsiders' imitation of the Caribbean creole language is often superficial—a poor mimesis of the accent without a command of the complexities of grammar or vocabulary. Such imitations seem intended to ridicule or put the Caribbean interlocutor on display.

And third, members of the Caribbean middle class have normally been prohibited by their parents from speaking these languages. These basilects are seen as "raw" and ignorant. Therefore, an outsider who speaks these languages uninvited by the Caribbean interlocutor accidentally implies that the interlocutor is ignorant and does not understand or speak respectable English. Hence, these potential linguistic vehicles of communitas can accidentally remind lower-status people of their social inferiority. Thus, even middle-class Jamaicans on the island hesitate to speak Patwa to people of subordinate classes for fear that they are insulting the poorer interlocutor by calling attention to the addressee's deficient command of "the Queen's English."

Up to this point in their explanation, I sensed a great similarity between the potential offense rendered by an African American speaking Caribbean basilects and by a white American speaking AAVE. For example, when a white American man calls me "bro," I read the gesture as either ignorant or ironic. I would interpret this speech as merely ignorant if the white man is prematurely signaling familiarity; he is trying to lower himself to what he assumes to be my already-low level in order to make friends. However, my friends and I do not tend to speak in that class register. If his intentions are to make fun of how he thinks I speak, he is signaling something other than friendship. There is no way for me to take it well.

However, my Harvard students offered me an additional and unfamiliar sociolinguistic lesson. Explaining why the middle-class, white Jamaican politician Edward Seaga was allowed to speak Patwa so freely and publicly, my Harvard students opined that only those who bring resources of value to the lower-class community—such as politicians or shopkeepers—are welcome to speak these languages to their lower-class interlocutors. In sum, although the proper use of basilect and its implication of interclass unity are not easy for even natives to execute, virtually any use of basilect by a nonnative is bound to be offensive and to hoist higher the flag of class or ethnic difference.

On the one hand, the explanations I received in my class at Harvard assume that the setting of these communications is in the Caribbean, where Patwa is a low-status medium of communication. On the other hand, at Howard, there was a white female undergraduate in the Department of History who had spent a semester in Jamaica and came back speaking apparently fluent Patwa. And she did so frequently in her circle of Caribbean Students Association friends, despite lacking any appreciable material resources to give to her interlocutors. This phenomenon was certainly a testament to her linguistic and metalinguistic gifts. But it also attests to a situational shift in the status of Patwa. Perhaps her endorsement of Caribbean difference from African Americans was regarded as a useful immaterial resource. As a barrier to the merging of African American and Caribbean identities, Patwa has become a high-status medium in the context of Howard. African American use of Patwa reduces its cache, while white participation increases it.

African Americans and Caribbeans at Howard often regarded each other as collective nemeses, and the struggles for status often concerned linguistic style. Just as white Americans both admire British English and resent it as an expression of intellectual and class superiority, so African Americans alternately admire and contest or correct Anglo-Caribbean and Anglo-African writing, speech, and table manners. Some Caribbean students at Howard report battles with African American instructors who, in the students' view, contemptuously corrected their British spelling or punctuation in class essays. The mastery of the language of the imperial master and of the slave master is perhaps the preeminent voluntarily attainable sign of intelligence and social worth among the oppressed and the recently decolonized. Southern Nigerian immigrants to the United States are also often deeply offended to hear the linguistic product of decades of education and intra-Nigerian competition dismissed by US Americans as incomprehensible or incorrect. These contests over spelling, grammar, and accent reflect a rivalry between groups with competing but equally hard-won markers of class superiority in their respective postimperial societies.

As Fanon ([1952] 2008, 1–23) points out, the colonized must learn the language of the colonizer in order to get respect from the colonizer and from the fellow colonized. Yet, just as there is a hierarchy of places and classes within the postimperial world, there is also a hierarchy of language varieties. Each can be used to assume prestige, to deny esteem, to patronize, and to exclude others from camaraderie. The loser in these linguistic microbattles for pride of place, in effect, has his or her costly cultural capital devalued or invalidated. However, these competitive battles never solve the real dilemma. For an intellectual from a dominated or stigmatized population who seeks esteem for his or her person or people, the choice of any language is fraught simultaneously with self-assertion and a potential confession of inferiority.

Table manners are another medium of interimperial competition and ambiguity. In the post–World War II generation, the Anglo-Caribbean etiquette of eating food with the tine-down fork in the left hand is the object of much conflicted judgment. To middle-class African Americans, it looks vulgar, but its presumably British origins might actually make it superior.

Thus, self-presentation at this crossroads of Black and black ethnic class diversity is full of dilemmas and pitfalls. While at Howard, Caribbean immigrants talk less about complexion differences than do their African American hosts, they, too, face dilemmas around the choice of language register and the display of high-class status. Any given choice potentially suggests a degree of embrace or distancing in relation to an interlocutor, and the multiple audiences of any given performance may interpret its meaning and implications for them differently. Moreover, as the long-term victims of stigmatization, most of these audiences are attentive to every potential source of offense. A sensitive and successful actor must be aware of the polysemic implications of any expressive choice.

The Floor beneath the Welcome Table

Black ethnic students at Howard move remarkably far across the DC landscape to reach other outposts of their respective ethnic groups in the area—to the off-campus apartments they typically share with coethnics; to the Nigerian-Ghanaian restaurant in the Adams Morgan neighborhood; to the Silver Spring, Maryland, night club that hosts Caribbean Students Association parties; to powwows in North Carolina, Virginia, and Maryland; and to the homes of Creole family friends or aunts in Columbia, Maryland.

But their knowledge of the nonethnic Black populations in between is often strategically flattened and essentialized. However many African American professors, physicians, and administrators they have met, many black immigrants identify the addled, homeless wanderers of the Georgia Avenue crack alley south of Howard as the typical African Americans. The carefully trimmed yards of the lower-middle-class row houses in the Petworth neighborhood north of Howard escape notice, as does the caravan of Mercedes and Cadillacs that ferry the African American upper-middle class from the Gold Coast, Montgomery County, and Prince George's County to Howard or past Howard to their downtown offices. Even African Americans from other states mistake the local drug addicts—and the local teenagers who (following a reported fashion) tuck their pants into their socks—for exemplars of the difference between their home states and Washington, DC, in general.

My Panamanian friend at Duke blames these misperceptions partly on the mass media, which, in her view, depict only two Washingtons. Hollywood's white Washington consists of Georgetown, suburban but tony Bethesda, and the (pre-Obama) White House, while Hollywood's Black Washington is a corner of Southeast Washington strewn with empty crack vials.

Even at the "Capstone of Negro Education," the image of the "typical" African American is a foil to the self-aggrandizement of various black and various Black subgroups. And my experience at Andover taught me why. People of African descent who know that they are as complex and capable as any other human being are forced to announce what makes them different from the normative Black person depicted in US American journalism, sociology, folklore, and film—a person who is designed to volunteer for his own disfranchisement.

Every person from a population so stigmatized must make a case for his or her exceptionality or take obtuse pride in his or her typicality. And every stigmatized group contains subpopulations that adopt each of these strategies. Indeed, a strategic vacillation between the two—or code-switching—is probably the norm in most populations in that vast gap between the most stigmatized and the least.

However, diaspora conditions create a special incentive for the stigmatized to idealize themselves in the idiom of "culture" and to infuse their cultures with the ideals of the host country. Hence, Brazilian transmigrant Gilberto Freyre described Brazil as a "racial democracy"; female Yoruba-American sociologist Oyeronkẹ Oyewumi (1997) described Yoruba culture as free of gender inequality; and Caribbean Americans, most elaborately of all, describe their "Caribbean culture" as categorically hardworking, free of racism, Anglophile, monogamous, and education oriented. Such ethnology is made plausible by the fact that, like heaven, the home country is out of reach for fact-finding by most of the target audience. These accounts of the culture "back home" also sometimes pander to the nonidealistic but unconscious wishes of the dominant class of the host country. In the case of Caribbean Americans, these wishes include respect for royalism, hereditary class hierarchy, and a certain degree of sympathy with the marginalization of African Americans.

This chapter, then, is not so much an effort to generalize about the attitudes and alliances that all black ethnics, or all members of any particular ethnic group, share. Rather, it concerns the structure of the *choices* presented by US racial binarism and by the symbolic, social, and physical architecture of the nation's leading historically Black university. Yet it also suggests some hypotheses about ethnogenesis generally. First, the primary agents of ethnogenesis and exponents of "cultures" are often émigrés or returnees. Second, they are often motivated by the experience of stigmatization abroad. Third, their accounts of the home "culture" often reflect a competition with rival populations eligible for the same socioeconomic niche in the host country. And, finally, these accounts of the home culture selectively, strategically, and often fictionally dramatize those ideals and wishes of the dominant class in the host country that would facilitate opportunity for the immigrant.

I conclude, then, with one narration of racial embrace and ethnic distancing, by a self-described "black Indian woman," whose maternal grandmother was an Aquinna Wampanoag from Connecticut. She also calls Africa "the motherland" and describes herself as "caramel-colored"—the "ideal" in her family. She has traveled in Africa, Latin America, and Asia. In other contexts, she might have defined her Indianness and hereditary affluence as her defining traits. However, her black immigrant interlocutors cast her in the same lot as the ostensibly deficient African American.

Sarah Johnson Page is a Yale legacy from New Haven who decided, instead, to attend all-female Mount Holyoke for college and historically Black Howard for graduate school, where, in 2002, she was earning her master's degree. Several of her relatives had also attended professional school at Howard. She says she chose Howard because it is less expensive than other schools, because white and Black companies recruit there, and because it would allow her to become professional without denying her "identity." Moreover, she reports, Howard has produced eight ambassadors, and she wants to join their company. Here she outlines her ambivalent place amid the ethnic and class diversity of the Howard campus:

> This might sound like [Lawrence] Otis Graham:[2] [Howard] is a lot more lower class than I'd expected. Lots of people are unfamiliar with Jack and Jill and vacations in Sag Harbor. I'm used to these things. Lots of students have low self-esteem. They're here because that's the only place they thought they could survive. Lots of students are really bright, but the grammar is colloquial. There's a time and a place for that, but we're in college. . . . . I love the urban street vernacular, because it's like speaking in code. . . . Some people here say I talk white. It breaks my heart. Some administrators even said that to me. . . .
>
> I'm also struck here by the relatively small number of African Americans. There are many Caribbeans [etc.]. . . . . I wish we had another term for us [native-born African Americans] that was exclusive. We don't [get] respect for the distinctive contribution that made this flood of immigration possible.

We've only had full citizenship in this country for forty years—two generations—and we've already [produced] astronauts, [we're] running companies.... Yet there's all this talk about "lazy African Americans." ... African Americans are very generous and welcoming, but I'd like to have a place where we can talk about *my* culture—like the blues, jazz, [etc.]. They enter our organizations and claim to be African American when it's useful, but they have their own exclusive organizations....

We have no "back home," unlike Africans [etc.]. When you live here and have been exposed to certain rights and opportunities, you're not a political refugee, not facing genocide. In your own home, naturally you're not going to settle for certain conditions....

You hear lots of "back home, back home" nostalgia. You have to remind them about the corruption, coups d'état, low literacy levels.... I've been to those countries. You have to remind them that, collectively, we represent only 13 percent of the national population and have done so much. Foreigners tend to grow in their respect for African Americans over time.

I love the camaraderie [at Howard]. At the Business School, my [heavily Caribbean and African] class has grown in "coopitition"—a combination of cooperation and competition. We're only as good as we all are. Some of my classmates have tutored me for free in areas where I'm not as strong. We're very caring, supportive. We recognize each other's value. Truly a thrilling experience. We've even had open discussions [about ethnic chauvinism], and they respect me for it.

Sometimes "black Indian," sometimes African American, and always unapologetically bourgeois, Ms. Page offers evidence that, for some students at HBCUs, race and ethnicity are less permanent states than situational emphases that are motivated at times by stigma, at times by material interest, and at times by love. Her words also suggest that the only people who are captive to other people's judgment of their collective worth are nonethnic African Americans, who have no well-established option for naming their own self-interested strategies of racial embrace and ethnic distancing. Yet the painful dilemma of black ethnics is palpable. They typically face stigma not only for their skin color but also for their geographically marginal origins. Whether or not they see the wisdom in alliance with others who are stigmatized for similar reasons, the sense of dignity and competency that derives from mastery over a "culture" with a real, imagined, or invented home of its own is an emotional anchor not easily replaced.

This chapter illustrates the nostalgic storytelling about "Caribbean culture" and the unflattering stereotypes about African Americans that bolster Caribbean American students' and faculty members' sense of collective worth—in opposition to their racial stigmatization—in US society. This chapter shows that what is described in Jamaica and Trinidad as "middle-class" values—such as respect for monogamous marriage, the exam school, home ownership, and speaking "the Queen's English"—is, in the United States, described as "Caribbean culture," as though working-class, lumpen, and oppositional culture were somehow foreign to the Caribbean and its diaspora and, at the same time, were the sum total of African American culture.

Thus, as Goffman points out, the stigmatized "stratify their own." The lesson of this chapter is not that Blackness is uniquely stigmatized. Rather, Blackness is stigmatized to such an extreme in US society that it illustrates in a paradigmatic way the range of responses that may also be found among all populations suffering hereditary stigma. These include Jews and Gypsies in Europe, Eta and Koreans in Japan, Hutus in interlacustrine East Africa, and so forth. But they also include all sorts of nonethnic populations made discreditable by their gender, age, class, regional background, and so forth. This chapter reveals, beyond Goffman's observations, the dynamics of embrace and distancing among those who cannot easily or fully escape stigma.

As in the case of the Hausa people in Ibadan during the 1950s, what is distinctive about the cases of ethnogenesis among Caribbean Americans is that it occurs far away from the homeland. What I have seen, in sum, is that the cultural self-representation of people far away from home is always dynamic, selective, situational, strategic, and responsive to the socioeconomic conditions and cultural values of the host country. Among those values in the United States is the profound stigmatization—vividly depicted in the public communications media and in daily talk—of Black people. Hence, it is the argument of this chapter that, for African-descended people from abroad, social articulation and the corollary forms of cultural self-representation are profoundly shaped by the situational advantages and disadvantages of association with the paradigm case of American racial stigma—the native-born, nonethnic African American.

To my mind, the Caribbean American case is a most extreme example of the competitive processes characterizing all ethnogenesis. However, it is strikingly parallel in its form and its objectives to two other phenomena treated in this ethnography: the "culture" making of partly African-descended Native Americans and of Louisiana Creoles of color, as well as the taste- and class-based self-construction of my own people.

This study has forced me to recognize the parallel tendency of the African Americans who call themselves "middle-class" to construct ourselves in opposition to the forms of diction, dress, décor, and cuisine that we imagine characterize the "ghetto" and, in my father's generation, to the Gullah/

Geechees. Of course, middle-class white Americans similarly cast "poor white trash" as their coracial constituent other. But for Black and white Americans alike, the public discussion of this petit bourgeois social climbing is embarrassing. We US Americans typically imagine ourselves as egalitarians. However, my encounter with black ethnics spotlights a phenomenon that begs for recognition. Hierarchy is an equal backdrop of "taste" and of the discourse of "cultures." Together, these cases suggest that no populations are more anxious than the middling ones—that is, the discreditable, as opposed to the fully credited and the fully discredited—to create, reify, and elaborate distinctions of "taste" and "cultures." They are the masters of ethnological schadenfreude.

I also argue here that universities are not just external analysts of cultural diversity. They produce it, and they heighten the competitive motives behind it. The university is a unique context in which to observe the performative strategies of embrace and distancing through which the middling shape the power/knowledge of domination.

The height of the slave trade and of the efforts to justify it coincided historically with the formation of the European and Euro-American nation-state. So Africans have played two preeminent roles in the symbolic self-fashioning of the nation-state in general. In the founding of the American republics, the French Revolution, German Romanticism, Abolitionism, and the US Civil War, the image of the African has served as either the opposite of the worthy citizen or the ultimate test case of the nation-state's democratic inclusiveness and egalitarianism. Since the late nineteenth-century apogee of pseudoscientific racism and the early twentieth-century Boasian reaction against it, no institution has been more active in the articulation of these symbolic roles than the university.

The next chapter concerns how black scholars at the HBCUs and the TWIs have debated the meaning of Africa in the global moral hierarchy.

6
Heaven and Hell:
American Africans and the Image of Home

What is Africa to me:
Copper sun or scarlet sea,
Jungle star or jungle track,
Strong bronzed men, or regal black
Women from whose loins I sprang
When the birds of Eden sang?
One three centuries removed
From the scenes his fathers loved,
Spicy grove, cinnamon tree,
What is Africa to me?
. . . .
In an old remembered way
Rain works on me night and day.

Quaint, outlandish heathen gods
Black men fashion out of rods,
Clay, and brittle bits of stone,
In a likeness like their own,
My conversion came high-priced;
I belong to Jesus Christ,
Preacher of humility;
Heathen gods are naught to me.

Father, Son, and Holy Ghost,
So I make an idle boast;
Jesus of the twice-turned cheek,
Lamb of God, although I speak
With my mouth thus, in my heart

> Do I play a double part.
> Ever at Thy glowing altar
> Must my heart grow sick and falter,
> Wishing He I served were black,
> Thinking then it would not lack
> Precedent of pain to guide it,
> Let who would or might deride it;
> Surely then this flesh would know
> Yours had borne a kindred woe.
> Lord, I fashion dark gods, too,
> Daring even to give You
> Dark despairing features where,
> Crowned with dark rebellious hair,
> Patience wavers just so much as
> Mortal grief compels, while touches
> Quick and hot, of anger, rise
> To smitten cheek and weary eyes.
> Lord, forgive me if my need
> Sometimes shapes a human creed.
> COUNTEE CULLEN, "Heritage" (1930)

The poem "Heritage," by Harvard alumnus Countee Cullen, is his most famous. It gives flesh to the dilemmas of a population cast as the symbols of darkness in the domain of European and Euro-American empire. That dilemma is most explicit for the African constituent other living in the belly of the beast, the African American, and his self-positioning in relation to Africa is the key question. Lest we forget, the other great empire of the Eastern Hemisphere—Islam—has been equally involved in the dehumanization of Africa and, amid its own dehumanization by the West (Said 1978), has had an especially difficult time living up to its own antiracist ideals. Today, Africa and her diaspora must look both ways—west and east—to contest our role as the world's constituent other.

Should we aspire to lightness and criticize our own darkness or invest in gods who look like us? Is it possible to make new gods in our own image that are not themselves enslaved by the need to contest and invert Europe's invention of blacks and whites as opposite kinds of people? This chapter articulates not only the African American dilemma but that of the people whom Nigerian American novelist Chimamanda Ngozi Adichie's character Mwombeki calls "American-African" (Adichie 2013a, 141). Mwombeki is Tanzanian and a "double major in engineering and political science" (140) who teaches the protagonist about the two separate organizations on their college campus—one enlisting "our brothers and sisters whose ancestors were slaves" and the other made up of African-born people who, even when they have American accents, typically eat African food at home and are slapped by their parents for getting a C or a B—. This chapter also concerns American Africans' articulation of an amplified dilemma. They are extremely diverse in their origins, natal lifeways, earnings, and reasons for immigration to the United States. However, among all immigrant groups in the United States, Africans are, on average, the most highly educated and the second-highest earning. Yet they come from the poorest continent. And their image is not their own.

Since the late eighteenth century, learned Europeans like Hegel and learned Euro-Americans like Thomas Jefferson have treated the enslaved African as the foil to their own aspirations to freedom and sought to explain why freedom-loving Europeans are still justified in enslaving Africans. American Africans at Howard seek to earn their living and articulate their own retort in the midst of an African American project to do the same. Like the Louisiana Creoles who articulate their collective ambition very differently in African American–dominated and white-dominated settings, so the American Africans at Howard and at TWIs answer their shared dilemma in very different ways.

This chapter, then, is a series of vignettes, a representational strategy motivated by three facts. First, American Africans are extremely diverse. They range from war refugees, famine victims, and Islamist militants to high-ranking professors and the student offspring of industrial magnates. Second, they and their relatives at home are key symbols—positive and negative—in so many peoples' self-understandings. And, third, Africans are the most highly educated of continent-of-origin groups in the United States, requiring me to give ample space to their own "literally-defined world." Overall, the trajectory of this fractal story acknowledges, first, the symbolic hell and, then, the symbolic heaven that American Africans and their interlocutors in the university have conjured out of real, earthly African lives.

This chapter is about the image of Africa in the self-making of not only African immigrants and transmigrants but also a greater circle of the dark and disenfranchised—Afro-Brazilians, Afro-Cubans, Cuban émigrés, African Americans, and immigrants from Guatemala and El Salvador, for whom Washington, DC, is likely to have been the first point of contact with African-inspired lifeways. The African student population in Howard's College of Arts and Sciences has plummeted since the 1980s, and, in inverse proportion, the population of African professors at Howard and African professionals in the DC area—many of them highly educated refugees from the declining fortunes of Nigeria—has skyrocketed. In particular, in 2002, Howard had become the North American headquarters of a Yoruba nationalist movement struggling for democracy in their homeland. At the same time, the West African religions of the Yoruba and Ashanti peoples were the focus of a cultural renaissance richly subsidized, debated, refigured, and canonized in a series of North American universities, especially in traditionally White institutions. This cosmopolitan renaissance has incorporated not just Latino Americans and African Americans but also local Ethiopians and Sudanese, who, before immigrating to the United States, probably had as little exposure to the Yoruba and the Ashanti gods as did the Central Americans. This renaissance is visible in both scholarship and daily life.

Like the ingenious political strategy of a once-discredited politician, Yoruba-Atlantic religion in particular changes the narrative on Blackness. However, like any collective identity, this superethnicity incorporates many of the ideals of the dominant, ethnoracially unmarked group. Moreover, it can be mobilized in projects of ethnic upward mobility within the existing hierarchy, or as a racialized declaration of independence from that hierarchy.

Earth

Africa is, in truth, neither heaven nor hell. Writes Adam Hochschild:

> Africa has too many corrupt statesmen, but such figures blight countries everywhere, from Afghanistan to Belarus. Yes, many African societies are deeply scarred by the heritage of masters and slaves, but so is Russia: some 150 years ago, most people there were serfs. . . . [O]ne would never guess that for all the continent's troubles, democratic elections are today far more common [there] than in the states of former Soviet Central Asia or the Arabian Peninsula. Or that Africa's economic growth has, for more than a decade and a half, been far higher than Europe's. (Hochschild 2012)

Likewise, the African-born population of the United States is full of surprises to those who know Africa through the television imagery of Tarzan movies, *Daktari*, *Mutual of Omaha's Wild Kingdom*, Save the Children, and even Alex Haley's *Roots*.

The third-greatest surprise is the rapidity of the recent growth in their population. By 1990, the 363,819 voluntary twentieth-century African immigrants to the United States were but a tiny percentage of the immigrants to the United States, but they had already exceeded in number the 361,100 Africans who arrived here in chains between 1619 and 1859 (Wish 1941; Eltis 2001; US Census Bureau 1999). Almost as shocking, between 1990 and 2007, the number of African-born people in the United States nearly quadrupled, reaching 1.4 million (Priority Africa Network 2011). Three-quarters have come in the past two decades, and almost half of the African-born population of the United States has entered since 2000. There were nearly 1.5 million of them in 2009 (McCabe 2011). Their leading countries of origin are Nigeria, Ethiopia, Egypt, and Kenya. They are concentrated on the East Coast of the United States, between New York City and Washington, DC, the last being the US metropolitan area with the highest concentration of African immigrants, whether they are measured as a proportion of the metropolitan area's entire population or as a proportion of that metropolitan area's black population. More than a few of them have worked or studied at Howard.

The second-greatest surprise for those of us who grew up on Tarzan movies is that African immigrants are significantly more educated on average than their fellow immigrants. Among the African-born, 47.7 percent have a bachelor's degree or higher, compared with only 26.8 percent of immigrants as a whole and 28.1 percent of native-born people. However, there is great heterogeneity from one national-origin population to another. For example, 60 percent of Nigerians in the United States have a bachelor's degree or higher, but 38.4 percent of Cape Verdeans and 37.5 percent of Somalis lack even a high school diploma. The incomes of African immigrants reflect these educational gaps. Overall, African immigrants are slightly more likely to live in poverty (18.5 percent) than immigrants overall (17.3 percent) and considerably more likely than native-born people (13.6 percent). However, only 10.6 percent of Nigerians in the United States live in poverty, in contrast to 49.9 percent of Somalis (McCabe 2011).

The greatest surprise is that, even though three-quarters of African immigrants reported their race as "Black" in 2009 (McCabe 2011), many of even the phenotypically blackest Africans—that is, southern Nigerians—were initially shocked to learn, upon arrival in the United States, that they are "Black." In Nigeria, it is more commonplace to think about tribe and tribalism than about race and racism. Moreover, especially since the country's oil boom and among the kind of people who emigrate, rapid individual class mobility has been regarded as normal and independent of ethnoracial background. The idea of a skin-color-based, collective struggle for equal opportunity does not immediately strike them as natural or necessary. To an equal and opposite degree, the naturalness and the necessity of this strategy are obvious to most African Americans. The resulting misunderstandings between Nigerians and African Americans are numerous. Relatedly, most Nigerians, Ethiopians, and Eritreans become "African" for the first time when they immigrate to the United States and must both embrace and redefine that category in reaction to Fanon's hierarchy of light to dark. In other words, they face a new struggle of their own.

The stories of Nigerians' first encounters with US racialism are often comical. For example, one Nigerian Igbo professor in Massachusetts told me about the day that his six-year-old son came home from school and announced with pride, "Guess what, Daddy! I'm Black!" The father furled his eyebrows, retracted his chin, and replied, "What is that?" The same professor told me that, during a trip back to Nigeria by another Nigerian American family, their child asked, "Daddy, where are the white people?" An obvious answer might have been: "There are hardly any of them here, so neither they nor their images are important reference points in our self-understanding." But I do not, in truth, know how the other father answered. It must also be said that there is something peculiar in this regard about the Nigerian experience since the oil boom. Kenyans, Zimbabweans, South Africans, Senegalese, and other Africans are still accustomed to a demographically and politically significant white presence in their countries, as well as the light-dark hierarchy, often as a daily reality. American race and racism cannot be as surprising an experience for them as it is for Nigerians.

Having grown up decades after decolonization and the so-called Indigenisation Decree of 1972, most of my Nigerian-diaspora friends report that they had never thought of themselves as "Black" (or "black") until they arrived in the United States or the United Kingdom.[1] That is, they had never thought of their skin color as a distinguishing mark or as the badge of any particular political affiliation, rank, or endogamous social group. During her lecture at Duke University in 2013, Chimamanda Ngozi Adichie, then thirty-six, reported that the first time an African American called her "sister," she thought, "I have three brothers, I know where they all are, and you're not one of them" (Adichie 2013b). And when she wrote a memoir reporting this initial noncognizance of her Blackness, her white editor deemed the claim too implausible to publish. In her brief time in the United States, she realized that she had already absorbed this country's negative stereotypes about Blackness and the sense of many black immigrants that success means moving away from it. She did not say so, but many black immigrants—such as Jamaican immigrant Leonard Bartlett—have mentioned the warnings they received from white people about the importance of avoiding African Americans, on account of our ostensible dangerousness, laziness, or irresponsibility—all linchpins of many white Americans' wishful thinking that their long monopoly on opportunity and power were perfectly fair and reasonable. Few black immigrants recognize the ulterior motive behind such white ethnological schadenfreude, and most ultimately elaborate their own genre of the same. However, after years of reading and experience, Adichie concluded, "I am happy to announce that I am happy to be Black, happy to be a sister."

In the United States, I am as mindful of others' reaction to my skin color as I am unmindful of it in Nigeria. There, I am more frequently judged by my eyeglasses than by the color of my skin. Like me when I first entered the Maret school, new Nigerian arrivals in the United States are shocked that they are not recognized primarily for what they regard as salient about themselves— their high education levels, high incomes, and the excellence of their diction relative to their social peers at home and, in their view, relative to most native-born Americans (see also Adichie 2013a). For such elite black immigrants, the precipitous drop into "Blackness" feels like hell. The reports they make from predominantly white communities and TWIs are particularly anxious.

My wife, Bunmi, is Nigerian. I met her during my first year out of Harvard College, during my stint as a Rotary Scholar at the University of Ibadan. We married eight years later, in 1990. Soon thereafter, I became an assistant professor at Harvard, and we moved to Cambridge. After five years in the shadow of the nation's leading TWIs—one at Princeton and the next four at Harvard—she clearly named her image in even the most enlightened reaches of the white American mind:

> Before my immigration to the United States . . . I was known as a Nigerian of the Yoruba ethnic group. I was also a Western-educated woman with certain privileges and high expectations. Since coming here, though, my identity has changed. I am now an "African woman." My culture, attitude, and experience are presumed to reflect all of Africa, a continent of 55 countries, 400 million people, and thousands of ethnic and linguistic groups. By definition, I am supposed to be poor, uneducated, and ridden with disease. . . .
>
> I grew up in a rural town in Nigeria. We had five primary schools and a high school. There was a post office and a small clinic. All these facilities have since expanded as Nigeria grew rich from its oil. . . .
>
> In high school, we studied Shakespeare, George Eliot, Jonathan Swift, the Brontë sisters, and Charles Dickens. Under British colonial rule, generations of Nigerians studied such writers to the exclusion of African authors. . . .
>
> I can understand the misconceptions of the average person. But in December 1993, Sen. Ernest Hollings (D[emocrat]) of South Carolina, returning from trade talks in Switzerland, jokingly implied that African leaders were cannibals.
>
> I was shocked to read this, not only because of the insult, but also because of what it implied about the great ignorance of the realities of our lives.
>
> Some of the worst riots in Nigeria have their roots in the disparity between the opulent lifestyles of the elite—the privileged diplomats who traveled to Geneva—and the austere lives forced on the rest of the population by the government. While a large percentage of the population is suffering, the elites are

> driving BMWs, Mercedes-Benzes, and Alfa Romeos. Their opulent houses are built with tall fences and staffed with servants, guards, and dogs....
>
> These rulers were the same ones characterized as starving cannibals. This could be said with impunity, because this is what being an African seems to mean in America.
>
> It does not matter that some of these "cannibals" are products of the world's best universities; neither does it seem to matter that they belong to the class that controls and distributes the resources of their countries.
>
> I am beginning to understand the differences between the myth of the African that I am in America and the Nigerian I consider myself to be. I spoke to my first Kenyan and tasted my first dish from Sierra Leone in this country. It was at a dinner given by an American friend who worried all evening that she had not prepared it the authentic way. I doubt I convinced her that I wouldn't know an authentic Sierra Leonean dish from her version. Both were as foreign to my palate as pizza.
>
> Even as I become accustomed to what Americans expect from me—do I know their friend in Mombasa, Kenya? Or perhaps an acquaintance in Ghana?—their stereotype of the silent and voiceless African woman remains alien to me. The women I grew up with were anything but silent.
>
> Yoruba women of southwestern Nigeria have a long history of organization and prosperity. Many of our grandmothers put our parents through college. Many own real estate and farms. They employ workers and commute home at the end of the day in luxury cars after they've closed their shops. In fact, women dominate the retail sector in Nigeria....
>
> To become an African woman is to struggle against the myths and misconceptions of African womanhood. Yes, I am an African, but I am a Nigerian first. That is the only honest claim I can make. I cannot speak for a continent. (Fatoye-Matory 1996)

Identified with a whole continent and its alleged misery, Bunmi has articulated an image of herself that had never been necessary in Nigeria. Africa is the most genetically diverse continent on the planet and one of the most culturally diverse. But by 2010, she says that she had also abandoned the aim implicit in her 1996 article—to change Western minds about Africa. She says that she would rather invest her energies in developing her home region. Disillusioned with the corruption of the Nigerian state, she places both her identity and her hopes for our children not in Nigeria but specifically in Ekiti State, where she says people tend to share the value that she and our family place on education, rather than, for example, on financial wealth. She hopes that Ekiti will become a safe haven, whenever our children need it, against the predations of race in America.

Hell

On Friday, May 17, 2002, my frequent host Daag called to apologize for not having telephoned as promised the previous Sunday. I hadn't called, either. I was too tired and had not grown accustomed to the normalcy of this kind of African in my Afro-Atlantic world. He was a tall and robust Shilluk man from Sudan, a site of racially coded oppression and ethnic proliferation far away from the imagination of most African Americans but strikingly parallel in its ambiguities and ambivalences, poised at the border between two worlds of social classification and stratification. He had failed to call because a Dinka countryman of his—Anyong Kout Deng—had gotten into a fight in an Eritrean-owned bar on Eighteenth Street, where, I later learned, the upstairs was called "Heaven" and the downstairs "Hell." Struck in the head with a bottle by an unidentified fellow black man, Anyong initially survived his struggle between heaven and hell, but the next day he woke up at 2:00 p.m., disoriented and crying for help because of a pain in his head. He was declared dead on arrival at the hospital, from intracranial bleeding. No one around Daag knew the cause of the fight.

In principle, Islam divides the world between believers and unbelievers, regardless of phenotype, and divides the unbelievers into protected and unprotected peoples, the second of which Muslims are free to enslave in the

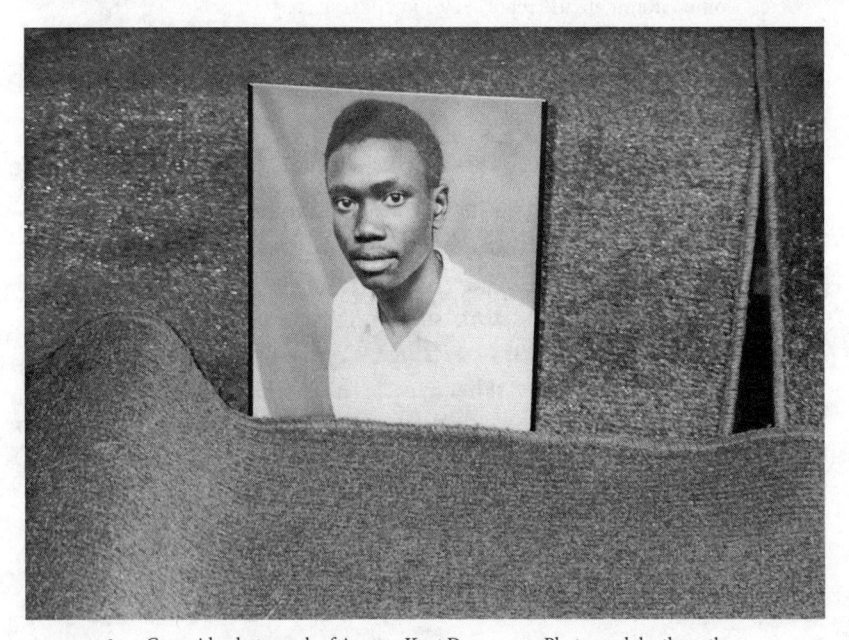

FIGURE 6.1. Graveside photograph of Anyong Kout Deng, 2002. Photograph by the author.

context of war, regardless of their phenotypes. Yet Bernard Lewis (1990) argues that Islam—in contrast to the Roman and Chinese empires—was the first truly global empire, in which radically different-looking types of people were brought together in close, regular interaction. So there was a potential for the emergence of a racial taxonomy, in many ways like the one that began in eighteenth-century Europe, reached its crescendo in nineteenth-century craniometry, and hardly flickered until the Nazis had used it to do their worst.

Moral equality among the believers is a powerful principle in the Islamic world. Yet, like the empires and religions that had preceded it, Islam took for granted the reality of slavery and of male superiority. However, Muslim and non-Muslim historians argue that Islam conferred rights upon slaves and women—and recommended forms of decency in behavior toward them— that were unprecedented. No more than the prior empires and religions did Islam specify the enslavement of any particular racial group or exclude any racial group from enslavement. Rather, all unbelievers were eligible for enslavement and capture, as were the children of Muslim slaves. Dhimmis, or people who agreed to the terms of Islamic rule and who paid the appropriate taxes, were exempted from enslavement as long as they continued to obey the rules laid down for them. These were usually "people of the book"— Christians and Jews. The best-documented forms of Islamic slavery were domestic and commercial (i.e., the enslavement of apprentices and workers in urban homes and businesses). But some enslaved people were soldiers, administrators, and household managers. Many of these were men who had been castrated from an early age.

Despite the egalitarian principles of Islam, there has long been de facto prejudice and differential treatment of people according to their appearance in the Islamic world. According to Lewis, early Islam hosted a discourse of Arab superiority to Persians, Turks, and Slavs. Moreover, *One Thousand and One Nights*, a book of West and South Asian tales first compiled during the Golden Age of Islam, from the eighth century to the twelfth, teems with stories about black slaves and menials cuckolding their masters with the masters' willing wives.

Eve Troutt Powell (2012) documents both the multiracial terrain of slavery and the phenotypical stratification of society generally in the late Ottoman Empire of the nineteenth and early twentieth centuries, as well as their echoes in the twenty-first century. In the nineteenth century, both the Caucasus and Sudan were slave-hunting grounds for the Ottomans. In this empire, Turks dominated Arabs, and elite men favored enslaved concubines from the Caucasus, while enslaved males from the Caucasus were disproportionately assigned to leadership positions. Despite their enslaved status, these Caucasian "Mamluk" soldiers and administrators dominated the indigenous Arab population of northeastern Africa. Enslaved Sudanese and Ethiopians were sometimes powerful but were generally at the bottom of the hierarchy, and their numbers grew sharply as a proportion of the empire's enslaved population over the course of the nineteenth century. During this same century, an Arab bourgeoisie arose in both Egypt and Sudan, eventually leading movements of independence from the Ottomans and the British. Yet they proudly continued the forms of domestic slavery that had characterized the Ottoman aristocracy, often attaching great sentiment to their relationships with the enslaved black concubines and eunuchs who had reared them. Post-nineteenth-century Arabic draws a close association between "black person" and "slave." The term *'abd* means both. This term is hurled contemptuously at Dinka, Shilluk, and other Sudanese war refugees in Cairo—people who fled wars in central and southern Sudan, which were partly motivated and certainly exacerbated by northern Sudanese Arabs' feelings of superiority to their non-Arab or non-Muslim countrymen. Hence, Africa and black Africans have faced hell on both the western and the eastern shores of the continent.

On the western shore, the encounter with Europe has also left the Yoruba, the Igbo, the Ashanti, the Wolof, the Kongo, and their descendants trapped and struggling for rank in a hierarchy of light to dark (Fanon [1952] 2008). In that hierarchy, neither whites nor Blacks are allowed to be completely human. They are represented and compelled to act like the dialectical and pathological creations of each other. Each group is stripped of half of its human qualities by this dialectic, in a process that Fanon calls "double narcissism." Whites declare themselves intellectual and Blacks physical. Whites project what is "dark" in them—sex, aggression, and unvarnished nature—on Blacks and then both fear and crave us. Many whites feel guilty about the oppression of Black people in our soi-disant democracy but must, in order to assuage their consciences, avow that Blacks are animals or, at the very least, people made dangerous by our desire for revenge.

Like Jews and other racially stigmatized peoples, observes Fanon, Black people cannot but see ourselves through white stereotypes, aware that we can always be discredited by one mistake, even when we outperform whites in an overall sense. The struggle is irresolvable, since even the most prodigious efforts at conformity to the white ideal can always be terminated by the sudden uncovering of one's inferior essence. If you give up, you confirm the stereotype, and if you keep trying, you will still ultimately prove the stereotype.

The degree to which this Fanonian model applies to the interaction between Africans and the Islamic world is not clear to me. But Said (1978) identifies what might be called a "double narcissism" between the West and the

Islamic world. And there are signs that Islamic North Africa suffers at the intersection of these two double narcissisms. Once they have sized me up as a sub-Saharan African, which they often do, many Moroccans and Egyptians whom I meet in Europe and the United States announce that they are "African like [me]." Yet the violence inflicted by Libyans and Egyptians upon the black Africans in their midst is astonishing. Amid their own struggles with triple consciousness, depending on the context, the embrace and the expiation of Africa seem equally—and well-precedented—human reactions.

The image of Africa in the African diaspora and in Africa itself is deeply connected to its image in Europe. Africa is the negative pole that Europe and most of the colonized, the formerly colonized, and the formerly enslaved have adopted as their antitype. For example, many black South Africans and Ethiopians define themselves in contrast to, superior to, and not really part of "Africa." But Africa also represents the romance of escape from worn-out Western models, as it did for Picasso and Brancusi. For many African Americans and Afro-Caribbeans in particular, Africa is the source of our shame. But it is also a place where we can imagine that people like us are or were once exempt from the burden of enslavement, colonization, segregation, double narcissism, and the toll they take on the spirit.

During the early twentieth century, after the passing of Booker T. Washington, few, if any, black leaders were more internationally known than African American W. E. B. Du Bois and Jamaican Marcus Garvey. They did not agree about much. However, they did agree that black unity and the uplift of Africa were indispensable preconditions to the redemption of the African diaspora. Africa was the Jerusalem toward which her scattered sons and daughters prayed, but it was also known as the land irredeemably cursed by Ham's indiscretion. Our heaven is also our hell, and the source of our salvation is also our tormentor.

The narrator of African American Countee Cullen's poem—first published as the poet earned his master's degree in English from Harvard—recounts the ambiguous heritage of the colonized and the enslaved. Though "conversion came high-priced," the worship of the white man's god held out a promise. Though unfulfilled, that promise is not forgotten, so it leaves a gaping hole of longing for a black god—not just a black god that preceded white oppression, but one who embodies triumph over white-imposed suffering and self-alienation. It is no stretch to see in this poem a secular meaning as well. The narrator's ambivalent regard of the white god is the obverse side of the embrace and distancing, the communitas and stratification that shape the behavior of the stigmatized toward their own. This ambivalence inspires the invention of new black gods, new fictions of a black idyll in some far-off place to rival the fictions of a white idyll that remains equally inaccessible. The heritage of the stigmatized is precariously bridged between heaven and hell, much like the "Africa" of the popular African-diaspora imagination. "Africa" is both the metonym of militant unity among those who face the stigma of blackness and the worst-case scenario from which we scatter in flight.

American African Schadenfreude and Last-Place Anxiety

It is a reasonable hypothesis that all middling or subordinate populations—and perhaps all proximate groups in a hierarchy—stereotype each other with a fervor that can be explained only by existential fear. But schadenfreude is an especially predictable response to the hell of suddenly being cast into last place. The irony is that Africans, the world's constituent other, immigrate to the United States and, in their new context, find someone else to substitute for them in the role.

Speaking to me as one of her own, one Nigerian pediatrician with a private practice in eastern Massachusetts told me, "The problem with [American] African children is that they identify excessively with African Americans." Her seemingly Olympian superiority complex recalled that of Daniel Patrick Moynihan and of many white Americans who stand in judgment on Black Americans. Indeed, one of her twins is brilliantly accomplished, but the pediatrician herself is twice divorced, the second time violently. Both of her daughters may have prevailed over US racism partly because they bore the parentally instilled psychological armor of believing themselves superior to the conventional victims of white American racism. I do not know what to make of the fact that, while her daughter attended Harvard Medical School, this same pediatrician urged her daughter to use my sister Yvedt—an African American, ironically—as a role model. Thinking of my own repeated misdiagnoses by white physicians at the Harvard University Health Service, who had also witnessed mountains of Black American decency and accomplishment around them, I pitied the African American children this pediatrician may have treated with her quick and stereotypical judgments about what ails them and how they deserved to be treated.

Illustrating the differences between Africans and African Americans, an Eritrean restaurateur on U Street expressed pity for African Americans in general and, demonstrating the nobility of his feeling, told me that he sometimes feeds the African American derelicts who wander into his restaurant. Many Africans feel misrepresented in the US media by the virtually uninterrupted representation of Africa in terms of wild animals, war, famine, dictatorship, and AIDS, and some suspect that this antipodean representation of a whole continent serves a psychological function for Americans. Recalling the fifty-dollar check they once sent to Save the Children, the sort of US Americans who relish this narrative also like to wag their heads and furl their brows in pity for their American African interlocutors, reassuring themselves of their collective white superiority and noblesse. It cannot fit into their mental worlds that the African to whom they are speaking is far wealthier and more highly educated than they. All of this passed through my head as I was addressed similarly by this restaurateur from the Horn of Africa, which is the preeminent source of African refugees from famines, wars, and murderous dictatorships. At such moments, I felt what Bunmi had felt throughout her first five years under the American gaze. People are quick to brand stigmatized populations with pitiful or unflattering generalizations, even when the observed think that the diversity of their coethnics is self-evident.

I heard the "tough love" version of American African schadenfreude from a Nigerian Igbo security guard *on Howard's campus*, who lamented that African Americans "don't value education." In America, he advised, "[A]ll you need to get ahead is education." He seemed unaware of the trend among his own coethnics in Nigeria that might be described identically. School and university attendance have reportedly declined sharply among Igbo males.

Another frequent interlocutor of mine was a Ghanaian security guard at the local CVS pharmacy, who regularly gave me lessons in Twi. He is an Ashanti from Kumasi, but he spoke of having built a big, beautiful house in Takoradi, thus alerting me, in a typically West African cultural idiom, that I should not measure his success by his currently low employment status. This sixty-five-year-old security guard confided that he is frustrated with some of my African American "brothers" who come into the store. One tried to steal about $200 worth of merchandise, he said. While my interlocutor held the thief for the police, he complained, another man just stood there watching. In his view, such thieves—and unhelpful bystanders—should be sent to Ghana or Nigeria. They would not survive, he said. They would be beaten to death or rescued only in the unlikely event that the police arrived in time. "Some of your brothers do not want to work," he concluded, after asking me if I was from the United States. He repeatedly said, "This is a good country. You work hard, you get ahead."

As my son Adu and I emerged from the CVS, we too could see what he saw: an apparently African American junky stood nodding against a light pole. I am certain that my Ghanaian tutor had seen similar sights at the end of many a workday, but unlike my son and me, this elderly Ghanaian sojourner believed that this junky typified—or at least embodied—what is wrong with the African American population as a whole. I, on the other hand, thought of the unwashed and often-unclothed individuals who wander West African marketplaces and sleep by smoldering trash heaps. I did not think it would be useful or logical to give him advice about his Ghanaian "brothers" based upon their example. While I begin with the assumption that my elderly Ghanaian interlocutor is an honest man, I would be as justified in attributing to his society a collective tolerance for bribery and other forms of poverty-generating corruption. Murderous vigilantism against hungry thieves in the market is hardly proof that Ghana provides a suitable moral model for Black America.

As they address me, such interlocutors often ask—with some insistent verbal nudging—whether I am not really from someplace else, my speech and accomplishments providing, in their view, some pretty firm evidence. They smile as though I should feel flattered, welcomed into their brotherhood of non–African American and, therefore, responsible citizenship. Such interlocutors often know my entire family and dozens of similar African American families at Howard. But they have a supraempirical stake in insisting that the junky is more representative of African Americanness than we are.

The stigmatized stratify their own because no one wants to be in last place.

Two of the Nigerian-born Yoruba contributors to *Problematizing Blackness: Self-Ethnographies by Black Immigrants to the United States* (2003) are philosopher Olufẹmi Taiwo and literary scholar Tẹjumọla Ọlaniyan, then professors at Seattle University and the University of Wisconsin at Madison, respectively. They well illustrate the ethnological schadenfreude that is the focus of this book. They are clearly and rightly critical of racism in the United States, one of the most galling aspects of which is the degrading and homogenizing representation of Africa in the US media and popular culture. The defensive response that they document in their "self-ethnographies," however, is premised on an idealized and generalized representation of African life, based upon the selective citation of their own nationality-, ethnicity-, gender-, class-, and age-specific experience, which they contrast with an equally homogenizing, unsubtle, and perhaps unintentionally degrading portrait of African Americans.

This response has much in common with the argument by Yoruba American sociologist Oyeronkẹ Oyewumi, who teaches at Stony Brook University, that, in contrast to Western society, where male-female difference allegedly determines and limits *every* role that a female can play in Western society, Yoruba culture and society are primordially and completely gender-free, such that there are *no* sex-specific role expectations beyond the immediate context of procreation (Oyewumi 1997). In all three of these arguments, the result is often a cartoonish contrast between Africans and Westerners, one that bears the marks of its diasporic origins, where the immigrant speaker must react defensively to the prejudices of the host population and, in making counteractive assertions, counts on the likelihood that the audience knows little or nothing about his or her homeland.

Taiwo (2003) begins by refuting the argument of African American conservative Shelby Steele that, nowadays, African American disadvantage results largely from "race holding"—that is, blaming all of their failures upon racism and, consequently, failing to act like responsible individuals in order the get ahead. Taiwo does not deny that African Americans engage in "race holding" but instead blames African American failings largely on *white American* race holding, which confines all blacks and Blacks to the same ceaseless, narrowly scripted, disadvantaged and race-specific tastes, opportunities, and roles. Whites and Black Americans treat anyone who steps out of these roles as odd and out of place. Even Black Americans demand that recently immigrated blacks join their typecast "army" in the fight against whites, without appreciating that black immigrants, based upon the example of Taiwo himself, grew up middle class and in societies free of racial typecasting. Taiwo repeatedly describes himself as an "individual," because, during his Nigerian upbringing, he performed a varied set of roles irreducible to race:

> All my life in Nigeria, I lived as a Yoruba, a Nigerian, an African, and a human being. I occupied, by turns, several different roles . . . Boy Scout . . . well-read African cultural nationalist . . . member of the Nigerian province of the worldwide communion of the Church of England who remains completely enamored of the well-crafted sermon and of church music, often given to impromptu chanting from memory of whole psalms, the *Te Deum* or the *Nunc Dimittis* . . . student leader of national repute . . . aspiring revolutionary . . . frustrated journalist . . . ardent football player of limited talent . . . budding spiritualist who has since stopped professing faith. (Taiwo 2003:41)

Of course, this is a valid and valuable retort to some unnamed racist's assumption that Taiwo's life was simple and confined to some race-specific or Africa-specific script. But it is also intended to demonstrate the "individuality" that Taiwo regards as a norm in his country, a form of "individuality" that he says contrasts with the "black individuality" that characterizes African Americans. As he defines it, this "black individuality" is not individuality at all; it is actually living one's whole life confined to race-specific and subordinate roles and options, much like Oyewumi's representation of the role of women in Western societies.

This portrait in contrast is shaped by a deliberate *silence* about the powerful and often oppressive forms of typecasting and collectivist ethics that shape identity and opportunity in Nigeria as well. They are less often racial than they are related to ethnicity, class, age, gender, religion, and family obligations and expectations. For example, access to contracts and even to the most basic infrastructural services in Nigeria is filtered through clientelism, ethnic nepotism and exclusion (i.e., "tribalism"), and disproportionate male power in the decision making of the state. Such phenomena indeed contribute to a conditional sort of individuality—that is, a nearly predatory use of state resources by state actors and collusion in such conduct by their citizen clients, all with the consequence of impoverishing the collective in one of the world's greatest oil-producing nations. However, these individually stolen collective resources must be redistributed among extended families and village communities, often under threat of mystical harm.

Taiwo's portrait of his Nigerian "individuality" is shaped by the same "logic of the trial" that drives southeastern Indian, Louisiana Creole, and Caribbean "culture" making. Portraits of the homeland and its "culture" that correct powerful outsiders' devaluation of the spokesperson selectively, strategically, and often fictionally dramatize those ideals of the dominant class that would facilitate opportunity for the spokesperson and then attribute those ideals to the spokesperson's group as a whole. However, Taiwo's selective portrait of opportunity and alleged freedom from collective constraints based upon a person's social category might also result from his taking for granted the privileges enjoyed by people of his particular ethnic group, class, age, gender, religion, and parentage—privileges that the bearers of some other collective identities in Nigeria may not be able to take for granted to the same degree. For example, a problem currently raging in Europe is the suffering of female prostitutes from Nigeria. They and their families, many of them from the Edo-speaking region, see the young women's gendered earning potential in Europe as a valuable source of support for the impoverished family. Many of these women and their families have knowingly agreed to enter into highly coercive, oathbound relationships with sex traffickers. The young women feel a sense of obligation to their families and ambitions that they believe can be fulfilled in this gender-specific way. On the other hand, their families feel a need and consider people of that gender and age suitable fulfillers of that need.

As Oyewumi and many others have correctly pointed out, Yoruba society sharply subordinates younger people to older people. However, contrary to her "either-or" portrait, people's roles—even beyond the moment of procreation—are also profoundly shaped by gender (see J. L. Matory 2003). For example, a woman is treated as a junior to everyone who was born to or married into her husband's family before she married in. She must defer to them. In the 1980s, when my wife, who is Yoruba, first drove her new car through her village, young people exclaimed—"Look, a woman who is like a man!" During the time of my immersion in Nigerian life, people have long spoken of "bottom power," the ways in which women use or must use sexual favors in order to access state financial resources that are accessible to their male counterparts without the requirement of a sexual exchange. Carole Boyce Davies points out that it may be her own class status—as, for example, the daughter of a prominent king—that enabled Oyewumi to underestimate the constraining force of gender in other Yoruba women's lives (J. L. Matory 2003). But it is equally clear that the "logic of the trial" is at work in her portrait of Yoruba society as "genderless." Such ideas are propagated far more credibly in TWIs, where Oyewumi's students and peers have fewer opportunities to evaluate the actual conduct, talk, and in situ reputation of Nigerian (often Yoruba) boyfriends, than at Howard.

In my observation, it is far more difficult for a Yoruba person to think of him- or herself as an individual in relation to the birth family than it is for most English-speaking Americans to do so. Families pressure their offspring to pursue certain careers rather than others, and once those offspring prosper, they are no longer fully free to spend their resources or even to conduct their marital or household affairs independently of the collective judgment or material demands of their birth families. Under pressure from their birth families, people regularly marry or refuse to marry based upon ethnic stereotypes and, among Igbo people, based upon caste.

Taiwo's immigrant representation of African personhood and agency will surprise most anthropological students of sub-Saharan thinking about the person, as well as most Nigerian immigrants, whose families at home feel strongly entitled to the immigrant's income. In the face of demands from brothers, sisters, cousins, nephews, and so forth, the virtue of individual responsibility is not a tenable counterargument. The type-based roles that shape and constrain most Nigerian lives defy Taiwo's repeated assertions of his own individuality. Such roles are evident in the words of Uncle Badejọ's mother on the eve of his departure for the United States: "Remember whose child you are. Do not step outside your proper place in the world." Taiwo may indeed think and act like an individual, unconstrained by the role expectations and prejudices of the Nigerian society in which he grew up, but he is, in that regard, hardly representative of Nigerians, and the sense of individuality that he asserts in the United States is probably not an effect of his Africanness, his Nigerianness, or his Yorubaness. In my observation, for the Yoruba people who want to do so, it is extremely difficult to define one's status, control one's resources, and apportion one's time independently of the demands of one's extended family, one's elders, and one's community. Conversely, these commitments often inspire socially unconstrained conduct in the national sphere and far away from home, resulting in phenomena—ranging from 419 scams to kleptocracy—of which few Nigerian Americans I know are proud. Indeed, most would say that these individualist behaviors violate their "culture."

African Americans may face a different set of dilemmas, but they result in no less complex and mutually contradictory a set of responses. As Mintz and Price ([1976] 1992) point out, there is perhaps no more compelling drive in African American life than the pursuit of individual self-expression in opposition to racist typecasting and confined opportunities. The varied results include some of the most creative and fast-changing expressive musical cultures on the planet, "badness" (i.e., deliberately exaggerated and often death-defying performances of the stereotypes projected onto us) and "John Henryism" (S. James 1994). The failure to perceive such human diversity among the stigmatized results from trained selectivity of perception and contrastive self-aggrandizement, not the rarity or invisibility of any of these phenomena among African Americans.

Ọlaniyan's diagnosis of African American psychopathology rests upon a contrast between Africans as a whole and African Americans as a whole even more cartoonish than Taiwo's. He argues that the reason that Africans and African Americans tend not to get along is that African Americans are—on account of our long experience of racism and of being outnumbered—unassertive, complacent, and deferential to whites.

By contrast, he says that Africans, who have grown up in predominantly black societies and have a "pragmatic" attitude toward the state, are essentially assertive. He gives the example that, even as an assistant professor in a TWI, he behaved with the confidence of a higher-ranking professor. This example surprised me because of the extreme importance that most Yoruba people in Nigeria, even in the setting of the university, attach to seniority. For example, at the University of Ibadan, between the 1980s and the present century, I have observed a norm of extreme deference by junior to senior professors, including bowing and enormous attention to whether a professor should be addressed as "Doctor," indicating a junior status, or "Professor," indicating a senior status. So intense is many Yoruba people's concern with seniority that a Yoruba professor who joined the Harvard faculty in the early 2000s bawled me out for addressing him by his first name. At the time, he was a newcomer to my institution, and both of us were full professors. However, he is some fifteen years my senior, and despite the fact that we met in the context of a US university where even the most junior lecturer typically calls a full professor by his or her first name, he apparently considers me Yoruba because of my marriage to a Yoruba woman and my long immersion in his

Nigerian networks. (By contrast, I considered him to be the one entering into *my* networks.) I do not recognize the Nigerian or Yoruba cultural precedents that Olaniyan identifies as the source of his confidence in violating seniority-based forms of social intercourse. However, there would be nothing intrinsically non-Nigerian or non-Yoruba about a person behaving as Olaniyan says that he behaved at Madison. Rather, most Yoruba people I know would recognize the ignoring of seniority as a shameless violation of local "cultural" ideals, the likes of which happen in every society all the time. In Yoruba, such bold defiance of recognized norms is called ṣakará. To declare abroad that such behavior would be normal in Nigeria—and even behaving that way in a US university department—might be described as further instances of ṣakará.

Equally surprising is Olaniyan's extraordinary unawareness, or self-flattering denial, of the coordinated African American self-assertion that has transformed US democracy over the past century and a half and made the flood African immigration possible. Olaniyan's observations about African American professors at the University of Wisconsin at Madison are quite different from my observations of their counterparts at Harvard, where, through excellent scholarship and bold strategy, African Americans have built one of the richest and most powerful departments on any US college campus. African American professors there—including Cornell West, Henry Louis Gates Jr., Peter Gomes, and I—were among the most outspoken professors on campus, and not just on issues of race. At Duke, African American professors are anything but deferential to whites. Indeed, we are found at virtually every level of the administrative hierarchy, and, for better or worse, at least two of us reportedly shout in the faces of our white colleagues and senior administrators regularly, though most of us would never do so. Even if Olaniyan is correct about his University of Wisconsin colleagues, his quickness to generalize, like that of anyone engaged in ethnological or racial schadenfreude, appears to flow less from a project of careful observation than from a project of self-promotion in a setting of racial hierarchy.

What I also wish to highlight in Taiwo's and Olaniyan's contrastive representations of African and African American conduct is not just their supraempirical content but also their striking—but not absolute—contrast to the representations of black self and black other that I heard in the self-presentations of my three fathers. Both Taiwo and Olaniyan know me, my wife is close friends with Taiwo, and Taiwo seems to know a great deal about Skip Gates's academic leadership. These could hardly be the limits of their knowledge to the contrary, but Taiwo's and Olaniyan's most thoughtful moments of public self-construction seem to reduce the great diversity of African American character and accomplishment to an antitype of their own aspirations. Perhaps Taiwo's and Ọlaniyan's self-ethnographies are signs of the times, an era different in both demography and ethos from the days of my three fathers. But the sort of ethnological schadenfreude these self-ethnographies represent is hardly unprecedented or unique to black America.

In Nigeria, the Nigerian diaspora, and native Black American alike, the dynamics of individualism and collectivism are considerably more complex than Taiwo allows. For example, immigration and the struggle of immigrants to evade the exorbitant demands for remittances entail a process of individualization, and this process is compounded by the experience of being an "exotic" (Manyika 2003, 74–75) or middle-class black. And, as Wright and others (Wright 1997; Wright, Taylor, and Moghaddam 1990) have pointed out, any degree of openness in the dominant group to upward mobility by the stigmatized greatly encourages individual striving. Such tokenism stabilizes existing social hierarchies that still rest on unequal opportunities for different population groups. By contrast, the virtually complete closure of the elite ranks to the disadvantaged (the likes of which preceded the civil rights movement and decolonization) encourages collective action against the system. Such collective action also peaks when some members of the disadvantaged group find the courage to announce their experience of discrimination and express anger about it. Not all situations are equally favorable to such announcements. One way of discouraging dissent among the discredited is promoting a token of the sort that African Americans call the "HNIC," the "head nigger in charge." When one of our own has been appointed by the powerful to represent or govern us, most of us do not want to embarrass him by complaining. Delighted by his own power, he is often even less constrained in his cruelty and less responsive to the hardships of the subordinated than the head white man had been. Such dynamics are as real in Yoruba as in African American life. Moreover, personal idiosyncrasy and diversity of interests are common in both populations.

Moreover, Taiwo's and Ọlaniyan's accounts assume the hyperreal infallibility of white values and performances. Taiwo appropriates the oft-stated white American ideal of "individualism," taking it for granted as an accurate description of white American conduct and as a value system morally preferable to collectivism. For his part, Ọlaniyan (2003, 60) says that a source of great antagonism between himself and African Americans is that Black Americans as a whole are worse at understanding his accent and pronouncing his name than are white Americans as a whole. Yet most of the African American examples he gives are "middle school kids," servers at "Burger King or McDonald's," and clients at the legal aid clinic where his wife works. As a professor in one of the finest African studies programs in the country, Ọlaniyan would certainly encounter a disproportionate number of whites who are more than casually acquainted with African languages and with the decoding of African orthographies, which is hardly a representative sample of white Americans.

The sample available to my wife and me is hardly unbiased, either, but in our East Coast environs, we have noticed no difference between white and Black Americans' competency at understanding Nigerian speech or reproducing Nigerian names. In fact, in our environment, we have greater occasion to speak of the frequency with which African Americans not only pronounce but adopt African names. And although Ọlaniyan is surely aware of the highly popular Afrocentrism movement, he believes that African Americans in general think negatively about Africa and avoid identifying with it (2003, 61–62). What I perceive in Black America is mainly a widespread and growing but romantic identification with Africa. There is clearly deep ambivalence among African Americans about Africa: to us, it is both heaven and hell. Ọlaniyan is not the only Nigerian, however, who fails to notice the frequency with which African Americans worship Africa, particularly Yoruba culture, partly because the "Africa" that we tend to worship is either unrecognizable or odious to these Nigerians themselves. It is a pagan, oppositional Africa—almost the opposite of the urban, Western-educated Africa that produced the Yoruba American professoriate and of the ideal Africa pursued by their Pentecostalized countrymen. In other words, African immigrants and their urban peers "back home" also tend to feel deeply ambivalent about Africa as well. The ideal to which they aspire and according to which they find African Americans wanting is a hyperreal white America, whose real-world imperfections have been erased.

The rise of anti–African American identity among American Africans coincides with the rise in the number of black immigrants who have come to stay. Particularly among Nigerian immigrants and professors, the prospect of returning permanently to a viable homeland has, to a great extent, died. A series of northern, non-Yoruba-dominated dictatorships starved the universities and presided over the cancerous growth of kleptocracy, a decline in health care, and an epidemic of home invasions, in which armed robbers break down the walls of elite homes and, while holding the homeowners at gunpoint, clear out all of the valuables. Taiwo and Ọlaniyan illustrate the process of ethnogenesis in a time when a previously temporary migrant population has sunk roots in North America. Under these conditions, many highly accomplished African Americans and highly accomplished American Africans have become proximate rivals, rather than the long-distance cheerleaders and role models that they were for each other in my fathers' day.

For prosperous immigrants who can afford to travel home often, these roots do not necessarily mean that ties with the homeland are cut. Prosperous transnationals can afford to take advantage of the structural conditions of life in the home country and the country of origin—for example, sending unruly children "back home" when necessary for schooling and discipline (Shani 2013). But in their family decision making, such transnational migrants are highly aware of the limited opportunities, social complications, and disconcerting value orientations found in both the homeland and the host society. Stories of perfection and of a superior culture "back home" are fictional and strategic, though the effective performance of ethnological schadenfreude relies on forgetfulness about this fact.

While these narratives of immigrant cultural superiority focus on native Black incompetency or incapacity, they occur against the backdrop of competition from highly competent and powerful African Americans at every professional level. While some down-on-their-luck Yoruba immigrants gratefully report the generosity and kindness of African Americans toward them, more such immigrants report cases in which African Americans in predominantly white settings "played the native game" and intervened to close an opportunity that the black immigrant deserved. Others simply report sadness about how difficult it has been to make African American friends. Ethnological schadenfreude can express last-place anxiety, the consciousness of a formidable rival, or a disappointment over the failure of an expected solidarity.

A Way Out

With their high concentration of African immigrants, Washington, DC, and Howard University host another genre of thinking about individualism, collectivism, and the alternatives to hell. This genre critically addresses the conditions of home and of the diaspora. It is both reflective and activist, eschewing idealism about the homeland. The following vignette examines another Yoruba philosopher's take on "culture," one articulated in the very different setting of its genesis—historically Black Howard University and Washington, DC.

Changes in the population of Nigerians at Howard have followed the changes in Nigeria's political and economic fortunes. Our oil crisis of 1973 and 1974, when US Americans lined up for gas, was for Nigerians an oil boom, which funded the studies of thousands of Nigerian students in the United States. They were expected to return home eventually, but the ultimate story is more complicated. They brought with them both government money and national pride, which, in addition to their intelligence, greatly impressed their peers at Howard. More than a decade after the oil boom/crisis, the African-born outnumbered the Caribbean-born students, a situation that has reversed since then. In 1987–88, 41.6 percent, or 839, of Howard's international students came from Africa, and the plurality of these from Nigeria. Only 36 percent, or 760, of the international students then came from the nearby Caribbean region (Diallo 1989; Feinberg 1988). One of the reasons that certain black immigrant populations, on average, perform well economically is that many members of those populations have come to the United States specifically in order to seek education and have remained after graduation.

The number of African-born students in Howard's College of Arts and Sciences fell with the decline of oil prices, but the massive theft of public resources by Nigerian military dictators and other public officials, the decline of Nigerian secondary education, and the post-1989 tuition surcharge also took their toll. In 2002, the spring party of the Howard University African Students Association was virtually empty, the small crowd dwarfed by the cavernous ballroom of the Blackburn Center. Most guests were supporters from the Caribbean Students Association. Adding insult to injury, the deejay was reportedly forced by complaints to reduce the amount of African music played.

By contrast, the generation of Nigerians who benefited from government-funded educations and were pushed out of Nigeria by crime and the northern military dictators' strangulation of the universities has become a significant presence at Howard and in DC's professional class. Their American-born children are an equally significant presence in elite TWIs and in the professional schools at Howard. In 2002, the annual convention of the North American chapter of the Ẹgbẹ́ Ọmọ Odùduà—a Yoruba nationalist organization—filled the Blackburn Center auditorium from wall to wall.

This organization was founded in the 1940s by Nigerian independence leader Ọbafẹmi Awolọwọ before he and his diasporic companions returned from England to lead Nigeria into independent nationhood. In Yoruba, its name means "The Club of Odudua's Children" and refers to the mythical first king and progenitor of all of the Yoruba monarchies and subethnic groups. Called "Odua" in Cuba, he is also one of the highest gods in the Afro-Cuban pantheon. The lead branch of this organization, Ẹgbẹ́ Ìṣọ̀kan Yorùbá—or Club of Yoruba Unity—is located in Washington, DC.

During my 2002 sojourn at Howard, the Washington-area branch led the US American diaspora of this Nigerian ethnic group in its Yoruba-nationalist struggle. The club fought against the northern Nigerian-, Muslim-, and Hausa-dominated military's rapacious grip on the state and against what many Yoruba people, from the south, regarded as the proclivity of this northern class to murder the opposition, including Nigeria's democratically Yoruba president-elect, Moshood Abiọla, in 1998. The meetings of the Washington branch alternated between the auditorium of Howard's School of Engineering and that of the University of the District of Columbia, on upper Connecticut Avenue. I often attended on- and off-campus meetings with Nigerian Yoruba professors, several of them major leaders of Ẹgbẹ́ Ọmọ Odùduà.

Candidates in Nigerian elections came to Washington and attended these meetings in order to solicit the club's endorsement, and the club sent delegates to Yorubaland to broker alliances among the diverse political organizations at home, such as the Odudua People's Congress, Afẹ́nifẹ́re (We Want What Is Good for People), Ẹgbẹ́ Ọmọ Odùduà, the Odudua Group, and so forth. These groups unite Christian and Muslim Yoruba people, and they advocate for the security, political unity, and self-determination of Yorubaland. However, virtually all of the meetings that I attended began and ended with Christian prayers. Ẹgbẹ́ Ìṣọ̀kan Yorùbá sponsored a Saturday-morning Yoruba-language class on the Howard campus for the children of members. Like many immigrant and transmigrant communities, these Yoruba organizers are focused on the finances of their transnational families and on the politics of the homeland. However, a sense of ongoing turmoil and ethnic grievance in their homeland made Yoruba intellectuals even more attentive to these issues than most immigrant ethnic groups.

It was not in Ibadan or Igboho (where I spent several years of study and field research in Nigeria) but in Washington that I first encountered the national flag of the Yoruba nation and the Yoruba anthem, which was sung at the beginning and end of every meeting.

Red, black, and green (after the colors of Marcus Garvey's Black nationalist flag), the Yoruba national flag bore at its center an image of the world-famous bronze bust, apparently representing a monarch, excavated in the early twentieth century by German art historian Leo Frobenius and accessioned by the British Museum.

I was connected to this crowd of highly educated Nigerians at multiple levels, as my parents had been introduced to each other by a Yoruba man—Uncle Badejọ—who had attended college with both of my parents and medical school with my father. I was also connected to them through my wife, who was active in the diasporic opposition to General Sani Abacha, a northern, Kanuri man who was then the military ruler of Nigeria. At the multiple meetings, the club would call together, from the entire mid-Atlantic seaboard, the most highly educated sector of the global Nigerian community. They planned their peaceful strategies against not only their northern Nigerian oppressors but also their Yoruba compatriots who, for better or worse, failed to defend the rights of their coethnics. Amid the latter challenge, graft was the suspected cause of much disloyalty.

FIGURE 6.2. The 2002 annual convention of the North American chapter of the Yoruba nationalist organization Ẹgbẹ́ Ọmọ Odùduà, held at Howard University's Blackburn Auditorium. Note the Yoruba national flag on the banner. It is a recent invention. Photograph by the author.

I was also connected to them by the fact that the president of Ẹgbẹ́ Ọmọ Odùduà at the time had grown up near Igboho, in Ọ̀yọ́ North, where I had conducted my predissertation field research. And as if that were not enough, I had administered the Yoruba-language competency test—in fulfillment of the university's foreign-language requirement—to his daughter at Harvard. This international leader of Yoruba politics and culture was also the chair of the Philosophy Department at Howard. Though he led an organization concerned largely, at that time, with ethnic autonomy at home, the greater part of his scholarly opus is devoted to pondering the possible terms of African and Black unity. He combines a vision of "traditional" African religion as heritage with an unabashed modern secularism rare among his followers. Nonetheless, his publications might profitably be read against the backdrop of his changing political projects—first in Nigeria and then in the United States.

I offer this account of our multiple layers of connection for two reasons. First, it gives flesh to the argument that "culture" and ethnicity unfold in cosmopolitan settings. Second, it offers a further counterpoint to the premise of Taiwo's autoethnography (that African Americans are more parochial than he is) and Ọlaniyan's autoethnographic report of social isolation between African Americans and American Africans). Ours is elite company, to be sure. But their experience of the intersection between African American and American African lives is no more representative than mine. Perhaps the difference between Taiwo and Ọlaniyan, on the one hand, and the Yoruba Howard philosopher and me, on the other, is the length of our exposure to the HBCU.

Our Howard colleague's first book, published while he was on the faculty of a prestigious Nigerian university, was an effort, after the fashion of British empiricism, to systematize the African conceptions of the person, destiny, and ethics through the analysis of the Nigerian Yoruba and Ghanaian Twi languages and of the related precolonial religious practices. The former happens also to be, in principle, the sacred language of Cuban-inspired Ocha and of African American Yoruba religion, while the latter is the sacred language of African American practitioners of Akan religion. The best-known African speakers of the Akan language group are of the Ashanti ethnic group in Ghana. His book and its title are intended to reconstruct the shared features of an "ultimate reality and meaning" that characterize "the Yoruba conception" of the world and, by extension, the African conception generally. In this philosopher's work, influences from Arab and Hausa cultures are treated as authentic, while Western influences are excluded as exogenous.

Ironically, the exemplars of African culture invoked by African American and Yoruba ethnicity entrepreneurs, like those employed in Lorenzo Dow Turner's research on the roots of Gullah/Geechee language, are selected from the catalogs of anglophone scholarship and mediated by the anglophone university system. Both colonized chiefly by the British and both, like the British, royalist in their forms of government, the Yoruba and the Akan play starring roles in the English-language ethnography and in the collections of the British Museum. The elevation and the pairing of the Yoruba and the Akan in university African and African-diaspora identity making are, in sum, tandem results of British imperialism. The Yoruba and the Akan are now authoritative references in the anglophone African and African-diaspora cultural nationalisms that have taken shape in Howard's shadow. There is nothing natural about such "syncretic" culture making, either.

The second half of this Yoruba American philosopher's book addresses the "contemporary African realities" that, in the professor's view, an authentically African "ultimate reality and meaning" must be mobilized to improve. He blames bourgeois Africans' selfish appropriation of their nations' wealth on a Western-style materialism that defies the authentically African premises of communalism and egalitarianism. He regards Africans of diverse ethnic groups as fundamentally alike with respect to this system of "ultimate reality and meaning" and therefore regards ethnicity itself as a smokescreen thrown up by the bourgeoisie in order to draw the people's attention away from the bourgeoisie's theft of the African nations' communal wealth. Following

Fanon, he regards culture as inherently dynamic and generated by collective struggle, rather than a thing of the past that justifies its own static retention. The upshot of this philosophical argument is that all Nigerians must unite in the service of national unity, self-determination, and communal uplift. The author is preoccupied ultimately with saving Nigeria and Africa from the exogenous values that have made Africans divide themselves up ethnically and destroy their own continent. In sum, while working and living in Africa, this professor retooled the religious ethnography of the British imperialists in the service of pan-Africanism and a critique of contemporary African class hierarchies.

After a series of brief appointments at predominantly white universities and colleges in the United States, this professor received a senior and tenured appointment at Howard. At the time that I knew him, his activism remained centered on fixing Nigeria, though the fix seemed to focus less on pan-Africanism than on the Nigerian dictatorship's unfairness to Yoruba people in particular and on the consequent need for Yoruba autonomy.

At the same time that his political activism sought to divide Nigeria into ethnic parts, his scholarship rationalized an expansion of his pan-Africanist program to the African diaspora. The prior emphasis of his opus—on the unity of diverse African and Nigerian ethnic groups—gave way to a focus on the unity of Africa with its diaspora. Once at Howard, his academic publications came to focus consistently on issues affecting Africans and African-diaspora people alike, such as sickle-cell anemia (a perennial focus of scientific and clinical work in Howard's medical complex), the compatibility of pan-African solidarity and antiracism, and the "kinship" among the intellectual heroes of Africa, the Caribbean, and the Black United States. He addresses and refutes the position of another African philosopher that "African continental elites" who visit the West have an experience and political interests entirely different from those of "the diaspora African." Their shared interests become obvious, argues the Howard philosopher, when those "African continental elites"—like this professor himself—come to the West and are forced to ask, "Why should I be treated this way?"

Thus, even the work of university scholars illustrates the contextuality of ethnic identity and of its performance. But the African scholar at the HBCU is, in fact, in two places at once. On the one hand, he is conscious of the realpolitik of interethnic division and hierarchy at home, and he longs for his own ethnic group to be free of domination by others. On the other, he is in the United States, where Hausa, Yoruba, and African Americans are all vulnerable to being "treated this way." He is at once in the diaspora, far away from the country of his birth and longing for its well-being, and in Black

America, a place of unavoidable stigma, misrecognition, and ultimately common struggle, a place where a common "culture" and reason for cooperation are not given but must dynamically and creatively be established. In his opus, indigenous religion is an ideal vector of both sentiments. Odudua, for example, is at once a symbol of Yoruba nationalism, transcending the Christian/Muslim divide in Nigeria, and a god in the sub-Saharan African religion with the most globally dispersed adherents. Treated as a secular hero, this god gives his name to the organization that this philosopher led, Ẹgbẹ́ Ọmọ Odùduà—the Association of Odudua's Children.

Yet the Yoruba scholars I met at Howard seemed unaware of the fervor of many African-diaspora people's pursuit of redemption through Africa and, particularly, through Yoruba "culture" and identity, which have now become an alternative standard of dignity and virtue for millions at the dark end of the global hierarchy.

For example, Ethiopian and ethnic Amhara Haile Gerima is legendary in the pan-African arts community for his film *Sankofa* (1993), which arguably clothes Gerima's own northeast African struggles for African-descended people's dignity in the attire of Yoruba, Akan, and, in sum, "black Atlantic" spirituality—the same cultural foundations articulated by the head of Ẹgbẹ́ Ọmọ Odùduà. However, Gerima does so with a more explicit awareness of his popular counterparts. Though I interviewed him at his film studio, just across and a block up Georgia Avenue from Howard, I did not ask him about his films. I simply told him of my interest in black ethnic diversity at Howard. It was not difficult to perceive the connection between his filmic vindication of Black collective pride and the autobiographical story that he spontaneously offered. He told me that, while his parents approved of his marriage to his classy African American bride, some of his countrymen did not. They complained, "Ah, he married a Negro [*baria*]," a term that these fellow Amharas, says Gerima, falsely conflate with "slave" and use to describe both darker-skinned Ethiopians and African Americans of any shade, much as many Arabs use the term '*abd* for both "slave" and "black people."[2]

In support of Gerima's observation, a Sudanese colleague told me that, during a visit to New York, the wife of Emperor Haile Selassie—himself an Amhara descended from another Ethiopian ethnic group, the Oromos—was once asked about the size of Ethiopia's population. When she replied, "About 5,000," the journalist replied with incredulity. She was then forced to acknowledge that the country was actually home to tens of millions, but "that's only if you count the Negroes." Yet, Gerima told me, even the phenotypically blackest of Ethiopians will say of him, "'Oh, he's married to a black woman,' as if she [the speaker] herself weren't black." Gerima seems to hint at the use of color references in women's competition for desirable mates.

He went on to add that, if he had married a Somali speaker—though also an occasional referent of the ethnonym "Habesha"—such critics would have said, "He married a nomad [*zel'lan*]," implying that she is uncivilized and derived from a people lacking a constitution and historical continuity. If he had married a Nigerian, they would have said, "He married an African." For Ethiopians, Africa is a "symbol of crucifixion, demonized." He observes that black South Africans similarly demonize other Africans and that, in the past, African Americans, too, used the term "African" as an expletive intended to terrorize the African-looking members of their own community. When African American freedmen founded Liberia in the mid-nineteenth century, they treated the Africans whose land they colonized with violence and contempt.

Although the Afrocentric movement of the 1980s greatly diminished it, this phenomenon is not dead. Gerima's testimony illustrates the imagination and creativity with which the stigmatized "stratify their own." They are highly aware of the alleged characteristics that stigmatize them all in the eyes of the dominant, ethnically unmarked audience, and they are anxious to distinguish themselves from populations that can be represented as more fully embodying those traits. Marx's anti-Semitic and anti-African tirade against Ferdinand Lassalle (Sperber 2013, 411) is another vivid example. This zero-sum flight from dishonor is the hell in which the stigmatized live their daily lives.

Yet symbolic inversion is an equally available and tempting reaction to stigma. For example, when they celebrate their historic expulsion of the invading Italians in the early 1940s, Ethiopians describe their nation as "the Black Lion" and declare metaphorically, "The black snake will kill you more surely than the white snake." Though it is sometimes derogatory, Gerima regards the term for "black" in this context, *tukwur*, as an indication of a chink in Ethiopia's otherwise anti-Negro ethos, a symbol of Ethiopia's African pride in having resisted white conquest. Such an interpretation accords with the motivation behind African Americans' vociferous devotion to the Ethiopian cause during that period. As in Latin America, so at these other cultural crossroads, references to blackness can justify the egalitarian embrace of one's oppressed fellows or, alternatively, a distancing from those who seem, on racial grounds, to deserve their oppression and marginalization more than the speaker does. One might add that, in 1963, Ethiopia hosted the founding of the Organisation of African Unity in Addis Ababa.

However, an Ethiopian student of mine at Duke and her parents view the matter differently. They emphasize that no Ethiopian would call him- or herself *tukwur*. For them, the more common symbolic inversion of Western assumptions is embedded in the following tale. My student told me,

> [M]any Ethiopians, particularly those immigrants of the royal or aristocratic families, would not only consider themselves as better than other Blacks and Africans, but Whites as well. Here, I would like to mention an old and very racist joke told by Ethiopians that goes as follows: God was cooking bread. The first batch he undercooked and threw it into Europe. The second batch he burned and placed it in West Africa. Finally, the third batch was just right and God placed it in Ethiopia. (student e-mail, December 2, 2013)

Outside of the context of its telling, it is difficult to interpret the implications of this tale. Whether it demonstrates that Ethiopians feel superior to whites and to blacks or instantiates how the stigmatized deflect dishonor onto both the constituent other and the normally unmarked, dominant party, it amplifies our grasp of how the stigmatized stratify their own. In any case, my student added that those young Ethiopian Americans who have heard it feel ashamed of the sentiments expressed in this tale.

In the end, Gerima seems to have regretted his candor. After our interview, he privately told my African American research assistant that he thought my project on black ethnic diversity was divisive. There is no point in highlighting interethnic conflict among African and African-descended peoples, which he mistakenly thought was my goal, when, in his view, "We Ethiopians don't even like each other." Every African people on the planet is, at this historical juncture, suspended painfully between the hope of its own sense of dignity and humanity and the hell of black people's collective symbolic role in the global self-aggrandizement of the white race.

Gerima's master work is as much an act of culture making as are Olaniyan's and Taiwo's "self-ethnographies." Yet rather than stratifying the stigmatized, he selectively highlights potential idioms of Black unity in Habesha culture, married an African American, and employs Afro-Atlantic religion as an allegory of Black unity, both naturalizing his marriage and denaturalizing the forms of ethnological schadenfreude that are common in northeast Africa. Plutarch's style of syncretism is no less plausible a strategy of culture making than is schadenfreude.

Gerima's widely celebrated film *Sankofa* (1993) tells the story of an alienated African American fashion model's surreal rediscovery of her West African past and of her power to overthrow racist oppression and its religious vehicle—Christianity. During her mystical journey into the slavery-ridden past, she is led by a fellow slave called Shango, who shares his name with the famous Yoruba-Atlantic god of lightning, royalty, and justice. The film's title refers to an ideograph used in the Adinkra funerary cloth of Ghana's Akan peoples, another African ethnic group celebrated by the British for their royal traditions and, in the influential Boasian and Herskovitsian ethnography, falsely but influentially canonized, along with the Yoruba and the Fon, as the chief demographic and cultural roots of black American civilization. The ideograph represents a mythical bird that looks backward while flying forward, serving as a visual proverb that reminds its viewers and wearers always to learn from the past. The eponymous film is perhaps the most celebrated and widely cited artistic expression of pan-Africanism of all time.

Heaven

A range of Howard intellectuals and activists have embraced Booker T. Washington's, Du Bois's, and Garvey's secular logic that redeeming Africa is a precondition to the redemption of the African diaspora as well. The will to unity among the stigmatized is exceptional but is commonest in the elite ranks of the stigmatized, whose lives are more dominated by immediate competition with the nonstigmatized than by immediate competition with other members of the stigmatized group. By speaking with authority about the unity of the stigmatized group, that elite reifies and dignifies a large constituency and burnishes its authority to speak for that constituency. The will to unity is least likely to appear where stigmatized populations with similar occupational skills and skill levels live and work near each other and therefore compete for the same limited resources, opportunities, and honors. Most real-world settings of avant-garde ethnogenesis combine such incentives for cooperation and competition among the stigmatized.

Low-ranking people also often take pride in the accomplishments of similar-looking people at high ranks and are willing to overlook ethnic or other hereditary differences. Sometimes they anticipate a broader trickle-down of resources, as when my father endorsed the priority given to light-skinned Howardites in the earliest assignments to medical residences at TWIs. And sometimes the common interests of the stigmatized loom larger than their differences of interest, as when the majority of Latinos, Asians and, very likely, American Indians voted for President Obama in 2007 and 2011.

However, this research has taught me that unity among the stigmatized is not a default. Rather, it is a project. Here I will discuss several Black projects of interethnic unity, advancing the hypothesis that the chief de facto index of ethnic unity is not "cultural" unanimity or political consensus but a place at the table where the diacritica of group membership are debated before an implicitly present white, or ethnoracially unmarked, audience. Any given declaration of a single correct "cultural" norm of group membership or behavior is an interested and competitive assertion of authority over the constituency, which is bound to be contested by rival claimants to speak for the group. And vigorous debate is perhaps the most important proof and realization of collective identity.

Historically, Howard has hosted great advocates for and connoisseurs of Africa. For example, in 1928 Harvard PhD and US diplomat Ralph Bunche founded Howard's Department of Political Science. Initially interested in comparing Brazilian and US race relations, he ultimately wrote a prize-winning Harvard dissertation on French colonial administration in Togoland (which is now called simply Togo) and Dahomey (now called Benin Republic). He did so at a time before anthropologist Melville J. Herskovits had reportedly made it difficult for African Americans, including Caribbean American Elliot Skinner, to conduct research in Africa. Bunche is most famous for winning the Nobel Peace Prize, which he received for negotiating an armistice between Israel and the Arab states in 1949. (Again, I shake my head in wonder at the usual black ethnic postulate that African Americans are lazy, parochial, unassertive, and unaccomplished.)

Bunche was also a fiery critic of colonialism in Africa. In an article derived from his dissertation, he wrote, "This great continent and its sweltering population are mere sacrific[i]al offerings on the altar of world imperialism" (Regents of University of California [2004] 2005). Elsewhere, he articulated his faith in Western education as the solution to African problems, though he could just as well have been speaking about the aspirations of Howard University for all Black people. He wrote, "When the natives acquire more educ[ation] in Western methods & a greater understanding of their latent powers, they should be able to wrench control of their country from the ruthless & greedy hands of the white exploiters. That day may not be as far distant as some imperialistic nations like to think". Indeed, Bunche taught at Howard under the university's first Black president, Mordecai Johnson. In Bunche's honor, Howard established the Ralph J. Bunche International Affairs Center in 1993.

Graham-cracker-colored himself, Bunche spoke of his white-looking and formerly enslaved grandmother much as he could have spoken of that Black president, who made a similar choice amid the heaven and hell of race in the Atlantic world. Like Johnson, Bunche's grandmother appeared Caucasian "on the outside," said Bunche, but she was "all black fervor inside" ("Ralph Bunche—Biographical").

At Howard, other leaders with multiple identity choices also chose unity with the stigmatized, making Africa the touchstone of that unity. For example, Trinidadian-born and Harlem-raised, the late Howard alumnus Stokely Carmichael is most famous for having popularized the slogan "Black Power." After moving to Guinea-Conakry in 1969, he changed his name to Kwame Turé—in honor of his pan-Africanist benefactors President Sékou Touré of Guinea-Conakry and President Kwame Nkrumah of Ghana. However, he frequently returned to the United States as the spokesman for the All-African People's Revolutionary Party, founded by Nkrumah. For years, he led the African Liberation Day rally every summer in Washington's Malcolm X Park—in the shadow of Howard's Meridian Hill Apartments dormitory, where my aunt Arnzie had lived. As a teenager, I often sat alongside the park's sculpted shrubbery, cascading fountains, streamers of incense, and a sea of African-clad Black Americans, absorbing Turé's rhythmic exhortations to transnational Black unity and "scientific socialism." It was here that my long-distance love for African animals, clothing, and art (a received combination that I only later recognized as problematic) morphed into a political pan-Africanism, which I preached to anyone who would listen, including my white classmates at Maret.

Others have revalorized their ancestral connection to Africa through genetics. Until recently, Dr. Rick Kittles was the director of the Molecular Genetics Unit at the Howard-based National Human Genome Center. The vision statement of the center is nonreductive and intellectually sound:

> The National Human Genome Center at Howard University is a comprehensive resource center for genomic research on African Americans and other African Diasporic populations, distinguished by a diverse social context for framing biology as well as the ethical, legal, and social implications of knowledge gained from the human genome project and research on genome variation.[3]

However, Kittles, along with Henry Louis Gates Jr., is among the principal promoters of the idea that African Americans can discover, by means of a genetic test, the African ethnic group from which their ancestors originated. Many scientists regard the evidence for such interpretations as dubious, but it is no surprise that this project reuniting the Black world spun off from Howard (see Bolnick et al. 2007).

Though Howard's prize library collection focuses on the Black world, the African art collection of early-twentieth-century philosophy professor and longtime chair Alain Locke has, over the years, undergone cycles of disappearance and intermittent reappearance in the public galleries of the Fine

Arts Building. On the other hand, since the 1960s, Howard has employed numerous fine arts professors—such as Ethiopian Skunder Boghossian, African Americans Lois Mailou Jones and Delilah Pierce, and Louisiana Creole Raymond Dobard—and trained numerous students who placed pan-African political sentiments and African ritual motifs at the center of their canvasses and wall-mounted carvings (Howard University Gallery of Art 2005). The scions of these great teachers are central to the art establishment in Trinidad. It should be noted, however, that, while the African diasporans tended to represent Africa and its ancestral powers through images of West and West Central African–style masks, Howard's Ethiopian artists tended to favor abstract motifs and figurative images associated with the Ethiopian Coptic Church.

In the late 1960s, my mother organized a public exhibition of their work on behalf of the Med Wives—the Women's Auxiliary of the Medico-Chirurgical Society of the District of Columbia. This may have been the moment when her own tastes in collecting shifted toward Africa and Haiti.

After Asians, African immigrants are the second most highly educated continent-of-origin group in the United States (McCabe 2011; Batalova 2011). As recently as 1994, they were the most highly educated (Speer 1994). After World War II, Uncle Badejọ came among a flood of Nigerians, Kenyans, Ghanaians, and others who pursued an education and access to the tools with which to return to and rebuild a beleaguered continent. Like the Kenyan father of Barack Obama and Lorraine Hansberry's fictional character Asagai in *A Raisin in the Sun*, Uncle Badejọ was princely, dignified, and ambitious—a walking balm to the racial shame of African Americans. Black America and Howard University in particular vicariously dreamed the dreams that these scholars and nation builders brought with them.

By then, Howard had already hosted generations of individual scholars committed to careful scholarship about Africa, building a bridge of respect and respectability between Africa and its diaspora across the morass of Little Black Sambo, Tarzan, Stepin Fetchit, and similar white lies. Among these bridge-builders were linguist and literary scholar Lorenzo Turner and Africanist historian William Leo Hansberry. The latter taught at Howard until 1959. Uncle Badejọ said that he found Hansberry—an African American guide to a future African statesman's learning about Africa—inspiring.

This bridge had a strong footing in Western universities and museums, but the traffic in ideas that crossed it moved far beyond the shore. Lorraine Hansberry was William Leo's niece. She penned the first drama by a black woman to be staged on Broadway, *A Raisin in the Sun* (1959). It then became a popular 1961 film and a perennial favorite of high school drama clubs. The play tells the story of a poor urban Black American family's struggle to retain its dignity and ethics in a system where racism, sexism, and class elitism seem to prevent even their most consistent efforts from paying off.

Amid the struggle between an education-oriented sister and a brother too upset by the system's denial of his manhood to think straight, there arises a cool character never before seen in North American drama—a sophisticated Nigerian Yoruba student who gave the lie to the half-naked, bug-eyed, and cowardly "Ubangis" whose invention served to highlight Tarzan's racially inherent bravery, intelligence, agility, and virility. Though casually dismissive of American feminism and insufficiently worried about his own potential for corruption when he returns to lead his people to nationhood, Joseph Asagai (whose suggestive name means "spear" in several southern Bantu languages and nothing at all in the West African Yoruba language) gives the sister, Beneatha Younger, the new confidence to wear her hair natural and to dream of a goal greater than integration into the white suburbs (Gascoigne 2011). My son Adu played the role of Asagai in the 2011 production of *A Raisin in the Sun* at the Durham School of the Arts.

Like me, Lorraine Hansberry had grown up in the shadow of Howard University, aware of ghetto privations but equipped to rise. We were also inspired to pull other Black people up as we climbed. The Talented Tenth is not rooted in thin air; it was founded and has always been funded by the pennies and the protests of sharecroppers, janitors, cooks, and maids. Indeed, critics of Hansberry's play complained that her real-estate-broker father was a slum lord. My father served many poor patients. My grandfather funded the graduate-school education of four daughters from the collection plates of a hundred tar-papered rural sanctuaries and drafty storefront churches. When my parents separated and the adversarial legal system had drained my father's bank account and eclipsed his better judgment, it was our housekeeper, Ms. Wellons, who lent my mother money to sustain the household.

Against this earthy backdrop and from an early age, I, like Hansberry, dreamed of a pan-African and African American–style "Africa," where the Zulu and the Yoruba shared a common role in my own pursuit of a Black heaven. I still have the tattered *Illustrated Book about Africa* (1959) that had been my teddy bear as I learned to read. Hansberry had the benefit of an Africanist historian for an uncle, so her eyes were presciently open to the unromantic realities of African slave traders and official corruption, but, with a change of pronouns, she could easily have been writing about me in her unfinished, partly autobiographical novel:

> In her emotions she was sprung from the Southern Zulu and the Central Pygmy, the Eastern Watusi and the treacherous slave-trading Western Ashanti

themselves. She was Kikuyu and Masai, ancient cousins of hers had made the exquisite forged sculpture at Benin, while surely even more ancient relatives sat upon the throne at Abu Simbel watching over the Nile. (Gascoigne 2011)

The extraordinary literacy of her references notwithstanding, she and I are both complicit in the circum-Atlantic project by which long-distance imaginations of the continental other—whether those visions are starry-eyed or opprobrious—serve in the making of the self (Roach 1996). We certainly imagine ourselves one with the human objects of our fantasy of a better self, but as Edwards (2003) points out regarding African Americans' use of France and the French colonial empire as an object lesson against US racism, one people's use of another as an object lesson can accidentally affirm the sanctimony of oppressors abroad. During the 1920s and 1930s, black Antilleans and Africans in France had to remind the likes of Howard University professor Alain Locke that racism remained alive and well in France and its empire.

Edward Said (1978) observed the self-aggrandizing motive behind Western stereotypes about "Orientals," as well as their politically oppressive implications. William Pietz (1985) and Valentin Mudimbe (1988) have made similar points about Western representations of Africa. Equally important, then, is the more proximate mutual gaze through which Africans and African Americans—in many ways the symbolic anchors of a global system of Western racism and non-Western resistance—lovingly distort and reinvent each other in projects of self-making. For example, the Gullah/Geechees have reinvented themselves in the image and service of Africa. But not every reinvention has been so congenial. Nonetheless, the form of this uncongeniality is perhaps diagnostic of the structural reality of all ethnicity in an age of long-distance, desensualized collective identity—where people fight out the authentic cultural definition of their peoples less and less through face-to-face performances and more and more through print media, the Internet, and film.

The 1960s were a transitional period in the consciousness of my family. When Black people were rare on television, the appearance of one of us on the little screen prompted a flurry of phone calls among the homes of my mother, her sisters, and their friends. "Turn to channel 4, quickly! There's a *Negro* on television!" They were both proud and afraid of the possibility of being embarrassed. On one occasion, I remember my aunt Marilyn's exclaiming, "Oh, no! Why did they have to put on someone so *dark*?" She was a product of Virginia Union College and Howard's School of Medicine in the 1940s. Later Marilyn and her family lived temporarily in Liberia, an experience that may have done little to challenge the framework of US racism. At that point in history, the descendants of US slaves still contemptuously dominated their African neighbors, much as refugees from the Shoah dominate their neighbors in Palestine. On the other hand, during the late 1960s, my youngest aunt, Arnzie, became a Black nationalist at Howard, bringing home to me Black nationalist slogans along with Hostess Twinkies and chocolate cupcakes. She herself often wore "African"-style paisley print blouses and gowns. By the early 1970s, Benin bronzes (which are typically cast, not forged), ebony carvings from Kenya, ivory busts from Nigeria, and Haitian teakwood statues had begun to compete with Japanese woodblock prints and abstract expressionism in our houses. During the same period, President Richard Nixon's journey to China and the traveling exhibition of Tutankhamun's riches turned the eyes and the travel itineraries of our African American neighbors to China and Egypt as well. But the overwhelming new influence on our home décor was African or Haitian, which meant something similar to us.

Yale undergraduates in the early 1970s, Marilyn's children Gloria and Thomas assembled gospel choirs from our grandfather's Church of God in Christ to perform in a concert benefiting famine-relief efforts in the Sahel. Having found her calling, in the late 1970s Gloria organized a for-profit reggae concert tour in Lagos and Ifẹ, Nigeria. During the planning, she borrowed hundreds of thousands of dollars from Arnzie and her husband, from Aunt Bundy, and from various friends of her parents. Arnzie was moved by the fervor of her love for Africa to accompany Gloria on this visit to the continent. She and her husband, John, both nephrologists, funded the concert tour with $200,000 from their savings.

Apparently hundreds of counterfeit tickets to the concert were in circulation, so there was no profit. Furthermore, my squeamish aunt Arnzie encountered flying tropical roaches in the luxurious Eko Hotel, the likes of which, I must admit, also disturbed me far beyond my future Nigerian wife's comprehension during my first year in Nigeria. For us, roaches were a viscerally frightening symbol of the ghetto. Arnzie and John lost all of their money—which Gloria then insisted was an investment rather than a loan. As new furnishings simultaneously appeared all around Marilyn's house, Arnzie had to sell the beautiful oceanfront plot where she and her husband had already, in their minds, built their dream house. Neither Arnzie's marriage nor her pan-African identity survived the debacle. Almost comically, she promptly refocused her identity on her Americanness and on her mother's alleged Native American ancestry. On a trip to the Southwest, she bought a papoose, which she hung above the fireplace in Mother Dear and Granddaddy's sunken waterfront living room. It remained there throughout the subsequent decades that the Anna Street house remained in the family.

From the time that he bought the Embassy of the People's Republic of Benin (Many African nations had chosen to place their embassies and ambassadors' residences in our neighborhood), my father flew the US flag from the monumental hollow-metal flagpole that came with the house. To my father, the flag mostly represented his connection to his own father, a veteran, whose coffin had been draped with such a flag before his burial. Somehow, my mother could not, or would not, find the original flag to return it to him after the divorce. In defiance, he bought a new one and displayed it atop the enormous flagpole left by the Beninese.

To me, his display represented a betrayal of all of the Black people who had been enslaved, hamstrung, and murdered under that flag, and of African American attorney Ted Landsmark, who, in 1976, was stabbed with a flagpole by antibusing rioters in front of Boston City Hall. From the mid-1970s onward, I have often worn African clothes, some of them brought to me by my sister from her art- and art history–inspired tours of Senegal, Ghana, and Nigeria. At my high school graduation party in 1978, I wore a handwoven robe that my father had received from a patient at Howard University Hospital—probably a Liberian, judging by the weave and the tailoring. Dad would not wear it, but he was content to let me do so, at least inside the yard or the house. On the other hand, out of fear for our safety, he forbade me to wear even the simplest African attire as we drove south toward Hilton Head Island, South Carolina. On that occasion, we were bound for a medical conference and retreat, completely unaware that the hosting island had been, before the resort developers displaced its owners, a capital of Gullah/Geechee society, and that nearby Sheldon, South Carolina, had become the site of Oyotunji, the Yoruba-revivalist village. African attire might not have been so out of place there.

As a Yale undergraduate and "Scholar of the House" at her Morse College dormitory, my sister received African travel funding that enabled her to acquire African textiles, photograph art and performance in West Africa, and create African-inspired, multimedia art that she displayed at the college and in our home. Over the years of her career as a surgical oncologist and her marriage to a husband less interested in unconventional travel, her Japanese art and our mother's extensive collection of antique fine china displaced her African art from the living room to the sun porch, and her own African-inspired art disappeared into the storage room. Some of the latter has since migrated to Duke's and my collection of African and African-inspired sacred art.

In the mid-1970s, Trinidadian American Howard alumnus Stokely Carmichael had drawn the connection, for me, between Black American liberation and anticolonialism. My subsequent years in Nigeria also helped to make me feel more American, but no less African. During my first sojourn to Nigeria, in 1982–83, the sudden insignificance of my blackness lifted off of my chest a boulder that I had never even known was there. But a number of experiences made me feel very American: among them, having to speak in a different language or a different accent all day, of having my cursive handwriting questioned, of encountering a doctor who judged my hepatitis A normal rather than terrifying, of missing ice cream sundaes and Mars bars, and of having "CIA" scrawled across my campaign poster when I ran, albeit successfully, for public relations officer of the postgraduate student organization. One female socialite, apparently assessing my potential as a toy boy, announced to the crowd at a high-society party in Ibadan, "African American men are so sexy, but so irresponsible!"

My Urhobo friend Andy found the remark as hilarious as I found it offensive. I doubted that she had ever had a relationship with an African American man. Even if she had received this information from Nigerian transmigrants, its ultimate source was clearly white American. To such an interested portraitist of African American men, it is simply unimaginable that, when my divorced mother and father accompanied me to Washington National Airport, Dad promptly paid my unexpected $500 overweight luggage charge, or that he called me in Ibadan every Sunday afternoon at Ms. Fabiyi's house. Equally unimaginable to her were the countless African men, such as our current president's father, who abandoned wives and children in the United States when they returned home to Africa. It dawns on me in hindsight that white American and European women also encounter excessively generalizing assumptions about their sexual irresponsibility when they travel to Africa. In the end, I came to feel that my combination of being American (including its crazy and heterogeneous components), of being Nigerian (with all of its crazy and heterogeneous components), and, ultimately, of being Brazilian (with its craziness and heterogeneity too) were all equally OK. Each family of behavioral and residential options provided me with its own forms of fun, strength, and reassurance. Most of the time, I can blend in with my hosts, and, by and large, the farther I am from white America, the less insulting and consequential the dominant local stereotypes about African Americans are.

Over the years of my pestering him with my pan-Africanism, my father recalled having told me repeatedly, "I didn't leave anything in Africa, and I'm not going back to Africa." Only once do I recall his having uttered these words as a statement of conviction. But in the intervening years, he quoted himself several times per year in contrition. He eventually traveled to post-apartheid South Africa in connection with the National Medical Association's efforts to contribute knowledge to the improvement of African health care and to eastern Nigeria, where Igbo colleagues at Howard have annually led weeks-long junkets of Howard physicians to provide surgical care to underserved populations there. He was vocally proud of his South African involvements. And in his waning years, he repeatedly sought my help in designing potential National Medical Association programs to make a further impact on public health in Africa.

During my teaching stint at Howard in 2002, I met several African American women—such as self-described "black Indian" Sarah Johnson Page—who vocally admired African men for their dignity and beauty. Such women were usually dark. In conversations about the period from the 1950s until the present, a number of dark African American women have told me they felt more appreciated by African and Caribbean men than by their African American male peers (though color discrimination is common in the Caribbean). More than a few such attractions ended in marriage. During medical school and an internship at Howard, my sister dated a Kenyan man, who treated me very deferentially, as though he were—I recognize in hindsight—dealing with a potential African in-law. I liked him. I do not know why my sister, in the end, did not. My somewhat idealistic but by no means naïve regard of Africa is an enduring legacy of my upbringing among the Howard-centered intelligentsia. That regard exists by virtue of a conscious and scholarly struggle against the massive degradation of Africa in European intellectual history and in the mass media. In this chapter, we have seen this culture-making strategy pursued by African Americans, Africans, and Caribbeans. Hence, as a reaction to collective stigma, ethnological schadenfreude is not inevitable. Among the other lessons of this tale are that the cultural repertoire of the African American bourgeoisie is cosmopolitan and that every ethnoracial identity—among immigrants and natives alike—has a history far more complex than the inheritance of an ethnically bounded and frozen past.

Yale showed my sister the way to Africa, and my search as a Harvard undergraduate for what made me African led me to the work of Roger Bastide and through Brazil to Nigeria in search of the Yoruba gods. Had she not met me, my wife says that she, like most Western-educated Yoruba people, would have continued to fear and avoid these beings and their priests. My continued research on Nigerian and Afro-Brazilian religions rewarded me with a tenured full professorship at Harvard and rewarded her with a new appreciation of gods that the American missionary Baptist church and her first-rate Western education had taught her to despise. She now maintains an altar for the goddess Ọṣun, who, now world-famous, came originally from Bunmi's hometown of Igede-Ekiti. Also striking in these events is the role of the TWIs in the articulation of a Black heaven.

Fellowship and Debate: The Gods of the Stigmatized

For me and for many others, the embrace of Africa and the valorization of the stigmatized have a sacred dimension. Between Africa and me, the first intercessor was the Holy Ghost. The "shouting" of the church mothers and their "speaking in tongues" was for me the height of every service in my maternal grandfather's Church of God in Christ. Melville J. Herskovits and Roger Bastide transmuted these epiphanies into symbols of my own Africanness and into a declaration of independence from white people's definitions of me. TWIs like Columbia, Northwestern, Yale, and Harvard have been more than instrumental in this style of African-diaspora identity and culture making. Along with music and dance, spirituality is usually central in the scholarly representation of the oppressed and in the entertainment, as well as the healing, of the oppressor. My focus on the religious connections between Africans and African Americans bears the mark of this view from the oppressor class.

For "ethnicity entrepreneurs," the advantage of the sacred—at least in the iterations that arise from the religions of "discontinuous revelation" (Thornton 1998), such as Judaism, Christianity, and Islam—is its deep frozenness. Thornton distinguishes these religions from those of "continuous revelation," such as African-inspired religions of spirit possession, in which divination or a god manifest in his or her priest can reveal new and authoritative truths at any moment. On the other hand, the anachronism of Abrahamic sacred symbols is proof of the revelation's primordiality, and such primordiality is the defining quality of the god of these religions. To declare that this god, its rules, and its signs change is normally also to run the risk of being killed for apostasy. Religion, at least after its dominant Western forms, is the preeminent form of "culture," a fact that still does not exempt it from extensive debate.

For Fanon ([1961] 2004), "culture" is the writing and painting by which elites express and shape the consciousness of the surrounding society. On the other hand, he believes that people's actual lifeways are essentially dynamic and constituted by the relations of domination and exchange that the political and economic system induces. For him, what anthropologists generally call "culture" is the set of customs, conceptions, and social arrangements that have been artificially frozen and reified by colonialists, sentimentalized by indigenous intellectuals, and embraced defensively in their frozen form by psychologically assaulted locals. Indeed, it follows that being convinced of the frozenness of one's culture and the boundedness of one's group is diagnostic of a dominated state. Fanon argues that the changing patterns of collective life among the dominated are actually shaped by long-term ambivalence and debate over the degree to which the dominated should imitate or revile the manners and the accomplishments of their oppressors. There is much truth in his observations.

For many of Howard's scholars and neighbors, "Africa" is the argument for trying something different—namely Black unity and dignity—and the focus of a debate over the defining standards of unified and dignified comportment. That "Africa" does take form in elite writing and painting, but it also takes form in the culinary, musical, and religious reinterpretations that elites appropriate as material embodiments of their deliberations about the boundaries and cultural diacritica of social groups.

Durkheim (1915) argued that gods are the apotheoses of society and of its internal divisions. So for him God is the overwhelming experience of human solidarity and interdependency, like a grand conscience that feels, to the average person, as real, as inescapable, and as indispensable to the human condition as is social cooperation itself. The following discussion takes up the question of what God and the gods look like to those who are driven by stigma both to stratify their own and to see a collective as the most reliable source of consolation and defense. In this study, however, there is ample reason to doubt the Durkheimian premise that "culture" and "religion" rest on long-term consensus. In my observation, debate is the substance of both. Such debate is often inspired by the tension between larger social groups and the smaller groups nested within them. While the unity of larger groups depends on Plutarchian syncretism, secession depends on the articulation of rival standards and symbols. Hierarchy inspires constant jockeying for position and, therefore, a further aspect of the debate—ethnological and class schadenfreude and retorts to it. This analysis focuses on the heaven and the hell embodied—among Africans and diasporans alike—in the God and gods of Africa.

The following is a discussion of African-inspired and especially "Yoruba"-identified religions around Howard's campus and the very different interpretation given to them by Yoruba American, African American, and Latino intellectuals on the campuses of TWIs. Like the forms of Louisiana Creoleness articulated at TWIs, the "Yoruba religion" articulated and debated at TWIs is detached from the political realities of the homeland but full of implications for the standards of supraethnic, or racial, unity in the broader population that employs Yoruba culture and religion as the preeminent signs and proof of Black and African worth. Far more than the Yoruba scholars at Howard, those at TWIs are driven by the consciousness of a white, or ethnoracially unmarked, audience and by the motive to establish and reinforce the image of Yoruba dignity, beauty, and orderliness. As usual, the "logic of the trial" generates a retort to the calumny and an image of this religion resembling those ideals of the dominant host society that will favor the progress of the speaker. Yet the defendants in this trial are diverse in class, gender, color, sexual orientation, and place of origin. Here I document the conflicting interests in a debate about the religious grounds of group belonging.

The African-inspired religions that I have studied for decades are well represented on and around Howard's campus. Indeed, like African art, they have, over the past half century, become a focus of African Americans', Afro-Caribbeans', Afro–Latin Americans', and Afro-Latinos' pursuit of racial self-esteem. At the same time, both African art and African religion are often a source of division, shame, and fear among large classes of people, especially among Africans and American Africans.

For example, the Orthodox Easter service of my dormitory's Eritrean housekeeping supervisor clarifies her difference from Ethiopians, but it could just as easily have proven the claim that Eritrean-Ethiopian unity is the more sacred and fundamental truth. On May 4, 2002, Adu and I attended the jam-packed all-night Orthodox Easter Eve service at the Universalist Church building at Sixteenth and S Streets, Northwest. The ritual might easily have demonstrated Habesha unity, since most of the service was, as it should be, in Ge'ez, the ancient liturgical language of the shared Orthodox church of Ethiopia and Eritrea.

FIGURE 6.3. A Habesha graduate of Howard with his family, 2002. The dress of the women at the center is the Habesha *kemis*. Photograph by the author.

However, my hostess and her many friends spent a good part of the evening—between hours of standing, sitting, call-and-response singing, kissing the Bible, and, for the morally pure, taking communion—teaching me Tigrinya, which is spoken by millions of Ethiopians but is the primary language of Eritrea.

A Haitian spiritualist advertised consultations in a storefront near campus, but a Haitian medical-school student in my building remained very discreet about his practice until assured of my respect for it. The nephew of a *manbo*, or initiated priestess of the Haitian religion known as Vodou, he was knowledgeable about herbs, sacred rituals, and the songs that activate their healing power. Practitioners regard the source of their deepest knowledge and the origin of their gods as *Ginen*, which is simultaneously the geographical Africa and a sacred underwater transmutation of that continent that encompasses the best of both Africa and Europe. He promised to bring me books and recordings of his practice that he normally kept far away in his family home in New York City.

He had chosen to attend Howard, even though his mother had endeavored to keep him away from what she regarded as the negative influence of his African American neighbors. But he was aware that the suspicion was, to a certain degree, mutual. Around Howard's campus, parlance signaling one's Christian faith is common, particularly among African Americans. "Have a blessed day!" was a common way of saying good-bye, and the wearing of watches and pendants with the inscription "WWJD" (for "What Would Jesus Do?") was common in 2002. My Haitian dormitory mate had undoubtedly grown up around people who regarded Vodou as comparable to AIDS in its stigmatizing character, but at Howard he had not felt marked out negatively for his Haitianness. Both of us, though, were aware of the half-joking, half-antagonistic rumor on campus that New Orleans Creoles practice "Voodoo." In the context of Christian Protestant hegemony and outspokenness on campus, my Haitian interlocutor's usual silence about his convictions and practices was deeply meaningful. The most maligned of the African-inspired religions, Haitian Vodou is a source of shame for many Haitians and a prominent referent of ethnological schadenfreude among African Americans, who tend to pass the racial contempt that we receive on to Haitians.

Yet, around the Atlantic perimeter, Yoruba religion is one of the preeminent symbols of black people's collective dignity and divinity. Consequently, the standards of its practice are among the most debated. That reality has its roots in a little-known elite struggle against racial stigma in British colonial West Africa. But that struggle and the "Yoruba" collective identity itself emerged from a startlingly circum-Atlantic array of symbolic resources and alliances, which is a major reason for its uniquely enduring and widespread persuasiveness in efforts to rally and redeem the stigmatized. Since the late nineteenth century, Yoruba religion has become a way of worshipping Africa writ large and the sacred embodiment of a supraterritorial African superethnicity, but one with greater purchase in the diaspora than in Yorubaland itself.

As I have argued elsewhere (J. L. Matory 1999), the Yoruba ethnic identity is not a survival of some primordial African past. What made Yoruba religion the diacritic of such a widely debated and therefore powerfully centripetal superethnicity was the timing and the ingenious ethnicity entrepreneurship of a Western-assimilated black class elite struggling, in the "logic of the trial," against racial stigmatization in nineteenth-century British colonial West Africa. A Western-educated population of Africans who had served as loyal functionaries to the British empire during much of the nineteenth century built Yoruba ethnicity and religion like a mighty fortress against the rising tide of colonial racism in the 1890s.

And this struggle was not merely local. It was one part and product of a transatlantic dialogue involving Afro-Brazilian and Afro-Cuban returnees to Lagos; missionary-educated Saro returnees from the British abolitionist colony of Freetown, Sierra Leone; and African American activists and journalists. The Lagosian Cultural Renaissance of the 1890s established an unprecedented documentary canon of "Yoruba" history and theology, which anglophone Afro-Latin merchants translated for the founder of Afro-Brazilian studies, Raymundo Nina Rodrigues, and the founder of Afro-Cuban studies, Fernando Ortiz. In turn, these scholars established the unique dignity of the "Yoruba" and their religion among the diverse African-inspired practices of the Americas and, indeed, made this ethnic group and its religions into symbols of national dignity in Brazil and Cuba. Consequently, Brazilian Candomblé and Cuban Santería/Ocha have thrived to this day among Brazilians and Cubans of all colors, expanded as symbols of healing and dignity among Latin Americans and US Latinos, and occupied a unique place of dignity in the Western academy's representation of sub-Saharan African "cultures." The later work of Melville J. Herskovits, Oseijeman Adefunmi I, and Robert Farris Thompson enshrined Yoruba religion as a classic among English-speaking African Americans as well.

There was no ethnic group that called itself "Yoruba" before the mid-nineteenth-century, and it probably did not become a *popular* self-identity until the beginning of the twentieth century. At the end of the eighteenth century and the beginning of the nineteenth, the decline of the Ọ̀yọ́ empire and the ascent of Dahomey threw tens of thousands of Ọ̀yọ́, Ìjẹ̀sà, Ẹ̀gbá, Ẹ̀gbádò, Ìjẹ̀bú, and Òkìtìpupa people into the transatlantic slave trade. At that time, none of these groups had shared a homogeneous lifestyle, and none had called themselves "Yoruba." Their language varieties were diverse and sometimes mutually incomprehensible. And despite the historical connections among their language varieties—like those among Spanish, Portuguese, and Italian—they had never considered themselves one people. Before the middle of the nineteenth century, the term "Yarriba" seems to have been the name that the Hausa and other northern peoples applied only to the subjects of the Ọyọ kingdom.

In this way, just like many groups of Africans who embarked at the same port, this range of peoples was first grouped together under what Gerhard Kubik (1979) calls a "trademark," a common label first applied by the people who bought and sold them. The Spanish called these and other related peoples the "Lucumí" (after the expression, in some dialects of what is now called "Yoruba," olùkù mi, meaning "my friend"), while the Portuguese called them "Nagôs" (after the term preferred by the slave-trading Fon rulers of the kingdom of Dahomey). The buyers in each American country tended to prefer one African nation or another in any given occupation, and the Roman Catholic Church organized its efforts to assemble and proselytize African converts around these categories.

Few people today are aware that, from 1830 onward, thousands of emancipated Afro-Brazilian and Afro-Cubans returned to the multicultural cities of the West African coast, introducing collective neo-African identity configurations without precedents in the daily lives of the Ọ̀yọ́, Ìjẹ̀ṣà, Ẹ̀gbá, Ẹ̀gbádò Ìjẹ̀bú, and Òkìtìpupa peoples. In the West African city of Porto-Novo, such Afro-Latin American returnees were the patrons of and interpreters for the French missionary Noel Baudin, whose extensive and Brazilian returnee-influenced but fantastical documentation of "Yorouba" religion became fundamental to Raymundo Nina Rodrigues's and Fernando Ortiz's subsequent understanding of the "African origins" of Brazilian Candomblé and Cuban Ocha.

The second major foundation in the construction of Yoruba culture and identity, from the middle of the nineteenth century, was the missionary activity of the rescued and returned captives from Freetown, or the Sàró (from "Sierra Leone"). Located in what is now Sierra Leone, Freetown was founded by the British at the end of the eighteenth century. From its inception, it became the home of exiled Jamaican maroons, Black loyalists to the British monarchy who fled during the US War of Independence, and the Black Poor from England. After 1808, when the British Royal Navy began to enforce British legislation against the slave trade, the Africans rescued from the slave ships, called "recaptives," were resettled in Freetown. A disproportionate number of these had come from Ọyọ and neighboring states. Together, the recaptives, the Jamaican Maroons, the Black American loyalists, and the Black Poor from England were called the "Krios" (from "Creoles"). They were converted and schooled by German, English, and African American missionaries. By the middle of the nineteenth century, the Krios had themselves produced a great number of Western-trained missionaries, physicians, lawyers, artisans, and successful merchants.

The Black Krio missionaries generated a standard language—designed to be understood in common by all of the potential Ọ̀yọ́, Ìjẹ̀ṣà, Ẹ̀gbá, Ẹ̀gbádò, Òkìtìpupa, and Ìjẹ̀bú converts. Between the middle and the end of the nineteenth century, these Krio missionaries also invented an orthographic standard that would become the foundation of the Yoruba literary canon. It was Ọyọ-descended black Krio missionary Samuel Ajayi Crowther who created this new, hybrid language and called it "Yoruba." The first publications in this language were a Bible and a dictionary, which were later employed as sources of orthography and of sacred information by orisha priests in Brazil and Cuba in the writing of catechisms and explanations of their religions.

Though intensely Westernized in their religion, behavior, and occupations, many Krios integrated into their Anglo-Yoruba culture some non-Christian religious institutions of Ọyọ inspiration, such as Egungun and the hunters' societies. Owing to their colonial education, which gave them opportunities that the indigenous Sierra Leoneans lacked, this emergent "Yoruba" ethnic group developed a clear sense of its collective superiority, and its hybrid culture became an object of imitation by neighboring African groups.

Many such Krios ultimately returned to or reestablished their ties with their hometowns in what would later become "Yorubaland." And many more "returned" to Lagos, where they joined the Afro-Latin American returnees as major sources of support to the British colonial enterprise in that future capital. Lagos came to be not only a capital of British colonialism in West Africa but also the capital of the emergent "Yoruba" identity. Note that this city lies far away from, and had never been subject to the rule of, the original referent of the Hausa term "Yarriba"—that is, the inland kingdom of Ọyọ.

The roots of the Lagosian Cultural Renaissance of the 1890s—the third major foundation of Yoruba identity and "culture"—lay in a disaster that befell this culturally hybrid elite. The massive construction of railroads in the United States flooded the global market with US farm products, sharply decreasing food prices, and creating a global economic crisis in the 1880s. The small-capital businesses of this Anglo-African and Latin American elite could no longer survive the competition with better-capitalized European firms. Moreover, improvements in British tropical medicine enabled white

British missionaries, physicians, and administrators to replace these loyal Anglo-African servants of British colonial interests. The economic interests of the white newcomers supported a tide of anti-African racism in Lagos, a new local hatred of whites, and, most important to our story, the Lagosian Cultural Renaissance—a revival (and culturally hybrid invention) of "African" clothes, names, marriage practices, historical accounts, and practices that came to be reified, documented, and known collectively as "Yoruba traditional religion." Through word and deed, the Lagosian Cultural Renaissance declared, "No, we are not inferior versions of you Britons but Africans with a superior legacy." This movement had German antecedents (in von Herder and the burgers' efforts to redeem the German speakers from French cultural hegemony) and participants. German missionaries in Freetown had been particularly active in the respectful documentation of the African languages spoken there.

Back-and-forth Afro-Brazilian traveler Martiniano do Bonfim conveyed the literature of the Lagosian Cultural Renaissance to Bahia, Brazil, and interpreted it for Nina Rodrigues, whose work is also cited by Fernando Ortiz amid his conversion to the cause of "Yoruba" dignity. Since then, without knowing it, the researchers, the patrons, and the selective protectors of African-inspired religion in the Americas have been unable to escape the transformative influence of the Lagosian Cultural Renaissance of the 1890s.

The sacred imagination of the Yoruba-Atlantic world and of Howard University remains indebted to the cultural nationalism of the Lagosian Cultural Renaissance and to the powerful impact that this defensive display of "Yoruba" dignity had on Latin American scholars and political elites. These elites have elevated and protected "Yoruba" religion—and the Afro-Latin American traditions recognized as its cognates—above all other African-inspired religious practices. These practices have thrived and expanded where Kongo, Cross-River, and Fon practices have suffered state persecution, marginalization, and near extinction.

On Eighteenth Street, surrounded by Ethiopian and Eritrean restaurants, Botánica Yemayá y Ochún was half a block south from Heaven and Hell. *Botánicas* are stores that sell healing herbs and sacred paraphernalia for the practice of popular Latino religions, especially those that are shaped by the profound African influences on the Caribbean, such as Caribbean Spiritism and the Cuban-inspired and Yoruba-affiliated Ocha religion, which is also called "Santería." Botánica Yemayá y Ochún took its name from two goddesses. Yemayá is the goddess of the ocean and the Cuban interpretation of the West African Yoruba goddess Yemọja, goddess of the River Ògùn. Ochún is the goddess of fresh water, gold, and honey. She is the Cuban interpretation of the Yoruba goddess of the River Ọṣun. Just beyond where Eighteenth Street curves and turns into Calvert Road, was Botánica San Francisco de Asís, named after a Roman Catholic saint equated in the syncretic iconography of these Caribbean religions with the Ocha and Nigerian Yoruba god of divination, Ifá.[4] These shops owe their generic name and their storefront format to the "botanical" shops that served the folk medicinal and spiritual needs of African American migrants from the South amid the blossoming of heterodox spirituality in the Harlem of the 1930s. When Latin American migrants to US cities adapted this institution to their own needs, the stores came to be called *botánicas*.

In 2002, Botánica Yemayá y Ochún was owned by a Guatemalan man and Botánica San Francisco de Asís by a black Puerto Rican woman who told me that she had been initiated in Nigeria as a *babalawo*, or divination priest, much to the chagrin of her Caribbean Hispanic counterparts in that divinatory priesthood. In the Cuban tradition of orisha worship, which dominates in Spanish-speaking Latin America and the United States, women cannot typically become *babalawo* diviners, and they only rarely perform even the simpler forms of orisha divination for others. Among all of these African-inspired priests, only this Afro–Puerto Rican babalawo professed to know and work with people from Howard. However, her botánica closed around 2005.

Nevertheless, until 2014, the Central American owner of the first botánica remained in good company. There is a considerable turnover in their locations, but numerous shops of this sort have long dotted Georgia Avenue, Park Road, and the nearby Maryland suburbs, serving, in Africanized fashion, the spiritual, health-related, financial, and legal needs of Washington's large Central American population. I would not be surprised if some of Howard's heavily Central American janitorial staff employ the services of these establishments.

In 2002, I also spent a good deal of time with a high-ranking African American professor and administrator at the School of Pharmacy. He took a kindly interest in my son and me, introducing us to a world of African American Yoruba and Akan devotees, who, in the largely Black middle-class precincts of upper Northwest Washington and during the celebration we attended, were more conspicuously concerned about Black gender relations and parenting than about race per se. In addressing my research questions, he observed that women and non-US black people predominate on the faculty and in the student body of the School of Pharmacy. But he emphasized their right to be there. No one should be excluded from the community and its full benefits on account of his or her national origins. His religiosity appeared to embody his cosmopolitan sense of Blackness and its membership.

He invited my son and me one evening to "A Celebration of Our Fathers." The aim of this gathering was to address current worries about the African American family by highlighting models of good fathering in multiple strands of the African American cultural heritage—both African and black Indian. The fact is that parenting by divorced or never-married mothers is increasingly common across all races in the United States, particularly among the poor. But African Americans—only partly for demographic reasons—have been the focus of the national anxiety about this issue. This sacred project is directed equally against some Black fathers' choice not to participate actively in rearing their children and against the false premise that this phenomenon is universal or traditional among Black men. Many African Americans have sought solutions in the form of cultural and religious reform. In the auditorium of the People's Congregational Church, a progressive African American

FIGURE 6.4. Altar of the Yoruba goddess Oshun at "A Celebration of Our Fathers," held in the auditorium of the People's Congregational Church in Washington, DC, 2002. Photograph by the author.

congregation in upper Northwest Washington, an African American priestess of Yoruba religion invited other priests of her religion and of Ghanaian-inspired Akan religion to preside over a dance ceremony, poetry recitation, and prayers celebrating Black fathers. At the center of the gathering was an altar to the Yoruba river goddess Oshun.

Half of the attendees and all of the priests wore West African clothing. But one African-descended man wore buckskin and Native American hair ornaments. The priests burned sagebrush and invoked Native American spiritual traditions as well.

Yet the HBCU and its surrounds are not the only scholarly venue in which dignity and proper conduct are negotiated in Yoruba terms. Indeed, the heated struggles over the meaning of Yorubaness in TWIs offer a further illustration that ethnic identity is not only situational, strategic, and protean but also, by its nature, debated. An ethnic group is defined less by insiders' consensus about its definitional boundaries, or cultural diacritica, than by the vigor and the venues of debates about potential diacritica. Culture is, to borrow Hebdige's felicitous phrase, a "struggle for the possession of the sign" (Hebdige 1979).

Howard's chair of philosophy articulated in writing a proposal for pan-African unity based upon Yoruba and Akan religion, an explicit alternative to Christianity and to the selfishness of African bourgeois elites. However, during this nadir of Nigerian military terror, even the philosophy chair's interest in Yoruba and Akan ancestral religions seemed abstract—remarkable but peripheral to the agenda of the community he led. In 2002, these scholars and professionals were preoccupied with Yoruba autonomy and the struggle against decades of northern and Hausa military domination. Most meetings began and closed with Muslim or Christian prayers. There were no prayers to the *oriṣa* gods.

If I were a Nigerian Yoruba, I would feel proud of the proliferation of my ancestors' gods around the Atlantic perimeter, but the Yoruba people who welcomed me to their community meetings in Washington seemed variously unaware of, uninterested in, and amused by the phenomenon. They laughed with pride and camaraderie about my speaking Yoruba and being married to a Yoruba woman, but they never responded to my excited talk about the millions of people, including Washingtonians, who imagine Yoruba people as scions of an African Mount Olympus.

Yoruba-Atlantic Identity and the TWI

What Thompson described as the "Yoruba Atlantic" is the set of ethnic groups, polities, and religious practices around the Atlantic perimeter propagating traditions that began in what is now southwestern Nigeria. It includes Brazilian Candomblé, Cuban Ocha (or Santería), and Trinidadian Shango. The Yoruba-Atlantic case illustrates the role of Western universities and other state-supported educational institutions, such as museums, in subsidizing the imagination of ethnic groupings rooted in faraway places and struggling to avoid last place.

The opportunities and incentives for Yoruba scholars at TWIs to profess expertise about "Yoruba" religion and art are altogether different from those of Howard's Yoruba scholars and activists. Like Louisiana Creole nationalism, Yoruba religion has found its most fertile ground far away from home, in TWIs. The liveliness with which Yoruba and non-Yoruba scholars debate the nature of this now circum-Atlantic religious identity reveals important truths about the nature of "culture" and ethnicity generally. TWIs offer honor and earnings for an expertise that Yoruba people embody, all the more so since Yale University professor Robert Farris Thompson, in the 1970s and 1980s, enshrined the study of Yoruba "culture" at the center of African and African American studies. There is a TWI diaspora of Yoruba religious studies scholars, art historians, philosophers, literary critics, and a sociologist deeply engaged in debate with non-Yoruba scholars and an old circum-Atlantic diaspora of priests over the nature of an extraterritorial Yoruba "culture."

Academic debates have long helped to create working ethnic identities on the ground. The "invention of traditions" literature documents this phenomenon well during the late nineteenth century (Hobsbawm and Ranger 1983). Less widely examined are the roles of diasporic scholars in creating national cultures and of bourgeois nationalist folklorists in the ethnic self-recognition of subaltern populations within the nation-state (J. L. Matory 2005a, 149–87, 199–207). Boas's anthropology department at Columbia inspired Brazilian anthropologist Gilberto Freyre's influential *mestiço*-nationalist manifesto, *The Masters and the Slaves* ([1933] 1986), at a time when the Brazilian establishment was still wedded to dreams of whitening the nation. Since Freyre organized the first Afro-Brazilian Congress in 1934, dozens of conferences have brought together priests and scholars intent on rethinking the role of Afro-Latin American religions in their host nation-states, reorganizing these religions internally, and establishing their relationship to communities beyond the nation-state. Several such conferences have had momentous effects, largely because they have helped to establish—by the standards of scholars and of the more powerful elites who fund them and take their counsel—which priests' practices are normal, which are best prohibited, and who legitimately speaks for the group. The initially research-based and eventually

Platonic relationships between scholars, on the one hand, and specific Afro-Brazilian, Afro-Cuban, and Haitian priests, on the other, have had parallel effects on the reproduction of Afro-Atlantic collective identities.

Sometimes the discussions in universities are distant from the current priorities of the general population, but, through their influence on the children of elites, the mass media, and forensic agencies, those discussions sometimes trickle down to the mainstream and have implications in nonacademic and ethnic leadership struggles. That the audience affects the character of the discussion is evident in the difference between the debates at Howard and those at Harvard, Yale, and Michigan. With the endorsement of elite TWIs and extravagantly illustrated catalogs of sacred art, the partisans of lofty debates about Yoruba-Atlantic religion have in many ways already become high priests of a new African superethnicity. In this final section of the chapter, I document an important venue of ethnogenetic debates—the TWI-sponsored world conferences that convene priests and scholars from the entire Atlantic and Caribbean perimeter. The ultimate effects of these debates among diasporic intellectuals have yet to be systematically explored, though I have made some initial observations elsewhere (J. L. Matory 2005a, 219–23).

The liveliness of these TWI-based debates about the nature of Yorubaness made it the only single African ethnic group in the yearlong 2011 Mellon-Sawyer Seminar series on Ethnicity in Africa to which an entire seminar was devoted. This debated ethnicity exemplifies the broader principle that "cultures" arise more from conflict than from consensus (J. L. Matory 2005a, 1994). Contrary to the view of Barth and Cohen that cultural diacritica clarify the boundaries between ethnic groups, I observe that, in real time, cultural diacritica are more often the subject of debate than of consensus. Ethnicity is less a fixed taxonomy than a situationally changing set of claims to prestige and prerogative. The cultural diacritica of any given ethnic identity are as diverse and changing as are the interests of the actors—ethnicity entrepreneurs—who use them to distinguish insiders from outsiders and to make interested demands for the distribution of resources and honors. Ethnicity is therefore structured less by consensus within the ethnic group about the intensionally defined differences between insiders and outsiders than by the debate among insiders and outsiders and by the shared venues of that debate. An ethnic group is a translocal field of debate within a global field of debate.

The TWI, or the ethnoracially marked university, is the authoritative venue for the debate and recognition of ethnic groups. Moreover, the loftiness of the venues—none being loftier than the conference rooms and lecture halls of the most ethnically unmarked universities—is a measure of the level of dignity achieved by an ethnic identity relative to its rivals in the race for distinction. The canonization of Yorubaness and its constituent debates have taken place not only at a series of regional universities but at the two preeminent universities in the world's greatest power (Harvard and Yale) and most recently at one of its most prestigious state universities (the University of Michigan at Ann Arbor), all of which are predominantly white, by a large margin. Even among TWIs, the stratified nature of these venues has shaped the nature of the debates and their tentative outcomes.

WHO IS YORUBA?

First, the temporal boundaries of Yorubaness are hotly contested. For example, the description "Yoruba art" is regularly applied to objects created by people who almost certainly never called or considered themselves "Yoruba," such as the pre-nineteenth-century objects depicted in Drewal, Pemberton, and Abiọdun's *Yoruba: Nine Centuries of African Art and Thought* (1989). In oral communications, some Nigerian Yoruba scholars, such as Wande Abimbọla and Oyeronkẹ Oyewumi, angrily dispute Robin Law's influential assertion that the Yoruba ethnic identity as we know it today was a mid-nineteenth-century invention. They argue, for example, that the ancientness of Odudua and of the Ifa divination system demonstrates the primordialness of Yoruba identity. I can only imagine what they think of J. D. Y. Peel's argument (2011) that Yoruba ethnogenesis is closely allied to Christianity.

In many ways, this debate is a struggle about who gets to speak for whom, a question with broad political implications. For example, are the Edo speakers descendants of the Yoruba or its progenitors, entitled to control over their own state and channel to oil revenues? Are Yoruba subregions or politicians who ally with northern political parties traitors to their ancestral family? Nor is it clear to me that all of the contemporary human and divine populations that Robert Farris Thompson calls the "Yoruba Atlantic" belong to the same ethnic group. But that is the point. The criteria by which one would judge the matter are protean, situational, strategic, and, above all, continually debated.

There is a rival claimant to the status of "nation" most influential in any given diaspora religion (e.g., Parés [2006] 2013). In Brazil, for example, the worshippers of the *vodum* gods, of the *inquice* gods, and of the *caboclo* Indian spirits experience the state-supported dominance of Candomblé's Yoruba-affiliated temples as a form of imperialism. In Cuba, the *orichas* embody the economic and cultural dominance of Havana and Matanzas over El Oriente, where the *fodunes* held an earlier pride of place.

RACE AND YORUBA-ATLANTIC ETHNICITY

Second, is race one of the qualifications of membership? And if so, which races qualify?

Black North American participation in orisha worship is often traced to the 1959 pilgrimage of Walter Serge King, a Detroit-born dancer with the Katherine Dunham Company, and of his friend Chris Oliana to Matanzas, Cuba, where they were initiated in Lucumí religion, the names of whose gods (orichas) clearly share common antecedents with the contemporary Nigerian oriṣa. King adopted the name Oseijiman Adefunmi I, founded an orisha temple in New York City, and, eventually, moved to the South Carolina Lowcountry, where he founded a "Yoruba" kingdom called Oyotunji in the town of Beaufort. For him and for many African American orisha worshippers, initiation in Cuban Ocha, or Santería, and especially in a North American adaptation of it that expurgated Roman Catholic "syncretism," represented a recovery of their African ancestral heritage and racial authenticity. Many such African Americans therefore consider the participation of whites in "the Religion" blasphemous and intrusive. However, according to Kamari Maxine Clarke (2004), Oyotunji residents who undertook pilgrimages to Nigeria were often called *oyinbo* (white people, Westerners). In turn, they branded westernized and non-oriṣa-worshipping Nigerians "white black people" (Clarke 2004, 14).

Since the early 1990s, large numbers of Central American and Mexican immigrants to US Latino neighborhoods have also adopted Lucumí religion, or Cuban Ocha, from their Caribbean Latino predecessors in the United States. Not only many white Cubans and Puerto Rican practitioners of Ocha, or *santeros*, but also many white and Indian-looking Mexican, Guatemalan, and Salvadoran *santeros* propagate the idea that African Americans tend to lack the speakers' collectively shared Latino racial acumen for Ocha spirit possession.

By contrast, Nigerian participants in this field of debate articulate a very different racial logic of boundary and connection. That is, Nigerian Christians increasingly abhor the religious practices of their precolonial ancestors and endeavor to erase them as touchstones of collective identity. For example, many Pentecostal Yoruba people nowadays remove references to the oriṣa gods from their family names and replace them with Christian references. In a parallel crosscutting of racial boundaries, internationally itinerant Nigerian priests, such as and Wande Abimbọla and the Epega dynasty, have served racially diverse Western Hemisphere clienteles with the understanding that Yoruba cosmogony charts the creation of humankind, not just black people. In the early twentieth century, a Yoruba Christian minister named David Ọnadele Epega founded a late-twentieth-century dynasty of priests of "Yoruba traditional religion." Citing the Black nationalist writings of Edward Wilmot Blyden among his sources of inspiration, Epega published several treatises on this religion. Several of his grandsons became orisha priests and have initiated other priests in Chicago, Florida, São Paulo, and probably elsewhere. They continue their grandfather's publishing legacy as well. Some African American devotees criticize the late Afọlabi A. Epega, one of the grandsons, for his promotion of white American initiate Philip John Neimark (J. L. Matory 2005a, 64). African American orisha worshippers and nonworshippers tend to regard whites' entry into the priesthood as a form of theft, made worse by the fact that, in the critics' view, the white-dominated society will reward white practitioners out of proportion with their talents and then marginalize the more deserving Black practitioners. Elvis Presley's lucrative adoption of a Black musical performance style is a frequent reference in these complaints. In Cuba, some people attribute the precedence of the Yoruba Cultural Association, with its junior legacy and lighter-skinned leadership, over the *Casa 10 de Octubre*, with its older legacy and darker-skinned leadership, to a similar phenomenon—Cuban government racism. It is partly against this backdrop that Cubans debate the relative legitimacy and authority of these two organizations' *letras del año*, or Ifá readings of the year.

In sum, these Nigerians, Latin Americans, Latino immigrants, and African Americans are making rival claims about whose participation in Yoruba religion is legitimate and authentic.

AFRICAN PURISM AND YORUBA-ATLANTIC ETHNICITY

Third, is hybridity or purism the normative grounds of Yoruba collective identity?

Most African and African-inspired sacred practices are proudly hybridizing, creating value and efficacy through cross-cultural imagery and the mimesis of connections, rather than divisions, between once geographically or socially separated populations. The roots of the Yoruba ethnic identity are themselves hybrid. In the hands of ethnicity entrepreneurs, "cultures" and "religions" tend to become idioms of recalcitrant difference and separation. Like other debates, the debate over purity and syncretism has implications not only for the collective dignity of the group but for the competition among potential leaders and spokespeople.

The Latin American worshippers of African- or Native American–inspired gods have long used the iconography of similar Roman Catholic saints to hide, represent, or embody and worship those gods. Arthur Ramos and his followers called this phenomenon "syncretism," a term that has come to encompass other types of cultural hybridity as well. Some worshippers and scholars describe this Roman Catholic iconography as a "mask," while others take the correlation between the saints and African-inspired gods of Haitian Vodou, Cuban Ocha, and Brazilian Candomblé and Umbanda more seriously.

In my argument, I have used the term "syncretism" with a different emphasis, which was earlier attributed to Plutarch—the unification of rival parties in response to a shared external threat and, by extension, the elaboration or resignification of signs in the service of such unification. Afro-Atlantic priests' correlation of the similar gods of the various Yoruba kingdoms, the Fon, the BaKongo, the Cuban *santeros*, the Brazilian *candomblecistas*, the Trinidadian Shango practitioners, and the Haitian *vodouisants* with each other is easily interpreted as another form of syncretism. And, with a hierarchical logic exceeding even that of Afro-Roman-Catholic syncretism, these intraracial syncretisms tend to treat the Ọyọ pantheon as the lingua franca or, as António Risério (1981) put it, the "metalanguage" of all these other Afro-Atlantic pantheons.

On the other hand, in the 1960s, African Americans like Oseijeman Adefunmi I spearheaded the effort to eliminate the Roman Catholic saints from the Latin American traditions that they had adopted through interaction with Latino immigrants and travel to Cuba. Influential Afro-Brazilian Candomblé priestess Stella de Azevedo and white Cuban American *santero* Ernesto Pichardo took up the same banner in the 1980s and 1990s, respectively. As the occasion of her most widely cited declaration against syncretism, Mãe Stella chose the Third Congress of Orișa Tradition and Culture, organized by the Caribbean Cultural Center and held at Hunter College in New York City.

Pichardo's greatest influence arose from his US Supreme Court case. In the early 1990s, Pichardo opened a public temple for the orichas in Hialeah, Florida, transforming a Cuban tradition that had, since the turn of the century, favored domestic practice and a high degree of secrecy. When embarrassed Cuban members of the Hialeah City Council endeavored to prohibit animal sacrifice, which Pichardo also vowed to bring out of the shadows, Pichardo took the city council all the way to the US Supreme Court and won his 1993 case for the constitutionally protected status of what he regards as a necessary and sacred practice. In the meantime, Nigerian *babalawo* diviner Wande Abimbọla has declared blood sacrifice a dispensable element of the religion that he and Pichardo putatively share. Abimbọla is willing to accommodate urban US sensitivities. Thus, both secrecy and animal sacrifice have also become touchstones of debate among priests about purity and standards.

In the Americas, orixá, oricha, and orisha worship is a highly competitive business. Both the Cuban American Ernesto Pichardo and the Cuban-descended African American John Mason are highly knowledgeable and celebrated *oriatés*, or non-*babalawo* divination priests. Both are re-Africanizers, seeking an end to Roman Catholic iconography in their religion. Moreover, they appear to be of equal age and initiatic seniority. And the broad influence of Pichardo's Supreme Court victory is matched by the influence of the orisha hymnal and catechisms-cum-ethnographies published by Mason's arch-ministry. Yet at a 1999 conference at Florida International University, Mason assailed Pichardo's authority and, during the question-and-answer period following a panel in which Pichardo had participated, repeatedly addressed Pichardo as "son." The motive was not immediately clear, but in private conversations there were hints that Mason felt that his race gave him a superior claim to authority in this African-inspired religion.

The syncretism/antisyncretism debate (Stewart and Shaw 1994; Palmié 1995) among worshippers has implications for both gerontocracy and Black dominance as diacritica of Yoruba-Atlantic identity. First, at the bridge between the nineteenth and the twentieth centuries, Afro-Brazilian *babalawo* and transatlantic merchant Martiniano Eliseu do Bonfim brought back from Lagos the motive and the authority to invent a "purely African" religious system that many Bahians found convincing (Matory 1999). Assertions that its priests and the merchants of its raw materials were racially pure bolstered their claims about the purity of their African religious practices. These discourses were directly indebted to Lagosian reactions to British racism in the 1890s and were similar in sentiment to the pride that my father's surgery chief felt in my father's unambiguously black accomplishments. Martiniano's system helped Eugênia Ana dos Santos, an initiate of the far older Casa Branca temple, to establish the towering reputation of the Ilê Axé Opô Afonjá temple. Though seniority is a strong principle of rank throughout the Yoruba-Atlantic, Mãe Aninha—as dos Santos is affectionately called—and her new temple catapulted to first place in prestige and influence over the older Casa Branca, Gantois, and Ilê Maroiá Laji temples of the Quêto (or Yoruba-affiliated) nation by instituting Martiniano's program of "African purity." Orisha worshippers from junior temples throughout the Americas—including the Italian converts from Umbanda to Candomblé in São Paulo and black North Americans—have also found "African purity" (i.e., the alleged mastery of a more African and, therefore, older tradition, such as Nigerian Ifa) a convincing symbolic means of skipping ahead in the queue of seniority among temples. Seniority and purity are principles that benefit different partners.

For similar reasons, the unity and the diversity of these traditions also benefit different parties. Members of genealogically deeper temples or temples whose leadership is threatened by the authority of itinerant African priests have an interest in dignifying the distinctiveness of their national traditions, including their Catholic-inspired divergences from contemporary Nigerian orisha worship. National or regional particularism buttresses their temples against contemporary Africans' claims of historical seniority in the overall Yoruba-Atlantic world.

This strategic pattern helps us to understand the passionate but seemingly unfashionable celebration of syncretism in the autobiography of Afro-Puerto Rican *santera* Marta Moreno Vega (2000). In 1981, she and Wande Abimbọla had organized at the University of Ifẹ the first World Conference of Orisha Tradition and Culture. Thus, for the first time in history, a conference brought together scholars and priests of orisha religion from Brazil, Cuba, Puerto Rico, Trinidad, the United States, and Nigeria. Nigerian Yoruba Christians, on the other hand, protested against the conference. A wave of US-influenced Pentecostalism has turned Yoruba Christians all the more radically against orişa worship and worshippers. A dozen such conferences have followed, albeit under increasingly factionalized leadership. As the leader of one series of conferences, Abimbọla is now regarded by some as the paramount leader of the global orisha-worshipping community and by some Latin Americans as the head of all "Yorubas" globally. Such an understanding of Abimbọla's role is clearly contested, and he himself denies any such personal pretensions. However, until now, no one else had to my knowledge ever been credited with such authority (J. L. Matory 2005a, 219–20).

At stake in the debate over the definition and worth of purity in these religions are also debates about the breadth and boundaries of the new world religion, as well as the worth of seniority as implied by any given logic of inclusion. Vega blames her withdrawal from the alliance with Abimbọla on his sexism. It is difficult not to see her subsequently enthusiastic endorsement of syncretism as a symbolic declaration of independence.

GENDER AND YORUBA-ATLANTIC ETHNICITY

Fourth and finally, are women subordinate in Yoruba-Atlantic religion and "culture," and should they, by tradition, be so?

Anthropologist and feminist heroine Ruth Landes (1940) influentially described the orixá priesthoods of Bahia, Brazil, as a "cult matriarchate," describing the ostensibly recent rise of male priests as a corruption of African tradition. By contrast, Afro-Cuban folklorist Rogelio Martínez Furé (2001) says of the Cuban Ocha tradition, "[T]here is a very well-defined gender structure: men carry out the most important responsibilities in the religion." He adds, "Women are subordinate at almost all levels of ritual life" (193; translation mine). For her part, Yoruba American sociologist Oyeronkẹ Oyewumi won brief but considerable recognition for declaring that there is no gender whatsoever in Yoruba culture or religion except what was imposed upon it by "colonialism." These conflicting positions about the role of gender in Yoruba-Atlantic "tradition" have been debated vigorously by hundreds of scholars and priests at a dozen conferences and numerous lectures and in an ever-growing number of publications—all with significant implications for the definition of belonging and the assignment of authority within this circum-Atlantic community. Also at stake are the defense of the community's reputation under the white gaze and individual scholars' pursuit of honor and evasion of stigma in the TWIs (see J. L. Matory 2003).

North American participants in these conferences tend to attribute the split between Vega and Abimbọla to Abimbọla's alleged sexism and to his putative inability to deal with a woman in an equal position of authority. Juana Elbein dos Santos, an Argentine-born Jewish woman deeply involved in the promotion Candomblé, opines that Abimbọla actually had trouble with the US sources of Vega's authority and financial backing. The explicit manifestation of this division was a disagreement over whether Ilé-Ifẹ̀, in Nigeria, is the Rome of the global orisha church or, instead, but one among seven equally holy sacred capitals. By the first logic, every other meeting of this world conference should take place in Ilé-Ifẹ̀. By the second logic, the meetings should take place in each of the six other capitals before returning to Ilé-Ifẹ̀. The decision would have equal implications for the relative rank of Abimbọla, on the one hand, and the overwhelmingly female leadership of the "great" Bahian temples, on the other. So the decision had gendered implications as well.

In Nigeria, *babalawo* diviners are almost all male, but a few, according to Abimbọla, are women. These women are eligible for this rank only after menopause, and they cannot "give birth to," or initiate, other *babalawo*. However, even this degree of gender flexibility disconcerts the large and highly organized community of Cuban *babalaos*, who declare that no woman or gay man can ever be a *babalao*, the Nigerian difference providing further proof to them that Cuban practice is truer to its ancient origins than is contemporary Nigerian practice and that contemporary Nigerians therefore have no right to assume seniority and corrective authority over the New World traditions. A lengthy online debate documents this controversy and the collective conscience of the antagonists. The debate over the validity of the Nigerian initiation of an Afro–Puerto Rican woman (not necessarily the former owner of Botánica Francisco de Asís) as a babalawo became a cause célèbre and the focus of a heated effervescence. The rivalry between the Nigerian and Nigerian-oriented babalawos and the Cuban and Cuban-oriented *babalaos* is even manifest in the subtly different color combinations used in their necklaces. In turn, the prominence of gay people in Cuban Ocha/Santería and Brazilian Candomblé, and any discussion of it, is abhorrent to most of the Nigerian scholars contributing to these debates over the legitimate boundaries of Yorubaness.

At a 2008 Harvard University conference on Ifa divination, which is the expertise of the *babalawo*, Yoruba American sociologist Oyeronkẹ Oyewumi challenged what she regarded as male supremacist *interpretations* of Ifa, such as Abimbọla's view that all witches (*àjẹ́*) are women (1997, 403), by contrasting the authenticity of what Ifa itself says with the implicit unreliability of what the *babalawo* diviners say. This contrast was for her a source of evidence that the Ifá divinatory texts, which some regard as the authoritative embodiment of Yoruba tradition and culture, do not avow that all witches are women. As with many of Oyewumi's assertions, debate could not proceed, as her position was premised on speculation about some plane of reality or moment in time to which no one had access. How, precisely, would one determine what Ifa says independently of what the *babalawo* and their intergenerationally transmitted oral recitations say? The strength of her rhetoric is that no one at a joint conference of priests and university scholars could refute her logic without appearing to question the existence of a disembodied and infallible spirit known as Ifa, which exists independently of its earthly interpretations.

With similar rhetorical craft, Oyewumi argued in *The Invention of Women* (1997) that the gender neutrality of pronouns, of most personal names, and of many other words in Yoruba proves that Yoruba culture once was and, in essence, still is free of both gender and power inequalities between males and females. Of course, any speaker of Yoruba could identify numerous terms in the language that do distinguish males from females—including ones that imply power asymmetry between the sexes: for example, *baálẹ̀* (nonroyal quarter or town chief [lit., father of the land]), *iyálé* (eldest wife of the house) and *baálé* (head of a residential compound [lit., father of the house]). It should be noted that female nonroyal quarter or town chiefs are so nonnormative that they, too, are called *baálẹ̀* and that the terms *baálé* and *iyálé* are distinguished from each other only by the gender of the referent. Yet in real social life, the persons described as "fathers of the house" rank far higher in the house than do the people called "mothers of the house" (J. L. Matory 2008, 539).

Moreover, a whole range of asymmetrical gender practices operate quite independently of the Yoruba lexicon. For example, polygyny has long been widely accepted, expected, and authorized by formal rituals in Yoruba society. Polyandry is not. Furthermore, amid the historical norm of viripatrilocal postmarital residence, every woman who marries is junior in rank to a child born in her new, postmarital residence even the day before her marriage. Yoruba men simply do not experience this sort of demotion during the normative life course. None of these phenomena is likely to be the product of Western colonial influences, but Oyewumi escapes the need to prove her point by declaring that all of the gendered terms and conduct currently present in Yoruba society must have emerged after "colonialism," a period that she dates variously—and confusingly—from the slave trade, from the beginning of the nineteenth century, and from European colonization, the last of which did not take place in the Ọyọ region, which is the setting of her argument, until the end of the nineteenth century. Conveniently, this vague and implicitly unchanging "precolonial" period is one to which Oyewumi and her various audiences have no documentary access. Naturally, though, her claims have provoked debate. An entire roundtable of Yoruba and non-Yoruba scholars of Yoruba life convened at the African Studies Association meeting in 2000 in order to refute her conclusions.

Whether or not her argument is credible in a scholarly sense, Oyewumi is, as the daughter of an important Yoruba monarch, a politically well-placed actor in the Yoruba-Atlantic field, and she possesses the rhetorical power to shift the debate over the authentic standards and diacritica of belonging to this superethnic identity. Hers is a direct challenge to the equally interested cultural diacritica advanced by Abimbọla. Yet their disagreement binds them in obligatory mutual respect. For example, Abimbọla cannot deny the transcendent existence of Ifa. Oyewunmi's and my debate unites us similarly in Yoruba-Atlantic belonging. Neither passion nor evidence will settle the matter.

Abimbọla has his own stake in some debatable postulates. For example, he views cowry-shell divination in Cuban Ocha and Brazilian Candomblé as lesser or poorly preserved forms of current West African forms of Ifa divination and as products of forgetfulness on the part of Cuban and Brazilian diviners (personal communication, November 9, 2010). At that 2008 conference at Harvard, several Nigerian male partisans of this view also told me that Ifa encompasses all Yoruba tradition and culture—in Africa and abroad—and is the authoritative version of Yoruba tradition and culture. These definitions of authentic Yoruba culture and ethnicity are highly empowering to Abimbọla and equally disempowering to the predominantly female and gay male leadership of many Western Hemisphere orisha traditions. The respect accorded to babalawos like Felisberto Sowzer and Martiniano do Bonfim in the first third of the twentieth century in Brazil is well known, and Braga (1988) reports a vague but enduring sense that male cowry-shell diviners in Brazil are regarded as superior to female cowry-shell diviners. He regards this sense as an implicit memory of Ifa. Currently, there are a few babalawos in Brazil who underwent initiation in Cuba or at the hands of Cuban immigrants to Brazil. They are concentrated in Rio de Janeiro and São Paulo and have little or no presence in Bahia, the heartland of the Candomblé religion. Yet the lack of controversy surrounding their presence is a measure of their marginality in current Afro-Brazilian religious networks. Moreover, there have never been many babalawos in Brazil, and Candomblé temples have long operated and conducted divinations quite independently of that class of diviners.

Controversy over the proper gender of sacred leadership is central to the daily conversations and lively sociality of Cuban and US orisha worshippers— even online. Priestesses of Santería/Ocha in Cuba and the United States hardly seem to divine for anyone but themselves, although, in the nineteenth and early twentieth centuries, there were several famous female Ocha diviners (*oriatés*) in Cuba. Nonetheless, Cuban *santeros* and *santeras* hotly contest the Cuban *babalaos*' androcentric claim to technical superiority over *santeros* and *oriatés*. *Santeros* say that their own competency and that of the *oriaté* diviners are simply different from that of *babalaos*. The principle that no woman can ever be a *babalao* is grudgingly accepted but resented by many Cuban and US *santeros*, including *oriatés*, but it is rumored that gay men have secretly become *babalaos*. Some Cuban Santería/Ocha temples, in principle, never call upon *babalaos*, as their competency is considered dispensable, and the skills of the largely male *oriaté* diviners are considered sufficient.

There are also West African counterparts to the disregard of the *babalawo* diviners' assertion of superiority. In Ọyọ North, where I conducted extensive field research among the female worshippers of Yemọja and the male and female worshippers of Ṣango, I never witnessed any interaction between these possession priests and the local community of *babalawo* diviners. They did not even attend each other's festivals. The worshippers of Yemọja and of Ṣango conducted all of their own divination, even on the most important matters.

Peel (1990) shows that, among orisa devotees, the *babalawo* diviners in nineteenth-century West Africa enjoyed the best rapport with the Christian missionaries. The epistemological styles of the pastor and the *babalawo* were more compatible than either style was with that of the possession priests. This fact may help us to understand why the *babalawo* have thrived more than the orisa worshippers in colonial and postcolonial Nigeria; why the *babalawo* have led the way in organizing the dwindling Nigerian orișa priesthoods in organizations such as Ìjọ Ọrúnmìlà and other church-like orișa-worshipping congregations; and perhaps even why the *babalaos* enjoy such prestige and state support in Havana. Indeed, the fact that Ifá and the *babalaos* have a weak and relatively recent presence in Cuba outside of the national capital causes me to think that Ifa's success—where it succeeds—is directly related to the forms of state-centered or Western power found most strongly in royal, national, and imperial capitals. Indeed, *babalawo* in Nigeria consciously claim powers duplicating those of monarchs. Their ostensible superiority is a reflection of state power.

Any given worshipper is entitled to decide whether such symbols and claims of sovereignty better serve that worshipper's spiritual needs. Despite its prestige and increasing dominance among orisha worshippers in both Cuba and Nigeria, Ifa is not a diacritic of Yoruba-Atlantic identity for everyone. Indeed, its role in the definition of Yorubaness is either implicitly or passionately debated in both countries, as well as in the US-based orisha-worshipping community. When I reported these facts at the Harvard conference on Ifa, the same attendees who had declared Ifa the exhaustive and authoritative account of Yoruba tradition and culture expressed incredulity and anger. It is our desire for each other's understanding and agreement, rather than our agreement, that indexes our degree of Yoruba-Atlantic belonging.

In sum, the controversial view that Ilé-Ifẹ̀ is the capital of this new world religion and that Ifa is its master text bears profound practical implications for the gender and complexion of leadership, as well as the validity of syncretism, in the Yoruba-Atlantic community. Whereas Abimbọla's interests lie in the lumping together of Yoruba-Atlantic identity, the leaders of old priestly lineages and the priestesses of the Western Hemisphere have a greater stake in territorial nationalism. Each position has a rationale based on its own definition of Yoruba culture.

Predictably, opinions about the proper place of homosexuality also unite the Yoruba-Atlantic transnation in debate. I have argued that the metaphors in West African Ọyọ-Yoruba religious parlance and attire represent the relationship between a god and a possession priest as similar to the relationship between a rider and a horse and between a husband and a wife. The Yoruba term *gùn* (to mount) can describe not only what a rider does to a horse and what a male animal does to a female animal in the sexual act but also what a god does to the possession priest. And the priest may be called a "wife" (*iyàwó*), a "mount" (*ẹlẹ́gùn*), or a "horse" (*ẹṣin*). These facts about the West African possession priesthood, which are transliterated in the parlance of Latin American orisha worshippers, help me to understand why men who are described by Ruth Landes (1940), for example, as "passive homosexuals" are so common in the possession priesthoods of Brazilian Candomblé and Cuban Santería. Indeed, in both of those traditions, males who are susceptible to spirit possession are regularly suspected of being "passive homosexuals" (*maricones* [Sp.]; *bichas* or *adés* [Port.]) (J. L. Matory [1994] 2005b). That is, in Brazil, Cuba, and the Cuban diaspora, a set of West African metaphors has been *reinterpreted* to encompass Latin American conceptions of gender, resulting in a Latin American inference that the kind of males who submit to spiritual "mounting" are also usually the kind of males who submit to sexual penetration. The added fact is that such men tend to feel at home in Candomblé and Santería/Ocha and are often highly respected as possession priests.

In response to my observation, Oyewumi (1997) accused me of calling the West African possession priests "drag queens" and "symbolic if not actual homosexuals," arguing to the contrary that homosexuality is foreign to "the Yoruba conception" (117). I have never said that West African Yoruba possession priests are any kind of homosexual, much less "drag queens." Oyewumi has various motives to distort my arguments. First, she would like for it to be known in the TWIs that her authority to speak of Yoruba culture is greater than mine, and, second, she wishes to defend her ethnic group against the pervasive suspicion that Africans are overly and inappropriately sexual. Similarly, Abimbọla has expressed to me in personal communications his offense at the idea of his religion being discussed in terms related to sex. Ọlajubu (2003, 14, 114) and Okome (2001) have also done so in writing. I reminded Abimbọla that virtually every religion on the planet is preoccupied with sex and that the Nigerian Ṣango and Yemọja priests who mentored me talked about it openly and jocularly (see also Matory 2008).

Sexual puritanism and especially the denial of indigenous homosexuality are nearly universal and defining features of the public self-representation of populations trying to prove their worth to their British colonizers and former colonizers. Hindu nationalists have long engaged in similar debates with Western scholars, which debates are an important de facto dimension of the "Indo-European civilisation" that binds them in mutual regard. Of course, these discourses have marginalizing and sometimes murderous implications for the same-sex-loving subpopulations of the nation. For example, in 1999, Yoruba cadets in the Nigerian Defence Academy were put on trial for alleged homosexual acts. This nationalist reaction to collective stigma also marginalizes the *wọ̀wọ̀*, a refined class of male homosexual entertainers that once existed in Ìjẹ̀bú-Yorùbá society and a more general class of anally penetrated men who were called *adódìí* among the Ìjẹ̀bú-Yorùbá as late as the mid-twentieth century. In 1989, I met a number of male-loving Yoruba men in London and now understand one of the reasons that they preferred to live there. An equally defensive, nostalgic, and frozen view of "the Yoruba conception" might disqualify Oyewumi herself for her choice to cut her hair short and to wear pantsuits or disqualify Abimbọla on account of his willingness to forgo animal sacrifice as an element of ritual practice. But sovereignty in any population means deciding who needs to be excluded, while feeling immune to exclusion by others. This is a lesson taught equally well by Native Americans who exclude their partly African-descended members from tribal citizenship.

The Nonethnic Audience and the Inducement to Ethnicity

In the end, these are not so much debates over the quality of the evidence or its syllogistic implications but instances of social positioning in response to stigma. The excluded always long for a space where they themselves can exclude and the stigmatized for a space where we can stigmatize. Some of the rhetorical positions in these debates are plausible only in the context of the diaspora and especially of the TWI, which is different in a number of ways from Howard. At Florida International University, Hunter College, Seattle University, and the University of Wisconsin at Madison, there are fewer people with research and personal experience in these religions and lifeways with the potential to contradict even the most arbitrary assertions by an American African about his or her African culture. Second, the ethnically unmarked but predominantly white audience constrains the dissent of American Africans who knew better and inspires a conspiracy of silence (J. L. Matory 2003). Unveiling the fraud of one's coethnic risks embarrassing the whole ethnically marked group. Moreover, if believed, some outlandish tales underline the "exotic" nature of the speaker's group and, thus, its deservingness of collective exemption from the stigma imposed upon similar-looking natives (see Manyika 2003). Third, by embodying just the right aspects of the dominant group's ideals, such "exotic" scholars hope to pry the door open just wide enough to get themselves in. Finally, these debates concern values of little importance or credibility to the majority of Nigerians in Nigeria and in most of the diaspora. Like most other debates in the TWIs, they do not depend for their efficacy on their immediate helpfulness to the non-white "folk." Rather, they score points by lapidating or obliterating a genealogy of antecedent positions within the Western academy about race, gender, rank, beauty, justice, and what makes a people a people. Though they make selective reference to the "folk," they are framed by the "habitus" (Bourdieu [1972] 1985), or the strategic dispositions, of the academy. They are positions by which people in particular disciplines strategically vie for leadership and articulate their dignity in an atmosphere of pervasive doubt. The most influential culture-makers vividly dream of a future ideal in the terms of a hyperreal past, which occasionally has powerful reverberations beyond the walls of the academy.

In between Heaven and Hell

If you start out from Howard University Hospital, at the southwest corner of the campus, you go eleven blocks west on U Street and three blocks up Eighteenth. There you find Heaven and Hell in one converted four-story Adams Morgan townhouse. Within this bar, bright neon signs identify the upstairs terrace as "Heaven" and the basement as "Hell." From Heaven you get a good view of the Bukom Café across the street, where Senegalese, Cameroonians, Nigerians, and Ghanaians together eat peppery meat, fish, and vegetable stews with rice and fried plantain or with doughy starches like fermented corn-based *kenke*, cassava-based *Ẹ̀bà/fùfú*, pounded yam, and *àmàlà*, made from rehydrated yam or plantain flour. After the house opens at around 4:00 p.m., you can also watch soccer together on the big screen; discuss boxing and baseball; drink Star, Gulder, or Tusker beer; and, on weekends, listen to live bands. The upbeat Nigerian juju and Congolese soukous contrast sharply with the melancholy minor chords and melisma of the Habesha music played at the parade of Ethiopian and Eritrean restaurants stretching back to Howard's campus and beyond.

My son Adu and I often dined at Bukom Café, in the midst of our circulation among of the Subway sandwich shop and the various purveyors of Trinidadian roti, Pakistani lamb dishes, Creole gumbo, and my own low-carb, high-vegetable concoctions at home. The Bukom requited our longing for Bunmi and Ayọ's company. It also reminded me of the sour *kenke* and peppery fried fish—a specialty of the Bukom neighborhood in Accra, Ghana—that I used to savor in the dark with the Ghanaian women street vendors on Victoria Island, Lagos, after my uncle Badejọ and his "Brazilian" wife had gone to bed. Ghana and Nigeria had exchanged human and culinary diasporas, sometimes violently, for decades, just as Yorubaland and Brazil had done for centuries. Even Accra has a Brazilian returnee neighborhood called "Tabom," meaning "It's Good" or "OK."

At Bukom's Washingtonian outpost, the televisions loudly broadcast several soccer games at once. Bored by the on-screen action, I would chat with the Ghanaian Yoruba owner and his teenage son, who felt overworked and overdisciplined on account of his parents' being immigrants and business owners. The father did not like his telling me so. I then predicted that Adu would have some comparable complaint about his African American father, and I have recently discovered that I was right. He recently called me a "helicopter dad." Perhaps for that reason, the semester we returned to Cambridge, he did get a perfect score on the Massachusetts Comprehensive Assessment System examinations (Guha 2003). His success was all the more remarkable because he was a year younger than the average student in his grade, since he had skipped the second year of kindergarten.

Like my Panamanian friend and me, Adu and the son of the restaurateur may one day thank their parents for the kick-start. However, while the restaurateur's son will likely attribute his future successes to the advantages of having an immigrant and non–African American upbringing, my son will attribute his advantages to his mother's being Nigerian. However, if I am credited, it is likely to be for my being a professor or belonging to some other nonethnic category to which millions of other responsible African American parents belong. Yet my parenting style could hardly be called anything but African American. While I worried that my helicoptering would make him neurotic, both the continual news of Black boys being shot down in the street and of the "achievement gap" reminded me of what all of my African American forebears told me: "If you are Black, you have to be twice as good to get half as far." Even in the absence of the deliberate oppression and psychological assault suffered by Black Americans, white Americans, too, worry about their own achievement gap in relation to the higher average standardized test scores of selected groups of European, Asian, and Asian American students. However, they seldom cognize this phenomenon in terms of collectively white incompetency, laziness, and family dysfunction.

As I write, I worry even more about the fact that my son grew up in predominantly white communities, where his peers, whose opinions most preoccupied him, unself-consciously regurgitated white American narratives about the nature of human diversity and social order, and where it was possible to receive his biracial friend's unfavorable comparison of a Black man with a large cheese pizza as sociology rather than absurdity. Unless he looks back like the Sankofa bird, Adu may forget about the lineage of African American men and women whose love and ferocious commitment to excellence culminated in his own success. He may forget that Blackness includes not just the possibility of acting out imposed stereotypes but also a long legacy of dogged struggle against stigma in pursuit of upward mobility.

Almost every time I am back in Washington, I drive past Heaven and Hell, reminded of another Africa and another borderland of racial and ethnic ambiguity, where, instead of thriving, like my son, a young Dinka man lost his life. In 2002, the Arab-dominated government of the Islamic

Republic of Sudan was still at war with the marginalized inhabitants of its southern provinces. Reports of rampant state-sponsored slave catching, rape, murder, and ethnic cleansing were common in the Western press but were denied by the government. Human rights advocates accused the government of racism, while the government denied that dark brown Arabs could logically be accused of racism toward the bitumen-black Christians and animists of the south. While they blamed the Zionists for the slander, I had no doubt that the northern Sudanese Arabs were trying to excoriate a bit of their own stigmatized blackness. Years later, in 2011, the Republic of South Sudan would, through a bilateral treaty and a popular vote, obtain its independence.

Despite their long struggle for collective dignity, the stigmatized people of South Sudan have themselves now found a most violent way to "stratify their own." Perhaps there is no irony there.

What I learned about the life and death of Anyong Kout Deng comes from my Shilluk friend Daag, three Dinka friends of Anyong's, and a northern Sudanese Arab named Ahmed Bashir, whom I met at Anyong's funeral. Daag lived in a neat Capitol Hill apartment and earned his living as a nighttime security guard at the Howard Law School and at the Blackburn student center. This gentle and cosmopolitan man revealed an identity ecumene of which Evans-Pritchard had sketched but the palest outlines.

Anyong had left home optimistic at a time of war and had initially lived and studied pharmacy in Perugia, Italy, before moving to Washington, DC. There, in 1997 and 1998, he continued his studies for a year and a half at the Howard University School of Pharmacy. However, he ran out of money and needed to pay $2,000 before he could resume his studies.

Anyong had no wife or child, so he shared an apartment in northern Virginia with two other young Dinkas. And it was the habit of some of these young single men, explained Daag, to get drunk and pick fights. Most of the southern Sudanese people in the Washington area, Daag said, are Dinka. When I asked why, he seemed perplexed by my guess that the Dinkas had been special victims of land grabs, enslavement, and even castration by Sudanese Arabs during two civil wars (1955–72, 1983–2005). Rather than agreeing as such, he said, "Yes, because they are in the area with lots of the nomadic." As he seemed unable to find a word that he thought I would understand, I asked, "Like the Baggara [Arabs]?"

"Yes, the Baggara," he replied.

Unlike me, Daag seemed not to blanket Arabs with the suspicion of abuse toward southern Sudanese or of indifference to their suffering. Daag told me that his own wife, who works for the United Nations, had just finished a vacation in Syria. She had then returned to her job in Pakistan and might soon be sent to Afghanistan.

In a way, Ahmed taught me a great deal, too. He spoke with an affected, thuggish street accent and said that he is the kind of northern Sudanese person to whom southerners run for refuge during times of war. According to him, the southern and northern Sudanese in Washington get along well, and he is a sort of intermediary between Washington-area southern Sudanese and the District of Columbia authorities. For example, he planned to talk with his friend, the chief detective in the DC police department, about Anyong's death. In the know, Ahmed identified the owner of Heaven and Hell as an Eritrean named Mahari.

On Saturday, May 11, 2002, Anyong apparently went to Hell and got drunk. Then some sort of fight ensued. At first, he left Hell but then changed his mind and went back to look for his antagonist. However, when he found and hit the wrong man, his victim and the victim's companions beat Anyong severely. One of them struck him on the side of his head with a bottle. Daag touched his own face to indicate where. Anyong fell out but got up again, saying that he was OK.

The bottle-wielding assailant left unidentified, though he was definitely a black man. Anyong's roommate who accompanied him to the club that night also took him home, where Anyong slept until afternoon and woke up wailing. Before long, his brain had drowned in blood.

The funeral was supposed to begin at 1:00 p.m. at the Evangelical Free Church on Gallows Road in Annandale, Virginia—a favorite of the southern Sudanese women in the Washington area. Like most of the men, Daag doesn't go often, but like most northern Shilluks, he was missionized by American Presbyterians. Most southern Shilluks, on the other hand, are Catholics.

Daag, Adu, and I did not reach the funeral until 2:00 p.m., the same time that Anyong had died.

When we reached the church, a Ugandan minister from Baltimore named Pastor Mike was preaching that Christians of faith were promised resurrection. In heaven, they would "take off the corruptible and put on the incorruptible." He endlessly repeated the theme that the Christian could hope for eternal life in heaven, where he or she would see dead loved ones again. A multiethnic southern Sudanese choir of a dozen people sang several songs in what Daag said was the colloquial Arabic spoken in southern Sudan. It is quite different from classical Arabic, which he and others had studied in the government schools in the south and in which one normally writes. The songs were call-and-response harmonies, with one female solo offering the brief call and the chorus responding. There was prayer with bowed heads and a brief sermon by the white pastor of the local congregation, who arrived a twenty minutes later than we. Sudanese people streamed in until the end, at about 2:30. Anyong had lived so briefly and so unknown by the people appointed to speak for him that there was nothing to fill this farewell but formulae.

The mourners' black polyester clothes had not been cut for their willowy bodies and looked especially shiny against their matte-black skin, which looked bleached by misery and cold, in contrast to the ebony brilliance of Alek Wek or Leni Riefenstahl's Nuba. The one young man in khaki- and brown-toned hip-hop attire stood out. The one white woman sat in the middle of the audience during the service and stood at the front toward the end, as though she were some kind of official.

Throughout, two young women kneeled in front of their chairs, three feet from the closed casket. The hefty sister of the deceased, who had come down from Connecticut, sat near them. She had not seen Anyong in several years. At the end, Pastor Mike organized a viewing of the body—family first and then section by section. Many cried. I saw that Anyong bore large, shiny scarifications along the sides of his face.

The funeral director was an African American with missing lower incisors, as though he had passed some nineteenth-century African test of bravery. He represented the W. H. Bacon Funeral Home, owned by Wanda C. Brown. On the funeral home's card, a line in Spanish reflected the changing demographics of Washington's inner city.

Anyong was buried in a plot near busy Braddock Road West, the cheapest section of Fairfax Memorial Park. A collection had been taken up in what Daag called "the community" to pay the $6,000 cost of the burial. The plot alone cost $1,500. Next to the grave was an awning with a row of chairs for the family underneath. Anyong's youthful photograph at first sat atop the casket and then, after the wind blew it over, on the ground in front of it.

Pastor Samuel from Virginia reminded us about our not seeing Anyong again until we all get to heaven. And Mr. Piyo Tem Kuag (Anyong's "uncle"—really his father's cousin; English translation of the highly specific terms of Sudanese kinship systems is difficult) made remarks in English and Dinka on behalf of the family. Before the casket was lowered, each family member was guided by Pastor Samuel to drop pinches of sand from a dustpan into the grave, this after his explanation that God made us from ashes and returns us to ashes before, in the end, we all go to heaven. The words sounded recorded and as ill-fitting as most of the mourner's clothes. By the third time I heard them, I wondered if even the pastors believed in this confusing postmortem itinerary. I did not hear the swell of weeping that usually follows this incantation in the Black American churches I know. So I looked for signs that these mourners had their own way of understanding this senseless waste of life. I longed to understand the graveside call-and-response songs, led by a woman who stood not in front but behind the first layer of the crowd.

Speechlessly, people milled around after the coffin was lowered and then stepped back as a crane lowered a huge, flat black stone to cover the coffin and a truckload of red earth was tipped over into the hole. All I learned from Pastor Francis was that this new practice of lidding the grave served to prevent people from stealing the coffin, which was costly and could otherwise be resold.

Daag dismissed my suspicion that the family would seek vengeance against the killer; there are laws here that will take care of the matter. In cases when a Shilluk family at home agrees to have handled in the "native court," the bereaved family would be entitled to ten cattle for the death, no matter what the dead person's gender, age, or historical free/slave status. He says that similar payments exist to compensate for deaths in Sharia courts, which can be used to decide such cases in northern Sudan. This much I knew how to ask, and Daag was perhaps being kind in not dismissing my questions as foolishly anachronistic, influenced as they were by Evans-Pritchard's classic ethnography of the Nuer. But in no other moment during my field research did I feel so distant in class and culture from my interlocutors—not from the Gullah/Geechees, the Occaneechi-Saponis, the Louisiana Creoles, the Trinidadians, the Habesha, or the Yoruba. I knew these populations as I was known, each of us an accustomed element in the other's taxonomy of self and constituent other. On the other hand, among these southern Sudanese, I had to fish to find the signs to which we felt a common emotional response or a matter of equal concern to debate over. Surely this was a matter of experience and familiarity. Thus, Anyong's people reminded me of the deep family resemblances between me and all of these older Afro-Atlantic populations (some of them only *possibly* Afro) who were burning rubber to distinguish themselves from people like me.

Fortunately, Daag's imagination about his connections to the Afro-Atlantic world and its dilemmas was richer than mine. After the funeral, at Daag's Capitol Hill apartment, Daag, Adu, and I watched *Guess Who's Coming to Dinner*, a 1967 film in which Bahamian-American actor Sidney Poitier plays the perfect, well-groomed, and unmistakably Black American fiancé—he is even a physician who leads innovative medical initiatives in Africa—and wins over the publicly liberal but hypocritically reluctant father of his white fiancée. Daag apparently likes the story enough to have bought a VHS copy. In the car on the way to his place, he had said that Sudanese frown upon one of their com-

HEAVEN AND HELL 443

FIGURE 6.5. Mourners at Anyong's funeral, Fairfax, Virginia, 2002. Photograph by the author.

patriots' marrying a white person, but everyone, he conceded, has to make his or her own decision. Daag also disapproves of the leading southern Sudanese figure in the United States—a professor of political science. However, the professor's marriage to a white woman is not the main reason. Rather, Daag disapproved of this highly accomplished and educated man because an "elder" such as he should show an interest in the affairs of "the community" and, therefore, appear at funerals like this. People are judged not just by their educational accomplishments, said Daag, but also by their conduct.

On the bookshelf in Daag's apartment was a statue of a brush-topped helmeted Greek spearman with his possibly exposed privates facing the rear of the bookshelf. Also on the walls were an ornately framed, French-looking gilt mirror, a Pakistani rug (brought from Pakistan by his wife), several model ships, and two clocks, one of them sharing a frame with a model ship. His artwork also included decorated ostrich eggs—one beaded with the then-current Sudanese national colors (red, green, black, and white) and the other of variegated colors.

Daag blamed former president Jaafar Nimeiri for the major problems in Sudan. Treaties in 1972 had promised autonomy to the south, but Nimeiri abrogated them, saying the treaties "are not the Koran or the Bible." Thus the second civil war began. Nimeiri also changed the flag to imitate those of the Arab countries. Before 1970, the flag had been blue, yellow, and green—much nicer, said Daag. The current flag, he agreed, was similar in color to the Palestinian flag. Daag also displayed on his apartment walls wooden African masks, photos of a bronze Baule mask from Côte d'Ivoire, of male and female Bamana *tyi wara* antelope sculptures and of a carved Dogon horseman from Mali, of a Yoruba *egungun* ancestral masquerade from Nigeria, and of a Yombe caryatid stool from the Democratic Republic of Congo. Daag's usual armchair was draped with a length of cloth printed with ancient Egyptian gold ankhs. In the corner, there is a piano bench upholstered with elephant motifs and designs resembling the Yoruba god Eshu and the Pueblo Kokopelli—both tricksters who crosscut boundaries and muddy the border between the expected and the unexpected. Daag also kept a lamp on top of the bench.

Daag's bookshelves were full of books belonging to him and his cousin—books on Sudanese politics and on Palestine, Arabs, and Israel; C. G. and Brenda Z. Seligman's *Pagan Tribes of the Nilotic Sudan* (1932), and Bob Woodward's *The Choice* (1996), about Bill Clinton's first presidential election. Near the kitchen, Daag displayed the Smithsonian catalog for the museum exhibition "Wrapped in Pride: Ghanaian Kente and African American Identity," which features on the cover Eliot Elisofon's photo of a gold- and kente-draped chief on the cover.

One of Daag's other books was *Feeling the Spirit* (1994), an anthology of the photos of *New York Times* photographer and HBCU graduate Chester Higgins. Most of these photos document West African–inspired religious phenomena in the Americas, though many of the photographed celebrants and priests look white. On the cover is the image of a white Brazilian woman dressed for and apparently possessed by Oxum, the Brazilian version of a goddess who, according to her Nigerian praise poetry (*oriki*) originated from my wife's town of Igede-Ekiti, Nigeria. Also featured in the book are photographs of Native Americans of partly African ancestry. This book appears to represent Higgins's own transoceanic superethnic self-construction as African, not just politically but also culturally and spiritually pan-African. In the postscript, Higgins honors his dead mother and, through her, proclaims himself a descendant of the Gullahs but is unashamed to call their original Gullah ancestor "thick-tongued"—a prejudicial but apparently affectionate reference to that ancestor's creole language variety.

Southern Sudanese identities and debates emerged historically at the interface of worlds that have been racialized as African and Arab. This fact, in addition to their distinctive appearance and their cattle culture, causes me to imagine them at a far remove from the Afro-Atlantic sources of my birth and of the dilemmas most central to my identities. To me, northeast Africans tend to look quite different from western Africans and African Americans—their lifeways, like their bodies, having been shaped by the convergence of a different set of populations, cultigens, and commercial networks. However, my imagination is clearly not the limit of Daag's or of filmmaker Haile Gerima's. And my own involuntary pursuit of what is frozen and fixed among them failed me. Howard's northeast African population reminds me that heaven and hell have Afro-Byzantine, Afro-Ottoman, and Afro-Arab axes, as well, with their own motives and means of embrace and distancing. However, Africans from these points of encounter find a convincing model for their own unsettled dilemmas in the icons and the "literally-defined world" of Howard and of the Afro-Atlantic peoples.

American Africans are among the richest and best-educated Americans, but they come from the poorest and one of the most culturally diverse continents. They are thus an apt metaphor of the heaven and the hell that dwell in every black body on the planet—at once the slave and the spirit of hope, rebellion, and freedom known best to the slave. Indeed, a person born to privilege could not imagine freedom without pondering the hope of the slave. The world's beacons of freedom—the United States and France—were, at the time that they propagated their most enduring noble ideals, major slave-trading and slaveholding nations. It is no surprise, then, that many elite American Africans—themselves cast by the world into symbolic abjection—are willing to redeem themselves at the expense of African Americans. Such is the nature of ethnological schadenfreude.

But, as American Africans at Howard demonstrate, Plutarchian syncretism is an equally plausible mode of culture making, and the choice between these strategies is shaped by context. Yes, people often identify themselves and their cultures according to the largest group that includes them and excludes the antagonist, as Evans-Pritchard would predict, but some people make a different ethical choice. The "literally-defined world" of the university is rich in the raw materials of multiple identity configurations. Howard hosts much ethnological schadenfreude. However, the loss of hope in the homeland, precarious economic times in the host country, and the predominantly white immediate audience create a very different set of motivations for American African professors at TWIs, generating highly influential debates about the cultural diacritica of a centripetal, supraethnic Yoruba identity. On the one hand, this identity configuration is far removed from the realities of most West African Yoruba lives, but it entails forms of self-exoticization that carry individual benefits for the scholar. On the other hand, Yoruba-Atlantic religion is a powerful allegory of reform in African-diasporan and white people's lives. Above all, the intensity of its internal debates demonstrates the strength of the interethnic community—American African, African American, Euro-American, Latin American, and Latino—that participates in them. During my investigation of Afro-Atlantic ethnic diversity, my Sudanese mentors at first seemed to offer one lesson. Even as we appear to disagree diametrically, the common assumptions shared by antagonists become obvious when they encounter populations whose arguments are unfamiliar. Yet under certain circumstances, such as their superior imagination or attention, these unfamiliar populations may recognize themselves in our debates.

Conclusion: "Through a Glass, Darkly"

> For now we see through a glass, darkly; but then face to face: now I know in part; but then shall I know even as also I am known.
>
> 1 CORINTHIANS 13:12

The global light-dark hierarchy needs black people as its anchor, just as every hierarchical system needs its constituent other—not just as the touchstone of middling populations' consent to the sovereignty of others but as a walking, breathing id, and occasionally superego, to the sovereign population. Cast in the role of the collective id, African Americans are experienced as an inherent danger to society. As the collective superego, we may be allowed to perform the role of Christlike victim and selfless servant to others. So it is difficult for the sovereign and the middling to recognize us when we step, or even stampede, out of these roles. When they are forced to notice us outside of these roles, we are a threat to their self-esteem and, in moments of even the most mundane disagreements and social conflicts, are quick to experience flashbacks and repressed memories of who we "really" are.

On the evening of February 26, 2012, an African American teenager was returning from the neighborhood convenience store to the home of his father's fiancée in Sanford, Florida. Wearing a hooded sweatshirt and armed only with a can of iced tea and a packet of Skittles candy, Trayvon Martin looked suspicious to Neighborhood Watch volunteer George Zimmerman, the son of a German American father and a Peruvian American mother with a small degree of African ancestry. Against the instructions of the 911 emergency police operator, Zimmerman followed the young Martin. By the end of their encounter, Zimmerman had shot the seventeen-year-old dead. Zimmerman claims that the unarmed boy had circled Zimmerman's vehicle aggressively and later, unprovoked, set upon him, requiring Zimmerman to defend himself with the gun he had been carrying all along. He seemed to be hunting for an excuse to use it. On the other hand, the person whom Martin called to express his own fear of the unidentified stranger pursuing him,

Haitian-American Rachel Jeantel, reported Martin's words that "a creepy-ass cracker" was following him. She quoted Martin's saying, "Oh, shit. The nigga [meaning 'person'] is behind me! . . . Why are you following me? . . . Get off! Get off!" A jury of five white women and an Afro-Latina woman who later said that she regretted succumbing to their pressure, acquitted Zimmerman of murder, suggesting that they preferred to believe his story over Jeantel's.

Since then, Zimmerman has been the subject of an ever-expanding list of revelations—a previous arrest for "resisting officer with violence," an accusation of antiblack racism by his cousin, and separate accusations of domestic violence by his estranged wife and his girlfriend (e.g., Capehart 2013).

In *Black Skin, White Masks* ([1952] 2008), Frantz Fanon coins the term "double narcissism" to describe the social psychology whereby whites fashion themselves the opposite of blacks by projecting all that is bad, wrong, and fearsome onto the black other and denying the multidimensionality of their white selves. The black subjects of this projection are also vulnerable to this pathological condition, imagining all that is good, right, and comforting in them onto whites, and thus participating in the denial of their own multidimensionality.

Paul's words in his first letter to the members of the young church at Corinth bespeak the difficulty of seeing the truth of the other, and they serve as an apt metaphor of racialized subjectivities. The subjects of *Stigma and Culture* are visually impaired by double narcissism. This book explores the subjectivity of the in-between—not only "exotic blacks" but also borderline whites like George Zimmerman and all populations in flight from last place. In the United States, their ambiguity often intensifies their reaction to African Americans. Borderline and other status-anxious whites—including the working-class Irish and Italians who disproportionately populate northern police forces, like the poor whites historically enlisted to police Black people in the South—often find it as difficult to cognize an innocent Black boy enjoying childish pleasures while walking back to where his father lived as they find it to see any implications about white men and boys in the fact that they commit the vast majority of mass murders in American workplaces, schools, and public buildings. It is as difficult for many whites and "wannabe" whites to recognize what is typically black about Uncle Badejọ, Elliot Skinner, my father, and me as it is for them to recognize what is typically white about settler colonialism, lynching, union shops closed to Black people, the suppression of minority voting rights, Wall Street fraud, *Hillbilly Hand Fishin'*, and fraternity gang rape.

For example, William J. Bennett—radio talk-show host and former secretary of education under President Ronald Reagan—said in 2005,

I do know that it's true that if you wanted to reduce crime, you could—if that were your sole purpose—you could abort every black baby in this country, and your crime rate would go down. . . . That would be an impossible, ridiculous and morally reprehensible thing to do, but your crime rate would go down. (quoted in Herbert 2005)

Bill Bennett was talking about my son Adu and my daughter Ayọ, the hope of my dreams. He was also talking about Trayvon Martin. Unable to imagine that a similar thought experiment could be applied to people of his own race, gender, and religion, Bennett attacked his critics and defended his remarks as his entitlement under the First Amendment to the US Constitution. All of the petty street crimes of poor Black teenagers put together would not rise up to the ankles of the combined holocaust that was the Atlantic slave trade, the near extermination of Native Americans, and the Shoah. Does the Constitution justify idle public talk about the problems that would be solved by the abortion of all Christian white children, including Bennett's two sons, John and Joseph? Would aborting them and all of their kind have been the worthy basis of a First Amendment-protected thought experiment?

Bennett grew up in the same city as I and is roughly halfway between my father's age and mine. He did not attend schools of the same rank as mine, but he chaired the National Endowment for the Humanities, which has funded my research and the activities of the center that I direct at Duke. He served in the same presidential administration as Black neoconservatives Clarence Thomas and Clarence Pendleton. How did the complex and varied swathe of humanity that looks roughly like us and our children come to be reduced, in the recesses of his imagination and among the themes that drive his talk-show improvisation, to criminality? Are our children not first human beings, even when they do commit crimes, and therefore deserving of a punishment *proportionate* to those crimes, rather than preemptive extermination? Would Bennett think it equally reasonable to consider a preemptive death penalty for a white child, or would he assume that only an unborn *white* child possesses too much potential goodness, love, wisdom, and generosity to be written off before birth? Why did he choose words with so little concern that parents like Clarence Thomas, Clarence Pendleton, and me could hear him talking about our children that way? And by what hyperreal assumptions did he assume that people of his race and gender are the standard of good behavior and the Olympian judges of other populations' right to life? In 2005, this former supervisor of the nation's entire educational system seems to take for granted that, unlike my children, the millions of white criminals across our great land

FIGURE C.1. Our family portrait, 2007. Photograph commissioned by the author.

enjoy the Jeffersonian presumption of the right to live. If only his opinion were unique. Every time a white person shoots down another unarmed Black boy, the comments pages of US newspapers fill up with anonymous affirmations of this very opinion, as do defense funds for the trained police officers who are often responsible for these deaths.

As a graduate of Williams College, the University of Texas, and Harvard Law School, Bennett is surely aware of the suggestive quality of his coyly Nazi-like rhetoric. I cannot help but imagine that he derived some deep satisfaction from miming for his lowbrow audience the momentary restoration of the white man to the throne from which people like them, for centuries, exercised the unchallenged power of life and death over Black people. He was flirting in the same direction as his boss Ronald Reagan, who began his 1980 presidential campaign in Philadelphia, Mississippi, where three young civil rights workers—James Chaney, Andrew Goodman, and Michael

Schwerner—were kidnapped, murdered, and buried under a dam by members of the Ku Klux Klan. In that Mississippi town, Reagan brought the crowd to its feet with the Confederate rallying cry "I believe in states' rights," the same words that southerners had used to defend slavery against the federal efforts to abolish it (Herbert 2005).

The Greek word in Paul's letter that has been translated as "glass" is ambiguous. It could mean "lens" or "mirror." Similarly, when status-anxious whites look through such a glass at the black constituent other, what they see could just as easily be an unveiled revelation of themselves, the savage they themselves fear being seen as, or the id that they cannot bear to acknowledge in themselves. They cannot see their own murderous fantasies of scapegoating for what they are. Black Americans tend to be more consciously thoughtful about these matters. Despite our best efforts to disprove or evade these narcissistic projections upon us, black people in the United States always have the sense of being seen through a glass darkly. The Trayvon Martin trial made an open discussion of the widespread anxiety among the parents of African American boys that, on some days, that glass is the scope of a white or even a wannabe white man's firearm.

My family recently had its own Trayvon Martin moment. Like many, this uncomfortable interracial encounter might be dismissed as a harmless mistake by goodwilled, color-blind people. Or it might be read as an instance of unconscious racism, in which a right-acting young Black man was prejudged "suspicious" and, even after proven innocent, subtly accused of not knowing his place. Like the man who innocently invited his new moose friend for a drink in the hunting lodge, many white readers will be surprised by the new friend's reaction to the moose heads on the wall.

Since moving to our mostly white Durham, North Carolina, neighborhood five years ago, we have been active socially and civically. My wife, our children, and I have been guests or hosts at numerous parties. Neighbors have toured our house, pre- and postrenovation. Indeed, it is one of the finest in the neighborhood. And my wife, Bunmi, volunteers in the neighborhood association. So everyone on our street knows us by face and by name. They know that our children are polite and that their colleges are top-tier. At the time of the incident, Ayọ was a rising senior at Harvard and Adu a rising sophomore at New York University, and Adu had done volunteer or paid work in several neighbors' homes.

Before her several-months-long vacation, our next-door neighbor asked Adu, then eighteen years old, to take care of her house. At 10:30 one night, having returned from working his two summer jobs, he stepped onto the neighbor's brightly lit front porch to get the watering can, which he took back to our yard to fill it from our spigot. Little did he know he had fallen under the suspicious gaze of a group gathered on another porch just twelve feet away.

Then three white men marched up onto our driveway to confront him.

"Can I help you?" Adu asked.

"Just wanted to see what was going on," one of them replied.

Standing in his own yard, my son answered, "I live right here. Z—— asked me to take care of her house."

"Oh, it's just Adu," announced one man.

Polite words were exchanged and, with Obama-esque equanimity, my son concluded, "No problem. I'm glad you're concerned about the safety of Z——'s house, too."

The story was so normal and yet so disturbing. The three white men were motivated by good, neighborly intentions. On the other hand, Adu was in danger, by no fault of his own.

I needed to talk to my neighbors—much as I hope this book will reach its black ethnic audience—to express the fear and pain that I felt, hoping that our shared discomfort would deepen rather than harm our friendship. That day, family and friends had again gathered on their porch to enjoy the homeowners' new granddaughter. A kind man, the grandfather made sure to introduce me all around. Spontaneously, his son—the baby's father—declared, "We had a little run-in with Adu the other day." The genial twenty-eight- or twenty-nine-year-old projected the out-loud confidence of the boss's son in the family business. They are tradesmen.

"It was bold!" he exclaimed with a laugh. "Eleven o'clock at night, this fella just walks RIGHT UP on the [vacationing neighbor's] porch, even with ALL OF US sitting over here on the porch! It was bold!"

The grandfather added, "It was funny!"

I said, "I don't think it was funny at all. I heard that everyone was polite, and I appreciate that. But the first thing I thought of was Trayvon, and I wanted to make sure that my boy was safe." And I had to ask: "Did any of the people who approached my son have guns? Because I know that a lot of the people on our street have guns." The grandfather assured me that they did not.

I struggled to keep my voice calm—to preserve our friendship with these good neighbors—but my upper lip quivered with instinctual fear for the life of my son and involuntary anger that this young father's words still implicitly blamed my son.

I remain baffled that my neighbors failed to recognize Adu from the start. I surely would have recognized their son on a brightly lit porch from twelve feet away. Yet members of dominant majority groups are often visually impaired when it comes to distinguishing minorities from one another. Even if they did not immediately recognize Adu, there were plenty of other exculpatory hints about who the tall young man on the porch might be. An empirically minded person who witnesses a young man walking straight up onto a brightly lit porch might see the actor as someone with nothing to hide, as someone who belongs on that porch. The recollection that they have a tall, young Black neighbor might have bolstered the impression of normalcy. Never mind the fact that we all knew Z—— had made similar arrangements with a young white male neighbor in the past and that that young neighbor was no longer around. Moreover, Z—— told me after the fact that she had informed the grandmother of the current arrangement with Adu. Yet, even days after my neighbor's son learned unambiguously who was on the porch that night and the entirely proper reason why, he persisted in recalling my son's behavior as "bold!" His psychology was as fixed in the same doubly narcissistic position as when the whole episode began. There was no sense that he recognized any error in his actions or that he felt embarrassed about them.

Did this young man's continued confidence in his judgment, his conduct, and his jovial words reflect youthful hubris? White-skin privilege? Being the boss's son? Or was it just insensitivity to what it's like to see a row of heads like your own mounted on the wall? I don't know. But this young white father still clearly felt qualified to judge the "boldness" of people like my son and deputized to check it when necessary. I had the strange feeling of being in another century.

I quietly lamented the endurance of the casual assumption—even among well-intentioned neighbors—that some young men are inherently suspicious. It was my neighbors who had been bold—not to mention mistaken—but they could not see it, and an apology for their insulting behavior was the last thing on their minds. I have good neighbors, but I was reminded that sometimes a right-acting young Black man pays for a neighbor's mistaken boldness with his life.

We have another white neighbor who, since we moved in, has extended us every kindness—helping to move trash bins on trash day, bag leaves, repair appliances, and so forth. He is not only kind but also witty and generous. Throughout the six years of our acquaintance, he and his wife have frequently invited us to their parties, where they serve a Bacchanalian array of homemade delicacies and top-drawer liquors. Yet, until two years after we had moved in, he never accepted an invitation to our parties or open houses.

By his own confession, he stocks his home with dozens of guns, both for hunting and in anticipation of self-defense. At the first party of ours that he attended, he cavalierly announced that, a year earlier, an off-duty police officer friend visiting his house had seen Adu and a Mexican American friend of his sitting and talking in that friend's parked car for two hours. (Adu says that it was, in fact, five minutes.) Our neighbor reported that the visitor told him, "Hey, there's two guys casing your house." Our neighbor then identified the "two guys" as my son and his Mexican American friend, who were standing next to us as this revelation unfolded.

This was one of the many occasions—dating back to that encounter with Adu's prekindergarten teacher—where I needed to address two audiences with equal urgency, correcting a well-intentioned white person's inappropriate remarks and fortifying my child against the potentially ill effects on his sense of self-worth.

I immediately urged our neighbor to tell the policeman that one of those "two guys" is currently a freshman at the University of North Carolina–Chapel Hill—the state's flagship public university—and that he had just won half a dozen prizes at his graduation from the city's finest public high school, Durham School of the Arts. Tell him, too, I said, that the other boy, my son Adu, is a freshman at New York University, a National Merit Scholar, and an AP Scholar with Distinction on account of his half dozen top scores on the precollegiate advanced placement examinations. Tell him that misjudgments like his have life-and-death consequences for boys who look like them and especially for those who look like my son.

Our neighbor tried to soften the blame on this policeman friend by saying that it was not the officer who used the word "casing" but our neighbor himself who had put those words into the officer's mouth. I said that, given the number of guns our neighbor has in his house and the number of recent cases of gun-toting white people's shooting Black boys based on a false judgment and an illegal self-deputization, this confession was hardly comforting. When I cited the shooting of Trayvon Martin, my neighbor concluded, "I think there was something more going on there than you're admitting." It was as automatic for him to suspect that the young Martin had it coming to him as it was for me to believe that an innocent child had died because a mentally imbalanced adult, programmed by US racism, had misrecognized him and overreacted.

What strikes me most about these experiences is the evidence of how long racially trained blindness persists amid goodwill and lengthy acquaintance. In each case, these white men told me their side of the story in a spirit of camaraderie, humor, and perhaps friendly teasing. Many Americans tease each other as a sign of trust and friendship, and such teasing often alludes to both the known vulnerabilities of its object and the competitive anxieties of the speaker. My family is better educated, our children attended more prestigious universities, and we live in a larger and finer house than any of these friendly white neighbors, all the more reason for them to stick it to us over the fact that our son is, in their doubly narcissistic mental world, easily mistaken for a criminal. What is actually funny is the racial narcissism by which our neighbor and his policeman friend could imagine that thieves parked in front of our house would be interested in his considerably smaller and less elegant house at all.

These two stories of double narcissism and white status anxiety illuminate the big picture surrounding the central theme of this book—the ethnological schadenfreude of black ethnics in the United States, the taste-based pursuit of class distinction among soi-disant "middle-class" Black people, and the proverbial "crabs in a barrel" phenomenon among all of these stigmatized populations. As much as they disappoint my early, naïve expectation that the oppressed would simply see themselves as one, these phenomena hardly ever caused me to fear for my life or for that of a family member. Only once during these investigations of black ethnicity—while surrounded by the reportedly knife-wielding dark Indian women at the Occaneechi-Saponi powwow—did I feel physically unsafe. The difference between most black ethnics and my white neighbors is that my dignity, my success, and my children's longevity offer immediate hope to most black ethnics, but not to my white neighbors. It is easier for whites to forget that we, too, are all ultimately in the same boat. Yet the Second Amendment "right to bear arms" and its subsequent judicial and popular interpretations contain a thinly veiled genocidal impulse in the DNA of settler colonies like the United States, South Africa, Australia, and Israel. In the wake of their monumental crimes of land expropriation, enslavement, and mass murder against the nonwhite inhabitants of their territories, the European-descended colonists live in a pressure cooker of suppressed guilt and fear of vengeance. Amid the double narcissism that colonialism and slavery have planted in the heart of these Herrenvolk democracies (Fredrickson 1982), whites are as quick to detect and react to signs of dark vengeance as Blacks and natives are to see the reenactments and reverberations of the initial white assault. Yet the overall system of racial hegemony works not mainly because of whites' continued armed suppression of Blacks but because, between these extremes of the light-dark hierarchy, there is a spectrum of hopefulness and hopelessness and of opportunities for one-upmanship instead of rebellion. Sovereignty always depends on the consent of the governed. Class and ethnological schadenfreude is not only a powerful motivator but also a mechanism of consent.

Discovery

When I began this research project in 1994 and until my immersion in the topic as a visiting professor at historically Black Howard University, I thought that immigrants of African ancestry to the United States and region-specific ethnic populations of African descent in the United States would, upon their encounter with the racial protocols of the US metropolis, embrace their Blackness, eschewing the nonbinary forms of racial identity that tend to prevail in most of their lands of origin. I had long recognized Blackness as a strategically essentialist concept (Spivak 1987) but still believed that this ideology, quintessential to the *longue-durée* US civil rights movement, from the late nineteenth century to the early 1970s, had proven itself the most obviously effective strategy of resistance to the forms of white supremacy that triumphed around the world during the first half of the twentieth century. At least at the level of political alliance, all people of African descent were, in my view, made essentially the same by virtue of our similar relationship to white colonizers, enslavers, and their descendants—descendants whose power was preserved by the inheritance of ill-gotten wealth, segregation, collusion against Black upward mobility, and strategies of divide and conquer.

At the level of "culture," I was convinced by the likes of W. E. B. Du Bois, Melville J. Herskovits, Roger Bastide, Fernando Ortiz, and Raymundo Nina Rodrigues that there were enough of a common ancestral past and enough contemporarily shared tastes and beliefs among African-descended populations to serve as emblems of mutual recognition and even as the backbeat of a good dance party. The frisson of our likeness in diversity had always excited me. What would life be without soca, soukous, and funk, not to mention north Indian classical, European baroque, and the existential lamentations of white American men like Jackson Browne, Bruce Springsteen, and James Taylor.

In my youth, I, like many Black nationalists during the 1960s and 1970s, came to see African-descended people who advertised their white or American Indian ancestry as self-hating and those who did not embrace the truth of our shared Africanness as "mentally enslaved," to quote the felicitous phrase of Jamaican immigrant Marcus Garvey. Like most nationalisms, mine smudged the divisions of class. It suppressed discussion of intergenerational class inequality among African-diaspora populations, much of it indexed to complexion. Though my racial nationalism celebrated "the people," it found culturally nationalist allies among dictators Black and white—ranging from Mobutu Sese Seko to the military rulers of Nigeria and Brazil in the 1970s. Its heroes were the "kings and queens of Africa" and many of its chief emblems the artistic and religious products of an enormous concentration of wealth, some of it subsidized by or derived from the Atlantic slave trade. Consider kente cloth and the cowry shell, a major currency of the slave trade, but one that copiously adorns gorgeous altars of the Yoruba-Atlantic and the raiment of diasporic pan-Africanism.

As I listened to and closely watched my interlocutors at Howard in 2002, I began to see more history, more dimensions, more irony, and more intriguing nuance in the forms of unity that I craved. Pan-African mutual identification among these populations seems to have reached its unsteady crescendo in the 1980s—as the cumulative result of the Garveyite movement and the Harlem Renaissance in the 1920s; *Afro-Cubanismo*; *Négritude* and the Brazilian *ciclo do negro* in the 1930s; the acceleration of black immigration to the United States; the US and Trinidadian Black Power movements in the 1960s and 1970s; the international popularity of reggae; the boom in Black admissions to TWIs; and the founding of Black studies programs in those same institutions during the 1970s. The 1980s witnessed a truly popular Afrocentrism movement and its "culturalization" of Blackness.

African dress, cornrows and dreadlocks, the Nation of Islam, Yoruba religion and Kwanzaa, African art, kente cloth stoles, cowries, and hip-hop—incubated in the African American and Caribbean ghettoes of New York—were the new face of Black collective identity, largely displacing the white-middle-class-looking "Sunday best" two-piece suit, the men's "skinny" haircut, and the ironed female tresses and bouffants that had dramatized Negro identity and dignity at the height of the Civil Rights Movement. The culturalization of Blackness had its holdouts, such as my father, who, until the early 1980s, prohibited the wearing of cornrows among his employees in the Ambulatory Care Division at Howard University Hospital and declared, albeit temporarily, that he had "left nothing in Africa" and wasn't "going back."[1] But the culturalization of Blackness also energized its dialectical antithesis, in the form of a public proliferation of *ethnic* identities subdividing black America. This dialectic is the immediate subject of this book.

Most of the stories in this book acknowledge the common experience of "invisibility" (Bryce-Laporte 1972) but highlight the pursuit of visibility by striving or upwardly mobile black populations in the United States. Our enormous and costly displays of conformity and "cultural goodwill"—or the faith of the nondominant in the cultural standards stipulated by the dominant class (Bourdieu [1979] 1984)—and our efforts to reassure whites with an energetic smile are seldom compensated with the degree of human recognition, opportunity, or reward that we expect. The extent of our efforts is always obscured by the shadow of the nightmare that whites have projected onto us as the constituent other. This book has detailed a range of our responses to this situation, highlighting the parallels between the pursuit of "culture," or self-cultivation through the display of taste, and the confabulation of "cultures." Both are competitive projects that occur in a hierarchical and racialized context.

Stigma and Culture started as a research project about black ethnic diversity, motivated by a cosmopolitan race love that was as blind as any territorial nationalism to class inequality and ethnic passions. In many ways, that project was a liberal handmaiden to Howard University's own self-image as the "Mecca" of "Negro" education and uplift. However, many of my interlocutors and teachers rejected encompassment in this Civil Rights–era common sense about the worth, efficacy, and cultural diacritica of Blackness as a unified peoplehood. Indeed, their preferred peoplehoods frequently constructed Black people like me as a constituent other.

As I heard my black ethnic interlocutors talk, I came to recognize the likeness of this ambivalent self-fashioning to the African American bourgeois self-making that I had witnessed and learned while growing up. We soi-disant "middle-class Black people" tend to see ourselves as advocates of the race but also as the distant superiors of its primary exemplars. Like many elites, we had long interacted with nonlocal populations and acquired an internationally hybrid set of expressive habits, including speech stripped of local accents, vocabulary, and contextual references but peppered with words and references from faraway places. That I am an anthropologist is but an extreme development of the cosmopolitanism of my family's class disposition and extreme proof that white America's definitions of us overlook our breadth. Curiosity about the rest of the black world was in my childhood diet. *The Illustrated Book about Africa* was my teddy bear.

This book, then, grew out of my curiosity about the African and Caribbean people in my midst. I had grown up with many of my interlocutors in this investigation. And while I thought we were more alike than different, they tended to think the opposite. I did not recognize myself in the mirror they held up to me, but in the nature of my discipline, I fell through the looking glass. By seeing how they saw me, I began to perceive similarities in the structure of our thinking about the other. In reaction to the awareness of a white gaze that stigmatized us all, my black ethnic interlocutors constructed me, in contrast to themselves, as the appropriate referent of this stigma. My family and I, on the other hand, had constructed lower-class Black people, in contrast to ourselves, as the appropriate referent of the stigma. Each of us—black ethnics and "middle-class" Black people alike—had preserved the option to embrace and advocate for the deficient black other, or to claim opportunity and access in a white-dominated world by virtue of our emphatic difference from that other. However, while their idiom of distinction was "culture" and ethnicity, my people's idiom was class and taste. In common, we experienced and, indeed, actively practiced what I have called the schadenfreude of the stigmatized—an existential plea against dehumanization that stratifies one's own and voluntarily dehumanizes another subpopulation of the stigmatized. This book is the two-way mirror that I now hold up to the people who have shared their lives with me. If the scalpel of this analysis is aimed toward the heart of their self-invention, it is also aimed toward my own. "Then shall I know even as also I am known."

The central theme in the stories I have told and in the analytical conclusions that I have reached is the management of stigma. What I have seen is a mode of schadenfreude, whereby a stigmatized population seeks relief from stigma by identifying a neighboring group as more worthy of the stigma. Race and racial stigma may not be identical in form or equally important everywhere. But collective stigma is universal, and the preeminent Anglo–North American form of racial stigma is perhaps its purest, the most widely accepted, and the most indelible form. Imperialist Europe constructed Africa and its people as the bottom of the ladder of humanity and itself as the top, giving everyone else the opportunity to climb a rung or two based upon proof of distance from this Africa. Ethnological schadenfreude achieves its crescendo in the last-place anxiety of the African-descended populations—including Africans themselves—that converged in the recently desegregated immigrant society of the United States.

And the university is not an incidental context of this investigation. It is a setting increasingly available, at least since the nineteenth century, to repair the class defects of individuals, as well as the collective stigma of the women, subaltern religions, subject nations and regions, oppressed races, and even physical disability categories whose loyal bourgeoisies the various universities have been chartered to train. "Cultures" are the ambivalent genre of middling and discreditable populations' assertion of conditional autonomy from and equality with their would-be overlords. For example, students at Gallaudet University in Washington, DC, which was founded to educate deaf students, actively propagate what is known as "deaf culture" and defend it against the perceived threats to its endurance as more deaf people receive cochlear implants, read lips, speak, or attend universities where the hearing predominate. It is not surprising that many Gallaudet students also stratify their own. In the post–Civil Rights era, they have demanded that their leadership be committed to the primacy of sign language, and in 2006 they rejected a deaf candidate for university president who could also speak because she was "not deaf enough" (de Vise 2011). Some accuse the "deaf culture" advocates of isolationism, a common adjunct to the making of subaltern "cultures," one that reflects the perhaps-mistaken premise that such "cultures" cannot survive in times or places where the dominant, unmarked lifeway is equally available. Such has long been the false conviction of the university-based study of the Gullah/Geechees' African "culture." But the truth is that "cultures" are articulated, and they survive because of their utility within a broader field of social hierarchy and competition. "Cultures" are the consent of the middling to the sovereignty of their ethnoracially unmarked betters, and universities play a central role in articulating what might be called—by extension of Bourdieu's term ([1979] 1984)—"cultural goodwill."

These stories about the role of racial stigma in ethnogenesis are presented as specific cases of a general phenomenon—the role of stigma in the genesis of ethnic groups and their "cultures." Amid the spread of egalitarian notions of citizenship, of universal human rights, and of anthropological "cultures" concept, something remains distinctive about the experience of populations historically stigmatized as inherently inferior—including Pygmies in equatorial Africa, Khoisan speakers in southern Africa, Irish Catholics in the British Isles, Jews, Muslims and Roma in Europe, Africans in the Americas, low-caste South Asians, Eta and Koreans in Japan, and so forth. However, that distinctive experience also highlights an important class dynamic equally long at work in the formation of all national, regional, religious, gender, and sexual orientation–based identities. Ethnogenesis is the collective flight from stigma.

This book addresses the productive role of one paradigmatically stigmatized group—African Americans—as the constituent other in the self-fashioning of the aspiring national or world citizen. Everyone is stigmatized to one degree or another, but it is always useful—psychologically and materially—to have fellow citizens who are even more stigmatized than you. The anxiousness to avoid last place in a hierarchy or contest for honor is an overwhelming motive among the stigmatized. However, at times it is also useful to reclaim one's most stigmatized neighbors as emblems of self-redefinition. I address here not just the lessons of race and ethnicity in a transnational world but also the lessons of the stigmatized for the theory of culture and ethnicity generally.

In an age of vast mobility and mass mediation, it is more obvious than ever before that "cultures" are a rationalization of difference in answer to disappointed aspirations and ambitions. Nostalgia is less the detailed recollection of the past than an imaginative index of one's dissatisfaction or disappointment with the present situation and a counterargument to its naturalness or legitimacy. Mutual imitation among proximate populations is virtually inevitable. Its avoidance requires powerful motives and great effort, but these motives and efforts are seldom successful at preserving discrete lifeways. They more successfully produce diacritical, or cosmetic, differences that competitively justify privileged access to the shared desiderata of multiple neighboring groups. Hence, the remembrance of things past is a prominent feature of the "culture" making described here. In this way, an ethnic group is a population that tends to share or can be induced to share similar disappointments and dissatisfactions in the context of even more broadly shared wants and needs. Hence, the attribution of a "culture" to a population is an index of its social inferiority.

The hallmark of these collectivizing portraits called "cultures" is that they capitulate to the fact that only the members of socially dominant and ethnoracially unmarked groups can come close to being treated as individuals. The dominant are credited with the power, capacity, and authority of free will in ways denied to the stigmatized and voluntarily ceded by the social climbers among them. No matter what they do, in the context of ethnography and of daily life, the stigmatized always represent a group, and the group's reputation affects them. In daily life, everything good they do allows them the momentary status of exceptions, but everything bad they do confirms the validity of the whole group's marginalization. To the degree that the description of a population is ethnography, as opposed to, say, biography or memoir, everything they do is subjected to explanation in terms of a collective norm, and collective norms define the meaning and realness of what they do. Only the collectively stigmatized need such "literally-defined" norms to legitimize themselves, to exempt them from the premise of their collective worthlessness. "Cultures" must be selected and described in such a way that makes the bearers of that "culture" collectively comprehensible and respectable according to the unnecessary-to-justify and therefore taken-for-granted norms of the dominant (consider also Asad 1986).

In turn, "cultures" selectively ratify those self-attributed virtues of the ethnoracially unmarked class that, if successfully claimed by the vulnerable middling group, would favor that middling group's social elevation. When the "culture" attributed to such a middling group does not fulfill this function, even the most factually honest ethnography tends to elicit the outrage of the referent population. A further dimension of the confabulation of "cultures" is competition for the approval of the ethnically unmarked dominant class through the highlighting of the discreditable group's collective *differences from the highly stereotyped constituent other* and often, concomitantly, the middling protagonist's repetition and exaggeration of the dominant class's stereotypes about the already discredited.

Yet because the legitimacy of "cultures" requires them to be "time-honored," the bearers of cultures can never catch up with the ever-changing but arbitrary tastes that mark out the legitimate rulers of the world. The shibboleths by which this unmarked social and economic elite defines its boundaries will always be inaccessible to the bearers of "cultures." When manifest in an ethnoracially discredited or discreditable person, the cultural omnivorousness that characterizes today's legitimate elites is likely to be dismissed as inauthentic or self-hating. For the bearers of "cultures," letting on to one's similarity to *any* other race or ethnic group entails the risk of losing the petty privileges and monopolies held by the corporate ethnic group.

The people who define "cultures" as such are typically university scholars of borderline white backgrounds or scholar-activists of the selfsame stigmatized population. These "culture" inventors and definers are middling classes that gain power and esteem by speaking for the population so collectivized. But in the real world, these inventors and definers have an equal stake in both dignifying that group and demonstrating their personal superiority to the people for whom they speak. That is, the "folk" cannot and must not conform to the standards of the ethnoracially unmarked group. Only the assimilé spokesperson can do that. Moreover, the typical present-day members of the "culture" never really live up to the frozen, nostalgic standards that the spokespeople have identified as the "real" culture. Whenever the "folk" speak up for themselves, they can be judged deficient by one standard or the other.

And, as Fanon ([1952] 2008) points out, the striving elites of the sort who canonize ethnic cultures often hate themselves and feel very ambivalent about those "cultures." They must inevitably sublimate their inner conflicts about the contradictions between the metropolitan cultures that they have mastered out of love and the ethnic cultures that they have, to a great extent, stopped practicing but profit by speaking for. Such spokespeople are dissenters within the metropolitan establishment. They are a loyal opposition with little popular support. The ethnographies they write serve the demands of elite peer review and tenure more than they usefully address the immediate interests and needs of the populations spoken for. But these native ethnologists create the terms in which elite whites and their executants—including the police and social workers—will deal with those populations and selectively authorize the reproduction of their lifeways.

Culturally hybrid and ambivalent elites play an outsize role in defining and propagating the cultural norms of any given ethnic group. These discreditable petty elites create cultures as bulwarks against the indignities of the day—against the put-downs of their class superiors and against the insurgent aspirations of their unacculturated class inferiors. These bulwarks are products of editing, borrowing, and reacting to the funhouse mirror of other groups' stereotypes about the collective self. A "culture" is a frozen moment of self-consciousness and self-assertion in an argument for collective autonomy and dignity amid the hierarchical global social configuration of the day, but it serves the personal interests of the scholar and emerges from the university-based habitus of the scholar. Therefore, popular ethnology and its scholarly prototypes are not neutral reports about self and other. They occur in the "logic of the trial" (Bourdieu [1979] 1984), through which the discreditable argue their claims to worth in the language of the dominant.

Stigma and Culture documents the "logic of the trial" under the conditions of the most extreme collective stigmatization, amid the movement of ambitious population from one system of racial stratification into another, which hosts a racialized constituent other. The backdrop is a factor that unites all of these Western-influenced racial systems—a Fanonian double narcissism that deprives each party of half of its humanity. No less than in other settings, ethnicity is protean, situational, economically motivated, and shaped by the interests of insider and outsider interlocutors of multiple classes.

Universities play an ambivalent role in this ethnogenesis. They defend the discreditable group but establish its legitimacy in the terms dictated by the ethnoracially unmarked dominant group, which also provide an opportunity for the assimilated native spokesperson to establish his or her superiority to his or her coethnic fellows.

In this study, we see several southeastern Indian tribes and Louisiana Creoles ambiguously reemerging, or emerging, from the binary Anglo-American sociocultural configuration of "race" in efforts by ethnicity entrepreneurs to establish them as distinct "cultures," entitled to the small privileges that some of their ancestors enjoyed before their induction into the dark side of segmented assimilation in the United States. More clearly, they are communities of debate. In their reaction to segmented assimilation, Caribbean immigrants offer the most extreme demonstration of the competitive and hierarchical nature of ethnogenesis. The Caribbean American confabulation of "culture" recapitulates the ambitions of the discreditable Caribbean "middle class" but reclassifies them as a "culture." Africans are the global embodiment of heaven and hell, for black people and everyone else. American Africans demonstrate how context—in this case, desegregation, long-term coresidence, and the difference between the HBCU and the TWI—affects the choice to unify with one's fellow oppressed people or to distinguish oneself selfishly.

Gullah/Geechee revivalists and nationalists, by contrast, identify an "African" cultural model for and measure of their collective dignity—either an alternative to or an inversion of the light-to-dark hierarchy of people, places, and languages that places them at the bottom of the US social hierarchy. They exemplify a pattern of oppositional self-dignification pioneered by African Americans and subsequently imitated by Latinos, Native Americans, gays, and deaf people in the United States. Globally, this manner of oppositional self-dignification has always been a rarity. But since the 1960s, this African American model of inverting the received light-dark hierarchy has been imitated by stigmatized populations all over the world. In its curriculum, its social organization, and the writings of its professors, Howard University both recapitulates the light-dark hierarchy and offers an alternative paradigm of worth—Africa.

The first of *Stigma and Culture*'s three anonymous readers asked, skeptically, why I need to be such a central character in the story that I tell. He or she hated the blending of genres as much as the other two loved it. In sum, *Stigma and Culture* is an account of others' multiple consciousness through the perspective of my own multiple consciousness. My father was a middle-class fraternity man at the nation's leading historically Black university and I the asthmatic son of privilege who, once I entered TWIs, became a complete outsider, dependent on grades rather than connections for my opportunities. As a condition of my material survival and academic success, I have gradually acquired what Du Bois ([1903] 2007) called "double consciousness." In a historical moment very different from Du Bois's, I am learning to be aware of how my person and my accomplishments are regarded by others of my own ambivalent race and class, and I simultaneously study how they are perceived by the dominant white society, which is torn between its current ideology of "color-blindness" and its structural addiction to both its own hyperreal infallibility and its Black foil.

What Afro-Panamanian-American and Washingtonian sociologist Roy Simón Bryce-Laporte (1972) described as the "invisibility" of black immigrants is an artifact of the discrepancy between, on the one hand, the self-awareness that the migrant brought from his or her homeland and, on the other, white and Black American expectations. I have made it my job here to understand what I might call the "triple consciousness" of my black ethnic neighbors and friends. For example, Caribbean Americans are made triply conscious by the inescapable awareness of (1) how they are perceived in their own class- and color-stratified West Indian homelands, (2) how white Americans perceive them, and (3) how African Americans perceive them.

The first analytical tool that I brought to this investigation was my own native-trained double consciousness. However, I have been made triply conscious by a wake-up call that many of these neighbors depend on the invisibility of friends and neighbors like me in order to bolster their own collective sense of self-worth. *Stigma and Culture* bears the lessons of the mutual gaze between "invisible" parties, both of whom are made more aware of the system by the fact that it is always stepping on our toes and we are often stepping on each others'.

The same reviewer who was disturbed by the centrality of autobiography in this text was also troubled by its changes of voice, which is necessitated by the fact that I am a product of the events that I recount and as much an object of analysis as an analyst. Because this ethnography is a dialogue and is about a dialogue, I could not rely on the stability or the objectivity of the third person. The lifeways that I describe here are neither fixed nor exterior to my own. I am talking about me and you, because there is no other way to write about the lessons of the fact that, on trial yourselves, you have put me on trial since long before I even knew about it.

Race, Class, and Culture in the Post-Reaganite Age

From his vantage, Du Bois saw ahead of him the century of the "color line." From my vantage, I have seen the emergence, since the 1980s, and the preeminence, in the twenty-first century, of the "ethnic line." The century of the ethnic line has at its backdrop extraordinary levels of human migration and the rapid mobility of capital. People can, in the idiom of ethnicity, advertise their virtues as workers to businesses in lands far away from home. Moreover, as nation-states provide fewer and fewer services, people increasingly rely on other forms of solidarity and mechanisms of resource distribution, including religion, extended family, and ethnic group.

The culturalization of Blackness and the magnification of black ethnicity in the 1980s have a further backdrop: the legal buttresses of Black unity had been destroyed by desegregation. This case parallels the religious transformation of Ibadan's Hausa community after the official decommissioning of its administrative quarter and its chiefly ruler in the 1950s. By the early 1970s, the United States had repealed the last of the laws that officially made people of African descent a distinct residential, commensal, educational, marital, and occupational group. Yet, like the Hausas' trade monopoly, unofficial motivations for Black American unity remained strong—in this case, the need to redress enduring unofficial discrimination in hiring and lending, and the enduring effects of past discrimination, such as inequality of accumulated educational and economic assets.

However, after desegregation, it became much easier for Black individuals with sizable cultural and economic assets to leave the Black community and opt out of the struggle for collective uplift. Indeed, the affirmative action policies implemented after the Civil Rights Movement have helped them to do so. Those already endowed with middle-class diction, manners, and taste could surge forward, all the more rapidly if they possessed light skin and European features. At a more basic level, the structure of pedagogy in the United States generally favors students who can isolate themselves in silence and who prefer the competitive display of intellectual distinction to cooperation with their peers. Such cooperation is often called "cheating" or "plagiarism."

Many American whites were outraged—and remain outraged—by the repeal of the laws, and the outlawing of many of the customs, that had, for centuries, favored whites and fixed Blacks in a status of poverty and dishonor. Southern white Democrats massively turned against their political party after Democratic president Lyndon Baines Johnson endorsed these reforms. Almost uniformly, southern whites flooded into the Republican Party, rewarding that party for its opposition to the Civil Rights Act of 1964 and the Voting Rights Act of 1965. During the 1970s, Democratic and Republican presidents supported affirmative action, which redressed the enduring effects of anti-Black laws and, to an even greater degree, discrimination against white women. However, these policies magnified the ire of many white American men, an anger that Republican politician Ronald Reagan and Republican political strategists Karl Rove and Lee Atwater turned into a political revolution. Not only did they successfully reinvigorate the Confederate conviction that the federal government is the enemy of white freedom, but they also mobilized old racist code phrases, like "states' rights" and invented new ones like "welfare queen," proclaiming white supremacy and Black unworthiness without even mentioning "biological" race.

In a 1981 interview, Republican Party strategist Lee Atwater explained the evolution of the Republican Party's southern strategy as follows:

> You start out in 1954 by saying, "Nigger, nigger, nigger." By 1968 you can't say "nigger"—that hurts you. Backfires. So you say stuff like forced busing, states' rights and all that stuff. You're getting so abstract now [that] you're talking about cutting taxes, and all these things you're talking about are totally economic things and a byproduct of them is [that] blacks get hurt worse than whites.
>
> And subconsciously maybe that is part of it. I'm not saying that. But I'm saying that if it is getting that abstract, and that coded, that we are doing away with the racial problem one way or the other. You follow me—because obviously sitting around saying, "We want to cut this," is much more abstract than

even the busing thing, and a hell of a lot more abstract than "Nigger, nigger." (quoted in Herbert 2005)

The Reagan Republicans canonized a new interpretation of Civil Rights discourse—that any state action that targets racial minorities for the redress of discrimination is itself an act of "reverse discrimination" against whites. Allied with this conviction was the emerging insistence that charges of continuing racial discrimination against Blacks and other minorities are nothing but products of exquisite fantasy (see Omi and Winant 1994; Bonilla-Silva 2010). Undeserving Black people were simply looking for an unearned handout. By the 1990s, Black people who interpreted their experience of misfortune, setback, or disappointed aspiration as consequences of racism were demagogues "playing the race card" and propagating vapid "identity politics," instead of honest dealing and "straight talk" about the real issues, Black social and "cultural" dysfunctionality—including female dominance, absentee fathers, laziness, disinterest in school, black-on-black violence, and the like.

This reasoning was equally useful to ambitious black and white ethnics. For borderline white Daniel Patrick Moynihan, this argument whitewashed the dysfunctionality of his own and other Irish working-class families and propagated the image that family dysfunction was quintessentially Black. This explanation also suspended reflection on what enduring social conditions still made it easier for the offspring of dysfunctional white-skinned families, like Moynihan himself, to earn enough money to take care of a family and to move up than it was for the offspring of dysfunctional black-skinned families to do so. What Omi and Winant call the "ethnicity theory" suggests that the reason for the continuing lag in Black upward mobility relative to white upward mobility lies in the intrinsic and superior individual talents that just happen to occur more often in white-skinned people than in black-skinned ones. The "ethnicity theory" eschews talk of racism, because, as Omi and Winant observe, it represents Black people not as a "race" but as just another "ethnic group." According to this "ethnicity theory," neither their biology nor their history requires the state to treat Blacks any differently from how it treats the Irish, the Italians, the Jews, or the Polish. They have all been treated alike.

Amid the Reaganite backlash against the Civil Rights Movement, white-skinned ethnics in the United States followed suit in their own self-positioning, rejecting their description as "white" and thus denying the history of unearned privileges that admission to the unmarked ethnoracial category had long held out to their not-quite-white immigrant ancestors. Instead of emphasizing their whiteness as the justifiable precondition to the relative ease of their admission to the post–World War II suburban middle class, they moved in the 1980s to emphasize their ethnic identities—as Irish, Italian, Jewish, and so forth (Alba 1990; also Sacks 1994; Ignatiev 1995; Roediger 1989). Such designations accentuated not a history of white racial privileging, whereby whites had benefited from opportunities denied to the enslaved Africans and their Jim Crowed descendants, but a history of tribulation, disadvantage, initiative, and heroic uphill battle whereby white immigrants had attained the American dream on their own independent pluck and merit. No, the wind had never been at *their* backs, either (Alba 1990).

In sum, part of the backdrop of the intensification of black ethnogenesis in the post–Civil Rights era was a differently motivated but almost as fervent proliferation of middle-class white ethnic identity in the 1980s. Ethnic revivalisms encourage each other across very different circumstances, just as the Arab Spring has, since 2010, put wind in the sails of Scottish nationalism. On the one hand, for black immigrants this ethnicization was most often a claim to "cultural" difference from African Americans and therefore greater entitlement to the rewards of citizenship. On the other hand, middle-class white re-ethnicization was a claim that their forebears had been treated no better than Blacks, and so, if Black people had not gotten ahead, it was Blacks' own intellectual and behavioral deficiencies that were to blame. By this argument, they defended their enduring advantages over African Americans. The new "European Americans" (Alba 1990) tend to be unaware of the lengths to which many of their forebears had gone in order to exclude Black people, on racial grounds, from US labor unions, fire departments, and police departments and oblivious to the racial favoritism that these forebears received from realtors, banks, and the Federal Housing Administration during the post–World War II suburbanization of the American middle class (e.g., Sacks 1994). Some simply pretend to be unaware of this history or simply take for granted that something about them and their ancestors makes them inherently more deserving than Blacks.

Moreover, the politicized Christian right in the United States—much like the politicized Islam of Iran and global Wahabism—declared itself a peoplehood under attack by the federal government. In reaction, these Christian insurgents selected elements of their religious and cultural legacy, declared those elements the fundamental principles of their respective religions, asserted the unique correctness and Americanness of those legacies, and demanded—through political and military activism—that everyone else conform.

Among the most important stakes, however, were clearly economic ones. The Christian fundamentalists have been objecting to what they regard as distortions in the distribution of national and global resources by powerful European and Euro-American states. Their insurgent reactions have articulated images of an original and therefore superior culture, whose God-givenness legitimates the restoration of the believers' privileged access to resources, such as the best jobs and cheap Middle Eastern oil. The believers' long history of suffering at the hands of unbelievers further ennobles their cause.

Yet such struggles—whether ethnic or religious—are hardly ever *purely* economic in nature. They are an appeal for personal and collective dignity when the partisans feel that their dignity has been undermined. So these white insurgents are often willing to cede the economic profits of their struggle to the business elites who will fund their campaigns, such as Halliburton and the Koch brothers. From William Buckley to Allan Bloom and William Bennett, the intellectual right has waged an allied battle of resistance against feminism and minority rights in the campus "culture wars." They and their white fundamentalist Christian allies have found a common home with business elites in the Republican Party.

Both this Reaganite reaction and the simultaneous Afrocentrism movement embody the trend toward "culture" and "values," at the expense of merely biological race, as the publicly acceptable coin of collective identity and worth. Yet Republicanism and Afrocentrism differ along a spectrum between the principles of individualism and collectivism in the distribution of benefits.

Black ethnics, too, have mobilized "culture" in diverse ways. Trinidadian American Kwame Turé's dashikis meant one thing. Quite different are the motives of black ethnics ambitious to enter the system at the most materially advantageous level (and afraid that their children will suffer the same long-term social immobility experienced by the sort of African Americans they meet in the ghetto and see on television). For both black and white ethnics, these arguments have two primary intended audiences—first, the ethnically unmarked white elite, who disproportionately control everyone's opportunities for upward mobility and, second, their own ethnic children. Despite evidence of discrimination, black ethnic parents assure their children, conformist behavior will be rewarded.

As Walter Benn Michaels (2006) points out, "diversity" has now replaced "equality" as the preeminent ideal in US public policy and polite conversation. In this discourse, "culture" becomes "a model of differences we can love." However, he laments, it undermines the solidarity among the exploited and the oppressed that could otherwise help to end the increasingly unfair extremes of economic inequality between the rich and the poor.

In a post-Reaganite age, there is one form of diversity that has become too rude to mention in polite company—race. Even the first Black president of the United States, Barack Obama, speaks publicly and consistently for the rights of gays and lesbians, Jews and women, but his comments about race and racism are rare and timid. And, when he does directly address African American audiences, it is never with the politician's usual promises of rewards for his or her most loyal constituency. Instead, it is often with some finger-wagging criticism about our poor parenting or some other alleged behavioral deficiency of ours. President Obama keeps his race-specific art in the private quarters of the White House, a further sign of his exquisite sensitivity to the possibility that if he mentions Black people or legitimizes our specific and even rightful demands, he will lose any chance of winning the hearts of the white majority and the civility of the Republicans. He knows that, if he fails to mention Black people's issues enough, he is likely to lose but a small measure of Black support (Kantor 2012). He seems willing to pay that price.

Cultures and Hierarchy

This is a story of populations at a cross-cultural convergence of ideas and amid rapid historical shifts in the significance given to race. My field site has been Howard University and its alumni networks, as well as several TWIs hosting similar black ethnic populations. These settings exemplify a multi-sited, circum-Atlantic world where African-descended populations with very different antecedent histories and notions about race interact. So my point is not that Black populations are identical to each other in their lifeways. Not even my home neighborhood was homogeneous in this way. For example, our foods, our ethnic identities, and even our degree of regard for the law varied. Rather, *Stigma and Culture* is a story about the role that discreditable populations play in each other's ethnogenesis and in the ethnoracially unmarked identity formation of the dominant class. My point is that the conceptual boundaries drawn around neighboring groups normally follow a supraempirical logic, shaped by motives that are normally hierarchical, strategic, and competitive.

Black people in the United States epitomize the "stratification of one's own" and the production of the "literally-defined worlds" among the stigmatized, just as well as the Central Asian Tungus epitomize shamanism and precolonial Hawaiians epitomize mana and taboo. African Americans also model for the world the will to turn stigma into pride and go head to head with Goliath. For the sizable and multiethnic class of black people at the center of this analysis, Western education is the hope of the slave and the answer to history's shame. In this book I have documented several of the subsidiary strategies of upward mobility ambivalently hosted by and debated at Howard University. Ethnicization is one of them.

The contemporary university is a major arbiter of ethnicity and its cultural boundaries. Subsidized by the university, "culture" is an insurgent discourse. Successively, Johann Gottfried von Herder, Gustav E. Klemm, E. B. Tylor, Franz Boas, and Alain Locke articulated the conceptual bases—*Geist, Kultur*, and "cultures"—for stigmatized and marginalized peoples to be represented as reasonably different from, rather than merely the permanent racial inferiors to or the historically less advanced versions of, French and English royals. Foundational to this concept was Herder's notion of a distinctively German *Geist*, the spiritual outcome of the German people's history and environment that made the Germans a people sui generis, and not merely a deficient version of a universal standard of civilization exemplified by the French nobility and, in von Herder's day, slavishly imitated by the locally born rulers of the German speakers. In the twentieth-century academy, many of the leading advocates of this idea of divergent but equally legitimate local lifeways, or "cultures," were not-so-white, or borderline, whites, such as Bronislaw Malinowski, Franz Boas, and Ruth Benedict. They were responding directly to the elite European and Euro-American conviction, rendered in the increasingly confident language of "science," that Slavs, Jews, Irish, and southern Europeans were racially inferior to Anglo-Saxons and other "Aryans." However, this genealogy of ideas is not inherently egalitarian in its uses or its effects. Indeed, it has become useful to a surprising range of class interests.

For example, Herder's ideas about a distinct German spirit included the notion that this spirit is polluted by interaction or intermarriage with foreigners—a notion that has been blamed for Nazi xenophobia and murderous anti-Semitism a century and a half later. Yet the monstrousness of Hitler's attempt to exterminate his fellow Europeans has made it too easy to forget the sense of German inferiority and stigmatization that he intended for his actions to avenge and reverse. Contemporary Americans tend to imagine Hitler and, by extension, all Germans as evil geniuses, machinelike in their technological superiority and organization. So it comes as a surprise that, in the eighteenth century, Benjamin Franklin did not even consider most Germans "white," and he lamented their racially polluting presence in Pennsylvania (Franklin [1751] 1918). The reason that Marx's nineteenth-century analyses of capitalism focused on the British economy was that he considered English society vastly more advanced economically and politically than his own native German society (Sperber 2013). The nineteenth-century German-speaking middle class also saw itself as laggards in the history of economic development, national unification, and republicanism in Europe. And on the twentieth-century battlefield, they remained perennial losers. As late as 1989, dear Christian German friends of mine sought my sympathy for the wrongdoing of their parents' generation with a tale reflecting their enduring sense of collective inferiority to the Jews. As one said,

> What happened was terrible, but you can sort of understand. Back then, a Jewish trader would come to the farm of a German farmer [*Bauer*] and tell him, "Oh, I can see that your cow is sick. I'll take it off your hands, just as a favor to you, before it dies." In his innocence, the farmer would sell the cow for a pittance. But then the Jewish trader would go on to the next *Bauer*'s farm and sell the cow [at a high price].

In 2014, highly educated German friends of mine both admired French culture and resented what they regard as French people's sense that their culture is superior to everyone else's, that French culture is *"the* culture"— *Die Kultur*. It is difficult not to imagine the glee that Hitler and many of his countrymen felt as they rolled their tanks so effortlessly down the Champs-Élysées. The misfortune of the French was a vindication of Germany's material interests and of its deficient self-esteem.

The usual vindication of a sense of inferiority is seldom the pursuit of a general equality. It is most often the pursuit of superiority to someone else and sometimes, only rarely, the upending of the hierarchy. On the face of it, Hitler's rambling autobiography, *Mein Kampf* (1927), presents his own crusade as a pursuit of equality. The tome begins with a lament about Germany's disempowered position relative to France and the rest of Europe, which Hitler blames on disunity among German speakers and on family dysfunction and lack of national pride among poor urban Germans (in contrast to the proud French working class). Germany's lack of colonies underlines the problem, and one of Hitler's goals is to make Germany the equal of other European nations through the acquisition of colonies.

This complex psychological dynamic strikingly parallels white American social psychology. The cinematic male heroes of the US as a world power—from George Bailey of *It's a Wonderful Life* to the title character of *Forrest Gump*—are loving, egalitarian, and naïve rubes, even as they are surrounded by willingly subordinate Blacks. Indeed, George Bailey's life is an idyll where not-quite-white Italian immigrants are given the chance to live lives of decent, comfortable citizenship. At the moment when things seem to be at their worst, an angel shows George what life would have been like if not for people like him. He and the movie audience are shown that, without George and the racially segmented access he gave whites and not-so-whites to affordable housing, Bedford Falls would have been a smoky hell where, to the chords of a grimacing Black jazz pianist, the people drown their sorrows in booze.

If the white American hero made a mistake that caused someone else a lot of harm—such as sending a drunk Irish uncle to pay a major bill or conducting the Vietnam War—it was always an innocent mistake, motivated by excessive trust, naïveté and goodwill. But the hero always overcomes the ingenious British-sounding, German, Russian, Asian, or Arab-terrorist evildoer by the sheer force of his innocent white American folk goodness. He explicitly reestablishes his autonomy from and equality to the richer, craftier, or more ruthless enemy. Unchallenged is the rightness—and ostensible kindliness—of his rule over Blacks. Perhaps American receptiveness to this German Romantic idea—"cultures"—lies partly in these parallel national histories and mindsets. As Mamdani (2001) points out in reference to the Hutus of Central Africa, people who conceive of themselves as potentially victimized are the most likely to become victimizers.

Surely, Alain Locke's and Franz Boas's application of the idea of cultural relativism is a great legacy and contribution to mutual understanding among peoples. But the current uses of the anthropological idea of "cultures" by black ethnics and white neoconservatives highlight the fact that hierarchy has never left its constitution. "Cultures" (particularly in cases where the term has a plural form) are not attributed to populations out of the blue. Like Herder's *Geister*, "cultures" are normally stipulations of a frozen essence that refutes the more insulting, conventional wisdom about a lesser or stigmatized people, the kind of people who are sufficiently organismic that they can be generalized about or who fear that they can be generalized about disadvantageously by superior populations. By contrast, the ethnically unmarked, dominant class is defined by its ever-inventive and ever-advancing "styles" and by its cosmopolitanism, with the assumption that objectivity, informed personal change, creativity, and freedom are the hallmarks of their higher echelon.

On the other hand, as they invoke culture and ethnic identity to deny the assumption that they are collectively inferior, soi-disant ethnic groups claim a timeless essence that is intended to supersede their momentarily downtrodden state. This self-construction may be understood as an instance of middle-class "cultural goodwill" toward the status quo (Bourdieu [1979] 1984, 318–71) or of the opposite—that is, as the anchor of an autonomous, alternative, and morally equal world. And public articulations of that essence do tend toward these two complementary extremes. Even when the ethnic group claims superiority to the dominant, unmarked lifeway, the ethnic "culture" is adapted to the comprehension and approval of that politically dominant audience. In either case, "cultures" are the credit of the discreditable, a weapon of the weak.

However, the idea of ethnicity is also easily used by the ethnic group's rivals or class superiors to represent the group as permanently unassimilable—as essentially foreign to full citizenship and to the upper ranks of authority. "Cultures," ethnicity, and the interethnic field of debate that constitutes them are also debates about the legitimacy of the current social hierarchy and about the place that the ethnically identified interlocutor deserves in that hierarchy.

Although the discreditable and discredited races are the *locus classicus* of "cultures," university- and anthropology-inspired conceptions of "cultures" are superseding race and continue to displace "class" as a legitimate vocabulary of human difference in the United States. Yet "culture" also encompasses and sublimates these other two idioms. Amid immigration and a crossracial ethnocultural revival in the United States, nonethnic African Americans are losing any legitimate claim of difference. African Americans cannot—unlike, say, Puerto Ricans, Jamaicans, and Jews—politely fly a flag of their own, form an organization excluding people without four US-born Black American grandparents, or even name themselves by a term that clearly separates them from dark Jamaican Americans or Nigerian Americans. Thus, much like "Africanness," "Blackness" and "African Americanness" are signifiers floating free of clear legal definition and ownership, categories subject to fantastic elaboration and appropriation by Blacks and non-Blacks alike.

For example, extensive media coverage has made the political and aesthetic forms of African American resistance to oppression world famous and widely imitated. As they revolt against their own forms of exclusion, non-Black marginalized and insurgent ethnic, class, and age groups across the United States and the world imitate the versions of Black American music, dress, and speech made available by the US mass media. However, those versions of Black American music, dress, and speech chosen for imitation are highly selected and stylized, as the paying consumers are not just African Americans looking to unify and liberate themselves but, even more often, young white Americans looking for a dramatic way to express their own frustration, sexual inadequacy, and rage, as well as those older white Americans who are gratified by evidence that Blacks deserve to be excluded. The selective and stylized image of African Americans that emerges in the mass media—with the grudging consent of the Black artists who will not be paid unless they perform that image—is a fun-house mirror closely related to the one that black ethnics held up to me as proof of their superiority.

Hence, ethnogenesis is not only strategic, competitive, and university-subsidized but also mass-mediated. The US film and music industries export across the globe a heavily scripted racial imaginary grounded largely in white Americans' changing idealizations and shock-value distortions of its historical encounter with Native Americans, Asians, Middle Easterners and especially Africans. These idealizations and distortions shape the rest of the world's perceptions of and interactions with each of these groups. Today's mass-media representation of Black American life is selectively defined by characters who have decided they cannot compete according to the standards set by school and the professions and have instead sought upward mobility or compensation by other means—hypersexuality, hair-trigger violence, hedonism, the unregulated and amoral pursuit of wealth, and an emphasis on style over substance. These are also the values of the ethnoracially unmarked capitalist elite, projected onto a dark scapegoat. Additionally, however, this popular media version of "Black" life dramatizes the impatience, lack of sublimation, and fearlessness of taste that the middle class wishes it, too, could risk.

The Black artists who are paid to produce these shock-value images for white, Asian, and increasingly Black magnates to sell are responding to a racially segmented job market with certain encumbrances and certain targeted opportunities for young Black men. Their performances serve the ontological needs of the dominant and dominated fractions of a largely white but ethnoracially unmarked elite—an elite that increasingly has no name or distinctive symbols of its own. Its defining cultural repertoire is eclectic and, indeed, global (Khan 2012). The "Black men" of media fame are but an element of the culturally unmarked elite's eclectic repertoire of diacritica.

In a related point, the long-distance, mass-mediated mutual transformation of ethnoracial groups involves a gendered dynamic. For white males, these media-constructed "Black men" are vicarious embodiments of raw masculine power, unbridled by feminism, school, or good manners. It is no accident that the men placed at the bottom of the global social hierarchy would also be granted a comparative advantage in the representation of masculinity. Across cultures, as Bourdieu ([1979] 1984, 383) suggests, men of the most dominated classes often strongly resist conformity to middle-class manners and behavioral ideals. In French, Euro-American, and African American class-dominated populations, such conformity is typically regarded as effeminate and, indeed, homosexual. Together, the imitation of middle-class manners by ambitious women of the dominated class and the flight from those manners by men of the dominated class normalize a sharp differentiation between masculine and feminine behaviors, far greater than the differentiation between the male and female behaviors of the middle class of any of these populations. The emerging norms of upper-class gender differentiation, though, beg for investigation. The gender gap in education is now greatest among families in the top 25 percent of the earnings distribution (Coontz 2012).

Black men's potential athletic and sexual dominance was once the threat that the white elite used to draw dominated white men into a cross-class white alliance and white women into a "protected" status (Hall 1983). Now, Black athletics and sexuality are major models of white male youth and working-class aspirations, as well as the occupations to which many would *confine* Black men in order to prevent competition in other fields. Even young Black men with the cultural capital to compete in other areas are sometimes persuaded to confine their endeavors to such professional trajectories, where they believe they will encounter the least white resistance and Black peer disapproval.

On Ethnological Schadenfreude, or the Middling Nature of "Culture"

In the United States, the process of ethnological schadenfreude usually employs the native-born African American as the constituent other. But ambitious native-born African Americans have identified Africans or other groups of African Americans as their constituent other. This process occurs against the backdrop of what I call the "hyperreal infallibility" of the dominant group, whereby the excellence of a small proportion of the dominant group is regarded as typical of the dominant group and the faults of an equal proportion of that group are treated as exceptional. It is understood that no individual member of the dominant group should be under the constant suspicion that he or she will ultimately manifest the faults of the worst of his or her group. Conversely, members of the constituent other are always under suspicion and must continually prove their innocence and cultural goodwill in order to receive the protections and opportunities guaranteed by default to members of the dominant group. The faults of a small proportion of the constituent other population are regarded as *typical* of that group, while the excellence of an equal proportion of this definitively subordinated group is treated as exceptional. Closely associated with this phenomenon is the difficulty that members of the dominant group experience in visually distinguishing one member of the constituent-other group from another.

During the 1980s, professional anthropologists initiated a slash-and-burn critique of the Tylorean and Boasian concept of "culture" that had previously been the stock-in-trade of US anthropology. This critique highlighted the tendency to posit a sharp self-other distinction between the observer's kind of people and that of the observed, a distinction that implied a hierarchy partly by denying the historical dynamism and internal heterogeneity of the observed population. The utility of the anthropological "cultures" concept in the self-making of black ethnics indeed relies on the premise that these ethnic groupings are internally homogeneous, demographically discrete, and historically unchanging. And if this self-attribution of otherness indexes black ethnics' social inferiority to the dominant and ethnically unmarked population, it still bears the advantage of distinguishing black ethnics from the constituent other—African Americans—who must, by this logic, be equally discrete, internally homogeneous and, indeed, bereft of the virtues that justify black ethnics' claims to the protections and opportunities that they think they should be conceded by the dominant group.

This book is not, however, another critique of the anthropological concept of "culture." Rather, it is a documentation of the social pragmatics of the term's real-world usage in the self-defense of the stigmatized and the discreditable. The concept of ethnological schadenfreude amplifies the current preoccupation of anthropology with the structures of unequal economic power and subaltern resistance to them. But it also illuminates the forms of popular consent on which inequality and domination rest. In their flight from last place, the discreditable often throw tacks on the road behind them. The monument of "culture" implicitly concedes their inferiority to the culturally unmarked, standard-setting dominant elite and explicitly defines a neighboring discreditable population in terms of its ostensible deficit of the elite standards that the ethnic culture has been confabulated to illustrate. In this regard, black ethnic "cultural" identities bear a striking resemblance to middling class identities, in that these classes, too, tend to highlight the speaker's likeness to the dominant class by highlighting the ostensible deficiencies of the next class down.

Moreover, the internal homogeneity that popular and professional ethnology projects onto "culture" recapitulates the conformism that is typical of the middle class. Upper classes are notoriously populated by idiosyncratic characters and their "bad" behavior. And despite the generalizing stereotypes projected upon them, the poor get fewer benefits from conformity to any given uniform standard. Therefore, they have less of a stake in such conformity. Careful students of the African diaspora note the explosion of idiosyncrasy, dynamism, and individualist self-expression that characterize lower-class African American dress, music, dance, and plastic arts (e.g., Mintz and Price [1976] 1992). By contrast, the middle classes of most African diaspora populations are more afraid to step out of line and thereby give evidence that we do not deserve the protections and opportunities that we have so tenuously and recently received. In this regard, we are different only in degree from other, nonblack middle classes, because we are more easily discreditable.

Like taste, "cultures" partake of the "logic of the trial." Racialized populations—the main referent of the discourse of "cultures"—are the exemplary defendants. No one but the hypothetically uppermost and the lowermost actor in a social hierarchy escapes the trial, since the first is constitutionally beyond reproach and the last, irredeemably excluded, has no choice but to defy the system and create his or her own hierarchy of values. However, because everyone feels stigmatized sometimes or with respect to some trait, such creative defiance keeps the system changing, a process of defiance for which Bourdieu's ([1979] 1984) theory of "distinction" seems unable to account.

In this process, the most stigmatized are also the most aesthetically creative of all. Whereas the dominant are born with the time to create refinement and the material surplus that makes rarity more valuable than quantity, the dominated are accorded at birth the social competency to define virility, passion, spirituality, nonconformity, and cathartic vulgarity and violence. With the least effort, the dominated are credited with a comparative advantage in the performance of these qualities for the vicarious delight of the dominant. At the same time, they are given too little credit for their displays of refinement and discretion. Whatever they do, they are sitting ducks for the situationally embarrassing accusation of vulgarity, criminality, or lack of sexual self-control. It takes psychological and social genius to play this game right. At this point in history, tens of millions of African Americans have shown themselves willing to "work twice as hard to get half the rewards" of refinement, while a handful of us have grown wealthy through the musical and cinematic performance of vulgarity for the cathartic benefit of the rest of the world. However, such performances make it more dangerous for the rest of us to walk down the street, drive to work, or even water the neighbors' plants.

"Cultures" are assertions of moral dignity among the racially stigmatized. However, the concept is now also used in the academy to describe the lifeways of dominant groups—such as white Americans and the personnel of the laboratory or the "corporate boardroom"—as "cultures," the effect of which is to relativize and take them down a peg from their status as universal measures of correctness and worth. Even this usage indexes the hierarchical and competitive context of culture making.

After reading the penultimate draft of this book, students in my fall 2013 graduate-level "Theories in Cultural Anthropology" class at Duke noted that the éminence grise behind every word of this tale of ethnological schadenfreude—nonbourgeois, native-born African Americans—lack a voice here. My self-ethnography complicates many white Americans' and black ethnics' anemic and homogenizing representations of African Americans by illustrating the cosmopolitan dilemmas, the accomplishments, and the foibles of the Black American middle class. But an ungenerous or undiscerning reader may still come away with the impression that the quarter of black Americans who live in poverty are, as one student put it, an "undifferentiated mass of felons."

If I have created that impression, a kind reader might give me credit for dramatic irony—producing a book that exemplifies the social phenomenon that it observes. However, that is not my intention.

Stigma and Culture is a story about how new and nondominant populations in a hierarchical setting respond to the imaginary presence of such a constituent other and then help to legitimize the subordination of others as they themselves seek the protections and opportunities enjoyed by the dominant group. This is a story of ethnicity and "culture" making as a strategy of self-presentation typical of discreditable or middling groups. However, it is a careless reader who will conclude that the constituent other is a physically real person or population. In fact, if my hypothesis is correct, it is a null set, a fiction created to support everyone's self-fashioning. Anyone pointed out as an antitype of someone's self-conception imagines him- or herself able to point downward at someone else—at some inferior mass of people who are in some way or another undesirable and who, in the end, set off the speaker and his or her group as worthy of the previously denied, doubted, or tenuous level of respect that the speaker deserves. The main character in most of the stories and jokes that I have repeated here is not a real person but a fiction.

This is a book not about the poor but about middling populations of the sort who attend universities and count on them as a route to upward mobility. These populations usually define themselves as of the race but above the race, bound to it and benefiting from its struggles but opposite the race with respect to those characteristics that qualify them for approval by the dominant status group. They are black, but being the most excellent of their kind makes them all the more excellent, an ego-gratifying equation that motivates the most degrading portraits of the coracial constituent other.

Yet it takes an overwhelming act of will to ignore the creativity and talent of the African American working class—from the agricultural genius of the Gullah/Geechees to hip-hop and the most imitated dialect in the country. Yet the greatest manifestation of this creativity and talent is survival itself. To suffer under the boot of so many for so long, be the last hired and the first fired, and still walk proud is an extraordinary human achievement. Their dilemmas far exceed whether to pay the heat or the car note this month. They include whether to rap about senseless violence and get a recording contract or rap about politics and get none. But the dilemmas and compromises of real people with almost no symbolic means of escaping last place are the subject of another book.

Among the readers who have generously offered their advice on this manuscript, there are Germans who think the term "scapegoating" would be better than "schadenfreude." Indeed, "schadenfreude" suggests a sense of glee over the misfortune of others, and those others are normally the social equals or superiors of the person who feels the schadenfreude.

Indeed, the displacement of guilt and pollution, or scapegoating, is an element of schadenfreude. He who feels schadenfreude must be able to imagine that he, too, could have fallen victim to the same misfortune—an imagination to which few black ethnics in the United States are long immune. Yet "scapegoating" lacks a reminder of the emotional motives behind it. There is a certain joy in the undoing of the other and, in that joy, an implicit acknowledgment that the object of the scapegoating is *equivalent* to the scapegoater: in black America, the object of ethnological schadenfreude is actually more likely a rival or a superior—in demographic strength, voting power, cultural influence, and knowledge of the local terrain—than an inferior. His or her undoing is titillating because it relieves the scapegoater of a rival and raises the relative worth of the scapegoater. These are among the reasons that black ethnics' reports about how African American values and behaviors differ from their own—like Black middle-class people's comments about working-class Black people's diction and behavior—are so often punctuated with harsh laughter.

Acknowledgments

> You may trod me in the very dirt
> But still, like dust, I'll rise.
> MAYA ANGELOU, "Still I Rise" (1978)

During the 1970s, I came to adult consciousness not in the "crabs in a barrel" world of the stigmatized but in Washington, DC's, most expensive private school, where I learned and believed the white liberal doctrine that sustained goodwill, simplicity, and honesty would prevail in the end. I was only half conscious of the defensive striving of my mother and the John Henryism of my father. I took them for granted because they were the norm in my Black Washington, which stretched from Amidon and Shepherd Elementary Schools to Maret and Sidwell Friends, from Federal Triangle to the North Portal Estates. The center of that world, however, was Howard University, the "Mecca" and the "Capstone of Negro Education."

Thanks to my mother, Auntie Arnzie, and Aunt Ruth, I never cognized the US American web of meaning in which my assertiveness was read as dangerous. My birth father and his generation ran interference: if there was a world beyond our means or our right of way, I was largely unaware of it. Thanks to them, cheese pizza was the least of my many choices. We were by no means the richest or the best-traveled family in our Black Washington. Only in hindsight do I now recognize the full significance of the fact that we were among the darkest, calling to mind the motives behind the academic drive of the dark Caribbean men and darker Nigerians who joined my father and his kind at Howard in the 1940s and 1950s. They had a lot to prove, and many in my generation internalized their model.

For a born pan-Africanist and protégé of three such fathers, this story of ethnological schadenfreude is an unhappy one. Looking back at my past and at the historically Black university that largely produced it, I learned that there is nothing natural or automatic about solidarity among oppressed races, ethnic groups, classes, disability groups, genders, or sexual orientation groups. Their solidarity is a triumph of imagination and hope. There is perhaps no ethnoracial population in the world that better illustrates the effects of last-place anxiety than people of African descent. But it is also for that reason that no other population so thoroughly demonstrates the genius to revolutionize aesthetic standards, name the unfairness of the system, and mobilize collectively to fight against it. Hence, Black people are not only the foremost constituent other but also the foremost model of resistance to stigma among women, Latino Americans, gays, and Muslims in the United States and one of the foremost models for stigmatized groups all over the world.

This study of downtrodden dirt and rising dust would not have been possible without the generous support of the Spencer Foundation and the welcome extended to me by Howard University, its faculty, its staff, its students, and its alumni in Washington, Maryland, Virginia, North Carolina, New Orleans, Trinidad, Jamaica, and Nigeria. I thank you all for the unmerited grace of your generosity and candor. I wish that space allowed me to mention you individually by name. Rose Powhatan and her family, Jimmy Cummings, Michelle Skeete, Cyril Buchanan, Myrtle Young, Diane Shelby, and Michelle Miller Morial perhaps best exemplify the kindness that Howardites extend to their own. As my welcoming hosts and critical readers, the History Department deserves special recognition. Its chairs during the period of my research, Ibrahim Sundiata and Emory Tolbert, facilitated my work in every way possible. I thank my brother-friend Chris Dunn for his profound insights into New Orleans life and for his many fruitful introductions. I also am grateful to Sybil Kein for being so generous with her time and her vast knowledge.

Knowing how difficult it is to find the time to teach, publish, and take care of one's family, I still stand in astonishment and gratitude to the friends who took the time to read the entire unedited manuscript and discuss it with me at length: Zoila Airall, Emily Bernard, and Kamela Heyward-Rotimi. A half dozen black-ethnic friends who also appear in this book have read the chapters pertaining to their people and given their most candid feedback, which has now become a part of this text. Your insights, your experiences, and your encouragement have enriched this book immeasurably. We often agreed but occasionally disagreed in our conclusions, but our debates are, to me, the most enlightening moments in this dialogue. I thank you here namelessly in order to keep your confidences. But you know who you are. The named and the unnamed among you are all coauthors of this book. However, I beg other

ACKNOWLEDGMENTS

readers not to blame you for any untruth or misjudgment that inadvertently appears among these pages.

In 2008, an early version of this manuscript became the substance of my Lewis Henry Morgan Lecture at the University of Rochester. I feel deeply humbled that the lecture series committee chose me for this honor, and I hope that I have suitably upheld the legacy of the series. If I have done so, no small credit goes to the faculty of Rochester's Department of Anthropology, who also read and discussed the manuscript with me at length. This would be a very different book without the benefit of their praise and their provocations, and those of my colleagues in the Department of Cultural Anthropology at Duke. The bibliographic suggestions and personal insights of Tom Gibson, Signithia Fordham, and the three anonymous readers for the University of Chicago Press, have been particularly helpful, but I take the blame for any misreading or neglect of critical issues. I thank you, my editor T. David Brent, and your assistants Priya Nelson (now an associate editor) and Ellen Kladky for your patience and encouragement.

Bunmi, you are in many ways my foremost coauthor. I count on you, like no other, for fair-minded criticism, reality checks, and dissent that compels me to rethink issues. Like my mother's and my father's, your voice is always in my head before and after I speak, and I judge my words reasonable only if I have considered your point of view. Little that I say is a duplication, but hardly anything I say fails to reflect your thoughts and deeds in my life. Ayọ and Adu, this book is also deeply informed by your experiences and words. *Stigma and Culture* is in many ways an extended rumination on the obstacles and prospects that you face in a world that is even more international than the space and time where I came of age. Although white America can no longer count on its apical role in the global hierarchy of light and dark, the United States and its racial pathologies remain powerful touchstones in the sorting of people and the assignment of opportunity all over the world. In a changing world, I hope you will fashion from your double and triple consciousness an independent moral compass. Thus bringing the gifts that our ancestors gave, you are the dream and the hope of the slave.

Stigma and Culture is dedicated to your grandmother, Deborah Love Matory; to your grandfather, William E. Matory Sr., MD; and to Howard University, where my love of Blackness was born.

Notes

Introduction

1. Of course, these dilemmas of identification and distancing occur between other groups as well. For example, many European immigrant groups conducted their self-Americanization on the model of the Irish, whose arrival preceded theirs (Barrett and Roediger 2005). Not quite white in Europe, Irish immigrants often murderously distinguished themselves from African Americans, who preceded them, and Italian immigrants who came later. Italian Americans often passed the abuse they received from the Irish on to African Americans. For some immigrants with Iberian surnames, Puerto Ricans became an antitype, or constituent other.. Upon immigration to the Boston area in the 1960s, one Portuguese immigrant friend of mine Anglicized his surname in order to avoid the job discrimination that he knew Puerto Rican immigrants suffered at the time.

2. *Piers Morgan Tonight*, Cable News Network, August 29, 2013.

3. Elizabeth M. Grieco, "Race and Hispanic Origin of the Foreign-Born Population in the United States: 2007," American Community Survey Reports, US Census Bureau, 7. The number of self-identified foreign-born black people in the United States continues to grow rapidly. By 2011, the number had grown to 3.6 million, or 9.2 percent of the black population of the United States (US Census Bureau, "Race: The Black Alone Population in the United States: 2011—People and Households," accessed October 25, 2013, http://www.census.gov/population/race/data/ppl-ball.html).

4. Elizabeth M. Grieco, "Race and Hispanic Origin of the Foreign-Born Population in the United States: 2007," American Community Survey Reports, US Census Bureau, 7.

5. Kent 2007; US Census Bureau, "Race—The Black Alone Population of the United States: 2011—People and Households," accessed October 25, 2013, http://www.census.gov/population/race/data/ppl-ball.html; Massey 2007, 245; Capps, McCabe, and Fix 2011, 2.

6. US Census Bureau, "Table 2. Region of Birth of the Foreign-Born Population: 1850 to 1930 and 1960 to 1990," Internet release date March 9, 1999, accessed March 31, 2010, http://www.census.gov/population/www/documentation/twps0029/tab02.html; US Census Bureau, "Table 3. Foreign-Born Population by World Region of Birth for the United States and Regions: 2000," in "The Foreign-Born Population: 2000, Census 2000 Brief," 6; "The Foreign-Born Population in the United States: 2010," *American Community Survey Reports*, US Census Bureau, issued May 2012, accessed October 25, 2012, http://www.census.gov/prod/2012pubs/acs-19.pdf.

7. *Global Affirmative Action in a Neo-liberal Age*, a film by the Center for African and African American Research at Duke University, 2013, caaar.duke.edu/films.

8. Wikipedia, "Flag of Cape Verde," accessed March 12, 2010.

9. Though I had begun my research with the assumption that Howard would permanently inculcate this lesson in "Black" solidarity and racial binarism, Howard ended up teaching me a very different lesson in 2002. The most important discovery of my research is that Howard works. My beloved Howard and my beloved Harvard have similar levels of behind-the-scenes conflict and resentment, which only occasionally erupt into public displays. Like Harvard, Howard trains, every year, thousands of people who heal the sick, run cities and nation-states, seek justice for the oppressed, save souls, or make millions on Wall Street. However, I inadvertently chose a topic that inspires much quiet pain—as much in me as in most Howard students, faculty, and staff, not to mention much of the Afro-Atlantic world. Indeed, at Harvard, some of the most painful divisions have centered on the ambivalence of a Euro-Atlantic ethnic group about its distinctive identity among whites—that is, the fear and guilt that many American Jews experience around Zionism.

10. I owe this insight to my wife, Olubunmi Fatoye-Matory, a sociologist of education and a Nigerian immigrant. The popularity of Frank McCourt's 1999 novel *Angela's Ashes*, of the eponymous film in 2000, and of Martin Scorsese's film *The Departed* attest to the Irish reputation for social dysfunction in the American imaginary (Clymer 2003).

11. I thank Kevin Yelvington for alerting me to this reference.

12. Landes and Margaret Mead, another student of Boas, also employed the anthropological concept of "culture" to demonstrate that the subordination of women is not universal or, therefore, natural and inevitable.

Chapter Two

1. Our house shared its name with a US government battleship that Union officers had burned in Norfolk Harbor to prevent its capture by the Confederate secessionists. A year later, however, the Confederates salvaged, rebuilt, and recommissioned it as an iron-clad ram called the CSS *Virginia*.

2. Franklin actually criticized the Howard University administration, contrasting its take-it-or-leave-it attitude to the solicitousness of the administration of North Carolina Central University. Harvard University officials often convey the similar impression that the university has done the faculty member a favor by hiring him or her (Y. Williams 1998).

3. These and subsequent enrollment statistics derive from the following documents provided by the Office of the Associate Vice President for Enrollment Management: "Enrollment of United States Citizens, Permanent Residents, and International Students for Academic Years 1976–77 to 2000–01," "Geographical Distribution of Students for the Academic Year 2000–01," and "Geographical Distribution of Enrolled Students by School/College for the Academic Year 2000–01."

4. "U.S. News College Compass: Best Colleges 2011," accessed March 2, 2011, http://colleges.usnews.rankingsandreviews.com/best-colleges/howard-university-1448.

5. In 2010, according to the Association of American Medical Colleges, the overall population of medical students remains majority male—53 percent male and 47 percent female ("Medical School Enrollment Shows Diversity Gains," October 13, 2010, accessed November 1, 2013, https://www.aamc.org/newsroom/newsreleases/2010/152932/101013.html).

Chapter Three

1. "Future Intellectuals: Lorenzo Dow Turner (PhD 1926)," *Integrating the Life of the Mind: African Americans at the University of Chicago, 1870–1940*, accessed April 17, 2010, http://www.lib.uchicago.edu/e/webexhibits/IntegratingTheLifeOfTheMind/LorenzoDowTurner.

2. For example, whereas historian Margaret Creel (1988) sees "possession-trance" as the telltale sign of an African "survival" in the ring shout, historian Sterling Stuckey (1987) sees its *circularity* as its main African feature and as a model of Black political organization.

3. Pollitzer 2005a, 3, 12; Turner [1949] 1973, ix, 5, 42, 240; DeCamp 1973, ix; Creel 1988, 3, 15, 97, 99, 100, 197, 240; Pinckney 2003, 2, 3, 7; National Park Service 2005, 13, 21, 39, 51–52, 70, 74, 79, 84; Pollitzer, 2005b, D1, D2, D4, D9, D10, D15, D20; Hargrove 2005, F5, F8–F9, F22, F23, F33, F37; Bascom 1941, 43, 47; Joyner 1985, 6, 9; Sengova 2006, 241; Curry 2001.

4. For an example from another part of the world, within language zones on the island of Malaita in the Solomon Islands, when people of different dialects interact, they often accentuate or exaggerate their dialectical differences in order to highlight their identities (David Akin, personal communication, 2008).

5. For good reason, the students of Gullah/Geechee rice culture are among the few Gullah/Geechee specialists to abandon the discourse of "isolation" (e.g., Wood 1974; Littlefield [1981] 1991; Rosengarten [1986] 1987; Carney 2001). Yet it had never been recognized, before my initial 2001 publication of this critique (see J. L. Matory 2001 and 2008), that the argument for the African origins of American rice culture actually contradicts this foremost causal principle in the wider literature. Chireau's (2003) analysis, too, is unusual and revealing: "The transmission of indigenous African traditions to first- and second-generation American blacks would have been *hindered* by the isolation and dispersal of these 'saltwater' [i.e., newly arrived] Africans" (53; emphasis mine). Her hypothesis diametrically contradicts the prevailing hypothesis but is just as intuitively persuasive.

6. This is not to imply that most Gullah/Geechees were reading or writing such books but that influential local experts of the Gullah/Geechees' most emblematically African or African-looking practices were, through their literacy and their use of the US Postal Service, in touch with a multicultural smorgasbord of ritual options.

7. Dale Rosengarten believes that Penn School and its missionary founders played some role in defending the landownership of the Gullah/Geechees' ancestors (personal communication, May 3, 2007), thus guaranteeing their relative freedom to dictate the terms of their commercial and symbolic interaction with non-Gullah/Geechee speakers.

8. One might make the further point that West African kingships, legal systems, monetary systems, and religions have, for the past five hundred years, been in mutually transformative dialogue with their European counterparts. See, for example, Pietz (1985) and Matory (unpublished manuscript).

9. Unlike many linguists, Mufwene and Gilman (1987) believe that Gullah language is not dying or decreolizing and that it is likely to survive as long as some predominantly Gullah-speaking residential communities remain intact. They report that Gullah language is changing and varies across generations but no more so than most non-Creole languages, and the trajectory of its changes is not toward English.

10. By the term "socially white," I mean that many such elites in northeastern Brazil are considered "white" (*branco*) on account of their wealth, education, and social networks, despite physical evidence of African ancestry. Here I refer to Charles Wagley's concept of "social race"

([1952] 1963). In Brazil, the "one-drop rule"—whereby "one drop" of African "blood" makes one "black"—does not usually apply. São Paulo's elite tends to have fewer African ancestors than do the elites of the northeast. The manner in which many *paulistas* are considered "white" would be more familiar to most people in the United States.

11. Mufwene (1991) concludes not that isolation is necessary for the endurance of Gullah language but that there must be some communities where enough Gullah people live together as neighbors that they "might need Gullah as a vernacular for in-group communication" (232).

Chapter Four

1. The name of the Haliwa is a neologism formed by the elision of the names of the two counties that they occupy—Halifax and Warren Counties. It does not appear to derive from any pre-Columbian term.
2. The efforts of the Cherokee nation to exclude its black citizens continue unabated in the District of Columbia federal court case *Cherokee Nation v. Raymond Nash*, which began in 2014.
3. E-mail from Nadia Zysman to J. Lorand Matory, September 8, 2014.
4. This theme is also taken up in the film *Imitation of Life* (1934 and 1959).

Chapter Five

1. Kasinitz (1992) coined the term "ethnicity entrepreneurs" to describe a then-new generation of Caribbean New Yorkers who were increasingly vocal about their Caribbeanness and made "their living by bridging the gap between the polity and the Caribbean community." He continues, "They hold formal leadership positions (sometimes self-created). . . . In many ways their position is less dependent on the Caribbean community than on the sponsorship of the political establishment. They capitalize on both the state's interest in supporting ethnic organizations and the needs of local politicians to make ties to the growing Caribbean community" (163–64). I apply the same term in an only slightly less metaphorical sense to businesspeople and others who employ ethnic identity strategically and often inventively in order to enhance their esteem and opportunities in an arena of competition.
2. Graham is the author of *Our Kind of People: Inside America's Black Upper Class* (1999).

Chapter Six

1. The Nigerian Enterprise Promotion Decree gave Nigerians "the exclusive right to the ownership of some enterprises and greater participation than hitherto in the equity ownership of others" (Inanga 1978, 31). This decree and the wealth-creating oil boom of the early 1970s eliminated whites, Indians, and Lebanese as major visible presences in the Nigerian marketplace and even more so in Nigerian society at large.
2. An Ethiopian graduate student at Duke and her parents tell me that *baria* is an insulting term that associates dark skin, characteristically sub-Saharan hair, and "non-Arab-looking" facial features with enslavement, servitude, and tenancy.
3. "Vision Statement," National Human Genome Center, http://www.genomecenter.howard.edu/intro.htm, accessed February 5, 2015.
4. For simplicity's sake, I do not normally include tone marks in single Yoruba words or names that would be unambiguous without them. I do, however, include accents marking the vowel sounds and stress patterns in words used by Romance-language speakers, as the absence

of these orthographic diacritica would actually misrepresent their pronunciation. It is the Cuban convention to transcribe the name of this god and of this divination system as Ifá, marking the stress on the last syllable. In Yoruba, the diacritic on Ifá marks the last syllable as high tone. I dispense with this diacritic in the West African context.

Conclusion

1. In 1981, an African American woman employee of American Airlines named Renee Rogers complained about a similar prohibition by her employer. She lost her case in the US District Court of New York (*Rogers v. American Airlines* 1981).

References

Abdel-Malek, Anouar. "Orientalism in Crisis." *Diogenes* 44 (Winter 1963): 103–40.
Abu-Lughod, Lila. "Writing against Culture." In *Recapturing Anthropology: Working in the Present*, edited by Richard G. Fox, 137–54, 161–2. Santa Fe, NM: School of American Research Press, 1991.
———. *Veiled Sentiments: Honor and Poetry in Bedouin Society*. Berkeley: University of California Press, 1986.
Adebọnọjọ, Badejọ Olurẹmilẹkun. *Itan Ido Ijẹbu*. Ikeja, Lagos State, Nigeria: John West Publications, 1990.
———. *My Life*. Ikẹja, Lagos State, Nigeria: John West Publications, [1994] 1996.
Adichie, Chimamanda Ngozi. *Americanah: A Novel*. New York: Alfred A. Knopf, 2013a.
———. "A Conversation with Chimamanda Ngozi Adichie." Duke University Center for African and African American Research, 2013b. http://caaar.duke.edu/films.
Ahmad, Sadaf. *Transforming Faith: The Story of Al-Huda and Islamic Revivalism among Urban Pakistani Women*. Syracuse, NY: Syracuse University Press, 2009.
Alba, Richard D. *Ethnic Identity: The Transformation of White America*. New Haven, CT: Yale University Press, 1990.
Alim, H. Samy, and Geneva Smitherman. "Obama's English." *New York Times*, September 9, 2012. Accessed October 31, 2012. http://www.nytimes.com/2012/09/09/opinion/sunday/obama-and-the-racial-politics-of-american-english.html?pagewanted=all&_r=0.
American Bible Society. *De Nyew Testament: The New Testament in Gullah Sea Island Creole with Marginal Text of the King James Version*. Translated by the Sea Island Translation Team in cooperation with Wycliffe Bible Translators. New York: American Bible Society, 2005.
Anderson, Benedict. *Imagined Communities: Reflections on the Origin and Spread of Nationalism*. Rev. ed. London: Verso, [1983] 1991.
Appadurai, Arjun. "Disjuncture and Difference in the Global Cultural Economy." *Public Culture* 2, no. 2 (1990): 1–24.
Asad, Talal. "On the Concept of Translation in British Anthropology." In *Writing Culture: The Poetics and Politics of Ethnography*, edited by James Clifford and George E. Marcus, 141–64. Berkeley: University of California Press, 1986.
Austin, J. L. *How to Do Things with Words*. Cambridge, MA: Harvard University Press, 1962.

Baker, Lee D. *From Savage to Negro: Anthropology and the Construction of Race, 1896–1954*. Berkeley: University of California Press, 1998.

———. *Anthropology and the Racial Politics of Culture*. Durham, NC: Duke University Press, 2010.

Balibar, Étienne, and Immanuel Wallerstein. *Race, Nation, Class: Ambiguous Identities*. London: Verso, 1991.

Barber, Karin. *I Could Speak until Tomorrow: Oriki, Women, and the Past in a Yoruba Town*. Washington, DC: Smithsonian Institution Press, 1991.

Barewa Old Boys Association. *List of Admissions to Barewa College, 1981–2000*. New ed., vol. 2. N.p., 2001.

Barrett, James R., and David R. Roediger. "The Irish and the 'Americanization' of the 'New Immigrants' in the Streets and in the Churches of the Urban United States, 1900–1930." *Journal of American Ethnic History* 24, no. 4 (2005): 3–33.

Barth, Fredrik. "Introduction." In *Ethnic Groups and Boundaries: The Social Organization of Culture Difference*, edited by Fredrik Barth, 9–38. Boston: Little, Brown, 1969.

Bascom, William R. "Acculturation among the Gullah Negroes." *American Anthropologist* 43, no. 1 (1941): 43–50.

Bashi, Vilna, and Antonio McDaniel. "A Theory of Immigration and Racial Stratification." *Journal of Black Studies* 27, no. 5(1997): 668–82.

Bastide, Roger. *African Civilizations in the New World*. Translated by Peter Green. New York: Harper and Row, [1967] 1971.

———. *Estudos Afro-Brasileiros*. São Paulo: Perspectiva, 1983.

Batalova, Jeanne. "Asian Immigrants in the United States." *Migration Information Source*, May 24, 2011. Accessed August 21, 2013. http://www.migrationpolicy.org/article/asian-immigrants-united-states.

Bateson, Gregory. *Naven, A Survey of the Problems Suggested by a Composite Picture of the Culture of a New Guinea Tribe Drawn from Three Points of View*. 2nd ed. Stanford, CA: Stanford University Press, [1936] 1958.

Boas, Franz. *Race, Language, and Culture*. Chicago: University of Chicago Press, 1940.

Bolnick, Deborah A., Duana Fullwiley, Troy Duster, Richard S. Cooper, Joan H. Fujimura, Jonathan Kahn, Jay S. Kaufman, Jonathan Marks, Ann Morning, Alondra Nelson, Pilar Ossorio, Jenny Reardon, Susan M. Reverby, Kimberly TallBear. "The Science and Business of Ancestry Testing." *Science* 318, no. 5849 (2007): 399–400.

Bolster, W. Jeffrey. *Black Jacks: African American Seamen in the Age of Sail*. Cambridge, MA: Harvard University Press, 1997.

Bonilla-Silva, Eduardo. *Racism without Racists: Color-Blind Racism and the Persistence of Racial Inequality in the United States*. 3rd ed. Lanham, UK: Rowman and Littlefield, 2010.

Bourdieu, Pierre. *Outline of a Theory of Practice*. Translated by Richard Nice. Cambridge: Cambridge University Press, [1972] 1985.

———. *Distinction: A Social Critique of Taste*. Translated by Richard Nice. Cambridge, MA: Harvard University Press, [1979] 1984.

Braga, Júlio Santana. *O jogo de búzios: Um estudo da advinhação no candomblé*. São Paulo: Editora Brasiliense, 1988.

Brasseaux, Carl A., Keith P. Fontenot, and Claude F. Oubre. *Creoles of Color in the Bayou Country*. Jackson: University Press of Mississippi, 1994.

Brint, Steven, Mark Riddle, Lori Turk-Bicakci, and Charles S. Levy. "From the Liberal to the

Practical Arts in American Colleges and Universities: Organizational Analysis and Curricular Change." *Journal of Higher Education* 76, no. 2(2005):151–80.

Bryce-Laporte, Ray Simón. "Black Immigrants: The Experience of Invisibility and Inequality." *Journal of Black Studies* 3, no. 1(1972): 29–56.

Bu, Liping. "Educational Exchange and Cultural Diplomacy in the Cold War." *Journal of American Studies* 33 (1999): 393–415.

Burton, Linda M., and Carol B. Stack. "'Breakfast at Elmo's': Adolescent Boys and Disruptive Politics in the Kinscripts Narrative." In *Open to Disruption: Time and Craft in the Practice of Slow Sociology*, edited by Anita Ilta Garey, Rosanna Hertz, and Margaret K. Nelson, 174–91. Nashville: Vanderbilt University Press, 2014.

Butler, Judith. *Bodies That Matter: On the Discursive Limits of Sex*. New York: Routledge, 1993.

Bush, George W. "Commencement Address at Yale University in New Haven, Connecticut." May 21, 2001. The American Presidency Project. Accessed 8 October 2010. http://www.presidency.ucsb.edu/ws/index.php?pid=45895.

Capehart, Jonathan. "George Zimmerman's Relevant Past." *Washington Post*, May 28, 2013. Accessed November 22, 2013. http://washingtonpost.com/blogs/post-partisan/wp/2013/05/28/george-zimmermans-relevant-past/.

Capps, Randy, Kristen McCabe, and Michael Fix. *New Streams: Black African Migration to the United States*. Migration Policy Institute, 2011. Accessed October 27, 2013. http://www.migrationpolicy.org/pubs/AfricanMigrationUS.pdf.

Carney, Judith A. *Black Rice: The African Origins of Rice Cultivation in the Americas*. Cambridge, MA: Harvard University Press, 2001.

Carter, Stephen L. *The Emperor of Ocean Park*. New York: Alfred A. Knopf, 2002.

Chireau, Yvonne P. *Black Magic: Religion and the African American Conjuring Tradition*. Berkeley: University of California Press, 2003.

Chua, Amy. *Battle Hymn of the Tiger Mother*. London: Penguin, 2011.

Clarke, Kamari Maxine. *Mapping Yoruba Networks: Power and Agency in the Making of Transnational Communities*. Durham, NC: Duke University Press, 2004.

Clarke, Kamari Maxine, and Deborah A. Thomas, eds. *Globalization and Race: Transformations in the Cultural Production of Blackness*. Durham, NC: Duke University Press, 2006.

Clifford, James. *The Predicament of Culture: Twentieth-Century Ethnography, Literature, and Art*. Cambridge, MA: Harvard University Press, 1988.

Clymer, Adam. "Daniel Patrick Moynihan Is Dead; Senator from Academia Was 76." *New York Times*, March 27, 2003.

Cohen, Abner. *Custom and Politics in Urban Africa: Mediating Conflict and Reshaping the State*. Berkeley: University of California Press, 1969.

Cole, Johnnetta Betsch. "An Interview with Johnnetta Betsch Cole." By Kevin A. Yelvington. *Current Anthropology* 44, no. 2 (2003): 275–88.

Coleman, James S. *The Adolescent Society: The Social Life of the Teenager and Its Impact on Education*. New York: Free Press, 1961.

Comaroff, John L., and Jean Comaroff. *Ethnicity, Inc.* Chicago: University of Chicago Press, 2009.

Coontz, Stephanie. "The Myth of Male Decline." *New York Times*, Sunday Review, September 29, 2012. http://www.newyorktimes.com/2012/09/30/opinion/sunday/the-myth-of-male-decline.html?pagewanted=all&_r=0.

Cooper, Carolyn. "Who Is Jamaica?" *New York Times*, August 5, 2012. Accessed October 25, 2012. http://www.nytimes.com/2012/08/06/opinion/who-is-jamaica.html.

Cose, Ellis. *Rage of a Privileged Class*. New York: HarperCollins, 1993.

———. *Envy of the World: On Being a Black Man in America*. New York: Washington Square, 2002.

Creel, Margaret Washington. *A Peculiar People: Slave Religion and Community-Culture among the Gullahs*. New York: New York University Press, 1988.

Crenshaw, Kimberlé. "Demarginalizing the Intersection of Race and Sex: A Black Feminist Critique of Antidiscrimination Doctrine, Feminist Theory, and Antiracist Politics." *University of Chicago Legal Forum*, 139–67 (1989).

Curry, Andrew. "The Gullahs' Last Stand?" *U.S. News and World Report* 130, no. 24 (2001): 40–41.

Davies, Scott. "Subcultural Explanations and Interpretations of School Deviance." *Aggression and Violent Behavior* 2 (1999): 191–202.

Davis, Natalie. "Women on Top: Symbolic Sexual Inversion and Political Disorder in Early Modern Europe." In *The Reversible World: Symbolic Inversion in Art and Society*, edited by Barbara A. Babcock, 147–90. Ithaca, NY: Cornell University Press, 1978.

Dawson, Michael C. *Behind the Mule: Race and Class in African-American Politics*. Princeton, NJ: Princeton University Press, 1994.

De Camp, David. Foreword to *Africanisms in the Gullah Dialect*, 3rd ed., by Lorenzo Dow Turner, v–xi. Ann Arbor: University of Michigan Press, 1973.

De Visé, Daniel. "Gallaudet University Adjusts to a Culture That Includes More Hearing Students." *Washington Post*, September 24, 2011. Accessed September 4, 2013. http://www.washingtonpost.com/local/education/gallaudet-university-adjusts-to-a-culture-that-includes-more-hearing-students/2011/09/23/gIQAC3W9tK_story.html.

Degler, Carl N. *Neither Black nor White: Slavery and Race Relations in Brazil and the United States*. Madison: University of Wisconsin Press, 1971.

Deleuze, Gilles, and Félix Guattari. *A Thousand Plateaus: Capitalism and Schizophrenia*. Trans. Brian Massumi. Minneapolis: University of Minnesota Press, [1980] 1987.

Desdunes, Rodolphe Lucien. *Our People and Our History: A Tribute to the Creole People of Color in Memory of the Great Men They Have Given Us and of the Good Works They Have Accomplished*. Baton Rouge: Louisiana State University Press, [1911] 1973.

Diallo, Anthony D. "Howard Seen as an International Mecca." *Washington Post*, January 5, 1989, DC6.

Dikötter, Frank. *The Construction of Racial Identities in China and Japan*. Honolulu: University of Hawai'i Press, 1997.

Domínguez, Virginia R. *White by Definition: Social Classification in Creole Louisiana*. New Brunswick, NJ: Rutgers University Press, 1986.

———. *People as Subject, People as Object: Selfhood and Peoplehood in Contemporary Israel*. Madison: University of Wisconsin Press, 1989.

Douglas, Mary. *Purity and Danger: An Analysis of Concepts of Pollution and Taboo*. London: Routledge and Kegan Paul, [1966] 1984.

Downes, David M. *The Delinquent Solution*. New York: Free Press, 1966.

Dromgoole, Will Allen. "The Malungeons." *Arena* 3 (1891): 470–79.

Du Bois, W. E. B. *The Souls of Black Folk*. Oxford: Oxford University Press, [1903] 2007.

———. "The Talented Tenth." 1903. Accessed October 31, 2012. http://teachingamericanhistory.org/library/document/the-talented-tenth/.

Durkheim, Émile. *The Elementary Forms of the Religious Life*. New York: Free Press, 1915.

Dutarque, John, Jr. Letter in the *South-Carolina Gazette*, 25 June to 2 July, 1763. In *Runaway Slave*

REFERENCES

Advertisements: A Documentary History from the 1730s to 1790, vol. 3, compiled by Lathan A. Windley, 231. Westport, CT: Greenwood, 1983.

Dzidzienyo, Anani, and Suzanne Oboler, eds. *Neither Enemies nor Friends: Latinos, Blacks, Afro-Latinos*. New York: Palgrave Macmillan, 2005.

Edwards, Brent Hayes. *The Practice of Diaspora: Literature, Translation, and the Rise of Black Internationalism*. Cambridge, MA: Harvard University Press, 2003.

Eidheim, Harald. "When Ethnic Identity Is a Social Stigma." In Barth, *Ethnic Groups and Boundaries*, 1969, 39–57.

Elder, Charles, Jr. "Giving Foreign Students a Hand." *Washington Post*, February 4, 1988, DC1.

Ellis, Col. A. B. *The Yoruba-Speaking Peoples of the Slave Coast of West Africa*. Chicago: Benin, [1894] 1964.

Eltis, David. "The Volume and Structure of the Transatlantic Slave Trade: A Reassessment." *William and Mary Quarterly*, 3rd ser., 58, no. 1 (January 2001): 17–46. Accessed April 15, 2010. http://www.historycooperative.org/journals/wm/58.1/eltis.html.

Eltis, David, Stephen D. Behrendt, David Richardson, and Herbert S. Klein, eds. *The Trans-Atlantic Slave Trade: A Database on CD-ROM*. Cambridge: Cambridge University Press, 1999.

Evans, Ben. "Black Caucus Questions Cherokee Vote." *Boston.com*, March 13, 2007. Accessed August 24, 2014. http://www.boston.com/news/nation/washington/articles/2007/03/13/black_caucus_questions_cherokee_vote/.

Evans-Pritchard, E. E. *The Nuer*. Oxford: Clarendon, 1940.

Fader, Ayala. *Mitzvah Girls: Bringing Up the Next Generation of Hasidic Jews in Brooklyn*. Princeton, NJ: Princeton University Press, 2009.

Family across the Sea. Directed by Tim Carrier. Produced by South Carolina Educational Television. San Francisco: California Newsreel, 1991.

Fanon, Frantz. *Black Skin, White Masks*. Translated by Richard Philcox. New York: Grove Press, [1952] 2008.

———. *Wretched of the Earth*. Translated by Richard Philcox. New York: Grove, [1961] 2004.

Fatoye-Matory, Bunmi. "I Am Not Just an African Woman." *Christian Science Monitor*, July 1, 1996.

Feinberg, Lawrence. "Hill Queries 2 D.C. Colleges on Foreign Students." *Washington Post*, April 15, 1988, D7.

Ferguson, Roderick A. *Aberrations in Black: Toward a Queer of Color Critique*. Minneapolis: University of Minnesota Press, 2003.

Fields, Barbara J. "Slavery, Race and Ideology in the United States of America." *New Left Review* 181 (1990): 95–118.

Fikes, Robert, Jr. "An Extensive List of Notable Black/Non-Black Interracial Couples, 1801–2001." *AfroCentric News*, 2000. Accessed October 30, 2005. http://www.afrocentricnews.com/html/interracial.html.

Fluehr-Lobban, Carolyn, and Kharyssa Rhodes. *Race and Identity in the Nile Valley: Ancient and Modern Perspectives*. Trenton, NJ: Red Sea, 2010.

Fordham, Signithia. *Blacked Out: Dilemmas of Race, Identity, and Success at Capital High*. Chicago: University of Chicago Press, 1996.

Fordham, Signithia, and John Ogbu. "Black Students' School Success: Coping with the Burden of 'Acting White.'" *Urban Review* 18, no. 3 (1986): 1–31.

Foucault, Michel. *Power/Knowledge: Selected Interviews and Other Writings, 1972–1977*. Edited and translated by Colin Gordon. New York: Pantheon, 1980.

Franklin, Benjamin. "Observations Concerning the Increase of Mankind, Peopling of Countries, &c." *Magazine of History with Notes and Queries* 16 ([1751] 1918): extra numbers 61–64.
Frazier, Edward Franklin. "Rejoinder [to Herskovits] by E. Franklin Frazier." *American Sociological Review* 8, no. 4 (1943): 394–402.
———. *Black Bourgeoisie*. New York: Free Press, [1957] 1997.
Fredrickson, George. *White Supremacy: A Comparative Study in American and South African History*. New York: Oxford University Press, 1982.
Freyre, Gilberto. *The Masters and the Slaves*. Translated by Samuel Putnam. Berkeley: University of California Press, [1933] 1986.
Fry, Peter. *Para Inglês Ver*. Rio de Janeiro: Zahar, 1982.
Fryer, Roland G. "Acting White." *Education Next* 6, no. 1 (2006). Hoover Institution. Accessed June 17, 2010. http://educationnext.org/actingwhite/.
Furé, Rogelio Martínez. "Comentarios." In *Culturas encontradas: Cuba y los Estados Unidos*, edited by Rafael Hernández and John H. Coatsworth, 189–94. Havana: Centro de Investigación y Desarrollo de la Cultura Cubana Juan Marinello; Cambridge, MA: David Rockefeller Center for Latin American Studies, 2001.
Gans, Herbert. "Race as Class." *Contexts* 4, no. 4 (2005): 17–21.
Gascoigne, Bamber. "Lorraine Hansberry (1930–1965)." *TimeSearch for Books and Writers*, 2011. Accessed December 2, 2011. http://www.kirjasto.sci.fi/corhans.htm.
Gasman, Marybeth. "Salvaging 'Academic Disaster Areas': The Black College Response to Christopher Jencks and David Riesman's 1967 *Harvard Educational Review* Article." *Journal of Higher Education* 77, no. 2 (2006): 317–52.
Gaspar, David Barry, and David P. Geggus, eds. *A Turbulent Time: The French Revolution and the Greater Caribbean*. Bloomington: Indiana University Press, 1997.
Gates, Henry Louis, Jr. "The Passing of Anatole Broyard." In *Thirteen Ways of Looking at a Black Man*, 180–214. New York: Random House, 1997.
———. "The Slave Kingdoms." Episode of *Wonders of the African World*. Public Broadcasting Service, 1999.
Gatto, John Taylor. *Dumbing Us Down: The Hidden Curriculum of Compulsory Schooling*. 2nd ed. Gabriola Island, BC: New Society, 2005.
Gbadegẹsin, Ṣẹgun. *African Philosophy: Traditional Yoruba Philosophy and Contemporary African Realities*. New York: Peter Lang, 1991.
———. *Kinship of the Dispossessed: Du Bois, Nkrumah, and the Foundations of Pan-Africanism*. New York: Routledge, 1996.
Gehman, Mary. *The Free People of Color of New Orleans: An Introduction*. New Orleans: Margaret Media, 1994.
Gilman, Sander L. *Freud, Race, and Gender*. Princeton, NJ: Princeton University Press, 1993.
Glaberson, William. "Who Is a Seminole, and Who Gets to Decide?" *New York Times*, January 29, 2001. Accessed September 9, 2011. http://www.nytimes.com/2001/01/29/us/who-is-a-seminole-and-who-gets-to-decide.html.
Goffman, Erving. *Stigma: Notes on the Management of Spoiled Identity*. Englewood Cliffs, NJ: Prentice-Hall, 1963.
Goldsmith, Arthur H., Darrick Hamilton, and William Darity Jr. "Shades of Discrimination: Skin-Tone and Wages." *American Economic Review* 98, no. 2 (2006): 242–45.
Gomez, Michael A. *Exchanging Our Country Marks: The Transformation of African Identities in the Colonial and Antebellum South*. Chapel Hill: University of North Carolina Press, 1998.
Gould, Stephen J. *The Mismeasure of Man*. NY: W. W. Norton, 1981.

Graham, Lawrence Otis. *Our Kind of People: Inside America's Black Upper Class*. New York: HarperCollins, 1999.

Grandison, Kenrick Ian. "Negotiated Space: The Black College Campus as a Cultural Record of Postbellum America." *American Quarterly* 51, no. 3 (1999): 529–79.

Guha, Auditi. "Third Grader Scores Perfect 40 on MCAS." *Cambridge Chronicle*, September 24, 2003.

Gupta, Akhil, and James Ferguson. *Anthropological Locations: Boundaries and Grounds of a Field Science*. Berkeley: University of California Press, 1997.

Guyer, Jane. *An African Niche Economy: Farming to Feed Ibadan, 1968–1988*. Edinburgh: Edinburgh University Press, 1997.

Hall, Jacqueline Dowd. "'The Mind that Burns in Each Body': Women, Rape, and Racial Violence." In *Powers of Desire: The Politics of Sexuality*, edited by Ann Snitow, Christine Stansell, and Sharon Thompson, 328–49. New York: Monthly Review Press, 1983.

Handler, Richard. *Nationalism and the Politics of Culture in Quebec*. Madison: University of Wisconsin Press, 1988.

Hannerz, Ulf. *Transnational Connections: Culture, People, Places*. London: Routledge, 1996.

Hargrove, Melissa D. "Overview and Synthesis of Scholarly Literature." Appendix F in *Low Country Gullah Culture Special Resource Study and Final Environmental Impact Statement* by the National Park Service, F1–F54. Atlanta: National Park Service Southeast Regional Office, 2005.

Harrison, Ira E., and Faye V. Harrison, eds. *African-American Pioneers in Anthropology*. Urbana: University of Illinois Press, 1999.

Hartigan, John. "Translating 'Race' and *Raza* between the United States and Mexico." *North American Dialogue* 16, no. 1 (2013): 29–41.

Hartman, Saidiya. *Lose Your Mother: A Journey along the Atlantic Slave Route*. New York: Farrar, Straus and Giroux, 2007.

Hazel, Forest. "Occaneechi-Saponi Descendants in the North Carolina Piedmont." *Southern Indian Studies* 40 (1991): 3–29.

Hebdige, Dick. *Subculture: The Meaning of Style*. London: Methuen, 1979.

Helg, Aline. "Race in Argentina and Cuba, 1880–1930." In *The Idea of Race in Latin America, 1870–1940*, edited by Richard Graham, 37–69. Austin: University of Texas Press, 1990.

Hernández, Katya Kateri. "Too Black to Be Latino/a: Blackness and Blacks as Foreigners in Latino Studies." *Latino Studies* 1, no. 1 (2003): 152–59.

Herbert, Bob. "Impossible, Ridiculous, Repugnant." *New York Times*, October 6, 2005.

Herskovits, Melville J. *The Myth of the Negro Past*. Boston: Beacon, [1941] 1958.

Herzfeld, Michael. *Anthropology through the Looking-Glass: Critical Ethnography in the Margins of Europe*. Cambridge: Cambridge University Press, 1989.

———. *Cultural Intimacy: Social Poetics in the Nation-State*. 2nd ed. New York: Routledge, [1997] 2005.

Higgins, Chester. *Feeling the Spirit: Searching the World for the People of Africa*. New York: Bantam Books, 1994.

Higman, B. W. "The Slave Family and Household in the British West Indies, 1800–1834." *Journal of Interdisciplinary History* 6, no. 2 (1975): 261–87.

Hintzen, Percy C. *West Indian in the West: Self-Representations in an Immigrant Community*. New York: New York University Press, 2001.

———. "Whiteness, Desire, Sexuality, and the Production of Black Subjectivities in British Guiana, Barbados, and the United States." In *Problematizing Blackness: Self-Ethnographies by*

Black Immigrants to the United States, edited by Percy C. Hintzen and Jean Muteba Rahier, 129–68. New York: Routledge, 2003.

Hintzen, Percy C., and Jean Muteba Rahier, eds. *Problematizing Blackness: Self-Ethnographies by Black Immigrants to the United States*. New York: Routledge, 2003.

Hirsch, Arnold R. "Simply a Matter of Black and White: The Transformation of Race and Politics in Twentieth-Century New Orleans." In *Creole New Orleans: Race and Americanization*, edited by Arnold R. Hirsch and Joseph Logsdon, 262–319. Baton Rouge: Louisiana State University Press, 1992.

Hirsch, Arnold R., and Joseph Logsdon, eds. *Creole New Orleans: Race and Americanization*. Baton Rouge: Louisiana State University Press, 1992.

Hobsbawm, Eric, and Terence Ranger, eds. *The Invention of Tradition*. Cambridge: Cambridge University Press, 1983.

Hochschild, Adam. "Assessing Africa." Review of *Of Africa*, by Wọle Ṣoyinka. *Sunday Book Review* of *New York Times*, November 4, 2012. Accessed November 13, 2013. http://www.nytimes.com/2012/11/04/books/review/of-africa-by-wole-soyinka.html?pagewanted=2&_r=0.

Hoetink, H. *Two Variants on Race Relations: A Contribution to the Sociology of Segmented Societies*. Oxford: Oxford University Press, 1967.

Holsey, Bayo. *Routes of Remembrance: Refashioning the Slave Trade in Ghana*. Chicago: University of Chicago Press, 2008.

Horowitz, Helen Lefkowitz. *Campus Life: Undergraduate Cultures from the End of the Eighteenth Century to the Present*. New York: Alfred A. Knopf, 1987.

Howard University. "Biennial Evaluation Report—FY 93–94." 1994. Accessed March 26, 2007. http://www.ed.gov/pub/Biennial/533.html.

———. *Facts*. Washington, DC: Howard University Office of Research and Planning, 2001.

———. *Facts*. Washington, DC: Howard University Office of Research and Planning, 2002.

Howard University Gallery of Art. *A Proud Continuum: Eight Decades of Art at Howard University*. Washington, DC: Howard University Gallery of Art, Division of Fine Arts, College of Arts and Sciences, 2005.

Hughes, Michael, and Bradley R. Hertel. "The Significance of Color Remains: A Study of Life Chances, Mate Selection, and Ethnic Consciousness among Black Americans." *Social Forces* 69, no. 1 (1990): 1105–20.

Hunt, Stephanie. "Disappearing Dialects." *Charleston Magazine*, February 2007, 140–47.

Huntington, Samuel P. *The Clash of Civilizations and the Remaking of the World Order*. New York: Simon and Schuster, 1997.

Ignatiev, Noel. *How the Irish Became White*. New York: Routledge, 1995.

Inanga, Eno L. "The First 'Indigenisation Decree' and the Dividend Policy of Nigerian Quoted Companies." *Journal of Modern African Studies* 16, no. 2 (1978): 319–28.

Integrating the Life of the Mind: African Americans at the University of Chicago 1870–1940. Future Intellectuals: Lorenzo Dow Turner (Ph.D. 1926). Web exhibit, Special Collections Research Center, University of Chicago Library. Accessed April 17, 2010. http://www.lib.uchicago.edu/e/webexhibits/IntergratingTheLifeOfTheMind/LorenzoDowTurner.html.

Jacques, Edna Bolling. Letter to the editor. *New York Times*, February 6, 2011, 7.

James, Sherman A. "John Henryism and the Health of African Americans." *Culture, Medicine, and Psychiatry* 18 (1994): 163–82.

James, Winston. *Holding Aloft the Banner of Ethiopia: Caribbean Radicalism in Early Twentieth-Century America*. London: Verso, 1998.

Jencks, Christopher, and David Riesman. "The American Negro College." *Harvard Educational Review* 37, no. 2 (1967a): 3–60.

———. "Four Responses and a Reply." *Harvard Educational Review* 37, no. 3 (1967b): 465–68.

Jensen, Jane McEldowney. "Creating a Continuum: An Anthropology of Postcompulsory Education." *Anthropology and Education Quarterly* 30, no. 4 (1999): 446–50.

Johnson, Samuel. *The History of the Yorubas*. Lagos: CSS Bookshops, [1897] 1921.

Jok, Jok Madut. "The Legacy of Race." In *Race and Identity in the Nile Valley: Ancient and Modern Perspectives*, edited by Carolyn Flueher-Lobban and Kharyssa Rhodes, 187–206. Trenton, NJ: Red Sea, 2004.

Jorge, Angela. "The Black Puerto Rican Woman in Contemporary American Society." In *The Puerto Rican Woman: Perspectives on Culture, History, and Society*, 2nd ed., edited by Edna Acosta-Belén, 180–87. New York: Praeger, 1979.

Journal of Blacks in Higher Education. "News and Views: The Destructive Faculty Feud at Virginia State University." *Journal of Blacks in Higher Education*, October 31, 2001, 9.

Joyner, Charles. *Down by the Riverside: A South Carolina Slave Community*. Urbana: University of Illinois Press, [1984] 1985.

———. "Gullah/Geechee Region Becomes a Cultural Heritage Corridor." *Heritage Matters: News of the Nation's Diverse Cultural Heritage*. Washington, DC: National Park Service, 2007.

Kantor, Jodi. "For First Black President, a Complex Calculus of Race." *New York Times*, October 21, 2012, 1, 22.

Kasinitz, Philip. *Caribbean New York: Black Immigrants and the Politics of Race*. Ithaca, NY: Cornell University Press, 1992.

Katz, William Loren. *Black Indians: A Hidden Heritage*. New York: Atheneum, 1984.

Kein, Sybil, ed. *Creole: The History and Legacy of Louisiana's Free People of Color*. Baton Rouge: Louisiana State University Press, 2000a.

———. Introduction to *Creole: The History and Legacy of Louisiana's Free People of Color*, edited by Sybil Kein, xiii–xxiv. Baton Rouge: Louisiana State University Press, 2000b.

———. "Louisiana Creole Food Culture: Afro-Caribbean Links." In *Creole: The History and Legacy of Louisiana's Free People of Color*, edited by Sybil Kein, 244–51. Baton Rouge: Louisiana State University Press, 2000c.

Kennedy, N. Brent. *The Melungeons: The Resurrection of a Proud People*. 2nd, rev. and corr. ed. Macon, GA: Mercer University Press, 1997.

Kennedy, Randall. *Nigger: The Strange Career of a Troublesome Word*. New York: Pantheon, 2002.

Kent, Mary Medeiros. "Immigration and America's Black Population." *Population Review Bulletin* 62, no. 4 (2007). Accessed October 25, 2007. http://www.prb.org/pdf07/62.4immigration.pdf.

Khan, Shamus. "The New Elitists." *New York Times*, Sunday Review, July 8, 2012.

Kristoff, Nicholas D. "Africans in China Are Finally Freed." *New York Times*, January 6, 1989.

———. "Japan Confronting Gruesome War Atrocity." *New York Times*, March 17, 1995, A1, A12.

Kroeber, Alfred Louis, and Clyde Kluckhohn. *Culture: A Critical Review of Concepts and Definitions*. Papers of the Peabody Museum of American Archaeology and Ethnology, Harvard University 47, no. 1 (1952).

Kubik, Gerhard. *Angolan Traits in Black Music, Games and Dances of Brazil: A Study of African Cultural Extensions Overseas*. Lisbon: Junta de Investigações Científicas do Ultramar / Centro de Antropologia Cultural, 1979.

Kummels, Ingrid, Claudia Rauhut, Stefan Rinke, and Birte Timm, eds. *Transatlantic Caribbean: Dialogues of People, Practice, Ideas*. Bielefield, Germany: Transcript Verlag, 2014.

Lamar, Jacob V. "Saying No to Lee Atwater." *Time*, March 20, 1989. Accessed March 26, 2007. http://www.time.com/time/magazine/article/0,9171,957283,00.html?promoid=googlep.

Landes, Ruth. "A Cult Matriarchate and Male Homosexuality." *Journal of Abnormal and Social Psychology* 35 (1940): 386–97.

The Language You Cry In. Directed by Alvaro Toepke and Angel Serrano. San Francisco: California Newsreel, 1998.

Lee-St. John, Jeninne. "The Cherokee Nation's New Battle." *Time*, June 21, 2007. http://www.time.com/time/printout/0,8816,1635873,00.html.

Lewis, Bernard. *Race and Slavery in the Middle East: An Historical Enquiry*. New York: Oxford University Press, 1990.

Lewontin, R. "The Apportionment of Human Diversity." *Evolutionary Biology* 6 (1972): 381–98.

Littlefield, Daniel C. *Rice and Slaves: Ethnicity and the Slave Trade in Colonial South Carolina*. Urbana: University of Illinois Press, [1981] 1991.

Locke, Alain Leroy. "The Concept of Race as Applied to Social Culture." *Howard Review* 1 (1924): 296–99.

Loller, Travis. "DNA Study Seeks Origin of Appalachia's Melungeons." Associated Press, May 25, 2012. Accessed May 26, 2012. http://news.yahoo.com/dna-study-seeks-origin-appalachias-melungeons-201144041.html.

Long, Carolyn Morrow. *Spiritual Merchants: Religion, Magic, and Commerce*. Knoxville: University of Tennessee Press, 2001.

Long, Richard A. "Gullah Culture Special Resource Statement of National Historical and Cultural Significance." In *Low Country Gullah Culture Special Resource Study and Final Environmental Impact Statement*, by the National Park Service, 101–3. Atlanta: National Park Service Southeast Regional Office, 2005.

Lott, Eric. *Love and Theft: Blackface Minstrelsy and the American Working Class*. New York: Oxford University Press, 1993.

Louisiana Writers' Project. *Gumbo Ya-Ya*. Boston: Houghton Mifflin, 1945.

Lovett, Laura L. "African and Cherokee by Choice: Race and Resistance under Legalized Segregation." In *Confounding the Color Line: The Indian-Black Experience in North America*, edited by James F. Brooks, 261–91. Lincoln: University of Nebraska Press, 2002.

Lowenstein, Roger. "The Inequality Conundrum." *New York Times Magazine*, June 10, 2007, 11, 12, 14.

Magolda, Peter M. "The Campus Tour: Ritual and Community in Higher Education." *Anthropology and Education Quarterly* 31, no. 1 (2000): 24–46.

———. "Saying Good-Bye: An Anthropological Examination of a Commencement Ritual." *Journal of College Student Development* 44, no. 6 (2003): 779–96.

Mahmood, Saba. *Politics of Piety: The Islamic Revival and the Feminist Subject*. Princeton, NJ: Princeton University Press, 2005.

Maillard, Kevin Noble. "The Pocahontas Exception: The Exemption of American Indian Ancestry from the Racial Purity Law." *Michigan Journal of Race and Law* 12, no. 107 (2007): 351–86.

Malinowski, Bronislaw. *The Argonauts of the Western Pacific: An Account of Native Enterprise and Adventure in the Archipelagoes of Melanesian New Guinea*. Prospect Heights, IL: Waveland, 1922.

Mamdani, Mahmood. *When Victims Become Killers: Colonialism, Nativism, and the Genocide in Rwanda*. Princeton, NJ: Princeton University Press, 2001.

Manyika, Sarah. "Oyinbo." In *Problematizing Blackness: Self-Ethnographies by Black Immigrants to the United States*, edited by Percy C. Hintzen and Jean Muteba Rahier, 65–83. New York: Routledge, 2003.

Martin, Douglas. "Pedro A. Sanjuan Dies at 82; Cleared US Path for African Envoys." *New York Times*, October 6, 2012. Accessed August 27, 2014. http://www.nytimes.com/2012/10/06/us/pedro-a-sanjuan-dies-at-82-cleared-us-path-for-african-envoys.html.

Massey, Douglas S., Margarita Mooney, Kimberly C. Torres, and Camille Z. Charles. "Black Immigrants and Black Natives Attending Selective Colleges and Universities in the United States." *American Journal of Education* 113 (February 2007): 249–71.

Masters, Brooke A. "Howard U. Lobbies to Remove Surcharge for Foreign Students." *Washington Post*, Metro Section, May 1, 1992, D1.

Matory, J. Lorand. *Sex and the Empire That Is No More: Gender and the Politics of Metaphor in Oyo Yoruba Religion*. 2nd ed. New York: Berghahn Books, [1994] 2005b.

———. "The English Professors of Brazil: On the Diasporic Roots of the Yoruba Nation." *Comparative Studies in Society and History* 41, no. 3 (1999): 72–103.

———. "Surpassing 'Survival': On the Urbanity of 'Traditional Religion' in the Afro-Atlantic World." *Black Scholar* 30, nos. 3–4 (2001): 36–43.

———. "Contradiction and Forgetting among the Yewésseys." *Transforming Anthropology* 10, no. 2 (2002): 2–12.

———. "Gendered Agendas: The Secrets Scholars Keep about Yoruba-Atlantic Religion." *Gender and Society* 15, no. 3 (2003): 408–38.

———. *Black Atlantic Religion: Tradition, Transnationalism, and Matriarchy in the Afro-Brazilian Candomblé*. Princeton, NJ: Princeton University Press, 2005a.

———. "The 'New World' Surrounds an Ocean: Theorizing the Live Dialogue between African and African American Cultures." In *Afro-Atlantic Dialogues: Anthropology in the Diaspora*, edited by Kevin A Yelvington, 151–96. Santa Fe, NM: School of American Research; Oxford: James Currey, 2006.

———. "The Illusion of Isolation: The Gullah/Geechees and the Political Economy of African Culture in the Americas." *Comparative Studies in Society and History* 50, no. 4 (2008): 949–80.

———. "Obituary: Elliot Percival Skinner (1924–2007)." *American Anthropologist* 111, no. 1 (2009): 125–30.

———. "Marx, Freud, and the Gods Black People Make: European Social Theory and the Real 'Fetish.'" Unpublished manuscript.

Matory, W. Earle, Jr., ed. *Ethnic Considerations in Facial Aesthetic Surgery*. Philadelphia: Lippincott-Raven, 1998.

McCabe, Kristen. "African Immigrants in the United States." *Migration Policy Source*, 2011. Accessed August 20, 2013. http://www.migrationinformation.org/article/african-immigrants-united-states.

McCourt, Frank. *Angela's Ashes: A Memoir*. New York: Scribner, 1996.

McDaniel, Anne, Thomas A. DiPrete, Claudia Buchmann, and Uri Shwed. *The Black Gender Gap in Educational Attainment: Historical Trends and Racial Comparison*. New York: Columbia University, Department of Sociology, 2009.

McKinnon, Susan. "Reading the Contested Contours of Nation through Contested Forms of Kinship and Marriage." Lecture, Department of Cultural Anthropology, Duke University, January 12, 2015.

McWhorter, John. H. *Winning the Race: Beyond the Crisis in Black America*. New York: Gotham Books, 2005.

———. "A Life Between." *New York Times*, October 15, 2010. Accessed March 13, 2011. http://www.nytimes.com/2010/10/17/books/review/McWhorter-t.html?pagewanted+print.

Métraux, Alfred. *Voodoo in Haiti*. 2nd ed. New York: Schocken Books, [1959] 1972.

Meinig, D. W. *The Shaping of America: A Geographical Perspective on 500 Years of History*. New Haven, CT: Yale University Press, 1986.

Michaels, Walter Benn. *The Trouble with Diversity: How We Learned to Love Identity and Ignore Inequality*. New York: Metropolitan Books, 2006.

Miller, Errol. *Men at Risk*. Kingston, Jamaica: Jamaica Publishing House, 1991.

Mills, Gary B. *The Forgotten People: Cane River's Creoles of Color*. Baton Rouge: Louisiana State University Press, 1977.

Mintz, Sidney W., and Richard Price. *The Birth of African-American Culture: An Anthropological Perspective*. Boston: Beacon, [1976] 1992.

Moffatt, Michael. *Coming of Age in New Jersey: College and American Culture*. New Brunswick, NJ: Rutgers University Press, 1989.

Morrison, Toni. "On the Backs of Blacks." In "The New Face of America," special edition, *Time*, Fall 1993.

Mudimbe, V.-Y. *The Invention of Africa: Gnosis, Philosophy, and the Order of Knowledge*. Bloomington: Indiana University Press, 1988.

Mufwene, Salikoko S. "Some Reasons Why Gullah Is Not Dying Yet." *English World-Wide* 12, no. 2 (1991): 215–43.

Mufwene, Salikoko S., and Charles Gilman. "How African Is Gullah, and Why?" *American Speech* 62, no. 2 (1987): 120–39.

Nathan, Rebekah. *My Freshman Year: What a Professor Learned by Becoming a Student*. Ithaca, NY: Cornell University Press, 2005.

National Park Service. *Low Country Gullah Culture Special Resource Study and Final Environmental Impact Statement*. Atlanta: National Park Service, Southeast Regional Office, 2005.

New York Times. "Head of Howard U. Announces Retirement." April 23, 1989. Accessed March 26, 2007. http://www.nytimes.com/1989/04/23/us/head-of-howard-u-announces-retirement.html.

———. "The Shame of the Cherokee Nation." Editorial, June 8, 2007a. Accessed March 9, 2011. http://www.nytimes.com/2007/06/08/opinion/08fri3.html?pagewanted=print.

———. "An Unjust Expulsion." Editorial, March 8, 2007b. Accessed March 29, 2007. http://www.nytimes.com/2007/03/08/opinion/08thu4.html?ex=1331010000&en=8b457ab3.

Nieves, Evelyn. "Putting to a Vote the Question 'Who Is Cherokee?'" *New York Times*, March 3, 2007. Accessed March 9, 2011. http://www.nytimes.com/2007/03/03/us/03cherokee.html.

Ogbu, John U. *Minority Education and Caste: The American System in Cross-Cultural Perspective*. New York: Academic, 1978.

———. *Black American Students in an Affluent Suburb: A Study in Academic Disengagement*. Written with the assistance of Astrid Davis. Mahwah, NJ: Lawrence Erlbaum Associates, 2003.

Ojo, Ọlatunji. "The Root Is Also Here: The Nondiaspora Foundations of Yoruba Ethnicity." In *Movements, Borders, and Identities in Africa*, edited by Toyin Falọla and Aribidesi Usman, 53–80. Rochester, NY: University of Rochester Press, 2009.

Okome, Mojubaolu. "African Women and Power: Reflections on the Perils of Unwarranted Cosmopolitanism." *JENDA: A Journal of Culture and African Women Studies* 1, no. 1 (2001). Accessed April 24, 2007. http://www.jendajournal.com/vol1.1/okome.html.

Ọlajubu, Oyeronke. *Women in the Yoruba Religious Sphere*. Albany: State University of New York Press, 2003.

Ọlaniyan, Tẹjumọla. "Economies of the Interstice." In *Problematizing Blackness: Self-Ethnographies by Black Immigrants to the United States*, edited by Percy C. Hintzen and Jean Muteba Rahier, 53–64. New York: Routledge, 2003.

Omi, Michael, and Howard Winant. *Racial Formation in the United States: From the 1960s to the 1990s*. 2nd ed. New York: Routledge, 1994.

Opala, Joseph A. "The Gullah: Rice, Slavery, and the Sierra Leone-American Connection." Online publication by the Gilder-Lehrman Center, Yale University, n.d. Accessed 2007. http://www.yale.edu/glc/Gullah/cont.htm.

Ortiz, Fernando. *Los negros brujos*. Miami: Ediciones Universal, [1906] 1973.

Oxford English Dictionary, Compact Edition. Complete text reproduced micrographically. New York: Oxford University Press, 1971.

Oyewumi, Oyeronkẹ. *The Invention of Women: Making an African Sense of Western Gender Discourse*. Minneapolis: University of Minnesota Press, 1997.

Palmié, Stephan. "Against Syncretism: 'Africanizing' and 'Cubanizing': Discourses in North American Òrìṣà Worship." In *Counterworks: Managing the Diversity of Knowledge*, edited by Richard Fardon, 73–104. London: Routledge, 1995.

———. *Wizards and Scientists: Explorations in Afro-Cuban Modernity*. Durham, NC: Duke University Press, 2002.

Parés, Luis Nicolau. *The Formation of Candomblé: Vodun History and Ritual in Brazil*. Translated by Richard Vernon in collaboration with the author. Chapel Hill: University of North Carolina Press, [2006] 2013.

Parry, Odette. *Male Underachievement in High School Education: In Jamaica, Barbados, and St. Vincent and the Grenadines*. Kingston, Jamaica: Canoe Press, 2000.

Peel, J. D. Y. "The Cultural Work of Yoruba Ethnogenesis." In *Pioneer, Patriot and Patriarch: Samuel Johnson and the Yoruba People*, by Toyin Falọla, 65–75. Madison: African Studies Program, University of Wisconsin, [1989] 1993.

———. "Islam, Christianity and the Unfinished Making of the Yoruba." Lecture at the Mellon-Sawyer Seminar on Ethnicity in Africa, University of Michigan at Ann Arbor, April 1–2, 2011.

Perry, Theresa. "Up from the Parched Earth: Toward a Theory of African-American Achievement." In *Young, Gifted, and Black: Promoting High Achievement among African-American Students*, by Theresa Perry, Claude Steele, and Asa G. Hilliard III, 1–108. Boston: Beacon, 2003.

Philips, John Edward. "The African Heritage of White America." In *Africanisms in American Culture*. Edited by Joseph E. Holloway, 225–239. Bloomington: Indiana University Press, 1990.

Pietz, William. "The Problem of the Fetish I." *Res: Journal of Anthropology and Aesthetics* 9 (1985): 5–17.

Pinckney, Roger. *Blue Roots: African-American Folk Magic of the Gullah People*. 2nd ed. Orangeburg, SC: Sandlapper, [1998] 2003.

Pollitzer, William S. *The Gullah People and Their African Heritage*. Athens: University of Georgia Press, [1999] 2005a.

———. "The Gullah People and Their African Heritage." Appendix D, author's synopsis of Pollitzer. In *Low Country Gullah Culture Special Resource Study and Final Environmental Impact Statement*. Atlanta: National Park Service, Southeast Regional Office, D1–D52, 2005b.

Ponterotto, Joseph G., J. Manuel Casas, Lisa A. Suzuki, and Charlene M. Alexander, eds. *Handbook of Multicultural Counseling*. 2nd ed. Thousand Oaks, CA: Sage, 2001.

Powell, Colin, with Joseph E. Persico. *My American Journey*. 1st rev. ed. New York: Ballantine Books, [1995] 2003.

Powell, Eve M. Troutt. *Tell This in My Memory: Stories of Enslavement from Egypt, Sudan, and the Ottoman Empire*. Stanford, CA: Stanford University Press, 2012.

Powers, Retha. "Student Power!" *Essence* 20, no. 4 (August 1989): 122.

Price, Sally, and Richard Price. *Maroon Arts: Cultural Vitality in the African Diaspora*. Boston: Beacon, 1999.

Priority Africa Network. *African Immigrants and Census 2010: A Resource Guide for Increased Participation of Africa-Born Communities*. Priority Africa Network, 2011. Accessed April 14, 2011. http://www.priorityafrica.org/Census_the_African_immigrant-FINAL.pdf.

Puckett, Newbell Niles. *Folk Beliefs of the Southern Negro*. New York: Dover, [1926] 1969.

"Ralph Bunche—Biographical." Nobelprize.org. Accessed April 3, 2010. http://nobelprize.org/nobel_prizes/peace/laureates/1950/bunche-bio.html.

Ranger, T. O. "The Invention of Tradition in Colonial Africa." In *The Invention of Tradition*. Edited by Eric Hobsbawm and Terence Ranger, 211–62. Cambridge: Cambridge University Press, 1983.

Regents of University of California. "'The Great Good That Is in Us': A Centenary Celebration of Ralph J. Bunche." Regents of the University of California. April [2004] 2005. Accessed April 3, 2010. http://www.library.ucla.edu/bunche/howard.html.

Reisman, Karl. "Cultural and Linguistic Ambiguity in a West Indian Village." In *Afro-American Anthropology*, edited by Norman E. Whitten and John F. Szwed, 129–44. New York: Free Press, 1970.

Rimer, Sarah, and Karen W. Arenson. "Top Colleges Take More Blacks, but Which Ones?" *New York Times*, June 24, 2004. Accessed March 11, 2011. http://www.nytimes.com/2004/06/24/us/top-colleges-take-more-blacks-but-which-ones.html.

Risério, António. *Carnaval Ijexá*. Salvador da Bahia: Corrupio, 1981.

Ritterhouse, Jennifer. "Reading, Intimacy, and the Role of Uncle Remus in White Southern Social Memory." *Journal of Southern History* 69 (August 2003): 585–622.

Roach, Joseph R. *Cities of the Dead: Circum-Atlantic Performance*. New York: Columbia University Press, 1996.

Robinson, Eugene. "The Rap *Revolución*: In Cuba, an Insistent Musical Voice Is Pounding Home Its Points and Protests." *Washington Post*, April 14, 2002, beginning on p. G1.

———. *Disintegration: The Splintering of Black America*. New York: Anchor Books / Random House, 2010.

Robinson, Pearl T., and Elliot P. Skinner. *Transformation and Resiliency in Africa: As Seen by Afro-American Scholars*. Washington, DC: Howard University Press, 1983.

Rodrigues, Raymundo Nina. *Os Africanos no Brasil*. São Paulo: Companhia Editora Nacional, [1905] 1945.

Roediger, David R. *The Wages of Whiteness: Race and the Making of the American Working Class*. London: Verso, 1989.

Rosengarten, Dale. *Row upon Row: Sea Grass Baskets of the South Carolina Lowcountry*. Columbia, SC: McKissick Museum of the University of South Carolina, [1986] 1987.

Rosengarten, Dale, Theodore Rosengarten, and Enid Schildkrout. *Grass Roots: African Origins of an American Art*. New York: Museum for African Art, 2008.

Rountree, Helen C. *Pocahontas's People: The Powhatan Indians of Virginia through Four Centuries*. Norman: University of Oklahoma Press, 1990.

Russell, Kathy, Midge Wilson, and Ronald Hall. *The Color Complex: The Politics of Skin Color among African Americans*. New York: Harcourt Brace Jovanovich, 1992.

Sacks, Karen B. "How Did Jews Become White Folks?" In *Race*, edited by Steven Gregory and Roger Sanjek, 78–102. New Brunswick, NJ: Rutgers University Press, 1994.

Sahlins, Marshall. *Culture and Practical Reason*. Chicago: University of Chicago Press, 1976.

Said, Edward W. *Orientalism*. New York: Vintage, 1978.

Sankofa. Directed by Haile Gerima. Washington, DC: Myphedus Films, 1993.

Schildkrout, Enid. *People of the Zongo: The Transformation of Ethnic Identities in Ghana*. Cambridge: Cambridge University Press, 1978.

Schudel, Matt. "Surgeon Helped Howard University Grow." *Washington Post*, February 15, 2009. Accessed October 27, 2013. http://articles.washingtonpost.com/2009-02-15/news/36855522 _1_william-earle-matory-surgery-emergency-care.

Scott, James C. *Weapons of the Weak: Everyday Forms of Peasant Resistance*. New Haven, CT: Yale University Press, 1985.

Sekora, John. "The Emergence of Negro Higher Education in America, A Review." *Race & Class* 10 (1968): 79–87. Accessed February 23, 2010. http://rac.sagepub.com.

Sengova, Joko. "'My Mother Dem Nyus to Plan Reis': Reflections on Gullah/Geechee Creole Communication, Connections, and the Construction of Cultural Identity." In *Afro-Atlantic Dialogues: Anthropology in the Diaspora*, edited by Kevin A. Yelvington, 211–48. Santa Fe, NM: School of American Research; Oxford: James Currey, 2006.

Severson, Kim. "Taxes Threaten an Island Culture in Georgia." *New York Times*, September 25, 2012. Accessed October 23, 2012. http://www.nytimes.com/2012/09/26/us/on-an-island-in -georgia-geechees-fear-losing-land.html.

Shack, William A., and Elliot P. Skinner. *Strangers in African Societies*. Berkeley: University of California Press, 1979.

Shani, Serah. "African Immigrant Parents, Transnational Lives, and Schooling in the United States: The Case of Ghanaians in New York City." Lecture at the Center for African and African American Research, Duke University, October 30, 2013.

Shumar, Wesley. "Making Strangers at Home, Anthropologists Studying Higher Education." *Journal of Higher Education* 75, no. 1 (2004): 23–41.

Sider, Gerald M. *Lumbee Indian Histories: Race, Ethnicity, and Indian Identity in the Southern United States*. Cambridge: Cambridge University Press, 1993.

Sinnette, Calvin H. "Howard University College of Medicine and the Education of Caribbean-Born Medical Doctors." *Journal of the National Medical Association* 86, no. 5 (1993): 389–92.

Skinner, Elliot P. "Ethnic Interaction in a British Guiana Rural Community: A Study in Secondary Acculturation and Group Dynamics." PhD diss., Columbia University, 1955.

———. "Strangers in West African Societies." *Africa* 33, no. 4 (October 1963): 307–20.

———. *The Mossi of Burkina Faso: Chiefs, Politicians, and Soldiers* (previously titled *The Mossi of Upper Volta: The Political Development of a Sudanese People*). Prospect Heights, IL: Waveland, [1964] 1989.

———, ed. *Peoples and Cultures of Africa: An Anthropological Reader*. Garden City, NY: American Museum of Natural History and Doubleday / Natural History Press, 1973.

———. *African Urban Life: The Transformation of Ouagadougou*. Princeton, NJ: Princeton University Press, 1974.

———. "Competition within Ethnic Systems in Africa." In *Ethnicity and Resource Competition in Plural Societies*, edited by Leo A. Despres, 131–57. The Hague: Mouton, 1975.

———. "The Dialectic between Diasporas and Homelands." In *Global Dimensions of the African Diaspora*, edited by Joseph E. Harris, 17–45. Washington, DC: Howard University Press, 1982.

———. *African Americans and U.S. Policy toward Africa: In Defense of Black Nationality, 1850–1924*. Washington, DC: Howard University Press, 1992.

Smith, M. G. *West Indian Family Structure*. Seattle: University of Washington, 1962.

Sobel, Mechal. *Trabelin' On: The Slave Journey to an Afro-Baptist Faith*. Princeton, NJ: Princeton University Press, [1979] 1988.

Southern, Eileen. *The Music of Black Americans: A History*. 2nd ed. New York: W. W. Norton, [1971] 1983.

Speer, Tibbett. "The Newest African Americans Aren't Black." *American Demographics* (January 1994): 9–10.

Sperber, Jonathan. *Karl Marx: A Nineteenth-Century Life*. New York: Liveright, 2013.

Spivak, Gayatri. *In Other Worlds: Essays in Cultural Politics*. New York: Methuen, 1987.

Stack, Carol. *All Our Kin: Strategies for Survival in a Black Community*. New York: Basic, 1970.

Stanley-Washington, Alessandra, and Jacob V. Lamar. "Saying No to Lee Atwater." *Time*, March 20, 1989. Accessed March 26, 2007. http://www.time.com/time/magazine/article/0,9171,957283,00.html?promoid=googlep.

Steele, Claude M. "A Threat in the Air: How Stereotypes Shape Intellectual Identity and Performance." *American Psychologist* 52, no. 6 (1997): L613–29.

Stewart, Charles, and Rosalind Shaw, eds. *Syncretism/Anti-Syncretism: The Politics of Religious Synthesis*. London: Routledge, 1994.

Stewart, Dafina Lazarus. "Being All of Me: Black Students Negotiating Multiple Identities." *Journal of Higher Education* 79, no. 2 (2008): 183–207.

Stinchcombe, Arthur L. *Rebellion in a High School*. Chicago: Quadrangle Books, 1964.

Strauss, Valerie, and Susan Kinzie. "Howard President to Retire Next Year." *Boston Globe*, April 28, 2007. Accessed August 27, 2014. http://www.boston.com/news/education/higher/articles/2007/04/28/howard_u_president_to_retire_next_year/.

Stuckey, Sterling. *Slave Culture: Nationalist Theory and the Foundations of Black America*. New York: Oxford University Press, 1987.

Sutton, Felix. *The Illustrated Book about Africa*. New York: Grosset and Dunlap, 1959.

Taiwo, Olufẹmi. "This Prison Called My Skin: On Being Black in America." In *Problematizing Blackness: Self-Ethnographies by Black Immigrants to the United States*, edited by Percy C. Hintzen and Jean Muteba Rahier, 35–51. New York: Routledge, 2003.

Tajfel, Henri, and John Turner. "An Integrative Theory of Intergroup Conflict." In *The Social Psychology of Intergroup Relations*, edited by William G. Austin and Stephen Worchel, 33–48. Monterey, CA: Brooks/Cole, 1979.

Tanenhaus, Sam. "In Texas Curriculum Fight, Identity Politics Leans Right." *New York Times*, March 20, 2010. Accessed September 15, 2010. http://www.nytimes.com/2010/03/21/weekinreview/21tanenhous.html?pagewanted=all.

Tate, Greg, ed. *Everything But the Burden: What White People Are Taking from Black Culture*. New York: Broadway Books, 2003.

Tatum, Beverly Daniel. *"Why Are All the Black Kids Sitting together in the Cafeteria?" and Other Conversations about Race*. New York: Basic Books, 2003.

REFERENCES

Thompson, Edgar T. "The Little Races." *American Anthropologist* 74, no. 5 (1972): 1295–1306.

Thornton, John K. *African and Africans in the Making of the Atlantic World, 1400–1800.* Cambridge: Cambridge University Press, 1998.

Timberg, Craig. "Academic Haven for Blacks Becomes Bias Battleground." *Washington Post*, September 6, 2000, A01.

Touré. *Who's Afraid of Post-Blackness? What It Means to Be Black Now.* New York: Free Press, 2011.

Treuer, David. "Kill the Indians, Then Copy Them." *New York Times*, September 30, 2012.

Turner, Lorenzo Dow. *Africanisms in the Gullah Dialect.* 3rd ed. Ann Arbor: University of Michigan Press, [1949] 1973.

Turner, Victor. *The Ritual Process: Structure and Anti-structure.* New York: Aldine de Gruyter, [1966] 1995.

US Census Bureau. "Table 2. Region of Birth of the Foreign-Born Population: 1850 to 1930 and 1960 to 1990." Internet release March 9, 1999. Accessed March 31, 2010. http://www.census.gov/population/www/documentation/twps0029/tab02.html.

———. Poverty, 2013 Highlights. http://www.census.gov/hhes/www/poverty/about/overview/index.html.

US Department of Labor, Office of Policy Planning and Research. "The Negro Family: The Case for National Action." Washington, DC: US Government Printing Office, 1965.

Vasconcelos, José. *La raza cósmica: Misión de la raza iberoamericana.* Paris: Agencia Mundial de Librería, 1925.

Vega, Marta Mareno. *The Altar of My Soul: The Living Traditions of Santería.* New York: One World, 2000.

Vlach, John Michael. *The Afro-American Tradition in Decorative Arts.* Athens: University of Georgia Press, [1978] 1990.

von Herder, Johann Gottfried. *Reflections on the Philosophy of the History of Mankind.* Translated by T. O. Churchill, abridged and edited by Frank E. Manuel. Chicago: University of Chicago Press, [1784–91] 1968.

Wagley, Charles. Introduction to *Race and Class in Rural Brazil*, edited by Charles Wagley, 7–15. New York: UNESCO, International Documents Service; Columbia University Press, [1952] 1963.

Wagner-Winkle, Rachelle. "The Perpetual Homelessness of College Experiences: Tensions between Home and Campus for African American Women." *Review of Higher Education* 33 (Fall 2009): 1–36.

Washington Post. "Psychologist Deborah Matory Dies." July 18, 1995. Accessed January 17, 2005. http://www.highbeam.com/doc.1P2-844046.html.

Waters, Mary C. *Ethnic Options: Choosing Identities in America.* Berkeley: University of California Press, 1990.

———. *Black Identities: West Indian Immigrant Dreams and American Realities.* New York: Russell Sage Foundation; Cambridge, MA: Harvard University Press, 1999.

Welsing, Frances Cress. *The Isis (Yssis) Papers.* Chicago: Third World, 1991.

Wikipedia. "Flag of Cape Verde." 2008. Accessed March 12, 2010. http://en.wikipedia.org/wiki/Flag_of_Cape_Verde.

Wilgoren, Debbi. "Howard Foreign Students Protest Rise in Tuition." *Washington Post*, March 8, 1990, DC1.

Williams, Brackette F. "A Class Act: Anthropology and the Race to Nation across Ethnic Terrain." *Annual Review of Anthropology* 18 (1989): 401–44.

Williams, Eric. *Inward Hunger: The Education of a Prime Minister.* Princeton, NJ: Markus Wiener, [1969] 2006.

Williams, Juan, and Dwayne Ashley. *I'll Find a Way or Make One: A Tribute to Historically Black Colleges and Universities.* New York: HarperCollins/Amistad, 2004.

Williams, Raymond. *The Country and the City.* Oxford: Oxford University Press, [1973] 1975.

Williams, Yohuru R. "A Series of Frustrations: John Hope Franklin's Troubled Tenure at Howard University, 1947–1956." *Negro History Bulletin* 61, nos. 3–4 (1998): 72–76.

Willie, Charles V., and Ronald R. Edmonds, eds. *Black Colleges in America: Challenge, Development, Survival.* New York: Teachers College Press, 1978.

Willis, Paul E. *Learning to Labor: How Working Class Kids Get Working Class Jobs.* New York: Columbia University Press, 1977.

Wilson, Jill. "African-Born Residents of the United States." Migration Policy Institute. Migration Information Source, August 2003. Accessed April 14, 2011. http://www.migrationinformation.org/usfocus/display.cfm?ID=147.

Wilson, William J. *The Declining Significance of Race: Blacks and Changing American Institutions.* Chicago: University of Chicago Press, 1978.

Winkle-Wagner, Rachelle. "The Perpetual Homelessness of College Experiences: Tensions between Home and Campus for African American Women." *Review of Higher Education* 33, no. 1 (2009): 1–36.

Wish, Harvey. "The Revival of the African Slave Trade in the United States, 1856–1860." *Mississippi Valley Historical Review* 27, no. 4 (1941): 569–88.

Wisnieski, Richard. "The Averted Gaze." *Anthropology and Education Quarterly* 31, no. 1 (2000): 5–23.

Wolf, Eric R. *Europe and the People without History.* Berkeley: University of California Press, 1982.

Wood, Peter H. *Black Majority: Negroes in Colonial South Carolina from 1670 through the Stono Rebellion.* New York: Alfred A. Knopf, 1974.

Woodson, Carter G. *The Mis-education of the Negro.* New York: AMS, [1969] 1977.

Wright, Stephen C. "Ambiguity, Social Influence, and Collective Action: Generating Collective Protest in Response to Tokenism." *Personality and Social Psychology Bulletin* 23, no. 12 (1997): 1277–90.

Wright, Stephen C., Donald M. Taylor, and Fathali M. Moghaddam. "Responding to Membership in a Disadvantaged Group: From Acceptance to Collective Protest." *Journal of Personality and Social Psychology* 58, no. 6 (1990): 994–1003.

Yancey, William L., Eugene P. Ericksen, and Richard N. Juliani. "Emergent Ethnicity: A Review and Reformulation." *American Sociological Review* 41, no. 3 (1976): 391–403.

Yelvington, Kevin A., ed. *Afro-Atlantic Dialogues: Anthropology in the Diaspora.* Santa Fe, NM: School of American Research Press; Oxford: James Currey, 2006.

Index

References to images appear in italics

Adebọnọjọ, Olubadejọ Olurẹmi, MD, 69, 75–82
Adebọnọjọ, Ọtunba Olubadejọ Olurẹmilẹkun, MD, 69, 75–82. *See also* Uncle Badejọ
Adebọnọjọ, Samuel Adegbesan, *Dagburewe* of Idọwa, Nigeria, 76
Adelaja, Eva Adebayọ, 76
Adichie, Chimamanda Ngozi, 371–72
affirmative action, 26, 305
    effects of, 466
    inclusion of Creoles of color and black Indians, 306
    political support for, 466
Africa
    African-identified religions, 412–15
    as both heaven and hell, 391
    and collective neo-African identity, 416
    image of, in self-making of groups, 369, 372
    pan-Africanism, 317, 357, 397, 401, 403, 481
    as world's constituent-other, 371
African Americans
    "acting white," 308, 309, 310
    Bourgeoisie, self-making of, 458
    complexion, status, and hierarchy, 146–47, 150
    as constituent-other, stigmatized as, 460, 477
    cultural nationalism, 69
    culture making, 410, 445
    education, views of, 308–9
    elite
        code-switching, 132
        neighborhoods of, 47
    identity
        as cast in the role of the collective id, 447
        dilemma of, 371
        diversity of, 330, 372
    as excluding African and Caribbean immigrants, 135
    as outsider, 2, 117
    overlap with Louisiana Creoles and Native tribes, 234
    pursuit of individual self-expression, 388
    as symbols, 372
    term as ambiguous, 326
    as trope, 135
    and vernacular speech, 135
middle-class, 3
    accomplishments and disproving anti-Black stereotypes, 332
    code-switching, 132, 345
    creativity of, 343
    and misbehavior of other African Americans, 332
native-born
    diversity of class, ancestry, values, and conduct, 6
    dynamics of individualism and collectivism, 390
    nonethnic system of Black fraternities, 122
    in relation to non-native-born Blacks, 327
    and stereotyping of others of higher or lower classes, 49
parents and parenting
    admonishment to prepare twice as well, 328
    myth of mothers' career preference for daughters, 329
and schadenfreude, 49
stereotyping of, 49, 333, 388
stigmatization of, 343, 460, 477
symbolic heaven and hell of, 372

African Americans (*continued*)
  tension between native-born and foreign-born, 327
  and white America
    defamation of, as constant reality, 120
    power and status, mimesis of elite white American manners, speech, and writing, 154
  women, education and employment of, 329
  working-class
    demand for conformity and intragroup homogeneity, 161
    and middle-class Black ethnics, 3
African American Vernacular English (AAVE), 106, 135, 181
Africans
  African-descended people, assumed unity of, 456
  continental
    as foil, 2, 3
    high education level of, 372
  culture-making, 410
  as embodiment of heaven and hell, 463
Africans, American
  diversity of, 372
  ethnological schadenfreude, 445
  and image of home, 370–446
  and metaphor of heaven and hell, 445
African Studies Association, Melville J. Herskovits Prize, 87
Afrocentrism, 188, 457
  and neoconservative backlash against affirmative action, 469
Afro-Cubanismo, 457
Afro-Cuban Santéria (or Ocha), 154, 191, 422, 427, 433
Akan
  Ashanti as most famous subgroup, 214, 219
  and English language ethnography, 396
AMA (American Medical Association), exclusion of African American physicians, 91
American Anthropological Association, and ethics, 89
American College of Surgeons (ACS), 99
American Indians, 5, 142
  of African descent
    culture-making of, 368
    debate as identity, complexion or culture, 231–306
    denial of ancestry for honor and profit, 230
    and colorism, 64, 93
    as communities of debate, 463
    education of, 249
    identity and debate
      modern-day ambivalence toward whites as well as Blacks, 260
      tensions between lighter- and darker-skinned bands, 256
    legal recognition of, role of museums and salvage anthropology in, 304
  Pamunkeys, 233, 261
  Piscataway/Piscatawa tribe, 7, 29, 237, 237
  in relation to Blacks
    animus toward African Americans, 244, 253, 255
    anti-Black racism, 248, 249
    fear of being redefined as "people of color," 256
    in past, enslaved Black people, 253
    seen as threat to recovering treaty rights, 255
  self-identity, disagreement over whether one can be both Black and Indian, 251
  southeastern
    discomfort around darker-skinned, 239–40
    racial component, 261
    summary, 248–49
  Virginia tribes
    denial of ancestry, 261
    efforts to distinguish themselves from African Americans, 257
    and last-place anxiety, 258
    opposition to intermarriage with Blacks, 260
  See also Native Americans; *and names of individual tribes*
American Medical Association (AMA), exclusion of African American physicians, 91
Anderson, Benedict, 182
anthropology, field of
  anthropologists, seen as "handmaidens of colonialism," 50–51
  "borderline whites," 122
  culture seen as comprehensive way of thinking and of conducting life, 282
  founding of, 51
  historical turn, 85
  idea of "cultures" as discrete and homogeneous largely dead in this field, 173
  lessons of the stigmatized, 65
  post–World War II, 8
  shifting perspectives over time, 50
  viewed, over time, 50
Arabs, 18, 19, 54, 398, 439, 444
Ashanti, as most famous subgroup of the Akan speakers, 214, 219
Association of Black Scientists and Engineers (ABSE), 279
Atwater, Lee, 163–64, 466–67
Aunt Arnzie (Carolyn Arnzietta Love), 142, 143, 146–47, 149–50, 329, 407, 481
Aunt Ruth (Ruth J. Wilsen), 481

INDEX

Aunt Yewande Adebọnọjọ (née Daniel), 80
Autocrat Social & Pleasure Club, *296*
autoethnography, defined, 3

Badejọ, Uncle, 69, 75–82, 93, 108, 148, 238, 394, 404. *See also* Adebọnọjọ, Olubadejọ Olurẹmi, MD
Bakke case, 123–24
Balibar, Étienne
   addressed role of race, 17
   on people in face-to-face competition, 32
Barbadians, 167
Barth, Fredrik
   on the cultural diacritica that define membership in ethnic groups, 304
   cultural difference and ethnic difference, 314
   theories on ethnicity, 38
Bastian, Adolf, concept of "cultures," 50
Bastide, Roger, 208, 410, 411, 456
Bateson, Gregory, 38, 42, 225
Benedict, Ruth, xi
   on divergent lifeways or cultures, 471
   legitimate cultures vs. inferior cultures, 471
Bennett, William J., 448–49, 450
binary hypodescent system, 22, 32
   Black race, 22
   unmarked, higher, non-Black race, 22
binary racial order, 4, 112
Black Americans
   bourgeoisie
      characteristics of, 68
      code-switching, 106
      names as cosmopolitan, transnational, 105
      role of ethnicity and transnationalism in the recent transformation of, 68
      self-love, self-loathing, and ambition, 68
   elites, and large-scale dilemmas of political identity faced by, 85
   identity
      as binary hypodescent system, 22–23
      elites and, 457
      as exemplar of negative stereotyping, 333
      loyalty and conformity demanded by, 111
   middle-class
      after affirmative action, 466
      child-rearing, 327–28
      dilemmas, accomplishments, and foibles of, 478
   unity, unofficial reasons for, enduring effects of past discrimination, 465
   views of, anemic portraits, 3
   working-class diction and behavior as inferior, 480
   See also African Americans
Black ethnics
   and African Americans, 329

Black Atlantic culture, 194
   Caribbeans' attempt to escape condition by invoking tie to Britain, 346
   as claiming more deserving of esteem than African Americans, 319
   and mobilization of "culture," 469
   responses to racial stigma, 230
   stereotyping of, 49
   strategic stereotyping of, 49
   view of African Americans as fictional foil to ambition and accomplishments of non-African Americans, 329
   view of native-born African Americans as a constitutent other, 54–55
Blackness
   collective identity, empirical challenges to, by immigration and by economic diversification, 9
   culturalization of, and proliferation of ethnic identities subdividing black America, 457
   as including stereotypes and struggle against stigma, 438
   as strategically essentialist project and essential to the US civil rights movement, 456
   as strategy of resistance to white supremacy, 456
   as symbol of exclusion and stigma, 122
   as terms without clear legal definition, 474
Black people
   Black identity, "Black any way you want to be," *133*, 133–34, 135, 161–70
   contradictory desires and expectations faced by, 286
   defined as any degree of African ancestry, independent of phenotype, 7, 22
   each bears the burden of representing his or her race, 117
   fear of confirming stereotypes propagated by the majority, 117
   foreign-born, belief in superiority over native-borne African Americans, 333
   foremost example of constituent-other but also foremost model of resistance to stigma, 482
   middle-class, and taste-based pursuit of class distinction, 455
   ongoing fear that shortcomings will always count more than successes, 117
   orthographic distinction, 22
      emic identity category and the "one-drop rule," 23
   as pertaining to a particular set of physical characteristics, 22
   and upward mobility in United States, 457

Black Power movement, 40, 188, 403, 457
    in Trinidad, 457
Black Skin, White Masks (Fanon [1952] 2008), 448
Boas, Franz, and cultural relativism, xi
    Boasian concept of "culture," 8, 15, 30, 278, 476
    on divergent lifeways or cultures, 471
    idea of cultural relativism, 473
    role in a "salvage anthropology," 51
Bonilla-Silva, Eduardo, 45, 467
Bourdieu, Pierre, 478
    class distinction in the dynamics of ethnicity, 314
    class hierarchy and ethnogenesis, 3
    on distinction, 42
    on ethnography, 76
    "in the logic of the trial," 76, 114, 115, 386
    portraits of cultures, 174
    taste as an idiom of class stratification, 36, 61
bourgeoisie
    Afro-Atlantic, 109
    Washington, DC, 143
Brazil, ix
    Candomblé, 91, 154, 193, 198, 227, 427
    ciclo do negro, 457
    research, ix
    valorization of miscegenation, 8
Brigham and Women's Hospital, 74
Brodhead, Richard, 130–31
Brown v. Board of Education, 159
Bryce-Laporte, Roy Simón, 111, 457, 464
Bunche, Ralph, 83, 320, 402
Bush, George H. W., 164
Bush, George W., 45, 130–31

Caribbeans
    and African Americans
        presumed superiority, 334
        similarity and superiority, 312
    ambivalent response of immigrants to stigmatization of Blackness, 65
    Caribbean Day Parade, 358, 359, 361
    color discrimination, 410
    cultural distinction and ethnic rivals, 342
    culture and middle-class values, 323
    culture making, 112, 365, 410
    and ethnogenesis
        the defining role of debate and contestation, 304
        ethnic difference, myth of, 323–32, 335–48; as being the best of one's (stigmatized) kind, 348
        ethnic sameness and difference, 348–60; language of, 360–64
        as the most extreme demonstration of the competitive and hierarchical nature of ethnogenesis, 463
    mythical anthropology of, and ethnic differentiation, 307–25, 335
    race and ethnic distinction, 313–15, 316–23, 342
    self-identity
        declare they are not African Americans, 46
        Jamaicans and Trinidadians, particularly, elaborated a fictional anthropology of difference from African Americans, 321
        and miscegenation, 8
        the mythological discourse of cultural difference under conditions of migration, racial stigmatization, and class similarity, 311–12
        and superiority, the tethering of the myth, 346
        willful propagation of "model minority" ideology, 331
    self-representation
        cultural difference and, in reaction to racial stigmatization, 311–12
        to establish distinction, 321
        not empirical but strategic and selective, 312
        "representing," 332–34; as honoring one's group, 332
    triple consciousness, 464
    views of African Americans
        narrative trope regarding, 318
        upwardly mobile effort to describe what favorably distinguishes them from African Americans, 314, 323
        view of parents not instilling ambition, 328–29
Carmichael, Stokely, 318, 408
Chaney, James, 450–51
Cherokees, 233
    citizenship rights of mixed-race descendants, 253, 262
Cherokee tribe, 203, 233, 245, 253–54, 255, 262
Chickahominy tribe, 34, 233, 242, 251, 253, 261, 263
China, 18, 19, 35, 407
Chisholm, Shirley, 318
Choctaws, 233, 255
churches, Indian, avoidance of Blacks, 257, 258
citizenship, US, boundaries of, 330
civil rights era, 459
    black ethnogenesis intensified, 114
    middle-class white ethnic identity in 1980s, 468
    Reagan Republicans canonized a new interpretation of civil rights discourse, 467–69
civil rights movement, 35, 67, 110, 188, 457
    and founding of Howard University, 78
    racial uplift vocabulary of, 67
    result, affirmative action policies implemented, 466

INDEX

some Indians allied with African Americans, 257
Civil War, 28, 186, 199, 206, 221
class
   class-specific sense of legacy, 68
   as framework, xi
   as idiom of distinction, 459
   status, signs of, 68
class and conformity, 477
classification systems, racial, 25
code-switching, as form of image management, 68–69, 130, 131, 132, 309
coding, to distinguish groups from African Americans, 68–69
Cohen, Abner, 37, 85, 314
Cohn, Bernard, ix
Cold War, 85
colonialism, 75, 87, 113, 448
   and gender role, 430
   as having planted a double narcissism, 455
colonization, 68, 188, 363, 456
   self-representation, worth, and colonizers, 435
color complex, 67–68
   defined, complexion-based discrimination among people of African descent, 67–68
colorism, 64, 93, 109, 136, 279, 301, 316
Columbia University, 82, 84, 108
   and founding of American cultural anthropology, 82, 88
   Skinner's training of anthropologists, 88
complexion
   complexion-based forms of exclusion, 147, 335
      American Indians of part-African descent, and revivalist claims of distinct cultures, 64–65
      Louisiana Creoles of color, and employment of discourse of culture to seek distinction and dividends, 64–65
      light-skinned
         and President Obama, 169
         privilege and elite status, 149–50
consciousness, double, 55, 71, 86, 464–65
consciousness, triple, 464
constituent-other, 2, 4
   Black American men, 66
   Black people foremost example, 482
   faults of the few seen as typical of that group, 476
   in hierarchical systems, 447
   and native-born African Americans, 476
   nondominant group as seeking protection of dominant group, 479
   is the nonethnic African American, 302
   projected onto blacks by whites, 457–58
   racialized, 463
   responses to, 458

Creoleness, diacritica of
   phenotype and "culture" debated, 272, 303
   reified as specific ethnic group, as a lifeway frozen in time, 301–2
   term is as ambiguous as it is contentious, 273
Creoles
   culture
      and African Americans, 268, 278, 303
      defining indices of, 269–71
      as distinct, 303
      and racism, 275
   as ethnic group, 30
   literature seen as cultural diacritica, 270
   flight from stigma, 274
   how they redraw their ethnic boundaries, 273–74
   how they stratify their own, 273–74
   identity
      as assertions of superiority as well as difference, 279
      colorism in, 279
      as ethnic category, 267–68
      meaning has changed over time and varies according to class and regional background of the speaker, 271
      and role of university, 235–36
   judgment based on phenotype, 274
   responses to skin color and phenotype, 274–75
   self-representation of, 5
   separate and different culture debate, 78, 303
   and southeastern Indian, assertions of African American inferiority common among, 242
   and southeastern Indian tribes
      charge of seeking sense of superiority to African Americans, 235
      focus on matrilineal ancestry, 274
      partial African ancestry of, 234
      as powerful illustration of role of stigma and interethnic hierarchy in ethnogenesis, 235
   variance in residential, territory of origin, linguistic, and phenotypical standards, 268
   See also Creoles, Louisiana
Creoles, Louisiana
   and African Americans, 271
   and fictional anthropology of difference, 321
   alleged convergence with Americans of African ancestry, 233
   alleged cultural difference from African Americans for honor and profit, 230
   ambiguity and Creole lore, 292–300
   boundaries of elite bear some resemblance to boundaries around African American elite, 271

Creoles, Louisiana (*continued*)
  college-educated, most described themselves as "Creole," 281
  as communities of debate, 463
  contradictory desires and expectations faced by, 287
  cuisine of, 282, 283, 284
  culturally coded boundaries are permeable, 273
  culture
    and Gothic storytelling, 292
    resist pressure to assimilate, 233
  debate as identity, complexion or culture, 231–306
  as ethnic group
    ambiguity as a cultural diacritic, 283
    class and education-level elements, 280–81
    double or triple consciousness of, 282
    as one defined by its own uncertainty about its distinctiveness, 282
    as one of rejection, reticence, and quiet pride, 282
    as separate or different culture, 282, 283, 303
    tensions implicit in, 280
    as an unsettled dialogue, 282
  hierarchy
    elite, and porous boundaries of inclusion, 271, 284
    separates urban from rural Creoles, 233
  identity
    ambiguity as implicit diacritic, 286–88
    continual debate among, 29–30
    culture making of, 368
    diversity of, 233, *277*
    and family genealogy, 293
    and light-skinned Black people, 267–68
    shown to be emerging from binary construction of race, 463
  motives by which Creoles and Indians group and regroup themselves, 235
  scholars, Raymond DuPlessis and Melissa Shapiro, 300
  social networks
    fluid movement between Creole and non-Creole African American networks, 280
    marriage patterns, 290–92
    membership and complexion, 289
    "paper bag test," 295
    principles of mate selection, 290–91
    and reputation for magical powers, 283–84
    schools, 288–89
    segregated schooling of, Catholic schools, 184
    Seventh Ward, 298–99
  speech, 284–85

Cuffe, Paul, 256
Cullen, Countee ("Heritage," 1930), 370–71
"culture"
  as assertions of moral dignity among the racially stigmatized, 478
  concept and definition
    anthropological concept of, 3, 8, 50
    black ethnic construction of, 115
    Boasian concept of, 4, 50, 176, 232
    confabulation of, as competitive, hierarchical, and racialized, 458
    displacing class as a vocabulary of human difference, 474
    as euphemism for race, 8
    as insurgent discourse, 471
    inventors and definers, 462
    as response to French cultural chauvinism, 51
    on term's adoption and use in the United States, 51
    Tylorean concept of, 176, 232
    usage of concept in defense of the stigmatized and discreditable, 477
  cultural difference and distinctiveness
    as multicultural, interclass dialogue, 226
    myths of: as social fictions, 334; as symbolic strategies of discipline, 334
  cultures and rules as fictions of fixity, 172–76
  and ethnic identity
    dialogical theory of, 226–30
    dialogic theory of, groups that seek honor and profit by denying ancestry, 230
    people as developing patterns of behavior that complement those of the populations they live beside, 226
  and ethnological schadenfreude, 476–80
  as fiction of fixity, 172–76
  and hierarchy, 470, 473
    and competition for approval through highlighting collective differences, 461–62
    culture making, indexing of the hierarchical and competitive context of, 478
    pursuit of as response to being viewed as the constituent-other, 457–58
    as source of mutual "othering" by subordinate and middling groups, 53, 54
  as idiom of distinction, 459
  not self-existent entities or "islands" of sui generis distinction and homogeneity, but intersection and convergence of translocal flows, 194
  pursuit of, as response to being viewed as constitutent-other, 457–58
  vs. color, 269–73

INDEX

culture, pursuit of, self-cultivation through display of taste is competitive and hierarchical, 458
culture making
　cultural diacritica as subject of debate, 423
　remembrance of things past as prominent feature of, 461
　role of diasporic scholars in creating national cultures is not well examined, 422
cultures, the stigmatized, the dominant, and the ethnoracially unmarked, 461

Davis, Miles, 81
Degler, Carl, 113
Deng, Anyong Kout, 378, *378*, 439–42, *443*
desegregation, 67, 465, 466
differences as useful, 226
differentiation, racial, xi
discrimination, racial
　and Hausa, discrimination and inequality of educational and economic assets, 465
　during post–World War II suburbanization, by realtors, banks, and Federal Housing Administration, 468
　as self-fulfilling prophecies, 330
diversity
　cultural, became rude to mention race or racism at all, 124
　at Howard University, 3
　as preeminent ideal, in post-Reaganite age, 469–70
　racial, black ethnic, 458
diversity, phenotypical
　associated with a moral, aesthetic, and social hierarchy, 25
　and discrimination, 24
Dole, Robert, 89
dominant group, x
　hyperreal infallibility of, 476
Dominicans, and Puerto Ricans as lazy, 343
Douglas, Mary, 283–84
Douglass, Frederick, 19, 45
Drew, Charles, 96–97
Du Bois, W. E. B., 12, 456
　Africanist diplomacy, 89
　call for Black unity and African uplift, 87–88, 401
　collaboration with Boas, 51
　and the "color line," 15, 465
　double consciousness, 86
　The Souls of Black Folk, 55
　and the "Talented Tenth" (and university), 136, 186
Duke University, 483
　African American graduates of, 134

Center for African and African American Research, 105, 133, 330
　the role of academic and nonacademic ethnology in the pursuit of honor and opportunity, 63
　and the southern (white) elite, 127
DuPlessis, Raymond, 269–72, 279, 280
　anger as revealing tensions implicit in Creole identity, 280
　definitions as nostalgia, 303

education
　Americans, Black and white, skeptical of academic intelligence, 118
　establishment of segregated schools, 249
　gender gap, 167–68
　as "the hope of the slave and the answer to history's shame," 470–71
emancipation, 188
empires, colonial, 85
endogamy, 236–37
Epps, Charles D., 79
Eritrea/Eritreans, 65, 264, 351, 354, 413, 414
Ethiopia/Ethiopians, 65, 156, 161, 167, 348, 354
ethnically unmarked
　competition for approval of, through stigmatization, 461–62
　debate and constrained dissent, 436
ethnic difference
　black, mythological anthropology includes premise that African Americans undervalue education339
　Caribbeans, 324, 343
　as performative ethnology, 316
　myths of, by the Caribbeans
　　includes underreporting racism there, 335
　　that not color at all that matters, but class, 335
ethnic distinction
　among Indians and Creoles, 231
　among non-American students, 132
　as defined by dialectical difference, 181
　diversity, 9, 61
　membership and secrecy, 273
　and racial embrace, in the university, 316–23
　vs. racial solidarity, xi, 1, 125
ethnic groups
　Black
　　and affirmation of superiority to native Black population, 54
　　of African descent, adoption of parlance of "culture" for exemption from racial stigma, 8
　　also mobilized "culture" in diverse ways, 469
　　appeal for exemption from stigma, 122

ethnic groups—Black (*continued*)
  attempt to distance themselves from African Americans, 123; dilemma faced by, 367
  diversity, 458
  otherness, and black ethnic social inferiority, 477
  similarity to African American peers, 123
  and the Tylorean/Boasian parlance of "cultures," 122
  collective practice and identity as strategic as they are habitual, 227
  conditions that cause emergence of, 183
  cultural features of are not fixed, 183
  difficulty with ethnological schadenfreude, 348
  distinction
    and competitive pursuit of earnings and honor, 304
    and issue of unity, similar adversity unites previously dissimilar parties, 313
    and rejection of discredited group members, 273
    self-representation, most common trope is "the lazy African American," 137
  food traditions, as diacritica of ethnic distinction, 262–63, 266–67
  as translocal debate within a global field of debate, 423
  white-skinned, self-positioning of, and denial of white racial privilege, 467–68
ethnic identity
  Black
    as reaction to risk of subordination, 14
    renaissance of, described, 64
  canonization of, 37
  can outlast apparent cultural assimilation, 278
  coethnics, 334
  cultural diacritica of are diverse and changing, 423
  and culture, dialogical theory of, 226–30
  as defined by anthropologists, 36–37
  emphasis on in 1980s, by Irish, Italian, and Jewish, 468
  ethnocultural revival, crossracial, and loss of legitimate claim to difference for African Americans, 474
  general theory, 226–30
  increasing emphasis of, in 1980s, 467–68
  matrilineal emphasis of, 294
  on motives by which Creoles and Indians group and regroup themselves, 235
  as protean and strategic invocations, 247
  as shaped by racial stigma, invention, and university scholars, 183
  and university discussions, 423
  as venues of debate about who belongs and who does not, 304
ethnicity
  as arising from pursuit or defense of a distinctive role, 226
  Black
    boundary-defining terms of, and the boundaries of Blackness as permeable, 122
    growth of, reveals economic changes, 110
    magnification of, in 1980s: buttresses of Black unity destroyed, 465; shared features of ethnogenesis, 110
    tends to correlate with upward mobility among African Americans, 351
  and claims to prestige and prerogative, 423
  as concept used by rivals to represent the group as unassimilable and essentially foreign, 474
  and culture, as idioms of resistance to racialism and of intraracial competition, 16
  deterritorialization of, 15
  emerges when one population has incentive to distinguish itself from a copresent population, 194
  ethnicization as strategy of upward mobility, 471
  as framework, xi
  as idiom of distinction, 459
  as protean, situational, and economically motivated, and shaped by the interests of insider and outsider interlocutors of middle classes, 463
  role of, 68
  stratifying articulations of, 68
  as structured by the debate among insiders and outsiders, 423
  theory, 467
ethnicity, black, 455
ethnicity and culture making, as strategy of self-presentation typical of discreditable or middling groups, 479
ethnicity entrepreneurs, 415, 426, 463
"ethnic line," 16, 465
ethnics, Black, tend to highlight speaker's likeness to the dominant class, 477
ethnogenesis, 6
  ambivalent role of universities in, 463
  as articulation of "culture"-based ethnic identities, 3
  Black, and the commoditization of ethnicity in a neoliberal age, 41
  as self-authorization in the "logic of the trial," 114
  and Caribbean Americans
    debate and one-upmanship, 306
    as most extreme example of the competitive element, 368

as collective flight from stigma, 460
as competitive and hierarchical process, 36, 65, 368
the competitive pursuit of honor and earnings is a major dynamic in ethno . . . and it relies on fiction of a constituent-other, 65
conflictual nature of, 304
"cultural," and imperialism, 14
debate as the phenomenal diacritic, 304
defining role of debate and contestation in, 304
hierarchical context of, 13
"literally-defined" debate, 234
racial context of, 13
role of education and debate, 235
role of race in, 15–16
as strategic, competitive, university-subsidized, and mass-mediated, 474
ethnography, xi, 3, 61, 85, 176
ethnological schadenfreude, 3, 4, 36, 46, 62, 65, 109, 320, 455, 459, 482
as competitive and hierarchical dimension of ethnogenesis, 36
described, 3
and forms of popular consent on which inequality and domination rest, 477
found at Howard University, 63
last-place anxiety of African-descended populations, 459
as "means of nosing one's way through the door," 172
as mechanism of consent, 455
and myth of superior culture "back home," 392
object of, in Black America, 480
one country toward another, 19
seen in highlighting deficiencies of the next class down, 477
solidarity among oppressed groups not automatic, 482
some Caribbean Americans as most extreme prototype of, 313
as "weapon of the weak" (Scott 1985), 320
when Caribbeans declare they are not African Americans, 46
ethnoracial identity
navigation of, 68
signaling of as competitive, to establish hierarchy, 315
standards of belonging as matter of debate, 287

Fanon, Frantz, 4
and ambivalent psychology of colonized and of recently independent elites, 68
culture, as customs frozen and reified by colonialists, 411
"double narcissism," 380, 381, 448, 463
on striving elites, 462

Fatoye-Matory, Olubunmi Elizabeth (Bunmi), 69, 74, 376, 377, 383, 410, 437, 450, 451, 483
Fields, Barbara J., 21, 182, 256
Florida Agricultural and Mechanical University, 94
Fordham, Signithia, 308, 309, 310, 311
"For now we see through a glass, darkly," 1 Corinthians 13:12, 70, 447, 451
Fort Dix school, integrated by President Eisenhower, 326
Foucault, Michel
and Foucauldian forms of resistance, 173
power/knowledge, 187
Franklin, John Hope, former Howard University History professor, descended from people enslaved by Choctaws, 255
Franklin, John Whittington, 255
Franklin, Shirley Clarke, 133
Frazier, E. Franklin, 44, 68, 196, 345
Freedmen's Hospital, 78, 94, 236. *See also* Howard University: divisions: Howard University Hospital
Freyre, Gilberto, 12, 51
fundamentalists, Christian
claim for restoration of privileged access to (economic) resources, 469
claims of politicized right, 468

Gallaudet University, and stratification of their own, 459–60
Gandhi (Mohandas Karamchand), Mahatma, 12
Gans, Herbert, 12–13
Garvey, Marcus, 30, 318, 394, 401, 456, 457
bold declaration of antagonism to colonialists, 87–88
Gates, Henry Louis, Jr., 33, 305, 320, 403
Gatto, John, and the "hidden curriculum," 124
gender
gap, 130
gap, educational, 167–68
stereotypes, 66–67
Germany, 471–72
Ghana, 31
Gibson, Thomas, xii
global economy, changing, 126–32
Goffman, Erving, 314
information-management as strategy of the discreditable, 243
rationality as the perfect "disidentifier," as cover for the discreditable and the discredited, 119
stigmatized crafting of a "literally defined world," 119
two further patterns of conduct among the stigmatized, 45
and "virtual identity," 42–43
Gold Coast, 142, 143, 252, 364

Goodman, Andrew, 450–51
Gospel at Colonus, 109
"Gospel at Colonus, The," (1985, opera), 70
gospel music, 70
Graham, Oscar Lewis, 68, 367
Greek-letter societies, 318
   Alpha Kappa Alphas, 147, 332
   Alpha Phi Alpha, 302
   Delta Sigma Theta, 147
   Kappa Alpha Psi, 302
   Omega Psi Phi, 141, 302
Guinier, Lani, 305
Gullah/Geechee
   culture
      and contrast with the Talented Tenth, 229
      dialogical genesis of, 190–91
      as evolving product of interaction, 192
      on the exemplary Africanness of, 196–99
      geographic area of defined, 177, 179, 195
      as Howard's foremost constituent-other, 176
      isolation as key explanation of cultural endurance, 200
      Janus face of, 186–90
      origin of terms, 194–96
      Penn Center on SC St. Helena Island, seen as heartland of the culture, 179–80, 186
      revision in cultural history of, 192
      revival of, 230
      role of universities in responding to this racial stigma and constituent-othering, 177
      role of university in study of, 228
      and the strategic and situational nature of ethnic identity, 227
   as ethnic group
      domestic, 5, 6
      and genesis of cultures: out-migration and return and cultural self-awareness, 192; seen as most African subculture and ethnic group, 183
      illustrates ambivalence essential to cultural nationalism, 176
      linguistic peculiarities of, 30
      nationalists' identification of "African" cultural model, 464
      political and cultural economy that has generated the emergence of, 228
      and results of securing federal recognition, 42
      seen as Black North America's most archaic, isolated ethnic group, 177
      transformation of into an ethnic group, 228
   ethnic identity
      as emerging from translocal interaction and stigma, 177
      a general theory, 226–30
      and genesis of cultures, at Howard University, 179–82
      and historical genesis of cultures and ethnic identities, 191
      reinvention, 406
      strategic and situational nature of, 227
   ethnogenesis
      and cultural diacritica that define membership in ethnic groups, 304
      illustrates prominence of schools and scholars in, 228

Haitians, 9, 343
Hamitic hypothesis of European colonialists, Tutsi chauvinism and Hutu rage, 19
Hansberry, Lorraine, 404–5
Hansberry, William Leo, 79, 404
Harlem Renaissance, 457
   literary movement at the roots of African American cultural nationalism, 51
Harvard College, 9, 307
Harvard Crimson, 23
Harvard University
   African American graduates of, 134
   Health Services, 72, 74
   instance of Creole self-declaration, 279
   as New Jerusalem of white America, 11
   and the northeastern white elite, 127
   tenure process, 117
   views of studious people, 131
HBCU (historically Black college or university)
   and the Black Bourgeois self, 170–72
   collective solidarity and upward mobility, 131
   complexion-based pecking order, 67–68
   contrasted with TWIs, 127
   education as weapon against white oppression, 131
   effect on community, 311
   freedom not to conform, 161
   Howard as preeminent, 11
   as *locus classicus* of self-fashioning, 122
   mission and appeal of, 157–61
   torn between two impulses, 116
   verbal and sartorial signs of class status, 68, 70–71
Heaven and Hell
   American Africans and the Image of Home, 370–446
   in between, 437–46
   on self-presentation of Eritreans, Ethiopians, Sudanese, Nigerian, 65
Hegel, Georg Wilhelm Friedrich, 372
hegemony, racial, one-upmanship instead of rebellion, 455
Hemings, Sally, 251
Herder, Johann Gottfried von

and concept of "cultures," 50
on German peoplehood, 182
notion of distinctively German *Geist*, 14, 51, 471
Herskovits, Melville J., 456
 founder of African studies in the United States, 83
 rejection of Skinner application to Northwestern University, 83
 student of Boas, 51
Herzfeld, Michael, 18, 273, 331
hierarchy, sociocultural, and the plea for collective exemption from last place, 15
Hitler, Adolph, and German sense of inferiority, 471
Hoetink, H., and the somatic norm image, 25, 289
Howard University
 administration, H. Patrick Swygert, 161–62, 163–64
 affiliates, 67
 campus
  "The crest of the Hill," *139*
  described, 137–41
  Founders Library, *138*; and world's premier collection of books about the black world, 138
  Freedmen's Hospital, 139
  "The Hill": as safe haven for Black elites, 142; as symbolic reflection of American racial history, 142
  map, *140*
  Ralph Bunche International Affairs Center, 83
  rich in lessons about communities of the stigmatized, 132
  surrounding community, 348–49, 437
  as symbolic reflection of American racial history, 142
  Towers dormitory, *60, 141*
  transformation and subdivision of identity categories, 166–67
 Commencement, *133*
  graduates, *134*
 curriculum
  Eurocentric foundations of, 154
  European and Euro-American standards of knowledge still central, 187
  highlights ambivalence inherent in all cultural nationalist projects, 178
  recapitulates light-dark hierarchy and offers alternative paradigm of worth, 464
 divisions
  Business School, 167
  College of Medicine, ix, 73, 94, 95, 98, 99
  Howard University Hospital, 30, 41, 78, 94, 98, 100, 105
  Law School, 108
 ethnic identity
  coethnics, 334
  Creole community, 269
  distinction and hierarchy, 316–23; Caribbeans as different from native-born Blacks, 312–13
  ethnic groups of African descent, 62
  ethnicization debated as a strategy of upward mobility, 471
 ethnogenesis, failure of Afrocentric Gullah/Geechee, 190
 field research, xii
 graduates and alumni
  alumnus, *312*
  John Hope Franklin, 255
 Greek-letter societies, past colorism in, 335
 The Hilltop, 93
 history
  emergence as preeminent training ground for Black leaders and professionals, 187
  foundation, 186–87
  growth of, in wake of desegregation, 162
  high expectations, 153–54
  historically Black, 456
  as the "Mecca" and "Capstone of Negro Education," 322, 481
  as Mecca of Black higher education, ix, 11, 481
  racial oppression as backdrop of its founding, 78
 role as university
  articulation of ethnic, genealogical, and cultural markers, xi
  as critical to recent genesis of the Gullah/Geechee ethnic identity, 181
  hypothesis that all American universities are communities of the stigmatized, 121
 role in supporting "the now quasi-ethnic or postethnic category 'international students,'" 166–67
 rural African American folkways as object of ambivalence, 186
 sacred imagination of as indebted to the cultural nationalism of the Lagosian Cultural Renaissance, 418
 schadenfreude among students, faculty, and alumni, 3
 School of Pharmacy, 419–20
 self-image as the "Mecca" of "Negro" education and uplift, 458
 self-presentation, undesirable styles of, 131
 Skinner's training of anthropologists, policy makers, 88
 sociocultural character of
  affiliates, 67, 73

Howard University—sociocultural character of (*continued*)
  African Americans' and Caribbeans' view of each other, 363
  "Black any way you want to be," 161–62
  cosmopolitanism and sophistication, 75
  on dating advantage of light-skinned, 169
  and the light-dark hierarchy, 464
state-based chauvinism, 264
status
  as the "Mecca" and "Capstone of Negro Education," 322, 481
  as "the Negro Oxford," 11
  as preeminent training ground for Black professionals, 11
student population
  black ethnic diversity at, 398
  black ethnics seek to distinguish themselves from the stereotypical image, 63
  black nationalism of student body, 154
  blacks as constituent-other for Central American workers at Howard, 137
  Caribbean Students' Association, 316, 318, 360
  complex dialectics of black ethnic identity at, 337
  complexion hierarchy and ethnic diversity, 137
  and consequences of intraclass competition, 322
  Creole community, 269
  Curtis Howe (pseudonym), 264, 265–66, 377; and Indian reservation as last stand of Jim Crow, 253
  diversity of black population, 168
  diversity of students, faculty, and administration, 136
  ethnoracial or subclass divisions within, 63
  female-to-male ratio, 167–68
  Hospital, 94, 457
  how affiliates represent themselves collectively in reaction to racial stigmatization in the United States, 312
  international students, animus toward, 165–66
  international students, representation of, 165
  Nigerian students, 393, 418
  as nurturing Blacks, Indians, and "Black-Indians," 250
  as pan-African melting pot, ix
  percent of foreign nationals, 167
  post–World War II era: largest convergence of Western-educated black people, 67; presence of "color complex," 67–68
  as preeminent training ground for the professional class, 187
  presence of black Caribbeans in student body, 228–29
  presence of New Orleans Creoles of color, 228–29
  principles of mate selection, 291–92
  protests against Atwater appointment, 164
  reasons for attending Howard, 162
  regarding international African and Caribbean peers, 123
  relative absence of ethnoracially unmarked population, 322
  sense of superiority among African and Caribbean peers, 229
  surcharge issue, 166
Hughes, Langston, 256
Huntington, Samuel P., 173
Hurston, Zora Neale, as liaison between Harlem Renaissance and founding of US cultural anthropology, 51
Hutus, 473

identity
  class, 3
  collective, 35
    alternative, 2
    Black, 457
    strategic interaction of class aspirations and, 87
  ethnic, 3
  fraught relationship among racial, class, and gender identity, 129
  role of debate, 45–46
  self, and skin color
    as dialectic of race, class, gender, and ethnicity, 169
    and the pull of ethnological schadenfreude, 169
identity-making, 53
Ifill, Gwen, 318
immigrants, black
  African and Caribbean, 1, 2, 5, 123
  interaction and self-presentation of, 57
  as new outsiders with fear of downward mobility, 123
  relationship to African Americans, 113
  entry into the United States, 111
  self-promotion over native-born African Americans, 113, 343–44
  and white American prejudices, 112
  See also specific groups
immigrants, white, 191
  sense of superiority over African Americans, 153
  use of negative stereotypes, 347
  See also specific groups
imperialism, 32, 254

INDEX

Indian treaty rights, in eastern United States, light-skinned claimants to and violent denial of part-black cousins' access to, 253
inferiority vs. superiority, 97–98, 472
intellectual right, 469
interethnic rivalry, 110
intergroup competition for resources, most important to maintain superiority over another group, 258–59
"invisible," the, demography of, 5
Irish, 10, 44, 119, 191, 203, 313, 322, 347, 448
Islam, 13, 19, 35, 188, 193, 356, 378–79
Italians, 347, 399, 448

Jack and Jill Club, 147, 280
Jackson, Jesse, 135
Jamaican-Americans
  Colin Powell on Jamaican superiority, 341, 343
  and negative generalization about African Americans, 49, 323
Jamaicans
  Kingston, Montego Bay, and Ocho Rios, 60
  mythological anthropology of, 341–43
  performance on standardized exams, 340
  Taino Indians of, 261, 337
Jeantel, Rachel, 447–48
Jefferson, Thomas, 1, 251
Jews
  Maret history teacher, 154
  "passing" and white-skinned ethnics, 43
  Shoah, 407, 449
  as stigmatized people, 154
  violin master, and condescension toward jazz, 153
  Western European deflection of stereotypes onto Eastern Europeans, 45
  working-class Jewish outsiders at the TWIs, 122
Jim Crow, 29, 87, 184, 233, 237, 302, 317, 334
  end of, 101, 142
  and the Indian reservation, 253
  segregation, grew more forceful in late nineteenth century, 257
John Henryism, 328
Johnson, Joyce Eleanor, 78
Johnson, Lyndon Baines, endorsement of reforms, 466
Journal of the National Medical Association, 99

Kennedy, Randall, 103
King, Martin Luther, Jr., 40, 320
Klemm, Gustav E., 471
  on collective lifeways, 51
  concept of "cultures," 50
Kluckhohn, Clyde, 51
Knights of Peter Claver, 295

Kroeber, Alfred Lewis, 51, 499
Ku Klux Klan, 237
  murder of three civil rights workers, 450–51

Landes, Ruth, 51, 429–30
last-place anxiety, 304
  as impulse to complicity, 258
  and people of African descent, 482
  schadenfreude and, 382–92
laws and legislation
  Civil Rights Act of 1964, 466
  Hart-Celler Immigration Act of 1965, 6, 40
  Indian Removal Act of 1830, 251
  "legal buttresses of Black unity" destroyed by desegregation, 465
  Plessy v. Ferguson case, and the "separate but equal" doctrine, 118
  Racial Integrity Act of 1924, 251
  Regents of the University of California v. Bakke (1978), undermined admissions policies giving preferential treatment, 123–24
  repeal of laws favoring whites, 466
  repeal of laws making people of African descent a distinct group, 465
  Voting Rights Act of 1965, 466
Lee, Spike, 320
legacy, as central theme of triumph over systematic obstacles, 77
Lewis Henry Morgan Lectures, ix, 483
Lewontin, Richard, 21
Lincoln University, 88
linguistic conventions, middle-class, seen as emasculating, 180–81
"little races," 7, 28, 29, 30
  Creole, 232–33
  debate over recovery of non-Black ethnic identity, 232
  endogamy within, 236–37
  ethnic groups as permeable, 304
  Indian, 232
  phenotype and collective self-definition of, 236
  and "salvage" ethnology, 285
  seen as existential threat, 280
Locke, Alain Leroy, 154, 406, 471
  cultural relativism, xi, 51, 473
  hierarchy as intrinsic to, 473
  doyen of the Harlem Renaissance, 79
"logic of the trial," 120, 477–78
Lumbee Indians, magical powers attributed to, 284
lynching, 448

Malcolm X, 318
Malinowski, Bronislaw, xi, 471
  on divergent lifeways or cultures, 471
  and pro-African apologetics, 87
Malveaux, Floyd, MD, 95

Malveaux, Myrna Ruiz, 95
Mamdani, Mahmood, 473
Manchester school, 85
Maret School, 104, 310
   views of studious people, 131
marginalization, 8, 9
Martin, Trayvon, 447–48, 449, 451, 452, 454
Marx, Karl, 45
   theory, 53
   view of British economy as superior, 471
mass media
   hyper-masculinity of Black men, 475
   image of cinematic male heroes and subordinate Blacks, 472
   selective nature of music, dress, and speech as distortions, 474–75
   television as propaganda machine, 116–17
   transformation of ethnoracial groups is gendered, 475
mass media images, of Indians and Blacks, and presumption of conformity, 330
Matory, Adu (son), 31, 59, 60, 66, 69, 73, 74, 96, 129–30, 141, 151–52, 153, 201, 238, 241, 242, 263, 275, 286, 328, 383, 405, 413, 437, 438, 440, 442, 449, 450, 451–54, 483
Matory, Ayọ Alexandra (daughter), 66, 74, 276, 328, 437, 449, 450, 451, 483
Matory, Deborah Love, 70, 93, 142, 146, 483
   academic career, 143, 144
   aesthetics, 404
   ambitions for her children, 146, 147–49
   appearance, style, and taste, 144, 146–47, 149
   bourgeoisie ethos, 145, 152
   divorce, 95–96, 145–46
   and Howard University, 143
   professional career, 144
      clinical psychologist, professor of psychology, 144
   "tiger parent," 153
Matory, J. Lorand, PhD
   academic career
      as anthropologist, 188
      divided between HBCU and TWI, 71
      Duke University, chair of African American Studies
      and director of Center for African and African American Research, 117–18
      and director of Lawrence Richardson Professor of Cultural Anthropology, 105, 320
   early life
      musical training, 328
      North Portal Estates, 96, 146, 151
      schools attended, Shepherd Elementary, Paul Junior High School, Congressional School, and Maret School, 70–71
      secondary schools, 68, 71
   family members, 68, 70, 75–115, 450
      fathers, 67–115
   Harvard College, 9, 72, 307, 376
   Harvard University, 11, 66, 72–73, 74, 310
      professor, 90
      received BA, 105
      teaching professor, 58, 63, 74
      tenured, full professorship, 105
      visiting professor from, 58
   Howard University
      History Department, 82
      living in dorm with Adu, 58–59
      reentered, 236
      visiting professor, 456
   New Orleans
      Creole shop, 298–99
      as honored guest of elite, 280
   Nigeria
      research, 394
      as second home, 69
   parents
      encouragement to study in the liberal professions, 93
      high expectations of, 71, 147–49
      Howard University–based networks, 90
      mother, 70, 93
   Phillips Academy
      issue of swimming test, 307–8, 342
      teaching, 307
   research
      African-descended population studied, 63, 316
      of Afro-Atlantic ethnic diversity, 446, 482
      in Black Atlantic world, 183
      black immigrants, triracial isolates, and Gullah/Geechees, 61
      Chickahominy powwow, 262
      on cultural categories, 316
      Duke University: class, "Theories in Cultural Anthropology," 478; director, Center for African and American Research, 117
      interpretation of cultures concept, 174
      Native Americans, 232–33
      New Orleans, Trinidad, Nigeria, and Jamaica, 63
      Occaneechi-Saponi powwow, 241–42
      as pan-Africanist, 409, 456, 481
      sources, 60–61
      Yoruba, 69
   University of Chicago, anthropology PhD, 105
   University of Rochester, Lewis Henry Morgan Lecture, 483
Matory, William Earle, Jr., MD, 100–103
   class of 1972 at Yale, 101
   death, 104

and Howard University, 101, 102
medical residencies, 102
professor of surgery, University of Massachusetts, 102
and Yale University, 101
Matory, William Earle, Sr., MD, 69, 95, 448, 483
death, 69–70, 90, 92
as deeply defined by networks of male friendship, 90, 93
divorce, 95–96, 102, 145–46
early life, 92, 148
business manager of the *Hilltop*, 93
undergraduate graduation with honors, 93
family life, 142
as father, 90
Howard University, ix, 3, 481
contribution to health care and medical training, 94
enrollment, 93
legacy as central theme, 77, 98
medical career
American College of Surgeons, 91
assistant dean for clinical affairs, 99–100
chair of Washington, DC, Board of Medicine, 91
comparison to John Henry legend, 90–91
director of emergency care, 98
first Black member of American Association of Surgery of Trauma, 99
full professor of surgery, 98
general surgery practice, 94
governor, American College of Surgeons, 99
Howard University Hospital, 99–100, 457
Medical Education for National Defense program, 98
medical societies and fraternities, 100
and National Medical Association, 98
as part of generation of firsts in leadership of non-Black medical establishment, 99
receives MD, 93
as surgeon and teacher, 90
training of medical students and professionals, 91
military service, captain in the US Air Force, 94
professional life, complexion-related exclusion, 94, 97
publications, 91
Matory, Yvedt Lové, 142
accomplishments of, 103–4
birth, 143
death, 104
musical training, 328
research, 154

Sidwell Friends, 103
surgical oncologist and professor of surgery at Harvard, 103
Yale, 103
Matory family, 450
bourgeois ethos of, 145
complexion-based forms of exclusion, 147
musical training, 328
North Portal Estates, 146
Mattaponis, 233
McWhorter, John, 45, 328
Medico-Chirurgical Society of District of Columbia, 144
miscegenation, 8
model minorities, mythology of, 330
Mooney, James, encouragement of tribes' performances, 258
Morehouse College, 120, 271
Morial, Ernest "Dutch," contrast in self-representation, 300–301
Motley, Judge Constance Baker, 318
Mount Zion Baptist Church, 151
Moynihan, Daniel Patrick, 119, 320, 467
mythologies, Black Atlantic
Brazilian "Ogum," 91
Caribbean child-rearing practices contrasted, 324
Cuban "Oggún," 91

Nanticokes, 29, 233, 252
National Association for the Advancement of Colored People (NAACP), 280
National Cathedral, 109
National Endowment for the Humanities, 449
nationalism, cultural
ambivalence inherent in, 178
Gullah/Geechee as example of its ambivalence, 176
Yoruba, 69
nationalism, racial, 456
Black, 68, 87, 154
independence movements
Africa, 67
Caribbean, 67
National Medical Association
attempt to extend services of, 98
organization of African American physicians, founded in 1895, 91
National Urban League, 280
nation-states, 77, 85, 182
Native Americans
claiming of treaty rights, 7
lost lifeways of, 51
near extermination of, 449
North Carolina populations
Cherokee, eastern band, 240

524 INDEX

Native Americans—North Carolina populations (*continued*)
    effort to deny recognition as both Black and Indian, 238, 245
    as heartland of the southeastern Indian populations, 240
    Lumbees, 245
    Melungeons, 240–41
    Occaneechi, resisting demand for "racial purity," 246–47
    segregated schooling of, 184
    Virginia tribes, 233
    "white-Indian" / "black-Indian" divide, 250
    See also American Indians
native ethnics, mixed race, dilemma faced by, 7
Négritude, 457
"Negro Ivy League" article, responding to incendiary article, Black academics mount defense; pub. of *Black Colleges in America*, 120
New York University, 84
Nigeria, ix
    and American race and racism, 375, 377
    Barewa College, 185
    changes in political and economic fortunes, 392–93
    complex dynamics of individualism and collectivism, 390
    elite, postcolonial, 31, 76
    gender roles and inequality, 430, 431
    Hausa community of Ibadan, 37–38, 41, 193, 224, 260, 368, 421, 465
    Idọwa, *Dagburewe* of, 76 (*see also* Adebọnojọ, Samuel Adegbesan)
    Igbo, 39, 79–80, 219, 313, 339, 410
    Lagos, 60, 80
    Lagosian Cultural Renaissance, 415, 417–18
    people of, 31, 69, 321
    religion, 412–15, 416
        debate over African purity, 429
        gender and metaphor, 434–35
        hybridity, 426
        as preeminent symbol of black people's collective dignity and divinity, 414
        and rival claims as to authentic participants, 422, 426
    student enrollees in the United States, 77
    Yoruba, 37–38, 39
        aesthetic preference, 275–76
        as classical reference in African American cultural nationalism, 69
Nigerian Civil War, also known as the Biafran War, 79–80
Noguera, Pedro, 112–13
North Portal Estates, 285
Nuer people, 314

Obama, Barack, 33, 67, 470
Occaneechi-Saponi, 7, 29, 233, 250
    assertions of African American inferiority, 242
    Derek, 238, 241, 243–44, 247–48, 249, 250
    as distinct community, 41
    identity as both Black and Indian, 242
    North Carolina powwow, 41–42
    powwow, 31, 41, *240*
    and long-awaited recognition, 238–39, 244
    self-identity
        insistence upon not being Black, 242
        shunning of African Americans, 241–42
    tribal history, 246–47
Odubọwale, Regina (née Odumọsu), 76
Odumọsu, J. J., 76
Ogbu, John, 47, 308
Ọlaniyan, 391
"one-drop" rule, 256
Opala, Joseph, 197, 214, 215, 221, 222
oppressed groups
    increasingly competitive relations among, 16
    solidarity not automatic, 482
òrìṣà àkúnlẹbọ, and Uncle Badejọ, 69
Orisha (òrìṣà), 419, 425, 428, 429, 433
Ortiz, Fernando, 456
outsiderness, 117
    immigrants and natives in the 1950s, 122
Oyewumi, Oyeronkẹ
    on gender roles, equality, and divination in Yoruba-Atlantic debate, 431–32
    misrepresentation, motive, and authority as spokesperson, 435
Oyotunji, Yoruba revivalist kingdom, 191–92

Pamunkey, 34, 156, 233, 258, 260, 266
Park, Robert, 44
Pendleton, Clarence, 449
People's Congregational Church, 420, *420*
Phi Alpha Theta History Honors, initiation ceremony, 187–89
Phillips Academy, 307
Piscataway/Piscatawa tribe
    Gabrielle Tayac, 252, 255
    powwow, 253
    recognition of, 233, 237, *237*, 238
Plecker, W. A., 251, 252
populations
    copresence, results in each group imitating the other, 194
    status insecurity, 3
    stigmatized as inferior, 460
postracialism, 26, 74
Powell, Colin, belief in West Indian superiority, 341, 345, 360
Prince George's County, MD, African American community with highest average income, 252

Protestants, white Anglo-Saxon, ethnicity and lifeways treated as unmarked norm, 173
Protestant whites, working-class, and working-class Jewish outsiders at the TWIs, 122a

Queen Quet, Gullah/Geechee nation, 220
Queen's Royal College, 184

race
  baiting, 163–64
  binarism and colorism, 316
  binary logic of identities, 111–12
  changing concepts of, 17–18
  and class, 17
  as class position in the global division of labor, 17
  concept, as bad science, 21
  as contradiction, 133–37
  debate regarding universality of race as social category, 16–17
  debunking of, by anthropologists, 8
  and ethnic identity, interaction of, 58
  as framework, xi
  nonbinary, in schools, 184
  other countries' terms for, 23–24
  in post-Reagan years, 465–70
  as of the race but above the race, 479
  racism across nations, 21–22
  tripartite classification, 30
  universality and endurance of, as central to today's political and scholarly debates, 16
  uses of, 182
  varying definitions of, 23–24
racism, in United States, 254, 329
  seen as thing of the past, 123
Rappahannocks, 233
Reagan, Ronald
  backlash against civil rights movement, 14, 26, 40, 466, 467–68
  code phrases and rhetoric, 66, 466
  government as enemy of white freedom, 466
  1980 presidential campaign, 450
  turned white anger into political revolution, 466
realpolitik, of African and Caribbean nation-states, often violently divisive, 110
"Redemption," as white supremacist term for the overthrow of Reconstruction, 251
Red Shirt, Oglala Dakota, 254
"representing"
  performing one's best to honor your group, 332
  pressure to represent the group well, 333
  racially stigmatized bear the burden of always representing or being represented by a group, 350

Republican Party
  promotion of antiblack stereotypes, 467
  regarding distribution of benefits, 469
  and southern white Democrats, 466
rhizomatic processes, 55–56, 61
Rice, Condoleezza, 89
Rodrigues, Raymundo Nina, 456
Rove, Karl, 466

Said, Edward, 4, 50, 406
Saint Albans School, 105, 106, 107
"Sankofa," 398, 400
santero art, Cuban, 152
Saponi Nation, Haliwa Saponi, 29, 78, 245, 249, 255. *See also* Occaneechi-Saponi
schadenfreude, ethnological
  achieves crescendo in last-place anxiety of African-descended populations in recently desegregated immigrant society of the United States, 459
  American African, and last-place anxiety, 382–92
  of black ethnics in the United States, 455
  conflicting tensions of race, class, and gender as central to, 169
  described, 3
  identification of other groups as worthy of stigma, 459
  motivator and mechanism of consent, 455
  scapegoating as element of, 479–80
  and stereotyping, 382
  of the stigmatized, 455, 459
  of West-Indian superiority, 345
schools, 70
  as sites of triage, 304
  white students, lack of seriousness among, 309–10
Schwerner, Michael, 450–51
segregation, 75, 456
  closing of union shops to Blacks, suppression of voting rights, 448
  educational institutions, 184, 325–26
  Federal Housing Administration, racial favoritism toward whites post–World War II, 468
  housing, 325–26
  racial exclusion of Blacks, 252, 468
  racist and demeaning signs, 118
  "red-lining" of neighborhoods, 92
  in stores, 147
self-definition in opposition to negative stereotype, xi
self-identification, racial, 32
self-representation, 11–15, 49, 169–70
Seminoles, 233, 253
sexism, 327

Shapiro, Melissa (pseudonym), 281
　attempts to revive and publicize a "separate" Louisiana Creole culture, 278–79
　as "Creole nationalist," 277–78
　definitions as nostalgia, 303
Shoah, 407, 449
Sidwell Friends School, 107
　Yvedt attends, 107
Skinner, Elliot Percival
　ambassadorial service, 84–85
　career, 82–89
　at Columbia University
　　position as Franz Boas Professor (Emeritus), 82, 84
　　stature as doyen of African American anthropology, 82
　early life, 82, 84, 85
　on the elite and mobile black populations around the Atlantic perimeter, 84
　professorships and academic honors, 88
　　fellowships, 88
　　first Black chair of any academic department in the Ivy League, 82
　　first Black tenured professor at Columbia, 82
　　as professor at Howard, 82
　　as visiting professor at Howard, 69
　research, 88
　　the black elites of the circum-Atlantic world, 82
　　contrasts political strategies of Marcus Garvey and W. E. B. Du Bois, 87–88
　self-identity
　　as American first and Trinidadian second, 85
　　as "a man in between," 84, 89, 448
　　only nonphysician among Matory's fathers, 82
　　as racial outsider, 87
　　wedding of pride and pragmatism, 85
　　wife Gwendolyn Mikell, 83
slavery
　Confederate defense of, 451, 456
　following Bacon's Rebellion, 256
　Gullah/Geechee descent from slaves, 195
　Islamic, 379
　multiracial terrain of, 379–80
　racism, and "document genocide," 251–64
　transatlantic slave trade, 188, 415–16, 449, 457
Smith, Emma (pseudonym)
　assertions of African American inferiority, 241–42
　as most vocal advocate of Indian superiority and difference from African Americans, 251, 253, 256, 261
Snowden, Frank, 79

Sonn, Franklin, 95
Speck, Frank G., encouragement of tribes' performances, 258
Spelman College, 120, 162
Spencer Foundation, 482
Steele, Claude, 332–33
stereotyping
　anti-Black, 43, 69, 286, 467
　by black ethnics, 75
　hip-hop music, hypermasculinity of male artists, 110
　trope of the lazy native, 137
　by whites, 75
stigma, 109
　ambition as stigmatized quality, 333–34
　Anglo-North American form of racial stigma is most pervasive and indelible, 459
　competitive flight from, 36
　of inferiority, 15, 109
　management of, 459
　racial, ix, 8
stigmatization
　antiblack prejudice, 43
　assimilation to white middle-class, 190
　by Black ethnics, 458
　management of, 459
　middle-class Blacks, 458
　perspective of, 121
　racial
　　Black people as a foremost example for stigmatized groups all over the world, 482
　　and "the desperation to escape it," 8
　　and racial "otherness," 8
　role of
　　and hierarchy in the genesis of ethnic groups, 65
　　and interethnic competition, 57
　　and segmented assimilation, 1
　　shapes the hidden curriculum, 177
　of slave ancestry, 116
　social positioning in response to, 436
　status anxiety, white, 455
　and stereotype, resistance to empirical correction, and demonstrating proximity to the elite, 322
stigmatized groups
　as constituent-other, 457–58, 460, 477
　construction of community around shared sense of superiority, 334
　the discreditable and the discredited, dense web of social connections often unites, 254
　dividends of exceptionalism, 345
　easier for whites to credit Blacks with physical gifts than with Black intellectual excellence, 118

INDEX

hurdles faced by, outperforming one's fellows, making them feel inferior, 333
as hyperaware, 118–19
and inversion of received light-dark hierarchy, 464
as most aesthetically creative, 478
on negotiation of distance, alliance, and dignity among, 137
"pragmatism" of, 300
racially stigmatized, must bear burden of representing or being represented by a group, 350–51
role of mass media, 116–17
seek to adopt language of ethnically unmarked dominant class, 119–20
strategy of, 119
stratification among, 4, 32, 45, 67–68
unenviable dilemmas of, 117
unity among is a project rather than a default, 401
and uses of fiction and image-management, 332
willingness to work twice as hard to get half the rewards, 478
Sudan/Sudanese
civil war, 19, 438–39
Deng, Anyong Kout, 378, *378*, 439–42, *443*
populations against one another, 19
self-presentation of, 65
Sudan as slave-hunting grounds for Ottomans, 379
Swygert, H. Patrick, xi, *133*, 133–34, 135, 161

Taiwo, Olufẹmi, 385, 390
taste, as idiom of distinction, 459
taxonomy, racial, 14
Thomas, Clarence, 449
"Three Fathers," charting role of color, class, and social background in pursuit of manhood, 66–70
Touré, Sékou, 403
transmigrants, 2
transnationalism, 56
role of, 68
Trinidad and Trinidadians, 84, 184
attempt to escape condition by proclaiming tie to Britain, 346
Howard engineer alumnus, *312*
interactions and discrimination based on color, 335–36
multi-racial and class-stratified, 84
not free of racism, 336
research in, 60
triracial isolates, 2, 7, 28, 29, 30, 240
Tureaud, A. P., 30
Turner, Lorenzo Dow, 182
academic career of, 177–78

Turner, Nat, 256
Turner, Victor, 85, 283–84
TWIs (traditionally white institutions)
as authoritative venue for the debate and recognition of ethnic groups, 423–24
debates about cultural diacritica, 445
as important venue shaping nature of debates about ethnogenesis, 424
as instrumental in African diaspora identity- and culture-making, 411
in post–civil rights era, may be only convenient and profitable places to assert Creole cultural distinction, 290
as world of the stigmatized, 161
Tylor, Edward Burnett, 471
culture concept critiqued, 476
Tylorean/Boasian "cultures," 304

Uncle Badejọ
academic and medical training, 78
autobiography, 78, 79, 80
board certification, 78
family, 78–81, 448
friendships, colleagues and peers, 79–80
at Howard University, 77
medical positions held, 79–80
return to Nigeria, 79–80
Yoruba celebration, 81–82
See also Adebọnojọ, Olubadejọ Olurẹmi, MD
universities, 126–32
class and identity-making, elite
as foremost pathway of outsiders seeking acceptance, 57
as guidance in the flight from social stigma, 57
promoting the concept of "cultures," 173
and class status
affirming and empowering the stigmatized, 173
among professors, 132
as arena for socially mobile middle classes
on careerism vs. the life of the mind, 125
class formation, ethnoracial, 124
cultures as patterns of collective life seen from the position of low rank, 175
helps ethnic and lower-class whites acquire diction, manners, and marital partners, 173
its denizens are also driven to "stratify their own," 172–73
like ethnic groups, universities exist in a field of competition for resources and rank, 132
mimicry of Oxford and Cambridge, 187
most founded in the service of stigmatized local elites, 119

universities—and class status (*continued*)
  as one of the main institutional generators of opportunity for the transnational Black bourgeoisie, 115
  "outsiders" in, most black natives and immigrants in the 1950s, 122
  post-slavery or postcolonial, 70
  role of producing and reifying collective identities in multiple ways, 315
  professors, like ethnic groups, exist in field of competition for resources and rank, 132
  scholars found it difficult to ignore the global political context of their studies, 83
  social order of, as compromise, 190
  as social triage and stratification, 155–57
  as triage system, sorting people out according to color, class, and ethnicity, 185
  as context in which the stigmatized seek to intellectualize their way out of the dilemmas of dishonor, 119
  as defining cultures, 462
  demographic, increasingly dominated by racial and gender outsiders, 121
  and ethnogenesis, 422
    ambivalent role, 463
  identity-making and ethnic identity
    advocate "culture" in the sense of conformity to the single ethnoracially unmarked standard of excellence, 178
    how primary identity categories can be changed by, 166
    key role in rearticulation and invention of ethnic identities, 58
    as major arbiter of ethnicity and cultural boundaries, 471
  role of
    in authorizing social categories, 304
    and the centrality of university education in defining the black bourgeoisie since World War II, 68
    most founded in service of stigmatized local elites, 119
    triage and social stratification, 155–57
  sociocultural character of, 13
  sociocultural nature of
    of authority, order, and "the rules," 174–75
    where class-marginal have a chance to elevate their fates, 173
  and the stigmatized, 56–57
    as exemplary world of the stigmatized, 56–57, 172–73
    as a literally defined world, 57, 64, 127, 132, 184, 234, 445, 461; stigmatized seek to improve own image and evade anticipated defamation, 120
    no perch safe from dishonor and stigma of not having published recently, 117
    as paradigmatic communities of the stigmatized, 120
  and upward mobility
    education as best chance for socially disadvantaged, 121
    often most reliable route to upward economic mobility for partly black Indians and triracial isolates, 29
    right-wing hostility toward, 189
    role in African and African-diaspora identity-making, 396
    role in defining the Black bourgeoisie, 68
    role in offering chance to the class-marginal to elevate their status, 173
University of Rochester, ix
  Lewis Henry Morgan Lectures, 483
upward mobility
  as abandonment or betrayal, 30
  Blackness and struggle against stigma, 438
  of black populations in the United States, overshadowed by white projection as the constituent-other, 457
  for Jewish immigrants, 121
  lag in Black upward mobility blamed on superior talents in white-skinned people, 467
  racial identity tends to correlate among African Americans, 351
  and resentment of downtrodden populations, 118
  white, generally associated with abandonment of marked ethnic and class identities, 350–51
US Constitution, First Amendment, 449

Virginia tribes, Native American, Curtis Howe (pseudonym), 264, 265–66, 337

Wagley, Charles, 487
Wallerstein, Immanuel, 18, 32
Washington, Booker T., 401
Washington, DC
  Black communities, 481
  Capitol Hill, gentrification of, 286
  Gold Coast, 142, 143, 252, 364
  Rock Creek Park, 46
Weber, Max, 53
Wessorts, 7, 29
West Indians, immigrants
  as contrasted with African Americans, 39, 323
  earnings of, 344–45
  ethnological schadenfreude of, 345

seeking to differentiate themselves from African Americans, 41
white people
  advantage, 291
  Americans, power and status in manners, speech, and writing, 154
  commitment to keep Blacks out of elite-producing institutions, 67
  elite
    ethnically unmarked who control opportunities for upward mobility, 469
    use of Black men's potential athletic and sexual dominance to draw white men into cross-class white alliance, 476
  as ethnoracially unmarked, xi, 286, 401
  and expectations of African Americans, discomfort with signs of ambition or superiority, 153
  and judgment as individuals, not as a class, 333
  as racially privileged, xi, 101
  white supremacy, 256, 456
whites, borderline, includes working-class Irish and Italians of northern police forces, 448
Wilder, Douglas, 278
Williams, Dr. Eric, 11, 69, 136–37
  historian, 82
  led Trinidad to independence, 229
Willis, Paul
  on the antischool culture of many working-class populations, 128, 152
  and demand for conformity, 161
Wilson, William Julius, 44–45, 320
Woodson, Carter G., 186
working-class, views of, 127–28
world system, racialized, xi

Xavier University, 283, x

Yale University, 101, 103
Yoruba, 457
  culture
    definition of, by scholars, 462
    and double narcissism, 380
    and principle that cultures arise more from conflict than from consensus, 423
    worship of, 391, 415
  ethnic identity
    and African purism, 426–29
    arising from the ethnicity entrepreneurship of black class elite, 415
    construction of, 193, 415
    debate over purity and syncretism, 426–27
    foundations of: arose from a disaster, 415, 417–18; missionary-educated returnees from Sierra Leone, 416–17; returnees to Lagos, 415–16
    and gender, 430–36
    judging criteria are protean, situational, and strategic, 424
    and "the logic of the trial," 415
    and the nonethnic audience, 436–37
    race and, 425
Yoruba-Atlantic Identity
  debates as powerful allegories of reform, 445
  hybrid roots of, 426
  and role of universities in, 65
  syncretism/antisyncretism debate as diacritica of, 428, 429
  and the TWI, as important venue of ethnogenetic debate, 421–22, 423
Yorubaland, 88, 394, 415
Young, Andrew, 79, 272, 319

Zimmerman, George, 447–48